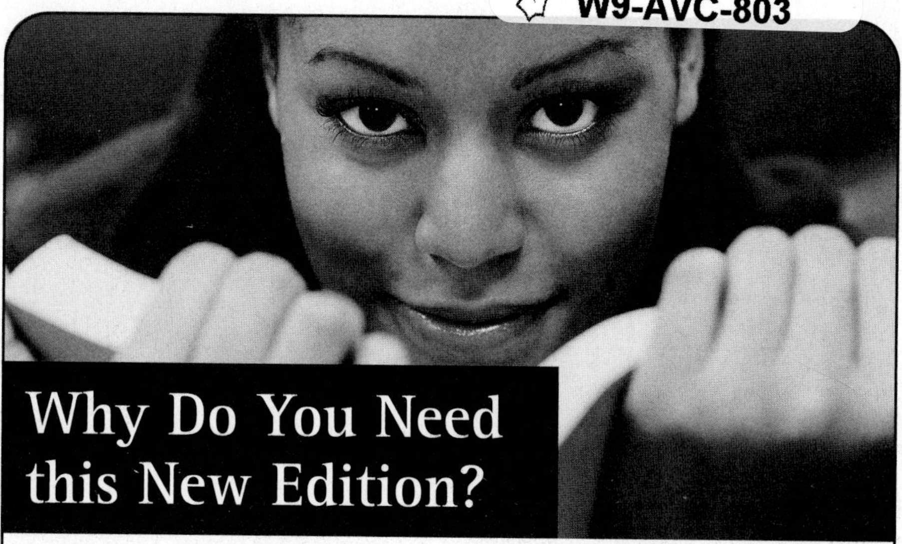

Why Do You Need this New Edition?

Why should you buy this new edition of *Patterns of Exposition?* Here are four good reasons!

1. **Thirteen new readings** address innovative, contemporary uses of rhetorical patterns and introduce writers representative of current trends and styles in nonfiction writing. These imaginative and often irreverent essays raise questions of value and ethical choices in today's society.
2. **Works by an expanded selection of writers**—including blogger Jennifer Graham, *New York Times* columnist Verlyn Klinkenborg, *New Yorker* writer Ian Frazier, and Pulitzer Prize winner Anne Fadiman—provide insights into contemporary issues and a wider range of viewpoints and subjects.
3. **An additional essay in Chapter 14, Combining Patterns**—"The Great TV Debate," by Jason Kelly—expands the emphasis on good writing that integrates multiple rhetorical patterns.
4. **More readings on argumentation and persuasion (Chapter 13)** provide more examples of this critical rhetorical pattern.

PEARSON

Patterns of Exposition

Nineteenth Edition

Robert A. Schwegler
University of Rhode Island

Longman

Boston Columbus Indianapolis New York San Francisco Upper Saddle River
Amsterdam Cape Town Dubai London Madrid Milan Munich Paris Montreal Toronto
Delhi Mexico City São Paulo Sydney Hong Kong Seoul Singapore Taipei Tokyo

Senior Sponsoring Editor: Virginia L. Blanford
Executive Marketing Manager: Sandra McGuire
Senior Supplements Editor: Donna Campion
Production Manager: Denise Phillip
Project Coordination, Text Design, and Electronic Page Makeup: Pre-PressPMG
Senior Cover Design Manager/Designer: Nancy Danahy
Cover Photo: © iStockphoto
Senior Manufacturing Buyer: Alfred C. Dorsey
Printer and Binder: R. R. Donnelley & Sons/Crawfordsville
Cover Printer: R. R. Donnelley & Sons/Crawfordsville

Library of Congress Cataloging-in-Publication Data
Patterns of exposition / Robert A. Schwegler.—19th ed.
p. cm.
Includes index.
ISBN 978-0-205-73177-0
1. College readers. 2. Exposition (Rhetoric) 3. English language—Rhetoric. I. Schwegler, Robert A. II. Title.
PE1417.P3954 2009
808'.0427—dc22
2009035356

1 2 3 4 5 6 7 8 9 10—DOC—12 11 10 09

Longman
is an imprint of

www.pearsonhighered.com

ISBN-13: 978-0-205-73177-0
ISBN-10: 0-205-73177-5

Contents

Thematic Contents

Politics and Leaders

Personality and Behavior

Nature and the Environment

Morals, Crime, and Punishment

Growing Up/Getting Old

Differences

Families and Children

Society and Social Change

Media

Essay Pairs

Preface

Instructors familiar with *Patterns of Exposition* will notice that this new edition retains the discussions of rhetorical patterns, student essay examples, and comprehensive chapters on reading and writing that have been well received in previous editions. And it continues the tradition of providing many new and interesting readings. The discussions of patterns of exposition and argument and the essays illustrating these strategies demonstrate the ways in which rhetorical patterns enable writers and readers to explore, understand, and take a stand on questions of culture, identity, and value in the college community, the workplace, and in society at large.

NEW TO THIS EDITION

You will find thirteen new readings in this edition, including selections by such widely known writers as Ian Frazier, Pat Conroy, Jonah Lehrer, Verlyn Klinkenborg, and Anne Fadiman. New voices, like that of Jennifer Graham on decorating a dorm room, are also represented here. These new selections both model patterns appropriately and reflect contemporary topics that students will find compelling.

THE CORE OF THIS BOOK

Chapter 1, "Reading as a Writer," introduces students to reading strategies especially useful for the essays in this text, for academic reading in general, and for turning reading into writing. The chapter pays particular attention to critical reading and reading for technique as well as reading for understanding. It introduces students to concrete reading strategies for use in composition courses, in other college courses, and beyond.

Chapter 2, "Ways of Writing," introduces students to the composing process and to a variety of useful techniques for discovering ideas and information, planning an essay, developing a thesis, drafting, and revising. The chapter also provides numerous student examples, including a student essay in draft and revised form. Our emphasis here and elsewhere in the text is on the practical: concrete writing strategies, specific suggestions, and concise illustrations.

Each chapter covering a pattern of exposition (or argument) begins with a discussion of the roles the particular pattern can play for writers and readers. The discussions provide a definition of the pattern; a paragraph example taken from the work of an accomplished, professional writer; a discussion of the various uses of the pattern ("Why Use . . . ?); suggestions for designing essays that employ the pattern ("Choosing a Strategy"); and techniques for developing the content of an essay as well as individual paragraphs and sentences ("Developing. . . .").

The first few essay selections in each chapter illustrate some of the many roles a pattern can play in organizing thought and expression within an essay or the roles a pattern can play in working with other rhetorical patterns to create an organized, purposeful, effective exposition (or argument).

Each chapter concludes with a cluster of essays focusing on "Issues and Ideas" of contemporary and (perhaps) enduring significance. The primary goal of these clusters is not simply to encourage students to think and write about the specific themes and issues, but to help students develop an awareness of rhetorical strategies as a critical tool for understanding differing perspectives and to demonstrate the variety of purposes a strategy can serve. It is precisely the broad similarity in subject matter and strategy among the essays in a cluster that serves to highlight for students the important differences and the varied models for expression the selections provide.

The questions at the end of each selection highlight important issues of meaning, technique, and style that help develop students' abilities as readers and the range of options available to them as they write. "Read to Write" activities follow the questions. The first activity in each set, labeled "Collaborating," offers students a chance to work with their classmates to develop ideas, essay plans, brief essays, and, occasionally, a collaboratively written essay. The second activity, labeled "Considering Audience," directs students' attention to readers' expectations and audience constraints. Some of the activities ask them to consider the likely reactions of readers to the essay presented in the text; other activities call for speculation about readers' reactions to different writing strategies. The third activity, "Developing an Essay," helps students view the sample essay in the text as a broad model for their own work—a model that they are encouraged to alter and develop in a fashion appropriate to their own perspectives and purposes. These activities provide practice in linking reading to writing—one of the primary focuses of the book as a whole. The "Writing Suggestions" at the end of each chapter include collaborative activities and offer further avenues for students to follow from reading into writing.

In choosing new essays and retaining those from previous editions, I have looked first for selections that are well written and insightful and that reward careful (re)reading, and then for selections that can serve as useful models for thought, organization, and expression. I have also drawn on suggestions from the text's instructor-users and have reviewed the responses of students. Although obviously I am unable to comply with all requests, I have seriously considered and fully appreciated all of them, and I have incorporated many suggestions into this new edition. I have responded, as well, to requests for added essays in some of the most heavily used chapters of the book.

The wealth of excellent and recent nonfiction writing reflecting the perspectives of many different cultural and social groups has made it possible for me to choose selections reflecting the intellectual ferment and challenge of our times. In drawing on this diversity, I have not tried to represent every identity in an unimaginative and rigid fashion but have instead tried to use it to create an exciting mixture of perspectives and backgrounds designed to encourage varied, engaged responses from students.

Because so many instructors find it useful, I continue to retain the table of contents listing pairs of essays. Each pair provides contrasts (or similarities) in theme, approach, and style that are worth studying. The essay pairs can form the focus of class discussion or writing assignments.

The "Further Readings: Combining Patterns" chapter provides contemporary selections to provoke discussion. The pieces also suggest some intriguing combinations of patterns and goals for writing essays that can be pursued in the hands of skilled and daring writers. The essays in this section can be used on their own or with the other chapters of the book.

Throughout *Patterns of Exposition,* Nineteenth Edition, I have tried to make possible the convenient use of all materials in whatever ways instructors think best for their own classes. With a few exceptions, only complete essays or freestanding units of larger works have been included. With their inevitable overlap of patterns, they are more complicated than excerpts illustrating single principles, but they are also more realistic examples of exposition and more useful for other classroom purposes. Versatility has been an important criterion in choosing materials.

Forty-six of the selections best liked in previous editions have been retained. Thirteen selections are new, and all but a few of these are anthologized for the first time.

The arrangement of essays is but one of the many workable orders; instructors can easily develop another if they so desire. The thematic table of contents and the table of essay pairs also suggest a variety of arrangements.

I have tried to vary the study questions—and undoubtedly have included far more than any one teacher will want—from the purely objective to those calling for some serious self-examination by students. (The Instructor's Manual supplements these materials.)

"A Guide to Terms," at the end of the book, briefly discusses matters from *Abstract* to *Unity* and refers whenever possible to the essays themselves for illustrations. Its location is designed to permit unity and easy access, and there are cross-references to it in the study questions following each selection.

In all respects—size, content, arrangement, format—I have tried to keep *Patterns of Exposition* uncluttered and easy to use.

ACKNOWLEDGMENTS

This edition of *Patterns of Exposition* is a truly collaborative effort, and I want to acknowledge and thank my collaborator: Nancy Newman Schwegler. I have benefitted immensely from her insights and efforts. Working with her has been a pleasure as well as a learning experience for me. Nancy Newman Schwegler has contributed much to prior editions of the text, but until recently I have not had a chance to acknowledge her contributions in a way they certainly deserve. Her insight, taste, and intelligence have helped make this book a continued success for instructors and students.

I would also like to thank Brian and Tara Schwegler for their advice on current social developments and cultural trends; Christopher Schwegler for tolerating this all; and Ashley Marie Schwegler for putting up with two authors in the house and making our lives a lot sunnier. And I want to thank Nancy Newman Schwegler for her love and support.

In addition, special thanks are due to the many users of this text and to the reviewers for this revision: Connie S. Adair, Marshalltown Community College; Jacqueline A. Blackwell, Thomas Nelson Community College; Paul Friskney, Cincinnati Christian University; Vicki Houser, Northeast State Community College; Lillie Miller Jackson, Southwest Tennessee Community College; and Kaushalya Jagasia, Illinois Valley Community College.

Robert A. Schwegler

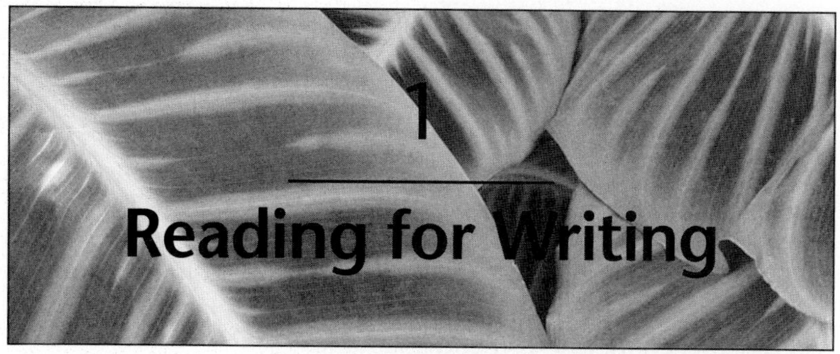

1 Reading for Writing

Reading and writing work together. Good writers draw ideas and information from their reading. They use reading to help understand an audience's likely reactions. They read to discover techniques of expression. They use critical reading as a springboard for their own writing. You can read for all of these purposes—understanding, critical response, and discovery of technique—or for only a few, depending on your goals as a writer.

To develop your skills as a reader and writer of expository and argumentative texts, you need to pay attention to three ways of approaching a text: reading for understanding, critical reading, and reading for technique. No matter what your approach, however, you need to pay attention to the elements of the **reading process: previewing, reading,** and **reviewing.** These elements are important whether you are reading **expository writing** (including essays, magazine articles, reports, memos, newspaper reports, and nonfiction books) or **argumentative writing** (including editorials, opinion essays, reports and proposals, policy statements, investigative reporting, or professional articles).

If you plunge right into reading, moving quickly through an article, essay, or book and then put it aside, you are missing important opportunities. Effective readers treat reading as a process consisting of **previewing, reading,** and **reviewing.** They develop techniques for each of these stages of the reading process.

PREVIEW YOUR READING

Previewing means "reading before you start reading." Newspapers provide headlines to tell you what to expect in an article. Books and articles have titles. Authors and editors often provide brief summaries at the beginning of a chapter or in a table of contents. Magazine editors often take key statements from an article and reprint them in large type within boxes where readers can see them as they flip through the pages. Paying attention to these features is important because the knowledge and expectation you bring to a text can affect how well you understand it.

Look for Help from the Editor or Writer

Writers and editors often provide you with considerable help for previewing. Titles are a good place to start. Many will tell you much about a work's contents and organization, as does the title of Don Aslett's book, *How Do I Clean the Moosehead? And 99 More Tough Questions About Housecleaning.*

A table of contents provides detailed information about the coverage and purpose of a work and perhaps even a summary of individual sections of the work. The table of contents for this book, for example, offers brief summaries of the essay selections, identifying the general topic of each and the writer's perspective. Here, for instance, is the entry for Catherine Seipp's essay, "Meet Today's Dad" (pp. 167–169).

> A conservative writer takes a satiric look at "Today's Dad," contrasting the contemporary version with "Yesterday's Dad" and finding the traditional model (and traditional values) superior in a number of ways.

Once you know that Seipp writes from the perspective of the cultural and political right (the selection comes from the conservative website *National Review Online*), you can read her essay with a greater appreciation of the origin and consequences of her ideas.

If an article or book does not have a table of contents, skim the text looking for headings and subheadings that reveal the writer's plan and the topics being discussed.

If an editor highlights important passages in an essay or article, pay attention to them. Here are three passages from an magazine article entitled "What Makes Sammy Walk?" that the editor chose to reprint in large type in the middle of a page.

Less than 70 percent of U.S. men are now full-time year-round workers.

"You don't have a social life," Dave's daughter says, "and you don't do anything."

"I just put in a proposal to cut my hours to thirty-two a week and take a 20 percent pay cut," says a woman. "It's been accepted. I'm so happy."

Look for Help from the Context

The kind of magazine, scholarly journal, or newspaper in which an essay appears can tell you important things about its outlook. Some publications have a reputation for publishing articles with a particular social, cultural, or political point of view. Look for any statements of the periodical's editorial outlook. Pay attention to the magazine's title and to the titles of the other articles it contains.

For books, look at the back cover or dust jacket. They may provide a brief summary of the contents or the writer's outlook. They may also offer quotations from reviewers that highlight a book's main points.

READ FOR UNDERSTANDING, CRITICAL RESPONSE, AND TECHNIQUE

The reading strategies you employ should vary according to your goals for reading: to understand, to respond critically, or to understand writing techniques. These goals can overlap, of course, but whenever you try to do too many things as you read, your effectiveness at each task suffers. For this reason, you may often need to read a selection more than once, concentrating on a different goal each time.

Understanding

When you read for understanding, you focus on ideas and information by asking questions as you read. You try to identify the main idea (**thesis**) and the line of reasoning that supports it. You explore meanings and values. Questions can help guide your reading.

What is this selection about?

Some essays focus on one topic throughout. Other essays, just as effective, discuss several related topics, such as the effect of television on attitudes towards violence and its consequences for family life.

Brent Staples's essay, "Just Walk on By," (pp. 50–54) presents a variety of examples and brief incidents, but they all illustrate how people reacted to the author's presence as a black man.

As a reader, you need to be able to identify the topic or related topics around which an essay is constructed. Avoid the temptation to pay attention only to ideas and information that interest you. You risk misunderstanding the real focus of the essay if you give selective attention to the elements that interest you.

- **Look for cues.** Writers frequently use a title, headings in the text, or direct statements as cues identifying an essay's topic or focus.

  Title: "Women, Men, and the Media"
  Heading: "Stereotypical Portrayals of Men and Women"
  Direct Statements: "But in what ways are our behaviors, especially those of children, shaped by the inaccurate and oversimplified portraits of men and women that populate the mass media?"

- **Make a list of topics.** Review what you have read and make a list of the topics or important ideas discussed in the essay. If the elements in your list fit clearly within a broader topic, state it; or if they do not, try stating their relationship in a way that identifies the essay's focus.

  local restaurants replaced by fast food
  small shops replaced by malls
  family farms turn into agribusinesses
  hardware stores replaced by home building centers
  small towns replaced by sprawling suburbs

  Overall Topic: change from small, individualized social organizations to large, more impersonal ones

- **Look for repetition.** Identify words, ideas, or subjects that appear repeatedly in the text. Such repetitions provide evidence of an essay's focus and may even be intentional signals provided by the writer. In his essay "Just Walk on By," (pp. 50–54) for example, Brent Staples uses words like "softy," "embarrassed," and "frightening" to refer to himself, his feelings, and his reaction to the incidents he describes. He uses a contrasting set of words like "fearsomeness," "dangerous," and "terror" to describe people's (mistaken) reactions to him and to other young black men like him.

What does this selection mean?

Expository writing offers conclusions and insights. Argumentative writing offers opinions or proposes a course of action. Much of the value of these kinds of writing lies in the insights, ideas, and opinions conveyed: What the writing means.

Sometimes direct statements announce the meaning(s) of an essay. Often, however, conclusions are presented less directly or even implied, requiring you to provide an answer to the question, "What does it mean?" Good writing generally offers more than one insight or conclusion, typically a main point and several related points. Identifying the main point is an important step for any reader trying to understand an essay.

- **Highlight direct statements.** While you read or when you have finished reading an essay, try highlighting or otherwise making note of conclusions, generalizations, or opinions stated directly to readers. These can include statements (or restatements) of an essay's main idea or *thesis* like the following.

> "Taboos, big or small, are always about having to respect somebody's (often irrational) boundary—or else."
>
> —Michael Ventura
> "Don't Even Think About It!"

> "I am a peace-loving woman. But several events in the past 10 years have convinced me I'm safer when I carry a pistol."
>
> —Linda Hasselstrom
> "A Peaceful Woman Explains Why She Carries a Pistol"

For many essays, a list of such statements would provide a rough but revealing outline of the writer's exploration of a subject or of the chain of argument supporting a thesis. Here is the list Shauna Benoit compiled from her reading of Cullen Murphy's essay, "Hello, Darkness" (pp. 291–294). Note how the list clarifies the way the writer has arranged the essay.

"The average American a hundred years ago was able to sleep 20 percent longer than the average American today."

"Other evidence seems to indicate that the rate of sleep loss is in fact accelerating."

"We are laboring under a large and increasingly burdensome 'sleep deficit'. . . ."

"Many commentators would blame it on what might be called the AWOL factor—that is, the American Way of Life. We are by nature a busy and ambitious people whom tectonic social forces . . . have turned into a race of laboratory rats on a treadmill going nowhere ever faster."

"Yet electricity's ubiquitous and seemingly most innocuous use—to power the common light bulb—could not help exacting a price in sleep."

"Whatever it is that we wish or are made to do—pursue leisure, earn a living—there are simply far more usable hours now in which to do it."

- **Look for repetition and emphasis.** Look for words, phrases, details, and ideas that the writer repeats throughout a text. They are cues to ideas or issues that receive special emphasis within the text—even if not all the repetition was consciously intended by the writer. Repetitions can help you interpret the meanings and values around which an essay has been constructed and can also act as evidence for your conclusions about the essay.
- **Pause and summarize.** As you read an essay you will likely pause at a number of "resting places," between sections or paragraphs, for example. When you pause, take a moment to summarize what the essay has already said and to predict what it will say next. Then read ahead to test the accuracy of your predictions as well as your understanding of the essay.

What is this selection's purpose?

Expository and argumentative writing each have general purposes: expository—to explain and explore; and argumentative—to convince and persuade. To understand an individual essay, you need to recognize its more specific purpose(s), however.

By taking purpose into account as you read, you can more easily grasp an essay's meaning and evaluate its likely effect on readers. Sometimes, writers state their purpose directly; at other times, you will need to pay attention to repeated phrases and ideas in a text to understand its purpose. Remember, too, that essays often have secondary purposes as well as primary ones.

How is the main idea developed or supported?
Once you have identified the main idea (thesis) and related ideas in an essay, you can pay attention to the distinction between them and the examples, information, and discussions that develop or support them. To do so, try keeping two questions in mind as you read: How is the main idea developed or supported? How adequate is the development/support?

Writers often make your job easier by using familiar words or phrases to signal supporting details, discussions, or examples. Here are a few of the most familiar.

for example	supports	in the case of
for instance	explains	sheds light on
contributes to	because	illustrates
justifies	as a consequence	explains

Critical Response

Critical reading questions and challenges a text. It treats the text as a starting point, not the final word on a subject or issue. It helps you develop your own ideas and conclusions and evaluate the ideas and information in a text. Critical reading also suggests directions for your own writing. Above all, critical reading calls for activity on your part.

- **Keeping a reading journal.** A **reading journal** is a notebook, folder, or computer file in which you keep your responses to reading: notes, questions, ideas, criticisms, and the like. Turning the fleeting ideas, questions, and responses that occur to you as you read into sentences in a journal helps you remember them and makes them available for later use, perhaps in an essay of your own.

  You can organize entries in a reading journal according to the particular selection, allotting a few pages to each article, chapter, or book, for example. Or you can organize the journal by categories, such as "Responses (and Objections) to Readings About New Roles for Men and Women" or "Quotations and Information for Use in My 'Dangers of Dieting' Paper."

  A reading journal can be particularly valuable when you plan to integrate sources into your writing. Are you looking for conclusions or perspectives that differ from yours? Summarize or quote any that you encounter and explore them in writing along with your own point of view so you can discover ways to incorporate both in an essay of your own (and jot down relevant information about your source.

- **Create marginal notes. Marginal notes** are the scribbles, jottings, abbreviations, and other annotations you make in the margins of a book or magazine. Typically, you make such annotations when something you read prompts a strong response that you can record in brief form. You may wish to use marginal notes to record agreements or disagreements with what the writer says, to highlight passages or techniques you admire, or to note important ideas and information.

  Your marginal notes are most likely to be of use to you when they indicate ways to turn the text or your response to it into material for your own writing, as with the following.

  No! Putting attractive people in an ad is not necessarily a way of using sex to sell.
  People can be attractive without being sexy, for example.
  And the people belong in the ad because they show how the product works. (They wear safety goggles, for example.)
  Would it be better to have ugly people? Or just plain-looking people? I bet audiences would be critical of that approach, too.

  To make your marginal annotations as useful as possible, try to give some variety to your responses. Consider making comments in categories like these.

  Interpretations of what the author is trying to say
  Questions you wish the author had answered
  Objections to the author's conclusions
  Counterarguments the writer fails to mention
  Notes on passages you find confusing
  Evaluations of the writer's conclusions or techniques of expression.

Technique

Reading for technique helps you identify and understand writing strategies you can adapt for your own work. Patterns of organization, ways to explore ideas, strategies for presenting supporting details, and ways to use words and sentences—reading for technique brings all of these to your attention.

The questions on "Expository (or Argumentative) Techniques" and "Diction and Vocabulary" following each selection in this book focus on technique. They help you develop your ability to analyze the techniques writers employ. They also suggest ways various techniques help writers achieve a range of purposes.

- **Pay attention to expository (and argumentative) patterns.** Writers use expository and argumentative patterns in varied ways: alone or in combination, for whole essays or sections of essays. The introductions to Chapters 4–14 in this book discuss patterns and their uses. The following questions can also help you identify patterns and the roles they play.
- **Turn to "A Guide to Terms."** "A Guide to Terms" at the end of this book (pp. 571–590) contains entries for important writing techniques, from subjects such as essay introductions and closings to creating emphasis and using the correct choice of words ("Diction") or sentence structure ("Syntax"). Before reading a selection in this book or elsewhere, turn to the Guide, choose an entry that interests you, and then read with attention to the technique described in the entry.

REVIEW

Take some time to review what you have read. Think of directions for your own writing that are suggested by your reading. Evaluate a text in whole or part, and consider any unanswered question you might wish to address.

One good place to start your review is with the kinds of questions that follow the essays in this text: Meanings and Values, Expository (or Argumentative) Techniques, and Diction or Vocabulary.

When you focus on meanings and values, you look back at the different topics covered in a text and the writer's conclusions about them.

When you focus on expository or argumentative techniques, you pay attention to overall patterns of organization and development, to opening and closing strategies, to paragraph and sentence techniques, to the use of detail and kinds of support and to patterns in words and groups of words.

- **Identify opportunities for writing.** By responding to your reading with questions like the following, you can identify opportunities for your own writing.
    1. What topics or issues does the writer address satisfactorily and completely? What questions are left unanswered, problems left unsolved, or issues left unresolved?
    2. Does the writer present a balanced perspective in offering conclusions or are important explanations and points of view left unconsidered?
    3. Does the writer reason fairly and provide adequate support for conclusions? Or is the writing clearly biased, omitting evidence or misrepresenting facts and distorting others' positions?
    4. Are there other kinds of information and experiences or different ideas and approaches that might lead to conclusions differing from those offered by the writer?

- **Evaluate a source's reliability and usefulness.** Evaluating the trustworthiness of a source and identifying its strengths and limitations are important parts of a review. Ask questions like these.
    1. What conclusions or generalizations does the source offer? Are they supported adequately or do they go beyond the facts presented in the text? Are they consistent with my knowledge of the topic?
    2. What is the reputation of the author, the publisher, or the publication in which the text appeared? Is the reputation one of thoroughness and balance or of bias and carelessness? How does this piece of writing compare with others on the topic?
    3. Are there any obvious errors? Which parts of the discussion are detailed and well documented?
    4. Does the text acknowledge and document its own sources? Does it appear to treat others' opinions fairly, presenting them in clear summaries or through quotations?

- **Evaluate electronic sources with special care.** Electronic sources such as Web pages and discussion groups pose some special problems—and opportunities. These sites can be rich and provocative sources of ideas and details. At the same time, electronic sites are often produced by individuals or organizations whose trustworthiness or bias are difficult to determine—unlike those for sources in scholarly journals, well-known magazines, or books from reputable publishers. Use questions like these to evaluate electronic sources.

1. Who is responsible for the site? Are there any obvious signs of bias or distortion, such as highly selective information or exaggerated language and points of view? In what ways does the site serve the interests of the person or organization that produced it, and how might this affect its reliability?
2. Are sources for information indicated clearly, or are details, examples, and ideas presented without attribution or documentation? Is information presented clearly and carefully? Are ideas and opinions explained thoroughly? Are alternate points of view acknowledged and discussed?

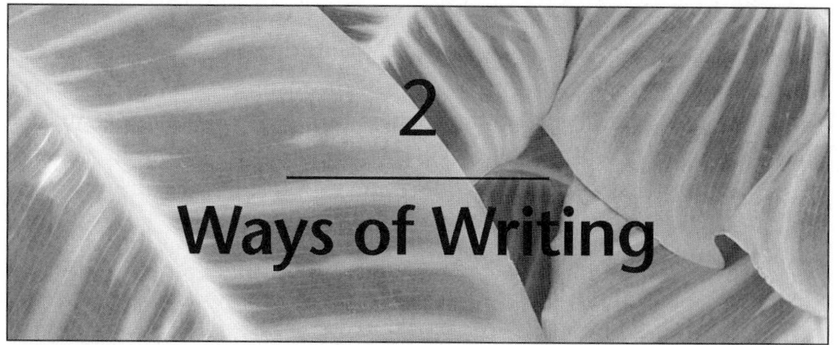

Confident writers know the importance of each of the stages of the composing process: discovering, drafting, revising, editing, and proofreading. They also know there is no single formula for all writing tasks, so they develop a variety of techniques. Making choices among strategies means paying attention to the needs of readers and the demands of a writing task.

The stages of the writing process may look regular and orderly: Discovering, Planning, Drafting, Revising, Editing, and Proofreading. The lines between these activities often blur, however. Writers often discover worthwhile new ideas as they draft and revise or amend an essay's plan based on readers' responses.

DISCOVERING

Most writing begins with an assignment or invitation: an essay for a college course, a report at work, or a call for submissions to a local newspaper, for example. Good writing can also be self-sponsored, growing from a writer's experiences and feelings and taking initial shape in the writer's journal or personal writing. Some of the best writers are those able to blend an understanding of task and audience with the impulse toward personal expression.

Look for the Assignment's Focus and Purpose—Nouns

When your writing begins with an assignment, make sure you have the exact wording—along with any explanatory comments from the person making the assignment.

Sometimes an assignment will announce a topic clearly. Often, however, assignments use nouns and noun phrases to introduce the various elements of the topic. Consider underlining any direct statements and associated nouns and noun phrases in your assignment. Then, draw on them as you write out the topic focus of the assignment. Student Rachel Baez underlined terms in the following assignment, then summarized it for herself.

> Many of the studies we have read about violent behavior among teens point to the influence of violent scenes on television and in movies. In the interviews we read, however, teenagers themselves point to different causes: social pressures, the personalities of individuals, drug and alcohol use, or a "desire for excitement and adventure." Analyze the differences among these explanations, tell which you find most convincing, and support your conclusions.

What do I see as the focus of this assignment? Two sets of explanations, one set in the studies and one set in the interviews.

Look for Purposes and Patterns in an Assignment—Verbs

The verbs and verb phrases in an assignment set goals (purposes) for your writing and may even suggest patterns for organizing and developing an essay. Verbs like *inform, explain, analyze, discuss,* and *show* suggest that your purpose will be *expository:* helping readers understand ideas, events, and information and offering carefully reasoned and supported conclusions about a subject. Words like *argue, persuade,* and *evaluate* suggest that your purpose will be argumentative: presenting reasoned arguments and supporting evidence designed to convince readers to share your opinion on an issue.

Underline such words in your assignment and write a purpose statement for your task, including information about the topic. When she went back to her assignment, here are the action words Rachel Baez underlined and the purpose statement she prepared.

> Many of the studies we have read about violent behavior among teens point to the influence of violent scenes on television and in movies. In the interviews we read, however, teenagers themselves point to different causes: social pressures, the personalities of individuals, drug and alcohol use, or a "desire for excitement and adventure." Analyze the differences among these explanations, tell which you find most convincing, and support your conclusions.

What are my purposes for this assignment? To give specific information about the differences, to offer my conclusion about the causes, and to give reasons and information that will help readers understand why my conclusions are reasonable.

Verbs and other words in the assignment may suggest (or require) patterns of exposition (or argument) for you to employ in all or part of an essay, alone or in combination with other patterns. Look for words like the following (or their synonyms) and consult the appropriate chapters in this book for ideas on using these patterns:

illustrate or provide *examples* (Chapter 3)
classify or *classification* (Chapter 4)
compare and *contrast* (Chapter 5)
create an *analogy* (Chapter 6)
analyze or explain a *process* or *process analysis* (Chapter 7)
analyze *cause* and *effect* (Chapter 8)
define or provide a *definition* (Chapter 9)
describe or create a *description* (Chapter 10)
narrate or use *narration* (Chapter 11)
reason *inductively* and *deductively* or use *induction* and *deduction* (Chapter 12)
argue or present an *argument* (Chapter 13)

Use these words, combined with information about your topic and purpose, to create a *design statement* for your writing, as did Rachel Baez.

I plan to begin with a section contrasting the sets of explanations for violent behavior among teens and indicating the specific differences. Then I will state clearly those I find convincing: media influence, social pressures, and the personalities of individuals. Finally, I will present examples and reasons why I think these are probably the most important causes for violent behavior.

Keep a Writing Journal

A *writing journal* (or *academic journal*) is a place (often a notebook or a computer file) in which you jot down ideas and discoveries, try out different perspectives on a topic, prepare rough drafts of paragraphs or essays, and note responses to readings or observations. Journals are not diaries: journals are starting places for public writing while diaries are places to record and keep your private observations.

This passage from Scott Giglio's journal, made in response to an article in his local newspaper, illustrates some of the ways journals can provide an imaginative start for the essay-writing process while at the same time be hard for anyone but the author to read.

> Article in PrJo 6/10/09 "Hispanics losing ground in employment" hadn't thought about this. Why? Article claims—uh, where is it—Census Bureau claims Hispanic families income down 5.1% more than others (can get rest of stats from article if impt. cut it out of paper) Ok Ok why happening and why important is this something to argue about or can I use it as part of paper on how people just seem to be same but lead diff. lives??

Ask Questions to Focus and Develop a Topic

Focusing questions help you identify goals or main ideas for your writing and may suggest general ways to divide a topic into parts and organize an essay around key points. They may even point toward a thesis around which you can build an essay (see pp. 18–20).

Here are some focusing questions that ask you to consider both your perspective on a topic and your readers' likely responses.

- What parts of this subject or ways of looking at it interest me the most? Is the subject as a whole interesting or does some part of it or specific way of looking at it seem more intriguing?
- What aspect of the subject is most likely to interest readers?
- What would I most like to learn about this subject? Would readers like to learn the same thing?
- What feelings about the subject do I want to share with readers? What knowledge, opinions, or insights do I want to share?
- How is my perspective different from the ones readers will likely bring with them?
- What are two (three? four?) fresh, unusual, unsettling, or controversial insights I have to share? Why may some readers have trouble understanding or accepting them?

PLANNING

Planning before you draft does not mean deciding ahead of time the exact order in which you will present each detail or idea. It does not mean determining at the start the precise conclusions you will offer and support in each paragraph. Why not?

For most writers, writing is itself a form of discovery. Putting sentences and paragraphs together brings ideas and information into often unanticipated relationships that create fresh perspectives worth sharing.

Nonetheless, if you begin writing without any plan, you are probably dooming yourself to false starts and long periods of inactivity when you try to decide what to say next—or whether to scrap the whole draft and start over.

Sometimes your exploration of a topic suggests a clear pattern and direction for your writing. Sometimes your **discovering** activities (pp. 13–16) suggest a point or **thesis** as a focus. And still other times, you have gathered so many ideas, opinions, and details that you need to move ahead before you are overwhelmed. All these are good times to begin planning.

Cluster and Diagram

Both clustering and diagramming (creating tree diagrams) lead to conceptual maps that group ideas to help you see relationships and develop focal points for your writing.

In **clustering** you develop ideas related to a central topic and link the ideas with lines to display how they are associated. Clustering encourages the interconnection of ideas. You may begin by developing a single idea into several seemingly unconnected nodes, but on further reflection recognize some connections you hadn't yet considered.

Begin by writing a concept, idea, or topic in the center of a page, and circle it. Then randomly jot down associations with the central idea, circling them and connecting them with lines to the center, like the spokes of a wheel. As you continue to generate ideas around the central focus, think about the interconnections among subsidiary ideas, and draw lines to show those.

You can also create clusters in cycles, each subsidiary idea becoming the central focus on a new page. You'll soon find that some clusters begin petering out once you've exhausted your fund of knowledge. Stand back and assess what you have. Is there enough to go on, without further consideration? If so, you may be ready to start some harder, more critical consideration of your paper's direction. If not, perhaps further strategies will open up additional ideas.

Tree diagrams resemble clusters, but their branches tend to be a little more linear, with few interconnections. Tree diagrams rely on the notion of subordination: each larger branch can lead to smaller and smaller branches. For this reason, tree diagramming can provide a useful way to visualize the components of your paper. You can even revise a tree diagram into a sort of preliminary outline (see p. 20) to use when deciding what to place in each paragraph of your paper.

Develop a Thesis

Perhaps the most important and useful planning technique involves focusing on what you want to say and do. In a finished essay, a **thesis statement** creates focus by announcing your main idea(s) to readers and helping organize supporting ideas, evidence, and discussions. An effective thesis statement is specific and limited; it announces and highlights the main idea without getting bogged down in details.

Specific: A good community exercise program makes provisions for four kinds of exercisers: people dedicated to fitness, people wanting to become fit, people struggling with health problems, and children building a base for a healthy lifestyle.

Vague: A community exercise program is good when it has room for people who want to exercise for all sorts of different reasons.

Limited: Extensive use of fossil fuels and widespread changes in agriculture have had significant effects on our climate in the last seventy-five years.

Too Broad: The last several centuries have seen massive changes in industrial production, in the use of fossil fuels, in transportation, in the development of cities, in agriculture, and in many other areas that have had an impact on our climate.

Direct: Despite all their protests to the contrary, people tend to value appearance, likelihood of success, and similarity of background in choosing a mate.

Bogged: People may say they look for spiritual qualities rather than looks in choosing a mate, yet research points out that they are more likely to be influenced by some traditional factors, and these are likely to include how a person looks, whether or not a person is likely to succeed financially or in social terms, and the extent to which the people's families, experiences, and social class are similar.

Effective thesis statements seldom start out specific, limited, and direct. They begin as **tentative thesis statements** that provide a focus for planning. As you draft and revise, they become clearer and more sharply focused, eventually taking final form in a finished essay.

Here are some techniques for developing a tentative thesis statement as part of your planning.

- ***List Your Conclusions and Evidence***
  Create a list of possible conclusions and evidence you wish to offer in an essay. Then sum them up in a **generalization,** which highlights the main idea linking them all.

  Support: Fashions in children's toys change quickly—sometimes several times a year.
  Support: Toy manufacturers must make product decisions a year before the toys appear in stores, so they need to predict trends a year ahead.
  Support: Bringing a new toy to market can cost millions of dollars.
  Support: Most new toys are not successes; many make very little money.
  Support: There are many well-managed and imaginative companies competing for business in the toy market.
  Generalization (Tentative Thesis): Manufacturing children's toys is a risky business.

- ***Create a Tentative Purpose Statement***
  Try writing yourself a note stating your potential topic along with your conclusions and possible goals for writing. To remain flexible and open to new ideas, you might begin your statement with a phrase like "I'd like to. . . ." or "I'm planning to. . . ."

> I'm planning to explain the reasons why many college students lose their motivation to work hard at their studies.
>
> —Bippin Kumar

> I'd like to tell what it felt like to be forced to leave my homeland, Haiti, so that my readers can understand why to leave something you love is to die a little.
>
> —Fredza Léger

Create a Rough Purpose/Thesis Outline

When you have in mind the various ideas and details you wish to present in an essay, create a **purpose/thesis outline** arranging the ideas and details in groups by clustering the details and summing up your conclusions and purpose for each section of an essay.

Here is Bippin Kumar's purpose outline for a paper exploring the reasons why college students may lose the motivation necessary to succeed at their studies.

1. Get readers' attention by mentioning the *bad habits* most of us have and that we may be able to correct on our own. (minor causes of the problem)

    lack of sleep

    disorganization

    distractions (television, video games, etc.)

2. Show how we are often responsible because of the choices we make and explain that we need to make wiser choices. (more serious causes)

    sports and other extracurricular activities

    friends and socializing

    Greek life

    letting ourselves get frustrated and angry over daily hassles (bookstores, commuting)

3. Conclude with problems that we can't avoid and that may require special planning or counseling to overcome. (more serious causes)

    work

    financial stresses

    family demands or problems

    lack of necessary skills

DRAFTING

Drafting involves a good deal more than setting pen to paper or fingers to keyboard and letting the words flow according to your plan. It means paying attention to the way each section of an essay relates to the other sections and to the central theme. It means making sure you begin and end the essay in ways that are clear, helpful, and interesting to readers. And it means making sure each section and each paragraph present sufficient, detailed information so that readers can understand your subject and have reasons to agree with your explanations and conclusions.

Drafting does not mean getting everything right the first time. Such a goal is likely to prove both exhausting and impossible to achieve. A much better goal is to draft with the most important features of an essay in mind and to work quickly enough so that you have sufficient time to revise later and then pay attention to details.

Keep Your Plan in Mind

As you draft, therefore, make sure that you introduce readers to your topic, indicate its importance, generate interest in it, and suggest the direction your essay will take. The essays in this collection can provide you with models of successful strategies for the beginnings of essays, and the *Introductions* entry in the Guide to Terms (at the back of the text, pp. 571–590) offers a detailed list of opening strategies. The Guide also provides advice about another important feature that should be a focus during drafting—your essay's conclusion.

Keep in mind the various sections you have planned for your essay, or keep at hand a copy of any planning strategies you have used, especially those that identify the planned parts of your essay, their general content, and their purposes.

Keep Your Focus (Thesis) in Mind

Most likely, you will also alter, revise, or change the main point (theme or thesis) of your essay as you write, and such changes often make for a better essay. By the time your essay is complete, moreover, you will also have to decide whether to announce your main point directly to readers in a concise **thesis statement** (see below), to present it less directly in a series of statements in the body of the essay, or to imply it through the details and arrangement of the paper. No matter which strategy you choose, you should have a relatively clear idea of your thesis before you begin drafting. Try stating your thesis to yourself in a tentative form. You can do this in several ways:

- Start with a phrase like "I want my readers to understand. . . ." or "The point of the whole essay is. . . ."
- Make up a title that embodies your main idea.

- Send an imaginary note to your readers: "By the time you are finished with this essay, I hope you will see (or agree with me) that. . . ."

If you want to share your knowledge of bicycling as a sport, for instance, you might try one or more of these thesis-building strategies, as in the following examples.

1. The point of the whole essay is that people can choose what kind of bicycle riders they want to be—recreational, competitive, or cross-country.
2. What Kind of Bicycle Rider Do You Want to Be?
3. By the time you finish this essay, I hope you will be able to choose the kind of bicycle riding—recreational, competitive, or cross-country—that is best for you.

A **tentative thesis statement** can guide your drafting by reminding you of your essay's main point. You can create a tentative thesis statement by summing up in a sentence or two your main point, the conclusion you plan to draw from the information and ideas you will present, or the proposition for which you plan to argue. You may eventually use a revised form of the tentative thesis statement in your completed essay as a way of announcing clearly to readers the main idea behind your writing.

For example, when Ken Chin was preparing a paper on different meanings of the phrase "recent immigrant," he used the following tentative thesis statement: "For some people, *recent immigrant* means a threat to their jobs or more strain on the resources of schools and social service agencies. For others it means fresh ideas and a broadening of our culture and outlook." In his final paper he used this thesis statement: "For some, *recent immigrant* means *cheap labor* or *higher taxes;* for others, it means *fresh ideas* and *a richer, more diverse culture.*"

Pay Attention to Sections

As you write, include statements that alert readers to the various sections, along with transitions marking the movement from one section to the next (or from paragraph to paragraph)(see "Guide to Terms": *Transitions*).

Make sure, too, that in making shifts in time, place, ideas, and content you do not confuse readers, but instead give them adequate indication of the shifts. Remember to provide readers with concrete, specific details and evidence that will give them the information they need about your topic, or the support necessary to make your explanations or arguments convincing.

Pay attention to the arrangement of your essay, especially to the patterns of exposition or argument you are employing. In any essay that classifies, for example, don't provide a detailed treatment of one category in the classification but skimpy treatment of the others—unless you have a special reason for doing so. Let your readers know, directly or indirectly, whatever pattern(s) you are employing. This will make them aware of your essay's design and will help to guide their attention to the key points you cover.

Make every effort to stick to your main idea (perhaps using your tentative thesis statement as a guide), and check to see that the parts of the essay are clearly related to and support the main idea. If you have trouble developing a section because you need more information, or because you can't express ideas as clearly as you want, make a note of the things that need to be done and then move on.

REVISING

When you shift your focus to revising, you pay special attention to the success with which your draft essay embodies your intentions and meets your readers' likely expectations. You examine the draft to see if it does a good job presenting insights, reasoning, and details. You look at the draft from a reader's perspective to see if the discussions are clear and informative, the reasoning is logical, and the examples and supporting details are related to the central theme.

Read for Revision

Revision starts with rereading—looking over your draft with a dual perspective: as an author and as a member of your potential audience. As you read for revision, keep track of the places that need more work and make note of the directions your rewriting might take, perhaps in the margins of your text. Most writers find it hard to read for revision directly from a computer screen, and they print a hard copy of their drafts on which to make notes.

Whether you are working with a handwritten text, an on-screen copy, or a printout from a word processor, you may find reading for revision most effective if you do it with a pencil or pen in hand to record your reactions and plans for revision.

Reading for revision can be even more effective when another writer does it for you (and you return the favor). Remember, collaborative readings of this sort are best done in a cooperative, rather than harshly critical, atmosphere. Your job and that of your reader(s) is to identify strengths as well as weaknesses and to suggest (if possible) ways to turn weaknesses into strong points. (For more about collaborative revising and editing, see pp. 29–30.)

Whether you are reading your own work or someone else's, you may find symbols (see box) useful shortcuts for making marginal comments to guide revision.

Reader Response Symbols

?	Could you explain this a bit more? I can't really understand this.
Add?	I would like to know more about this. I think you could use more detail here.
Leave out?	This information or this passage may not be necessary. You have already said this.
Missing?	Did you leave something out? I think there is a gap in the information, explanation, or argument here.
Confusing?	I have trouble following this explanation/ argument. The information here is presented in a confusing manner.
Reorganize?	I think this section (or paper) would be more effective if you presented it in a different order.
Interesting, Good, Effective, etc.	Your writing really works here. I like it.

You may be tempted to revise as you read, and for sentences or paragraphs that need a quick fix, this approach is often adequate. In most cases, however, your revisions need to go beyond tinkering with words and sentences if they are to lead to real improvement. You will need to pay attention to the overall focus, to the need for additional paragraphs presenting detailed evidence, and to the arrangement of the steps in an explanation or argument. To see the need for such large-scale changes, you need to read the draft paying attention to the essay as a whole, something you cannot do if you stop frequently to rework the parts. In addition, it makes little sense to correct the flaws in a sentence if you realize later on that the entire paragraph ought to be dropped.

Read with Questions

One good way to read for revision is to prepare questions that will focus your attention as you read—questions appropriate for your topic, your purposes, your pattern(s) of exposition or argument, and your intended readers. Following are some possible questions to help you evaluate your draft.

Revision Checklist

General

Does my essay have a clear topic and focus?
Does it stick to the topic and focus throughout?
How have I signaled the topic and focus to readers?
Is the essay divided into parts? What are they?
Are the parts clearly identified for readers?

Thesis and theme

Does the essay have a thesis statement? Is it clearly stated?
Is the thesis statement in the best possible location?
Should the thesis statement be more (or less) specific?
Are all the different parts of the essay clearly related to the thesis statement or the central theme?
In what ways have I reminded readers of the thesis or theme in the course of the essay? Do I need to remind them more often or in other ways?

Introductions and conclusions

Does my introduction make the topic clear? Does it interest readers in what I will have to say?
Does my introduction give readers some indication of the arrangement of the essay and its purpose(s)?
Does the conclusion help tie together the main points of the essay or remind readers of the significance of the information and ideas I have presented?
Does my conclusion have a clear purpose or have I ended the essay without any clear strategy?

Information and ideas

Have I presented enough information and enough details so that readers will feel they have learned something worthwhile about the topic?

At what specific places would the essay be improved if I added more information?

What information can be cut because it is repetitive, uninteresting, or unrelated to the topic or theme of the essay?

Is my information fresh and worth sharing? Do I need to do more thinking or research so that the content of my essay is worth sharing?

Do the examples and details I present support my conclusions in a convincing way? Do I need to explain them more fully?

Would more research or thinking enable me to offer better support? What kinds of support would readers find helpful?

Have I learned something new or worthwhile about my topic and communicated it to readers?

Sentences and paragraphs

Have I divided the essay into paragraphs that help readers identify shifts in topic, stages in an explanation, steps in a line of reasoning, key ideas, or important segments of information?

Does each paragraph make its topic or purpose clear to readers?

Which short paragraphs need greater development through the addition of details or explanations?

Which long paragraphs could be trimmed or divided?

Do the sentences reflect what I want to say? Which sentences could be clearer?

Are the sentences varied in length? Do they provide appropriate emphasis to key ideas?

Can I word the explanations or arguments more clearly?

Can I use more vivid and concrete language?

Would the paper benefit from more complicated or imaginative language? From simpler, more direct wording?

Readers' perspective

In what ways are my readers likely to view this topic or argument? Have I taken their perspectives into account?

What do I want my readers to learn from this essay? What opinion do I want them to share? What do I want them to do?

Have I considered what my readers are likely to know or believe and how this will shape their response to my purpose(s) for writing?

Sample Student Essay

Here is the draft of an essay Sarah Lake produced in response to an assignment asking her to write about a community of some sort, taking the perspective of an outsider trying to understand how the community works and what kinds of relationships people in the community form. The marginal comments on the paper are notes she has addressed to the classmates (peer readers) who will be responding to her paper with revision suggestions.

Welcome to the Gym!

As I stepped up to the door to the field house I saw myself in the reflection from the door. I had chosen mesh shorts, a white v-neck T-shirt, and tattered old sneakers in hope to "fit in" with the crowd. Luckily, I still possess the Ram sticker on the back of my I.D. I was all set. I was in. A cheery eyed student asked for my I.D., and pointed me towards the training room. So far, so good, I thought. My only hopes were that the gym was going to be a great place.

I've tried to make this interesting. Is it?

This is the community I studied. Is my purpose clear?

The smell was rather distinct; one part sweat, one part machine oil, and one part cleaner, or maybe it was the chlorine coming from the pool. Surprisingly, it was a rather welcoming smell. The kind of smell that says "Come on in, have fun, workout, sweat, be hot and sticky and smelly, it's O.K." I liked what it had to say, so I continued on, farther into the training room. As I stepped inside to the training room, heavy breathing and strenuous shouts of "One!, Two!, Three!" could be heard. The shouting seemed common, and went unnoticed by regulars. Weightlifters, mostly men, would grunt, scream, moan, and sometimes yell in agony as they tried to lift weights two, three times the weight they could handle. Their heads turned a tomato red and looked as if they were about to explode. Their veins,

I added a lot of detail. Does it work?

like thick rope, popped through the skin on their necks, arms, and legs. Due to the fact that I'm not a weightlifter or a man, I surely don't understand the meaning behind this behavior. It looked rather painful and it wasn't very flattering to them, but it was entertaining.

I squirmed my way through the machines, and people, and found myself a spot on one of the stair masters. I curiously stared at the screen in front of me. Blinking letters zoomed across the screen reading enter your weight and then press enter. Enter my weight? That's a lot to ask of a girl. I thought about it, and even considered lying to the machine, but reality set in, I realized it was just a machine. Why lie to a machine? I punched in my weight, and continued to answer the questions the screen produced.

As I started my workout, I began to gaze around and inspect everyone's interaction with each other. "Rules of the Gym" were listed on the wall and were followed by everyone. Everyone respected everyone and everything. On the other hand rules for socializing weren't posted, but underlying rules seemed to be understood. Socializing while working out or better yet, while in motion was not encouraged. Talking only took place while one was motionless or waiting for a machine. It seemed as if it took so much concentration to work out that no one could even talk while doing so. I, on the other hand, couldn't wait to talk when I got finished. I felt like I had gone through withdrawal. I needed some sort of outlet to make the time go by and my workout faster so I turned from people behavior watching to people's attire watching.

I think my punctuation and grammar got a bit out of control at times in this draft. Help!

Gym attire was rather diverse. Some wore the typical workout uniform, which consisted of tight spandex. It included tops, tops over tops, bottoms, bottoms over bottoms, etc., etc. Others wore outfits very similar to my own which was very comforting. My favorite outfit (I'm being sarcastic) was on a young woman, about 21, who turned more heads in twenty minutes than most supermodels do in their careers. It consisted of, from top to bottom: a bright pink scrunchie (one of those cloth elastics), a black headband, a bright pink jog bra, black lycra spandex, covered by a workout g-string, also bright pink in color. As I worked my eyes down to her legs and then to her feet I noticed she had boxing sneakers on. Smashing, was the only word to describe her ensemble.

Is this too much detail?

Peer Response

Before you revise (or in between successive drafts), getting a look at your work through another's eyes can help you spot strengths and weaknesses and identify steps you can take to improve your essay. To do this, ask a person or a group of people to read and comment on the strengths and weaknesses of your draft essay. Ask them, too, to suggest ways the writing might be improved. Their comments are most likely to be useful if you ask them to respond to specific questions (like those in the list on pp. 25–27) and to make concrete suggestions for improvement.

Here are some comments students Tonya Williams and Dave Cisneros made on Sarah Lake's essay.

Does this essay have a clear and interesting thesis statement or generalization?

TONYA: I don't see any thesis statement. The assignment asked us to make a generalization about the community. What is yours?

DAVE: In the planning materials you shared with us, you talked about the reasons people were exercising. Could you add a generalization about the motivations of people in this community?

Does this essay provide detailed examples that support or explain the essay's thesis statement or generalization?

TONYA: I like some of the pictures of gym life that you provide, but I don't see how they fit with any kind of generalization. The last example probably talks too much about clothes.

DAVE: I suggest cutting the last paragraph. It doesn't fit with the rest of the paper.

Are the sentences clear and effective? How might they be improved?

TONYA: A lot of the sentences begin with "I," so the paper seems to focus on you rather than the community you are exploring.

DAVE: I like the way you write. I think your sentences are easy to read in general. At times, though, the paper seems a bit informal. I'm not sure whether the writing is too informal in style or whether you are focusing more on your personal feelings than on the kinds of observations and conclusions you are trying to explain.

Are there any places the grammar and spelling might be improved?

TONYA: I think you have some grammar problems, especially fragments and run-ons. I put a question mark next to these on the paper.

DAVE: I noticed a few spelling problems and other small errors. I tried to mark them, but I may have missed a few.

EDITING, PROOFREADING, AND FINAL REVISION

After you have carefully rewritten your essay at least one time and perhaps several, you can focus on editing and on the final revision. In creating your finished paper, pay special attention to matters such as the style and clarity of sentences and paragraphs as well as correctness in grammar and usage. Before you hand in your final draft, carefully correct any typographical errors along with any mistakes in spelling or expression that remain.

Here is the final version of Sarah Lake's paper, including some revisions that she made during a last reading and some editing before she typed the final copy. In revising, Sarah took into account the comments of her classmates and those her instructor wrote on a copy of her draft. In addition, she went back to her planning document for ideas she left out of the draft, and she developed these ideas at some length in the revised version of the paper. The comments in the margin of the paper below have been added to highlight features of the essay.

Welcome to the Gym:
A Community of Worriers

As I stepped up to the door of the field house, I saw my reflection in the glass, and I started worrying. I had chosen mesh shorts, a white V-necked T-shirt, and tattered old sneakers in hopes of fitting in with the community I planned to observe: people exercising for fitness inside the gym. I was worrying about how well I would fit in. After my visit, I realized I fit in quite well. Not only had I dressed appropriately, but I was also worried, and worrying about appearance seemed to be one trait everybody at the gym shared. <u>It seems to be the attribute that defines this community and ties its members together.</u>

Moves from personal experience to the conclusion that will be explored in the essay. Thesis statement

As I stepped inside the training room I heard heavy breathing and strenuous shouts of "One! Two! Three!" Weightlifters, mostly men, were grunting, screaming, moaning, and yelling in agony as they tried to lift weights two, three times more than they could handle. Their heads turned tomato red, and they looked as if they were about to explode. I'm neither a man nor a weightlifter, and I had no idea why they were trying to overexert themselves, or so it seemed to me.

Paragraph presents observations

When I spoke with several of the weightlifters, they admitted that for many people who spend time lifting weights, appearance is a primary concern. They claimed that many male weightlifters begin exercising because they feel inferior about their physical appearance or because they want to get that "He-man" or "Caveman" look that they consider an ideal for men. Though the men I talked to said that they, personally, weren't that anxious about the way they looked, they also admitted that they felt that potential dates pay more attention to a man who has "bulked up." I asked why they felt it was important to have a muscular and masculine appearance in today's society, especially when a lot of people (women especially) talk about the need for men to be "sensitive." I was surprised by the answers because they seemed to reveal worry and insecurity—which was surprising coming from a group of very well-muscled college men. The weightlifters said they thought sensitivity was a good thing, and they claimed to work toward it in their relationships. They also said that sensitivity grows out of self-confidence,

Evidence supports overall thesis

Observations likely to surprise and intrigue reader

and that for men self-confidence often comes through physical fitness and athletic ability.

Though the weightlifters seemed sincere, as a woman I felt rather awed by their appearance and kept waiting for one of them to knock one of the female exercisers over the head and drag her back to his cave. This thought made me shift my attention to the women, most of whom were working on machines like Stair Masters, stationary bicycles, or Nautilus. To enter into the women's part of this community, I squirmed my way through the machines and people, and I found a spot on one of the Stair Masters. I stared curiously at the screen in front of me. Blinking letters zoomed across the screen asking me to enter my weight. "Enter my weight," I thought. "That's a lot to ask of a girl." I even thought about lying, but then I got embarrassed about lying to a machine. Later, when I shared this worry with some of the women at the gym, I realized they shared my apprehension and a lot of my other worries.

Transition to second set of observations

Personal experience supports thesis

Observations act as evidence for thesis

Like the men, the women shared many concerns about their appearance, especially about their attractiveness and about the relationship of appearance to self-confidence. They spoke of how the *Baywatch* girls are the ideals of appearance for women in our society, and of how they felt a need to compete with the "Barbies" of this world, even though such an appearance is unrealistic for the average woman. They also talked about having a kind of balance scale in their heads. As their weight increases, they feel less attractive, and as their weight decreases, they feel more attractive. They pointed out how magazines, TV programs, and movies seem to equate thinness with attractiveness and link attractiveness to self-confidence. Though they admitted that working women with responsibilities as wives and mothers might not have time or energy to work out in a gym, they worried about how their self-confidence might

Summarizes interviews

suffer if they didn't have the opportunity to exercise to control their weight.

After my time on the Stair Master came to an end and I had finished talking to the members of the gym community, I left, feeling as though I fit in. I was a worrier and I had dressed like many of the women. On my way out, however, I passed a woman dressed in a daring pink and black outfit who began turning heads as soon as she walked in the door. I started worrying again, and I knew the people in the gym were now worrying even more about their looks.

Conclusion echoes main point

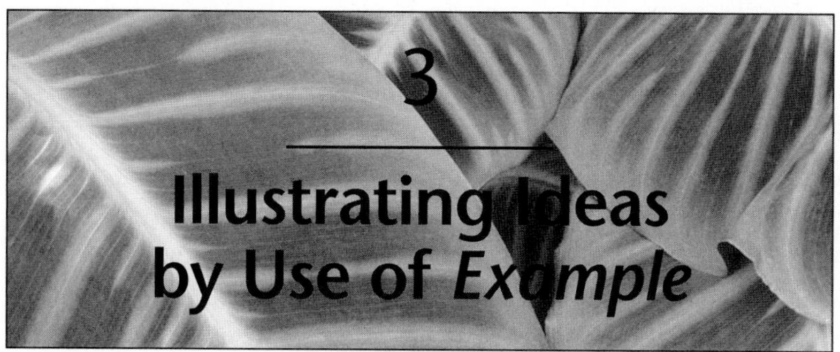

3 Illustrating Ideas by Use of *Example*

The use of examples to illustrate an idea under discussion is the most common, and frequently the most efficient, pattern of exposition. It is a method we use almost instinctively; for instance, instead of talking in generalities about the qualities of a good city manager, we cite Angela Lopes as an example. We may go further and illustrate her virtues as a manager by a specific account of her handling a crucial situation during the last power shortage or hurricane. In this way, we put our abstract ideas into concrete form—making them clearer and more convincing. As readers, we look for examples as well, often responding to general statements with a silently voiced question, "For instance?" and expecting the writer to provide us with appropriate specifics.

Examples can be short or long: a brief illustration within a sentence or a fully developed instance filling a paragraph or more. They can appear singly, or they can work together in clusters, as in the following paragraph where brief examples serve to make a generalization vivid and convincing.

> *There were many superstitions regarding food.* Dropping a fork meant that company would be coming. If we were to take a second helping of potatoes while we still had some left on our plate, someone always predicted that a person more hungry than we were would drop in during the day. Every housewife believed that food from a tin can had to be removed immediately after opening, or it would become deadly poison within a few seconds. My mother always ran across the room to dump the contents immediately.
>
> —Lewis Hill, "Black Cats and Horse Hairs"

Generality

Example 1
Example 2
Example 3
Example 4

Whether making an explanation clear, a generality more convincing, or an argument more persuasive, examples work in the same way. They make the general more specific, the abstract more concrete, and in so doing they illustrate a sound principle of writing.

WHY USE EXAMPLES?

Examples clarify by showing readers what a general statement means in terms of individual events, people, or ideas. By pointing out students who use "lucky" pens to take a test, lawyers who wear "special" ties or shoes to a big day in court, and engineers who begin a new project with a special breakfast, a writer can aid understanding of the statement, "Even educated people often make superstition part of their everyday lives."

On the other hand, lack of clear illustrations may leave readers with only a hazy conception of the points the writer has tried to make. Even worse, readers may try to supply examples from their own knowledge or experience, leading them to an impression different from that intended by the author. Since writers are the ones trying to communicate, clarity is primarily their responsibility.

Not only do good examples put into clear form what otherwise might remain vague and abstract, but they also serve to make generalizations and conclusions convincing. Not every generality requires supporting examples, of course. An audience with even a passing familiarity with films probably does not need extended examples to understand and accept the statement, "Action films are characterized by physical violence, explosions, chase scenes, and broadly drawn characters." Conclusions about unfamiliar or complicated subjects, technical discussions, and perspectives that may be difficult for readers to share initially usually call for examples. College instructors, for instance, will usually look for examples to render an interpretation convincing; business and public audiences will search reports and memorandums for examples that make the writer's judgments plausible.

With something specific for readers to visualize, a statement becomes more convincing—but convincing within certain limitations.

If you use the Volvo as an example of Swedish manufacturing, the reader is probably aware that this car may not be entirely typical. For ordinary purposes of explanation, the Volvo example could make its point convincingly enough. In supporting an argument, however, you need either to choose an example that is clearly typical or to present several examples to show that you have represented the situation fairly.

CHOOSING A STRATEGY

As a writer, you need to recognize not only places where individual examples can aid your writing but also occasions when your ideas might be most effectively presented through the use of examples as the primary strategy for an essay. If you have a fresh, unusual, or surprising conclusion to offer readers, consider using examples in a **thesis-and-support strategy.** Announce your thesis (perspective, interpretation) to readers, then offer evidence of its reasonableness in the form of varied, carefully developed examples, as illustrated in the following plan for an essay.

Tentative Thesis Modern technology offers many creative outlets for writers, musicians, and artists.

Supporting Point Cable television provides opportunities for creative work through the large number of television programs on its schedule.

Example: It provides work for scriptwriters of all kinds: dramatic, documentary, news, sports, and comedy.

Example: It creates opportunities for actors, cinematographers, and directors.

Example: It produces programs calling for original music, art, and graphics.

Supporting Point Software development calls for creative artists as well as software engineers.

Example: Games require scriptwriters, artistic designers, graphic artists, and composers (for music to accompany the action).

Example: Office programs require graphic design; home and landscape design programs involve artistic and graphic design; educational software calls for writers and designers (sometimes even music).

Supporting Point The World Wide Web provides the means to create and distribute works of art without significant financial resources.

Example: Composers and performers can create musical works without hiring performers or renting a studio and distribute their work on the Web.

Example: Desktop publishing allows writers to create printed copies of their novels, essays, and other writing without the expense or difficulty of working with publishers and printers.

Example: Design programs and drawing/painting programs let visual artists create without having to maintain a studio or buy expensive materials, and the Web gives them a way to advertise and distribute their work.

If an extended, especially detailed example covers all aspects of your topic that need explaining or provides a particularly appropriate instance of your main idea, consider using a **representative example strategy.** A representative example needs to be interesting in itself because it will serve as the main focus of the writing, preceded or followed (or both) by the main idea it illustrates.

In this chapter, Andy Rooney's "In and of Ourselves We Trust" (pp. 47–48) provides a particularly successful instance of a representative example (stopping at a red light when no one is around) followed by the writer's conclusion that "the whole structure of our society depends on mutual trust, not distrust."

CHOOSING EXAMPLES

Successful writers select and use examples cautiously, keeping in mind their readers and their own specific purposes for communicating. To be effective, an example must be pertinent to the chief qualities of the generality it illustrates. In writing about horror films, for instance, you might offer this interpretation: "The films generally have contemporary settings, yet most reinforce traditional, even old-fashioned, roles for both men and women." To be pertinent, examples would need to address the various elements of this thesis, including the contrast between the contemporary setting and the old-fashioned values, the roles of both men and women, and exceptions to the conclusion (the interpretation applies to "most" horror films, but not all).

Examples should be representative as well, presenting in a fair manner the range of situations, people, or ideas to which a generality applies. In discussing a new approach to education, you should be ready to consider it in terms of urban and rural as well as suburban communities. Your interpretation of a play, film, novel, or recording should take into account the work as a whole, not simply those parts corresponding most directly to your thesis. If you wish readers to adopt your perspective, you should choose examples that represent any important differences among their outlooks, often the product of differences in background, gender, ethnicity, or education.

It is possible to provide too many examples and make them too long, but for most writers, the opposite is usually the problem. We frequently underestimate the number of examples needed because we pay attention only to those that come to mind most readily. Almost any part of a subject can provide potential examples, however. With your generality or thesis in mind, look for representative events, situations, quotations, or people; typical attitudes, opinions, or ideas; and characteristic physical and emotional details. Make a conscious effort to draw examples from a variety of sources.

- *Your Experiences:* Draw on your involvement with the topic. For an essay on work, draw on jobs you have held. For an essay on sports, think of your experiences (pleasant and unpleasant) as an athlete or spectator. For a report on health care, begin with your own broken bones, doctor's appointments, sessions in the dentist's chair, and trips to the hospital either as patient or visitor.
- *Your Reading:* Add to your knowledge of a topic by searching a library catalog or using an Internet search engine. Choose articles and reports that expand your understanding and suggest the ways others may respond to your conclusions. Draw examples (including statistics) from your reading, being careful to acknowledge your sources using whatever documentation strategies your audience considers appropriate (such as the Modern Language Association or American Psychological Association styles).
- *Other People:* Think about other people whose experiences are consistent with your conclusions: the neighbor whose job history

reflects a changing view of loyalty to an employer or your cousin whose reliance on the Internet for shopping illustrates changing patterns of consumption.

- *One from a Group:* When your thesis or generalization applies to a wide variety of people, situations, organizations, or experiences, you may be tempted to provide numerous examples as a way of representing the group as a whole but instead end up with a cluster of indistinct, ineffective illustrations. Instead, consider focusing on one or two examples and presenting them in extended detail that explains and supports your conclusions. To illustrate the features of science fiction movies, for example, turn to one or two films likely to be familiar to your readers.

There is no set length for effective examples. They can be as short as a few words or as long as several paragraphs in length, depending on the purpose they serve. For a thesis-and-support essay, however, a paragraph of four to six sentences provides a good measure.

Each paragraph supporting your main idea should provide several brief examples (as in the sample paragraph on p. 35) or several sentences presenting the example and discussing it in detail. Writers often overestimate how much their readers know about a subject and offer examples lacking in important ideas and information, as in the following student example from a paper for a course on public health policy.

> Nonprescription drugs are still drugs and can be dangerous if misused. Many people make themselves ill by doubling or tripling the dosage of nonprescription drugs in order to get a greater effect.

When her instructor and fellow students pointed out the lack of information in this paragraph, the writer realized that she could have included examples of the toxic effects of high dosages of aspirin and other painkillers, of allergic reactions to excessive intake of vitamin and mineral supplements, and of physical damage that can result from overuse of digestive remedies—examples her readers would have found informative and useful.

Remember, a good example must be either instantly obvious to readers or fully developed so that they learn exactly what it illustrates, and how. Sometimes, however, illustration may be provided best by something other than a real-life example—a fictional anecdote, an analogy, or perhaps a parable that demonstrates the general idea. Here even greater care is needed to be sure these examples are both precise and clear.

Student Essay

If you looked back over the events in your life, how would you interpret them? Would you be able to state the perspective or idea that ties them together? The generality that runs through them? How would you select and present examples to illustrate the generality and help readers understand and share your perspective?

Adrian Boykin's experiences as a stutterer and his struggles to deal with the impediment shaped many of the events in his life, and he is able to share an understanding of his experiences and his perspective through carefully selected examples in the essay that follows.

Overcoming an Impediment: A Rite of Passage

Adrian Boykin

"Sp, sp, sp, sp spit it out already Adrian!" These were among the insults I received from classmates throughout elementary and junior high school. Inheriting the stuttering, dominantly linked phenotype from my father's side of my family has affected my speech, and in turn my relationships, since I first began to speak.

Dramatic opening

Thesis statement

Starting when I was only eight years old and in the third grade, I took speech lessons at school in an attempt to overcome a speech impediment. The trait dates back to my great-grandfather. In the last four generations, many Boykin men have expressed a stutter, while others, such as my younger brother, have not. Throughout childhood I often encountered a block in my speech at the first word of each sentence when beginning to speak. From third grade through my freshman year in high school, I participated in monthly, one-on-one speech classes. Through my working diligently with a speech specialist, I have, for the most part, been able to overcome this genetic defect successfully and speak without impediment.

Short examples of how his family has been affected

As a stutterer, it is difficult to explain to a nonstutterer why we sometimes just can't get the words out. Speaking in a casual one-on-one situation has never been a problem for me. Only in stressful situations

Background explanation of stuttering

where a large group of people were gathered, or in a setting where everyone is attempting to speak, did my speech impediment become evident. At these times I would compare the first word of my sentence to ice cream that has been in the freezer for a month on the coldest setting. No matter how hard you try to get a full scoop out of the container, only small tastes of the ice cream will come out. Unfortunately, for the stutterer, that small, unfulfilling taste of ice cream is the first syllable of the stutterer's first word. Repeatedly.

Uses an analogy to explain—see Chapter 4

The problems I encountered with speech never rivaled what my dad experienced growing up. Unable to answer the telephone, speak in class, or even speak without incessant stuttering at the dinner table, my father attended a summer camp in Michigan for three months each summer, four summers in a row, with the hopes of correcting his impediment. Today, though he still often stutters momentarily at the beginning of his sentences, he is a successful custom furniture designer and businessman. About ten years ago, still having difficulty speaking in front of groups, Dad completed the Toastmasters speaking course. Because his speech impediment hindered his social development for so many years and in so many ways, he was determined to never let my impediment hold me back socially.

Examples of how his father's life was affected

Because children are often cruel, I was picked on many times by my peers in elementary and junior high school for stuttering. Friends often made fun of me by imitating the stutter I had at the beginning of my sentences. Furthermore, I grew up watching television shows such as *In Living Color* and movies such as *Harlem Nights* and *Billy Madison,* which depict people with speech impediments as being stupid outcasts or class clowns. Looking back at these television shows and movies, I sometimes ask myself why dehumanization of stutterers is tolerated by the public. Racist stabs at minorities are viewed as disgusting and intolerable by the masses, but attacks and mockery aimed at stutterers are seen as hilarious.

Short examples of how stuttering made him feel in elementary school and junior high school

Fortunately, my speech impediment was never something that hindered me from experiencing all the things that other students with normal speech experienced. Because my father knew firsthand what it was like to have a speech impediment, he made sure that I was given therapy to correct my stutter. My father first sent me to a speech therapist affiliated with my elementary school in Denver. Only eight years old, I saw speech therapy as a fun way to get out of class and meet another boy, Michael, who also had a "block in his throat." Attending therapy with another child helped me get away from the feeling that I was alone in my speech problem. During speech class, though, I really never concentrated on Michael. What I remember is my therapist, Mrs. Rainart. "Wow," I always thought, "she is the nicest lady, and pretty too!" This was better than playing with G.I. Joes! By fifth grade, the main reason I liked going to therapy was because I liked seeing her.

Extended example

Elementary school—relationships with another stutterer and with therapist

Fifth grade was a time of physical change and of change in how I looked at the girls. Mrs. Rainart's milky white teeth and spiral, burgundy-colored hair made speech therapy more than tolerable for me. You know how elementary school children all have a crush on a teacher at one time or another? I guess that teacher was Mrs. Rainart for me.

Extended example

Begins to develop new kinds of relationships—successfully

My mother got a job in Boulder with Celestial Seasonings Tea Company when I was eleven. As a result we moved to a house in a suburb called Broomfield, wherein my father promptly found me another speech therapist in Boulder. The change in scenery made me nervous. Entering Birch Elementary School, I had to make all new friends. Fortunately, everyone at Birch was really nice. My confidence was soaring, and I was convinced that I no longer needed to go to some stupid speech class.

Then came my worst-ever stuttering experience. For my seventh-grade birthday, my parents let me have a party for both my boyfriends and my girlfriends. The

Extended example

night started well, with my friends and I boogying down to the latest Michael Jackson album. I was wearing my nicest polyester shirt to go with my loafers and tight Wranglers. My parents interrupted our disco party for cake, ice cream, and presents.

With the speech impediment seemingly gone, I started socializing with the group while I was opening my gifts. My girlfriend, Emily, gave me the coolest Michael Jordan poster. I began to tell Emily how much I appreciated her gift, when out of nowhere, a heavy encompassing piece of cake got stuck in my throat, and I could only stutter to Emily. I ran to the sink to get water when I realized it wasn't the cake that wasn't letting me speak, but that frickin' stutter. Trying to regain my composure, I went back into the family room and said to Emily, "Th, th, th, th." Once more, I tried to thank Emily, "Th, th, th, th."

Junior high school stuttering undermines relationships

Embarrassed, I could not speak, but only heard the laughter of ten wild seventh graders reverberating throughout the room. My good friend Shawn, always quick-witted, decided to slash open my wound a little further and promptly pour a tablespoon of salt on it. He said clearly and loudly, "Dang, Adrian speaks about as well as a cat barks."

More than anything, my stuttering as a child pushed me to aspire to excel socially. Throughout high school, I struggled to become a class leader whom others admired as someone who would express the concerns and wants of the school and group.

High school stuttering pushes him to excel

At the end of my junior year, my speech impediment was rarely noticeable. Furthermore, I wanted to prove to myself that I could speak in the most pressure-packed situations without a problem. Thus, I decided to run for senior class vice president. I gave my election speech in front of my senior class of about 300 and Broomfield High School's faculty. Approaching the podium, I was nervous, but confident in my speech. Usually having difficulties with my first word, I concentrated on my therapy tactics. "Keep it slow in the first

Extended example

Meets and overcomes challenges

Develops new relationships and self-confidence

word," I reminded myself. "Breathe deeply and imagine being in a one-on-one conversation." The sweat flowing in large beads down my back, I delivered a strong, stutter-free, three-minute speech. The crowd could not concentrate on my impediment because there was none. My classmates were forced to concentrate on the content of my speech. The next day I was given word of my election as class vice president.

During my senior year I realized that I was no longer getting any comments about my speech. I also started using my techniques learned from seven years of speech therapy without thinking about them. I had not been in a dusty brown, eight-by-twelve cubicle for three years. Even better, there was no reason for me to ever foresee going back. My father and I sat down and discussed our impediment from time to time, but his assistance was all I would need.

No longer needs speech therapy

By the time I graduated from high school, I had overcome the biggest fear of my speech impediment. Speaking in front of large groups was no longer a time where my speech impediment would reveal itself. As the senior class vice president, I was responsible for giving the closing address at graduation, probably the most high-pressure speech of all. For three weeks I rehearsed my graduation speech.

Extended example

On his own—biggest challenge

The biggest speech of my life was delivered in front of 2,000 friends, classmates, faculty, and family. The football stadium stands were packed like a Mexican piñata for a Cinco de Mayo celebration. Over 2,000 were in attendance, all to hear my closing address. Walking into the stadium, I looked at the happy but tightly squeezed crowd and realized that this was going to be a special moment in my eighteen-year-old life. More than the high school graduation that the class was celebrating, I was celebrating my ability to speak in front of crowds.

For the following two hours I tried listening intently to all of the other speeches. I found myself getting very nervous, but my stutter did not once come to my mind as being a problem. I was only nervous because I was soon going to be on the biggest stage I had ever been on before. Principal Martin gave a short address after we received our diplomas. He then said, "Ladies and gentlemen, the closing address will be given by Class Vice President Adrian Boykin."

I looked to the crowd, started slowly, and let my voice flow continuously and smoothly, similar to an eagle soaring through the sky. As I concluded, I looked into the dots of faces in the crowd and my eyes met my father's.

Throwing my graduation cap into the still, windless sky, I celebrated a rite of passage.

Builds to climax emphasizing his victory over the impediment and the barriers it creates

ANDY ROONEY

ANDREW A. ROONEY was born in 1920 in Albany, New York. Drafted into the army while still a student at Colgate University, he served in the European theater of operations as a *Stars and Stripes* reporter. After the war Rooney began what has been a prolific and illustrious career as a writer-producer for various television networks—chiefly for CBS—and has won numerous awards, including the Writers Guild Award for Best Script of the Year (six times—more than any other writer in the history of the medium) and three National Academy Emmy awards. The author of a number of magazine articles in publications like *Esquire, Harper's,* and *Playboy,* Rooney is nonetheless probably most familiar for his regular appearances as a commentator on the television program *60 Minutes.* Rooney also writes a syndicated column, which appears in more than 250 newspapers, and has lectured on documentary writing at various universities. His most recent books are *My War* (1995), Sincerely, Andy Rooney (1999), *Common Nonsense* (2002), *Years of Minutes* (2003) and *Out of My Mind* (2006). He lives in Rowayton, Connecticut.

In and of Ourselves We Trust

"In and of Ourselves We Trust" was one of Rooney's syndicated columns. Rooney's piece uses one simple example to illustrate a generality. He draws from it a far-reaching set of conclusions: that we have a "contract" with each other to stop for red lights—and further, that our whole system of trust depends on everyone doing the right thing.

Last night I was driving from Harrisburg to Lewisburg, Pa., a distance of about 80 miles. It was late, I was late, and if anyone asked me how fast I was driving, I'd have to plead the Fifth Amendment to avoid self-incrimination. 1

At one point along an open highway, I came to a crossroads with a traffic light. I was alone on the road by now, but as I approached the light, it turned red, and I braked to a halt. I looked left, right, and behind me. Nothing. Not a car, no suggestion of headlights, but there I sat, waiting for the light to change, the only human being, for at least a mile in any direction. 2

I started wondering why I refused to run the light. I was not afraid of being arrested, because there was obviously no cop anywhere 3 around and there certainly would have been no danger in going through it.

Much later that night, after I'd met with a group in Lewisburg and had climbed into bed near midnight, the question of why I'd stopped for that light came back to me. I think I stopped because it's part of a contract we all have with each other. It's not only the law, but it's an agreement we have, and we trust each other to honor it: We don't go through red lights. Like most of us, I'm more apt to be restrained from doing something bad by the social convention that disapproves of it than by any law against it. 4

It's amazing that we ever trust each other to do the right thing, isn't it? And we do, too. Trust is our first inclination. We have to make a deliberate decision to mistrust someone or to be suspicious or skeptical. 5

It's a darn good thing, too, because the whole structure of our society depends on mutual trust, not distrust. This whole thing we have going for us would fall apart if we didn't trust each other most of the time. In Italy they have an awful time getting any money for the government because many people just plain don't pay their income tax. Here, the Internal Revenue Service makes some gestures toward enforcing the law, but mostly they just have to trust that we'll pay what we owe. There has often been talk of a tax revolt in this country, most recently among unemployed auto workers in Michigan, and our government pretty much admits that if there were a widespread tax revolt here, they wouldn't be able to do any thing about it. 6

We do what we say we'll do. We show up when we say we'll show up. 7

I was so proud of myself for stopping for that red light. And inasmuch as no one would ever have known what a good person I was on the road from Harrisburg to Lewisburg, I had to tell someone. 8

Meanings and Values

1. Explain the concept of a "contract we all have with each other" (Par. 4). How is the "agreement" achieved (Par. 4)?
2. Why do you suppose exceeding the speed limit (Par. 1) would not also be included in the "contract"? Or is there some other reason for Rooney's apparent inconsistency?
3. Explain the significance of the title of this selection.

Expository Techniques

1. How does the example of the red light "work" for readers? How does an analysis of this example help us better understand each other?
2. What other uses of example do you find in the selection?
3. What, if anything, do the brief examples in Paragraph 6 add to this piece? (See "Guide to Terms": *Evaluation.*)

Diction and Vocabulary

1. Does it seem to you that the diction and vocabulary levels of this selection are appropriate for the purpose intended? Why or why not? (Guide: *Diction.*)
2. Could this be classified as a formal essay? Why or why not? (Guide: *Essay.*)
3. Rooney uses the word "trust" six times in Paragraphs 4–6. How effective is the repetition of such a word? Why might Rooney have chosen this strategy?

Read to Write

1. **Collaborating:** Working in groups of three, list several examples that could help convey a main idea similar to the generality Rooney advances in his essay. Then, together, write a brief essay using these examples and employing a casual tone of voice similar to Rooney's.
2. **Considering Audience:** Andy Rooney often appears on television as an oral commentator on events and social behavior. The style of this essay is more similar in some ways to spoken language than written language. How effective is this style for the essay's audience? Why is it or isn't it effective? Rewrite Rooney's essay in a more formal style and analyze the effectiveness of your new version.
3. **Developing an Essay:** Choose an experience that revealed to you something about your personal characteristics, the traits of family or friends, or the "character" of a larger cultural or social group to which you belong. Using Rooney's essay as a model, use this experience as an example to illustrate a generality about your subject, and draw also on briefer examples in the course of your essay.

(NOTE: Suggestions for topics requiring development by use of EXAMPLE are on pp. 75–76 at the end of this chapter.)

BRENT STAPLES

BRENT STAPLES was born in 1951 in Chester, Pennsylvania. He received his B.A. in 1973 from Widener University and his Ph.D. (in psychology) in 1982 from the University of Chicago. He is a member of the *New York Times* editorial board, writing on matters of culture and society. He was formerly a reporter for the *Chicago Sun Times* and an editor of the *New York Times Book Review.* Staples is the author of *Parallel Time* (1994), a memoir.

Just Walk on By

The power of examples to enable a reader to see through someone else's eyes is evident in this selection. Though many of the examples in the essay draw on a reader's sympathy, their main purpose appears to be explanatory; hence, the author accompanies them with detailed discussions. The result is a piece that is both enlightening and moving.

My first victim was a woman—white, well dressed, probably in her early twenties. I came upon her late one evening on a deserted street in Hyde Park, a relatively affluent neighborhood in an otherwise mean, impoverished section of Chicago. As I swung onto the avenue behind her, there seemed to be a discreet, uninflammatory distance between us. Not so. She cast back a worried glance. To her, the youngish black man—a broad six feet two inches with a beard and billowing hair, both hands shoved into the pockets of a bulky military jacket—seemed menacingly close. After a few more quick glimpses, she picked up her pace and was soon running in earnest. Within seconds she disappeared into a cross street. 1

That was more than a decade ago. I was 22 years old, a graduate student newly arrived at the University of Chicago. It was in the echo of that terrified woman's footfalls that I first began to know the unwieldy inheritance I'd come into—the ability to alter public space in ugly ways. It was clear that she thought herself the quarry of a mugger, a rapist, or worse. Suffering a bout of insomnia, however, I was stalking sleep, not defenseless wayfarers. As a softy who is scarcely able to take a knife to a raw chicken—let alone hold it to a person's throat—I was surprised, embarrassed, and dismayed all at once. Her flight made me feel like an accomplice in tyranny. It also made it clear that I was indistinguishable from the muggers who occasionally 2 seeped into the area from the surrounding ghetto. That first encounter, and those that followed, signified that a vast, unnerving gulf lay between nighttime pedestrians—particularly women—and me. And I soon gathered that being perceived as dangerous is a hazard in itself. I only needed to turn a corner into a dicey situation, or crowd some frightened, armed person in a foyer somewhere, or make an errant move after being pulled over by a policeman. Where fear and weapons meet—and they often do in urban America—there is always the possibility of death.

In the first year, my first away from my hometown, I was to become thoroughly familiar with the language of fear. At dark, shadowy intersections in Chicago, I could cross in front of a car stopped at a traffic light and elicit the *thunk, thunk, thunk, thunk* of the driver—black, white, male, or female—hammering down the door locks. On less traveled streets after dark, I grew accustomed to but never comfortable with people who crossed to the other side of the street rather than pass me. Then there were the standard unpleasantries with police, doormen, bouncers, cab drivers, and others whose business it is to screen out troublesome individuals *before* there is any nastiness. 3

I moved to New York nearly two years ago and I have remained an avid night walker. In central Manhattan, the near-constant crowd cover minimized tense one-on-one street encounters. Elsewhere—visiting friends in SoHo, where sidewalks are narrow and tightly spaced buildings shut out the sky—things can get very taut indeed. 4

Black men have a firm place in New York mugging literature. Norman Podhoretz in his famed (or infamous) 1963 essay, "My Negro Problem—And Ours," recalls growing up in terror of black males; they "were tougher than we were, more ruthless," he writes—and as an adult on the Upper West Side of Manhattan, he continues, he cannot constrain his nervousness when he meets black men on certain streets. Similarly, a decade later, the essayist and novelist Edward Hoagland extols a New York where once "Negro bitterness bore down mainly on other Negroes." Where some see mere panhandlers, Hoagland sees "a mugger who is clearly screwing up his nerve to do more than just *ask* for money." But Hoagland has "the New Yorker's quick-hunch posture for broken-field maneuvering," and the bad guy swerves away. 5

I often witness that "hunch posture," from women after dark on the warrenlike streets of Brooklyn where I live. They seem to set their faces on neutral and, with their purse straps strung across their chests bandolier style, they forge ahead as though bracing themselves 6 against being tackled. I understand, of course, that the danger they perceive is not a hallucination. Women are particularly vulnerable to street violence, and young black males are drastically overrepresented among the perpetrators of that violence. Yet these truths are no solace against the kind of alienation that comes of being ever the suspect, against being set apart, a fearsome entity with whom pedestrians avoid making eye contact.

It is not altogether clear to me how I reached the ripe old age of 7
22 without being conscious of the lethality nighttime pedestrians attributed to me. Perhaps it was because in Chester, Pennsylvania, the small, angry industrial town where I came of age in the 1960s, I was scarcely noticeable against a backdrop of gang warfare, street knifing, and murders. I grew up one of the good boys, had perhaps a half-dozen fist fights. In retrospect, my shyness of combat has clear sources.

Many things go into the making of a young thug. One of those 8
things is the consummation of the male romance with the power to intimidate. An infant discovers that random flailings send the baby bottle flying out of the crib and crashing to the floor. Delighted, the joyful babe repeats those motions again and again, seeking to duplicate the feat. Just so, I recall the points at which some of my boyhood friends were finally seduced by the perception of themselves as tough guys. When a mark cowered and surrendered his money without resistance, myth and reality merged—and paid off. It is, after all, only manly to embrace the power to frighten and intimidate. We, as men, are not supposed to give an inch of our lane on the highway; we are to seize the fighter's edge in work and in play and even in love; we are to be valiant in the face of hostile forces.

Unfortunately, poor and powerless young men seem to 9
take all this nonsense literally. As a boy, I saw countless tough guys locked away; I have since buried several. They were babies, really—a teenage cousin, a brother of 22, a childhood friend in his mid-twenties—all gone down in episodes of bravado played out in the streets. I came to doubt the virtues of intimidation early on. I chose, perhaps even unconsciously, to remain a shadow—timid, but a survivor.

The fearsomeness mistakenly attributed to me in public places 10
often has a perilous flavor. The most frightening of these confusions occurred in the late 1970s and early 1980s when I worked as a journalist in Chicago. One day, rushing into the office of a magazine I was writing for, with a deadline story in hand, I was mistaken for a

burglar. The office manager called security and, with an ad hoc posse, pursued me through the labyrinthine halls, nearly to my editor's door. I had no way of proving who I was. I could only move briskly toward the company of someone who knew me.

Another time I was on assignment for a local paper and killing time before an interview. I entered a jewelry store on the city's affluent Near North Side. The proprietor excused herself and returned with an enormous red Doberman pinscher straining at the end of a leash. She stood, the dog extended toward me, silent to my questions, her eyes bulging nearly out of her head. I took a cursory look around, nodded, and bade her good night. Relatively speaking, however, I never fared as badly as another black male journalist. He went to nearby Waukegan, Illinois, a couple of summers ago to work on a story about a murderer who was born there. Mistaking the reporter for the killer, police hauled him from his car at gunpoint and but for his press credentials would probably have tried to book him. Such episodes are not uncommon. Black men trade tales like this all the time. 11

In "My Negro Problem—And Ours," Podhoretz writes that the hatred he feels for blacks makes itself known to him through a variety of avenues—one being his discomfort with that "special brand of paranoid touchiness" to which he says blacks are prone. No doubt he is speaking here of black men. In time, I learned to smother the rage I felt at so often being taken for a criminal. Not to do so would surely have led to madness—via that special "paranoid touchiness" that so annoyed Podhoretz at the time he wrote the essay. 12

I began to take precautions to make myself less threatening. I move about with care, particularly late in the evening. I give a wide berth to nervous people on subway platforms during the wee hours, particularly when I have exchanged business clothes for jeans. If I happen to be entering a building behind some people who appear skittish, I may walk by, letting them clear the lobby before I return, so as not to seem to be following them. I have been calm and extremely congenial on those rare occasions when I've been pulled over by the police. 13

And on late-evening constitutionals along streets less traveled by, I employ what has proved to be an excellent tension-reducing measure: I whistle melodies from Beethoven and Vivaldi and the more popular classical composers. Even steely New Yorkers hunching toward nighttime destinations seem to relax, and occasionally they even join in the tune. Virtually everybody seems to sense that a mugger wouldn't be warbling bright, sunny selections 14 from Vivaldi's *Four Seasons.* It is my equivalent of the cowbell that hikers wear when they know they are in bear country.

Meanings and Values

1. Identify the contradictions the author presents through the example in the first two paragraphs.
2. Can any of the contradictions in the opening paragraphs be considered ironic? Please explain. (See "Guide to Terms": *Irony.*)

Expository Techniques

1. Identify each of the major (two sentences or more) examples in this essay.
2. Select three major examples and discuss what important purposes they play in the essay.
3. This essay was first published in 1986. Are the examples still relevant and accurate? If not, how would you suggest changing them?

Diction and Vocabulary

1. What words does Staples use in Paragraph 9 to highlight the contrast between the ideas expressed in this paragraph and those presented in Paragraph 8? (Guide: *Diction.*)
2. If you do not know the meaning of some of the following words, look them up in a dictionary: *affluent, impoverished, discreet* (Par. 1); *quarry, wayfarers, indistinguishable* (2); *taut* (4); *infamous* (5); *bandolier* (6); *lethality, retrospect* (7); *consummation* (8); *bravado* (9); *perilous* (10); *constitutionals* (14).

Read to Write

1. **Collaborating:** Young African American males are not the only group from whom specific kinds of behavior are expected—or whose behavior often contradicts expectations, as in Staples's case. Working with a group of classmates, identify two other social groups from whom certain kinds of behavior (positive or negative) are often expected. Choose one of the social groups, and drawing from the your general knowledge or experiences, write collaboratively two paragraph-length examples of actions or events that demonstrate behaviors contrary to the expected behaviors you listed.
2. **Considering Audience:** This essay was first published in 1986. How are readers' attitudes likely to have changed since then? In what

ways are they likely to have remained the same? Prepare a paragraph-length introduction to this essay in which you explain how readers' reactions are likely to have changed or not changed since it first appeared.

3. **Developing an Essay:** Using Staples's approach of developing a generalization through examples, develop an essay in which you explain how people have consistently misjudged or misunderstood you (or someone you know).

(NOTE: Suggestions for essays requiring development by EXAMPLE are on pp. 75–76 at the end of this section.)

JONAH LEHRER

As an undergraduate, JONAH LEHRER attended Columbia University. From there he went to Oxford University as a Rhodes Scholar. Currently, he is editor-at-large for *Seed* magazine and blogs at *The Frontal Cortex*. He has worked in the lab of Nobel Prize-winning neuroscientist Eric Kandel—and in the kitchens of Le Cirque 2000 and Le Bernardin. His writing has appeared in *The New Yorker, Nature, Wired*, the *Washington Post*, the *Boston Globe, NPR*, and *NOVAScienceNow*. Lehrer's two books are *Proust Was a Neuroscientist* (2007) and *How We Decide* (2009). In *How We Decide*, Lehrer explains how our best decisions make use of both emotion and reason.

The Uses of Reason

Despite its somewhat dull sounding title, "The Uses of Reason" tells a dramatic story about firefighters that has been told before (most notably in Norman Maclean's *Young Men and Fire*) for a variety of purposes. Lehrer uses it as an example to explain an important generalization about the role of reason in decisions made in highly emotional situations. The story loses none of its power when used as an example; indeed, it adds to the forcefulness of the generalization Lehrer draws from it.

The summer of 1949 had been long and dry in Montana; the grassy highlands were like tinder. On the afternoon of August 5—the hottest day ever recorded in the area—a stray bolt of lightning set the ground on fire. A parachute brigade of firefighters, known as smokejumpers, was dispatched to put out the blaze. Wag Dodge, a veteran with nine years of smokejumping experience, was in charge. When the jumpers took off from Missoula in a C-47, a military transport plane left over from World War II, they were told that the fire was small, just a few burning acres in the Mann Gulch river valley. As the plane approached the fire, the jumpers could see the smoke in the distance. The hot wind blew it straight across the sky. 1

Mann Gulch is a place of geological contradiction. It is where the Rocky Mountains meet the Great Plains, pine trees give way to prairie grass, and the steep cliffs drop onto the steppes of the Midwest. The gulch is just over three miles long, but it marks the border between these two different terrains. 2

The fire began on the Rockies' side, on the western edge of the gulch. By the time the firefighters arrived at the gulch, the blaze had grown out of control. The surrounding hills had all been burned; the 3 landscape was littered with the skeletons of pine trees. Dodge moved his men over to the grassy side of the gulch and told them to head downhill, toward the placid Missouri River. Dodge didn't trust this blaze. He wanted to be near water; he knew this fire could crown.

Crowns occur when flames get so high they reach into the top branches of trees. Once that happens, the fire has too much fuel. Hot embers begin to swirl in the air, spreading the fire across the prairie. The smokejumpers used to joke that the only way to control a crown fire was to pray like hell for rain. Norman Maclean, in his seminal history *Young Men and Fire*, described what it was like to be close to such a fire: 4

> It sounds like a train coming too fast around a curve and may get so high-keyed that the crew cannot understand what their foreman is trying to do to save them. Sometimes, when the timber thins out, it sounds as if the train were clicking across a bridge, sometimes it hits an open clearing and becomes hushed as if going through a tunnel, but when the burning cones swirl through the air and fall on the other side of the clearing, the new fire sounds as if it were the train coming out of the tunnel, belching black unburned smoke. The unburned smoke boils up until it reaches oxygen, then bursts into gigantic flames on top of its cloud of smoke in the sky. The new [novice] firefighter, seeing black smoke rise from the ground and then at the top of the sky turn into flames, thinks that natural law has been reversed.

Dodge looked at the dry grass and the dry pine needles. He felt the hot wind and the hot sun. The conditions were making him nervous. To make matters worse, the men had no map of the terrain. They were also without a radio, since the parachute on the radio pack had failed to open and the transmitter had been smashed on the rocks. The small crew of smokejumpers was all alone with this fire; there was nothing between them and it but a river and a thick tangle of ponderosa pine and Douglas fir trees. And so the jumpers set down their packs and watched the blaze from across the canyon. When the wind parted the smoke, as it did occasionally, they could see inside the fire as the flames leaped from tree to tree. 5

It was now five o'clock—a dangerous time to fight wilderness fires because the twilight wind can shift without warning. The breeze had been blowing the flames up the canyon, away from the river. But then, suddenly, the wind reversed. Dodge saw the ash swirl in the air. He saw the top of the flames flicker and wave. And then he saw the fire leap across the gulch and spark the grass on his side. 6

That's when the updraft began. Fierce winds began to howl through the canyon, blowing straight toward the men. Dodge could only watch as the fire became an inferno. He was suddenly staring at a wall of flame two hundred feet tall and three hundred feet deep 7 on the edge of the prairie. In a matter of seconds, the flames began to devour the grass on the slope. The fire ran toward the smokejumpers at thirty miles per hour, incinerating everything in its path. At the fire's center, the temperature was more than two thousand degrees, hot enough to melt rock.

Dodge screamed at his men to retreat. It was already too late to 8
run to the river, since the fire was blocking their path. Each man dropped his fifty pounds of gear and started running up the brutally steep canyon walls, trying to get to the top of the ridge and escape the blowup. Because heat rises, a fire that starts burning on flat prairie accelerates when it hits a slope. On a 50 percent grade, a fire will move nine times faster than it does on level land. The slopes at Mann Gulch are 76 percent.

When the fire first crossed the gulch, Dodge and his crew had a 9
two-hundred-yard head start. After a few minutes of running, Dodge could feel the fierce heat on his back. He glanced over his shoulder and saw that the fire was now fewer than fifty yards away and gaining. The air began to lose its oxygen. The fire was sucking the wind dry. That's when Dodge realized the blaze couldn't be outrun. The hill was too steep, and the flames were too fast.

So Dodge stopped running. He stood perfectly still as the fire 10
accelerated toward him. Then he started yelling at his men to do the same. He knew they were racing toward their own immolation and that in fewer than thirty seconds the fire would run them over, like a freight train without brakes. But nobody stopped. Perhaps the men couldn't hear Dodge over the deafening roar of flames. Or perhaps they couldn't bear the idea of stopping. When confronted with a menacing fire, the most basic instinct is to run away. Dodge was telling the men to stand still.

But Dodge wasn't committing suicide. In a fit of desperate cre- 11
ativity, he came up with an escape plan. He quickly lit a match and ignited the ground in front of him. He watched as those flames raced away from him, up the canyon walls. Then Dodge stepped into the ashes of this smaller fire, so that he was surrounded by a thin buffer of burned land. He lay down on the still smoldering embers. He wet his handkerchief with some water from his canteen and clutched the cloth to his mouth. He closed his eyes tight and tried to inhale the thin ether of oxygen remaining near the ground. Then he waited for the fire to pass around him. After several terrifying minutes, Dodge emerged from the ashes virtually unscathed.

Thirteen smokejumpers were killed by the Mann Gulch fire. 12
Only two men in the crew besides Dodge managed to survive, and that was because they found a shallow crevice in the rocky hillside.

As Dodge had predicted, the flames were almost impossible to outrun. White crosses still mark the spots where the men died; all of the crosses are below the ridge.

Dodge's escape fire is now a standard firefighting technique. It has saved the lives of countless firefighters trapped by swift blazes. At the time, however, Dodge's plan seemed like sheer madness. His men could think only about fleeing the flames, and yet their leader was starting a new fire. Robert Sallee, a first-year smokejumper who survived the blaze, later said he'd thought that "Dodge had gone nuts, just plain old nuts." 13

But Dodge was perfectly sane. In the heat of the moment he managed to make a very smart decision. The question, for those of us looking back on it, is how? What allowed him to resist the urge to flee? Why didn't he follow the rest of his crew up the gulch? Part of the answer is experience. Most of the smokejumpers were teenagers working summer jobs. They had fought only a few fires, and none of them had ever seen a fire like that. Dodge, on the other hand, was a grizzled veteran of the forest service; he knew what prairie flames were capable of. Once the fire crossed the gulch, Dodge realized that it was only a matter of time before the men were caught by the hungry flames. The slopes were too steep and the wind was too fierce and the grass was too dry; the blaze would beat them to the top. Besides, even if the men managed to reach the top of the mountain, they were still trapped. The ridge was covered with high, dry grass that hadn't been trimmed by cattle. It would burn in an instant. 14

For Dodge, it must have been a moment of unspeakable horror: to know that there was nowhere to go; to realize that his men were running to their deaths and that the wall of flame would consume them all. But Dodge's fear wasn't what saved him. In fact, the overwhelming terror of the situation was part of the problem. After the fire started burning uphill, all of the smokejumpers became fixated on getting to the ridge, even though the ridge was too far away for them to reach. Walter Rumsey, a first-year smokejumper, later recounted what was going through his mind when he saw Dodge stop running and get out his matchbook. "I remember thinking that that was a very good idea," Rumsey said, "but I don't remember what I thought it was good for . . . I kept thinking the ridge—if I can make it. On the ridge I will be safe." William Hellman, the second in command, looked at Dodge's escape fire and reportedly said, "To hell with that, I'm getting out of here." Hellman did reach the ridge, the only smokejumper who managed to do so, but he died the next day from third-degree burns that covered his entire body. The rest of the men acted the same way. When Dodge was asked during the investigation why none of the smokejumpers 15 followed his orders to stop running, he just shook his head. "They didn't seem to pay any attention," he said. "That is the part I didn't understand. They seemed to have something on their minds—all headed in one direction . . . They just wanted to get to the top."

Dodge's men were in the grip of panic. The problem with panic is that it narrows one's thoughts. It reduces awareness to the most essential facts, the most basic instincts. This means that when a person is being chased by a fire, all he or she can think about is running from the fire. 16

This is known as perceptual narrowing. In one study, people were put one at a time in a pressure chamber and told that the pressure would slowly be increased until it simulated that of a sixty-foot dive. While inside the pressure chamber, the subject was asked to perform two simple visual tasks. One task was to respond to blinking lights in the center of the subject's visual field, and the other involved responding to blinking lights in his peripheral vision. As expected, each of the subjects inside the pressure chamber exhibited all the usual signs of panic—a racing pulse, elevated blood pressure, and a surge of adrenaline. These symptoms affected performance in a very telling way. Although the people in the pressure chamber performed just as well as control subjects did on the central visual task, those in the pressure chamber were twice as likely to miss the stimuli in their peripheral vision. Their view of the world literally shrank. 17

The tragedy of Mann Gulch holds an important lesson about the mind. Dodge survived the fire because he was able to beat back his emotions. Once he realized that his fear had exhausted its usefulness—it told him to run, but there was nowhere to go—Dodge was able to resist its primal urges. Instead, he turned to his conscious mind, which is uniquely capable of deliberate and creative thought. While automatic emotions focus on the most immediate variables, the rational brain is able to expand the list of possibilities. As the neuroscientist Joseph LeDoux says, "The advantage of the emotional brain is that by allowing evolution to do the thinking for you at first, you basically buy the time that you need to think about the situation and do the most reasonable thing." And so Dodge stopped running. If he was going to survive the fire, he needed to think. 18

Meanings and Values

1. According to this essay, what are the uses of reason? List them, and be ready to explain each.

2. What is the generality explained in this essay?
3. In what ways was fear "part of the problem" (Par. 15)?

Expository Techniques

1a. Where in the essay does the writer indicate that the events are an extended example used to illustrate a generalization?

b. How does the writer signal this expository purpose? Does he do so successfully? (See "Guide to Terms": *Evaluation.*)

2. What technique does the writer use at the beginning of Paragraph 10 to create a strong contrast with the preceding paragraphs?
3. Explain how the contrast between Paragraphs 7–9 and 10 reflects the overall theme (generality) presented in the essay. (Guide: *Unity.*)

Diction and Vocabulary

1. What words does the writer use in Paragraphs 7–9 to emphasize the intensity of the events and the corresponding strong emotions they provoke in the firefighters? (Guide: *Diction.*)
2. If you do not know the meaning of some of the following words, look them up in a dictionary: *tinder* (Par. 1); *updraft* (7); *immolation* (10); *unscathed* (11); *grizzled* (14); *perceptual, peripheral* (17).

Read to Write

1. **Collaborating:** Working in a group, pool your experiences to create a list of emotional situations in which the ability to think carefully and rationally would be a benefit. Next, create a list of strategies people can use to help them think rationally when emotions threaten to overcome them.
2. **Considering Audience:** Readers are likely to have many different ideas about the importance or unimportance of emotions in decision making and behavior. Beginning with the insights offered by "The Uses of Reason," make two lists: one about the positive roles emotions can play and one about the negative roles emotions can play.
3. **Developing an Essay:** Use the lists you developed in #2 as a basis for an essay on the roles of emotion—one that takes into account readers' likely perspectives on the topic. Develop and explain your own generalization through examples, but acknowledge that other people may have different outlooks.

(Note: Suggestions for topics requiring development by example are on pp. 75–76 at the end of this section.)

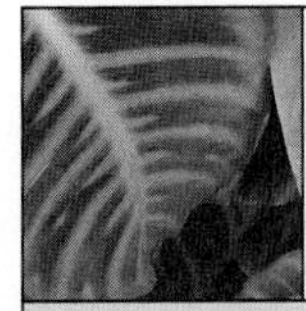

Issues and Ideas

Identities

- Wil Haygood, *Underground Dads*
- Alan Buczynski, *Iron Bonding*
- Mary Karr, *Dysfunctional Nation*

Discovering (or constructing) our identities—the attitudes, feelings, and ways of behaving that make us individuals—is an ongoing job for most people. Personal identity is a favorite topic for writers, too, because it plays an important role in determining what we believe and how we act.

Though they may agree on its importance, writers are just as likely to disagree about the meaning of "identity" and to argue over whether each of us has one true identity or many different ones. For some, identity is the sum of what we are as individuals, the product of our unique experiences and personal outlooks. For others, it is part of the "character" we share with people who are shaped by similar social and cultural forces. For still others, an identity is a role we construct for ourselves and play in specific settings or for particular purposes, and we are likely to have more than one identity.

The first two essays in this chapter (by Andy Rooney and Brent Staples) alert readers to some of the perspectives that shape our lives. The three essays that follow (by Wil Haygood, Alan Buczynski, and Mary Karr) offer generalities and examples that focus more specifically on the various ways we discover, construct, use, and struggle with our various identities.

WIL HAYGOOD

After graduating from college, WIL HAYGOOD began his career as a writer with the *Charlestown Gazette* and the *Pittsburgh Post-Gazette.* He then spent seventeen years with the *Boston Globe* as a staff writer and currently writes for the Style section of the *Washington Post.* His four nonfiction books are *Two on the River* (1987), *King of Cats: The Life and Times of Adam Clayton Powell, Jr.* (1993), *The Haygoods of Columbus: A Love Story* (1997), and *In Black and White: The Life of Sammy Davis, Jr.* (2003).

Underground Dads

Parents generally play key roles in shaping our identities, but what happens to someone who has not one parent or two, but a number of people who fill the role? Using as examples the men who acted as "underground fathers" for him, Haygood explains how unconventional parenting of the kind he experienced as a boy can be loving, supportive, and successful. This essay first appeared in the *New York Times Magazine.*

For years, while growing up, I shamelessly told my playmates that 1
I didn't have a father. In my neighborhood, where men went to work with lunch pails, my friends thought there was a gaping hole in my household. My father never came to the park with me to toss a softball, never came to see me in any of my school plays. I'd explain to friends, with the simplicity of explaining to someone that there are, in some woods, no deer, that I just had no father. My friends looked at me and squinted. My mother and father had divorced shortly after my birth. As the years rolled by, however, I did not have the chance to turn into the pitiful little black boy who had been abandoned by his father. There was a reason: other men showed up. They were warm, honest (at least as far as my eyes could see) and big-hearted. They were the good black men in the shadows, the men who taught me right from wrong, who taught me how to behave, who told me, by their very actions, that they expected me to do good things in life.

There are heartbreaking statistics tossed about regarding single- 2
parent black households these days, about children growing up fatherless. Those statistics must be considered. But how do you count the other men, the ones who show up—with perfect timing, with a kind of soft-stepping loveliness—to give a hand, to take a boy to

watch airplanes lift off, to show a young boy the beauty of planting tomatoes in the ground and to tell a child that all of life is not misery?

In my life, there was Jerry, who hauled junk. He had a lean body and a sweet smile. He walked like a cowboy, all bowlegged, swinging his shoulders. It was almost a strut. The sound of his pickup truck rumbling down our alley in Columbus, Ohio, could raise me from sleep. 3

When he wasn't hauling junk, Jerry fixed things. More than once, he fixed my red bicycle. The gears were always slipping; the chain could turn into a tangled mess. Hearing pain in my voice, Jerry would instruct me to leave my bike on our front porch. In our neighborhood, in the 60s, no one would steal your bike from your porch. Jerry promised me he'd pick it up, and he always did. He never lied to me, and he cautioned me not to tell lies. He was, off and on, my mother's boyfriend. At raucous family gatherings, he'd pull me aside and explain to me the importance of honesty, of doing what one promised to do. 4

And there was Jimmy, my grandfather, who all his life paid his bills the day they arrived: that was a mighty lesson in itself—it taught me a work ethic. He held two jobs, and there were times when he allowed me to accompany him on his night job, when he cleaned a Greek restaurant on the north side of Columbus. Often he'd mop the place twice, as if trying to win some award. He frightened me too. It was not because he was mean. It was because he had exacting standards, and there were times when I didn't measure up to those standards. He didn't like shortcutters. His instructions, on anything, were to be carried out to the letter. He believed in independence, doing as much for yourself as you possibly could. It should not have surprised me when, one morning while having stomach pains, he chose not to wait for a taxi and instead walked the mile to the local hospital, where he died a week later of stomach cancer. 5

My uncles provided plenty of good background music when I was coming of age. Uncle Henry took me fishing. He'd phone the night before. "Be ready. Seven o'clock." I'd trail him through woods—as a son does a father—until we found our fishing hole. We'd sit for hours. He taught me patience and an appreciation of the outdoors, of nature. He talked, incessantly, of family—his family, my family, the family of friends. The man had a reverence for family. I knew to listen. 6

I think these underground fathers simply appear, decade to decade, flowing through the generations. Hardly everywhere, and hardly, to be sure, in enough places, but there. As mystical, sometimes, as fate when fate is sweet. 7

Sometimes I think that all these men who have swept in and out of my life still couldn't replace a good, warm father. But inasmuch as I've never known a good, warm father, the men who entered my life, who taught me right from wrong, who did things they were not asked to do, have become unforgettable. I know of the cold statistics out there. And yet, the mountain of father-son literature does not haunt me. I've known good black men. 8

Meanings and Values

1. What are some of the important things that fathers are supposed to teach their sons? Why in Paragraph 1 does Haygood compare a boy without a father to woods without deer?
2. Twice in the essay Haygood mentions "good black men." Why do you think he makes race an issue with this reference?
3. In the beginning of Paragraph 2, Haygood speaks of "heartbreaking statistics tossed about regarding single-parent households. . . ." He says that these figures must be considered, yet he goes on to talk about households such as his, where "good black men" have helped raise children. Why does he mention such statistics if he does not plan to focus on them in the essay?

Expository Techniques

1. What examples does the author present of fatherly acts he experienced while growing up?
2. Would the examples of fatherly acts be sufficient to convince most readers that the writer should not be pitied for the lack of a father in his home? (See "Guide to Terms": *Evaluation.*)
3. Why does Haygood list several men who had an effect on his life and attitudes? Would his essay have been more effective if he had built it around one representative example of an influential man?

Diction and Vocabulary

1. Why does the writer use the words "gaping hole" to describe his friends' image of his household? Is this a figure of speech? (Guide: *Figures of Speech.*)
2. How does the word "shamelessly" (Par. 1) help define the image of himself the writer presents to readers? What other words and phrases does he employ to shape his audience's responses to himself?

READ TO WRITE

1. **Collaborating:** Prepare a list of men (not including your biological or adoptive father) who have had a profound impact on your life. Note also their relationship to you. Share your list with two other students in your class. Compare the roles that these men have had in shaping you into an adult. Write a two-page essay analyzing the similarities and differences between the adult males in your life and those in the lives of your classmates.
2. **Considering Audience:** Haygood's essay may strike chords in readers who have been raised without a father at home. However, even readers who have had fathers in their daily lives are likely to respond strongly to this essay. Why would both groups of readers understand the points Haygood makes? What similarities exist between children raised with fathers as a daily presence and those without? What are important differences, if any? Consider the varied ways in which readers might react to this essay based on their upbringing. Prepare a short essay explaining the different reactions readers might have to Haygood's essay.
3. **Developing an Essay:** Haygood mentions his mother briefly in Paragraph 1 of his essay; however, he does not discuss her effect on his life or the expectations he held for her. Make a list of the traditional "teaching" responsibilities of mothers and of fathers. Using these responsibilities as examples, prepare an essay supporting or refuting the notion that one person can take on the roles of both parents.

(NOTE: Suggestions for topics requiring development by use of EXAMPLE are on pp. 75–76 at the end of this chapter.)

ALAN BUCZYNSKI

ALAN BUCZYNSKI is a construction worker and a writer who lives in the Detroit area.

Iron Bonding

Newspaper columns, magazine articles, and everyday conversations are often filled with generalities about the different ways men and women behave. This essay looks at the emotional life of men, offering a working person's perspective rather than that of the intellectuals and professional people often associated with the "men's movement." The essay first appeared in the *New York Times Magazine.*

"I just don't get it." We were up on the iron, about 120 feet, waiting for the gang below to swing up another beam. Sweat from under Ron's hard hat dripped on the beam we were sitting on and evaporated immediately, like water thrown on a sauna stove. We were talking about the "men's movement" and "wildman weekends." 1

"I mean," he continued, "if they want to get dirty and sweat and cuss and pound on things, why don't they just get real jobs and get paid for it?" Below, the crane growled, the next piece lifting skyward. 2

I replied: "Nah, Ron, that isn't the point. They don't want to sweat every day, just sometimes." 3

He said: "Man, if you only sweat when you want to, I don't call that real sweatin." 4

Although my degree is in English, I am an ironworker by trade; my girlfriend, Patti, is a graduate student in English literature. Like a tennis ball volleyed by two players with distinctly different styles, I am bounced between blue-collar maulers and precise academicians. My conversations range from fishing to Foucault, derricks to deconstruction. There is very little overlap, but when it does occur it is generally the academics who are curious about the working life. 5

Patti and I were at a dinner party. The question of communication between men had arisen. Becky, the host, is a persistent interrogator: "What do you and Ron talk about?" 6

I said, "Well, we talk about work, drinking, ah, women." 7

Becky asked, "Do you guys ever say, 'I love you' to each other?" This smelled mightily of Robert Bly and the men's movement. 8

I replied: "Certainly. All the time." 9

I am still dissatisfied with this answer. Not because it was a lie, but because it was perceived as one. 10

The notion prevails that men's emotional communication skills are less advanced than that of chimpanzees, that we can no more communicate with one another than can earthworms. 11

Ironworkers as a group may well validate this theory. We are not a very articulate bunch. Most of us have only a basic education. Construction sites are extremely noisy, and much of our communication takes place via hand signals. There is little premium placed on words that don't stem from our own jargon. Conversations can be blunt. 12

Bly's approach, of adapting a fable for instruction, may instinctively mimic the way men communicate. Ironworkers are otherwise very direct, yet when emotional issues arise we speak to one another in allegory and parable. One of my co-workers, Cliff, is a good storyteller, with an understated delivery: "The old man got home one night, drunk, real messed up and got to roughhousing with the cat. Old Smoke, well she laid into him, scratched him good. Out comes the shotgun. The old man loads up, chases Smoke into the front yard and blam! Off goes the gun. My Mom and my sisters and me we're all screamin'. Smoke comes walkin' in the side door. Seems the old man blew away the wrong cat, the neighbor's Siamese. Red lights were flashin' against the house, fur was splattered all over the lawn, the cops cuffed my old man and he's hollerin' and man, I'll tell you, I was cryin'." 13

Now, we didn't all get up from our beers and go over and hug him. This was a story, not therapy. Cliff is amiable, but tough, more inclined to solving any perceived injustices with his fists than verbal banter, but I don't need to see him cry to know that he can. He has before, and he can tell a story about it without shame, without any disclaimers about being "just a kid," and that's enough for me. 14

Ron and I have worked together for nine years and are as close as 29 is to 30. We have worked through heat and cold and seen each other injured in the stupidest of accidents. One February we were working inside a plant, erecting steel with a little crane; it was near the end of the day, and I was tired. I hooked onto a piece and, while still holding the load cable, signaled the operator "up." My thumb was promptly sucked into the sheave of the crane. I screamed, and the operator came down on the load, releasing my thumb. It hurt. A lot. Water started leaking from my eyes. The gang gathered around while Ron tugged gently at my work glove, everyone curious whether my thumb would come off with the glove or stay on my hand. 15

"O.K., man, relax, just relax," Ron said. "See if you can move it." Ron held my hand. The thumb had a neat crease right down the center, lengthwise. All the capillaries on one side had burst and were turning remarkable colors. My new thumbnail was on back order and would arrive in about five months. I wiggled the thumb, an eighth of an inch, a quarter, a half. 16

"You're O.K., man, it's still yours and it ain't broke. Let's go back to work." 17

Afterwards, in the bar, while I wrapped my hand around a cold beer to keep the swelling and pain down, Ron hoisted his bottle in a toast: "That," he said, "was the best scream I ever heard, real authentic, like you were in actual pain, like you were really *scared*." 18

If this wasn't exactly Wind in His Hair howling eternal friendship for Dances with Wolves, I still understood what Ron was saying. It's more like a 7-year-old boy putting a frog down the back of a little girl's dress because he has a crush on her. It's a backward way of showing affection, of saying "I love you," but it's the only way we know. We should have outgrown it, and hordes of men are now paying thousands of dollars to sweat and stink and pound and grieve together to try and do just that. Maybe it works, maybe it doesn't. But no matter how cryptic, how Byzantine, how weird and weary the way it travels, the message still manages to get through. 19

Meanings and Values

1. According to the writer, how do men communicate with each other on emotional matters?
2. Buczynski concludes that "no matter how cryptic, how Byzantine, how weird and weary the way it travels, the message still manages to get through" (Par. 19). Does he convince you that this generality is well-founded? Why or why not?

Expository Techniques

1. Identify those places in the essay where the generality being illustrated is stated more or less directly. Would presenting the generality as a thesis statement in the opening paragraphs make the essay more effective? (See "Guide to Terms": *Thesis; Evaluation.*)
2. What strategy does the writer use in Paragraphs 1–10 to open the essay? (Guide: *Introduction.*)

3. Identify the main examples Buczynski uses and then discuss the effectiveness of each. (Guide: *Evaluation.*)

Diction and Vocabulary

1. Discuss how the simile in the third sentence of the opening paragraph, "like water thrown on a sauna stove," heightens the contrast between iron workers and people involved in the "men's movement." (Guide: *Figures of Speech.*)
2. Explain how the word choice in Paragraph 5 emphasizes contrasts between academics and blue-collar workers. (Guide: *Diction; Emphasis.*)
3. If you do not know the meaning of any of the following words, look them up in a dictionary: *maulers* (Par. 5); *interrogator* (6); *articulate* (12); *allegory, parable* (13); *disclaimers* (14).

Read to Write

1. **Collaborating:** Working in a small group, discuss the roles of stories, especially allegories or parables, in communicating emotions within your college environment. How do you, as college students, share emotions? Can you think of particular stories that helped you share such feelings? Has there been a significant event on campus that has generated such stories? Write a list of such events and stories that might be good examples for use in an expository essay about communicating.
2. **Considering Audience:** How do the communication and self-disclosure examples help this writer to establish an identity? Does the reader need some prior understanding of "blue-collar" workers to understand Buczynski's piece? With what other examples of male camaraderie and emotion sharing are Americans familiar? How about examples of female identity building and emotion sharing?
3. **Developing an Essay:** Using "Iron Bonding" as a model, use examples to create an essay explaining the communication strategies of a particular group of people with which you are familiar.

(NOTE: Suggestions for topics requring development by use of EXAMPLE are on pp. 75–76 at the end of this section.)

MARY KARR

MARY KARR'S highly praised memoir of her Texas childhood and unusual family, *The Liar's Club,* was first published in 1995. It won a PEN Prize and is frequently cited as among the best of the many moving and insightful accounts of growing up that have appeared in recent years. Her memoir of teenage years, *Cherry* (2000) has also been widely praised. Karr, who teaches creative writing at Syracuse University, has also published several volumes of poetry, including *Abacus* (1987), *The Devil's Tour* (1993), and *Sinners Welcome* (2006).

Dysfunctional Nation

To make the point that her dysfunctional family was far from unique, Karr draws examples from the many stories of other families she heard on a tour to promote her memoir. She suggests, in addition, that growing up in such a setting may not prevent a person from achieving a healthy identity and sense of self as an adult.

When I set out on a book tour to promote the memoir about my less-than-perfect Texas clan, I did so with soul-sucking dread. Surely we'd be held up as grotesques, my beloveds and I. Instead, I shoved into bookstores where sometimes hundreds of people stood claiming to identify with my story, which fact stunned me. 1

For one thing, my artist mother had been married seven times, twice to my Texas oil-worker daddy, who was Nos. 5 and 7. Both of my parents drank hard enough to hit some jackpots. Both were well armed. (The tile man who came to redo my mother's kitchen last spring pried more than one .22 slug from the wall.) 2

Yet in towns across this country I sat at various bookstore tables till near closing and heard people posit that reading about my tribe brought not slack-jawed horror, but recognition. Maybe these peoples' family lives differed from mine in terms of surface pyrotechnics—houses set afire and fortunes squandered. But the feelings didn't. After eight weeks of travel, I ginned up this working definition for a dysfunctional family: any family with more than one person in it. 3

Even the most perfect-looking clan seemed to suffer a rough patch. "I'm from one of these Donna Reed households you always wanted to belong to," said the elegant woman in Chicago. But her doctor daddy got saddled with a wicked malpractice suit, a few more martinis than usual got poured from his silver shaker every night. Rumor was he took up with his nurse. 4

What happened? "We worked it out. It passed." But not before 5
his Cadillac plowed over her bicycle one drunken night and her mother threatened divorce. Like me, she'd lain awake listening to her parents storm around in the masks of monsters and felt the metaphorical foundations of her house tremble, hopeless to prop it all up.

Not all folks reported such rough times as mere blips on the 6
family time line. In fact, I met dozens of people from way more chaotic households than mine. One guy's drug-dealer parents allegedly dragged him across several borders with bags of heroin taped under his Doctor Denton sleeper. Another woman had, at age 5, watched her alcoholic mother stick her head in a noose and step off a kitchen stool while the girl fought to shield her toddler brother's eyes. Surely many don't survive such childhoods intact (or they don't go to book signings because they're too busy being serial killers). But the myth that such a childhood condemns you to a life curled up in the back ward of a mental institution dissolved for me. On the surface, people seemed to have got over their troubled upbringings.

The female therapist in a Portland bookstore talked specifically 7
about the power of narrative in her life. She'd been raised by a chronic schizophrenic. On a given day, her school clothes were selected by God himself talking to her mother through scalp implants. The girl got good at worming her way into the homes of neighbors and any halfway decent teacher. In college, she fought depression with counseling she continued for nearly 10 years.

At 50, happily married, she wore a Burberry raincoat and toted 8
a briefcase of fine leather. She showed no visible signs of trauma. The real miracle? She was in fairly close touch with her mother, whose psychosis had diminished with new medications.

In part, this woman claimed to have survived through stories. 9
Traditional therapy, of course, starts with retelling family dramas. Talk about it, in the old wisdom, and the hurt eventually recedes. From narratives about her childhood, a self eventually emerged. Her tendency otherwise would have been to lop herself off from her own past, to make a false self for navigating the world. But false selves rarely withstand the real blows life delivers, hence, her need for stories, her own and other peoples'.

In our longing for some assurance that we're behaving O.K. in- 10
side fairly isolated families, personal experience has assumed some new power. Just as the novel form once took up experiences of urban, industrialized society that weren't being handled in epic poems

or epistles, so memoir—with its single, intensely personal voice—wrestles subjects in a way readers of late find compelling. The good ones I've read confirm my experience in a flawed family. They reassure the same way belonging to a community reassures.

My bookstore chats did the same. On the road, I came to believe that our families are working, albeit in new forms. People go on birthing babies and burying dead and loving those with whom they've shared deeply wretched patches of history. We do this partly by telling stories, in voices that seek neither to deny family struggles nor to make demons of our beloveds. 11

Meanings and Values

1. What conclusion about families does Karr offer in Paragraph 3? What examples does she provide to illustrate and support this generality?
2. Does Karr believe our identities and well being are primarily determined by our family backgrounds? If so, where in the essay does she make this point? If not, what else does she believe shapes who we are?

Expository Techniques

1. Explain how the statement, "On the surface, people seemed to have got over their troubled upbringings" (Par. 6), serves both to separate the two halves of the essay and to link them (see "Guide to Terms": *Transition*). In what ways does the second half of the essay answer questions suggested by the statement?
2. In what specific ways does the example in the second half of the essay (Pars. 7–9) and the way it is presented differ from the examples in the first half? How much space does the writer devote to presenting the later example and how much to commenting on and interpreting it?
3. What strategy does the writer employ to conclude the essay? (Guide: *Closings*.)

Diction and Vocabulary

1. Karr uses a number of vivid phrases in the course of the essay: "soul-sucking dread" (Par. 1); "drank hard enough to hit some jackpots" (2); "in the masks of monsters" and "the metaphorical foundations of her house" (5). Tell what each of these phrases means and what it contributes to the essay's effectiveness.

2. If you do not know the meaning of any of the following words, look them up in a dictionary: *memoir, grotesques* (Par. 1); *pyrotechnics, squandered, ginned, dysfunctional* (3); *trauma, psychosis* (8); *epistles* (10); *albeit* (11).

READ TO WRITE

1. **Collaborating:** Karr's essay touches on a variety of subjects, including storytelling, alcoholism, and family relationships. Make a list of all the subjects she mentions, and then choose two that you find most interesting. Then for each subject, make a list of topics or issues you might wish to explore in an essay of your own. Share your list with a group of classmates, asking them to identify topics they find most intriguing. Do the same for their lists, and, as a group, decide which topics are the most compelling and why.
2. **Considering Audience:** Other than the ones Karr discusses, what situations, relationships, or social forces make it hard for people to establish healthy identities? How many of these is the average person likely to encounter in his or her life? How many are they likely to know about from other people's experiences? How do people learn about such matters if not from their own experiences? Prepare a short essay discussing why readers in general would be likely to be comfortable or uncomfortable with an essay that presents examples of each type of negative situation, relationship, or social force. Include an explanation of why different groups of readers might react in different ways.
3. **Developing an Essay:** Karr begins her essay by describing a situation that surprised her by turning out to be the opposite of what she expected. Use this strategy to begin an essay of your own, and then go on to explore what you learned through the experience (just as Karr does).

(NOTE: Suggestions for topics requiring development by use of EXAMPLE follow.)

Writing Suggestions for Chapter 3

EXAMPLE

Use one of the following statements or another suggested by them as your central theme. Develop it into a unified composition, using examples from history, current events, or personal experience to illustrate your ideas. Be sure to have your reader-audience clearly in mind, as well as your specific purpose for the communication.

1. Successful businesses keep employees at their highest level of competence.
2. In an age of working mothers, fathers spend considerable time and effort helping raise the children.
3. Family life can create considerable stress.
4. Laws holding parents responsible for their children's crimes would (or would not) result in serious injustices.
5. Letting people decide for themselves which laws to obey and which to ignore would result in anarchy.
6. Many people find horror movies entertaining.
7. Service professions are often personally rewarding.
8. Religion in the United States is not dying.
9. Democracy is not always the best form of government.
10. A successful career is worth the sacrifices it requires.
11. "An ounce of prevention is worth a pound of cure."
12. The general quality of television commercials may be improving (or deteriorating).
13. An expensive car can be a poor investment.
14. "Some books are to be tasted; others swallowed; and some few to be chewed *and* digested." (Francis Bacon, English scientist-author, 1561–1626)
15. Most people are superstitious in one way or another.
16. Relationships within the family are much more important than relationships outside the family.

Collaborative Exercise

Working in a group, begin with the statement "Many people find horror movies entertaining," and ask each person to identify two examples to illustrate and support the generality advanced in the statement. (This task will probably require each group member to do some research.) After the examples have been collected, group members should present them, and the group as a whole should vote for those that best illustrate the generality. Each group member should then create a short essay using the examples to explain and support the statement. (Statements 7, 10, 12, and 13 also lend themselves well to this activity.)

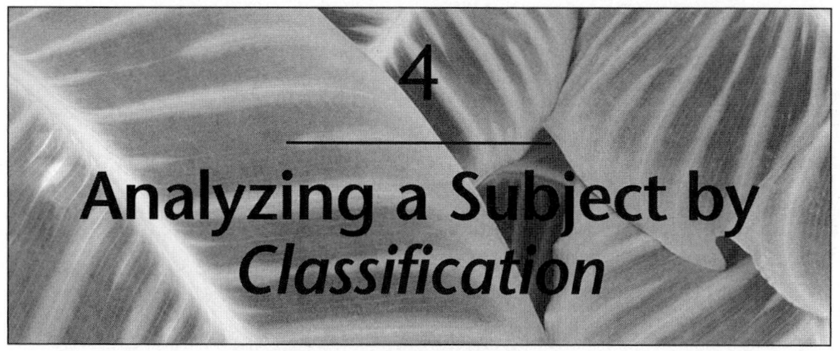

4
Analyzing a Subject by *Classification*

People naturally like to sort and classify things. A young child, moving into a new dresser of her own, will put handkerchiefs together, socks and underwear in separate stacks, and hair clips in a pretty holder for the dresser top. Another young child may classify animals as those with legs, those with wings, and those with neither. As they get older, they may find schoolteachers have ways of classifying *them,* not only into reading or math groups, but periodically on the basis of "A," "B," or "C" papers. On errands to the grocery store, they discover macaroni in the same department as spaghetti, pork chops somewhere near the ham, and apples just down from the miniature carrots (themselves part of larger groups like "carrots" and "root vegetables"). In reading the local newspaper, they observe that its staff has done some classifying for them, putting most of the comics together and seldom mixing sports stories with news of social affairs and marriage announcements (classifications based in turn on traditional categories of behavior). Eventually, they find courses neatly classified in college catalogs, and they know enough not to look for biology courses under "Social Science" or "Arts and Letters."

Classification also helps writers and readers sort through and understand detailed information or ideas. It groups people, ideas, objects, experiences, or concepts according to shared qualities and helps point out patterns of relationships among them. For example, if you were writing an article to help people understand their personal characteristics, you might draw on the ancient Indian concept of "ayurveda," as does the author of the following paragraph.

> The three ayurvedic types (or doshas) are vata, pitta, and kapha. Vatas (space and air) are creative, thin people with light bones and dark hair and eyes who are light sleepers, dislike routine, and tend toward fear and anxiety when they're under stress. Pittas (fire and water) are medium built, light-eyed, oily-skinned people who enjoy routine, make good leaders and initiators, are opinionated, and tend toward anger and frustration when they're under stress. Kaphas (water and earth) are amply built, thick-skinned and thick-haired people who are good at running projects, love leisure, sleep soundly, and tend to avoid difficult situations.
>
> —Lynette Lamb, "Living the Ayurvedic Way"

WHY USE CLASSIFICATION?

A classification creates groups on the basis of shared characteristics. It is a useful strategy when you are dealing with facts, events, or ideas whose differences are worth detailed examination. Many subjects that you may need to write and think about will remain a hodgepodge of facts and opinions unless you can find some system of analyzing the material, dividing the subject into categories, and classifying individual elements into those categories. The two patterns, **division** and **classification,** or *dividing* and *grouping,* move in different directions, at least to begin with. But when put in use for analysis and understanding, the two processes become inevitable companions that lead to a system of classification you can employ in your writing.

Expository writing both explains and informs, and classification is a pattern that enables writers to bring clarity to discussions of complicated subjects. Exercise programs, undergraduate majors, investment strategies, personal computers, ways to prepare for tests, even used cars—all these come in various types that are worth understanding. So, too, do other possible subjects for writing: behavior patterns; literary or anthropological theories; careers in engineering, business, or communications; management techniques; or environmental policies.

When readers encounter a classification, however, they expect more than a simple identification of categories. They look for an explanation of the qualities that distinguish each category and an explanation of the overall arrangement of the categories. In short, they expect the writer to provide a conclusion—a thesis—about the categories themselves, perhaps an explanation of why the subject falls into a particular set of categories or what implications the pattern of sorting has. A conclusion helps readers decide what to do with the information being presented; it helps them choose among alternatives, understand the specific uses of each set of policies or products; or grasp the implications of different psychological perspectives and social groupings.

CHOOSING A STRATEGY

If you choose to employ classification as a strategy for sharing information and ideas, your readers will expect you to take them into account from the beginning. They will want to know what information you are going to present and why it is important to them. They will expect you to make clear the purpose for your classification and the main idea or thesis tying it together.

From the start, therefore, you need to focus clearly on a **principle of classification,** that is, the quality that members of each group share and what distinguishes them from the members of other groups. The simplest classifications form two groups, those with a particular quality and those without it: vegetarians and meat-eaters, closed-end mutual funds and open-ended funds, introverts and extroverts, environmentally sensitive policies and environmentally destructive policies. But such simple classifications often break down, usually because the differences among groups are matters of degree or level (varying levels of environmental sensitivity; different degrees of strictness in adhering to a vegetarian diet) and not absolute.

In creating a classification, then, choose a strategy that reflects your purpose for writing while allowing you to maintain clear and logical distinctions among the categories. If your purpose is to help people understand dietary options available to them—vegan, ovo-lacto-vegetarian, avoidance of all meat except fish, and meat eating, for example—then your categories should be built around the kinds of food that people choose to include or avoid in their diet. In addition, the principle of classification should be consistent throughout the categories and complete with respect to the subject being investigated.

It would not be logical to divide movies into categories such as action films, science fiction films, romantic films, political films, serious films, and entertaining films because the principles of classification are not consistent and the categories therefore overlap: romantic films can be serious, entertaining, or both, for example. Likewise, it would not make sense to limit discussion of religious practices in North America to those of Christians, Jews, and

Muslims because to do so would exclude, for example, the many people who identify themselves as Buddhists and Hindus. A more limited system might be appropriate, however, when discussing the religious backgrounds of residents in a particular region (southwest Louisiana, rural Mexico) or from a particular cultural or ethnic group (Hungarians, Native Americans in Alaska or northern Canada). Although your classification system need not be exhaustive, it should at the same time not omit significant numbers of whatever behaviors, people, or ideas you are planning to discuss.

In many cases, the pattern of classification you choose will also serve to organize your writing, as the following tentative plan for an essay illustrates.

Tentative Thesis

People who love sports but have only limited athletic talent need not give up their dreams of a career in professional sports because being a player is only one of many career paths.

Category

Name: administrators. Definition: people involved in management of sports teams. Members: managers, coaches, public relations specialists, personnel managers.

Category

Name: medical staff. Definition: people concerned with physical and mental health of athletes. Members: trainers, team doctors, sports psychologists.

Category

Name: facilities staff. Definition: people who create and maintain sports facilities. Members: sports architects and designers, engineers, groundskeepers, facilities managers.

Category

Name: equipment specialists. Definition: people who design, manufacture, and sell sports equipment. Members: designers, testers, advertisers, manufacturing engineers, sales representatives.

A plan like this could logically include players' agents and legal representatives, people who work in financing sports, and people who arrange travel for sports teams. But although this would be a logical classification, it would be far too detailed for most readers. You should therefore limit the number of categories you present in an essay to avoid overwhelming and confusing your readers, but make sure you do not leave out any categories that are essential to the subject.

Any plan like this seems almost absurdly obvious, of course—*after* the planning is done. It appears less obvious, however, to inexperienced writers who are dealing with a jumble of information they must explain to someone else. This is when writers should be aware of the patterns at their disposal, and one of the most useful of these, alone or combined with others, is classification.

DEVELOPING CATEGORIES

At the center of any essay employing classification are the paragraphs that present, explain, and illustrate categories. There is no single strategy for presenting categories, and the way you approach the task should vary according to your subject and purpose for writing. Nonetheless, many writers find the following techniques useful for alerting readers to the structure of an essay, structuring the presentation of categories, and making sure they present each category with enough explanatory detail.

- *Use Transitions:* You can make effective use of transitional terms to signal the beginning of a new category.

type	sort	trait	segment
category	kind	species	characteristic
class	aspect	element	component
part	subcategory	subset	group

- *Name the Categories:* To help identify categories and also help readers remember them, try giving each a name when you explain it. The names can be purely descriptive ("supporters/opponents/compromisers of the policy") or they can be somewhat imaginative ("lookers/browsers/testers/buyers").
- *Provide Detailed Examples:* To help readers visualize and understand each category, consider providing at least one extended example or a cluster of shorter ones. By making the examples detailed and specific, you help explain the categories while making them more memorable.
- *Explain:* Remind readers of the principle of classification, of the qualities that characterize a category, and of the ways it differs from other categories. Let them know, too, how the categories are related: Do they represent differing or contradictory approaches

to a problem? Are they different products with similar functions? Will readers be faced with sharply differing options or a gradual range of choices?

Here is how one student, Hung Bui, put these techniques to work in a paragraph.

> Cigarettes play an even larger role in the lives of the next group, habitual smokers. They cannot quit as readily as the casual smoker can because of one key factor: habit. When the phone rings, they quickly grab an ashtray and cigarettes and chat. When having a cup of coffee in the morning, they simply must have a cigarette because "the coffee won't taste as good without it." And always, without fail, a good meal is followed by a good cigarette. Habitual smokers also smoke on a regular basis—a pack or two a day, never more, never less. They become irritated when they discover they are down to their last cigarette and rush to buy another pack. They also play games by buying only packs instead of cartons, rationalizing that because cigarettes aren't always on hand, they can't be smoking too much. They are constantly trying to cut down and tell everyone so, but never actually do, because in reality, smoking is an essential part of their lives.

Student Essay

Whenever you are learning, you do so in stages, from beginner, to novice, to (perhaps) expert. Heather Farnum applied these stages to a task she knew well (playing the piano) and came up with a system of classification that readers can apply to musicians in general and extend to other learners as well.

Piano Recitals

by Heather Farnum

Last night while I was sitting at the piano and relaxing by playing some old recital pieces, memories of playing in piano recitals as a child and high school student came flooding back to me. I remember looking at each pianist intently, watching how she or he presented a piece, and imagining myself sitting at the piano and playing in a similar way. I watched how each presented a selection—whether or not the person gave feeling to the music and was comfortable with playing it. Most of all, I watched how the pianist interpreted a piece, for

Begins with anecdote introducing the topic and creating interest

there are several quite different ways to interpret the same selection for an audience.

Thesis statement

Novice pianists, intermediate pianists, and top-class pianists all approach the job of interpretation in different and characteristic ways. You can help me explain these differences if you will imagine a stage in a brightly lit church hall or school auditorium. Stretched across the stage is a grand piano, set up so the audience of parents, friends, and fellow students can see the recitalist.

Category 1 example

The first person to walk tentatively across the stage to polite applause is a novice pianist. Like all novices, this one either rushes through the piece or plays much too slowly. He bobs his head up and down trying to maintain the tempo, messes up notes, and plays too loudly or too softly, but seldom in between.

Another example (detailed)

The best example of a novice pianist I can recall is Stephany Cody, a girl of about 7. For her first recital, Stephany played "Twinkle, Twinkle, Little Star" as loudly as she could, bobbing her head throughout the familiar piece. Every time she reached the "twinkle, twinkle, little star" she speeded up because she knew that part best. However, when she reached "up above the sky so gray," she slowed way down as she struggled through the less familiar notes.

Category 2 example

Next across the stage is an intermediate pianist. Sitting down, she strives for a professional look in form and stature. Unlike the novice pianist, she has control over dynamics, yet she is more tense because she is more aware of the things she needs to do and the things that can go wrong.

Another example (detailed)

John Cody (Stephany's ten-year-old brother) comes to my mind as an image of the intermediate pianist. For one of his recitals, John played a piece called "Festival of Arragon." He sat down at the piano with a serious disposition, like a professional. When he began playing, however, his form fell apart. His shoulders sagged and he held his head at an awkward angle because he was paying more attention to the correct tempo and the correct shade of loudness or softness than to the image he was presenting of himself and the music.

Last across the stage is an advanced pianist. She (or he) sits in a relaxed yet formal manner at the piano. When she plays, the dynamics and shades of sound are balanced and put the piece on display rather than the pianist. The tempo is even and steady, and the audience senses a performer in control with a strong stage presence.

Category 3 example

My piano teacher, Ann Fitch, remains in my mind as an image of the advanced pianist. Whenever she sits at the piano, she is calm and relaxed; her disposition alone makes the audience feel relaxed and at ease—ready for the piece to begin. She plays with tempos and rhythms that are steady and gradual. Most of all, however, she makes the audience members feel they are living the music.

Another example (detailed)

An advanced pianist like Ann goes even further with her performance. She plays with a mood and a stage presence that enable listeners to share the pianist's emotions. A top-flight pianist can convey feelings of love, romance, anger, sadness, depression, and excitement and arrange them in ways that guide listeners to the heart of the music without overwhelming them. Finally, if advanced pianists have a secret, it is that they keep four questions always in mind:

Example continues

1. What is the tempo I want to follow for this piece?
2. What mood do I wish to present?
3. What emotions do I want to convey?
4. How can I play so that the audience can live the piece of music at the same time I do?

In place of a conventional conclusion—a list of things all pianists should keep in mind

MATT CARMICHAEL

MATT CARMICHAEL is a writer and activist living in the United Kingdom. He teaches at the Roundhay School in Leeds.

Get Radical. Get Some Rest

Tiredness isn't one kind of thing, this writer explains. It is many kinds of things, and they are bad for us and for our planet, too. The essay calls for "a reevaluation of tiredness—all the different kinds" in order to move beyond the negative effects.

In *Prozac Nation,* a memoir that struck a chord with millions of readers, Elizabeth Wurtzel writes, "I don't want any more of this try, try again stuff. I just want out. I've had it. I am so tired; I am 20 and I am already exhausted." Despite the fact that we are surrounded by labor-saving devices, despite the elevation of convenience and comfort above almost all other values, a profound sense of tiredness seems to be one of the defining features of modern life. And our world is as exhausted as we are. Our ecosystems are stretched far beyond their limits, and social structures like families and communities battle for survival. 1

The natural response to tiredness is to rest. Modern consumer culture, however, doesn't like rest; "time is money," we are told. Every second saved by a dishwasher or a car must be paid back double in longer working hours. In the gym, exercise (which is freely available in the nearest park) is sold at exclusive rates so that we can do it while we're watching television. Even rest itself is commercialized and repackaged as "leisure." 2

Returning to truly replenishing forms of rest would demand a reevaluation of tiredness—all the different kinds, each of which leads to negative personal, social, and ecological consequences. In doing so, we would address the problem of unsustainability, which is, after all, the essence of tiredness. 3

When we are tired, we know we cannot carry on in the same way for long. In evaluating all the ways we're tired, we confront what makes life unsustainable. For us, and for our world. 4

First there's *sleepiness.* When we do not sleep properly, our brains run on depleted energy; compassion, creativity, imagination, and reason are lost, and the reptilian fight-or-flight brain takes over. 5

Some psychiatrists have suggested that depression is a symptom of sleep loss, rather than the other way around. A shortage of sleep is associated with obesity, road accidents, torture, and war.

In ecological terms, 24-hour culture means more emissions and more consumption of the earth's limited resources; we find ways to justify new runways, new wars, space tourism, and drilling for oil under melting arctic ice. 6

The solution, of course, is sleep. When the emperor of Persia asked his Sufi master how best to renew his soul, he was told to sleep as much as possible because "The longer you sleep, the less you will oppress!" We sacrifice sleep for time, but that time becomes less fulfilling—and robs the earth of resources. 7

Another kind of tiredness is *fatigue*: a tiredness of activity. We live in a hyperactive culture where more is continually demanded of us. Unions have to fight to maintain vacation allowances and workday limits. Life proceeds at a pace that belongs not to the human scale, but to the industrial scale. Fossil fuels allow us to travel great distances at inhuman speeds without feeling tired. The tiredness we would have felt does not disappear, but is displaced onto the ecosystems that support our existence. It turns out that the toddler who observed the airplane "scratching the sky" was right. 8

I used to look askance at evangelical Christian athletes who would not compete on a Sunday. Now I think we should follow their example. We are tempted to avoid rest because we think we will produce more, but what we produce is less wonderful. 9

We should also consider *ennui*, which is tiredness of stasis. Ennui is all about that feeling of being stuck in a rut, of going nowhere. It is extraordinary that in our hyperactive society so many people are bored. Bored young people hang around the streets causing trouble. Bored soldiers commit acts of atrocity in military prisons. Workers are forced to choose between the boredom of the production line and the boredom of unemployment. Television, computer games, and prescription drugs temporarily screen us from the effects of boredom, but it comes back to haunt us in poor mental health, addiction, crime, and disease. 10

It seems logical that the antidote to ennui is activity. However, as we have seen, we are very active—even hyperactive. We need to replace activities that isolate mind from body with activities that involve the whole person in a valuable process. There are many sources of wisdom to help us here. Gandhi viewed work as sacred. Dutch historian Johan Huizinga showed how play is fundamental to human welfare, and the Kama Sutra explores the spiritual significance of sex. 11

Martial arts generally developed as forms of meditation, ritualizing movement in order to replenish body and mind. In agriculture, one alternative to a static monoculture is crop rotation: Moving the crop replenishes the soil.

Perhaps the most prevalent form of tiredness in our society is *satiation*, tiredness of consumption. Our society has an obesity problem that extends far beyond the body mass index. Shopping is a chief "leisure activity." We continue to consume rapaciously because we are wedded to ownership, but the real effects of satiation are unwelcome. They first show up in the environment, where the raw materials for all this consumption must be found. Then they appear in unequal societies and unjust legislation that favors the obscenely wealthy. 12

The answer is sacrifice. Every year Muslims fast during daylight hours for the month of Ramadan. This is a striking example of the use of sacrifice for the benefit of an entire community. Christians and Jews tithe. Sikhs practice hospitality and share food; monks take vows of poverty; vegetarians and vegans refrain from eating meat; ethical consumers refuse to buy the shiny trinkets that are constantly advertised. 13

We are increasingly aware that capitalism is failing to make sense for our lives; money is not making us happy. But many of us who are ready to change are not aware of any alternative. So we carry on rushing around, making money, buying temporary happiness. 14

In a culture so dependent on activity—on consuming, producing, and achieving—rest becomes a radical form of protest and a catalyst for change. 15

Meanings and Values

1. Name the kinds of tiredness this essay discusses.
2. For each kind of tiredness, describe briefly its negative effects on our world.
3. Explain what the writer means when he says, "unsustainability . . . [is] the essence of tiredness" (Par. 3).

Expository Techniques

1. In presenting each category, the writer provides a definition, describes a problem, and offers a solution. Identify the sentences that perform these tasks in Paragraphs 5–7, 10–11, and 12–13.

2. What strategy does the writer use to begin this essay? (See "Guide to Terms": *Introductions.*)
3. In which paragraph does the writer announce the overall theme of the essay? What is it? (Guide: *Unity.*)

Diction and Vocabulary

1. What use does the writer make of irony in Paragraphs 1–2 to help readers understand the special nature of tiredness in our lives. (Guide: *Irony.*)
2. If you do not know the meaning of some of the following words, look them up in a dictionary: *ecosystems* (Par. 1); *Sufi* (7); *fatigue* (8); *askance* (9); *ennui, stasis* (10); *static* (11); *satiation* (12).

Read to Write

1. **Collaborating.** Carmichael takes a feeling that most of us would start by viewing as personal and treats it as a widespread, social trait. Take one of these three feelings, and, working in a group, split it into categories that can be viewed both as personal and social: anger, love, or amusement.
2. **Considering Audience.** Readers today are familiar with explanations that include our attitudes toward the environment. Prepare a short discussion of kinds of behaviors based on their effects on the environment.
3. **Developing an Essay.** Carmichael's essay classifies feelings and actions that are generally negative along with their negative effects. While we often encounter explanations that highlight the negative, we encounter those that highlight the positive less often. Looking at positive ideas, behaviors, and feelings can make for good, insightful writing, however. Draw on your own knowledge or experience for an essay of your own, classifying positive behaviors and effects.

(NOTE: Suggestions for topics requiring development by use of CLASSIFICATION are on pp. 118–119 at the end of this section.)

SALMAN AKHTAR

Born in Lucknow, India, SALMAN AKHTAR trained as a psychiatrist and is now a professor at Jefferson Medical College in Philadelphia. Akhtar writes about psychology and psychiatry (more than thirty books) and is a poet as well, having published six collections of poems in both English and his native Urdu. He comes from a family of poets and songwriters, and he is related to several directors of Bollywood movies. His most recent books are *Freud Along the Ganges* (2005) and *Objects of Our Desire: Exploring Our Intimate Connections with the Things Around Us* (2007).

Remembering the Dead

In this selection from *Objects of Our Desire*, the author explores our use of classification to help us in the process of mourning. We often react to the death of a loved one or family member, he tells us, by sorting out the possessions left behind.

Perhaps no item has the power to evoke nostalgia more than one left behind by a loved one who has died. These legacies are heart-wrenching reminders of our loss, yet they play an important role in helping us establish a meaningful continuity between the dead and the living. They become bridges across the chasm of time and generations and ultimately serve life-enhancing purposes. Proust's description of his reaction to the death of his sweetheart, Albertine, testifies to the power physical objects have to create nostalgia in a time of mourning. He writes: 1

> If all of a sudden I thought of her room, her room in which the bed stood empty, of her piano, her motorcar, I lost all my strength, I shut my eyes, let my head droop upon my shoulder like a person who is about to faint . . . . I stepped across the room with endless precautions, I took up a position from which I could not see Albertine's chair, the pianola upon the pedals of which she used to press her golden slippers, nor a single one of the things which she had used and all of which, in the secret language which my memory had imparted to them, seemed to be seeking to give me a fresh translation, a different version, to announce to me for a second time the news of her departure.

After the initial disbelief and pain, the mourner is able to face the reality of her loss. Now the possessions of the deceased are divided into three categories: things that are thrown away, things that are given away, and things that are passed on as mementos and 2 family heirlooms to the next generation. Most everyday items—toothbrushes, underwear, old household items—belong in the first category. The better-preserved garments and utensils figure in the second category. And precious china, jewelry, fine furniture, and objects of unique personal importance (e.g., journals, letters, a stamp collection, a handwritten manuscript) belong in the third category.

Sorting the deceased's possessions along these lines is an important step in the mourning process. Disposing of the everyday items can be the most difficult, as these are often the most intimate reminders of a person's existence. Emptying the closets and clearing out the medicine chest seems to erase them more completely than the reality of death. In grief, some may take years to remove these items. Others may hastily and immediately dispose of a dead relative's physical possessions. Both reactions suggest that the bereaved is having difficulty facing the pain of loss. By quickly throwing things away, she rapidly bypasses this pain and doesn't allow it to simmer, as it should in normally progressing grief. By keeping things for a long time, she postpones pain. Both these manners of handling things left by a dead person show an anguished reaction to loss. Both imply a difficulty in coming to grips with the changed realities consequent upon loss and the emotions stirred up by it. 3

In Judith Guest's *Ordinary People*, the saga of a suburban family coming apart under the strain of the accidental death of a teenage son, the room of the dead boy is kept "frozen" in time. Months pass, but nothing is changed, not one item moved or disposed of. In Anne Tyler's *The Accidental Tourist*, a description of the opposite phenomenon appears. The book's protagonist, who has lost his son in a freak shooting accident, throws away all the latter's possessions. His wife chides him: 4

> When Ethan died, you emptied his closet and his bureau as if you couldn't be rid of him soon enough. You kept offering people his junk in the basement, stilts and sleds and skateboards, and you couldn't understand why they didn't accept them . . . . There's something so muffled about the way you experience things, I mean love or grief or anything; it's like you are trying to slip through life unchanged.

The possessions in the third category—those items that will be passed down as keepsakes—connect us to our loved ones in two different ways: as ordinary mementos or as "linking objects." Mementos are owned proudly and used in a realistic way. Their connection with the deceased gradually becomes dim in the mind of the survivors. As a result, the survivors experience a comfortable sense of ownership of such objects. For instance, a young woman who receives 5 her late grandmother's china may happily use it for serving dinner on festive occasions as a way to fondly remember her beloved relative.

While some items symbolize our love for the deceased, others become "linking objects," depositories of our intense love-hate attitude toward the deceased. These objects stir up searing emotional pain, dread, or fear. This pain and dread can be so severe that a "linking object" is kept hidden and removed from day-to-day contact. A peculiarly ambivalent attitude develops with regard to it. On the one hand, it cannot be seen or used due to the unpleasant feelings it evokes. On the other hand, it cannot be thrown away because doing so becomes tantamount to "murdering" its former owner. As a result, the object—say, a camera or a wristwatch—is kept safely but unused and out of sight. The survivor always knows its whereabouts even though she might ignore it for considerable lengths of time. The object exists as a frozen reservoir of feelings. 6

When mourning goes well, however, old objects help establish meaningful continuity between the dead and the living. They become bridges across the chasm of time and serve life-enhancing purposes. For instance, after his father's death, Vamik Volkan, a distinguished psychoanalyst, chose to keep his father's diary and his citizenship papers. Both items help nurture Vamik's identity as a Cypriot and his connection to his father. Stamped with his father's photograph, the citizenship papers resound with the turbulent history of his native island and of his family. Cherished and affirming, these documents, hanging on his wall, help nurture his identity and connection to his father. 7

Though their effect on us differs remarkably, the fact is that all such bequeathed objects exert an enormous amount of power over us. Sometimes this effect is laden with the anguish of loss and other times with the pride of legacy. Such objects are hardly emotion free. That much one can say with certainty. 8

Meanings and Values

1. In the opening paragraph, the writer offers a thesis statement that applies to each of the categories discussed in the essay. What is it? (See "Guide to Terms": *Thesis, Unity.*)
2. The essay explores three main categories. Are there any obvious or useful categories the writer does not explore? If so, what are they?
3. What does the writer mean when he refers to an object as "a frozen reservoir of feelings" (Par. 3)?

Expository Techniques

1. Where in the essay does the writer first introduce the main categories? Why does he do so here rather than later in the essay?
2. Where in the essay does the writer introduce his discussion of each of the major categories? Does he provide a detailed discussion of the second category? If not, is the essay weakened by this omission? (Guide: *Evaluation.*)
3. What words or phrases does he use to introduce each category? Should he introduce the categories more clearly? Why, or why not. (Guide: *Evaluation.*)

Diction and Vocabulary

1. In the course of the essay, Akhtar uses these phrases which suggest visual images. Explain what they mean and tell whether you think they are appropriate or inappropriate, and why: "bridges across the chasm of time and generations" (Par. 1); "Their connection becomes dim in the mind of the survivors" (5); "The object exists as a frozen reservoir of feelings" (6).
2. If you do not know the meaning of some of these words, look them up in a dictionary: *bereaved* (Par. 3); *mementos* (5); *ambivalent, tantamount* (6); *Cypriot* (7); *bequeathed* (8).

Read to Write

1. **Collaborating:** Working with a group of fellow students, list objects from your childhood that fall into three categories: things you have kept, things you wish you had kept, and things you are glad you no longer have. Subdivide these categories if you can. If you cannot come up with a satisfactory list for the group, then make up your own lists and discuss them as a group. Look over the list(s) and decide what the objects in each category (or subcategory) have in common, either their traits or your attitudes toward the objects, for example.
2. **Considering Audience:** How are readers who have lost people close to them likely to respond to this essay. Are people who have not experienced the deaths of people important to them likely to respond in different ways? Why, or why not?
3. **Developing an Essay:** Choose another set of categories based on experiences that some readers may have had to a greater extent than others: victory in sports, for example, or time before an audience as a performer or musician. Develop an essay explaining different categories of experiences so that people who have not encountered it to any great extent can still understand.

(Note: Suggestions for topics requiring development by use of CLASSIFICATION are on pp. 118–119 at the end of this chapter.)

MICHAEL VENTURA

MICHAEL VENTURA worked as an editor for the *Austin Sun* and the *Los Angeles Weekly* (which he cofounded). He has been a columnist for the *Austin Chronicle* and the *Los Angeles Village View*. His books include *The Mollyhawk Poems* (1977); *Night Time, Losing Time* (1989); and *The Zoo Where You're Fed to God* (1994). His most recent book is a novel, *The Death of Frank Sinatra* (2000).

Don't Even Think About It!

In this essay, Michael Ventura explains how taboos, which many readers might associate with primitive societies or superstitions, help shape the things we do in our daily lives. By showing how many different kinds of taboos we routinely observe (more categories than readers usually encounter in an essay), Ventura demonstrates their prevalence and importance. The concrete examples that Ventura provides help keep the numerous categories from seeming overwhelming and abstract. The illustrations also help readers recognize taboos in their own behavior.

Taboos come in all sizes. Big taboos: when I was a kid in the Italian neighborhoods of Brooklyn, to insult someone's mother meant a brutal fight—the kind of fight no one interferes with until one of the combatants goes down and stays down. Little taboos: until the sixties, it was an insult to use someone's first name without asking or being offered permission. Personal taboos: Cyrano de Bergerac would not tolerate the mention of his enormous nose. Taboos peculiar to one city: in Brooklyn (again), when the Dodgers were still at Ebbets Field, if you rooted for the Yankees you kept it to yourself unless you wanted a brawl. Taboos, big or small, are always about having to respect somebody's (often irrational) boundary—or else. 1

There are taboos shared within one family: my father did not feel free to speak to us of his grandmother's suicide until his father died. Taboos within intellectual elites: try putting a serious metaphysical or spiritual slant on a "think-piece" (as we call them in the trade) written for the *New York Times*, the *Washington Post*, or most big name magazines—it won't be printed. Taboos in the corporate and legal worlds: if you're male, you had best wear suits of somber colors, or you're not likely to be taken seriously; if you're female, you have to strike a very uneasy balance between the attractive and the prim, and even then you might not be taken seriously. Cultural 2

Michael Ventura, "Taboo: Don't Even Think About It!" *Psychology Today*, January/February 1998. Reprinted with permission from *Psychology Today* Magazine, taboos: in the Jim Crow days in the South, a black man who spoke with familiarity to a white woman might be beaten, driven out of town, or (as was not uncommon) lynched.

Unclassifiable taboos: in Afghanistan, as I write this, it is a sin— 3
punishable by beatings and imprisonment—to fly a kite. Sexual taboos: there are few communities on this planet where two men can walk down a street holding hands without being harassed or even arrested; in Afghanistan (a great place for taboos these days) the Taliban would stone them to death. Gender taboos: how many American corporations (or institutions of any kind) promote women to power? National taboos: until the seventies, a divorced person could not run for major public office in America (it wasn't until 1981 that our first and only divorced president, Ronald Reagan, took office); today, no professed atheist would dare try for the presidency. And most readers of this article probably approve, as I do, of this comparatively recent taboo: even the most rabid bigot must avoid saying "nigger," "spic," or "kike" during, say, a job interview—and the most macho sexist must avoid words like "broad."

Notice that nearly all of our taboos, big and small, public and in- 4
timate, involve silence—keeping one's silence, or paying a price for not keeping it. Yet keeping silent has its own price: for then silence begins to fill the heart, until silence becomes the heart—a heart swelling with restraint until it bursts in frustration, anger, even madness.

The taboos hardest on the soul are those which fester in our 5
intimacies—taboos known only to the people involved, taboos that can make us feel alone even with those to whom we're closest. One of the deep pains of marriage—one that also plagues brothers and sisters, parents and children, even close friends—is that as we grow more intimate, certain silences often become more necessary. We discover taboo areas, both in ourselves and in the other, that cannot be transgressed without paying an awful price. If we speak of them, we may endanger the relationship; but if we do not speak, if we do not violate the taboo, the relationship may become static and tense, until the silence takes on a life of its own. Such silences are corrosive. They eat at the innards of intimacy until, often, the silence itself causes the very rupture or break-up that we've tried to avoid by keeping silent.

The Cannibal in Us All

You may measure how many taboos constrict you, how many taboos 6
you've surrendered to—at home, at parties, at work, with your lover or your family—by how much of yourself you must suppress. You

may measure your life, in these realms, by what you cannot say, do, admit—cannot and must not, and for no better reason than that your actions or words would disrupt your established order. By this measure, most of us are living within as complex and strictured a system of taboos as the aborigines who gave us the word in the first place. You can see how fitting it is that the word "taboo" comes from a part of the world where cannibalism is said to be practiced to this day: the islands off eastern Australia—Polynesia, New Zealand, Melanesia. Until 1777, when Captain James Cook published an account of his first world voyage, Europe and colonial America had many taboos but no word that precisely meant taboo. Cook introduced this useful word to the West. Its instant popularity, quick assimilation into most European languages, and constant usage since, are testimony to how much of our lives the word describes. Before the word came to us, we'd ostracized, coerced, exiled, tormented, and murdered each other for myriad infractions (as we still do), but we never had a satisfying, precise word for our reasons.

We needed cannibals to give us a word to describe our behav- 7
ior, so how "civilized" are we, really? We do things differently from those cannibals, on the surface, but is the nature of what we do all that different? We don't cook each other for ceremonial dinners, at least not physically (though therapists can testify that our ceremonial seasons, like Christmas and Thanksgiving, draw lots of business—something's cooking). But we stockpile weapons that can cook the entire world, and we organize our national priorities around their "necessity," and it's a national political taboo to seriously cut spending for those planet-cookers. If that's "progress," it's lost on me. In China it's taboo to be a Christian, in Israel it's taboo to be a Moslem, in Syria it's taboo to be a Jew, in much of the United States it's still taboo to be an atheist, while in American academia it's taboo to be deeply religious. Our headlines are full of this stuff. So it's hardly surprising that a cannibal's word still describes much of our behavior.

I'm not denying the necessity of every society to set limits and 8
invent taboos (some rational, some not) simply in order to get on with the day—and to try to contain the constant, crazy, never-to-be-escaped longings that blossom in our sleep and distract or compel us while awake. Such longings are why even a comparatively tiny desert tribe like the ancient Hebrews needed commandments and laws against coveting each other's wives, stealing, killing, committing incest. That the tribe hadn't seen violent, sexy movies, hadn't listened to rock 'n' roll, hadn't been bombarded with ads featuring

half-naked models, and hadn't watched too much TV. They didn't need to. Like us, they had their hearts, desires, and dreams to instruct them how to be very, very naughty. The taboo underlying all others is that we must not live by the dictates of our irrational hearts—as though we haven't forgiven each other, or ourselves, for having hearts.

If there's a taboo against something, it's usually because a considerable number of people desire to do it. The very taboos that we employ to protect us from each other and ourselves, are a map of our secret natures. When you know a culture's taboos (or an individual's, or a family's) you know its secrets—you know what it really wants. 9

Favorite Taboos

It's hard to keep a human being from his or her desire, taboo or not. We've always been very clever, very resourceful, when it comes to sneaking around our taboos. The Aztecs killed virgins and called it religion. The Europeans enslaved blacks and called it economics. Americans tease each other sexually and call it fashion. 10

If we can't kill and screw and steal and betray to our heart's desire, and, in general, violate every taboo in sight—well, we can at least watch other people do it. Or read about it. Or listen to it. As we have done, since ancient times, through every form of religion and entertainment. The appeal of taboos and our inability to escape our longing for transgression (whether or not we ourselves transgress) are why so many people who call themselves honest and law-abiding spend so much time with movies, operas, soaps, garish trials, novels, songs, Biblical tales, tribal myths, folk stories, and Shakespeare—virtually all of which, both the great and the trivial, are about those who dare to violate taboos. It's a little unsettling when you think about it: the very stuff we say we most object to is the fundamental material of what we call culture. 11

That's one reason that fundamentalists of all religions are so hostile to the arts. But fundamentalists partake of taboos in the sneakiest fashion of all. Senator Jesse Helms led the fight against the National Endowment for the Arts because he couldn't get the (vastly overrated) homosexual art of Robert Mapplethorpe or the most extreme performance artists out of his mind—he didn't and doesn't want to. He, like all fundamentalists, will vigorously oppose such art and all it stands for until he dies, because his very opposition gives him permission to concentrate on taboo acts. The Taliban of 12

Afghanistan will ride around in jeeps toting guns, searching out any woman who dares show an inch of facial skin or wear white socks (Taliban boys consider white socks provocative), and when they find such a woman they'll jail and beat her—because their so-called righteousness gives them permission to obsess on their taboos. Pat Robertson and his ilk will fuss and rage about any moral "deviation," any taboo violation they can find, because that's the only way they can give themselves permission to entertain the taboos. They get to not have their taboo cake, yet eat it too.

We are all guilty of this to some extent. Why else have outlaws from Antigone to Robin Hood to Jesse James to John Gotti become folk heroes? Oedipus killed his father and slept with his mother, and we've been performing that play for 2500 years because he is the ultimate violator of our deepest taboos. Aristotle said we watch such plays for "catharsis," to purge our desires and fears in a moment of revelation. Baloney. Ideas like "catharsis" are an intellectual game, to glossy-up our sins. What's closer to the truth is that we need Oedipus to stand in for us. We can't have changed much in 2500 years, if we still keep him alive in our hearts to enact our darkest taboos for us. Clearly, the very survival of Oedipus as an instantly recognizable name tells us that we still want to kill our fathers and screw our mothers (or vice versa). 13

A Country of Broken Taboos

Taboos are a special paradox for Americans. However much we may long for tradition and order, our longings are subverted by the inescapable fact that our country was founded upon a break with tradition and a challenge to order—which is to say, the United States was founded upon the violation of taboos. Specifically, this country was founded upon the violation of Europe's most suffocating taboo: its feudal suppression (still enforced in 1776, when America declared its independence) of the voices of the common people. We were the first nation on earth to write into law that any human being has the right to say anything, and that even the government is (theoretically) not allowed to silence you. 14

At the time, Europe was a continent of state-enforced religions, where royalty's word was law and all other words could be crushed by law. (Again: taboo was a matter of enforced silence.) We were the first nation to postulate verbal freedom for everyone. All our other freedoms depend upon verbal freedom; no matter how badly and how often we've failed that ideal, it still remains our ideal. 15

Once we broke Europe's verbal taboos, it was only a matter of time before other traditional taboos fell too. As the writer Albert Murray has put it, Americans could not afford piety in their new homeland: "You can't be over respectful of established forms; you're trying to get through the wilderness of Kentucky." Thus, from the moment the Pilgrims landed, our famous puritanism faced an inherent contradiction. How could we domesticate the wilderness of this continent; how could peasants and rejects and "commoners" form a strong and viable nation; how could we develop all the new social forms and technologies necessary to blend all the disparate peoples who came here—without violating those same Puritan taboos which are so ingrained, to this day, in our national character? 16

It can't be over-emphasized that America's fundamental stance against both the taboos of Europe and the taboos of our own Puritans, was our insistence upon freedom of speech. America led the attack against silence. And it is through that freedom, the freedom to break the silence, that we've destroyed so many other taboos. Especially during the last 40 years, we've broken the silence that surrounded ancient taboos of enormous significance. Incest, child abuse, wife-battering, homosexuality, and some (by no means all) forms of racial and gender oppression, are not merely spoken of, and spoken against, they're shouted about from the rooftops. Many breathe easier because of this inevitable result of free speech. In certain sections of our large cities, for the first time in modern history, gay people can live openly and without fear. The feminist movement has made previously forbidden or hidden behaviors both speakable and doable. The National Organization of Women can rail against the Promise Keepers all they want (and they have some good reasons), but when you get a million working-class guys crying and hugging in public, the stoic mask of the American male has definitely cracked. And I'm old enough to remember when it was shocking for women to speak about wanting a career. Now virtually all affluent young women are expected to want a career. 17

Fifty years ago, not one important world or national leader was black. Now there are more people of color in positions of influence than ever. Bad marriages can be dissolved without social stigma. Children born out of wedlock are not damned as "bastards" for something that wasn't their fault. And those of us who've experienced incest and abuse have finally found a voice, and through our voices we've achieved a certain amount of liberation from shame and pain. 18

These boons are rooted in our decidedly un-Puritan freedom of speech. But we left those Puritans behind a long time ago—for the 19 breaking of silence is the fundamental political basis of our nation, and no taboo is safe when people have the right to speak.

Keeper of Your Silence

In the process, though, we've lost the sanctity of silence. We've lost the sense of dark but sacred power inherent in sex, in nature, even in crime. Perhaps that is the price of our new freedoms. 20

It's also true that by breaking the silence we've thrown ourselves into a state of society's structure. Without them, that structure has undeniably weakened. We are faced with shoring up the weakened parts, inventing new ways of being together that have pattern and order—for we cannot live without some pattern and order—but aren't so restrictive. Without sexual taboos, for instance, what are the social boundaries between men and women? When are they breached? What is offensive? Nobody's sure. Everybody's making mistakes. This is so excruciating that many are nostalgic for some of the old taboos. But once a taboo is broken, then for good or ill it's very hard, perhaps impossible, to reinstate it. 21

But there is another, subtler confusion: yes, enormous taboos have fallen, but many taboos, equally important, remain. And, both as individuals and as a society, we're strained enough, confused enough, by the results of doing away with so many taboos in so short a time, that maybe we're not terribly eager for our remaining taboos to fall. We may sincerely desire that, but maybe we're tired, fed up, scared. Many people would rather our taboos remain intact for a couple of generations while we get our act together again, and perhaps they have a point. But the price of taboos remains what it's always been: silence and constriction. 22

What do we see, when we pass each other on the street, but many faces molded by the price paid for keeping the silences of the taboos that remain—spirits confined within their own, and their society's, silences? Even this brief essay on our public and intimate strictures is enough to demonstrate that we are still a primitive race, bounded by fear and prejudice, with taboos looming in every direction—no matter how much we like to brag and/or bitch that modern life is liberating us from all the old boundaries. The word taboo still says much more about us than most prefer to admit. 23

What is the keeper of your silence? The answer to that question is your own guide to your personal taboos. How must you confine yourself in order to get through your day at the job, or to be acceptable in your social circle? The answer to that is your map of your 24 society's taboos. What makes you most afraid to speak? What desire, what word, what possibility, freezes and fevers you at the same time, making any sincere communication out of the question? What makes you vanish into your secret? That's your taboo, baby. You're still in the room, maybe even still smiling, still talking, but not really—what's really happened is that you've vanished down some hole in yourself, and you'll stay there until you're sure the threat to your taboo is gone and it's safe to come out again. If, that is, you've ever come out in the first place. Some never have.

What utterance, what hint, what insinuation, can quiet a room of family or friends? What makes people change the subject? What makes those at a dinner party dismiss a remark as though it wasn't said, or dismiss a person as though he or she wasn't really there? We've all seen conversations suddenly go dead, and just as suddenly divert around a particular person or subject, leaving them behind in the dead space, because something has been said or implied that skirts a silently shared taboo. If that happens to you often, don't kid yourself that you're living in a "free" society. Because you're only as free as your freedom from taboos—not on some grand abstract level, but in your day-to-day life. 25

It is probably inherent in the human condition that there are no "last" taboos. Or perhaps it just feels that way because we have such a long way to go. But at least we can know where to look; right in front of our eyes, in the recesses of our speechlessness, in the depths of our silences. And there is nothing for it but to confront the keepers of our silence. Either that, or to submit to being lost, as most of us silently are, without admitting it to each other or to ourselves—lost in a maze of taboos. 26

Meanings and Values

1. Ventura says, "Taboos, big or small, are always about having to respect somebody's (often irrational) boundary—or else" (Par. 1). Do you agree with this definition of the word "taboo"? Why, or why not? Why do you think that we must honor other people's boundaries? What does "or else" mean?
2. Explain the connection that Ventura makes in Paragraph 5 between silence and taboos. How does silence impact us personally and in relationships?
3. Why does much of our popular culture violate many societal taboos? How do the media encourage this?

Expository Techniques

1. Ventura places taboos into many categories. Some are broad (e.g., "big taboos" and "little taboos") while others are very specific (i.e., "corporate taboos" and "language taboos"). Does he deliberately give equal standing to specific taboos? If so, why?
2. Beginning in Paragraph 14, Ventura explains how enforced silence led to a whole series of taboos. What are some of the subcategories of taboos that disappeared with the American practice of free speech, and what connection does Ventura make between these subcategories and Americans' willingness to talk?

Diction and Vocabulary

1. Ventura uses the expression "social stigma" in Paragraph 18 in conjunction with dissolved marriages. He uses the words "shame" and "pain" connected to incest and abuse. Why does he use such words when he is comparing American society before its willingness to speak openly with contemporary, more open American society? (See "Guide to Terms": *Diction.*)
2. Why does Ventura provide us with the etymology (history) of the word "taboo" and an explanation of its assimilation into languages (Par. 6)?
3. If you do not know the meaning of some of the following words, look them up in a dictionary: *assimilation, ostracized, coerced* (Par. 6); *garish* (10); *catharsis* (13); *piety, disparate* (16); *stoic* (17).

Read to Write

1. **Collaborating:** Ventura makes clear his opinion that taboos, though a reflection of human nature, are dangerous to society because they cause us to be silent about many horrible things that may be happening in our lives. Can you think of cases in which silence and taboos might be positive? In a small group, create a list of such instances, and as a team prepare a short essay classifying and explaining these taboos.
2. **Considering Audience:** Society's taboos about premarital and extramarital sex are less strong now than they were in the first half of the twentieth century. Other taboos have changed as well. Consider an audience reading this essay in the 1960s. What parts of the discussion and examples might have worked well for most readers at the time? What taboos were probably no longer as forceful for these readers as they might have been for readers earlier in the century? Prepare an essay examining how one or more taboos changed during the course of the century.
3. **Developing an Essay:** Look over one or more editions of a local newspaper. Identify and list some issues or behaviors that the articles treat as taboos. Separate the items in the list into categories. Adding

further examples from your experience and knowledge, develop the list into an essay on the way newspapers and similar media such as magazines reinforce or undermine taboos. You might also examine the various kinds of news programs on television (both "hard" and "soft" news) and write about the way they treat taboos.

(NOTE: Suggestions for topics requiring development by use of CLASSIFICATION are on pp. 118–119 at the end of this chapter.)

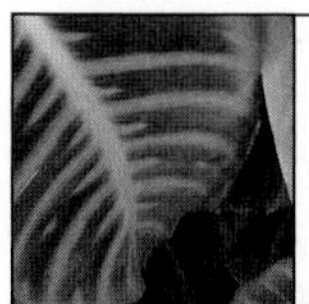

Issues and Ideas

Images of Sight and Sound

- Alissa Quart, *Cinema of the In-Crowd*
- Brenda Peterson, *Life Is a Musical*

Every day on television, in films, through songs, in magazine articles, and in countless other places we encounter images of people like us and also images of people whose lives are unfamiliar to us except as we encounter them through these images. Because images have the power to shape perceptions, relationships, and values, we need to recognize they can sometimes represent accurately and yet sometimes simplify and distort.

But what is an image? This is an easy question to answer for visual media like films, television, advertisements, and posters. It is a representation of a person's actions, attitudes, character traits, and relationships. The image can represent the person as an individual or as a typical member of a group. When the image is constructed simply from the traits of a group (often negative traits), we can refer to it as a stereotype. Negative (and often hurtful) stereotypes are quite familiar: the bimbo, the less-than-intelligent "jock," the absent-minded professor, or the violent gang member.

People frequently share traits with other members of a group, of course, but a stereotype erases individual differences. When all we know about a group comes from stereotypic images, especially negative ones, we need to be aware of the limitations of our understanding and look for more accurate images. In "Cinema of the In Crowd," Alissa Quart explores how stereotypes in teen movies sometimes fulfill—and sometimes upend—our expectations.

The images we receive through music, literature, and other forms of reading can be a bit harder to describe. In representing relationships, feelings, and values, these media present us with definitions of appropriate (or inappropriate) behavior and attitudes. These, in turn, can shape our perceptions, self-understanding, values, and relationships. Many of the images we receive through music can be positive and useful, as Brenda Peterson points out in "Life Is a Musical."

Images are not simply given to us by others. We can create them as well, especially in this age of recorders, cameras, and computers. Brenda Peterson's discussion of the way her family uses music to create and maintain its identity and the ways she integrates collections of songs into her own life are particularly interesting illustrations of how we can create images of ourselves (and others)—images that may act as creative responses to those thrust upon us every day.

ALISSA QUART

ALISSA QUART attended Brown University and the Columbia University School of Journalism. Her articles have appeared in numerous periodicals, including the *New York Times, The Nation, Elle, Film Comment,* and *Salon.* She has published two books: *Branded: The Buying and Selling of Teenagers* (2003) and *Hothause Kids: The Dilemma of the Gifted Child* (2006).

Cinema of the In-Crowd

This selection from *Branded* uses classification (and numerous examples) to look at a perennial favorite of filmgoers: the teenage film. Any classification of this sort is a look backward at films that have already appeared in theaters, of course, just as this essay looks back from 2003. At the same time, thinking about films in this way helps us as readers to understand new films, especially those created since 2003. It even encourages us to create new categories.

I was thirteen when I first understood what a teen film was. Knowledge arrived in the form of *The Breakfast Club.* 1

The characters include an indulged clotheshorse, a driven nerd, a vacant jock, a splenetic stoner, and an attention-deprived Goth. It was 1985, and the film was the *Ulysses* of its director, that maestro of puberty John Hughes, taking place as it did during a day of detention in the school library. At first the film's kids are mere types. The jock eats six turkey sandwiches for lunch, the nerd toadies up to the supervising teacher. The stoner sneers at the princess for being a virgin, bringing her own sushi, and having a drunk, rich mother. The jock accuses the loser of lying about his abuse—that his father burns the stoner with lit cigarettes. 2

But suddenly the quintet comes together, dancing, implausibly, to new wave music that emanates from an invisible stereo. Limbered up, they tell all. The nerd (Anthony Michael Hall) announces that he brought a gun to school to off himself—he was failing shop and thus screwing up his GPA. The jock (Emilio Estevez) lets it be known that he taped a geek's "buns together," imagining that doing so would finally convince his macho father he was a real man. 3

The nerd, lean with a scraggly mop of blonde hair and buggy eyes, recognizes that his day of inclusion and quasi-Method acting will end as soon as detention does. Near tears, as if recalling his 4 grade-grubbing harridan mom waiting for him at home, the nerd announces that they will all "become their parents": "It's unavoidable. . . . It just happens." "When you grow up, your heart dies," answers the Goth (Ally Sheedy), glittery-eyed and black-clad, excited by her own bleakness.

5 At thirteen, I suspected my heart would die also, sooner rather than later. It's embarrassing to admit now, but the film spoke to me. Sure, it's overacted and broad, like a summer-stock theater production. But it also has the ring of a diary entry, of what life is really like when our parents or teachers leave the room. Raging against high school cliques and hierarchies, it puts forth an appealingly sappy proposition: that all strata of kids should unite against two common enemies, their parents and a future of soulless-ness.

BRINGING IT ON

6 Fifteen years later, few popular teen films would depict such moments of veracity, or have responsible, liberal reflexes to guide them. Teen blockbusters—among them *Clueless, Bring It On, She's All That, Legally Blonde,* and *Varsity Blues*—had become the stories of insiders: sports stars, beauties, rich kids, and cheerleaders. These kids live in the blondest, richest suburbs, suburbs without seasons. The characters have abs so hard and defined they seem to have replaced personalities. It's difficult to feel affection for these studs and sylphs and even harder to pity them. . . . After visiting this cinematic life-world, one misses John Hughes. In fact, Hughes seems the apotheosis of teen film integrity.

7 The new films' fascination with the high school in-crowd echoes the marketing recommendations of Teenage Research Unlimited, a youth marketing agency whose clients include Sony and Coca-Cola. TRU's goal is to snag the shoppers of the in-crowd, called channelers or influencers—"the cream of the crop," those "that know their status and revel in it," as the TRU spokesman has said. "If you can attract them, you have scored. The biggest kiss of death is for you to be a cool brand in the mind of the conformers." The taste of the popular kids will reverberate downward.

8 In *Varsity Blues,* the hero is an influencer, a star quarterback (James Van Der Beek, formerly of *Dawson's Creek*). At the center of *She's All That* is an influencer, the senior class president and soccer star played by the canine-ishly handsome Freddie Prinze Jr. The heroine of *Legally Blonde* is a Bel Airhead beauty queen named Elle Woods. Elle, played by Reese Witherspoon, is the best-loved, prettiest, blondest

sorority girl at California University (this invented institution of higher learning happens to be an allusion to the college in the teen television show *Beverly Hills 90210*). When Elle goes to Harvard Law School, however, she is an outcast—because of the very qualities that made her so popular at CU. But she regains her influencer status at Harvard by applying her CU sensibility to a major law case. Her master stroke: keeping secret the shameful liposuction of her legal client, an aerobics instructor.

In *Bring It On,* the heroine is not just a cheerleader but a cheerleading *captain,* Torrance, played by Kirsten Dunst. Torrance struggles to keep her kingdom of cruel, anorexic simps happy—the resulting cheer-meets and cheer-offs are suffused with dialogue so excessively acid it resembles exchanges between drag queens in a mock cat fight. When one of the cheerleaders asks the team's hired choreographer why everyone has to go on a diet, he replies, "Because we're cheerleaders. We throw people in the air. And fat people don't go as high." When Torrance smiles winsomely at her crush while he watches her do her routine from the bleachers, her teammates are quick to judge. "You were having cheer-sex with him!" they say, aghast. 9

As a viewer shaped by an earlier teen film era, in which most films carried a whiff of after-school-special decency, I figured I knew what was coming in *Bring It On.* I expected Torrance to learn a lesson of some sort by the film's close, presumably some humanist nostrum about how girls of normal body mass are people, too. No such primer is doled out. Torrance doesn't muse about why she relies on pep and looks to get by but continues to let them work for her. (As for the film's box office, *Bring It On* appeals not just to lascivious boys but also to the prurient-older-man rental market; and no wonder, given the lithe teenagers performing deep splits and high kicks, their bodies encased in super-tight shirts, jog bras, colored panties, and even sudsy wet bikinis, the latter in the name of a car wash for, um, charity). *Bring It On's* screen teens are more often than not what critic Pauline Kael termed "un-people." *Most* of the kids in teen films are. Where in a former era the pubescent stars might have evinced personal fragility, they are now brittle and paper-thin. Where they once were confronted with real-life difficulties, they now have contests, social machinations, and makeovers. 10

The in-crowd wasn't always given the benefit of the doubt. Once, the in-crowd were ice princesses and authoritarian despots: the girls in 1989's *Heathers* or the malevolent pranksters who think 11 drenching a freak in pig's blood is funny, pace *Carrie.* In the former, the film's entirely unpleasant torturers, the all-named-Heather clones with upturned noses and flowing manes, answer the question "Why are you such a megabitch?" with the riposte "Because I can be." One of the Heathers demands that Veronica (played by a still *compos mentis* Winona Ryder) hold their hair while they vomit and that she join them in tormenting her former grade-geek friends. So when Veronica's gun-toting hipster boyfriend J.D. (Christian Slater) poisons one of the Heathers, our heroine's joining an offing of the gorgeous tyrants is something of a no-brainer. J.D. puts kitchen pipe cleanser into a hangover cure, and then Veronica willingly forges that Heather's suicide note. The two repeat the murder routine with two more of the school's vicious snobs. One can't help but notice that the dying villains of *Heathers* are boys and girls who would now be the heroes of teen films. In fact, the popular kids' brand consciousness—Veronica curses them as "Swatch dogs and Diet Coke heads"—is part of their villainy. Viewers are asked to hate these iniquitous snots to the extent that they might think the popular teens *do* deserve death by industrial-strength drain cleaner rather than sympathy or worship.

And, of course, the outsiders that do exist in the films today are 12 never as radically kooky as Ally Sheedy's character in *The Breakfast Club,* who shakes a head full of dandruff on her own drawing of a wintry landscape to make snow. If they start out disaffected and shunned, like the heroine of *She's All That,* for instance, we can be assured their marginality is only momentary—a quick costume change will seamlessly transform them into insiders in Act II.

The move toward the in-crowd emerges from an ever-increasing 13 need to appeal to huge audiences. With films opening on twice as many screens as they did twenty years ago, expensive television ad campaigns and an aversion to risk have become the norm. Films are no longer allowed to accrue audiences slowly; for the most part, if they don't open with a bang, they die. And studios have decreed that teens in particular must be herded into the theaters on opening weekend or else. The twelve-to-twenty-four-year-old niche may constitute only 18 percent of the public, but it makes up 37 percent of the film-going public. This is also the demographic that buys tie-ins: Studios are increasingly engaging in a "synergetic" cross-marketing agenda by hawking soundtracks and other products. With so much of a sales burden now riding on teen cinema, it's not a surprise that films have shrugged off their loser characters; after all, outcasts are less likely to sell clothes or music than their popular peers.

Meanings and Values

1. Identify each of the categories of films discussed in this selection.
2. What different sets of categories does the writer introduce in the course of this essay?
3. According to the writer, what are then main differences between the films of the 1980s and more recent films?
4. What elements of the film *Bring It On* does the writer find objectionable?

Expository Techniques

1. What techniques does the author use to announce the categories in the essay to readers?
2. Identify the strategy the author uses to begin this selection, and explain how it is connected to the rest of the discussion. (See "Guide to Terms": *Introductions.*)
3. The writer spends considerable time discussing the role played by Ally Sheedy in *The Breakfast Club.* What role does this extended discussion play in the essay?

Diction and Vocabulary

1. Identify particular words or groups of words the author uses in Paragraphs 9–10 to highlight what she considers objectionable features of *Bring It On.* (Guide: *Diction.*)
2. Identify those words or groups of words the author uses to convey and emphasize her evaluation of *Heathers.* (Guide: *Diction, Emphasis.*)
3. If you do not know the meaning of some of these words, look them up in a dictionary: *splenetic, toadies* (Par. 2); *implausibly, emanates* (3); *harridan* (4); *sappy* (5); *veracity, apotheosis* (6); *reverberate* (7); *aghast* (9); *nostrum, lascivious, prurient, lithe* (10); *despots, malevolent, riposte, iniquitous* (11); *disaffected, marginality* (12); *constitute* (13).

Read to Write

1. **Collaborating:** Working with a group of writers, make a list of types of films, recordings, television shows or other components of popular culture that you feel can be understood and explained through

classification. Then identify one or more sets of categories that help understand your subject. Finally, make a list of the sets of categories and each subcategory you might decide to include in an essay.

2. **Considering Audience:** Take the topic and categories you identified in question 1, above, and still working in a group, create four possible thesis statements, one each for each of these potential audiences: people from 18–25, 26–40, 41–60, and 61 or older.
3. **Developing an Essay:** Choose one of the audiences from question 2, above, and create an essay of your own using either the possible thesis statement you developed in a group or one you developed on your own.

(NOTE: Suggestions for topics requiring development by analysis of DEFINITION are on pp. 118–119 at the end of this chapter.)

BRENDA PETERSON

BRENDA PETERSON, a novelist and essayist, was born in 1950 in a forest ranger station in the Sierra Nevada Mountains. As a child she lived in many different places, especially in the Southeast. Currently, she lives in Seattle. Peterson received a B.A. in 1972 from the University of California-Davis. From 1972 to 1976 she worked as an editorial assistant at the *New Yorker* magazine. She has taught creative writing at Arizona State University and now works as an environmental writer. Her novels include *River of Light* (1978), *Becoming the Enemy* (1988), *Duck and Cover* (1991), and *Animal Heart* (2004). Her essays have been collected in *Living by Water: Essays on Life, Land and Spirit* (1990); *Nature and Other Mothers* (1992); *Sister Stories: Taking the Journey Together* (1996); *Between Species* (2003); and *Fact to Face* (2004).

Life Is a Musical

In this essay, Peterson offers several closely related classifications as a way of exploring the ways music can (and ought to) enrich and heal our emotional lives. This essay was first published in *Nature and Other Mothers.*

When the day is too gray, when the typewriter is too loud, after a lovers' quarrel, when a sister calls with another family horror story, when the phone never stops and those unanswered messages blink on my machine like angry, red eyes—I tune out my life and turn up the music. Not my favorite public radio station but my own personal frequency—I have my own soul's station. It is somewhere on the dial between Mozart's *Magic Flute,* the gospel-stomping tiger growl of Miss Aretha Franklin, Motown's deep dance 'n' strut, and the singing story of Broadway musicals. 1

Whether Katie Webster's Swamp Boogie Queen singing "Try a Little Tenderness," or a South American samba, whether it's the Persuasions crooning "Let It Be" or that throbbing baritone solo "Other Pleasures" from *Aspects of Love,* my musical solace is so complete it surrounds me in a mellifluous bubble like a placenta of sound. To paraphrase the visionary Stevie Wonder, I have learned to survive by making sound tracks in my own particular key of life. 2

For years now I've made what I call "tapes against terror" to hide me away from the noisy yak and call of the outside world. These homemade productions are dubbed Mermaid Music; sometimes 3

I send them to friends for birthdays and feel the pleasure of playing personal disc jockey to accompany their lives too. Among my siblings, we now exchange music tapes instead of letters. It is particularly gratifying to hear my nieces and nephews singing along to my tapes, as another generation inherits our family frequency.

I trace making my musical escapes to a childhood of moving around. As we packed the cardboard boxes with our every belonging—sometimes we hadn't even bothered to unpack our dresses from those convenient hanging garment containers provided by the last moving company—the singing began. From every corner of the emptying house, we'd hear the harmonies: my father a walking bass as he heaved-ho in the basement; my mother's soprano sometimes shrill and sharp as the breaking glass in the kitchen; my little brother between pure falsetto and a tenor so perfect we knew he'd stopped packing his room simply to sing; my sisters and I weaving between soprano and first and second alto from our bedrooms as we traded and swapped possessions for our next life. At last gathered in the clean, white space that was once our house, we'd hold hands and sing "Auld Lang Syne." Piling into the station wagon, with the cat in a wooden box with slats for air holes, Mother would shift into a rousing hymn, "We'll Leave It All Behind," or sometimes, if she was mutinously happy to hightail it out of some small "burg" as she called them, she'd lead us into "Shuffle Off to Buffalo," substituting wherever we were moving for the last word. "Chattanooga Choo Choo" and "California, Here We Come" were her standard favorites for leave-taking. If, as we drove past our schools and our friends' houses for the last time, the harmonies in the backseat faltered, Mother might remind us that choirs of angels never stayed long in one place singing because the whole world needed music. Father might suggest some slower songs, as long as they weren't sad. 4

In all the shifting landscapes and faces of my childhood, what stays the same is the music. First, there was my mother's music, which seems now to have entered effortlessly into her children's minds as if we were tiny tape recorders: the mild, sweetly suave Mills Brothers, Mitch Miller's upbeat swing, the close sibling harmonies of the Andrews Sisters, and always the church music, the heartfelt Sunday singing, which is the only thing I ever miss since leaving that tight fellowship of Southern Baptist believers. 5

Ever since I can remember—certainly I have flashes of being bounced around in the floating dark of my mother's womb as she tap-danced on the church organ pedals, sang at the top of her voice, and boogied across the keys—there has been this music. It is the 6 only counterpoint to, the only salvation from a sermon that paralyzes the soul into submitting to a jealous God. From the beginning, music was an alternative to that hellfire terror. I can still hear it: a preacher's voice, first a boom, then a purr that raises into a hiss and howl to summon that holy hurricane of fire and brimstone. But after enduring the scourge of sins, there came the choir. Cooing and shushing, mercy at last fell upon those of us left on an Earth that this God had long ago abandoned. Listening to the full-bodied harmonies, I could close my eyes and heretically wonder, Wasn't Heaven still here?

Yessss, hallelujah, still here. . . . Hush, can't you hear? the choir murmured like so many mammies' lullabies. Then silence as a small woman stepped forward, her rapt vibrato shimmering like humid heat lightning right before rain. Or a baritone dropping his woes and his dulcet voice low as a cello, caressing a whole congregation. If we were blessed that Sunday, there might be a shorter sermon and a "songfest" with harmonies we could hear in our heads, syncopating, counterpointing in a lovely braid of bright sound that beckoned us. *Sing now, brothers and sisters.* And we were many voices making one song. The fundamental fear was gone; weren't we already angels in Heaven? 7

Now that I am forty and have been what my family pityingly refers to as "settled-down" for ten years, now that I am so far backslid from the fellowship of the Southern Baptist believers, now that I no longer even make top ten on my mother's prayer list, now that the terror of Hell has been replaced by the terror of living, I still find myself calling upon my homemade choirs to accompany me in my car, to surround my study or kitchen and sing back the demons of daily life. Sometimes I've even caught myself slipping another tape against terror into the stereo and singing a distracted riff of my mother's favorite, "We'll Leave It All Behind." 8

During the recent holy war between the United States and Iraq, with the apocalyptic rhetoric about "Satan" and "infidels" eerily reminiscent of southern revivals—Mermaid Music was working long hours to meet my own and my friends' wartime demands. To offset NPR's daily interviews with military experts commenting on the allied video-war air strikes with the zealous aplomb of sportscasters, I'd surrender to the tender tenor of Aaron Neville singing "With God on Our Side" or "Will the Circle Be Unbroken?" As I drove along freeways where phosphorescent orange bumper stickers shouted USA KICKS BUTT! or OPERATION DESERT STORM, as if it were a souvenir banner of a hot vacation spot, I wondered that there was 9 no music for the Gulf War. Where were the songs like "My Buddy" or "It's a Long Way to Tipperary"?

During the last days of the war, I relied upon Bach's Violin 10
Concerto in D Minor, the fierce longing of Jacqueline DePres's cello, Fauré's Requiem and, as always, Mozart. On a particularly bad day, between the Pentagon press conferences—men with pointers, target maps, smart-bomb videos, and a doublespeak war doggerel that called bombing "servicing a target"—I made a beeline to my public library and checked out every musical from *Oklahoma* to *Miss Saigon.* I made a tape entitled "Life Is a Musical" and divided it into three sections: (1) Love Found in Strange Places, (2) Love Lost Everywhere, and (3) Love Returns. It was astonishing how songs from vastly different time periods and places segued together. My favorite storyline riff is "Empty Chairs at Empty Tables," from *Les Misérables* to "The American Dream" from *Miss Saigon* to "Carefully Taught" from *South Pacific* to "Don't Cry for Me, Argentina," from *Evita* to "Bring Him Home" from *Les Misérables.* When I sent copies out to a select group of musicals-loving friends, it was as if we were all together at a candlelight mass or cross-continent communion, trying to imagine a war where no bombs fell.

Playing my own tapes against terror is a way to document and 11
summon back the necessities that mothered them. For example, "My Funny Valentine," with its Billie Holiday/Sarah Vaughan/Ella Fitzgerald/Alberta Hunter blues and ebullience is still a favorite, long after that lover has gone. Upon hearing that an old friend had bone cancer, I made him a tape called "Music to Heal By," which included the Delta Rhythm Boys' version of "Dry Bones." My friend wrote to say it was the first time he'd laughed in a long time. Now he's making his own tapes. After a writer friend of mine drank herself to death, I felt so bereft—since, after all, we'd planned to retire to the Black Hole Nursing Home for Wayward Writers together—that I made a tape called "The Ten Commandments of Love, or Southern Baptists Beware!" It's every song I ever slow-danced to or memorized in the sweaty backseat of a borrowed car as my date and I broke Sunday school rules on Saturday night. Declared by my siblings and southern pals to have gone into "metal" (their word for platinum or gold), it includes Etta James's soaring "At Last," Sam Cooke's silky "Wonderful World," and a steamy duet of "634–5789" with Robert Cray and Tina Turner. It's a great tape for getting in the mood.

Since ancient times, the Chinese have believed that certain 12
sounds can balance and heal. In acupressure, for example, each organ has a sound. Listening to a healthy heart, an astute healer can

hear laughter or, if there is disease, wind. The gallbladder shouts; the stomach speaks in a singsong, sometimes overly sympathetic voice; and the kidney, ever the perfectionist, groans. Sighs can be a sign of liver ailments, and the pitch of a person's voice can tell a story of that body's health just as well as a tongue. In some Taoist practices to enhance longevity, re-creating the sounds of certain organs can strengthen and tone them. For example, the *whuuuh whuuuh* sound of the kidney can revitalize the adrenals, fortifying the immune system. If one cannot take time to sing in the key of every organ, I'd suggest Chinese wind chimes like the ones that grace my back porch. When a strong salt wind blows off the beach, my chimes, which are perfectly pitched to a five-element Chinese scale, play an impromptu arpeggio—a momentary transport to some monastic garden, a Shangri-la of sound. Scientific studies report that the actual sound of nature resonates at the level of eight hertz; by comparison, a refrigerator reverberates at eighty hertz. Is it any wonder some of us need to return to a musical womb to retreat from such technological onslaughts to our nervous systems?

In fact, our time in the womb is not at all quiet; it is a noisy 13
symphony of voices, lower-tract rumbles, whirrings like waterfalls, and white noise. One of my friends found that if she played a tape of the roar of her sturdy Kirby vacuum cleaner, the sound immediately put her boisterous newborn twins to sleep. I have another friend whose entire house is wall-to-wall egg cartons, which absorb sound as well as enhance his audiophilic tendencies. I've visited houses that sound like living inside an aquarium, where pleasant underwater burbles from elaborate tropical fish tanks drown out the world. I've also entered homes where cuckoo clocks, grandfather chimes, and deep gongs count the hours so that I felt I was inside a ticking time bomb. Consciously or unconsciously we all make sound tracks to underscore our lives.

Mermaid Music has allowed me to enter a reverie of song, a 14
backstage "smaller-than-life" sojourn away from all the stresses. Right now I'm at work on two dance tapes for a summer roll-up-the-rug party. Entitled "Bop till You Drop" and "Bad Girls," the tapes defy all hearers not to kick up their heels with such all-time hits as "Heat Wave" and "I Heard It Through the Grapevine," as well as the ever-popular "R-E-S-P-E-C-T." Of course, I've had request for sequels and am at work on "Life Is a Musical II" divided into (1) "Falling," (2) "Feeling," and (3) "Forever Ruined/Recovery." It flows from "People Will Say We're in Love" to "Happy Talk" to "Just You Wait, Henry Higgins!"

My siblings say I should sell my tapes against terror on late-night TV in the company of such classics as Veg-O-Matics and "Elvis Lives" medleys. The idea fills me with horror. After all, there are copyright violations cops who come like revenuers in the dark of the night to bust local moonshiners and music makers. I'd rather stay strictly small-time and nonprofit, like that long-ago lullaby service I had in college, a trio of nannies against nightmares. But if anyone out there in music land is making his or her own tapes against terror, I'd be open to an exchange. After all, it's better than bombs through the mail or collecting baseball cards. 15

So tune in, and maybe we'll find ourselves on the same frequency. On this lifelong Freeway of Love, I just want to be an Earth Angel with my Magic Flute. Because after all, Everybody Plays the Fool and Ain't Nobody's Business If I Do. 16

Meanings and Values

1. In a paragraph of your own, summarize what this essay has to say about music, human emotions, and the relationship between them.
2. What subject or subjects is Peterson classifying in this essay?
3. Explain what the writer means by the phrase "my soul's station" (Par. 1).

Expository Techniques

1. Which paragraph announces the purpose and theme of the essay? (See "Guide to Terms": *Purpose; Unity.*) Can this essay be said to have a thesis statement? If so, where is it? (Guide: *Thesis.*)
2. What pattern other than classification does the writer employ in Paragraph 4? (Hint: see Chapter 8.)
3. What different subjects does Peterson classify in this essay? How, if at all, does the writer keep these different classifications from overlapping in a confusing manner? Would this essay be more effective if the writer had concentrated on only one or two of the classifications? Explain. (Guide: *Evaluation.*)
4. What is the function of the clauses that open the first sentence in the essay? (Guide: *Syntax; Introductions.*)

Diction and Vocabulary

1. Identify the extended comparison in Paragraph 12 and explain its relation to the central theme of the essay. (Guide: *Figures of Speech; Unity.*)

2. Identify those paragraphs in the essay that begin with transition words indicating that they will further develop the topic or ideas of the preceding paragraph. Discuss whether the transition words serve effectively to link paragraphs and ideas within the essay. (Guide: *Transition.*)

3. If you do not know the meaning of some of the following words, look them up in the dictionary: *solace, mellifluous, placenta* (Par. 2); *falsetto* (4); *suave* (5); *heretically* (6); *dulcet* (7); *riff* (8); *eerily, zealous, aplomb* (9); *segued* (10); *ebullience* (11); *astute* (12); *audiophilic* (13).

READ TO WRITE

1. **Collaborating:** Working in a group, list several types or categories of music. Then list the types of experiences, moods, or activities each group member associates with the different types of music. Note any similarities or patterns the group observes in the relationship between the kinds of music and the responses or uses of the music. Collectively plan an essay explaining the kinds of music and the typical responses to them. Consider drawing on this plan for an essay of your own.

2. **Considering Audience:** How effective are Peterson's examples for a young adult audience today? For an audience in some other age group? Write an essay on a plan similar to Peterson's but using musical examples directed at a particular age or cultural group with which you are familiar.

3. **Developing an Essay:** Drawing strategies from Peterson's essay, prepare an essay of your own, classifying tastes in art, movies, sports, or some other area of cultural or social activity. Try to explain why differences in people's tastes can be understood on the basis of differences in character, background, or some other factor.

(NOTE: Suggestions for topics requiring development by use of CLASSIFICATION follow.)

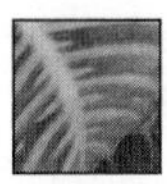

Writing Suggestions for Chapter 4

Classification

Use division and classification (into at least three categories) as your basic method of analyzing one of the following subjects from an interesting point of view. (Your instructor may have good reason to place limitations on your choice of subject.) Narrow the topic as necessary to enable you to do a thorough job.

1. College students
2. College teachers
3. Athletes
4. Coaches
5. Salespeople
6. Hunters (or fishers)
7. Parents
8. Drug users
9. Police officers
10. Summer (or part-time) jobs
11. Sailing vessels
12. Game show hosts
13. Friends
14. Careers
15. Horses (or other animals)
16. Television programs
17. Motivations for study
18. Methods of studying for exams
19. Lies
20. Selling techniques
21. Tastes in clothes
22. Contemporary music or films
23. Love
24. Ways to spend money
25. Attitudes toward life
26. Fast foods (or junk foods)
27. Smokers
28. Investments
29. Actors
30. Books or magazines

Collaborative Exercises

1. Working in a group, prepare a classification essay on college life using numbers 1–4 in the preceding exercise as the major sections for your classification. Assign group members to divide each of the four sections into two or three subcategories and to prepare a section of an essay explaining these subcategories. Then prepare a collaboratively written essay linking each section with clear transitions and unifying the whole with

a central idea on which all members of the group agree. (See "Guide to Terms": *Unity.*)

2. As a group, create three or more categories from the subject "careers" (see number 14). Have each member of the group research one of the types of careers and then create a collaboratively written essay with an appropriate introduction, conclusion, thesis, and transitions.

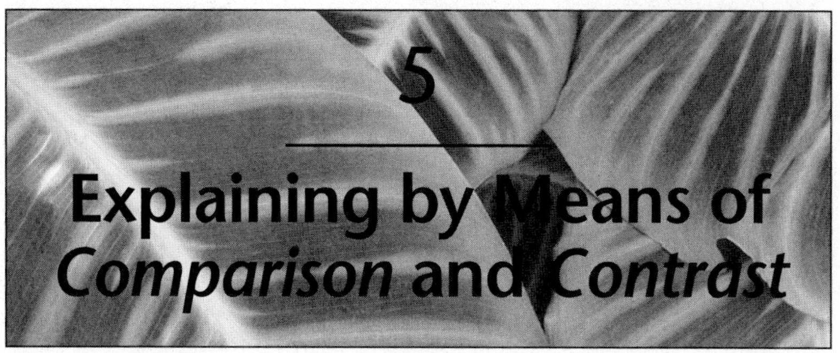

5

Explaining by Means of *Comparison and Contrast*

One of the first expository methods we used as children was **comparison,** noticing similarities of objects, qualities, and actions, or **contrast,** noticing their differences. We compared the color of the new puppies with that of their mother, contrasted a parent's height with our own. Then the process became more complicated. Now we employ it frequently in college essay examinations or term papers when we compare or contrast forms of government, reproductive systems of animals, or ethical philosophies of humans. In the business or professional world, we prepare important reports based on comparison and contrast—between kinds of equipment for purchase, the personnel policies of different departments, or precedents in legal matters. Nearly all people use the process of comparison (meaning both *comparing* and *contrasting*) many times a day—in choosing a head of lettuce, in deciding what to wear to school, in selecting a house, or a friend, or a religion.

In expository writing, brief comparisons—a sentence or two—may serve to alert readers to similarities or highlight differences. Longer comparisons need to do more; they need to explore the subject and convey the writer's perspective. For a longer comparison or contrast that explains or explores ideas, you need an ordered plan to avoid having a mere list of characteristics or a frustrating jumble of similarities and differences. You also need to give attention to all the important points of similarity (or difference). The following paragraph accomplishes all these things.

> We really are terribly confused about our relationship with nature. On the one hand, we like to live in houses that are tidy and clean, and

> if nature should be rude enough to enter—in the form of a bat in the attic, or a mouse in the kitchen, or a cockroach crawling along the skirting boards—we stalk it with the blood-lust of a tabby cat; we resort to chemical warfare. In fact, we judge people harshly if their house is full of dust and dirt. And yet, on the other hand, we just as obsessively bring nature indoors. We touch a switch and light floods the room. We turn a dial and suddenly it feels like summer or winter. We live in a perpetual breeze or bake of our devising. We buy posters and calendars with photographs of nature. We hang paintings of landscapes on our walls. We scent everything that touches our lives. We fill our houses with flowers and pets. We try hard to remove ourselves from all the dramas and sensations of nature, and yet without them we feel lost and disconnected. So, subconsciously, we bring them right back indoors again. Then we obsessively visit nature—we go swimming, jogging, or cross-country skiing, we take strolls in a park. Confusing, isn't it?
>
> —Diane Ackerman, *Deep Play*

WHY USE COMPARISON?

Highlighting similarities and differences is the most obvious use for comparison, but merely a starting point for effective writing. Whenever you employ the pattern, therefore, make sure you give it a worthwhile purpose. You can contrast llamas with potbellied pigs, for example, but your efforts will likely seem silly or trivial unless tied to some larger goal such as their relatively suitability as pets.

The question of purpose is especially important in a formal, full-scale analysis by comparison and contrast where the pattern lends shape to an entire essay. Sometimes the purpose may be merely to reveal *surprising or frequently overlooked likenesses and differences,* with the goal of adding to readers' knowledge, satisfying their curiosity, or developing their self-awareness. For example, an essay on generational differences over responsibility for housework might explain that younger people are more likely to share the work of cooking and cleaning, but that all generations seem to be maintaining traditional gender differences in the responsibility of home maintenance. Mark Twain, in the selection "Two Ways of Seeing a River" (pp. 132–133), contrasts his view of the Mississippi as a young man with his perspective as an experienced river pilot. In doing so, he helps readers understand how radically experience and changes in attitude can affect our perceptions of the external world—even making the same stretch of scenery appear a different place.

The aim may be to show *the superiority* of one thing over another. Or it may be to *explain* and *evaluate,* as in a discussion of alternatives or of differing points of view on an issue. For instance, you might examine competing proposals for an antismoking campaign, one designed by teenagers and the other by advertising professionals, evaluating the strengths and limitations of each.

The purpose could be to explain the *unfamiliar* (wedding customs in Ethiopia) by comparing it to the *familiar* (wedding customs in Kansas). Or it could be to support and explore a thesis, as is the case with several of the essays in this chapter. Alice Walker ("Am I Blue?" pp. 154–158), for example, uses comparison to advance the thesis that animals have emotional lives similar to those of humans. Catherine Seipp ("Meet Today's Dad," pp. 167–169) uses contrast between "Today's Dad" and "Yesterday's Dad" to explain why she believes the current version is "a model to avoid."

CHOOSING A STRATEGY

To take a comparison beyond the obvious and develop knowledge and insight worth sharing with readers, you need to begin by identifying **points of comparison** (or **points of contrast**), both major and minor. Some important points of comparison will be apparent to you (and your readers) from the outset, and therefore should be part of your analysis. Others will be less apparent, though not necessarily less important. Including them will enable you to provide a fresh or more thorough perspective, adding to your reader's understanding. Consider using the following questions to identify and explore points of comparison, adapted, of course, to the particular demands of your subjects.

What are the similar (or different) **physical aspects** (shape, color, size, texture, movement) of the subjects you are analyzing?

Parts and Processes (elements and their relationships, methods of operation, instructions)?
Benefits (individual, social, political, environmental)?
Problems (dangers, difficulties, limitations)?
Costs (financial, emotional, political)?
Uses (personal, social, environmental; to provide benefits, to create relationships, to accomplish a particular goal)?

As you develop responses to questions like these, keep in mind that you are trying to develop fresh insights both for yourself and your readers. Consider using questions like these to help you develop such a perspective.

What similarities (or differences) are readers likely to consider. . . .

Intriguing or surprising?
Useful or worth learning about?
Quite different from what they expected before they began reading?
Significant enough to make them more likely to consider different opinions on an issue or approaches to a problem?
Important enough to guide their choice among alternative policies, products, or conclusions?

The points of comparison you choose, along with your tentative thesis, your purpose for writing, and the complexity of your materials, will usually suggest an arrangement for your writing. The number of subjects making up any comparison (two or more) and the likelihood that you will be exploring multiple points of comparison along with their supporting details mean that you should plan the organization of an essay carefully and remember to make this arrangement clear to readers.

One of the two basic methods of comparison is to present all the information on the two (or more) subjects, one at a time, and to summarize by combining their most important similarities and differences. Here is a subject-by-subject plan for an essay.

Subject-by-Subject Pattern

Introduction
Subjects: Bella Costa Medical Center (curing illness) and Foothills Regional Health Complex (creating wellness)
Tentative Thesis: Today's health care dilemmas have gone beyond choices among insurance plans to choices between two very different kinds of medical treatment: one focused on curing illness (represented by Bella Costa M.C.), the other focused on creating wellness (represented by Foothills R.H.C.).
Subject 1: Bella Costa Medical Center
- Feature 1: Traditional medicine—curing illness
- Feature 2: Large hospital, newest equipment

Feature 3: Large staff of physicians
Feature 4: Emphasis on drugs, surgery, physical therapy

Subject 2: Foothills Regional Health Complex
Feature 1: Preventive medicine—creating wellness
Feature 2: Small hospital, limited facilities, local clinics
Feature 3: Some physicians, other staff including nutritionists, exercise specialists, and alternative therapists
Feature 4: Emphasis on diet, exercise, alternative therapies (acupuncture, holistic medicine), healthy lifestyle

Conclusion (summary): Summarize reasons for choosing either one and suggest that personal preferences may play an important role.

This method may be desirable if there are few points to compare, or if the individual points are less important than the overall picture they present.

However, if there are several points of comparison to be considered, or if the points are of individual importance, alternation of the material would be a better arrangement.

Point-by-Point Pattern

Subjects: *The Mummy* (1932) starring Boris Karloff
The Mummy (1999) starring Brendan Fraser

Tentative Thesis: The original version of *The Mummy* (1932) takes itself and the horror movie form seriously and provides an often scary portrait of evil. The remake (1999) takes itself only half-seriously and gently pokes fun at the conventions of the horror movie, so it is only occasionally scary and conveys no sense of evil.

Subject 1: Original version of *The Mummy*
Feature 1 (acting): Boris Karloff, serious acting style, dramatic scenes and speeches
Feature 2 (script): Provides motivation for characters, emphasizes force of evil desires
Feature 3 (special effects): Support story line, emphasize unnatural desires and presence of evil

Subject 2: Remake of *The Mummy*
Feature 1 (acting): Brendan Fraser, comic or ironic acting style, action scenes and physical comedy
Feature 2 (script): Little motivation for characters, highlights stereotypes and conventions of horror movies

Feature 3 (special effects): Call attention to themselves, emphasize unreal and exaggerated elements of horror stories

Conclusion (summary):

Original and remake show changing attitudes toward the horror movie as a portrait of evil.

Often the subject matter or the purpose itself will suggest a more casual treatment, or some combination or variation of the two basic methods. We might present the complete information on the first subject, then summarize it point by point within the complete information on the second. And although expository comparisons and contrasts are frequently handled together, it is sometimes best to present all similarities first, then all differences—or vice versa, depending on the emphasis desired. In any basic use of comparison, the important thing is to have a plan that suits the purpose and material, thoughtfully worked out in advance.

DEVELOPING COMPARISONS

In writing an essay using comparison as a primary pattern of exposition, keep these two important tasks in mind: 1) take care that your comparisons are logical and arranged in a manner that will be clear to your readers, and 2) provide detailed explanations of the similarities and differences in order to support your conclusions.

Above all, your comparison needs to be *logical.* A logical comparison or contrast can be made only between subjects of the same general type. (Analogy, a special form of comparison used for another purpose, is discussed in the next chapter.) For example, contrasting modern medicine (prescription drugs, surgery) and traditional medicine (herbal remedies, acupuncture) could be useful or meaningful, but little would be gained by contrasting surgery and carpentry.

Transition words and phrases are a big help with both logic and the arrangement of an essay, reminding you of an essay's plan as you write and signaling the arrangement to readers. Some transition words identify the elements of a subject, some indicate logical relationships or highlight the place of a paragraph in the overall organization, and some identify conclusions and supporting detail.

Elements of a Subject: trait, characteristic, element, part, segment, unit, feature

Logical Relationships and Arrangement: in comparison, in contrast, on the other side, on the other hand, likewise, moreover, similarly, in the same (or different) manner, in addition, then, further, yet, but, however, nonetheless, first, second, third, although, still

Conclusions and Supporting Detail: in conclusion, to sum up, finally, for example, for instance

Paragraphs are especially important in writing that compares or contrasts. Typically, they are devoted to one of the major steps in the exposition, often to one of the main points of comparison. In focusing on points of similarity or dissimilarity, be thorough. Provide facts, concrete details, and examples. Consider those that support your conclusions or recommendations as well as those that provide contrary evidence. Remember, too, that effective comparisons serve a purpose, so include details that support your overall thesis and further the purpose for which you are writing.

Student Essay

In the following essay, Amy Bell uses comparison as a pattern of thinking: a way to raise questions about and explore her topic. She inquires into the "truthfulness" of two pieces of writing that claim to be portrayals of events that really happened, and in so doing she raises questions about what really constitutes "truth" in writing. Amy uses comparison effectively in her own writing both as a way of representing her thinking and as a way of helping readers understand the many detailed similarities and differences she analyzes.

Perception of Truth

by Amy Bell

"The following motion picture is based on a true story." How many times have you seen this on the movie screen and thought, "Yeah, right, 'true' story my foot"? We all know that the movie producers/directors take huge liberties with the facts and portray events differently from the way they actually occurred. The same is true in non-fiction writing. Each author chooses what information to give to the reader and what information to withhold. In doing this the "truth" is blurred and the

Focuses on general topic/issue to be explored

author's personal bias emerges. Truman Capote and Norman Mailer are both hailed as authors who succeeded in writing "true-story" novels. In describing Norman Mailer's *The Executioner's Song*, critics have said he is "our greatest chronicler" and "the best journalist in the country" (Mailer cover). Critics have described Truman Capote's *In Cold Blood* as a "superbly written 'true account'" and "the best documentary of an American crime" (Capote cover). All of these book reviews imply that Mailer and Capote gave only the truth in their books. However, this is not possible. Mailer's and Capote's personal opinions also must be in these novels. So which novel is more truthful? This question cannot be answered. How can we ever know what information these authors changed or what information they left out completely? However, it is possible to show which novel creates a greater impression of truth. Truman Capote's novel, *In Cold Blood*, seems more truthful than Mailer's *The Executioner's Song*. The impression of truth in these novels was partly created by the way in which each author portrayed the murderer in his story.

Focuses on specific topic of essay

Purpose of essay—to be accomplished by comparing and contrasting

Thesis statement

General plan for essay—compare the works

Norman Mailer and Truman Capote both had unlimited access to the facts about the murderers, Gary Gilmore and Perry Smith [respectively]. In researching Gilmore, Mailer collected interview manuscripts, court records, and documents. He also conducted nearly 300 interviews, which added up to a manuscript of 15,000 pages (Mailer 1020). Capote also collected numerous official records and conducted interviews (Capote acknowledgments page). Capote and Mailer used carefully selected bits of truth from this multitude of information to portray their murderers differently.

Background—both Mailer and Capote

One obvious way in which Mailer and Capote described the murderers was to directly quote them. Norman Mailer put a numerous amount of quotations from Gilmore in his novel. Nearly forty letters written by Gilmore to his girlfriend Nicole were printed in the book. Mailer also included a great deal of interviews between Gilmore and his two lawyers. A lot of "truth" is

Feature 1: Quotations

Discussion of Mailer

divulged because so much personal information about Gilmore is given. However, for the reader this truth becomes blurred because of Gilmore's contradicting feelings and intense emotions. For instance, in one letter Gilmore writes to Nicole he says, "I saw a simple, quiet Truth, a profound, deep, and personal Truth of beauty and love" (qtd. in Mailer 345). It would seem that through these words the reader might see who the "true" Gary is. However, in the next letter the reader is bombarded with ". . . these chickens——t pricks. Give a motherf——er a little authority and they think they have to start taking privileges away from people . . . bunch of slack-jawed . . . gurgling . . . punks" (Mailer 348). Gilmore's variety of raving emotions weaves in and out of the letters in the book, leaving the reader wary of believing anything Gilmore says. Norman Mailer gives us too much information from an unreliable Gilmore, and in doing so there seems to be less truth.

Supporting details

Interpretation of details

Capote also quotes his murderer, Perry Smith; however, he uses fewer, carefully selected quotations. Capote only uses enough quotations to give an ample description of Smith. This creates less confusion for the reader about Smith. Smith could have been just as confusing to understand as Gilmore was; after all, Smith did kill four people without knowing why he did it. For example, Capote includes a few carefully selected quotations to describe Smith's childhood. Smith is describing the brutality of the nuns in an orphanage he lived in as a child: "She woke me up. She had a flashlight, and she hit me with it. Hit me and hit me. And when the flashlight broke, she went on hitting me in the dark" (qtd. in Capote 93). This well-chosen quotation gives the reader an understanding of Smith's childhood and gives a glimpse into the mind of Smith. Capote tells the reader who Smith is, instead of the reader having to figure out who Smith is by sorting through hundreds of Smith's thoughts. Capote gives us what he thinks the truth about Smith is, and he does it in such a way that the reader is compelled to believe it.

Feature 1: Quotations

Discussion of Capote

Supporting details

Interpretation of details

One way to make a story more believable and truthful is to give equal weight to everyone's side of the story. Mailer thoroughly gives Gilmore's side of the story; however, the stories of the victims are hardly mentioned. In chapters twelve and fifteen of part four, Mailer gives a basic description of the lives of the Bushnells and the Jensens. He only devotes about twenty pages out of 1,000 pages to these people. Also, Mailer's description of these people is not an intimate one. He gives an overview of their lives in a distant, journalistic style. Mailer writes, "It was at Utah State that Colleen was introduced to her future husband, Max Jensen" (Mailer 212). This is simply a description, and the voices and feelings of Max and Colleen are not seen.

Feature 2: Equal weight in presentation

Discussion of Mailer

Conclusion followed by supporting details

Capote, on the other hand, gives an equal amount of time to everyone's side of the story. In the first chapter, "Last to See Them Alive," Capote describes the Clutter family while also describing Dick [Smith's accomplice] and Perry [Smith]. Capote shows each member of the Clutter family, their relationships with each other and with the community. Capote includes a lot of dialogue between members of the family, so that the reader can see the murder victims as real people. The following is a conversation between Nancy Clutter and her brother, Kenyon. [Nancy speaks first.]

Feature 2: Equal weight in presentation

Discussion of Capote

Conclusion followed by supporting details

"I keep smelling cigarette smoke."

"On your breath?" inquired Kenyon.

"No funny one. Yours." (Capote 19)

In this interplay between brother and sister the reader can relate to the Clutters as human beings and not just as murder victims. Capote gives an in-depth, intimate description of every person's side of the story. For the reader this creates a perception that Capote was less biased, and therefore the story seems truthful.

Interpretation of details

Using basic logic, it would seem that Mailer probably wrote down more "truth" in a 1,000-page book than Capote wrote in a meager 350-page book. However, the amount of truth and the perception of truth are two very different things. Truman Capote's *In Cold Blood*

Summary conclusion: Capote <u>seems</u> more truthful

gives a greater perception of truth than Norman Mailer's *The Executioner's Song*. Then again, this statement is merely my opinion. As the author of this essay, I selected only the "appropriate" bits of information from these two novels to give my reader(s) my perception of what "truth" is.

Works Cited

Capote, Truman. *In Cold Blood*. New York: Modern Library, 1965. Print.

Mailer, Norman. *The Executioner's Song*. New York: Warner, 1979. Print.

MARK TWAIN

MARK TWAIN was the pen name of Samuel Clemens (1835–1910). He was born in Missouri and became the first author of importance to emerge from "beyond the Mississippi." Although best known for bringing humor, realism, and Western local color to American fiction, Mark Twain wanted to be remembered as a philosopher and social critic. Still widely read, in most languages and in all parts of the world, are his numerous short stories (his "tall tales," in particular), autobiographical accounts, and novels, especially *Adventures of Huckleberry Finn* (1884). Ernest Hemingway called the last "the best book we've had," an appraisal with which many critics agree.

Two Ways of Seeing a River

"Two Ways of Seeing a River" (editor's title) is from Mark Twain's "Old Times on the Mississippi," which was later expanded and published in book form as *Life on the Mississippi* (1883). It is autobiographical. The prose of this selection is vivid, as is all of Mark Twain's writing, but considerably more reflective in tone than most.

Now when I had mastered the language of this water and had come to know every trifling feature that bordered the great river as familiarly as I knew the letters of the alphabet, I had made a valuable acquisition. But I had lost something, too. I had lost something which could never be restored to me while I lived. All the grace, the beauty, the poetry, had gone out of the majestic river! I still kept in mind a certain wonderful sunset which I witnessed when steamboating was new to me. A broad expanse of the river was turned to blood; in the middle distance the red hue brightened into gold, through which a solitary log came floating, black and conspicuous; in one place a long, slanting mark lay sparkling upon the water; in another the surface was broken by boiling, tumbling rings that were as many-tinted as an opal; where the ruddy flush was faintest was a smooth spot that was covered with graceful circles and radiating lines, ever so delicately traced; the shore on our left was densely wooded, and the somber shadow that fell from this forest was broken in one place by a long, ruffled trail that shone like silver; and high above the forest wall a clean-stemmed dead tree waved a single leafy bough that glowed like a flame in the unobstructed splendor that was flowing from the sun. There were graceful curves, reflected images, woody heights, soft distances, and over 1 the whole scene, far and near, the dissolving lights drifted steadily, enriching it every passing moment with new marvels of coloring.

I stood like one bewitched. I drank it in, in a speechless rapture. 2
The world was new to me and I had never seen anything like this at home. But as I have said, a day came when I began to cease from noting the glories and the charms which the moon and the sun and the twilight wrought upon the river's face; another day came when I ceased altogether to note them. Then, if that sunset scene had been repeated, I should have looked upon it without rapture and should have commented upon it inwardly after this fashion: "This sun means that we are going to have wind tomorrow; that floating log means that the river is rising, small thanks to it; that slanting mark on the water refers to a bluff reef which is going to kill somebody's steamboat one of these nights, if it keeps on stretching out like that; those tumbling 'boils' show a dissolving bar and a changing channel there; the lines and circles in the slick water over yonder are a warning that that troublesome place is shoaling up dangerously; that silver streak in the shadow of the forest is the 'break' from a new snag and he has located himself in the very best place he could have found to fish for steamboats; that tall dead tree, with a single living branch, is not going to last long, and then how is a body ever going to get through this blind place at night without the friendly old landmark?"

No, the romance and beauty were all gone from the river. All 3
the value any feature of it had for me now was the amount of usefulness it could furnish toward compassing the safe piloting of a steamboat. Since those days, I have pitied doctors from my heart. What does the lovely flush in a beauty's cheek mean to a doctor but a "break" that ripples above some deadly disease? Are not all her visible charms sown thick with what are to him the signs and symbols of hidden decay? Does he ever see her beauty at all, or doesn't he simply view her professionally and comment upon her unwholesome condition all to himself? And doesn't he sometimes wonder whether he has gained most or lost most by learning his trade?

Meanings and Values

1. What is the point of view in Paragraph 1? (See "Guide to Terms": *Point of View.*) Where, and how, does it change in Paragraph 2? Why is the shift important to the author's contrast?
2. Show how the noticeable change of tone between Paragraphs 1 and 2 is related to the change in point of view. (Guide: *Style/Tone.*)

Specifically, what changes in style accompany the shift in tone and attitude? How effectively do they all relate to the central theme itself? (Remember that such effects seldom just "happen"; the writer *makes* them happen.)

3. Is the first paragraph primarily objective or subjective? (Guide: *Objective/Subjective.*) How about the latter part of Paragraph 2? Are your answers related to point of view? If so, how?
4. Do you think the last sentence refers only to doctors? Why, or why not?

Expository Techniques

1. Where do you find a second comparison or contrast? Which is it? Is the comparison/contrast made within itself, with something external, or both? Explain.
2. Is the second comparison/contrast closely enough related to the major contrast to justify its use? Why, or why not?
3. In developing the numerous points of the major contrast, would an alternating, point-to-point system have been better? Why, or why not? Show how the author uses organization within the groups to assist in the overall contrast.
4. What is the most noteworthy feature of syntax in Paragraphs 1 and 2? (Guide: *Syntax.*) How effectively does it perform the function intended?
5. What is gained by the apparently deliberate decision to use rhetorical questions only toward the end? (Guide: *Rhetorical Questions.*)

Diction and Vocabulary

1. In what ways do the word choices in Paragraph 1 differ from those in Paragraph 2? (Guide: *Diction.*)
2. Compare the quality of metaphors in the quotation of Paragraph 2 with the quality of those preceding it. (Guide: *Figures of Speech.*) Is the difference justified? Why, or why not?

Read to Write

1. **Collaborate:** We spend much of our lives preparing for work, working, and thinking about work. As Twain's essay points out, moreover, work shapes the way we perceive things and respond to them. Work can therefore be an excellent source of writing topics that are interesting to both writers and readers. Working in a group, add five more questions about work to the following list, and then use it to help generate possible topics for an essay: How do specific kinds of work shape perceptions and values? Are people's outlooks likely to vary according to the kinds of jobs they hold (or want to hold)? How

do my work habits, preferences, or experiences set me apart from others (or bring me closer)?

2. **Considering Audience:** Would readers of Twain's era, used to traveling by steamboat, horse-drawn carriage, steam-powered trains, and horseback, respond differently than readers of today to this essay? Write a brief essay of your own (1–3 paragraphs) explaining why readers might or might not respond differently. In doing so, consider the ways in which modern means of transportation affect our perceptions and values.

3. **Developing an Essay:** Twain's essay not only describes two scenes but also explains what changes in outlook and experience make them seem different. Prepare an essay of your own with a similar purpose. Choose a scene or event that you have observed more than once and from differing perspectives. Explain to readers the ways in which the scene appeared different and what it was about your perceptions that accounted for the difference.

(NOTE: Suggestions for topics requiring development by use of COMPARISON and CONTRAST are on pp. 172–173, at the end of this chapter.)

BRUCE CATTON

BRUCE CATTON (1899–1978) was a Civil War specialist whose early career included reporting for various newspapers. In 1954 he received both the Pulitzer Prize for historical work and the National Book Award. He served as director of information for the United States Department of Commerce and wrote many books, including *Mr. Lincoln's Army* (1951), *Glory Road* (1952), *A Stillness at Appomattox* (1953), *The Hallowed Ground* (1956), *America Goes to War* (1958), *The Coming Fury* (1961), *Terrible Swift Sword* (1963), *Never Call Retreat* (1966), *Waiting for the Morning Train: An American Boyhood* (1972), and *Gettysburg: The Final Fury* (1974). For five years, Catton edited *American Heritage.*

Grant and Lee: A Study in Contrasts

"Grant and Lee: A Study in Contrasts" was written as a chapter of *The American Story,* a collection of essays by noted historians. In this study, as in most of his other writing, Catton does more than recount the facts of history: he shows the significance within them. It is a carefully constructed essay, using contrast and comparison as the entire framework for his explanation.

When Ulysses S. Grant and Robert E. Lee met in the parlor of a modest house at Appomattox Court House, Virginia, on April 9, 1865, to work out the terms for the surrender of Lee's Army of Northern Virginia, a great chapter in American life came to a close, and a great new chapter began. 1

These men were bringing the Civil War to its virtual finish. To be sure, other armies had yet to surrender, and for a few days the fugitive Confederate government would struggle desperately and vainly, trying to find some way to go on living now that its chief support was gone. But in effect it was all over when Grant and Lee signed the papers. And the little room where they wrote out the terms was the scene of one of the most poignant, dramatic contrasts in American history. 2

They were two strong men these oddly different generals, and they represented the strengths of two conflicting currents that, through them, had come into final collision. 3

Back of Robert E. Lee was the notion that the old aristocratic concept might somehow survive and be dominant in American life. 4

Lee was tidewater Virginia, and in his background were family, culture, and tradition . . . the age of chivalry transplanted to a New World which was making its own legends and its own myths. He embodied a way of life that had come down through the age of knighthood and the English country squire. America was a land that was beginning all over again, dedicated to nothing much more complicated than the rather hazy belief that all men had equal rights and should have an equal chance in the world. In such a land Lee stood for the feeling that it was somehow of advantage to human society to have a pronounced inequality in the social structure. There should be a leisure class, backed by ownership of land; in turn, society itself should be keyed to the land as the chief source of wealth and influence. It would bring forth (according to this ideal) a class of men with a strong sense of obligation to the community; men who lived not to gain advantage for themselves, but to meet the solemn obligations which had been laid on them by the very fact that they were privileged. From them the country would get its leadership; to them it could look for the higher values—of thought, of conduct, or personal deportment—to give it strength and virtue. 5

Lee embodied the noblest element of this aristocratic ideal. Through him, the landed nobility justified itself. For four years, the Southern states had fought a desperate war to uphold the ideals for which Lee stood. In the end, it almost seemed as if the Confederacy fought for Lee; as if he himself was the Confederacy . . . the best thing that the way of life for which the Confederacy stood could ever have to offer. He had passed into legend before Appomattox. Thousands of tired, underfed, poorly clothed Confederate soldiers, long since past the simple enthusiasm of the early days of the struggle, somehow considered Lee the symbol of everything for which they had been willing to die. But they could not quite put this feeling into words. If the Lost Cause, sanctified by so much heroism and so many deaths, had a living justification, its justification was General Lee. 6

Grant, the son of a tanner on the Western frontier, was everything Lee was not. He had come up the hard way and embodied nothing in particular except the eternal toughness and sinewy fiber of the men who grew up beyond the mountains. He was one of a body of men who owed reverence and obeisance to no one, who were self-reliant to a fault, who cared hardly anything for the past but who had a sharp eye for the future. 7

These frontier men were the precise opposites of the tidewater aristocrats. Back of them, in the great surge that had taken people over the Alleghenies and into the opening Western country, there 8 was a deep, implicit dissatisfaction with a past that had settled into grooves. They stood for democracy, not from any reasoned conclusion about the proper ordering of human society, but simply because they had grown up in the middle of democracy and knew how it worked. Their society might have privileges, but they would be privileges each man had won for himself. Forms and patterns meant nothing. No man was born to anything, except perhaps to a chance to show how far he could rise. Life was competition.

Yet along with this feeling had come a deep sense of belonging 9
to a national community. The Westerner who developed a farm, opened a shop, or set up in business as a trader could hope to prosper only as his own community prospered—and his community ran from the Atlantic to the Pacific and from Canada down to Mexico. If the land was settled, with towns and highways and accessible markets, he could better himself. He saw his fate in terms of the nation's own destiny. As its horizons expanded, so did his. He had, in other words, an acute dollars-and-cents stake in the continued growth and development of his country.

And that, perhaps, is where the contrast between Grant and Lee 10
becomes most striking. The Virginia aristocrat, inevitably, saw himself in relation to his own region. He lived in a static society which could endure almost anything except change. Instinctively, his first loyalty would go to the locality in which that society existed. He would fight to the limit of endurance to defend it, because in defending it he was defending everything that gave his own life its deepest meaning.

The Westerner, on the other hand, would fight with an equal 11
tenacity for the broader concept of society. He fought so because everything he lived by was tied to growth, expansion, and a constantly widening horizon. What he lived by would survive or fall with the nation itself. He could not possibly stand by unmoved in the face of an attempt to destroy the Union. He would combat it with everything he had, because he could only see it as an effort to cut the ground out from under his feet.

So Grant and Lee were in complete contrast, representing two 12
diametrically opposed elements in American life. Grant was the modern man emerging; beyond him, ready to come on the stage, was the great age of steel and machinery, of crowded cities and a restless burgeoning vitality. Lee might have ridden down from the old age of chivalry, lance in hand, silken banner fluttering over his head. Each man was the perfect champion of his cause, drawing both his strengths and his weaknesses from the people he led.

Yet it was not all contrast, after all. Different as they were—in background, in personality, in underlying aspiration—these two great soldiers had much in common. Under everything else, they were marvelous fighters. Furthermore, their fighting qualities were really very much alike. 13

Each man had, to begin with, the great virtue of utter tenacity and fidelity. Grant fought his way down the Mississippi Valley in spite of acute personal discouragement and profound military handicaps. Lee hung on in the trenches at Petersburg after hope itself had died. In each man there was an indomitable quality . . . the born fighter's refusal to give up as long as he can still remain on his feet and lift his two fists. 14

Daring and resourcefulness they had, too: the ability to think faster and move faster than the enemy. These were the qualities which gave Lee the dazzling campaigns of Second Manassas and Chancellorsville and won Vicksburg for Grant. 15

Lastly, and perhaps greatest of all, there was the ability, at the end, to turn quickly from war to peace once the fighting was over. Out of the way these two men behaved at Appomattox came the possibility of a peace of reconciliation. It was a possibility not wholly realized, in the years to come, but which did, in the end, help the two sections to become one nation again . . . after a war whose bitterness might have seemed to make such a reunion wholly impossible. No part of either man's life became him more than the part he played in their brief meeting in the McLean house at Appomattox. Their behavior there put all succeeding generations of Americans in their debt. Two great Americans, Grant and Lee—very different, yet under everything very much alike. Their encounter at Appomattox was one of the great moments of American history. 16

Meanings and Values

1. Clarify the assertions that through Lee "the landed nobility justified itself" and that "if the Lost Cause . . . had a living justification," it was General Lee (Par. 6). Why are these assertions pertinent to the central theme?
2. Does it seem reasonable that "thousands of tired, underfed, poorly clothed Confederate soldiers" (Par. 6) had been willing to fight for

the aristocratic system in which they would never have had even a chance to be aristocrats? Why or why not? Can you think of more likely reasons why they were willing to fight?

3. What countries of the world have recently been so torn by internal war and bitterness that reunion has seemed, or still seems, impossible? Do you see any basic differences between the trouble in those countries and that in America at the time of the Civil War?
4. The author calls Lee a symbol (Par. 6). Was Grant also a symbol? If so, of what? (See "Guide to Terms": *Symbol.*) How would you classify this kind of symbolism?

Expository Techniques

1. Make an informal list of paragraph numbers from 3 to 16, and note by each number whether the paragraph is devoted primarily to Lee, to Grant, or to direct comparison or contrast of the two. This chart will show you Catton's basic pattern of development. (Notice, for instance, how the broad information of Paragraphs 4–6 and 7–9 seems almost to "funnel" down through the narrower summaries in Paragraphs 10 and 11 into Paragraph 12, where the converging elements meet and the contrast is made specific.)
2. What new technique of development is started in Paragraph 13?
3. What is gained, or lost, by using one sentence for Paragraph 3? For Paragraph 4?
4. How many paragraphs does the introduction comprise? How successfully does it fulfill the three basic requirements of a good introduction? (Guide: *Introductions.*)
5. Show how Catton has constructed the beginning of each paragraph so that there is a smooth transition from the one preceding it. (Guide: *Transition.*)
6. What seems to be the author's attitude toward Grant and Lee? Show how his tone reflects this attitude. (Guide: *Style/Tone.*)

Diction and Vocabulary

1. Why would a use of colloquialisms have been inconsistent with the tone of this writing?
2. List or mark all metaphors in Paragraphs 1, 3, 5, 7–11, and 16. (Guide: *Figures of Speech.*) Comment on their general effectiveness.
3. If you are not already familiar with the following words, study their meanings as given in the dictionary and as used in this essay: *virtual, poignant* (Par. 2); *concept* (4); *sinewy, obeisance* (7); *implicit* (8); *tenacity* (11); *diametrically, burgeoning* (12); *aspiration* (13); *fidelity, profound, indomitable* (14); *succeeding* (16).

Read to Write

1. **Collaborating:** Catton focuses on a dramatic moment in history and explains its long-range significance. Drawing on his approach, list some dramatic moments in history. In a group, compare your lists. Does your definition of "dramatic moment" match those of other group members? Decide as a group on one moment you all agree is dramatic and, in a short essay, explain its long-range significance.
2. **Considering Audience:** Ask yourself how much you knew about the topic of "Grant and Lee" before you began reading the essay, then go through the text and highlight sections that present information that was new to you. To what extent do you think that your initial knowledge of the topic was similar to that of most readers? Why? Study the ways Catton introduces information that most readers are likely to be unfamiliar with, and identify techniques you could use to present new information in your own writing.
3. **Developing an Essay:** One special achievement of Catton's "Grant and Lee: A Study in Contrasts" is its portrait of the two generals as embodiments of contrasting societies and cultures. Consider using this strategy in an essay offering a contrast between ideas, values, or cultures by means of a contrast between people who embody the differences. The strategy can be applied to a wide variety of subjects, not simply to public or political ones. You might use it to talk about different parenting strategies, for example, or about various religious beliefs or value systems.

(Note: Suggestions for topics requiring development by means of COMPARISON and CONTRAST are on pp. 172–173 at the end of this chapter.)

PHILLIP LOPATE

PHILLIP LOPATE was born in New York City in 1943, received a B.A. from Columbia University in 1964 and a doctorate from Union Graduate School in 1979. His essays have appeared in a wide range of publications including *The New York Times* and *The New York Times Book Review, House and Garden, Vogue,* and *Film Quarterly.* His essay collections include *Portrait of My Body* (1996) and *Totally Tenderly Tragically* (1998). Lopate's most recent novel is *Two Marriages* (2008), and his exploration of New York City's coastline, *Waterfront: A Walk around Mahattan,* was published in 2005.

A Nonsmoker with a Smoker

In this essay, which first appeared in *New Age Journal,* Lopate uses comparison and contrast to explore his own ambiguous feelings about smoking—and about his relationship with a smoker. In the course of the essay, he touches on many aspects of the smoking/nonsmoking conflict, yet he offers a personal perspective often lost in the public controversy.

Last Saturday night my girlfriend, Helen, and I went to a dinner party in the Houston suburbs. We did not know our hosts, but were invited on account of Helen's chum Barry, whose birthday party it was. We had barely stepped into the house and met the other guests, seated on a U-shaped couch under an A-framed ceiling, when Helen lit a cigarette. The hostess froze. "Uh, could you please not smoke in here? If you have to, we'd appreciate your using the terrace. We're both sort of allergic." 1

Helen smiled understandingly and moved toward the glass doors leading to the backyard in a typically ladylike way, as though merely wanting to get a better look at the garden. But I knew from that gracious "Southern" smile of hers that she was miffed. 2

As soon as Helen had stepped outside, the hostess explained that they had just moved into this house, and that it had taken weeks to air out because of the previous owner's tenacious cigar smoke. A paradigmatically awkward conversation about tobacco ensued: like testifying sinners, two people came forward with confessions about kicking the nasty weed; our scientist-host cited a recent study of indoor air pollution levels; a woman lawyer brought up the latest California legislation 3 protecting nonsmokers; a roly-poly real estate agent admitted that, though he had given up smokes, he still sat in the smoking section of airplanes because "you meet a more interesting type of person there"—a remark his wife did not find amusing. Helen's friend Barry gallantly joined her outside. I did not, as I should have; I felt paralyzed.

For one thing, I wasn't sure which side I was on. I have never been a smoker. My parents both chain-smoked, so I grew up accustomed to cloudy interiors and ever since have been tolerant of other people's nicotine urges. To be perfectly honest, I'm not crazy about inhaling smoke, particularly when I've got a cold, but that irritating inconvenience pales beside the damage that would be done to my pluralistic worldview if I did not defend smokers' rights. 4

On the other hand, a part of me wished Helen *would* stop smoking. That part seemed to get a satisfaction out of the group's "banishing" her: they were doing the dirty work of expressing my disapproval. 5

As soon as I realized this, I joined her in the garden. Presently a second guest strolled out to share a forbidden toke, then a third. Our hostess ultimately had to collect the mutineers with an announcement that dinner was served. 6

At the table, Helen appeared to be having such a good time, joking with our hosts and everyone else, that I was unprepared for the change that came over her as soon as we were alone in the car afterward. "I will never go back to that house!" she declared. "Those people have no concept of manners or hospitality, humiliating me the moment I stepped in the door. And that phony line about 'sort of allergic'!" 7

Normally, Helen is forbearance personified. Say anything that touches her about smoking, however, and you touch the rawest of nerves. I remembered the last time I foolishly suggested that she "think seriously" about stopping. I had just read one of those newspaper articles about the increased possibility of heart attacks, lung cancer, and birth deformities among women smokers, and I was worried for her. My concern must have been maladroitly expressed, because she burst into tears. 8

"Can't we even talk about this without your getting so sensitive?" I had asked. 9

"You don't understand. Nonsmokers never understand that it is a real addiction. I've tried quitting, and it was hell. Do you want me to go around for months mean and cranky outside and angry inside? You're right, I'm sensitive, because I'm threatened with 10 having taken away from me the thing that gives me the most pleasure in life, day in, day out," she said. I shot her a look: careful, now. "Well, practically the most pleasure. You know what I mean." I didn't. But I knew enough to drop it.

I love Helen, and if she wants to smoke, knowing the risks in- 11
volved, that remains her choice. Besides, she wouldn't quit just because I wanted her to; she's not that docile, and that's part of what I love about her. Sometimes I wonder why I even keep thinking about her quitting. What's it to me personally? Certainly I feel protective of her health, but I also have selfish motives. I don't like the way her lips taste when she's smoked a lot. I associate her smoking with nervousness, and when she lights up several cigarettes in a row, I get jittery watching her. Crazy as this may sound, I also find myself becoming jealous of her cigarettes. Occasionally, when I go to her house and we're sitting on the couch together, if I see Helen eyeing the pack I make her kiss me first, so that my lips can engage hers (still fresh) before the competition's. It's almost as though there were another lover in the room—a lover who was around long before I entered the picture, and who pleases her in mysterious ways I cannot.

A lit cigarette puts a distance between us: it's like a weapon in 12
her hand, awakening in me a primitive fear of being burnt. The memory is not so primitive, actually. My father used to smoke absentmindedly, letting the ash grow like a caterpillar eating every leaf in its path, until gravity finally toppled it. Once, when I was about nine, my father and I were standing in line at a bakery, and he accidentally dropped a lit ash down my back. Ever since, I've inwardly winced and been on guard around these little waving torches, which epitomize to me the dangers of intimacy.

I've worked hard to understand from the outside the satisfaction 13
of smoking. I've even smoked "sympathetic" cigarettes, just to see what the other person was experiencing. But it's not the same as being hooked. How can I really empathize with the frightened but stubborn look Helen gets in her eyes when, despite the fact we're a little late going somewhere, she turns to me in the car and says, "I need to buy a pack of cigarettes first"? I feel a wave of pity for her. We are both embarrassed by this forced recognition of her frailty—the "indignity," as she herself puts it, of being controlled by something outside her will.

I try to imagine myself in that position, but a certain smugness 14
keeps getting in the way (I don't have that problem and *am I glad*). We pay a price for our smugness. So often it flip-flops into envy: the outsiders wish to be included in the sufferings and highs of others,

as if to say that only by relinquishing control and surrendering to some dangerous habit, some vice or dependency, would one be able to experience "real life."

15 Over the years I have become a sucker for cigarette romanticism. Few Hollywood gestures move me as much as the one in *Now Voyager,* when Paul Henreid lights two cigarettes, one for himself, the other for Bette Davis: these form a beautiful fatalistic bridge between them, a complicitous understanding like the realization that their love is based on the inevitability of separation. I am all the more admiring of this worldly cigarette gallantry because its experiential basis escapes me.

16 The same sort of fascination occurs when I come across a literary description of nicotine addiction, like this passage in Mailer's *Tough Guys Don't Dance:* "Over and over again I gave them up, a hundred times over the years, but I always went back. For in my dreams, sooner or later, I struck a match, brought flame to the tip, then took in all my hunger for existence with the first puff. I felt impaled on desire itself—those fiends trapped in my chest and screaming for one drag."

17 "Impaled on desire itself"! Such writing evokes a longing in me for the centering of self that tobacco seems to bestow on its faithful. Clearly, there is something attractive about having this umbilical relation to the universe—this curling pillar, this spiral staircase, this prayer of smoke that mediates between the smoker's inner substance and the alien ether. Inwardness of the nicotine trance, sad wisdom ("every pleasure has its price"), beauty of ritual, squandered health—all those romantic meanings we read into the famous photographic icons of fifties saints, Albert Camus or James Agee or James Dean or Carson McCullers puffing away, in a sense they're true. Like all people who return from a brush with death, smokers have gained a certain power. They know their "coffin nails." With Helen, each cigarette is a measuring of the perishable, an enactment of her mortality, from filter to end-tip in fewer than five minutes. I could not stand to be reminded of my own death so often.

Meanings and Values

1. Tell why you think the writer made the title say *with* rather than *and.*
2. Does the writer's portrayal of the party (Pars. 1–6) make Helen's anger (7) seem justified? Why or why not?

3. To what parts of this essay might smokers and nonsmokers react in different ways? How might their reactions differ? Be specific in answering this question.
4. What conclusion about smoking, if any, does the writer reach in the last paragraph of the essay?

Expository Techniques

1. The focus of the essay shifts at the end of Paragraph 3. What role does the last sentence in the paragraph play, and in what way does the focus shift?
2. How would you characterize the tone and style in Paragraph 1? In Paragraph 3? (See "Guide to Terms": *Style/Tone.*) What contrast does the writer emphasize through the differences in tone and style?
3. To what extent does the focus of Paragraphs 7–11 lie on the question of smoking versus not smoking, and to what extent does it focus on the relationship between the writer and Helen? Be ready to defend your answer with specific evidence from the text.
4. What is being compared in Paragraph 11? How is this comparison related to the overall pattern of comparison in the essay?
5. In what ways do Paragraphs 13 and 14 contrast with 15 and 16?
6. State in your own words the contrast the author makes in the last two sentences of the essay. Do these sentences make an effective conclusion? (Guide: *Closings; Evaluation.*)

Diction and Vocabulary

1. Identify the informal diction in Paragraph 1 and the formal diction in Paragraph 3. (Guide: *Diction.*) Why has the writer created these contrasts in diction? (Hint: see "Expository Techniques.")
2. Identify the similes in Paragraph 12, and tell what they suggest about the effect of smoking on personal relationships. (Guide: *Figures of Speech.*)
3. Explain how cigarettes act as symbols in Paragraph 15. (Guide: *Symbol.*)
4. Identify the metaphors in Paragraph 15. Discuss their meaning and their effect, both as individual metaphors and as a cluster. (Guide: *Figures of Speech.*)
5. If you do not know the meaning of some of the following words, look them up in a dictionary: *tenacious, paradigmatically, ensued* (Par. 3); *pluralistic* (4); *toke* (6); *forbearance, maladroitly* (8); *epitomize* (12); *fatalistic, complicitious* (15).

Read to Write

1. **Collaborating:** In his essay, Lopate views behaviors and attitudes not so much as matters of choice but as outgrowths of our experiences,

personalities, and interactions with others. Follow Lopate's approach and explore in freewriting (see pp. 142–145) a pattern of behavior (perhaps one you disapprove of) by looking at the motivations of someone who engages in it and by exploring your own reactions to the behavior. Then turn your freewriting into two lists, one of motivations and one of reactions, and share your lists with a partner. Then write a short response to your partner's lists, indicating the extent to which you agree or disagree with the items on them.

2. **Considering Audience:** Compare and contrast how smokers and nonsmokers might react to this essay. Will they think Lopate is fair to both groups? Write notes for a short essay outlining the differing perspectives of two people on a similar conflict or issue such as wearing helmets while driving motorcycles or using seatbelts in cars and trucks.

3. **Developing an Essay:** Even familiar issues and controversies can be a source of new understanding for you and your readers when you take a personal approach to them and write with an expository purpose. Explore some potential subjects by asking questions like these: If smoking, wearing a fur coat, or some other activity or belief offends you, should you let the person doing the activity know about your feelings? What steps can you take to communicate your feelings without offending the other person? Should you worry about upsetting the other person?

(NOTE: Suggestions for topics requiring development by use of COMPARISON and CONTRAST are on pp. 172–173 at the end of this chapter.)

BILL McKIBBEN

BILL MCKIBBEN grew up in Lexington, Massachusetts and attended Harvard University, where he was editor of the *Harvard Crimson* newspaper. After college he became a staff writer for the *New Yorker* magazine. When he left the magazine, he moved to the Adirondack Mountains in New York to work as a writer. He has published numerous books beginning with *The End of Nature* (1989) and *The Age of Missing Information* (1992) and including, most recently, *Deep Economy: The Wealth of Communities and the Durable Future* (2007) and *The Bill McKibben Reader* (2008). He has written articles for many magazines, including *The Atlantic Monthly, Harper's, Rolling Stone,* and *Outside.*

Old MacDonald Had a Farmer's Market

To most Americans, Henry David Thoreau represents an ideal of self-sufficiency, simplicity, and independence for living on his own on the shores of rural Walden Pond, as recorded in his book, *Walden* (1854). McKibben contrasts this view of Thoreau with the reality of Thoreau's life in a nineteenth-century community. He also takes a further step, comparing the earlier ideas of community and individuality with our modern views, explaining why our modern concepts may be hiding an important truth: "we're built to rely on each other."

1 Generations of college freshmen, asked to read *Walden,* have sputtered with indignation when they learned that Henry David went back to Concord for dinner with his family every week or two. He's *cheating*; his grand experiment is a fraud. This outrage is a useful tactic; it prevents them from having to grapple with the most important (and perhaps the most difficult) book in the American canon, one that asks impossibly searching questions about the emptiness of a consumer economy, the vacuity of an information-soaked era. But it also points to something else: Thoreau, our apostle of solitary, individual self-reliance, out in his cabin with his hoe and his beans, the most determinedly asocial man of his time—nonetheless was immersed to his community to a degree few people today can comprehend.

2 Consider the sheer number of people who happened to drop by the cabin of an obscure eccentric. "I had three chairs in my house; one for solitude, two for friendship, three for society," he writes.

Often more visitors came than could sit—sometimes twenty or thirty at a time. "Half-witted men from the almshouse," busybodies who "pried into my cupboard and bed when I was out," a French-Canadian woodchopper, a runaway slave "whom I helped to forward toward the north star," doctors, lawyers, the old and infirm and the timid, the self-styled reformers. It's not that Thoreau was necessarily a cheerful host—there were visitors "who did not know when their visit had terminated, though I went about my business again, answering them from greater and greater remoteness." Instead, it was simply a visiting age—as most of human history has been a visiting age, and every human culture a visiting culture.

Until ours. I doubt if many people reading these words have 3 had a spontaneous visit from a neighbor in the past week—less than a fifth and Americans report visiting regularly with friends and neighbors, and the percentage is declining steadily. The number of close friends that an American claims has dropped steadily for the last fifty years too; three-quarters of us don't know our *next-door neighbors*. Even the people who share our houses are becoming strangers: *The Wall Street Journal* reported recently that "major builders and top architects are walling off space. They're touting one-person 'internet alcoves,' locked-door 'away rooms,' and his-and-her offices on opposite ends of the house." The new floor plans, says the director of research for the National Association of Home Builders, are "good for the dysfunctional family." Or, as another executive put it, these are the perfect homes for "families that don't want anything to do with one another." Compared to these guys, Thoreau with his three-chair cabin was practically Martha Stewart.

Every culture has its pathologies, and ours is self-reliance. 4 From some mix of our frontier past, our *Little House on the Prairie* heritage, our Thoreauvian desire for solitude, and our amazing wealth we've derived a level of independence never seen before on this round earth. We've built an economy where we need no one else; with a credit card, you can harvest the world's bounty from the privacy of your room. And we've built a culture much the same—the dream houses those architects build, needless to say, come with a plasma screen in every room. As long as we can go on earning good money in our own tiny niche, we don't need a helping hand from a soul—save, of course, from the invisible hand that cups us all in its benign grip.

There are a couple of problems with this fine scenario, of 5 course. One is: we're miserable. Reported levels of happiness and life-satisfaction are locked in long-term one-way declines, almost certainly *because* of this lack of connection. Does this sound subjective and airy? Find one of the tens of millions of Americans who don't belong to *anything* and convince them to join a church, a softball league, a bird-watching group. In the next year their mortality—the risk that they will die in the next year—falls by half.

The other trouble is that our self-reliance is actually a reliance on cheap fossil fuel and the economy it's built. Take that away—either because we start to run out of oil, or because global warming forces us to stop using it in current quantities—and our vaunted independence will start to lurch like a Hummer with four flat tires. Just think for a moment about that world and then decide if you want to live on an acre all your own in the outermost ring of suburbs. 6

The idea of self-reliance is so deep in our psyches, however, that even when we attempt to escape from the unhappy and unsustainable cul-de-sac of our society, we're likely to turn toward yet more "independence." The "back-to-the-land" movement, for instance, often added the words "by myself." Think about how proudly a certain kind of person talks about his "off-the-grid" life—he makes his own energy and grows his own food, he can deal with whatever the world throws at him. One such person may be left-wing in politics (à la Scott and Helen Nearing); another may be conservative. But they are united in their lack of need for the larger world. Not even to school their kids—they'll take care of that as well. 7

Such folks are admirable, of course—they have a wide variety of skills now missing in most Americans; they're able to amuse themselves; they work hard. But as an ideal, especially an economic ideal, that radical self-reliance strikes me as being almost as empty as the consumer society from which it dissents. Consider, for instance, the idea of growing all your own food. It's clearly better than relying on food from thousands of miles away—from our current industrialized food economy, which figures "it's always summer somewhere" and so orders take-out from that distant field every night of the year. Compared with that, an enormous garden and a root cellar full of all you'll need for the winter is virtue incarnate. But if you believe in many of the (entirely plausible) horror stories about what's to come—peak oil, climate change—then the world ends with you standing shotgun in hand above your vegetable patch, protecting your carrots from the poaching urban horde. 8

Contrast that with another vision, one taking shape in at least a few places around the country: a matrix of small farmers growing food for their local areas. Farmers' markets are the fastest-growing 9 part of our food economy, with sales showing double-digit growth annually. Partly that's because people want good food (all kinds of people: immigrants and ethnic Americans tend to be the most avid farmers' market shoppers). And partly it's because they want more *company*. One team of sociologists reported recently that shoppers at farmers' markets engaged in ten times more conversations per visit than customers in supermarkets. I spent the past winter eating only from my valley; a little of the food I grew myself, but the idea of my experiment was to see what remained of the agricultural infrastructure that had once supported this place. And the payoff was not only a delicious six months, but also a deep network of new friends, a much stronger sense of the cultural geography of my place.

Or consider energy. Since the 1970s, a particular breed of noble 10
ex-hippie has been building "off-the-grid" homes, often relying on solar panels. This has been important work—they've figured out many of the techniques and technologies that we desperately need to get free of our climate change predicament. But the most exciting new gadget is a home-scale inverter, one that allows you to send the power your rooftop generates down the line instead of down into the basement. Where the isolated system has a stack of batteries, the grid-tied solar panel uses the whole region's electric system as its battery: my electric meter spins merrily backward all afternoon because while the sun shines I'm a utility; then at night I draw from somewhere else. It's a two-way flow, in the same way that the internet allows ideas to bounce in many directions.

You can do the same kind of calculation with almost any com- 11
modity. Music doesn't need to come from Nashville or Hollywood on a small disc, for instance. But you don't have to produce it all yourself either. More fun to join with the neighbors, to make music together or to listen to the local stars. A hundred years ago, Iowa had 1,300 opera houses. Radio doesn't need to come from the ClearChannel headquarters in some Texas office park; new low-power FM lets valleys make their own. Even currency can become a joint local project—all it takes is the trust that underwrites any system of money. In hundreds of communities, people are trying to build that trust locally, with money that only works within the region.

Thinking this way won't be easy. We're used to independence 12
as the prime virtue—so used to it that three quarters of American Christians believe the phrase "God helps those who help themselves" comes from the Bible, instead of Ben Franklin. "Love your neighbor as yourself" is harder advice, but sweeter and more sage. We don't need to live on communes (though more and more old

people are finding themselves enrolling in "retirement communities" that are gray-haired, upscale versions). But we will, I think, need to figure out how to stop relying on both oil and ourselves, and instead learn the lesson that the other primates and the other human cultures never forgot: we're built to rely on each other.

Meanings and Values

1. State what the writer considers as our culture's pathology.
2. a. Explain why you think most readers would be likely at first to agree or disagree with the writer's opinions about the pathology.

   b. What reasons does the writer offer readers for agreeing with his point of view?
3. What are the ecological effects of self-reliance, according to this essay?

Expository Techniques

1. Specify the examples this essay offers of our culture's pathology. Include examples the writer offers of the negative effects of this pathology.
2. What words does the writer use in the opening sentences of Paragraphs 3, 6, 9, and 10 to emphasize comparisons or contrasts? (See "Guide to Terms": *Diction.*)
3. Which paragraphs does McKibben devote primarily to discussing the past and which to the present?

Diction and Vocabulary

1. Identify the transition words or repeated words and phrases the writer uses in Paragraphs 2, 3, and 5–10 to identify the different topics he is explaining and to indicate the stages of his explanation. (Guide: *Diction.*)
2. Identify the following figures of speech and discuss their use: *allusion* (Par. 3); *simile* (6), and *allusion* (7) (Guide: *Figures of Speech*).
3. If you do not know the meaning of some of the following words, look them up in a dictionary: *indignation, vacuity, asocial* (Par. 1); *eccentric, almshouse* (2); *spontaneous, alcoves* (3); *bounty, niche, benign* (4); *scenario,* (5); *psyches, cul-de-sac* (7); *incarnate, poaching* (8); *matrix, infrastructure* (9); *predicament* (10); *sage* (12).

Read to Write

1. **Collaborating:** Working in a group, survey each individual to see how often each week they drop by to visit someone unannounced.

Then see how often their families do the same. Write together a brief report summarizing the visiting habits of your group.

2. **Considering Audience:** Some readers are likely to have a negative opinion of McKibben's view of "self-reliance." Others may agree with his outlook. Write two paragraphs, each one summarizing the different reactions readers may have and explaining the probable reasons behind these reactions.

3. **Developing an Essay:** McKibben looks at two different and often contrasting values: self-reliance and community. Choose another pair: nationalism and internationalism, for example; humility and reasonable pride; self-interest and charity; hard work and leisure; or any others you consider important. Create an essay comparing and contrasting these values, paying special attention to their positive and negative outcomes for our society.

(NOTE: Suggestions for topics requiring development by means of COMPARISON and CONTRAST are on pp. 172–173 at the end of this chapter.)

ALICE WALKER

ALICE WALKER was born in Georgia in 1944, the youngest in a family of eight. Her parents were sharecroppers, and she attended rural schools as a child, going on eventually to attend Spelman College and Sarah Lawrence College, from which she graduated. She worked as an editor of *Ms.* magazine and taught at several colleges. At present she teaches at the University of California, Berkeley and lives in northern California. Her work as a poet, novelist, and essayist has been highly acclaimed, and one of her novels, *The Color Purple* (1982), received both a Pulitzer Prize and the American Book Award for fiction. Some of her other works are *Her Blue Body Everything We Know: Earthling Poems 1989–1990* (1991) (poems); *In Love and Trouble* (1973) (short stories); *Meridian* (1976), *The Temple of My Familiar* (1989), *Possessing the Secret of Joy* (1992), and *By the Light of My Father's Smile* (1998) (novels); *In Search of Our Mothers' Gardens* (1983), *Living by the Word* (1988), and *The Same River Twice: Honoring the Difficult* (1996) (essays); *The Way Forward Is with a Broken Heart* (2000) (stories); *We are the Ones We Have Been Waiting For* (2006) (nonfiction); and *Devil's My Enemy* (2008) (fiction).

Am I Blue?

Humans and horses might seem at first so different that any comparison would have to take the form of an analogy—a pairing of essentially unlike subjects whose limited similarities can be used for explanatory purposes (see Chapter 4). Walker's strategy in this essay from *Living by the Word* is just the opposite, however. She explains that despite their obvious differences, humans and animals are essentially alike, at least in important matters such as the capacity to love and to communicate.

"Ain't these tears in these eyes tellin' you?" 1

For about three years my companion and I rented a small house in the country that stood on the edge of a large meadow that appeared to run from the end of our deck straight into the mountains. The mountains, however, were quite far away, and between us and them there was, in fact, a town. It was one of the many pleasant aspects of the house that you never really were aware of this. 2

It was a house of many windows, low, wide, nearly floor to ceiling in the living room, which faced the meadow, and it was from one of these that I first saw our closest neighbor, a large white horse, 3 cropping grass, flipping its mane, and ambling about—not over the entire meadow, which stretched well out of sight of the house, but over the five or so fenced-in acres that were next to the twenty-odd that we had rented. I soon learned that the horse, whose name was Blue, belonged to a man who lived in another town, but was boarded by our neighbors next door. Occasionally, one of the children, usually a stocky teenager, but sometimes a much younger girl or boy, could be seen riding Blue. They would appear in the meadow, climb up on his back, ride furiously for ten or fifteen minutes, then get off, slap Blue on the flanks, and not be seen again for a month or more.

There were many apple trees in our yard, and one by the fence 4
that Blue could almost reach. We were soon in the habit of feeding him apples, which he relished, especially because by the middle of summer the meadow grasses—so green and succulent since January—had dried out from lack of rain, and Blue stumbled about munching the dried stalks half-heartedly. Sometimes he would stand very still just by the apple tree, and when one of us came out he would whinny, snort loudly, or stamp the ground. This meant, of course: I want an apple.

It was quite wonderful to pick a few apples, or collect those that 5
had fallen to the ground overnight, and patiently hold them, one by one, up to his large, toothy mouth. I remained as thrilled as a child by his flexible dark lips, huge, cubelike teeth that crunched the apples, core and all, with such finality, and his high, broad-breasted *enormity;* beside which, I felt small indeed. When I was a child, I used to ride horses, and was especially friendly with one named Nan until the day I was riding and my brother deliberately spooked her and I was thrown, head first, against the trunk of a tree. When I came to, I was in bed and my mother was bending worriedly over me; we silently agreed that perhaps horseback riding was not the safest sport for me. Since then I have walked, and prefer walking to horseback riding—but I had forgotten the depth of feeling one could see in horses' eyes.

I was therefore unprepared for the expression in Blue's. Blue 6
was lonely. Blue was horribly lonely and bored. I was not shocked that this should be the case; five acres to tramp by yourself, endlessly, even in the most beautiful of meadows—and his was—cannot provide many interesting events, and once rainy season turned to dry that was about it. No, I was shocked that I had forgotten that human animals and nonhuman animals can communicate quite well; if we are brought up around animals as children we take this for granted. By the time we are adults we no longer remember. However, the animals have not changed. They are in fact *completed*

creations (at least they seem to be, so much more than we) who are not likely to change; it is their nature to express themselves. What else are they going to express? And they do. And, generally speaking, they are ignored.

After giving Blue the apples, I would wander back to the house, 7
aware that he was observing me. Were more apples not forthcoming then? Was that to be his sole entertainment for the day? My partner's small son had decided he wanted to learn how to piece a quilt; we worked in silence on our respective squares as I thought. . . .

Well, about slavery: about white children, who were raised by 8
black people, who knew their first all-accepting love from black women, and then, when they were twelve or so, were told they must "forget" the deep levels of communication between themselves and "mammy" that they knew. Later they would be able to relate quite calmly, "My old mammy was sold to another good family." "My old mammy was_____ ______." Fill in the blank. Many more years later a white woman would say: "I can't understand these Negroes, these blacks. What do they want? They're so different from us."

And about the Indians, considered to be "like animals" by the 9
"settlers" (a very benign euphemism for what they actually were), who did not understand their description as a compliment.

And about the thousands of American men who marry 10
Japanese, Korean, Filipina, and other non-English-speaking women and of how happy they report they are, "*blissfully,*" until their brides learn to speak English, at which point the marriages tend to fall apart. What then did the men see, when they looked into the eyes of the women they married, before they could speak English? Apparently only their own reflections.

I thought of society's impatience with the young. "Why are they 11
playing the music so loud?" Perhaps the children have listened to much of the music of oppressed people their parents danced to before they were born, with its passionate but soft cries for acceptance and love, and they have wondered why their parents failed to hear.

I do not know how long Blue had inhabited his five beautiful, 12
boring acres before we moved into our house; a year after we had arrived—and had also traveled to other valleys, other cities, other worlds—he was still there.

But then, in our second year at the house, something happened 13
in Blue's life. One morning, looking out the window at the fog that lay like a ribbon over the meadow, I saw another horse, a brown one, at the other end of Blue's field. Blue appeared to be afraid of it, and for several days made no attempt to go near. We went away for

a week. When we returned, Blue had decided to make friends and the two horses ambled or galloped along together, and Blue did not come nearly as often to the fence underneath the apple tree.

When he did, bringing his new friend with him, there was a different look in his eyes. A look of independence, of self-possession, of inalienable *horse*ness. His friend eventually became pregnant. For months and months there was, it seemed to me, a mutual feeling between me and the horses of justice, of peace. I fed apples to them both. The look in Blue's eyes was one of unabashed "this is *it*ness." 14

It did not, however, last forever. One day, after a visit to the city, 15
I went out to give Blue some apples. He stood waiting, or so I thought, though not beneath the tree. When I shook the tree and jumped back from the shower of apples, he made no move. I carried some over to him. He managed to half-crunch one. The rest he let fall to the ground. I dreaded looking into his eyes—because I had of course noticed that Brown, his partner, had gone—but I did look. If I had been born into slavery, and my partner had been sold or killed, my eyes would have looked like that. The children next door explained that Blue's partner had been "put with him" (the same expression that old people used, I had noticed, when speaking of an ancestor during slavery who had been impregnated by her owner) so that they could mate and she conceive. Since that was accomplished, she had been taken back by her owner, who lived somewhere else.

Will she be back? I asked. 16

They didn't know. 17

Blue was like a crazed person. Blue *was,* to me, a crazed person. 18
He galloped furiously, as if he were being ridden, around and around his five beautiful acres. He whinnied until he couldn't. He tore at the ground with his hooves. He butted himself against his single shade tree. He looked always and always toward the road down which his partner had gone. And then, occasionally, when he came up for apples, or I took apples to him, he looked at me. It was a look so piercing, so full of grief, a look so *human,* I almost laughed (I felt too sad to cry) to think there are people who do not know that animals suffer. People like me who have forgotten, and daily forget, all that animals try to tell us. "Everything you do to us will happen to you; we are your teachers, as you are ours. We are one lesson" is essentially it, I think. There are those who never once have even considered animals' rights: those who have been taught that animals actually want to be used and abused by us, as small children "love" to be frightened, or women "love" to be mutilated and raped. . . . They are the great-grandchildren of those who honestly thought, because

someone taught them this: "Women can't think," And "niggers can't faint." But most disturbing of all, in Blue's large brown eyes was a new look, more painful than the look of despair: the look of disgust with human beings, with life; the look of hatred. And it was odd what the look of hatred did. It gave him, for the first time, the look of a beast. And what that meant was that he had put up a barrier within to protect himself from further violence; all the apples in the world wouldn't change that fact.

And so Blue remained, a beautiful part of our landscape, very peaceful to look at from the window, white against the grass. Once a friend came to visit and said, looking out on the soothing view: "And it *would* have to be a white horse; the very image of freedom." And I thought, yes, the animals are forced to become for us merely "images" of what they once so beautifully expressed. And we are used to drinking milk from containers showing "contented" cows, whose real lives we want to hear nothing about, eating eggs and drumsticks from "happy" hens, and munching hamburgers advertised by bulls of integrity who seem to command their fate. 19

As we talked of freedom and justice one day for all, we sat down to steaks. I am eating misery, I thought, as I took the first bite. And spit it out. 20

Meanings and Values

1. In which paragraphs does Walker describe what she believes to be Blue's thoughts and feelings?
2. According to Walker, in what ways is Blue similar to a human? In what ways is he different? To what other groups does the author compare Blue and his relationships with humans in Paragraphs 8–11?
3. What thematic purposes are served by the following phrases:
   a. "human animals and nonhuman animals" (Par. 6)
   b. "who did not understand their description as a compliment" (Par. 9)
   c. "Am I Blue?" (title)
   d. "If I had been born into slavery, and my partner had been sold or killed, my eyes would have looked like that." (Par. 15)
   e. "It gave him, for the first time, the look of a beast." (Par. 18)

Expository Techniques

1. Why do you think Walker chose to wait until near the end of the essay (Par. 18) for a detailed discussion of its theme? (See "Guide to Terms": *Unity.*) To what extent does the placement of this discussion give the essay an expository rather than an argumentative purpose? (Guide: *Argument.*)
2. Discuss how the "'images'" presented in Paragraph 19 can be regarded as ironic symbols. (Guide: *Symbol; Irony.*)
3. Describe the way Walker alters the tempo of the sentences and builds to a climax in the concluding paragraph of the essay. (Guide: *Closings.*)
4. Some readers might consider the ending effective. Others might consider it overly dramatic or distasteful. Explain which reaction you consider most appropriate. (Guide: *Evaluation.*)

Diction and Vocabulary

1. Describe the ways in which Walker uses syntax and figurative language (simile) for thematic purposes in this passage: "Blue was like a crazed person. Blue *was,* to me, a crazed person" (Par. 18). (Guide: *Syntax; Figures of Speech.*)
2. In speaking of the "'settlers,'" Walker says that this term is "a very benign euphemism for what they actually were" (Par. 9). What does she mean by this comment? What other terms might be applied to them (from Walker's point of view)? Why might she have chosen not to use such terms?
3. The title of this essay is taken from a song of the same name. In terms of the content of the essay, to what ideas or themes does it refer? Can it be considered a paradox? (Guide: *Paradox.*) The quotation from the song that opens the essay points to some of the ideas discussed in the essay. What are they?

Read to Write

1. **Collaborating:** Working in groups of four, discuss different animals that you have known. What have you learned from these animals? Can you apply what you have learned to your human relationships? To your understanding of human nature? How would you contrast the behavior of animals in specific situations with typical human behavior in such situations? As a group, plan an essay comparing and contrasting likely animal and human behavior in a set of situations you have chosen.
2. **Considering Audience:** Walker repeatedly refers to expressions and feelings seemingly conveyed through Blue's eyes. How might readers who have their own pets react to Walker's descriptions of the animal's eyes? How might readers without pets react? Will readers who have

pets understand Walker's comparison of animal owners and slave owners better than non-pet owners? Will most pet owners be offended by such a comparison? Who, if anyone, might be offended by the conclusions Walker draws about Blue's and other animals' feelings and intelligence? In two to three paragraphs, offer your answers to some or all of these questions as a way of describing readers' likely reactions to Walker's essay.

3. **Developing an Essay:** Walker's essay moves from obvious differences to surprising similarities, getting there through careful observation and comparison of horses and humans. Apply this pattern to a topic of your own choosing, using it to express hidden similarities you have already noticed or to reveal similarities as you write.

(NOTE: Suggestions for topics requiring development by means of COMPARISON and CONTRAST are on pp. 172–173 at the end of this chapter.)

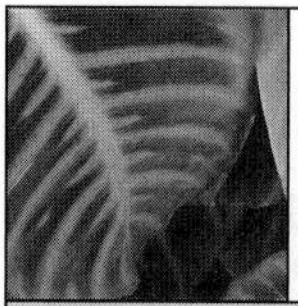

Issues and Ideas

Gender Differences

- Nicholas Wade, *Method and Madness: How Men and Women Think*
- Catherine Seipp, *Meet Today's Dad*

We understand our world by differences: wealthy, less wealthy, and a lot less wealthy; black, white, and brown; educated and uneducated; female and male. We come to understand who and what we are by learning who and what we are not.

One way we understand and deal with the world is through the difference between male and female, a distinction grounded in biological differences but extended to issues of emotion, intellectual ability, relationships, values, and social rules. These differences are maintained in various ways: through clothing styles, social organizations, sports teams, men's/women's publications, names (Kate/Carl), and kinship systems (aunt/uncle).

But how many of these differences are "real" and how many "imagined" or constructed by social custom? Just how different are men and women, and are their differences significant ones with important consequences?

As expository patterns, comparison and contrast parallel the identification of gender differences and similarities. Nicholas Wade makes good use of the pattern to explore surprising similarities that complicate, or even call into question, differences that many readers may consider obvious and unchanging.

Nicholas Wade looks to science, specifically brain research, for hard evidence of gender contrasts. He finds evidence of real contrasts, but not simple ones. And the implications for behavior and social organization are even more complex and sometimes contradictory. In contrast, Catherine Seipp looks at attempts to construct new patterns of male behavior as driven by political and social ideologies that ignore both tradition and (perhaps) biology, with unfortunate results.

NICHOLAS WADE

NICHOLAS WADE is a journalist who writes about science and scientific discoveries. He was born in Britain and educated at Eton and King's College, Cambridge. His books include *A World Beyond Healing* (1987), *Noble Dues* (1981), *The Ultimate Experiment* (1977), and *Before the Dawn: Recovering the Last History of Our Ancestors.* He has also edited a series of books for young people on nature and science.

Method and Madness: How Men and Women Think

We often look to science for firm answers to hard questions but get responses that are complex and raise as many questions as they answer. Looking over current research, the author of this essay reports that although there are clearly differences between men's and women's brains, what the differences mean is not that apparent. At times the research confirms stereotypes, but just as often it challenges them. What is clear in this essay is the writer's effective use of comparison and contrast as strategies for explaining the complicated relationships among biology, behavior, and gender.

The human brain, according to an emerging new body of scientific research, comes in two different varieties, maybe as different as the accompanying physique. Men, when they are lost, instinctually fall back on their in-built navigational skills, honed from far-off days of tracking large prey miles from home. Women, by contrast, tend to find their way by the simpler methods of remembering local landmarks or even asking help from strangers. 1

Men excel on psychological tests that require the imaginary twisting in space of a three-dimensional object. The skill seems to help with higher math, where the topmost ranks are thronged with male minds like Andrew Wiles of Princeton, who proclaimed almost a year ago that he had proved Fermat's Last Theorem and will surely get around to publishing the proof almost any day now. 2

Some feminist ideologues assert that all minds are created equal and women would be just as good at math if they weren't discouraged in school. But Camilla Benbow, a psychologist at Iowa State University, has spent years assessing biases like male math teachers or parents who favor boys. She concludes that boys' superiority at math is mostly innate. 3

But women, the new studies assert, have the edge in most other ways, like perceptual speed, verbal fluency and communications 4 skills. They also have sharper hearing than men, and excel in taste, smell and touch, and in fine coordination of hand and eye. If Martians arrived and gave job interviews, it seems likely they would direct men to competitive sports and manual labor and staff most professions, diplomacy and government with women.

The measurement of intellectual differences is a field with a 5 long and mostly disgraceful past. I.Q. tests have been regularly misused, sometimes even concocted, in support of prevailing prejudices. Distinguished male anatomists used to argue that women were less intelligent because their brains weighed less, neglecting to correct for the strong influence of body weight on brain weight.

The present studies of sex differences are venturing on ground 6 where self-deception and prejudice are constant dangers. The science is difficult and the results prone to misinterpretation. Still, the budding science seems free so far of obvious error. For one thing, many of the field's leading practitioners happen to be women, perhaps because male academics in this controversial field have had their lives made miserable by militant feminists.

For another, the study of brain sex differences does not depend 7 on just one kind of subvertible measure but draws on several different disciplines, including biology and anatomy. As is described in a new book, *Eve's Rib*, by Robert Pool, and the earlier *Brain Sex*, by Anne Moir and David Jessel, the foundations of the field have been carefully laid in animal research. Experiments with rats show that exposure in the womb to testosterone indelibly imprints a male pattern of behavior; without testosterone, the rat's brain is female.

In human fetuses, too, the sex hormones seem to mold a male 8 and female version of the brain, each subtly different in organization and behavior. The best evidence comes from girls with a rare genetic anomaly who are exposed in the womb to more testosterone than normal; they grow up doing better than their unaffected sisters on the tests that boys are typically good at. There's also some evidence, not yet confirmed, that male and female brains may be somewhat differently structured, with the two cerebral hemispheres being more specialized and less well interconnected in men than in women.

If the human brain exists in male and female versions, as modu- 9 lated in the womb, that would explain what every parent knows, that boys and girls prefer different patterns of play regardless of well-meaning efforts to impose unisex toys on both.

The human mind being very versatile, however, any genetic 10 propensities are far from decisive. In math, for example, the average girl is pretty much as good as the average boy. Only among the few students at the peak of math ability do boys predominate. Within the loose framework set by the genes, education makes an enormous difference. In Japan, boys exceed girls on the mental rotation tests, just as in America. But the Japanese girls outscore American boys. Maybe Japanese kids are just smarter or, more likely, just better taught, Japan being a country where education is taken seriously and parents and teachers consistently push children to excel.

There are some obvious cautions to draw about the social and political implications that might one day flow from brain sex research. One is that differences between individuals of the same sex often far exceed the slight differences between the sexes as two population groups: "If I were going into combat, I would prefer to have Martina Navratilova at my side than Robert Reich," says Patricia Ireland, president of the National Organization for Women. Even if men in general excel in math, an individual woman could still be better than most men. 11

On the other hand, if the brains of men and women really are organized differently, it's possible the sexes both prefer and excel at different occupations, perhaps those with more or less competition or social interaction. "In a world of scrupulous gender equality, equal numbers of girls and boys would be educated and trained for . . . all the professions. . . . [Hiring would proceed] until half of every workplace was made up of men and half, women," says Judith Lorber in *Paradoxes of Gender,* a new work of feminist theory. That premise does not hold if there are real intellectual differences between the sexes; the test of equal opportunity, when all unfair barriers to women have fallen, will not necessarily be equal outcomes. 12

Greek mythology tells that Tiresias, having lived both as a man and a woman for some complicated reason, was asked to settle a dispute between Zeus and Hera as to which gender enjoyed sex more. He replied there was no contest—it was 10 times better for women. Whereupon Hera struck him blind for his insolence and Zeus in compensation gave him the gift of foresight. Like Tiresias, the brain sex researchers are uncovering some impolitic truths, potent enough to shake Mount Olympus some day. 13

Meanings and Values

1. Paragraph 6 addresses current studies of sex difference as well as Wade's belief that much of the scientific research on the subject has been misinterpreted. Wade goes on to say, "Many of the field's

leading practitioners happen to be women, perhaps because male academics in this controversial field have had their lives made miserable by militant feminists." What point is Wade trying to make here? In what ways is the comment related to his statements about the misinterpretation of the data? Is his comment about feminists a conscious exaggeration? Why, or why not?

2. Why is Tiresias (Par. 13) a good choice for Wade's essay? (See "Guide to Terms": *Figures of Speech, Allusion.*)

3. Does Wade imply that one sex has a better way of thinking? Why, or why not? Is he neutral in his choice of evidence? Explain. What are the attributes people traditionally value in each of the sexes? In which paragraphs does Wade address these attributes?

Expository Techniques

1. Wade's first five paragraphs include several comparison/contrast examples. Why might he have begun his essay this way? Is this an effective introduction for the piece? (Guide: *Introductions; Evaluation.*)

2. In Paragraph 10, the writer uses a comparison within a comparison when he addresses the differences between Japanese boys and girls as well as American boys and girls, and then continues by comparing Japanese students overall to American students overall. Why might he have chosen this technique? What point is he trying to make through this use of "dual" comparison?

Diction and Vocabulary

1. How would you classify Wade's style and tone in this selection? (Guide: *Tone; Style.*) Are his word choices effective tools for communicating a message and a mood? (Guide: *Diction.*) Do you consider his use of phrases like "militant feminists" appropriate? Why, or why not?

2. This article first appeared in *The New York Times* in 1994. Was the level of difficulty of the vocabulary appropriate for the audience? Why, or why not?

3. If you do not know the meaning of some of the following words, look them up in a dictionary: *ideologue* (Par. 3); *indelibly* (7); *modulated* (9); *propensities* (10).

Read to Write

1. **Collaborating:** Working in a group, make a list of what most people consider the major differences between men and women. As a group, decide how justified these generalizations are. Then choose three items from the list that all group members feel are reasonably

justified and plan a comparison/contrast paper analyzing and explaining these differences. Make sure you include supporting details and examples in your plan.

2. **Considering Audience:** Are Wade's choices of comparison/contrast examples accessible for male and female readers of a variety of ages? Why, or why not? Is his concluding story of Tiresias effective? Rewrite the conclusion of the essay (Par. 13) using a different story or example that might be more accessible for modern readers.

3. **Developing an Essay:** Wade discusses how we identify ourselves based on gender as well as how we compare ourselves to the opposite gender. He says, "The present studies of sex differences are venturing on ground where self-deception and prejudice are constant dangers" (Par. 6). What does he mean by this sentence? Prepare an essay discussing the kind of self-deception to which Wade refers. Consider how men and women typically see their gender in relation to the other gender. Think also about some clichés we often use in discussing gender differences.

(NOTE: Suggestions for topics requiring development by use of COMPARISON and CONTRAST are on pp. 172–173 at the end of this chapter.)

CATHERINE SEIPP

CATHERINE SEIPP was born in Winnipeg, Manitoba, but grew up in Los Alamitos, California. She attended UCLA, graduating with a B.A. in English and experience working on the *Daily Bruin* and writing book reviews for the *Los Angeles Times.* She has been a fashion editor and columnist, a media critic, a freelance magazine writer, and a blogger. Her writing (online and print) has appeared in *Mediaweek, TV Guide, Reason, Salon, American Journalism Review, Buzz, Wall Street Journal, Forbes, Weekly Standard,* and *New York Press,* among many other places. Her blog is *Cathy's World.*

Meet Today's Dad

In this essay, which first appeared in *National Review Online,* Seipp provides a double contrast, looking at what she calls "Today's Dad" in contrast to both mothers and "Yesterday's Dad." Her purpose is likewise twofold: to explain and to criticize the behaviors of "Today's Dad." In keeping with her satiric purpose, she employs mild exaggeration, stereotyping, and irony, but she does not allow these techniques to overwhelm her detailed examples or her explanatory purpose.

I live in the groovy Silver Lake section of Los Angeles, which is home to not only bohemians and gays but also to families who, although they voted against vouchers, still don't want their kids sitting in a classroom filled with the masses; my neighborhood has one of the few public elementary schools in L.A. where most of the kids are middle class and speak English at home. We also have around half-a-dozen preschools within just a couple of miles. Because of all this, my neighborhood is also home to an earnest creature we locals know as Silver Lake Dad. 1

Often this is a guy whose wife slaves away at an office job so dreamy artistic dad can pursue his dreamy artistic dreams. Sometimes he's divorced; by his "I [HEART] Being a Dad" bumper stickers shall ye know him. And although he and his comrades seem particularly common around here, they seem to populate hip urban centers across the country. Silver Lake Dad is just the local version of a new paternal species I think of as Today's Dad. 2

By now it's something of a cliché that men often feel they deserve a medal for what women do as a matter of course. To borrow Samuel Johnson's observation about women preachers, seeing a 3 man take care of children is sometimes like seeing a dog walk on its hind legs: It is not done well, but you are surprised to see it done at all.

Not that Today's Dad isn't helpful. On Halloween, he comes up with the best costumes, or trails along with a cooler of gin-and-tonics while bossy mom plans the trick-or-treating route. But while Today's Dad is certainly involved in his children's lives, his child-care skills aren't always quite as honed as he imagines. 4

Not long ago at Trader Joe's (a Today's Dad hotspot) I saw one of these guys in action. He was bearded (natch), wearing a faded t-shirt advertising some sort of worthy event, and making a big fuss about pork chops with his son: "OK, we'll bread them and bake them! We'll make a project out of it!" The boy looked about four and was standing up in the shopping cart the way the cart warnings always say not to do. 5

Someone came over to chat with this dad, who said he was organizing an antiwar peace vigil. "Good for you!" said the friend. At which point Today's Dad smiled and nodded, accepting the benediction with that serenely self-satisfied expression I notice these guys often assume. It's sort of like the expression men get when playing air guitar—lower lip sucked in, head bobbing up and down—only without the eyes closed shut in ecstasy. 6

Now the problem here was that even though I could see this dad was reveling in his fab daditude, like many guys he found it difficult to do two things at once—like watch a child while chatting with another adult. Men in charge of small children are like women and parallel parking: Attention must be paid or something's going to get dented. Because at this point, the son was really bouncing around in that cart, to the continued obliviousness of his father and the father's friend. The two men were too busy congratulating themselves on their moral rectitude to notice. 7

"Sir," I felt like saying, "your child and various pork products are about to spill themselves upon the ground." But I didn't. Because I know from experience that sensitive Today's Dad types are quick to dismiss women like me as Mean Ladies. 8

Now although Today's Dad is a character who is galling enough in real life, he really rankles when you see him in the concentrated modern pop-culture version. Take the popular WB drama *Everwood,* whose season finale ended with sensitive, bearded (what is with these guys and facial hair?) Dr. Brown informing his teenage son's pregnant ex-girlfriend that she was not to 9 tell the son about this unfortunate turn of events. Because that would rob the boy—who's 17—of the precious last few moments of his childhood.

There was a time when the duties of a father would have in- 10
cluded telling a son in such a situation to grow up and be a man. But then Dr. Brown (who speaks in pitch-perfect Today's Dad lingo) always describes himself as a parent, never as a father.

I once went to a press conference for a sitcom about a working 11
mom and stay-at-home dad. The show runners chuckled happily about how their own kids ran wild around the free food that's always in TV-production offices—taking bites out of cookies, then setting them back on the tray. Gee, that's cute. And it reminds me of another thing I've noticed about Today's Dad: He's fun, he's warm, and he can't be bothered to enforce proper behavior.

I know, I know; I sound cranky. Blame it on 14-plus years of 12
single Mom-dom. I'm addicted to *Everwood,* but the episode where Dr. Brown's single-mom neighbor is working herself into the ground with extra waitressing shifts, while her ex-husband just got a new $120,000 job *and no one ever says anything about child support* really got me.

O.K., so Today's Dad is a fully involved partner in all aspects of 13
the modern child-rearing process, from toting baby around in a backpack at cocktail parties to screaming at third graders on the soccer field. The thing is that, as we all know, in real life the day-in, day-out toting and chauffeuring generally falls to Mom.

My ex-husband was a great diaper-changer, but he left when 14
our daughter was just ten months old. Money became so tight that I was grateful when my own father, who like most men of his generation had never changed a diaper in his life, helped out with babysitting and eventually came to live with us. Before he changed his granddaughter's first diaper, he had to steel himself for a week by staring at dog droppings on the street. And he has no tolerance for contemporary children's lax table manners.

When my daughter had a bad day at school recently—her 15
English teacher had called her a racist for writing a paper arguing that affirmative action isn't necessary for women—Grandpa still didn't cut her any slack at dinner. "We're going to have to make a videotape of this so you can see where you're going wrong with your fork-twirling skills," he said. "We'll call it, The Racist Eating Spaghetti." Still, over the years I've come to appreciate his retro, Yesterday's Dad ways.

Meanings and Values

1. What negative traits does Seipp identify in "Today's Dad"? What positive traits, if any, does she identify?
2. In what ways can the purpose of this essay be considered satiric? (See "Guide to Terms": *Satire.*)
3. What evidence does the essay provide of the writer's political and social outlook? How would you characterize this outlook? Explain why you think that comments reflecting her political and social values add to or detract from the effectiveness of the essay (Guide: *Evaluation.*)

Expository Techniques

1. Where in the essay does the writer first introduce the subject of her essay? Where does she first introduce the patterns of behavior she wishes to contrast with her subject's typical behaviors?
2. Can the extended example in Paragraphs 5–8 be considered a *representative example* (see Ch. 3, "Example," p. 46) that sums up the characteristics of "Today's Dad"? Why, or why not? If so, what roles do the examples in Paragraphs 9–14 play?
3. The writer uses herself as a character in this essay—a *persona*. (Guide: *Persona.*) Where does she employ this technique? How does this technique aid in conveying and explaining her perspective and her values? How, if at all, does the tone of the persona's comments differ from the overall tone of the essay? (Guide: *Style/Tone.*)

Diction and Vocabulary

1. Identify the references to famous people, well-known places, or cultural phenomena in Paragraphs 3, 5, and 9 and explain the use the writer makes of them.
2. This essay uses *verbal irony* (consisting of both *understatement* and *sarcasm*) (Guide: *Irony*) to explain and criticize. Identify one example of each technique and discuss how the writer uses it.
3. If you do not know the meaning of some of the following words, look them up in a dictionary: *bohemians* (Par. 1); *ye, paternal* (2); *honed* (4); *vigil, benediction* (6); *obliviousness, rectitude* (7); *lax* (14).

Read to Write

1. **Collaborating:** In a group, discuss the range of fathers (or mothers) that you or your friends had as children. Prepare a list of these people and the nurturing (or nonnurturing) roles they played. Extend your list by indicating which of these roles the group believes are best played by women or by men, or by either older people or

younger people. Indicate if there are any roles that can be played by only one gender or age group. Then develop at least three tentative thesis statements for essays on the many different kinds of fathers (or mothers) that people in our society need to grow up healthy and emotionally well balanced.

2. **Considering Audience:** Are most readers likely to view Seipp's views on fatherhood sympathetically? Why, or why not? Make a list of different kinds of readers who might be sympathetic and those who might be unsympathetic. Which groups does Seipp seem to address in this essay? Write out a brief plan for revising her essay to increase its appeal to groups that might be unsympathetic.

3. **Developing an Essay:** Using Seipp's essay as a starting point, prepare an essay of your own describing the range of mothers or fathers (or relatives) necessary for good social, emotional, and moral development of a child in our society. Or discuss the range of friendships you consider necessary for developing values like compassion, empathy, tolerance, and generosity.

(NOTE: Suggestions for essays requiring development by COMPARISON and CONTRAST follow.)

Writing Suggestions for Chapter 5

Comparison and Contrast

1. Base your central theme on one of the following, and develop your composition primarily by use of comparison and/or contrast. Use examples liberally for clarity and concreteness, chosen always with your purpose and reader-audience in mind.

    1. Two kinds of families
    2. Two Internet search engines
    3. The innate qualities needed for success in two different careers
    4. Dog people versus cat people
    5. Two musicians
    6. Two radio personalities
    7. Two methods of parental handling of teenage problems
    8. Two family attitudes toward the practice of religion
    9. Two "moods" of the same town at different times
    10. The personalities (or atmospheres) of two cities or towns of similar size
    11. Two politicians with different leadership styles
    12. Careers versus jobs
    13. Two different attitudes toward the same thing or activity: one "practical," the other romantic or aesthetic
    14. The beliefs and practices of two religions or denominations concerning one aspect of religion
    15. Two courses on the same subject: one in high school and one in college
    16. The differing styles of two players of some sport or game
    17. The hazards of frontier life and those of life today
    18. Two companies with very different styles or business philosophies
    19. Two recent movies or music videos
    20. Two magazines focusing on similar subjects but directed at different audiences
    21. The "rewards" of two different kinds of jobs

2. Comparison can be a way of exploring a topic in order to explain it to others. To make this work in your own writing, start by choosing a topic that interests you. Then compare or contrast the elements that make it up by using one or more of these comparative strategies: past and present; good and bad; useful and frivolous; kind and unkind; traditional and innovative; honest and dishonest; honorable and dishonorable; self-serving and dedicated to others; public and private; business

and government; old and young; before and after; or momentary and long-lasting.

3. When we make choices among events or other forms of entertainment and learning, we often compare them to decide which to attend or recommend to friends. Choose two of the following, and prepare an essay explaining the differences between them to guide reader's choices.

films	television shows	music DVDs or songs	books
comics	graphic novels	theater performances	anime
parks	musical groups	sporting events	outdoor experiences

4. Alice Walker (see pp. 154–158) demonstrates that things we often regard as different (humans and animals) are often very much alike in important ways. Think about things, people, events, values, or experiences that most people consider very different, and create an essay explaining the important ways in which they are the same. Or do the opposite: Demonstrate how subjects, feelings, or ideas that many people thing are the same are actually very different.

Collaborative Exercises

1. Choose a partner, and using topic number 19 from writing suggestion 1, write an essay comparing and contrasting two movies or music videos. Each member of the team should be responsible for researching one of the movies or videos.
2. Working with a partner, choose a topic on which you have differing perspectives and prepare an essay, each writing a section of the essay reflecting his or her own perspective. Combine the sections into a draft, then revise each other's section so that the essay reads as a smooth, consistent, and logical whole.

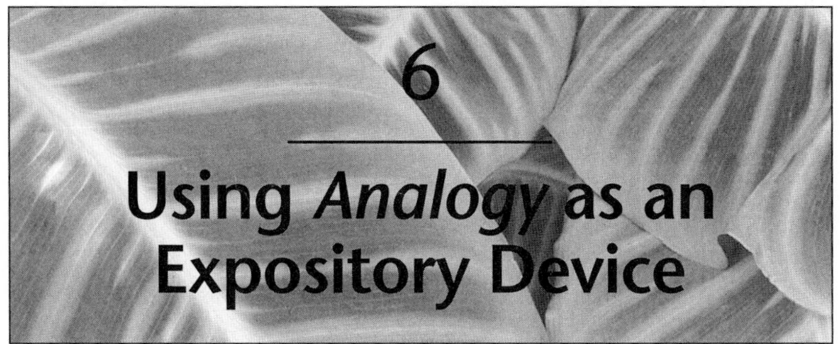

6

Using *Analogy* as an Expository Device

Analogy is a special form of comparison you can use to explain something abstract or difficult to understand. You can show its similarity to something concrete or something easier to understand. A much less commonly used technique than comparison (and contrast), analogy is, nonetheless, a highly efficient means of explaining difficult concepts or giving added force to explanations.

When you use comparison as an explanatory strategy, you need to make sure both subjects belong to the same general class of things, and you assume that readers will be more or less equally interested in both subjects. This is not the case with analogy. In analogy, you and your readers are really concerned only with one of the subjects; the second serves just to help explain the first. The two subjects, which may have little in common, also do not belong to the same class of things. The few elements they do share, however, are what give analogy the power to explain—and even to speculate about how things *might* be.

Certainly, for example, the universe is nothing like raisin bread—or so any reasonable person would think. But an analogy between the two can help explain a very difficult concept, as the following paragraph illustrates.

> If distant galaxies are really receding from the earth, and if more distant galaxies are receding faster than nearby ones, a remarkable picture of the universe emerges. Imagine that the galaxies were raisins scattered through a rising lump of bread dough. As the dough expanded, the raisins would be carried farther and farther apart from each other. If you were standing on one of the raisins, how would things look? You

wouldn't feel any motion yourself, of course, just as you don't feel the effects of the earth's motion around the sun, but you would notice that your nearest neighbor was moving away from you. This motion would be due to the fact that the dough between you and your nearest neighbor would be expanding, pushing the two of you apart.

—James Trefil, *The Dark Side of the Universe*

WHY USE ANALOGY?

In an analogy, you compare two things that are similar in some specifics but otherwise unlike. You can use this strategy to explain a complex, abstract, or unusual subject in familiar and easy-to-understand terms. Or you can use it to speculate about possible interpretations and consequences. For example, to explain how an electromagnetic field transmits radio signals from a station's transmitter to the radio in a listener's home or car, the physicist Richard Feynman asked his readers to imagine two corks floating in a pool of water. If we jiggle one cork, he pointed out, the waves in the water transmit the influence of our action and the second cork begins to jiggle, too. Like the water, an electromagnetic field transmits energy from sender to receiver in the form of waves—electromagnetic waves—conveying radio signals, a television picture, a radar image, or even plain light.

Analogy is not limited to scientific subjects, however. You can use it to explain and support your conclusions about other kinds of topics as well. For instance, a music critic, trying to explain her conclusion that jazz has influenced and will continue to influence modern music of all kinds, compares the jazz tradition to a tune that plays in the back of your mind all day, affecting your mood, the rhythm of your walk, and your tone of voice. Jazz, she explains, is a presence in the minds of composers and performers that shapes their choice of harmonies and rhythms, influences the tone of their compositions and the choice of instruments, and makes "hipness" (a mixture of sophistication, intensity, and emotional distancing) an attitude to which many of them aspire.

CHOOSING A STRATEGY

For a writer, the choice between using a brief analogy or an extended analogy is a significant one. A brief analogy, a sentence or two in length, can serve as an illustration or explanation of a difficult point or concept. To explain the need for a wide selection of college courses and the need for balance in a course of study, you might draw an analogy to a cafeteria, which serves desserts as well as meat, vegetables, and potatoes, allowing for various combinations adding up to balanced, full-course meals. If you wanted to extend this analogy to explain issues of curriculum and course choice in depth, however, you might run into problems with logic and with the adequacy of the particular analogy as an explanatory tool. Which courses, for example, should be classified as "desserts," and would all teachers and students agree on the classification? Does the concept of a well-balanced meal offer an adequate framework for understanding the specific kinds of balance appropriate for course choices?

An extended analogy, if carefully chosen for its logic and the points of comparison it offers, can serve as a framework for detailed explanation. In addition, it can offer a way to gain a fresh perspective on a problem, a controversy, or a puzzling phenomenon. For example, we often unconsciously draw on what we learn about relationships through family life in order to develop relationships within social organizations. Thus although businesses and other organizations are certainly different from families in many ways, there are still enough similarities to make an analogy worthwhile. Such an analogy asks readers to adopt a creative, "as if" perspective: let us examine the conflicts within an organization *as if* they were arguments among various members of a family to see whether the conflicts might be resolved in ways similar to those that work successfully in families. An analogy like this can be extended logically and consistently to explore a relatively broad topic, and it provides reasons for considering seriously the conclusions or interpretations the writer offers.

Analogies can take many different forms, and this flexibility is one of their appeals for both writers and readers. When you use an extended analogy to structure an essay, however, consider adopting a point-by-point arrangement to avoid confusing readers with too many comparisons at once. This is the approach taken in the following plan for an essay.

Tentative thesis: We can better understand corporations by viewing them as if they were large, extended families.

Point 1: Employee ranks are similar to family roles (CEOs, board members = grandparents; VPs = parents; and so on).

Point 2: Different parts of the company are similar to different parts of an extended family (main office = nuclear family; branch offices = families of uncles, aunts, cousins, and so forth).

Point 3: Conflicts over resources within a company are similar to rivalry among cousins or struggles over a will.

Point 4: Struggles over advancement within a company is similar to sibling rivalry.

Point 5: Training programs aim to help employees work together for the good of the company while family therapy tries to help maintain healthy relationships that preserve the family.

Point 6, 7, 8. . . . (if necessary)

DEVELOPING ANALOGIES

Simply stating an analogy and the specific grounds of similarity is seldom enough to make it an effective strategy, especially in the case of an extended analogy. The analogy needs to be clear to readers and developed in enough detail so that it provides convincing explanations and support for the writer's conclusions.

For an analogy to be effective, readers need to be familiar enough with the easier subject so that it really helps explain the more difficult one. Or the easier subject must be one that readers can understand with minimal discussion. An explanation of the human circulatory system, including the heart and arteries, in terms of a pump forcing water through the pipes of a plumbing system would be easily apprehended by readers. The analogy could be carried further to liken the effect of cholesterol deposits on the inner walls of the arteries to that of mineral deposits that accumulate inside water pipes and eventually close them entirely.

It is not enough for you as a writer simply to state an analogy, leaving for readers the job of understanding its significance. You need to explain both the analogy itself and its implications so that readers view it in the same way you do. To say that the world is like an overcrowded lifeboat will mean little in itself. You need also to explain that the lifeboat is in danger of sinking unless the number of passengers is reduced or the craft gains extra flotation power. And then you need to point out the implications: the world is overpopulated, and we must either limit population growth or increase our ability to sustain and feed people—without destroying the environment and, in effect, sinking the boat in which we are traveling.

Student Essay

People often use sports analogies to explain relationships and events in their lives. Kevin Nomura heard such analogies when he was growing up, especially comparisons between life and baseball. His essay draws on baseball for an extended analogy, but he uses it for a surprising purpose: to show how the analogy *fails* to explain much about life. Nonetheless, his essay makes effective use of analogy as a pattern and develops each element of the comparison in interesting, effective, and humorous detail.

Life Isn't Like Baseball

by Kevin Nomura

My father loves baseball. So does my mom. My sister was a star softball player in high school, and she is the regular shortstop on her college team. When my father tried to sign me up for Little League, however, I let him know that I would rather be playing soccer or tennis. It was about this time that he started trying to convince me that "life is like baseball." I wasn't convinced the first time he told me and I'm still not. Let me explain why.

Introduces the analogy

Thesis statement

Striking Out. People who think life is like baseball often talk about "striking out," "staying ahead on the count," or "taking a big swing." When you are up to bat in baseball, you get a lot of chances—not just three strikes but also four balls and any number of fouled-off pitches. I have made some serious mistakes at work, at school, and in my love life, but while I have been lucky enough to get an occasional second chance, I have never gotten any more. When I have failed at something, I have never failed as completely, as obviously, and as publicly as a baseball player does striking out. I suppose that getting booed off the stage is like striking out, but when I sang off-tune in my high school's production of *Bye, Bye Birdie,* no one yelled at me or called me back to the dugout (woops, dressing room). Instead my parents told me they were proud of me no matter what, and the director told me ways to get through my part of the song fast.

First element of the analogy

Why the comparison is illogical

An inaccurate example

Second element of the analogy

Questions pointing out why the analogy is faulty

Hitting a Home Run. People seldom strike out in real life, and they do not hit home runs either. When baseball fans talk about "hitting a home run" at work or in some other activity, they mean accomplishing something dramatic whose success and importance no one can deny. Who has a job that is big enough or important enough to allow for a home run? Can the manager of a McDonald's hit a home run? Can a clerk in a department store or a steelworker do it? Who has a job that allows for dramatic and significant achievement? Can a teacher create brilliant students overnight or an artist become famous for one drawing rather than a lifetime of careful, patient effort? I don't think so, or only so seldom that such an achievement is unrealistic for us mortals.

Third element of the analogy

Questions and examples that highlight the usefulness of the analogy

Like a Spitball. People who believe that life is like baseball often ignore those parts of the game that don't fit very well with everyday experience or that are not very pleasant. Is life like a spitball? Are successful people the ones who load things up with petroleum jelly or scuff them with emery boards, then lie when confronted with evidence—and boast about their deception afterwards? And if some do, should we pretend their actions are good sport and hold them up as examples for the kids? Should we praise people for "stealing" and put the biggest thieves in the record books? Should we treat every botched move—every balk—as a serious error and a public humiliation? Would you like it if a slight slip on your part automatically allowed your competitors to advance a base and maybe even bring home the winning run?

Conclusion—maintains humorous tone of the essay

I realize that I probably haven't convinced any real baseball fans to stop seeing life in terms of their game. I also realize that people will go on talking about "taking a good cut" or "winding up too long before the pitch." My younger brother says he agrees with me, but then he thinks life is a slap shot.

LAN SAMANTHA CHANG

LAN SAMANTHA CHANG is a novelist and director of the Iowa Writer's Workshop at the University of Iowa. She was born (in 1965) in Appleton, Wisconsin, where she lived until she left to attend college at Yale University. She also studied at Harvard, the University of Iowa, and Stanford University. She has been a creative writing instructor at Harvard University and the Bread Loaf Writer's Conference as well as fiction editor for the *Harvard Review*. Her short fiction has appeared in a variety of publications, including *Atlantic Monthly* and *Ploughshares*. Her books of fiction are *Hunger: A Novella and Stories* (1998) and *Inheritance* (novel) (2004).

Like Robinson Crusoe

This essay first appeared in *Prime Times: Writers on Their Favorite TV Shows* (1994). In it, Lan Samantha Chang introduces a variety of related analogies, many built around the television show *Gilligan's Island*, to explain her family's experiences as immigrants from China and to explore her feelings and her search for a "place" in which she belongs.

Desolate, my mother said. It was her first impression of the town where she would live for more than forty years. She took one step onto a pavement sheathed in ice and raised her eyes to view the narrow layer of snow-rimmed cars and houses, the edge of human evidence against the stark white sky. No people could be seen; they had stayed in against the cold. Only my father was there to welcome her. He had come weeks before, to begin his job, and now he brought my mother and sisters into the house that he had rented. It was February 1964, and my family began its life in Appleton, Wisconsin. 1

I have lived in seven states, on both coasts and in between, but in some vivid recess of my mind, I still believe I am a child in Appleton, sitting at the kitchen table with my mother. It is a quiet winter day. My sisters are at school and my mother is cleaning, sorting, and chopping vegetables to make the Chinese meals my father cannot do without. The outsized Midwestern green peppers are transformed to neat, bite-sized pieces in her hands. As she works, my mother describes the places she has lived. She was born in Shanghai, but her family moved two dozen times while seeking safety from the Japanese invasion and the civil war that followed. So 2 she speaks about Chongqing, the wartime capital, sweltering in the summer heat, and she describes the constant threat of Japanese bombers. She recalls the perfect year in Hong Kong, surrounded by palm trees and the ocean's reassuring blue. Later, she lived in Shanghai on the eve of the Nationalist collapse, a time of galloping inflation, of avenues clogged with refugees on foot and bicycle and in automobiles, terrifying days light-softened in spring sun, her last glimpse of mainland China before the Communists moved into the city, driving her and my father and thousands of others to an island in the sea.

Chongqing, Shanghai. Beijing, where my father was born. 3
These were only names to me, but they were vivid, living cities in my parents' recollections; they were the true and real world, the world left behind. My parents fled Shanghai expecting to return, but in the months after the Communist victory, the bamboo curtain tightened. Gunboats patrolled the waters. Travel ceased. Mail halted, save a trickle of letters through Hong Kong. My mother and father heard nothing from the people they had left, and the move to Appleton detached them from all family. I was born into a house of people living in exile, a tiny island of Chinese memories and customs, surrounded by vast shimmering fields of alfalfa, corn, and soybeans, by the fertile smell of dairy cows that drifted to our neighborhood on summer nights. The faraway cities, the friends my parents had known, were sealed in ice.

What does a family in exile watch on television? We had the 4
same programs as our neighbors, but we watched them as outsiders, stealthily, seriously, spying on the culture that the TV characters revealed so easily, took for granted. We watched each joke, each gesture, and each turn of phrase. It was from television that my grandmother learned English. It was a television sitcom that inspired my American name. My parents named me after Samantha Stephens, the domestic witch who held the power to change her circumstances in a flash. My mother hoped that I would bring our family such a rapid transformation.

After school, my sisters and I were permitted to watch televi- 5
sion until dinner. Our time slot ensured us a steady diet of sitcom reruns. I can remember a prolonged interest in *The Flintstones* and a brief dalliance with *The Brady Bunch*, but more than anything, we watched *Gilligan's Island*. Our repeated viewings of this show went on for years, from grade school through junior high and into high school. We would switch channels to catch another episode. The

show ran twice and sometimes three times daily. I must have watched more than three thousand episodes of *Gilligan's Island* before leaving home for college, an average of thirty viewings per episode. For years, I found this fact embarrassing and astounding. How was it possible that we could continue to find this old sitcom, once described by the *San Francisco Chronicle* as "a new low in the networks' estimate of public intelligence," so endlessly absorbing? Why is *Gilligan* the one television show whose episodes I still remember word for word?

Now, twenty years away from Appleton, our prolonged attachment to the castaways makes better sense. The brief sea trip, the storm of change, the spinning wheel of disorientation in space and time, were elements of our own story. The seven members of my family—my maternal grandmother, my parents, my sisters, and myself—lived surrounded by "native" Americans, their speech slow, their hair blond, their customs alien. Our isolation was broken only by an occasional visit from my uncles, or a friend of the family traveling to Chicago, guest stars stopping at our way station for a home-cooked meal and an evening of reminiscence. When these visitors arrived, I saw my parents' past lives bloom before them—my father's witty Mandarin puns, the unusual snacks hand-carried from some distant Chinatown grocer—but inevitably, the visitor would leave, and we would be left alone to continue and make do. 6

Our cultural alienation varied according to our generation. My grandmother's homesickness was perhaps the most acute. Her age rendered her more nostalgic, less adaptive. Unlike my parents, who could look forward to a future as Americans, she had only her past in a country now closed off to her. Having reached the age when she found herself naturally turning to the past, she was obliged to reach through a geographical as well as temporal remove. The focus of her nostalgia settled on certain missing foods. Like poor Gilligan, who squandered two of his three magic wishes on ice cream, my grandmother lay awake thinking about the dishes she had once eaten and loved: the tiny seafood dumplings in Shanghai; savory chicken wrapped in lotus leaves, a specialty of Hangzhou; the flavor of a certain pepper grown only in Sichuan. These lost dishes took on the poignancy and power of her lost youth. 7

My parents, plunged into a new setting in midlife, spent their time and energy adapting to the change. They settled in the new country, but knew the value of the old. Each day they ventured out to work and make our family's future; at the same time, they upheld 8 the values of the past. They tried to make the foods my grandmother missed. They found a butcher willing to sell us the unpopular cuts she liked. They were able to re-create, with some effort, the paper-thin spring roll wrappers. Certain staples were acutely missed and difficult to make. My mother still recalls their struggles to make tofu. They drove out into the country and rang the doorbell of a soybean farmer, from whom they bought two bushels of beans (I remember the empty baskets in the garage). The traditional method required grinding, but my parents had no grinder, so they used an electric mixer to beat the soybeans into milk. They worked away at it for hours, burning up one mixer's motor in the process. My father, a chemist, devised a way to curdle soybean milk with salt. They wrapped the curds into cheesecloth and pressed it in the refrigerator. The final product was, my grandmother said, "good." Having nothing to compare it with, I was reluctant to agree.

Born in Appleton, I was doubly ignorant: I knew nothing of China, but I knew little of America outside our home. I grew up into the space between two ignorances. My confusion was profound. It never occurred to me that I found *Gilligan* soothing because its characters' lives were similar to my American life. After all, I was a native Appletonian. But I was first of all a resident of my family's island, a living museum, a repository for mixed-up cultural adaptations. I can remember watching an episode featuring the Professor's hand-cranked phonograph, then turning off the television and going outside to fly kites using a Chinese-style kite-flying reel that my father had constructed from an old telephone dial and the parts of fishing rods. I would watch the castaways serve pancake syrup made from tropical trees and then I'd sit down to a real dinner made of Southern-style "salt chicken" my parents had cured on the back porch. My grandmother, who often caught the episodes while watching over a pot of brewing ginseng roots, praised the Professor's efforts to treat Gilligan's eyes by concocting a keptibora berry extract. She said, "Sometimes homemade medicine can work better than those foreign doctors." 9

I was intrigued and troubled by the way that *Gilligan* preserved the shadow of my parents' war. The original series, which ran from 1964 to 1967, presented a time in which the memories of World War II's Pacific battles were not long past. In one episode, the castaways stumbled upon a hidden munitions pit. Another episode guest-starred Vito Scotti as a deranged Japanese soldier who had survived on the Pacific islands for twenty years without knowing 10 the war had ended. This particular episode left me uneasy. I felt uncomfortable with the comical portrayal of the Asian accent, his mannerisms, and his bottle-top glasses. But I felt even more disturbed by the idea of the poor, deluded man, insisting on his own version of the war, unaware that the world had gone on without him.

Of course, time does not stand still. We were caught in its flow, through the Cold War, through feminism and Watergate. My family adapted. My mother studied American customs as carefully as she had once memorized the history of the dynasties. She kept a box of file cards listing what Americans liked to eat (large cuts of meat, sweet and sour dishes) and what they did not like (rice gruel, tofu, fish with eyes and shrimp with the shells on). She earned a second degree and became a piano teacher. My father became a Packers fan. He set up a woodworking room in the basement and made our furniture. He built standing lamps bearing the characters for longevity. He built walnut end tables with the characters for "big good luck," finished and sealed under glass. 11

We grew into an accomplished, noisy family with a strong sense of identity and rich blood, squeezed into a house that was too small for us. My older sisters remember us as happy, striving. But when I think of my childhood, I remember a certain sadness in the house. It stole in on the long blue shadows of our winter evenings. It was folded into the embroidered coverlets my mother kept beneath her bed. Once, while we were cleaning, my mother showed me the basement storage bin where she and my father had stacked the dusty suitcases they had brought from overseas. There, carefully wrapped in an old sheet, my father kept the long, blue silk jacket his mother had made for him when he was a young man. His mother had been left behind; he had not heard from his parents since leaving the country in 1949. This separation lay at the heart of our sadness. We were one of many families who shape this country of transplanted people, holding the long, unspoken sorrow of those cut off from what they have known. 12

I believe we each lived on our own island. My father enveloped himself in privacy, remembering the people he had left; my mother regretted the lost dreams of her own youth. They were not entirely unhappy; it was not so simple. They were each of them a separate being, isolated, exiled by their separate losses. I was an exile as well—not a political or geographical exile, like my parents, but a child holding on to the secret, mutinous loneliness of one who is about to leave. My island was Appleton. I did not belong in town, 13 and there was not enough room for me to continue in our family's makeshift world. I knew that I was meant to leave our home. In a few years, I would pack my own suitcase and leave to see the world. I would come back to visit, never to stay.

But at the time, my stay in Appleton felt interminable. Each day, I would trudge home from junior high school, where I was justifiably despised for being arrogant, a "brain," awkward, and friendless. I would be in an indignant, lonely frame of mind. The drifts of snow, which seemed to fall so thickly in those days, piled high around the house, glowed violet in the deepening dusk. Inside, when I took off my coat, I could feel the cold pressing through the windows. My sisters and I would sit in the room adjacent to the kitchen and watch television with all the lights turned on. Every day, the castaways attempted a new plan to escape. They all desired to leave, the insufferable Mr. Howell and the impossible Mary Ann. I watched carefully and seldom laughed. I found the castaways' frustration unsurprising. In every episode, they tried to leave the island, and every time, their plans were foiled. No one was getting anywhere. 14

And then the world changed. I remember the Chinese Ping-Pong players on television. After this time of tentative outreaches, of Ping-Pong diplomacy, my oldest sister graduated and went out into the world, like a milkweed seed traveling on the wind in search of a fertile place. In September 1978, Mao died. We heard it on the evening news. My parents grew very quiet when his death was announced. I asked, "Who is Mao?" Soon afterward, my second sister left home for college. My father wrote to the mainland government for information about the whereabouts of his family. He learned their addresses and made contact with his sisters—his parents and brother had died—and in 1982 he made the long trip back through time and across the world to see them again. In 1983, I left Wisconsin to attend Thurston Howell's rival school and I stopped watching television for many years. 15

The world is so open now. There is an Asian grocery less than two miles from my parents' house; even the supermarkets carry tofu made with local beans. In downtown Appleton, a crowded restaurant serves authentic Chinese dishes. My parents go to Lunar New Year parties with a local Chinese club. Nor need we content ourselves with China brought to us; now we can fly there ourselves. My sister and I traveled to Beijing to meet my father's sisters. We brought back for my father his own kite-flying rod and a brightly painted silk kite shaped like a butterfly with twirling eyes. He liked 16 the gift, although he did not use it. He has grown less sorrowful and less nostalgic, having rediscovered some old friends and reconnected with them safely, as adults. He has found a way off his island.

17 I have now lived away from Appleton for half my life. I moved to Connecticut, then Massachusetts, Iowa, California, New Jersey. In my travels I have not found a home. It occurs to me now, once more in Massachusetts, that I have been entirely conditioned by my childhood in the Midwest, my desires shaped to a non-specified place-longing. No sooner do I settle in one town than I begin to daydream about somewhere else. But I know there is no perfect place. It is clear that I belong not to a place but to my far-flung family, my tightly knit and fractious group of former exiles.

18 On a recent visit to Wisconsin, while I was sitting with my mother, an episode of *Gilligan's Island* came on. My mother and I were cutting up the vegetables for dinner. We sat in our old places, with the winter light at the window just as it had been when I was a child.

19 The castaways were still ensnared, still waiting to be saved. In one episode, Mr. Howell lost $3 million to Gilligan, betting over a makeshift putting green. I discovered I could still remember the lines. But now I understood one of the jokes for the first time. "I'm having trouble adjusting to this oyster shell putter," Mr. Howell said. Lovey replied, "Why, of course, it's because there's no *r* in the month." Watching a typical exchange between Gilligan and the Skipper in their skimpy bamboo hut, I enjoyed the Skipper's exaggerated mugging, the good-natured, slapstick humor. Why hadn't I seen this, in all those years?

20 I asked my mother whether she thought *Gilligan* was funny. Through all those years she'd caught the show from a distance, too busy, or unwilling, to sit with us for hours.

21 She laid down her paring knife. She was not watching the TV but looking through her spectacles at some memory I couldn't see. "Yes," she said.

22 "Why is it funny to you?"

23 "The show is funny because the characters were in an absurd situation," she replied. "They were unable to change with their environment."

24 "What is the difference between something funny and something sad?"

25 She did not answer. For a moment I felt that I had been transported to those years when my parents did not know if they would

ever be allowed to see the mainland. How many times did my parents dream that they were in China and wake up back in the Midwest, precisely where they had been? Where did they dream of being now? Finally, my mother smiled. She replied, "Some might say that problems are only sad if they don't work out. Sad times can only become funny when they're seen from far away."

Meanings and Values

1. What roles did television play in the life of the author's family, and what effects did it have on the family as a whole or specific members of the family? (See especially Paragraphs 4 and 5.)
2. What is the "island in the sea" (Par. 2)? Why might the author have chosen to call it an "island" rather than referring to it by its (well-known) name? In what ways is the "island in the sea" linked to other islands mentioned in the essay: "a tiny island of Chinese memories and customs" (Par. 3); "each . . . our own island" (Par. 13); "Appleton" (Par. 13); and *Gilligan's Island*?
3. What answer(s) does the essay offer to this question: "Why is *Gilligan* the one television show whose episodes I still remember word for word?" (Par. 5).
4. Explain what Paragraph 23 seems to say about an important difference between the author's family and the characters in *Gilligan's Island*.

Expository Techniques

1. What role in the organization of the essay does the rhetorical question at the end of Paragraph 5 play? (See "Guide to Terms": *Rhetorical Questions.*)
2. Where in the essay does the author first introduce and explain the main analogy she explores in the essay? Explain why you think she did not choose to introduce the analogy at the very beginning of the essay? What other analogies does the author offer in the essay (including the title)? How are they related (or unrelated) to the main analogy?
3. Identify the similarities in organization and emphasis shared by Paragraphs 7, 9, and 14. (Guide: *Emphasis.*) Explain what you think the author is trying to accomplish through the organization of these paragraphs.

DICTION AND VOCABULARY

1. Identify the words the author uses in Paragraph 1 to describe the town in ways that justify her mother's use of the word *"Desolate."*
2. To what kind of scene is the word "shimmering" often applied in a common (or clichéd) phrase? (Guide: *Clichés.*) What specific analogy does use of the word in Paragraph 3 introduce or reinforce? Do you consider this use of the word effective or ineffective? Why? (Guide: *Evaluation.*)
3. If you do not know the meaning of some of the following words, consult a dictionary: *stealthily* (Par. 4); *dalliance* (5); *disorientation, reminiscence* (6); *savory, poignancy* (7); *staples, curdle* (8); *cured* (9); *munitions* (10); *dynasties, characters* (11); *mutinous* (13); *interminable, indignant* (14); *fractious* (17); *mugging* (19).

READ TO WRITE

1. **Collaborating:** Break into groups of four. Discuss family relationships and experiences similar to those Chang describes that you and your classmates have had. Plan an essay using representative experiences from each member of the group. Be sure to choose the experiences carefully so that the analogy that develops from each can be connected through transitions to develop a coherent essay.
2. **Considering Audience:** Much of this essay focuses on immigrant experience and the perspectives and history of members of a particular cultural, ethnic group. As a consequence, the writer spends some time explaining experiences and outlooks with which readers may be unfamiliar. Prepare an essay similar in style and use of analogy to Chang's that draws on sources of experiences and feelings that readers are more likely to share: youth sports, vacation travel, high school, or popular music, for example.
3. **Developing an Essay:** As the basis for the main analogy in her essay, Chang uses episodes in a television show that come to embody ideas, values, feelings, and experiences. Use a similar source of analogies for an essay of your own that explores and explains your own experiences or ones you share with your readers.

(NOTE: Suggestions for topics requiring development by use of ANALOGY are on pp. 213–214 at the end of this chapter.)

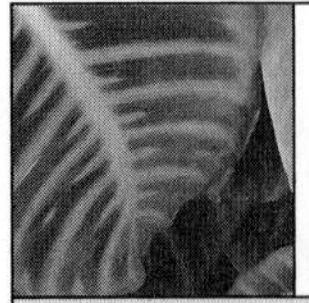

Issues and Ideas

Humans and Animals

- Tom Wolfe, *O Rotten Gotham—Sliding Down into the Behavioral Sink*
- Barbara Kingsolver, *High Tide in Tuscon*

Like most people, you have probably spent considerable time and effort trying to understand how people behave and how they maintain (or fail to maintain) relationships with each other. One way to do this is through careful observation of social interaction. Yet the complexity of human behavior often makes it difficult to isolate the patterns that can explain our relationships or predict our actions.

For this reason, scientists and other students of human behavior often look for explanatory patterns in studies of plants, animals, or natural processes. Historians sometimes discuss a civilization in terms of its germination, growth, flowering, and decay, for example. A sociologist may use a concept like "entropy" (from physics) to explain a society's decline into chaos, and an anthropologist may turn to biology and natural history to explain our reluctance to abandon settings that once held meaning for us.

To borrow such explanatory patterns is to make use of analogy: explaining complex behaviors by those behaviors that seem simpler and easier to understand (though they may, in truth, be just as difficult and complicated). The risk in borrowing explanatory patterns is that they may oversimplify relationships (bees can represent hardworking groups, but bee societies are certainly less complex than human ones) or that they may be mostly inappropriate (we can talk of a friendship "blossoming" while we know that it has few other similarities to plants or plant life).

In reading the discussions of human behavior in Tom Wolfe's "O Rotten Gotham" and Barbara Kingsolver's "High Tide in Tucson," therefore, pay attention to how the writers use analogy as an effective expository strategy, and also to the ways they use it as a tool for understanding. Bear in mind that an explanation that is rhetorically successful may still take unfounded logical leaps or leave important questions unanswered.

TOM WOLFE

TOM WOLFE was born in 1931 and grew up in Richmond, Virginia, graduated from Washington and Lee University, and took his doctorate at Yale. After working for several years as a reporter for the *Washington Post,* he joined the staff of the *New York Herald Tribune* in 1962. He has won two Washington Newspaper Guild Awards, one for humor and the other for foreign news. Wolfe has been a regular contributor to *New York, Esquire,* and other magazines. His books include *The Kandy-Kolored Tangerine-Flake Streamline Baby* (1965), *The Electric Kool-Aid Acid Test* (1968), *The Pump House Gang* (1968), *Radical Chic and Mau-Mauing the Flak Catchers* (1970), *The New Journalism* (1973), *The Right Stuff* (1977), *In Our Time* (1980), *From Bauhaus to Our House* (1981), *The Bonfire of the Vanities* (1986), *A Man in Full* (1999), *Hooking Up* (2000), *I Am Charlotte Simmons* (2004), and *Back to Blood* (2009).

O Rotten Gotham—Sliding Down into the Behavioral Sink

"O Rotten Gotham—Sliding Down into the Behavioral Sink," as used here, is excerpted from a longer selection by that title in Wolfe's book *The Pump House Gang* (1968). Here, as he frequently does, the author investigates an important aspect of modern life—seriously, but in his characteristic and seemingly freewheeling style. It is a style that is sometimes ridiculed by scholars but is far more often admired. (Wolfe, as the serious student will discover, is always in complete control of his materials and methods, using them to create certain effects to reinforce his ideas.) In this piece, his analogy is particularly noteworthy for the extensive usage he is able to get from it.

I just spent two days with Edward T. Hall, an anthropologist, watching thousands of my fellow New Yorkers short-circuiting themselves into hot little twitching death balls with jolts of their own adrenalin. Dr. Hall says it is overcrowding that does it. Overcrowding gets the adrenalin going, and the adrenalin gets them hyped up. And here they are, hyped up, turning bilious, nephritic, a queer, autistic, sadistic, barren, batty, sloppy, hot-in-the-pants, chancred-on-the-flankers, leering, puling, numb—the usual in New York, in other words, and God knows what else. Dr. Hall has the 1 theory that overcrowding has already thrown New York into a state of behavioral sink. Behavioral sink is a term from ethology, which is the study of how animals relate to their environment. Among animals, the sink winds up with a "population collapse" or "massive die-off." O Rotten Gotham.

It got to be easy to look at New Yorkers as animals, especially looking down from some place like a balcony at Grand Central at the rush hour Friday afternoon. The floor was filled with the poor white humans, running around, dodging, blinking their eyes, making a sound like a pen full of starlings or rats or something. 2

"Listen to them skid," says Dr. Hall. 3

He was right. The poor old etiolate animals were out there skidding on their rubber soles. You could hear it once he pointed it out. They stop short to keep from hitting somebody or because they are disoriented and they suddenly stop and look around, and they skid on their rubber-soled shoes, and a screech goes up. They pour out onto the floor down the escalators from the Pan-Am Building, from 42nd Street, from Lexington Avenue, up out of subways, down into subways, railroad trains, up into helicopters— 4

"You can also hear the helicopters all the way down here," says Dr. Hall. The sound of the helicopters using the roof of the Pan-Am Building nearly fifty stories up beats right through. "If it weren't for this ceiling"—he is referring to the very high ceiling in Grand Central—"this place would be unbearable with this kind of crowding. And yet they'll probably never 'waste' space like this again." 5

They screech! And the adrenal glands in all those poor white animals enlarge, micrometer by micrometer, to the size of cantaloupes. Dr. Hall pulls a Minox camera out of a holster he has on his belt and starts shooting away at the human scurry. The Sink! 6

Dr. Hall has the Minox up to his eye—he is a slender man, calm, 52 years old, young-looking, an anthropologist who has worked with Navajos, Hopis, Spanish-Americans, Negroes, Trukese. He was the most important anthropologist in the government during the crucial years of the foreign aid program, the 1950s. He directed both the Point Four training program and the Human Relations Area Files. He wrote *The Silent Language* and *The Hidden Dimension,* two books that are picking up the kind of "underground" following his friend Marshall McLuhan started picking up about five years ago. He teaches at the Illinois Institute of Technology, lives with his wife, Mildred, in a high-ceilinged town house on one of the last great residential streets in downtown Chicago, Astor Street; he has a 7 grown son and daughter, loves good food, good wine, the relaxed, civilized life—but comes to New York with a Minox at his eye to record!—perfect—The Sink.

We really got down in there by walking down into the Lexington Avenue line subway stop under Grand Central. We inhaled those nice big fluffy fumes of human sweat, urine, effluvia, and sebaceous secretions. One old female human was already stroked out on the upper level, on a stretcher, with two policemen standing by. The other humans barely looked at her. They rushed into line. They bellied each other, haunch to paunch, down the stairs. Human heads shone through the gratings. The species North European tried to create bubbles of space around themselves, about a foot and a half in diameter— 8

"See, he's reacting against the line," says Dr. Hall. 9

—but the species Mediterranean presses on in. The hell with bubbles of space. The species North European resents that, this male human behind him presses forward toward the booth . . . breathing on him, he's disgusted, he pulls out of the line entirely, the species Mediterranean resents him for resenting it, and neither of them realizes what the hell they are getting irritable about exactly. And in all of them the old adrenals grow another micrometer. 10

Dr. Hall whips out the Minox. Too perfect! The bottom of The Sink. 11

It is the sheer overcrowding, such as occurs in the business sections of Manhattan five days a week and in Harlem, Bedford-Stuyvesant, southeast Bronx every day—sheer overcrowding is converting New Yorkers into animals in a sink pen. Dr. Hall's argument runs as follows: all animals, including birds, seem to have a built-in inherited requirement to have a certain amount of territory, space, to lead their lives in. Even if they have all the food they need, and there are no predatory animals threatening them, they cannot tolerate crowding beyond a certain point. No more than two hundred wild Norway rats can survive on a quarter acre of ground, for example, even when they are given all the food they can eat. They just die off. 12

But why? To find out, ethologists have run experiments on all sorts of animals, from stickleback crabs to Sika deer. In one major experiment, an ethologist named John Calhoun put some domesticated white Norway rats in a pen with four sections to it, connected by ramps. Calhoun knew from previous experiments that the rats tend to split up into groups of ten to twelve and that the pen, therefore, would hold forty to forty-eight rats comfortably, assuming 13 they formed four equal groups. He allowed them to reproduce until there were eighty rats, balanced between male and female, but did not let it get any more crowded. He kept them supplied with plenty of food, water, and nesting materials. In other words, all their more obvious needs were taken care of. A less obvious need—space—was not. To the human eye, the pen did not even look especially crowded. But to the rats, it was crowded beyond endurance.

The entire colony was soon plunged into a profound behavioral 14
sink. "The sink," said Calhoun, "is the outcome of any behavioral process that collects animals together in unusually great numbers. The unhealthy connotations of the term are not accidental: a behavioral sink does act to aggravate all forms of pathology that can be found within a group."

For a start, long before the rat population reached eighty, a sta- 15
tus hierarchy had developed in the pen. Two dominant male rats took over the two end sections, acquired harems of eight to ten females each, and forced the rest of the rats into the two middle pens. All the overcrowding took place in the middle pens. That was where the "sink" hit. The aristocrat rats at the end grew bigger, sleeker, healthier, and more secure the whole time.

In The Sink, meanwhile, nest building, courting, sex behavior, 16
reproduction, social organization, health—all of it went to pieces. Normally, Norway rats have a mating ritual in which the male chases the female, the female ducks down into a burrow and sticks her head up to watch the male. He performs a little dance outside the burrow, then she comes out, and he mounts her, usually for a few seconds. When The Sink set in, however, no more than three males—the dominant males in the middle sections—kept up the old customs. The rest tried everything from satyrism to homosexuality or else gave up on sex altogether. Some of the subordinate males spent all their time chasing females. Three or four might chase one female at the same time, and instead of stopping at the burrow entrance for the ritual, they would charge right in. Once mounted, they would hold on for minutes instead of the usual seconds.

Homosexuality rose sharply. So did bisexuality. Some males 17
would mount anything—males, females, babies, senescent rats, anything. Still other males dropped sexual activity altogether, wouldn't fight and, in fact, would hardly move except when the other rats slept. Occasionally, a female from the aristocrat rats' harems would come over the ramps and into the middle sections to sample life in The Sink. When she had had enough, she would run back up the

ramp. Sink males would give chase up to the top of the ramp, which is to say, to the very edge of the aristocratic preserve. But one glance from one of the king rats would stop them cold and they would return to The Sink.

The slumming females from the harems had their adventures and then returned to a placid, healthy life. Females in The Sink, however, were ravaged, physically and psychologically. Pregnant rats had trouble continuing pregnancy. The rate of miscarriages increased significantly, and females started dying from tumors and other disorders of the mammary glands, sex organs, uterus, ovaries, and Fallopian tubes. Typically, their kidneys, livers, and adrenals were also enlarged or diseased or showed other signs associated with stress. 18

Child-rearing became totally disorganized. The females lost the interest or the stamina to build nests and did not keep them up if they did build them. In the general filth and confusion, they would not put themselves out to save offspring they were momentarily separated from. Frantic, even sadistic competition among the males was going on all around them and rendering their lives chaotic. The males began unprovoked and senseless assaults upon one another, often in the form of tail-biting. Ordinarily, rats will suppress this kind of behavior when it crops up. In The Sink, male rats gave up all policing and just looked out for themselves. The "pecking order" among males in The Sink was never stable. Normally, male rats set up a three-class structure. Under the pressure of overcrowding, however, they broke up into all sorts of unstable subclasses, cliques, packs—and constantly pushed, probed, explored, tested one another's power. Anyone was fair game, except for the aristocrats in the end pens. 19

Calhoun kept the population down to eighty, so that the next stage, "population collapse" or "massive die-off," did not occur. But the autopsies showed that the pattern—as in the diseases among the female rats—was already there. 20

The classic study of die-off was John J. Christian's study of Sika deer on James Island in the Chesapeake Bay, west of Cambridge, Maryland. Four or five of the deer had been released on the island, which was 280 acres and uninhabited, in 1916. By 1955 they had bred freely into a herd of 280 to 300. The population density was only about one deer per acre at this point, but Christian knew that this was already too high for the Sikas' inborn space requirements, and something would give before long. For two years the number of 21 deer remained 280 to 300. But suddenly, in 1958, over half the deer died; 161 carcasses were recovered. In 1959 more deer died and the population steadied at about 80.

In two years, two-thirds of the herd had died. Why? It was not starvation. In fact, all the deer collected were in excellent condition, with well-developed muscles, shining coats, and fat deposits between the muscles. In practically all the deer, however, the adrenal glands had enlarged by 50 percent. Christian concluded that the die-off was due to "shock following severe metabolic disturbance, probably as a result of prolonged adrenocortical hyperactivity. . . . There was no evidence of infection, starvation, or other obvious cause to explain the mass mortality." In other words, the constant stress of overpopulation, plus the normal stress of the cold of the winter, had kept the adrenalin flowing so constantly in the deer that their systems were depleted of blood sugar and they died of shock. 22

Well, the white humans are still skidding and darting across the floor of Grand Central. Dr. Hall listens a moment longer to the skidding and the darting noises, and then says, "You know, I've been on commuter trains here after everyone has been through one of these rushes, and I'll tell you, there is enough acid flowing in the stomachs in every car to dissolve the rails underneath." 23

Just a little invisible acid bath for the linings to round off the day. The ulcers the acids cause, of course, are the one disease people have already been taught to associate with the stress of city life. But overcrowding, as Dr. Hall sees it, raises a lot more hell with the body than just ulcers. In everyday life in New York—just the usual, getting to work, working in massively congested areas like 42nd Street between Fifth Avenue and Lexington, especially now that the Pan-Am Building is set in there, working in cubicles such as those in the editorial offices at Time-Life, Inc., which Dr. Hall cites as typical of New York's poor handling of space, working in cubicles with low ceilings and, often, no access to a window, while construction crews all over Manhattan drive everybody up the Masonite wall with air-pressure generators with noises up to the boil-a-brain decibel level, than rushing to get home, piling into subways and trains, fighting for time and for space, the usual day in New York—the whole now-normal thing keeps shooting jolts of adrenalin into the body, breaking down the body's defenses and winding up with the work-a-daddy human animal stroked out at the breakfast table with his head apoplexed like a cauliflower out of his $6.95 semi-spread Pima-cotton shirt, and nosed over into a plate of No-Kolresto egg 24 substitute, signing off with the black thrombosis, cancer, kidney, liver, or stomach failure, and the adrenals ooze to a halt, the size of eggplants in July.

One of the people whose work Dr. Hall is interested in on this 25
score is Rene Dubos at the Rockefeller Institute. Dubos's work indicates that specific organisms, such as the tuberculosis bacillus or a pneumonia virus, can seldom be considered "the cause" of a disease. The germ or virus, apparently, has to work in combination with other things that have already broken the body down in some way—such as the old adrenal hyperactivity. Dr. Hall would like to see some autopsy studies made to record the size of adrenal glands in New York, especially of people crowded into slums and people who go through the full rush-hour-work-rush-hour cycle every day. He is afraid that until there is some clinical, statistical data on how overcrowding actually ravages the human body, no one will be willing to do anything about it. Even in so obvious a thing as air pollution, the pattern is familiar. Until people can actually see the smoke or smell the sulphur or feel the sting in their eyes, politicians will not get excited about it, even though it is well known that many of the lethal substances polluting the air are invisible and odorless. For one thing, most politicians are like the aristocrat rats. They are insulated from The Sink by practically sultanic buffers—limousines, chauffeurs, secretaries, aides-de-camp, doormen, shuttered houses, high-floor apartments. They almost never ride subways, fight rush hours, much less live in the slums or work in the Pan-Am Building.

Meanings and Values

1. Who are members of the "species Mediterranean"? The "species North European"? What could account for their differences in space requirements (Pars. 8–10)?
2. Is this writing primarily objective or subjective? (See "Guide to Terms": *Objective/Subjective.*) Why?
3. Do you get the impression that the author is being unkind, "making fun" of the harried New Yorkers? How, if at all, does he prevent such an impression?

Expository Techniques

1. Is this analogy a success, or does the author work it too hard? Be prepared to defend your answer. (Guide: *Evaluation.*)

2. What are the benefits of the frequent return to what Dr. Hall is doing or saying (e.g., in Pars. 3, 5, 7, 9, 11, and 23)?
3. Paragraph 12 has a useful function beyond the simple information it provides—a sort of organic relation to the coming development. Explain how this is accomplished.
4. The preceding two questions highlight the ways Wolfe deals with problems of transition in this essay. (Guide: *Transition.*) How are such issues also matters of coherence? (Guide: *Coherence.*)
5. Analyze stylistic differences, with resulting effects, between the following sections of the essay (Guide: *Style/Tone*):
   a. The description of chaos at Grand Central and the information about Dr. Hall in Paragraph 7
   b. The Grand Central scene and the account of the laboratory experiment with rats in Paragraphs 8–20
   c. The Grand Central scene and the final paragraph
6. What is gained or lost by the unusual length and design of the last sentence of Paragraph 24? (We can be sure that it did not "just happen" to Wolfe—and equally sure that a sentence of such length would be disastrous in most writing.) (Guide: *Syntax.*)

Diction and Vocabulary

1. What is the significance of the word "Gotham"?
2. Why do you think the author refers to "my fellow New Yorkers" in the first sentence? What would have been the effect had he not taken such a step?
3. Why does he consistently, after Paragraph 2, refer to the people as "poor white humans," "poor human animals," etc.?
4. In Paragraph 14 he refers to the connotations of the word "sink." What are its possible connotations? (Guide: *Connotation/Denotation.*)
5. Cite examples of verbal irony to be found in Paragraphs 5, 8, and 24.
6. Consult your dictionary as needed for full understanding of the following words: *autistic, puling* (Par.1); *etiolate* (4); *effluvia, sebaceous* (8); *pathology* (14); *satyrism* (16); *senescent* (17); *decibel, thrombosis* (24); *lethal* (25).

Read to Write

1. **Collaborating:** One especially effective technique Wolfe employs in this essay is observation—specifically the overall view afforded by a balcony high above the main hall of Grand Central Station. With a team of three other people, choose a location that will provide you with a broad overview of human actions and behavior. Go to that spot with notebooks in hand and individually, without discussion,

write your observations. Return to the classroom and compare your notes. What similarities in behavior did you all observe? What different activities and images stood out in your minds? Write a short analysis of your collective observations. Be sure to include an explanation of the behaviors noticeable to all of you and reasons why other behaviors stood out to individual observers.

2. **Considering Audience:** Would this essay have a strong effect on readers raised in a rural area? What aspects of this essay might help someone from a farming environment relate to this? What other behaviors could be addressed to make this more accessible to audiences from rural areas? Choose a particular animal behavior that could be analogous to human activity in rural locations and create a plan for an essay based on the analogy.

3. **Developing an Essay:** Popular magazines can provide good summaries of contemporary research as can specialized encyclopedias and general interest books. Choose a theory or some research you think is insightful and use it to help explain common behaviors, perhaps some that you have observed in the manner described in the "collaborating" question. Prepare an essay built around two or more explanatory theories as Wolfe does in his essay.

(NOTE: Suggestions for topics requiring development by use of ANALOGY are on pp. 213–214 at the end of this chapter.)

BARBARA KINGSOLVER

BARBARA KINGSOLVER was born in 1955 in Annapolis, Maryland, and raised in eastern Kentucky. She studied biology at DePauw University (B.A., 1977) and the University of Arizona (M.S., 1981) and worked as a scientist and scientific writer before beginning her career as a writer of fiction and essays. Her highly acclaimed books include *The Bean Trees* (1988), *Animal Dreams* (1990), and *Pigs in Heaven* (1993) (novels); *Homeland and Other Stories* (1989) (stories); *Another America* (1992) (poetry); *High Tide in Tucson: Essays from Now or Never* (1996) (essays); *The Poisonwood Bible* (1998) (novel); *Prodigal Summer* (2000) (novel); *Small Wonder* (2002) (essays); and *Animal, Vegetable, Miracle* (2007) (nonfiction).

High Tide in Tucson

This essay, from Kingsolver's book with the same title, is built around a surprising and imaginative analogy. It offers a different and more optimistic perspective on modern society and behavior than Tom Wolfe does in the preceding essay ("O Rotten Gotham"), yet, like Wolfe, the author draws heavily on scientific research for her explanations.

A hermit crab lives in my house. Here in the desert he's hiding out from local animal ordinances, at minimum, and maybe even the international laws of native-species transport. For sure, he's an outlaw against nature. So be it. 1

He arrived as a stowaway two Octobers ago. I had spent a week in the Bahamas, and while I was there, wishing my daughter could see those sparkling blue bays and sandy covers, I did exactly what she would have done: I collected shells. Spiky murexes, smooth purple moon shells, ancient-looking whelks sand-blasted by the tide—I tucked them in the pockets of my shirt and shorts until my lumpy, suspect hemlines gave me away, like a refugee smuggling the family fortune. When it was time to go home, I rinsed my loot in the sink and packed it carefully into a plastic carton, then nested it deep in my suitcase for the journey to Arizona. 2

I got home in the middle of the night, but couldn't wait till morning to show my hand. I set the carton on the coffee table for my daughter to open. In the dark living room her face glowed, in the way of antique stories about children and treasure. With perfect 3 delicacy she laid the shells out on the table, counting, sorting, designating scientific categories like yellow-striped pinky, Barnacle Bill's pocketbook. . . . Yeek! She let loose a sudden yelp, dropped her booty, and ran to the far end of the room. The largest, knottiest whelk had begun to move around. First it extended one long red talon of a leg, tap-tap-tapping like a blind man's cane. Then came half a dozen more red legs, plus a pair of eyes on stalks, and a purple claw that snapped open and shut in a way that could not mean We come in Friendship.

Who could blame this creature? It had fallen asleep to the sound of the Caribbean tide and awakened on a coffee table in Tucson, Arizona, where the nearest standing water source of any real account was the municipal sewage-treatment plant. 4

With red stiletto legs splayed in all directions, it lunged and jerked its huge shell this way and that, reminding me of the scene I make whenever I'm moved to rearrange the living-room sofa by myself. Then, while we watched in stunned reverence, the strange beast found its bearings and began to reveal a determined, crabby grace. It felt its way to the edge of the table and eased itself over, not falling bang to the floor but hanging suspended underneath within the long grasp of its ice-tong legs, lifting any two or three at a time while many others still held in place. In this remarkable fashion it scrambled around the underside of the table's rim, swift and sure and fearless like a rock climber's dream. 5

If you ask me, when something extraordinary shows up in your life in the middle of the night, you give it a name and make it the best home you can. 6

The business of naming involved a grasp of hermit-crab gender that was way out of our league. But our household had a deficit of males, so my daughter and I chose Buster, for balance. We gave him a terrarium with clean gravel and a small cactus plant dug out of the yard and a big cockleshell full of tap water. All this seemed to suit him fine. To my astonishment our local pet store carried a product called Vitaminized Hermit Crab Cakes. Tempting enough (till you read the ingredients) but we passed, since our household leans more toward the recycling ethic. We give him leftovers. Buster's rapture is the day I drag the unidentifiable things in cottage cheese containers out of the back of the fridge. 7

We've also learned to give him a continually changing assortment of seashells, which he tries on and casts off like Cinderella's stepsisters preening for the ball. He'll sometimes try to squeeze into ludicrous outfits too small to contain him (who can't relate?). In 8 other moods, he will disappear into a conch the size of my two fists and sit for a day, immobilized by the weight of upward mobility. He is in every way the perfect housemate: quiet, entertaining, and willing to eat up the trash. He went to school for first-grade show-and-tell, and was such a hit the principal called up to congratulate me (I think) for being a broad-minded mother.

It was a long time, though, before we began to understand the 9
content of Buster's character. He required more patient observation than we were in the habit of giving to a small, cold-blooded life. As months went by, we would periodically notice with great disappointment that Buster seemed to be dead. Or not entirely dead, but ill, or maybe suffering the crab equivalent of the blues. He would burrow into a gravelly corner, shrink deep into his shell, and not move, for days and days. We'd take him out to play, dunk him in water, offer him a new frock—nothing. He wanted to be still.

Life being what it is, we'd eventually quit prodding our sick 10
friend to cheer up, and would move on to the next stage of a difficult friendship: neglect. We'd ignore him wholesale, only to realize at some point later on that he'd lapsed into hyperactivity. We'd find him ceaselessly patrolling the four corners of his world, turning over rocks, rooting out and dragging around truly disgusting pork-chop bones, digging up his cactus and replanting it on its head. At night when the household fell silent I would lie in bed listening to his methodical pebbly racket from the opposite end of the house. Buster was manic-depressive.

I wondered if he might be responding to the moon. I'm partial 11
to lunar cycles, ever since I learned as a teenager that human females in their natural state—which is to say, sleeping outdoors—arrive at menses in synchrony and ovulate with the full moon. My imagination remains captive to that primordial village: the comradely grumpiness of new-moon days, when the entire world at once would go on PMS alert. And the compensation that would turn up two weeks later on a wild wind, under that great round headlamp, driving both men and women to distraction with the overt prospect of conception. The surface of the land literally rises and falls—as much as fifty centimeters!—as the moon passes over, and we clay-footed mortals fall like dominoes before the swell. It's no surprise at all if a full moon inspires lyricists to corny love songs, or inmates to slamming themselves against barred windows. A hermit crab hardly seems this impetuous, but animals are notoriously responsive to the full moon: wolves howl; roosters announce daybreak all

night. Luna moths, Arctic loons, and lunatics have a sole inspiration in common. Buster's insomniac restlessness seemed likely to be a part of the worldwide full-moon fellowship.

But it wasn't, exactly. The full moon didn't shine on either end of his cycle, the high or the low. We tried to keep track, but it soon became clear: Buster marched to his own drum. The cyclic force that moved him remained as mysterious to us as his true gender and the workings of his crustacean soul. 12

Buster's aquarium occupies a spot on our kitchen counter right next to the coffeepot, and so it became my habit to begin mornings with chin in hands, pondering the oceanic mysteries while awaiting percolation. Finally, I remembered something. Years ago when I was a graduate student of animal behavior, I passed my days reading about the likes of animals' internal clocks. Temperature, photoperiod, the rise and fall of hormones—all these influences have been teased apart like so many threads from the rope that pulls every creature to its regulated destiny. But one story takes the cake. F. A. Brown, a researcher who is more or less the grandfather of the biological clock, set about in 1954 to track the cycles of intertidal oysters. He scooped his subjects from the clammy coast of Connecticut and moved them into the basement of a laboratory in landlocked Illinois. For the first fifteen days in their new aquariums, the oysters kept right up with their normal intertidal behavior: they spent time shut away in their shells, and time with their mouths wide open, siphoning their briny bath for the plankton that sustained them, as the tides ebbed and flowed on the distant Connecticut shore. In the next two weeks, they made a mystifying shift. They still carried out their cycles in unison, and were regular as the tides, but their high-tide behavior didn't coincide with high tide in Connecticut, or for that matter California, or any other tidal charts known to science. It dawned on the researchers after some calculations that the oysters were responding to high tide in Chicago. Never mind that the gentle mollusks lived in glass boxes in the basement of a steel-and-cement building. Nor that Chicago has no ocean. In the circumstances, the oysters were doing their best. 13

When Buster is running around for all he's worth, I can only presume it's high tide in Tucson. With or without evidence, I'm romantic enough to believe it. This is the lesson of Buster, the poetry that camps outside the halls of science: Jump for joy, hallelujah. Even a desert has tides. 14

When I was twenty-two, I donned the shell of a tiny yellow Renault and drove with all I owned from Kentucky to Tucson. I was 15 a typical young American, striking out. I had no earthly notion that I was bringing on myself a calamity of the magnitude of the one that befell poor Buster. I am the commonest kind of North American refugee: I believe I like it here, far-flung from my original home. I've come to love the desert that bristles and breathes and sleeps outside my windows. In the course of seventeen years I've embedded myself in a family here—neighbors, colleagues, friends I can't foresee living without, and a child who is native to this ground, with loves of her own. I'm here for good, it seems.

And yet I never cease to long in my bones for what I left behind. 16
I open my eyes on every new day expecting that a creek will run through my backyard under broad-leafed maples, and that my mother will be whistling in the kitchen. Behind the howl of coyotes, I'm listening for meadowlarks, I sometimes ache to be rocked in the bosom of the blood relations and busybodies of my childhood. Particularly in my years as a mother without a mate, I have deeply missed the safety net of extended family.

In a city of half a million I still really look at every face, anticipat- 17
ing recognition, because I grew up in a town where every face meant something to me. I have trouble remembering to lock the doors. Wariness of strangers I learned the hard way. When I was new to the city, I let a man into my house one hot afternoon because he seemed in dire need of a drink of water; when I turned from the kitchen sink I found sharpened steel shoved against my belly. And so I know, I know. But I cultivate suspicion with as much difficulty as I force tomatoes to grow in the drought-stricken hardpan of my strange backyard. No creek runs here, but I'm still listening to secret tides, living as if I belonged to an earlier place: not Kentucky, necessarily, but a welcoming earth and a human family. A forest. A species.

In my life I've had frightening losses and unfathomable gifts: A 18
knife in my stomach. The death of an unborn child. Sunrise in a rain forest. A stupendous column of blue butterflies rising from a Greek monastery. A car that spontaneously caught fire while I was driving it. The end of a marriage, followed by a year in which I could barely understand how to keep living. The discovery, just weeks ago when I rose from my desk and walked into the kitchen, of three strangers industriously relieving my house of its contents.

I persuaded the strangers to put down the things they were hold- 19
ing (what a bizarre tableau of anti-Magi they made, these three unwise men, bearing a camera, an electric guitar, and a Singer sewing machine), and to leave my home, pronto. My daughter asked excitedly when she got home from school, "Mom, did you say bad

words?" (I told her this was the very occasion that bad words exist for.) The police said, variously, that I was lucky, foolhardy, and "a brave lady." But it's not good luck to be invaded, and neither foolish nor brave to stand your ground. It's only the way life goes, and I did it, just as years ago I fought off the knife; mourned the lost child; bore witness to the rain forest; claimed the blue butterflies as Holy Spirit in my private pantheon; got out of the burning car; survived the divorce by putting one foot in front of the other and taking good care of my child. On most important occasions, I cannot think how to respond, I simply do. What does it mean, anyway, to be an animal in human clothing? We carry around these big brains of ours like the crown jewels, but mostly I find that millions of years of evolution have prepared me for one thing only: to follow internal rhythms. To walk upright, to protect my loved ones, to cooperate with my family group—however broadly I care to define it—to do whatever will help us thrive. Obviously, some habits that saw us through the millennia are proving hazardous in a modern context: for example, the yen to consume carbohydrates and fat whenever they cross our path, or the proclivity for unchecked reproduction. But it's surely worth forgiving ourselves these tendencies a little, in light of the fact that they are what got us here. Like Buster, we are creatures of inexplicable cravings. Thinking isn't everything. The way I stock my refrigerator would amuse a level-headed interplanetary observer, who would see I'm responding not to real necessity but to the dread of famine honed in the African savannah. I can laugh at my Rhodesian Ridgeback as she furtively sniffs the houseplants for a place to bury bones, and circles to beat down the grass before lying on my kitchen floor. But she and I are exactly the same kind of hairpin.

We humans have to grant the presence of some past adaptations, 20
even in their unforgivable extremes, if only to admit they are permanent rocks in the steam we're obliged to navigate. It's easy to speculate and hard to prove, ever, that genes control our behaviors. Yet we are persistently, excruciatingly adept at many things that seem no more useful to modern life than the tracking of tides in a desert. At recognizing insider/outsider status, for example, starting with white vs. black and grading straight into distinctions so fine as to baffle the bystander—Serb and Bosnian, Hutu and Tutsi, Crip and Blood. We hold that children learn discrimination from their parents, but they learn it fiercely and well, world without end. Recite it by rote like a multiplication table. Take it to heart, though it's neither helpful nor appropriate, anymore than it is to hire the taller of two men applying for a position as bank clerk, though statistically we're likely to do that

too. Deference to the physical superlative, a preference for the scent of our own clan: a thousand anachronisms dance down the strands of our DNA from a hidebound tribal past, guiding us toward the glories of survival, and some vainglories as well. If we resent being bound by these ropes, the best hope is to seize them out like snakes, by the throat, look them in the eye and own up to their venom.

But we rarely do, silly egghead of a species that we are. We invent the most outlandish intellectual grounds to justify discrimination. We tap our toes to chaste love songs about the silvery moon without recognizing them as hymns to copulation. We can dress up our drives, put them in three-piece suits or ballet slippers, but still they drive us. The wonder of it is that our culture attaches almost unequivocal shame to our animal nature, believing brute urges must be hurtful, violent things. But it's no less an animal instinct that leads us to marry (species that benefit from monogamy tend to practice it); to organize a neighborhood cleanup campaign (rare and doomed is the creature that fouls its nest); to improvise and enforce morality (many primates socialize their young to be cooperative and ostracize adults who won't share food). 21

It's starting to look as if the most shameful tradition of Western civilization is our need to deny we are animals. In just a few centuries of setting ourselves apart as landlords of the Garden of Eden, exempt from the natural order and entitled to hold dominion, we have managed to behave like so-called animals anyway, and on top of it to wreck most of what took three billion years to assemble. Air, water, earth, and fire—so much of our own element so vastly contaminated, we endanger our own future. Apparently we never owned the place after all. Like every other animal, we're locked into our niche: the mercury in the ocean, the pesticides on the soybean fields, all comes home to our breastfed babies. In the silent spring we are learning it's easier to escape from a chain gang than a food chain. Possibly we will have the sense to begin a new century by renewing our membership in the Animal Kingdom. 22

Not long ago I went backpacking in the Eagle Tail Mountains. This range is a trackless wilderness in western Arizona that most people would call Godforsaken, taking for granted God's preference for loamy topsoil and regular precipitation. Whoever created the Eagle Tails had dry heat on the agenda, and a thing for volcanic rock. Also cactus, twisted mesquites, and five-alarm sunsets. The hiker's program in a desert like this is dire and blunt: carry in enough water to keep you alive till you can find a water source: then fill your bottles and head for the next one, or straight back out. 23

Experts warn adventurers in this region, without irony, to drink their water while they're still alive, as it won't help later.

Several canyons looked promising for springs on our topographical map, but turned up dry. Finally, at the top of a narrow, overgrown gorge we found a blessed tinaja, a deep, shaded hollow in the rock about the size of four or five claw-foot tubs, holding water. After we drank our fill, my friends struck out again, but I opted to stay and spend the day in the hospitable place that had slaked our thirst. On either side of the natural water tank, two shallow caves in the canyon wall faced each other, only a few dozen steps apart. By crossing from one to the other at noon, a person could spend the whole day here in shady comfort—or in colder weather, follow the winter sun. Anticipating a morning of reading, I pulled *Angle of Repose* out of my pack and looked for a place to settle on the flat, dusty floor of the west-facing shelter. Instead, my eyes were startled by a smooth corn-grinding stone. It sat in the exact center of its rock bowl, as if the Hohokam woman or man who used this mortar and pestle had walked off and left them there an hour ago. The Hohokam disappeared from the earth in A.D. 1450. It was inconceivable to me that no one had been here since then, but that may have been the case—that is the point of trackless wilderness. I picked up the grinding stone. The size and weight and smooth, balanced perfection of it in my hand filled me at once with a longing to possess it. In its time, this excellent stone was the most treasured thing in a life, a family, maybe the whole neighborhood. To whom it still belonged. I replaced it in the rock depression, which also felt smooth to my touch. Because my eyes now understood how to look at it, the ground under my feet came alive with worked flint chips and pottery shards. I walked across to the other cave and found its floor just as lively with historic debris. Hidden under brittlebush and catclaw I found another grinding stone, this one some distance from the depression in the cave floor that once answered its pressure daily, for the grinding of corn or mesquite beans. 24

For a whole day I marveled at this place, running my fingers over the knife edges of dark flint chips, trying to fit together thick red pieces of shattered clay jars, biting my lower lip like a child concentrating on a puzzle. I tried to guess the size of whole pots from the curve of the broken pieces: some seemed as small as my two cupped hands, and some maybe as big as a bucket. The sun scorched my neck, reminding me to follow the shade across to the other shelter. Bees hummed at the edge of the water hole, nosing up to the water, their abdomens pulsing like tiny hydraulic pumps; by late 25 afternoon they rimmed the pool completely, a collar of busy lace. Off and on, the lazy hand of a hot breeze shuffled the white leaves of the brittlebush. Once I looked up to see a screaming pair of red-tailed hawks mating in midair, and once a clatter of hooves warned me to hold still. A bighorn ram emerged through the brush, his head bent low under his hefty cornice, and ambled by me with nothing on his mind so much as a cool drink.

How long can a pestle stone lie still in the center of its mortar? 26
That long ago—that recently—people lived here. Here, exactly, and not one valley over, or two, or twelve, because this place had all a person needs: shelter, food, and permanent water. They organized their lives around a catchment basin in a granite boulder, conforming their desires to the earth's charities; they never expected the opposite. The stories I grew up with lauded Moses for striking the rock and bringing forth the bubbling stream. But the stories of the Hohokam—oh, how they must have praised that good rock.

At dusk my friends returned with wonderful tales of the 27
ground they had covered. We camped for the night, refilled our canteens, and hiked back to the land of plumbing and a fair guarantee of longevity. But I treasure my memory of the day I lingered near water and covered no ground. I can't think of a day in my life in which I've had such a clear fix on what it means to be human.

Want is a thing that unfurls unbidden like fungus, opening 28
large upon itself, stopless, filling the sky. But *needs,* from one day to the next, are few enough to fit in a bucket, with room enough left to rattle like brittlebush in a dry wind.

For each of us—furred, feathered, or skinned alive—the whole 29
earth balances on the single precarious point of our own survival. In the best of times, I hold in mind the need to care for things beyond the self: poetry, humanity, grace. In other times, when it seems difficult merely to survive and be happy about it, the condition of my thought tastes as simple as this: let me be a good animal today. I've spent months at a stretch, even years, with that taste in my mouth, and have found that it serves.

But it seems a wide gulf to cross, from the raw, green passion 30
for survival to the dispassionate, considered state of human grace. How does the animal mind construct a poetry for the modern artifice in which we now reside? Often I feel as disoriented as poor Buster, unprepared for the life that zooms headlong past my line of sight. This clutter of human paraphernalia and counterfeit necessities—what does it have to do with the genuine business of life on earth? It feels strange to me to be living in a box, hiding from the steadying

influence of the moon; wearing the hide of a cow, which is supposed to be dyed to match God-knows-what, on my feet; making promises over the telephone about things I will do at a precise hour next *year.* (I always feel the urge to add, as my grandmother does, "Lord willing and the creeks don't rise!") I find it impossible to think, with a straight face, about what colors ought not to be worn after Labor Day. I can become hysterical over the fact that someone, somewhere, invented a thing called the mushroom scrubber, and that many other people undoubtedly feel they *need* to possess one. It's completely usual for me to get up in the morning, take a look around, and laugh out loud.

Strangest of all, I am carrying on with all of this in a desert, two thousand miles from my verdant childhood home. I am disembodied. No one here remembers how I was before I grew to my present height. I'm called upon to reinvent my own childhood time and again; in the process, I wonder how I can ever know the truth about who I am. If someone had told me what I was headed for in that little Renault—that I was stowing away in a shell, bound to wake up to an alien life on a persistently foreign shore—I surely would not have done it. But no one warned me. My culture, as I understand it, values independence above all things—in part to ensure a mobile labor force, grease for the machine of a capitalist economy. Our fairy tale commands: Little Pig, go out and seek your fortune! So I did. 31

Many years ago I read that the Tohono O'odham, who dwell in the deserts near here, traditionally bury the umbilicus of a newborn son or daughter somewhere close to home and plant a tree over it, to hold the child in place. In a sentimental frame of mind, I did the same when my own baby's cord fell off. I'm staring at the tree right now, as I write—a lovely thing grown huge outside my window, home to woodpeckers, its boughs overarching the house, as dissimilar from the sapling I planted seven years ago as my present life is from the tidy future I'd mapped out for us all when my baby was born. She will roam light-years from the base of that tree. I have no doubt of it. I can only hope she's growing as the tree is, absorbing strength and rhythms and a trust in the seasons, so she will always be able to listen for home. 32

I feel remorse about Buster's monumental relocation; it's a weighty responsibility to have thrown someone else's life into permanent chaos. But as for my own, I can't be sorry I made the trip. Most of what I learned in the old place seems to suffice for the new: if the seasons like Chicago tides come at ridiculous times and I have to plant in September instead of May, and if I have to make up 33 family from scratch, what matters is that I do have sisters and tomato plants, the essential things. Like Buster, I'm inclined to see the material backdrop of my life as mostly immaterial, compared with what moves inside of me. I hold on to my adopted shore, chanting private vows: wherever I am, let me never forget to distinguish *want* from *need.* Let me be a good animal today. Let me dance in the waves of my private tide, the habits of survival and love.

Every one of us is called upon, probably many times, to start a 34 new life. A frightening diagnosis, a marriage, a move, loss of a job or a limb or a loved one, a graduation, bringing a new baby home: it's impossible to think at first how this all will be possible. Eventually, what moves it all forward is the subterranean ebb and flow of being alive among the living.

In my own worst seasons I've come back from the colorless 35 world of despair by forcing myself to look hard, for a long time, at a single glorious thing: a flame of red geranium outside my bedroom window. And then another: my daughter in a yellow dress. And another: the perfect outline of a full, dark sphere behind the crescent moon. Until I learned to be in love with my life again. Like a stroke victim retraining new parts of the brain to grasp lost skills, I have taught myself joy, over and over again.

It's not such a wide gulf to cross, then, from survival to poetry. 36 We hold fast to the old passions of endurance that buckle and creak beneath us, dovetailed, tight as a good wooden boat to carry us onward. And onward full tilt we go, pitched and wrecked and absurdly resolute, driven in spite of everything to make good on a new shore. To be hopeful, to embrace one possibility after another—that is surely the basic instinct. Baser even than hate, the thing with teeth, which can be stilled with a tone of voice or stunned by beauty. If the whole world of the living has to turn on the single point of remaining alive, that pointed endurance is the poetry of hope. The thing with feathers.

What a stroke of luck. What a singular brute feat of outrageous 37 fortune: to be born to citizenship in the Animal Kingdom. We love and we lose, go back to the start and do it right over again. For every heavy forebrain solemnly cataloging the facts of a harsh landscape, there's a rush of intuition behind it crying out: High tide! Time to move out into the glorious debris. Time to take this life for what it is.

Meanings and Values

1. In Paragraph 22, Kingsolver says, "It's starting to look as if the most shameful tradition of Western civilization is our need to deny we are animals." In what ways, according to the essay, are we like other animals?
2. What are the superficial ways Buster resembles humans (see Pars. 5, 8, 9, and 10)? What are the important (even profound) similarities (see Pars. 11, 12, 15, 19, 30, and 33)?
3. Paragraphs 15–19 of this essay are devoted to some of the disruptions and problems created by contemporary ways of living. What answers or responses to these problems does the writer offer in Paragraph 19? How do the problems and the responses help unify the essay? (See "Guide to Terms": *Unity.*)

Expository Techniques

1. At what point in the essay does Kingsolver first make an analogy between the hermit crab and herself?
2. For what purposes does the author raise, and then dismiss, the comparison of hermit crab behaviors and those of humans and other animals in terms of their correspondence to cycles of the moon? (In answering this question, consider both the scientific reasons and those related to the purpose and design of her essay.)
3. The writer divides this essay into four parts (Pars. 1–14, 15–22, 23–28, and 29–37). Explain the content and purpose of each part, and tell why you think she chose to put them in this particular order. (Guide: *Purpose.*)
4. Discuss how the contrast between "wants" and "needs" at the end of Paragraph 28 serves as a transition to the next paragraph and those that follow. (Guide: *Transition.*)
5. Discuss how the question "What does it mean, anyway, to be an animal in human clothing?" (Par. 19) acts as a transition both within the paragraph and within the essay as a whole. (Guide: *Transition.*) Can the passage be considered a rhetorical question? Why? (Guide: *Rhetorical Questions.*)
6. Kingsolver introduces some briefer analogies in Paragraphs 32 and 36. What are they? Do they undermine or add to the effectiveness of the larger analogy around which the essay is constructed? In what ways? (Guide: *Evaluation.*)

Diction and Vocabulary

1. Discuss how the repetition of the word "tide" and related words helps to unify this essay. (Guide: *Unity.*)

2. In many places, Kingsolver mixes styles and kinds of vocabulary (diction) in imaginative ways. Examine Paragraph 11 and note the instances in which she has chosen scientific terms and phrases rather than familiar, less formal wording. What seems to be the reason for her word choices? Do the same for instances of notably informal language. (Guide: *Diction; Colloquial Expressions.*) What effect does the mixed diction in the paragraph have on its overall style and tone? (Guide: *Style/Tone.*) How does the mixture serve, or fail to serve, the author's purposes?

3. If you do not know the meaning of any of the following words, look them up in a dictionary: *murexes, whelks,* (Par. 2); *deficit, terrarium, cockleshell* (7); *preening, ludicrous* (8); *hyperactivity* (10); *menses, synchrony, ovulate, lyricists, impetuous* (11); *crustacean* (12); *siphoning, briny, ebbed* (13); *tableau, pantheon, yen, proclivity, furtively* (19); *deference, anachronisms, vainglories* (20); *copulation, ostracize* (21); *topographical* (24); *lauded* (26); *longevity* (27); *dispassionate* (30); *verdant* (31); *umbilicus* (32).

Read to Write

1. **Collaborating:** As mentioned in question 3 of Expository Techniques, Kingsolver divides this essay into four parts (Pars. 1–14, 15–22, 23–28, and 29–37). In a group, have each member individually focus on the analogies presented in one of these sections and critique the effectiveness of them. Compare your critiques. Do you all have similar responses to the quality of the analogies as well as the writing overall? Why or why not? Individually, write a short essay answering this question.

2. **Considering Audience:** The theme of this essay is easy to perceive for a reader who has had major life changes. Kingsolver shares her life shifts openly and relates them directly to Buster's environmental changes. Yet this piece is also effective for people who have experienced little changes in their lives. Why? Point to specific paragraphs to explain your response.

3. **Developing an Essay:** Comparing your behavior to that of a pet, as Kingsolver does, can have several advantages for you as a writer. You probably observed a pet's behavior in detail over a long period of time more carefully than you observed the activities of any other animal. You have seen the pet react to the same or similar situations that you have encountered. Follow Kingsolver's lead and prepare an essay on human and animal behavior based on your experiences with a pet.

(Note: Suggestions for topics requiring development by use of ANALOGY follow.)

Writing Suggestions for Chapter 6

Analogy

In any normal situation, the analogy is chosen to help explain a theme-idea that already exists—such as those in the first group below. But for imagination and fresh insight, you may wish to work from the other direction, to develop a theme that fits a preselected analogy-symbol.

1a. State a central theme about one of the following general topics or a suitable one of your own, and develop it into a composition by use of an analogy of your own choosing.

   a. A well-organized school system
   b. Starting a new business or other enterprise
   c. The long-range value of programs for underprivileged children
   d. Learning a new skill
   e. The need for cooperation in solving environmental problems
   f. Dealing with stress

b. Select an analogy-symbol from the list below and fashion a theme that it can illustrate. Develop your composition as instructed.

   a. A freeway at commuting time
   b. Building a bridge across a river
   c. A merry-go-round
   d. A wedding or a divorce
   e. A car wash
   f. The tending of a garden
   g. An animal predator stalking prey
   h. A baseball game
   i. A juggling act
   j. An airport

2. Some topics are hard for most readers to understand without analogies to more familiar subjects. Think about some knowledge you have gained through study in the natural sciences (chemistry, biology, physics, or physical anthropology, for example) or in the social sciences (sociology, psychology, or economics, for instance). Prepare an essay that uses one or more analogies to explain a subject from your studies for readers who have little experience with it. You do not need

to structure the entire essay around a single analogy; you can use several different ones in the course of the essay.

3. To understand our everyday lives, we often think about them in terms of an analogy: my job is like a march through the desert; our relationship is like a hurricane; working with this organization is like walking around in the dark; being part of this political campaign has been like taking a roller coaster ride. Most often, we state such analogies (or just think about them). Choose one that you often use or think of one to describe your experiences. Develop it into an essay that helps readers either understand their own lives or learn something about experiences they have not had.

4. At the library, find a book that explains a complicated topic to the average reader, such as one that explains recent developments in astronomy, genetics or human DNA, or ecology. Look for a section that makes use of analogies, and prepare a paper discussing the ways the writer uses analogies to explain and explore. (You may wish to choose a Web site that make similar use of analogies.)

Collaborative Activities

1. Working with a partner, choose a topic from a–f in Exercise 1a on page 213, and decide on an appropriate analogy. One member of the pair should outline the points that need to be made about the theme. The other member should outline comparative (analogous) details. Combine the two outlines, and write a well-developed essay from the combined plan.

2. In groups of three or more, come up with an appropriate analogy for the theme of "adapting to college life in the freshman year." Members should brainstorm to determine the best point of analogy. Once you determine that as a group, each member should provide one point of expansion that fits the analogy, and group members should then write essays of their own drawing on material developed by the group and adding their own ideas and examples.

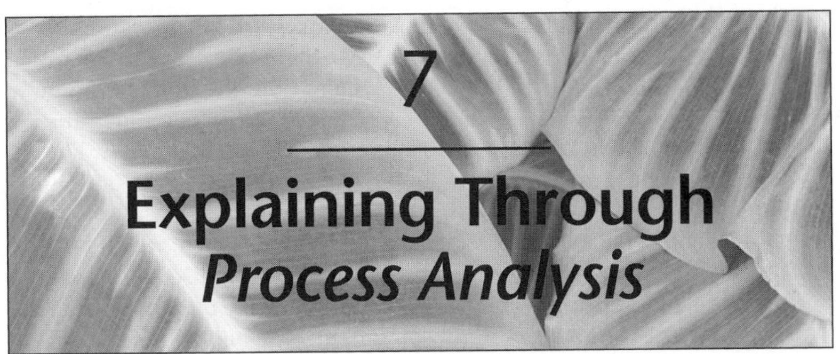

Process analysis focuses on *how* something happens. As an expository pattern, it appears most frequently in *instructions* that tell us how to do something, or in *explanations* that explain how something is or was done. Instructions can range from the simple and everyday to the complex and challenging: from the directions for using a new appliance or piece of electronic equipment to a detailed plan showing how to make the United Nations more effective. Effective instructions do more than simply list the steps to be taken. They generally provide detailed justification for individual steps or for the plan as a whole, and they take into account readers' background knowledge and abilities.

Explanations, on the other hand, might explain the stages of a wide variety of operations or actions, of mental or evolutionary process—how stress affects judgment and health, how volcanoes cause earthquakes and mudslides, or how digital telephones work. Effective explanations take into account the things readers want or need to know about, but they can also appeal to curiosity and imagination. You can speculate how space exploration might work or how societies might be better organized.

The following process analysis by L. Rust Hills shows how process analysis can be used in imaginative ways to talk about everyday matters. It takes the form of a set of directions, and though it is short, it is a whole essay in miniature. The second example is an explanation that helps readers understand some of the reasons hurricanes can be so dangerous.

This is admittedly not a problem qualitatively on the order of what to do about the proliferation of nuclear weaponry, but quantitatively it disturbs a great deal of Mankind—all those millions, in fact, who've ever used a bar of soap—except, of course, me. I've solved the problem of what to do about those troublesome, wasteful, messy little soap ends, and I'm ready now to deliver my solution to a grateful world.

The solution depends on a fact not commonly known, which I discovered in the shower. Archimedes made his great discovery about displacement ("Eureka!" and all that) in the bathtub, but I made mine in the shower. It is not commonly known that if, when you soap yourself, you hold *the same side* of the bar of soap cupped in the palm of your hand, that side will, after a few days, become curved and rounded, while the side of the bar you're soaping yourself *with* will become flat. (In between showers or baths, leave the bar curved side down so it won't stick to whatever it's resting on.) When the bar diminishes sufficiently, the flat side can be pressed onto a new bar of soap and will adhere sufficiently overnight to become, with the next day's use, a just slightly oversized new bar, ready to be treated in the same way as the one that came before it, in perpetuity, one bar after another, down through the length of your days on earth, with never a nasty soap end to trouble you ever again. Eureka, and now on to those nuclear weapons. Man is at his best, I feel, when in his problem-solving mode.

—L. Rust Hills, "What to Do About Soap Ends"

It's not the wind, though, that's the most dangerous part of a hurricane. It's the water, especially when something called the "storm surge" occurs. As the low-pressure eye of the hurricane sits over the ocean, the sea level literally rises into a dome of water. For every inch drop in barometric pressure, the ocean rises a foot higher. Now, out at sea, that means nothing. The rise is not even noticeable. But when that mound of water starts moving toward land, the situation becomes crucial. As the water approaches a shallow beach, the dome of water rises. It may rise ten to fifteen feet in an hour and span fifty miles. Like a marine bulldozer, the surge may rise up twenty feet high, crash onto land, and wash everything away. Then with six- to eight-foot waves riding atop this mound of water, the storm surge destroys buildings, trees, cars, and anything else in its path. It's this storm surge that accounts for 90 percent of the deaths during a hurricane.

—Ira Flatow, "Storm Surge"

WHY USE PROCESS ANALYSIS?

In almost every part of our lives, we rely on **instructions.** They help us cook a meal, repair a car, get to a vacation spot, perform an experiment, and calculate income tax. Essays offering instruction appear in newspapers, magazines, and books on topics from fashion, fitness, and sports to technology, pets, and personal relationships.

We turn to **explanations** not when we want to do things but when we want to understand how things work. Explanations can focus on mechanical or technical subjects (how computer operating systems work), on social matters (how societies create groups of insiders and outsiders), on psychological topics (how stress builds up), or on natural subjects (how cancer cells take over from normal cells).

Process analysis can have imaginative uses as well, helping us speculate about building floating cities, changing our diets for better health, or considering steps that might close the ozone hole over the South Pole. Writers sometimes explain a process in order to amuse or criticize—analyzing with a critical eye some aspects of behavior (as do Kilbourne and Mitford in this chapter) or looking at some surprising natural phenomenon. And process analysis often appears in combination with other expository patterns. You might use it to help readers understand the steps by which a cause (such as meditating) leads to an effect (reduced physical and mental stress), for example. Or you might explain differences in the processes of forming social relationships as part of an essay contrasting the behaviors of men and women.

Expository writing built around process analysis generally responds to a need for information and understanding. The need may be immediate (how to prepare for an upcoming sales meeting or an exam). It may be practical or helpful (understanding the ways our bodies respond to stress; strategies for incorporating a healthy diet and exercise into a busy schedule). Or it may be a matter of curiosity or a desire for understanding (discovering how puppeteers in Indonesia create hours-long shows that appeal to both children and adults; investigating the ways our brains process information).

CHOOSING A STRATEGY

Having encountered instructions and explanations many times before, your readers will probably expect you to employ some basic strategies. For example, they will expect the opening of a set of instructions to announce its purpose, establish the need for a step-by-step explanation of the process, and indicate any materials needed to accomplish it. The way you choose to accomplish these things should vary from situation to situation and topic to topic, however. If you are addressing a need your readers can readily recognize, such as finding effective ways to take a test, make a speech, or apply for a student loan, you might begin with a brief example of how important such knowledge is. Or you might even state the need directly: "Would you like to know how to give a speech without getting so flustered that you forget half of what you planned to say?" or "Wouldn't you like to know how to get a student loan without all the hassle and paperwork most people encounter?"

In many instances, however, you will have to convince readers that they ought to be interested in the instructions you are offering. This is the situation Heather Kaye faced when she decided to tell readers how to play the game "Bones." In response, she created an opening paragraph reminding her readers how often they get bored and telling them of the simple equipment they will need to pass the time with an amusing game.

> When boredom strikes, what can you do if you are tired of computer games, don't like chess, and don't have the money or time to go to a movie? Just collect a pad of paper, a pen, six dice, and a friend, and you are ready to play a game called "Bones." Bones provides fun and excitement, and you don't have to be Einstein to learn how to play. It is a game of chance and luck, laughter and friendship.

For an explanation, however, you may need to appeal to readers' curiosity or their desire for understanding (practical or otherwise). Emphasizing the mystery, adventure, or even oddity of a process will engage most readers' curiosity: What bodily processes allow pearl divers to stay underwater for several minutes when most of us can hold our breath for only ten or twenty seconds? How do bats produce a kind of "radar" that enables them to fly in the dark and catch minute insects? When you appeal to readers' desire for understanding, you will be most likely to succeed when you suggest a practical dimension for the knowledge. For instance, some readers interested in the natural world may be interested in the complex stages of the honey-making process. Yet to attract the majority of readers you may need to suggest that such knowledge can help them understand honey's virtues as a sweetener or choose among different kinds of honey as they shop.

Most process analyses are organized into simple, chronological units, either the *steps* involved in accomplishing the task or the *stages* of operation. In planning a set of instructions, begin by breaking it down into steps, approaching the activity as if you were doing it for the first time so that you do not leave out any necessary elements that have become so routine you might easily overlook them. Then create an organization that will help readers keep track of the many steps, perhaps dividing the task into several units, each containing smaller steps. Consider building your plan around a framework like the following.

Introduction: Need for the information, materials, statement of purpose
Step 1: Explanations, details
  Substeps 1, 2, 3. . . . (if any)
Step 2: Explanations, details
  Substeps 1, 2, 3. . . .
Step 3: Explanations, details
  Substeps 1, 2, 3. . . .
Summary (if necessary)

In planning an explanation, identify the various stages or components, including any that overlap, and create an organization that presents them in an easy-to-follow, logical order. If the process is complex, divide it into major components and subdivide each in turn, just as the following rough plan does.

Introduction (tentative thesis identifying need for the information): Because most people do not understand the amount of energy, natural resources, and human effort needed to create paper, they use it wastefully; understanding the process and the resources it requires is an important first step for all of us concerned with preserving our environment.
Stage 1: Bringing together natural resources
  a. Wood—logging
  b. Water—drawing from rivers or lakes
  c. Fuel for heat and power (oil, gas, or electric)
Stage 2: Turning logs into pulp
  a. Grinding up logs (uses water and power) *or*
  b. Breaking wood into pulp using chemicals
Stage 3: Turning pulp into paper
  a. Paper machine
    1. Feeding pulp into machine
    2. Using heated screen to congeal pulp into a mushy sheet of paper

b. Dryer
   1. Using heat to further congeal pulp
   2. Using rollers to stretch and thin the sheet (consumes energy)

Stage 4: Turning paper into paper products (energy and labor intensive)
   a. Creating giant rolls of paper
   b. Cutting and folding rolls of paper into tissues, newsprint, pads, paper towels, and other everyday products

Maintaining the exact order of a process is sometimes of greatest importance, as in a recipe. But occasionally the organization of an analysis may present problems. You may need to interrupt the step-by-step format to give descriptions, definitions, and other explanatory asides. Some processes may even defy a strict chronological treatment because several things occur simultaneously. In explaining the operating process of a gasoline engine, for example, you would be unable to convey at once everything that happens at the same time. Instead, you would need to present the material in *general* stages, each with subdivisions, so your readers could see each stage by itself yet also become aware of interacting relationships.

DEVELOPING A PROCESS ANALYSIS

In developing the paragraphs and sentences that make up an explanation of a process, you also need to pay attention to your readers' expectations. When you are presenting instructions, your readers will expect you to tell them of any necessary materials and will look for frequent summaries to allow them to check if they have followed the steps correctly. They will benefit from warnings of special difficulties they may encounter or any dangers the procedure entails. In addition, they will appreciate words of encouragement ("The procedure may seem strange, but it *will* work") or reminders of the goal of the process ("No pain, no gain: the only way to a flat tummy is through the hard work of repeating these exercises").

Effective explanations and instructions alike often have a visual element. Drawings can show how the parts of a mechanism fit together or help readers recognize the differences among the elements of a natural process, such as the growth of an insect or the eruption of a volcano. Pictures can help readers identify ingredients or components and show them what a finished product will look like.

To guide readers through the steps or stages of a process, to remind them of changes that will occur, or to highlight the sequence of events, consider using words that point out relationships among the various elements.

Words identifying different stages—*step, event, element, component, phase, state, feature, occurrence*
Words emphasizing relationships in time—*after, next, while, first, second, third, fourth, concurrently, the next week, later, preceding, following*
Words indicating changes—*becomes, varies, transforms, causes, completes, alters, revises, uncovers, synthesizes, cures, builds*

Make sure you include enough details to allow readers to visualize the steps or stages of the process, but not so many that the details become confusing. Present major steps (or stages) in considerable detail, minor ones in less. If you choose to write in the second person (*you*), as in a set of directions ("You should then blend the ingredients"), make sure you use this point of view consistently and do not shift to the first person (*I* or *we*) or the third person (*he, she, it,* or *they*) without good reason. If you choose the first person or third person for your perspective, make sure likewise that your presentation is consistent.

Student Essay

Losing weight is not easy for most people, nor is the process a simple one, as Karin Gaffney explains in the essay that follows. As a result, she provided detailed explanations along with her dieting instructions so that readers can understand not only *how* to diet but also *why* they should follow certain steps and avoid others.

Losing Weight
by Karin Gaffney

Across the board, regardless of age, gender, race, or background, most people spend time trying to lose weight (Williamson et al.). Some people want to lose only five or ten pounds while others worry about getting rid of seventy-five pounds or more. As a result, weight loss is both a universal concern and a highly individualized matter.

Losing weight must mean a lot to Americans. After all, they spend over three billion dollars on weight-loss programs each year ("Rating" 353). If you think you need to diet, think again. Many people think they are overweight because they compare themselves to impossibly thin models or imagine themselves in the slimmest of new fashions. So if you think you need to diet, consult a doctor and other reliable sources of health information. Then go to a good weight-loss program—if you really need one.

Why should you be careful about going on a diet? A study in 1988 by the Centers for Disease Control concluded that any change of weight either up or down led to a higher rate of heart disease in the people studied ("Losing" 350). This does not necessarily mean that you should forget about dieting, however, because weight loss can also help you avoid other health problems ("Losing" 348, 350).

To lose weight, some people turn to commercial diets and hospital programs, yet the majority rely on self-help. For those people who are trying to lose weight on their own, I can offer some general advice along with a simple weight-loss program. The simple advice is no different from what most of us have already heard, but it probably still needs to be repeated: 1) cut down on high-fat foods, 2) eat moderate portions of healthy foods, and 3) get regular exercise. Above all, consult your doctor not only to determine whether you should diet but to make sure your dietary and exercise programs are appropriate for you (and not for the models and athletes who appear on exercise tapes or talk about their health and muscle-power diets in magazines).

A person who is overweight probably has a diet heavy in fat (Beitz 281). A calorie of fat in food becomes part of body fat much more easily than does a calorie of carbohydrate, which is easily burned as energy (Delaney 46). In other words, the body often keeps the fat it takes in, but the carbohydrates it uses up. Moreover, a gram of fat has about 2.25 times as many calories as one gram of carbohydrate or protein does (Beitz 281).

The first step in a healthy weight-loss plan is to reduce the fat in your diet. If you eliminate high-fat foods such as ice creams, cheese, hamburgers, and butter from your diet, your body will respond immediately to the change. Low-fat substitutes, such as low-fat milk, can also have a positive effect, as can steps like cutting the fat off meat or taking the skin off poultry ("Losing" 352).

The second step is to eat more foods that are low in fat but high in fiber and carbohydrates. Here are several choices:

1. Potatoes (baked, not fried, and without butter or sour cream)
2. Beans (pinto, kidney, lentil, and so on)
3. Whole grains (cereals, pastas, breads)
4. Fresh fruits
5. Skim milk (and skim milk products)

When you eat foods like these, your blood sugar levels stabilize and you get "filled up," yet you take in only about one-half the number of calories that fatty alternatives provide (Delaney 44–45).

The third step is to snack wisely. Limit your snacks, of course, and choose from foods like the following: string cheese, corn-on-the-cob (without butter), vegetables, angel food cake, pita bread, soft pretzels, fruits, bagels, nonfat yogurt, juice, animal crackers, or fig bars ("30 Low Fat" 3). Food companies have also been adding fat-free items to grocery shelves in recent years, so when you shop, look for low-fat frozen desserts, low-fat cookies, and the like.

The fourth step is to exercise regularly. Exercise can burn up to 200–300 calories per day (Delaney 46). You may also be surprised to learn that exercise can decrease your weight even if you do not radically change your eating habits. Regular exercise increases basal metabolism, the energy needed just to stay alive. One-half of the calories in a person's diet, for example, can go to basal metabolism. Exercise can increase the basal metabolism rate so that a person can lose more calories by just living and breathing. The amount of muscle a person has also affects basal metabolism. A person with more muscle has a higher basal metabolism and burns up more of the calories in food through this means ("Losing" 357).

Your exercise routine does not have to be strenuous or exhausting like that of an Olympic trainee. Moderate exercise, such as one half-hour to an hour of good-paced walking, is beneficial. If you need an incentive to start your exercise program, remember that a person who goes from a nonexerciser to a moderate exerciser will notice the results more than someone going from moderate to advanced. There are other side benefits to exercise as well. For example, people who exercise regularly develop adult diabetes 40 percent less frequently than nonexercisers do ("Losing" 351).

The fifth step is to set reasonable goals for weight loss. Concentrate on losing a pound or two at a time, and try to maintain this small weight loss before continuing ("Losing" 350). This approach will help make you confident of your ability to lose weight and help you avoid the yo-yo effect of losing a lot of weight, then gaining it right back.

The final step is to keep several key points in mind.

1. Make eating right and exercising (not dieting) the focus of your attention and effort.
2. Concentrate on maintaining your healthy lifestyle so that you can make your weight loss permanent and benefit over the long term from good eating and exercise habits.
3. Remember that you are an individual and that the advice offered here may or may not apply to you. Always consult a doctor who knows you and your medical history.

Works Cited

Beitz, Donald C. "Nutrition." *McGraw-Hill Yearbook of Science and Technology.* New York: McGraw, 1993. Print.

Delaney, Lisa. "The 'No-Hunger' Weight-Loss Plan." *Prevention* Sept. 1993: 43–46. Print.

"Losing Weight: What Works, What Doesn't." *Consumer Reports* June 1993: 347–52. Print.

"Rating the Diets." *Consumer Reports* June 1993: 353–57. Print.

"30 Low Fat Foods to Grab." *Thinline* Sept./Oct. 1993: 3. Print.

Williamson, David F., Mary K. Serdula, Robert F. Auclay, Alan Levy, and Tim Byers. "Weight Loss Attempts in Adults: Goals, Duration, and Rate of Weight Loss." *American Journal of Public Health* Sept. 1992: 82–89. Print.

JOE BUHLER AND RON GRAHAM

JOE BUHLER, a professor of mathematics at Reed College, has published many scholarly articles as well as essays for more general audiences. Among the latter are essays on science, juggling, and the game Go.

RON GRAHAM is associated with Bell Labs in Murray Hill, New Jersey, and has had a distinguished career as a mathematician. He has published many articles in his field of research and his work has been honored with membership in the National Academy of Sciences. He is a past president of the International Jugglers' Association.

Give Juggling a Hand!

This instructional essay, a particularly compact explanation of an intriguing activity, was first published in *The Sciences.* It reflects the authors' enjoyment of juggling as well as their expertise. By providing some historical background, clear directions, and interesting explanations, the writers make the activity seem as enjoyable to readers as it is to them.

Nothing could be simpler than a game of catch. But just add another ball or two and the game turns magical—the juggled balls take on a life of their own. Suddenly, simple motions and common objects blur into one stunning display after another. 1

In recent years, juggling has experienced a renaissance. Street performers and skilled amateurs are practicing the ancient art in parks, back yards, and on campuses around the globe. Membership in the largely amateur International Jugglers' Association (IJA) has more than doubled since 1979. 2

Juggling is actually 4000 years young. In Egypt, Asia, and the Americas, it was once associated with religious ritual. In medieval Europe, wandering minstrels often juggled; the term derives from these *jongleurs.* 3

Amazing jugglers imported from the Orient—in particular the "East Indian" Ramo Samee, who was said to string beads in his mouth while turning rings with his fingers and toes, and the Japanese artist Takashima, who manipulated a cotton ball with a stick held in his teeth—convinced 19th-century Europeans that juggling could be extraordinary show business. 4

Perhaps the greatest juggler of all time was variety-show virtu- 5
oso Enrico Rastelli. By his death in 1931, he had taught himself to
juggle eight clubs, eight plates or ten balls; he could even bounce
three balls continuously on his head.

Most people assume that a skilled juggler can manage up to 6
20 objects. In fact, even five-ball juggling is very difficult and requires about a year to master. Only a few jugglers worldwide
have perfected seven-ball routines. At the 1986 IJA competition,
one entrant separately juggled nine rings, eight balls, and seven
clubs.

Jugglers use a bewildering variety of objects, including bowl- 7
ing balls, whips, plastic swimming pools, cube puzzles, fruit,
flaming torches, and playing cards. Performers trying for the
largest number of objects usually choose rings, which allow a
tighter traffic pattern and are stable when thrown to great heights.
Several jugglers can manage ten or 11 rings, and some are trying
for 12 or 13.

Clubs are the most visually pleasing objects to juggle. They're 8
especially suited for passing back and forth between performers.
Because they take up a lot of space when they rotate and must be
caught at one end, juggling even five is tricky. Almost nobody can
manage seven, even for a few seconds.

Throughout history, all jugglers—from South Sea Islanders to 9
Aztec Indians—have used the same fundamental patterns:

The Cascade. Here, each ball travels from one hand to the other 10
and back again, following a looping path that looks like a figure
eight lying on its side. The juggler starts with two balls in his right
hand, using a scooping motion and releasing a ball when his throwing hand is level with his navel. As the first ball reaches its highest
point, the other hand scoops and releases a second ball, and as that
one reaches *its* apogee, he throws the third. Skilled jugglers can keep
three, five, or even seven balls going in a cascade, but never four or
six. With an even number, balls collide at the intersection of the figure eight.

The Shower. In this more difficult pattern, the balls follow a cir- 11
cular path as they are thrown upward by the right hand, caught by
the left and quickly passed back to the right. Since the right does all
the long-distance throwing, the shower is inherently asymmetrical
and, therefore, inefficient; it is difficult with more than three objects.

The Fountain. This figure allows for a large number of balls. In a 12
four-ball fountain, each hand juggles two balls independently in a
circular motion. For symmetry, the number of balls is usually even.

If the hands throw alternately and the two patterns interlock, it is surprisingly hard to discern that the fountain is made of two separate components and not one.

Because gravity causes objects to accelerate as they fall, a juggler has only a short time to catch and throw one ball before another drops into his hand—even if he throws high. A juggler who throws a ball eight feet in the air, for example, must catch it 1.4 seconds later, but throwing it four times that high only doubles the flight time. 13

The best way to understand juggling is to learn to do it yourself. Some people get the hang of the three-ball cascade in minutes, although most need at least a few days. Limit your sessions to ten minutes rather than frustrate yourself with a two-hour binge. 14

Step 1: One Ball. Practice throwing a ball from your right hand to your left and back, letting the ball rise to just above your head. Make the ball follow the path of a figure eight lying on its side, by "scooping" the ball and releasing it near the navel. Catch the ball at the side of your body, then repeat the sequence. 15

Step 2: Two Balls. Put one in each hand. Throw the ball in the left hand as in Step 1, and then, just as the ball passes its high point, throw the right-hand ball. Avoid releasing the second throw too early or tossing the balls to unequal heights. 16

At first it may be difficult to catch the balls. Don't worry. Focus instead on the accuracy and height of the throws. Catching will come naturally as soon as the throws are on target. If things seem hectic, try higher throws. 17

Step 3: Two Balls Reversed. Reverse the order of throws so that the sequence is right, then left. 18

Step 4: Three Balls. Now put two balls in your right hand and one in your left. Try to complete Step 2 while simply holding the extra ball. Pause, then do Step 3. 19

The third ball can make it difficult to catch the second throw. To solve this, throw the third ball just after the second reaches its high point. The sequence is thus right, left, right. At first it may be tough to persuade your right hand to make its second throw. Remember: catches are irrelevant in the beginning. Throw high, accurately and slowly. Don't rush the tempo, and don't forget the figure-eight pattern. 20

Once you've mastered the three-ball cascade you'll want to try other patterns. A juggler is never finished: there is always one more ball. 21

MEANINGS AND VALUES

1. Are readers in general likely to find the topic of this essay interesting? Why or why not? How do the authors encourage readers to consider juggling an amusing or worthwhile activity? Are these reasons presented directly or indirectly?
2. People often think juggling is difficult because it *looks* difficult. What do the writers say about the process to convince readers that they can master it?
3. What purposes are served by the historical background in Paragraphs 3, 4, and 5? (See "Guide to Terms": *Purpose.*)

EXPOSITORY TECHNIQUES

1. What technique do Buhler and Graham use to begin the essay? To conclude it? What makes these techniques successful (or unsuccessful) in this particular essay? (Guide: *Introductions; Closings.*)
2. Why do the authors describe different juggling patterns before they provide specific advice on beginning to juggle? Would the selection be more effective or less effective if the order were reversed? (Guide: *Evaluation.*)
3. Which expository patterns, other than PROCESS ANALYSIS, do the authors use to make juggling readily understandable and to help readers believe that they can master it?

DICTION AND VOCABULARY

1. Tell how the diction and vocabulary choices in Paragraphs 10–12 help make juggling seem simple. (Guide: *Diction.*)
2. How does the diction in Paragraphs 14–20 contribute to the message that getting started with juggling is not as difficult as most readers might think?
3. If you do not know the meaning of some of the following terms, look them up in a dictionary: *renaissance* (Par 2); *virtuoso* (5); *cascade* (10).

READ TO WRITE

1. **Collaborating:** Physical activities can be difficult or challenging, but so can mental, social, or artistic activities. Working in a group, discuss activities you undertake with some success that others might find difficult, and list as many as you can. From the list, choose several that you and other group members are interested in writing or reading about. Note which ones you might be able to explain in ways that will intrigue readers and teach them something useful. Choose one as the topic for an essay and, as a group, prepare a plan for the essay.

2. **Considering Audience:** In the first seven paragraphs of their essay, Buhler and Graham offer a variety of information about juggling. Looking at each paragraph, describe the kinds of readers who might find the information it presents particularly interesting. Explain why you think these paragraphs are successful or unsuccessful in appealing to a wide range of readers.
3. **Developing an Essay:** Many sports and hobbies can seem difficult or mystifying. Drawing on Buhler and Graham's essay as a model, create a set of instructions to simplify a seemingly challenging, dangerous, or mysterious sport or activity. Make the activity interesting and encourage readers to try it.

(NOTE: Suggestions for topics requiring developing by use of PROCESS ANALYSIS are on pp. 262–263 at the end of this chapter.)

JENNIFER GRAHAM

JENNIFER GRAHAM is a freelance writer and an editor for the Web site *eHow: How to Do Just About Everything.* She has a master's degree in sociology.

How to Decorate a Dorm Room on a Budget

This selection was first published online at *eHow*, and like many electronic publications, it differs somewhat in format and style from print publications. It makes use of blocks of text instead of traditional paragraphs and makes greater use of headings. Yet it is a good example of process analysis used for instructions, and it contains all the elements we might expect from a clear exposition. The mingling of traditional and contemporary elements of expression makes for interesting (and perhaps helpful) reading.

Introduction

You have ventured into your college dorm room to see that it is drab, white and uninspired. This is a common problem on university and college campuses around the nation. It can be difficult to get excited about the move knowing that, as a college student, very little of your budget can go to room decorations. The good news is that your room does not have to remain plain and boring. By following the steps in this article, you will be able to put together a fun and stylish dorm room on a college student's budget.

Instructions

Difficulty: Moderately Easy

Choosing a Theme

Thing's You'll Need

Reversible Comforter
Fabric
Drapery Rod
Beads
Glitter
Plastic Crates

Jennifer Graham. "How to Decorate a Dorm Room on a Budget." Courtesy of eHow.com. http://www.eHow.com.

Bulletin or White Board
Newspaper Ads
Construction Paper
Photos from Home

Steps

Step One

Choose a reversible comforter from a discount store. The bed is the 1
focal point of any dorm room. It should be decorated that way. Choose a color scheme that represents your personality. A reversible comforter can be changed to suit your mood, but it will still have the same color and theme that works with the entire room.

Step Two

Venture to your local craft store. Look for bargains on fabrics that fit 2
in with your color scheme. Mix and match the colors. The fabric can be used in various ways. First, you might want to get a large swatch of plain fabric in one color to tack over one wall in your room. Most dorms will not allow you to paint, but this is a way to add a pop of color without damaging the walls. Purchase a drapery rod (after you have measured your window). You can easily drape fabric over the rod to make your windows stand out from the wall.

Step Three

Purchase beads or glitter that match your theme while you are at the 3
craft store. They will be used later.

Step Four

Choose distinct but budget-friendly crates or baskets from a local 4
discount store. They can be used to store things, but they can also be stacked on top of one another for an easy bedside table. Often, the crates/baskets come in all shapes and sizes. The main thing, again, is to stick with your theme. If you can find them in colors that compliment your comforter, it's all the better.

Step Five

Purchase an inexpensive bulletin or white board. These are often on 5
sale in the summer before school starts at office supply stores. Besides being able to put pictures and things on the board, you can also take your glitter and beads. Glue them around the edges of the board adding interest. This can also be done around the edges of your fabric on the windows. This will tie everything together. Now you have the base of the room, and it's time to add accessories.

Tips & Warnings

By sticking with a common theme and colors, the room will feel more organized and polished.

Remember your roommate! Shop together for a bonding experience.

Adding Accessories and Style

Steps

Step One
Decorate your room with accessories to make it feel more like home. 6
The best thing to do is to get out your local paper. Look at the classifieds and the weekly circulars of the major stores like Target. Look for garage sales and thrift stores in your area. These can be gold mines for accessories. See if you can find funky glasses or vases that match the color scheme you have chosen. These can be placed on your dresser, desk or windowsill to add touches of color.

Step Two
Check out the poster sale at your university during the first week of 7
classes. Most schools provide this for their students. You can find pretty inexpensive art. Look for modern pieces that will coordinate with you comforter on your bed. They don't necessarily have to be framed. Find cute tacks at your office supply store. Use sticky tack. One major piece will draw attention and not clutter the walls.

Step Three
Search for an inexpensive floor rug. Dorm rooms will have tile or 8
outdated carpet. By finding a cute rug that goes with your color scheme, you can cover this flaw. Make floor as stylish as the rest of the room. This ties everything together.

Projects

Steps

Step One
Hunt for garage sales around your city. Garage sales can be great for 9
small pieces of inexpensive furniture such as a small table, chair or ottoman. Keep in mind you don't have a lot of space! However, small items can be great buys. Often, with just a coat of paint, they can look brand new.

Step Two

Choose photos that remind you of friends and family at home. Make 10 cheap frames out of construction paper that coordinate with your theme colors. These can be placed in a cute collage on your bulletin board or over your desk. You can have ties to home right there in your room.

Step Three

Scour the sales in your newspaper to find a good deal on a nice 11 lamp. Lighting is one of the major problems in dorm rooms. The fluorescent glow makes the room feel very institutional. However, soft, ambient lighting can turn the space into a cozy haven.

Step Four

Sit back and enjoy your new space. Remember, your dorm room will 12 only be home for a little while, but it is important to relax in your space. Enjoy it while you can.

MEANINGS AND VALUES

1. According to the title, this essay will give instructions for two things. What are they?
2. Section three talks about "Choosing a Theme" and follows this heading with a list of "Things You'll Need." Look over the list, and then explain what the writer means by "theme." Why do you think she choose not to explain the term? Explain why you think she made the right choice (or not) in leaving out an explanation.
3. What evidence is there that this essay is directed (intentionally or unintentionally) at women? Does it exclude men as readers? Why or why not?

EXPOSITORY TECHNIQUES

1. The essay provides several sets of "steps" as instructions. How does the author prevent these several sets from becoming confusing for readers?
2. a. This is a very compact set of instructions. Some readers might prefer more detail, especially if they have little experience decorating. Take a careful look at section 4, step Two, and tell what explanatory or instructional details the writer might have added.

   b. Does leaving these details out harm the essay, or is their omission appropriate for the audience and the medium (Web site)? (See "Guide to Terms": *Evaluation.*)

3. What opening and closing strategies does the writer employ (section 1; section 7, step four)? (Guide: *Introductions, Closings.*)

Diction and Vocabulary

1. Look at the diction and sentence structure in section 6, step two. Describe how the choices in vocabulary and sentence structure make this explanation likely to be accessible to most readers. (Guide: *Diction.*)
2. What are "funky glasses" (section 6, step one)? "cute tacks" (section 6, step two)? What is an "ottoman" (section 7, step one)? a "cute collage" (section 7, step two)?

Read to Write

1. **Collaborating:** Working with a group of writers, make a list of the steps necessary to accomplish some relatively everyday tasks that nonetheless remains a mystery to many people (making cookies, hitting a baseball, or diving into a pool, for example). After you have completed the list, prepare another one outlining a different set of steps for accomplishing the same thing (do it for a third time, too, if you are able). Finally, try to integrate the different sets of steps into an outline for an essay that combines both sets of directions.
2. **Considering Audience:** Look over Graham's essay to see what assumptions she makes about the gender, background, social class, and values of her audience. Write a paragraph summarizing these assumptions. Then specify a different audience and write a paragraph indicating what changes would need to be made in the essay (if any) to better meet the needs and outlook of the second audience.
3. **Developing an Essay:** Using an arrangement similar to Graham's, prepare an essay offering instructions for another task readers are likely to encounter in their daily lives (it could be another decorating task). If you wish, adopt an approach like Graham uses for an essay that will appear online.

(NOTE: Suggestions for topics requiring development by PROCESS ANALYSIS are on pp. 262–263 at the end of this chapter.)

SRIDHAR PAPPU

SRIDHAR PAPPU currently is a correspondent for *The Atlantic Monthly,* based out of New York. At the time of this article's publication, he was a staff writer for *The Chicago Reader.* In addition to stints as a reporter and staff writer at *Money* and *Sports Illustrated,* Pappu served as a media columnist for *The New York Observer* from June 2001 to February 2004. Pappu holds a B.S. and M.S. from Northwestern University's Medill School of Journalism and resides in the Park Slope section of Brooklyn, New York.

Deranged Marriage

This essay was published in *Life as We Know It: A Collection of Personal Essays from Salon.com.* In it, Sridhar Pappu describes a process of "courtship" and marriage likely to be unfamiliar to many readers. What makes this analysis of a process even more interesting is that in the particular events Pappu presents, the process doesn't work—though it is clear that it has worked for other people for many years.

In the days before last Christmas, a girl I had never met or spoken to called me to see if I wanted to marry her. It wasn't the girl, really, but her family. And they didn't call me, exactly. They called my mother. 1

Thus began a series of events that concluded on a Saturday night in January with me sitting in the dark, sobbing into a pillowcase, drinking a bottle of He'brew beer that I'd saved from a friend's Hanukkah party, and listening to Merle Haggard. I had taken on the antiquated custom of arranged marriage, in its modern incarnation, and it had beaten me into a state of previously unfathomable self-pity that happened to include very bad beer. 2

This was new terrain for me. I am Indian by birth, but I grew up as a white kid in southwest Ohio. I drank beer in open fields in high school and still consider my greatest adolescent achievement the night I walked into the homecoming dance with the prettiest girl in my senior class. I worship Johnny Bench. And until last December, the prospect of an arranged marriage was an abstract idea to me, the appropriate narrative vein for someone else's story; my grandparents', my parents', even my sister's, but never my own. 3

Of course, I had distaste for all of it: a feeling, which informed every John Hughes movie I ever saw, that any kind of outside involvement in finding that "someone" was, well, wrong. I can say truthfully 4 now that I felt the right girl would just come to me on, say, the Wilson Avenue Bridge in Chicago, or within the basement-level environs of the old Knitting Factory in New York. Tabula rasa. I'm here.

5 I believed my future would be spent in apartments on the Upper East Side or in Greenwich Village, where, my hands shoved into the pockets of a tweed sports coat, I would find myself asking a waiflike brunet why she was leaving me or coming back to me, or if she had ever loved me at all. I saw my brows furrowed and my eyes drawn close. "Jenny," I'd say, "what's this all about?"

6 The fact of the matter is that I have passed through nearly half of my twenties without experiencing anything close to that exchange, and I realize that, on some level, the idea of an arranged marriage has always been with me. It has served as both an emboldening force against loneliness, and the precise cause of that loneliness, since it has hovered in the background as Plan B while I have searched for nothing less than the perfect girl.

7 Which brings us to the events of the past few months.

8 It all began with my hesitant approval of my mother's decision to start "the process." I did this without knowing precisely where or to whom that process might lead. Arranged marriage has changed a great deal since it was shipped to this country in the late 1960s, having been forced to embrace the exterior trappings of a world that it is designed to circumvent. There are (or can be) phone calls, dates, and months of courtship, supposedly meant to give the participants access to traits, qualities, and annoying habits not obvious at first glance. More important, these new aspects of the ritual seek to first simulate, then stimulate the intermittent passion, the plain pining, experienced in unmatched love.

9 My own faux dating started with a match to a girl from Louisiana that never got past the picture-viewing stage, then moved to a match with a soon-to-be-graduating medical school student from Florida. Nearly giddy in the days before Christmas, my mother and father called to say that, yes, "this one" was pretty, and soon, in a hotel room in Boston, they showed me her picture—with résumé.

10 The photograph showed her standing in profile, her face turned just slightly. She was wearing a sari with her hands placed over one another in an attempt to display a kind of grace. Her vita said her career goals include a "fellowship in gastroenterology" and listed her interests as "Languages, Literature" as well as travel and running. It went on to say that she enjoyed "people, social and fun loving." My father said she'd be coming to Chicago on the residency-interview trail in January, and that was when I could meet her.

"For now," said my father as I sat on the edge of the bed, pretending to only half-listen while watching *The Sopranos,* "we're going to just concentrate on doctors." 11

I met her two weeks later on a cold, sunless day. She had on a long, dark coat and a blue shawl, and a smile—bright and assured and unironic—that made her seem irreducibly pretty. We were, I felt, what a young couple should look like: well dressed and unwrinkled, what Eudora Welty once described as a "matched team—like professional, Spanish dancers wearing masks." 12

We spent seven hours together—beginning with a tense el ride and a tenser, chitchatty lunch at the Berghoff meant to create casualness where there was none. Of course, the easiest way for characters in any story to address the large, overarching dilemmas and issues (Why am I with you? What is going on between the two of us? How can I make things better?) is to talk about them, which, initiated by her, is what we did. 13

"Are your parents traditional?" she asked as we walked around the Art Institute. 14

"I guess they have traditional ideas," I said. "My dad likes to play the liberal, but my mom's the real heavy. They're pretty great, though. I dunno. I mean, what do you mean by 'traditional'?" 15

"I guess," she said, "I mean, what do they expect out of this?" 16

"I'm not sure," I said, and I wasn't. 17

"What do you expect out of this?" 18

"I don't know," I said, taken by her matter-of-factness. "How about you?" 19

She went on to tell me that her parents first brought up the idea a year ago, saying that as long as she was going to visit these cities, she "might as well" begin to meet "these" boys. 20

Listening to this, I felt my limbs entirely weaken and my head grow light. I thought about the Cincinnati Bengals' inability to keep their lead against the San Francisco 49ers in the 1989 Super Bowl, about the need for the Cincinnati Reds to pick up another quality starting pitcher. I saw my picture pasted on a bulletin board along with those of other earnest, nearsighted young Indian men. How did my looks rate next to theirs? My clothes? My hair? How did she feel when I told her that I felt unnerved around large groups of Indian people, that most of my close friends were Jewish? 21

I wanted to go home, but of course I didn't. Instead, I finished the museum tour with her and walked north up Michigan Avenue, talking to her about city politics in Chicago and Miami. She told me 22 that she loved Cuban coffee, and I said that my father had raised my sister and me to drink Maxwell House black. She said there was nothing so pretty as a Florida sunset, but that she wanted to live in a place with hip, young professionals. I didn't ask but was pretty certain that she really, really liked *Friends.*

"So, Sridhar," she said before we entered a Starbucks, "what else?" 23

"About me," I replied, "or about this?" 24

"About this," she said. "What are your concerns?" 25

That night in my notebook, I would write that I was "gripped by an acute sensation to hold her and only let go 30 or 40 years later." I know, yeech. But I suppose that a good deal of me had thought this was a moment of real definition, where she could see something that set me apart from the rest of the Sanjays and Ajays, the would-be radiologists and software engineers. The future had in fact unfolded. Now it just needed ironing out. 26

Inside, over a tall mocha and a tall house coffee, we spoke about our problems with the process and what we expected from a potential spouse. She said she didn't want to get married for two more years, and that she wanted to move to Houston. Proximity, she said, was a definite issue. I expressed the sentiment that part of me didn't feel Indian enough, that I wanted someone not entirely freaked out by my intention to eventually write a novel. 27

Smitten is the word for what I felt. In the course of the day I had premonitions of attending her medical school graduation in May, of buying a fixer-upper in Houston's Rice Village with a large sunporch and a home office in the attic. Premature feelings perhaps, but not entirely out of line with the heightened sense that comes with these things, where every word choice, every pause, every action takes on 400 to 500 additional pounds in emotional weight. 28

I told her that I'd like to see her before she left town, and she said that she felt the same. When I called her two days later, however, she said seeing me again wasn't possible, that she had gone ahead and made plans with other people. "I guess," she said, "it's just not going to happen." 29

A pretty good piece of dialogue for someone who is not a writer, good enough to plunge me into a rueful weekend of darkness and "Mama Tried." 30

Since then, however, in talks with my parents and my sister, I have come to see this experience for what it was: the first match, the initial act in a process that seeks to remove the randomness from life, that deals with affection directly and is meant to eliminate the 31 ambiguities and missed signals that plague us once we enter the love life of adults.

I'm not sure if it will ever "happen" for me, not in this way. But for now I'm willing to try. 32

Meanings and Values

1. What is the process Sridhar Pappu describes in this essay?
2. What do the imagined events described in Paragraph 5 reveal about the writer's cultural and social values?
3. How does the process Pappu presents differ from more traditional versions of the process? Can these differences account for the reactions he describes in Paragraph 2? Why, or why not?

Expository Techniques

1. Describe the strategy Pappu uses to open the essay. (See "Guide to Terms": *Introductions.*)
2. Is the opening to the essay likely to be effective in getting the attention of most readers? Why, or why not? (Guide: *Evaluation.*)
3. Why does the writer describe the failure of the process in Paragraph 2?
4. Where in the essay does the presentation of the process begin? Why do you think the writer waits so long to begin the presentation?

Diction and Vocabulary

1. Why does the writer use the phrase "faux dating"? Is the meaning of this phrase likely to be apparent to most readers? Why, or why not?
2. At several points in the essay, the writer includes quotations from himself and from other people. For what purposes does he include these quotations?

Read to Write

1. **Collaborating:** Working with a group of writers, make a list of activities that your parents and other people from earlier generations accomplish in ways different from those that are common or fashionable today. Make a list of the differences among present and past (or "traditional") processes. Then choose one process, and summarize the differences between present and past versions in a paragraph or two.

2. **Considering Audience:** Choose one of the processes from activity 1, above, and explore in writing what people from different age groups need to know about the values and ideas that shape each different version of the process.
3. **Developing an Essay:** Write an essay about the topic you explored in activity 2, presenting different versions of the process, and explain it to both contemporary and "traditional" audiences.

(NOTE: Suggestions for topics requiring development by analysis of PROCESS ANALYSIS are on pp. 262–263 at the end of this chapter.)

IAN FRAZIER

IAN FRAZIER was born in Cleveland, Ohio in 1951. He graduated from Harvard University in 1973 and soon after joined the staff of *The New Yorker,* where he wrote for the "Talk of the Town" section and published a variety of feature stories and humorous articles. He is known both for his success as a humorist and for employing a matter-of-fact, first-person narrative style when discussing topics that range from personal hobbies to history and life in the American West. Some of his other notable works include *Dating Your Mom* (1986), *Nobody Better, Better than Nobody* (1987), *Great Plains* (1989), *Family* (1994), *Coyote vs. Acme* (1996), *On the Rez* (2000), *The Fish's Eye* (2002), and *Lamentations of the Father* (2008).

How to Operate the Shower Curtain

One technique of humorous writing is to take a simple activity and explain it in such extensive, often irrelevant detail, that the explanation becomes ridiculous and funny. This technique pokes fun at the kinds of silly or pompous instructions and similar forms of writing we often encounter as well as the kinds of foolish situations we often find ourselves in. Sometimes writing of this sort includes parody, taking the form of serious writing but with exaggerated or outlandish content. That is the case with this essay from *The New Yorker*. It takes the form of a set of instructions but overstates them and includes loosely related details that poke fun at contemporary habits and customs while pointing out that we sometimes rely on written instructions when simple common sense might provide better guidance.

Dear Guest: The shower curtain in this bathroom has been purchased with care at a reputable "big box" store in order to provide maximum convenience in showering. After you have read these instructions, you will find with a little practice that our shower curtain is as easy to use as the one you have at home. 1

You'll note that the shower curtain consists of several parts. 2
The top hem, closest to the ceiling, contains a series of regularly spaced holes designed for the insertion of shower-curtain rings. As this part receives much of the everyday strain of usage, it must be handled correctly. Grasp the shower curtain by its leading edge and gently pull until it is flush with the wall. Step into the tub, if you have not already done so. Then take the other edge of shower curtain and cautiously pull it in opposite direction until it, too,

adjoins the wall. A little moisture between shower curtain and wall tiles will help curtain to stick.

Keep in mind that normal bathing will cause you unavoidably to bump against shower curtain, which may cling to you for a moment owing to the natural adhesiveness of water. Some guests find the sensation of wet plastic on their naked flesh upsetting, and overreact to it. Instead, pinch the shower curtain between your thumb and forefinger near where it is adhering to you and simply move away from it until it is disengaged. Then, with the ends of your fingers, push it back to where it is supposed to be. 3

If shower curtain reattaches itself to you, repeat process above. Under certain atmospheric conditions, a convection effect creates air currents outside shower curtain which will press it against you on all sides no matter what you do. If this happens, stand directly under showerhead until bathroom microclimate stabilizes. 4

Many guests are surprised to learn that all water pipes in our system run off a single riser. This means that the opening of any hot or cold tap, or the flushing of a toilet, interrupts flow to shower. If you find water becoming extremely hot (or cold), exit tub promptly while using a sweeping motion with one arm to push shower curtain aside. 5

REMEMBER TO KEEP SHOWER CURTAIN *INSIDE* TUB AT ALL TIMES! Failure to do this may result in baseboard rot, wallpaper mildew, destruction of living-room ceiling below, and possible dripping onto catered refreshments at social event in your honor that you are about to attend. So be careful! 6

This shower curtain comes equipped with small magnets in the shape of disks which have been sewn into the bottom hem at intervals. These serve no purpose whatsoever and may be ignored. Please do not tamper with them. The vertical lines, or pleats, which you may have wondered about, are there for a simple reason: user safety. If you have to move from the tub fast, as outlined above, the easy accordion-type folding motion of the pleats makes that possible. The gray substance in some of the inner pleat folds is a kind of insignificant mildew, less toxic than what is found on some foreign cheeses. 7

When detaching shower curtain from clinging to you or when exiting tub during a change in water temperature, bear in mind that there are seventeen mostly empty plastic bottles of shampoo on tub edge next to wall. These bottles have accumulated in this area over time. Many have been set upside down in order to concentrate the last amounts of fluid in their cap mechanisms, and are 8 balanced lightly. Inadvertent contact with a thigh or knee can cause all the bottles to be knocked over and to tumble into the tub or behind it. If this should somehow happen, we ask that you kindly pick the bottles up and put them back in the same order in which you found them. Thank you.

While picking up the bottles, a guest occasionally will lose his 9 or her balance temporarily, and, in even rarer cases, fall. If you find this occurring, remember that panic is the enemy here. Let your body go limp, while reminding yourself that the shower curtain is not designed to bear your weight. Grabbing onto it will only complicate the situation.

If, in a "worst case" scenario, you do take hold of the shower 10 curtain, and the curtain rings tear through the holes in the upper hem as you were warned they might, remain motionless and relaxed in the position in which you come to rest. If subsequently you hear a knock on the bathroom door, respond to any questions by saying either "Fine" or "No, I'm fine." When the questioner goes away, stand up, turn off shower, and lay shower curtain flat on floor and up against tub so you can see the extent of the damage. With a sharp object—a nail file, a pen, or your teeth—make new holes in top hem next to the ones that tore through.

Now lift shower curtain with both hands and reattach it to 11 shower-curtain rings by unclipping, inserting, and reclipping them. If during this process the shower curtain slides down and again goes onto you, reach behind you to shelf under medicine cabinet, take nail file or curved fingernail scissors, and perform short, brisk slashing jabs on shower curtain to cut it back. It can always be repaired later with safety pins or adhesive tape from your toiletries kit.

At this point, you may prefer to get the shower curtain out of 12 your way entirely by gathering it up with both arms and ripping it down with a sharp yank. Now place it in the waste receptacle next to the john. In order that anyone who might be overhearing you will know that you are still all right, sing "Fat Bottomed Girls," by Queen, as loudly as necessary. While waiting for tub to fill, wedge shower curtain into waste receptacle more firmly by treading it underfoot with a regular high-knee action as if marching in place.

We are happy to have you as our guest. There are many 13 choices you could have made, but you are here, and we appreciate that. Operating the shower curtain is kind of tricky. Nobody is denying that. If you do not wish to deal with it, or if you would rather skip the whole subject for reasons you do not care to reveal, we accept your decision. You did not ask to be born. There is no need ever to touch the shower curtain again. If you would like to receive assistance, pound on the door, weep inconsolably, and someone will be along.

Meanings and Values

1. At what point in this essay did you first become aware that it is not to be taken seriously, that it is, in fact, a parody? What specifically made you doubt the seriousness of the selection?
2. Choose two passages from the essay that can be considered examples of irony, and explain what makes them ironic. (See "Guide to Terms": *Irony.*)
3. This essay pokes fun at more than one subject. Review Paragraphs 3–6 carefully and identify as many targets of the humor as you can (including the "speaker" or persona in the essay, who seems to take simple things far too seriously). (Guide: *Persona.*)

Expository Techniques

1. One important technique in this essay is the creation of a persona, the person in the essay appears to be addressing the reader ("Dear Guest:" Par. 1) but who is in fact separate from the actual writer of the essay. Make a list of the apparent character traits and values of this persona. Indicate those which the essay appears to make fun of or criticize. (Guide: *Persona.*)
2. To what extent do the techniques in this essay move beyond simple humor into satire? Be ready to explain your answer by referring to specific sections of the text. For a definition of satire, see Guide: *Satire.*
3. Exaggeration is a frequent technique in humor and satire. Identify the exaggerations in Paragraphs 8–10 and tell for what purpose the writer seems to be using them. (Guide: *Purpose.*)

Diction and Vocabulary

1. The vocabulary in this selection often seems to be more formal and technical that the subject requires. Identify any such terms in Paragraph 2. (Guide: *Diction.*) Explain how the writer uses these terms to poke fun at the speaker (persona), readers who take the piece seriously, or both. (Guide: *Persona.*)
2. The last sentence in Paragraph 6 uses several words and phrases to poke fun at people who take cleanliness to extremes and at people

who may fail to see a contrast between their cultural sophistication and their other values. What are these passages? State their meaning in your own words.

3. If you do not know the meaning of some of the following words, look them up in a dictionary: *reputable* (Par. 1); *hem* (2); *adhering* (3); *atmospheric, microclimate* (4); *riser* (5); *inconsolably* (13).

READ TO WRITE

1. **Collaborating:** Many of the experiences described in this essay are likely to have happened to readers, though few readers are likely to have experienced them all. Working with a group, identify those things that have happened to one or more members. Then decide if the essay can be considered somewhat realistic despite its exaggerations and humor.
2. **Considering Audience:** This essay takes experiences that most of us have encountered and looks at them humorously. Make a list of similar common experiences and explain why they are worth treating with humor or satire.
3. **Developing an Essay:** Following Frazier's example, create an essay using process analysis and a speaker, or persona, whose explanations are worth criticizing, or at least not worth taking seriously.

(NOTE: Suggestions for topics requiring development by use of PROCESS ANALYSIS are on pp. 262–263 at the end of this chapter.)

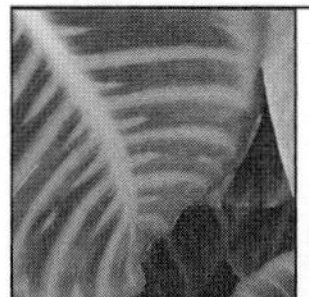

Issues and Ideas

Advertising and Appearances

- Jean E. Kilbourne, *Beauty . . . And the Beast of Advertising*
- Jessica Mitford, *To Dispel Fears of Live Burial*

Do appearances count? When they come to us on television, in movies, or through advertisements, they do—at least, that is what the essays that follow suggest. In addition, we are often ready to pay a good deal to keep up appearances, both while we are alive and after we die.

Jean E. Kilbourne offers a sharply critical analysis of the images of physical appearance and of behavior that dominate various media and have influenced our attitudes toward our bodies, our values, and our behaviors in harmful ways. She focuses especially on the ways women participate in and are affected by this process, but her conclusions also apply to society at large.

Jessica Mitford's treatment of our fascination with appearances has an even harder edge. She offers a bitingly satiric and humorous view of our concern with the appearance of the dead, a form of manipulation that amounts almost to a denial of the reality of death. Though she puts primary blame on the funeral industry for creating and maintaining this obsession with false appearances, she includes in her indictment all of us who willingly tolerate the sham process.

Taken together, these essays demonstrate the importance of media images in contemporary life and suggest ways of interpreting and analyzing these images that can lead to further writing.

JEAN E. KILBOURNE

JEAN E. KILBOURNE is a media critic whose award-winning films *Still Killing Us Softly* and *Calling the Shots* explore the relationships between media and advertising images and our values and behaviors. She lectures regularly on alcohol and cigarette advertising, images of women in advertising, and related issues.

Beauty . . . And the Beast of Advertising

In this essay, first published in *Media & Values* in 1989, Kilbourne analyzes the ways media images shape perceptions and values, particularly those of women. This essay blends a number of patterns, including definition, process analysis, and cause-and-effect analysis.

"You're a Halston woman from the very beginning," the advertisement proclaims. The model stares provocatively at the viewer, her long blonde hair waving around her face, her bare chest partially covered by two curved bottles that give the illusion of breasts and a cleavage. 1

The average American is accustomed to blue-eyed blondes seductively touting a variety of products. In this case, however, the blonde is about five years old. 2

Advertising is an over $100 billion a year industry and affects all of us throughout our lives. We are each exposed to over 2,000 ads a day, constituting perhaps the most powerful educational force in society. The average adult will spend one and one-half years of his/her life watching television commercials. But the ads sell a great deal more than products. They sell values, images and concepts of success and worth, love and sexuality, popularity and normalcy. They tell us who we are and who we should be. Sometimes they sell addictions. 3

Advertising's foundation and economic lifeblood is the mass media, and the primary purpose of the mass media is to deliver an audience to advertisers, just as the primary purpose of television programs is to deliver an audience for commercials. 4

Adolescents are particularly vulnerable, however, because they are new and inexperienced consumers and are the prime targets of many advertisements. They are in the process of learning their 5 values and roles and developing their self-concepts. Most teenagers are sensitive to peer pressure and find it difficult to resist or even question the dominant cultural messages perpetuated and reinforced by the media. Mass communication has made possible a kind of nationally distributed peer pressure that erodes private and individual values and standards.

But what does society, and especially teenagers, learn from the advertising messages that proliferate in the mass media? On the most obvious level they learn the stereotypes. Advertising creates a mythical, WASP-oriented world in which no one is ever ugly, overweight, poor, struggling or disabled either physically or mentally (unless you count the housewives who talk to little men in toilet bowls, animated germs in drains or muscle-bound giants clad in white clothing). And it is a world in which people talk only about products. 6

Housewives or Sex Objects

The aspect of advertising most in need of analysis and change is the portrayal of women. Scientific studies and the most casual viewing yield the same conclusion: Women are shown almost exclusively as housewives or sex objects. 7

The housewife, pathologically obsessed by cleanliness and lemon-fresh scents, debates cleaning products with herself and worries about her husband's "ring around the collar." 8

The sex object is a mannequin, a shell. Conventional beauty is her only attribute. She has no lines or wrinkles (which would indicate she had the bad taste and poor judgment to grow older), no scars or blemishes—indeed, she has no pores. She is thin, generally tall and long-legged, and, above all, she is young. All "beautiful" women in advertisements (including minority women), regardless of product or audience, conform to this norm. Women are constantly exhorted to emulate this ideal, to feel ashamed and guilty if they fail, and to feel that their desirability and lovability are contingent upon physical perfection. 9

Creating Artificiality

The image is artificial and can only be achieved artificially (even the "natural look" requires much preparation and expense). Beauty is something that comes from without; more than one million dollars is 10 spent every hour on cosmetics. Desperate to conform to an ideal and impossible standard, many women go to great lengths to manipulate and change their faces and bodies. A woman is conditioned to view her face as a mask and her body as an object, as *things* separate from and more important than her real self, constantly in need of alteration, improvement, and disguise. She is made to feel dissatisfied with and ashamed of herself, whether she tries to achieve "the look" or not. Objectified constantly by others, she learns to objectify herself. (It is interesting to note that one in five college-age women have an eating disorder.)

"When *Glamour* magazine surveyed its readers in 1984, 75 percent felt too heavy and only 15 percent felt just right. Nearly half of those who were actually underweight reported feeling too fat and wanting to diet. Among a sample of college women, 40 percent felt overweight when only 12 percent actually were too heavy," according to Rita Freedman in her book *Beauty Bound.* 11

There is evidence that this preoccupation with weight begins at ever-earlier ages for women. According to a recent article in *New Age Journal,* "Even grade-school girls are succumbing to sticklike standards of beauty enforced by a relentless parade of wasp-waisted fashion models, movie stars, and pop idols." A study by a University of California professor showed that nearly 80 percent of fourth-grade girls in the Bay Area are watching their weight. 12

A recent *Wall Street Journal* survey of students in four Chicago-area schools found that more than half the fourth-grade girls were dieting and three-quarters felt they were overweight. One student said, "We don't expect boys to be that handsome. We take them as they are." Another added, "But boys expect girls to be perfect and beautiful. And skinny." 13

Dr. Steven Levenkron, author of *The Best Little Girl in the World,* the story of an anorexic, says his blood pressure soars every time he opens a magazine and finds an ad for women's fashions. "If I had my way," he said, "every one of them would have to carry a line saying, 'Caution: This model may be hazardous to your health.'" 14

Women are also dismembered in commercials, their bodies separated into parts in need of change or improvement. If a woman has "acceptable" breasts, then she must also be sure that her legs are worth watching, her hips slim, her feet sexy, and that her buttocks look nude under her clothes ("like I'm not wearin' nothin'"). This image is difficult and costly to achieve and impossible to maintain (unless you buy the product)—no one is flawless and everyone ages. 15

Growing older is the great taboo. Women are encouraged to remain little girls ("because innocence is sexier than you think"), to be passive and dependent, never too mature. The contradictory message—"sensual, but not too far from innocence"—places women in a double bind; somehow we are supposed to be both sexy and virginal, experienced and naïve, seductive and chaste. The disparagement of maturity is, of course, insulting and frustrating to adult women, and the implication that little girls are seductive is dangerous to real children.

Influencing Sexual Attitudes

Young people also learn a great deal about sexual attitudes from the media and from advertising in particular. Advertising's approach to sex is pornographic; it reduces people to objects and de-emphasizes human contact and individuality. This reduction of sexuality to a dirty joke and of people to objects is the real obscenity of the culture. Although the sexual sell, overt and subliminal, is at a fevered pitch in most commercials, there is at the same time a notable absence of sex as an important and profound human activity. 16

There have been some changes in the images of women. Indeed, a "new woman" has emerged in commercials in recent years. She is generally presented as superwoman, who manages to do all the work at home and on the job (with the help of a product, of course, not of her husband or children or friends), or as the liberated woman, who owes her independence and self-esteem to the products she uses. These new images do not represent any real progress but rather create a myth of progress, an illusion that reduces complex sociopolitical problems to mundane personal ones. 17

Advertising images do not cause these problems, but they contribute to them by creating a climate in which the marketing of women's bodies—the sexual sell and dismemberment, distorted body image ideal and children as sex objects—is seen as acceptable. 18

This is the real tragedy, that many women internalize these stereotypes and learn their "limitations," thus establishing a self-fulfilling prophecy. If one accepts these mythical and degrading images, to some extent one actualizes them. By remaining unaware of the profound seriousness of the ubiquitous influence, the redundant message and the subliminal impact of advertisements, we ignore one of the most powerful "educational" forces in the culture—one that greatly affects our self-images, our ability to relate to each other, 19 and effectively destroys any awareness and action that might help to change that climate.

Meanings and Values

1. According to the writer, what does advertising tell women they should be, and by what process does it convey this message? Does the beginning of Paragraph 18 accurately summarize the process the writer has been analyzing? If not, what is missing from the summary? Would the essay be stronger if the missing information were included? Why or why not? (See "Guide to Terms": *Evaluation.*)
2. Who or what is the "new woman" (Par. 7)? Why does the writer believe that this image does "not represent any real progress"? Why would the absence of any discussion of the "new woman" weaken the expository purpose of the selection? (Guide: *Purpose.*)
3. At several places in the essay, Kilbourne discusses the consequences of advertising on teenagers while in much of the rest of the essay she focuses on women. Does the focus on teenagers undermine the unity of the essay? Why, or why not? (Guide: *Unity.*)

Expository Techniques

1. What strategy does Kilbourne use to begin her essay (Pars. 1–2)? (Guide: *Introductions.*) Can the opening of this essay be considered ironic? Why, or why not? (Guide: *Irony.*) What strategy does she use to conclude the essay? (Guide: *Closings.*)
2. What kinds of evidence does the author provide to support her conclusions about the process of advertising and its consequences? Which kind of evidence do you consider most effective, and which seems least effective? Why? (Guide: *Evaluation.*)
3. Discuss how Kilbourne varies sentence length (and structure) to achieve emphasis in Paragraphs 3, 9, and 15. (Guide: *Emphasis; Syntax.*)

Diction and Vocabulary

1. Where in the essay does the writer use numbers to present information? Be specific. Why can these numbers be considered a form of concrete diction? (Guide: *Concrete/Abstract; Diction.*) What do they contribute to the effects of the various passages in which they appear?
2. If you do not know the meaning of some of the following words, look them up in a dictionary: *provocatively, cleavage* (Par. 1); *touting* (2);

stereotypes, WASP (6); *pathologically* (8); *mannequin, attribute, exhorted, contingent* (9); *anorexic* (14); *sensual, disparagement* (15); *overt, subliminal* (16); *mundane* (17); *ubiquitous, redundant* (19).

READ TO WRITE

1. **Collaborating:** Working with a group of classmates, spend some time observing advertisements on television or analyzing them in magazines. Take notes on the process by which they achieve their effects as well as the effects themselves. Discuss the notes and arrive at a focus and a thesis for a possible essay.
2. **Considering Audience:** Read (or reread) Brent Staples's essay, "Just Walk on By" (pp. 50–55), for another example of an essay that begins with a reversal of readers' expectations. Create an opening for an essay of your own with a reversal of readers' expectations similar to the ones created by Kilbourne and Staples.
3. **Developing an Essay:** Using Kilbourne's essay as a model, discuss the process of advertising as it affects a group or groups other than women in general. Feel free to take a positive view of advertising in contrast to Kilbourne's generally negative perspective.

(NOTE: Suggestions for topics requiring development by means of PROCESS ANALYSIS are on pp. 262–263 at the end of this chapter.)

JESSICA MITFORD

JESSICA MITFORD was born in 1917, the daughter of an English peer. Her brother was sent to Eton, but she and her six sisters were educated at home by their mother. At the age of nineteen Mitford left home, eventually making her way to the United States in 1939. She made her home in San Francisco and became an American citizen in 1944. She did not begin her writing career until she was thirty-eight. Her books are *Lifeitselfmanship* (1956); her autobiography, *Daughters and Rebels* (1960); the bestseller *The American Way of Death* (1963); *The Trial of Dr. Spock* (1969); *Kind and Usual Punishment* (1973), a devastating study of the American penal system; *A Fine Old Conflict* (1977); and *Poison Penmanship* (1979). Mitford's articles have appeared in the *Atlantic, Harper's,* and *McCall's.*

To Dispel Fears of Live Burial

"To Dispel Fears of Live Burial" (editor's title) is a portion of *The American Way of Death,* a book described in the *New York Times* as a "savagely witty and well-documented exposé." The "savagely witty" style, evident in this selection, does not obscure the fact of its being a tightly organized, step-by-step process analysis.

Embalming is indeed a most extraordinary procedure, and one must wonder at the docility of Americans who each year pay hundreds of millions of dollars for its perpetuation, blissfully ignorant of what it is all about, what is done, how it is done. Not one in ten thousand has any idea of what actually takes place. Books on the subject are extremely hard to come by. They are not to be found in most libraries or bookshops. 1

In an era when huge television audiences watch surgical operations in the comfort of their living rooms, when, thanks to the animated cartoon, the geography of the digestive system has become familiar territory even to the nursery school set, in a land where the satisfaction of curiosity about almost all matters is a national pastime, the secrecy surrounding embalming can, surely, hardly be attributed to the inherent gruesomeness of the subject. Custom in this regard has within this century suffered a complete reversal. In the early days of American embalming, when it was performed in the home of the deceased, it was almost mandatory for some relative to stay by the embalmer's side and witness the procedure. Today, family members 2 who might wish to be in attendance would certainly be dissuaded by the funeral director. All others, except apprentices, are excluded by law from the preparation room.

A close look at what does actually take place may explain in large measure the undertaker's intractable reticence concerning a procedure that has become his major *raison d'être.* Is it possible he fears that public information about embalming might lead patrons to wonder if they really want this service? If the funeral men are loath to discuss the subject outside the trade, the reader may, understandably, be equally loath to go on reading at this point. For those who have the stomach for it, let us part the formaldehyde curtain. . . . 3

The body is first laid out in the undertaker's morgue—or rather, Mr. Jones is reposing in the preparation room—to be readied to bid the world farewell. 4

The preparation room in any of the better funeral establishments has the tiled and sterile look of a surgery, and indeed the embalmer-restorative artist who does his chores there is beginning to adopt the term "dermasurgeon" (appropriately corrupted by some mortician-writers as "demisurgeon") to describe his calling. His equipment, consisting of scalpels, scissors, augers, forceps, clamps, needles, pumps, tubes, bowls and basins, is crudely imitative of the surgeon's as is his technique, acquired in a nine- or twelve-month post-high-school course in an embalming school. He is supplied by an advanced chemical industry with a bewildering array of fluids, sprays, pastes, oils, powders, creams, to fix or soften tissue, shrink or distend it as needed, dry it here, restore the moisture there. There are cosmetics, waxes and paints, to fill and cover features, even plaster of Paris to replace entire limbs. There are ingenious aids to prop and stabilize the cadaver: A Vari-Pose Head Rest, the Edwards Arm and Hand Positioner, the Repose Block (to support the shoulders during the embalming), and the Throop Foot Positioner, which resembles an old-fashioned stocks. 5

Mr. John H. Eckels, president of the Eckels College of Mortuary Science, thus describes the first part of the embalming procedure: "In the hands of a skilled practitioner, this work may be done in a comparatively short time and without mutilating the body other than by slight incision—so slight that it scarcely would cause serious inconvenience if made upon a living person. It is necessary to remove the blood, and doing this not only helps in the disinfecting, but removes the principal cause of disfigurements due to discoloration." 6

Another textbook discusses the all-important time element: "The earlier this is done, the better, for every hour that elapses between death and embalming will add to the problems and complications encountered. . . ." Just how soon should one get going on the embalming? The author tells us, "On the basis of such scanty information made available to this profession through its rudimentary and haphazard system of technical research, we must conclude that the best results are to be obtained if the subject is embalmed before life is completely extinct—that is, before cellular death has occurred. In the average case, this would mean within an hour after somatic death." For those who feel that there is something a little rudimentary, not to say haphazard, about this advice, a comforting thought is offered by another writer. Speaking of fears entertained in early days of premature burial, he points out, "One of the effects of embalming by chemical injection, however, has been to dispel fears of live burial." How true; once the blood is removed, chances of live burial are indeed remote. 7

To return to Mr. Jones, the blood is drained out through the veins and replaced by embalming fluid pumped in through the arteries. As noted in *The Principles and Practices of Embalming,* "Every operator has a favorite injection and drainage point—a fact which becomes a handicap only if he fails or refuses to forsake his favorites when conditions demand it." Typical favorites are the carotid artery, femoral artery, jugular vein, subclavian vein. There are various choices of embalming fluid. If Flextone is used, it will produce a "mild, flexible rigidity. The skin retains a velvety softness, the tissues are rubbery and pliable. Ideal for women and children." It may be blended with B. and G. Products Company's Lyf-Lyk tint, which is guaranteed to reproduce "nature's own skin texture . . . the velvety appearance of living tissue." Suntone comes in three separate tints: Suntan; Special Cosmetic Tint, a pink shade "especially indicated for young female subjects"; and Regular Cosmetic Tint, moderately pink. 8

About three to six gallons of dyed and perfumed solution of formaldehyde, glycerin, borax, phenol, alcohol, and water are soon circulating through Mr. Jones, whose mouth has been sewn together with a "needle directed upward between the upper lip and gum and brought out through the left nostril," with the corners raised slightly "for a more pleasant expression." If he should be bucktoothed, his teeth are cleaned with Bon Ami and coated with colorless nail polish. His eyes, meanwhile, are closed with flesh-tinted eye caps and eye cement. 9

The next step is to have at Mr. Jones with a thing called a trocar. 10
This is a long, hollow needle attached to a tube. It is jabbed into the abdomen, poked around the entrails and chest cavity, the contents of which are pumped out and replaced with "cavity fluid." This done, and the hole in the abdomen sewn up, Mr. Jones's face is heavily creamed (to protect the skin from burns which may be caused by leakage of the chemicals), and he is covered with a sheet and left unmolested for a while. But not for long—there is more, much more, in store for him. He has been embalmed, but not yet restored, and the best time to start the restorative work is eight to ten hours after embalming, when the tissues have become firm and dry.

The object of all this attention to the corpse, it must be remem- 11
bered, is to make it presentable for viewing in an attitude of healthy repose. "Our customs require the presentation of our dead in the semblance of normality . . . unmarred by the ravages of illness, disease or mutilation," says Mr. J. Sheridan Mayer in his *Restorative Art.* This is rather a large order since few people die in the full bloom of health, unravaged by illness and unmarked by some disfigurement. The funeral industry is equal to the challenge: "In some cases the gruesome appearance of a mutilated or disease-ridden subject may be quite discouraging. The task of restoration may seem impossible and shake the confidence of the embalmer. This is the time for intestinal fortitude and determination. Once the formative work is begun and affected tissues are cleaned or removed, all doubts of success vanish. It is surprising and gratifying to discover the results which may be obtained."

The embalmer, having allowed an appropriate interval to 12
elapse, returns to the attack, but now he brings into play the skill and equipment of sculptor and cosmetician. Is a hand missing? Casting one in plaster of Paris is a simple matter. "For replacement purposes, only a cast of the back of the hand is necessary; this is within the ability of the average operator and is quite adequate." If a lip or two, a nose or an ear should be missing, the embalmer has at hand a variety of restorative waxes with which to model replacements. Pores and skin texture are simulated by stippling with a little brush, and over this cosmetics are laid on. Head off? Decapitation cases are rather routinely handled. Ragged edges are trimmed, and head joined to torso with a series of splints, wires and sutures. It is a good idea to have a little something at the neck—a scarf or high collar—when time for viewing comes. Swollen mouth? Cut out tissue as needed from inside the lips. If too much is removed, the surface contour can easily be restored by padding with cotton. Swollen

necks and cheeks are reduced by removing tissue through vertical incisions made down each side of the neck. "When the deceased is casketed, the pillow will hide the suture incisions . . . as an extra precaution against leakage, the suture may be painted with liquid sealer."

The opposite condition is more likely to present itself—that of emaciation. His hypodermic syringe now loaded with massage cream, the embalmer seeks out and fills the hollowed and sunken areas by injection. In this procedure the backs of the hands and fingers and the under-chin area should not be neglected. 13

Positioning the lips is a problem that recurrently challenges the ingenuity of the embalmer. Closed too tightly, they tend to give a stern, even disapproving expression. Ideally, embalmers feel, the lips should give the impression of being ever so slightly parted, the upper lip protruding slightly for a more youthful appearance. This takes some engineering, however, as the lips tend to drift apart. Lip drift can sometimes be remedied by pushing one or two straight pins through the inner margin of the lower lip and then inserting them between the two front upper teeth. If Mr. Jones happens to have no teeth, the pins can just as easily be anchored in his Armstrong Face Former and Denture Replacer. Another method to maintain lip closure is to dislocate the lower jaw, which is then held in its new position by a wire run through holes which have been drilled through the upper and lower jaws at the midline. As the French are fond of saying, *il faut souffrir pour être belle.*[6] 14

If Mr. Jones has died of jaundice, the embalming fluid will very likely turn him green. Does this deter the embalmer? Not if he has intestinal fortitude. Masking pastes and cosmetics are heavily laid on, burial garments and casket interiors are color-correlated with particular care, and Jones is displayed beneath rose-colored lights. Friends will say, "How *well* he looks." Death by carbon monoxide, on the other hand, can be rather a good thing from the embalmer's viewpoint: "One advantage is the fact that this type of discoloration is an exaggerated form of a natural pink coloration." This is nice because the healthy glow is already present and needs but little attention. 15

The patching and filling completed, Mr. Jones is now shaved, washed and dressed. Cream-based cosmetic, available in pink, flesh, 16

[6]"You have to suffer if you want to be beautiful" (editor's note).

suntan, brunette and blond, is applied to his hands and face, his hair is shampooed and combed (and, in the case of Mrs. Jones, set), his hands manicured. For the horny-handed son of toil special care must be taken; cream should be applied to remove ingrained grime, and the nails cleaned. "If he were not in the habit of having them manicured in life, trimming and shaping is advised for better appearance—never questioned by kin."

Jones is now ready for casketing (this is the present participle of the verb "to casket"). In this operation, his right shoulder should be depressed slightly "to turn the body a bit to the right and soften the appearance of lying flat on the back." Positioning the hands is a matter of importance, and special rubber positioning blocks may be used. The hands should be cupped slightly for a more lifelike, relaxed appearance. Proper placement of the body requires a delicate sense of balance. It should lie as high as possible in the casket, yet not so high that the lid, when lowered, will hit the nose. On the other hand, we are cautioned, placing the body too low "creates the impression that the body is in a box." 17

Jones is next wheeled into the appointed slumber room where a few last touches may be added—his favorite pipe placed in his hand or, if he was a great reader, a book propped into position. (In the case of little Master Jones a Teddy bear may be clutched.) Here he will hold open house for a few days, visiting hours 10 A.M. to 9 P.M. 18

Meanings and Values

1. What is the author's tone? (See "Guide to Terms": *Style/Tone.*) What does the tone reveal about the writer's attitude toward the intense concern with the appearance of the dead exhibited by embalmers (and other people)?
2. Why was it formerly "almost mandatory" for some relative to witness the embalming procedure (Par. 2)?
3. Do you believe that public information about this procedure would cost mortuaries much embalming business (Par. 3)? Why, or why not? Why *do* people subject their dead to such a process?
4. Use the three-part system of evaluation found under *Evaluation* in the "Guide to Terms" to judge the success of this process analysis.

Expository Techniques

1. What is the central theme? (Guide: *Unity.*) Which parts of the writing, if any, do not contribute to the theme, thus damaging unity? Which contribute to unity?
2. Beginning with Paragraph 4, list or mark the transitional devices that help to bridge paragraphs. (Guide: *Transition.*) Briefly explain how coherence is aided by such interparagraph transitions.
3. In this selection, far more than in most, emphasis can best be studied in connection with style. In fact, the two are almost indistinguishable here, and few, if any, of the other methods of achieving emphasis are used at all. (Guide: *Emphasis; Style/Tone.*) Consider each of the following stylistic qualities (some may overlap; others are included in diction) and illustrate, by examples, how each creates emphasis.
   a. Number and selection of details—for example, the equipment and "aids" (Par. 5)
   b. Understatement—for example, the "chances of live burial" (Par. 7)
   c. Special use of quotations—for example, "that the body is in a box" (Par. 17)
   d. Sarcasm and/or other forms of irony—for example, "How *well* he looks" (Par. 15) (Guide: *Irony.*)

Diction and Vocabulary

1. Much of the essay's unique style (with resulting emphasis) comes from qualities of diction. Use examples to illustrate the following. (Some may be identical to those of the preceding answer, but they need not be.)
   a. Choice of common, low-key words to achieve sarcasm through understatement—for example, "This is nice. . . ." (Par. 15)
   b. Terms of violence—for example, "returns to the attack" (Par. 12)
   c. Terms of the living—for example, "will hold open house" (Par. 18)
   d. The continuing use of "Mr. Jones"
2. Illustrate the meaning of "connotation" with examples of the quotations from morticians. (Guide: *Connotation/Denotation.*) Are these also examples of "euphemism"?
3. Use the dictionary as needed to understand the meanings of the following words: docility, perpetuation (Par. 1); *inherent, mandatory* (2); *intractable, reticence, raison d'être* (3); *ingenious* (5); *rudimentary, cellular, somatic* (7); *carotid artery, femoral artery, subclavian vein* (8); *semblance* (11); *simulated, stippling, sutures* (12); *emaciation* (13); *dispel* (7, title).

READ TO WRITE

1. **Collaborating:** Working in a group, think of any other common practices in which we alter appearances to hide reality or create a new reality. Choose one practice and analyze it in detail as the potential subject for an essay.
2. **Considering Audience:** Many of the processes Mitford describes would be likely to upset or offend many readers, yet she presents them in a way that does not do so except to help readers regard them critically. Choose one such passage and discuss in writing the techniques Mitford employs to present the subject critically but without making it seem distasteful to most readers.
3. **Developing an Essay:** Mitford presents an unpleasant subject—dead bodies—in such detail that it becomes intriguing (her humor helps here, too). Use a similar strategy in your own writing about a subject that readers might at first consider distasteful or boring.

(NOTE: Suggestions for topics requiring development by PROCESS ANALYSIS follow.)

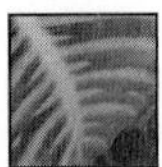

Writing Suggestions for Chapter 7

Analogy

From one of the following topics, develop a central theme into an informational process analysis, showing:

1. How you selected a college
2. How you selected your future career or major field of study
3. How your family selected a home
4. How an unusual sport is played
5. How religious faith is achieved
6. How gasoline is made
7. How the air (or water) in ______ becomes polluted
8. How lightning kills
9. How foreign policy is made
10. How political campaigns are financed
11. How ______ was rebuilt
12. How fruit blossoms are pollinated
13. How a computer chip is designed or made

Everyday Uses

1. Choose a useful everyday activity that you can do well but that others often do poorly (or are unable to accomplish), and create an essay that uses process analysis to share your skills with readers.
2. Choose an activity at which you excel but others don't. Share your pleasure at this skill through an essay that uses process analysis to explain your ability and suggests ways that others might develop a similar skill.

Collaborative Exercises

1. As a group, write an informative paper on the process of completing a collaborative project. Consider how you plan team meetings, team tasks, team evaluations, and so on.

2. For topics 2a–h, have each member of a group write the directional process for a different audience-reader. Predefine each person's audience profile using an audience profile sheet.
   a. How to do any of the processes suggested by topics 1a–e (This treatment will require a different viewpoint, one that is completely objective, and it may require a different organization.)
   b. How to overcome shyness
   c. How to overcome stage fright
   d. How to make the best use of study time
   e. How to write a college composition
   f. How to sell an ugly house
   g. How to prepare livestock or any other entry for a fair
   h. How to start a club (or some other kind of recurring activity)

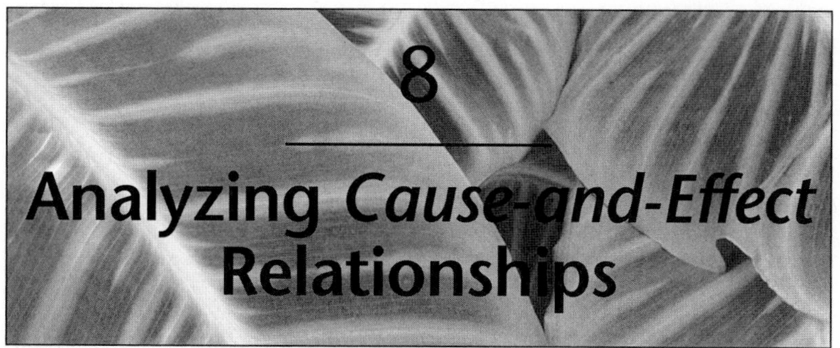

8

Analyzing *Cause-and-Effect* Relationships

Writing built around cause-effect analysis addresses questions like "Why did that happen?" and "What is likely to happen next?" It can grow from simple curiosity about the *why* of events or from a practical desire to avoid unpleasant or unforeseen consequences. Above all, cause-effect analysis focuses on relationships, the links between one phenomenon and another. When you employ the pattern in expository writing, you need to do more than identify possible causes or consequences. You need to establish a reasonable relationship among them by showing how both logic and the available evidence point to the relationship. After all, two things that often occur together, such as storms and tornadoes, are not *necessarily* related. Since many storms occur without the accompaniment of tornadoes, a cause-effect analysis would focus first on identifying those kinds of storms frequently associated with the appearance of tornadoes, then isolate specific causal features that can be demonstrably linked to funnel clouds and destructive winds.

A search for cause and effect can be rigorously scientific ("Researchers debate possible links between caffeine consumption and heart disease") or it can be personal ("Why do I always end up arguing with my parents over things we all know are unimportant?"). It can take the form of causal analysis, trying to identify all the links in a causal chain: remote causes, necessary conditions, and direct causes to immediate effects and more distant consequences. Or it can identify the many conditions and forces that work together in no particular pattern to shape a person's life, create a particular situation, or help bring about events.

Most expository uses of the pattern do not require scientific rigor, however. For social or cultural events, like the growth of a political movement or the rise of a new form of art, we can seldom hope to pinpoint exact causes and effects. Instead, we can identify the roots of contemporary phenomena and develop an awareness of the kinds of changes that may be going on today. This is the kind of explanation provided by the following paragraph, which looks at the early development of a popular kind of music.

> Rap started in the discos, not the midtown glitter palaces like Studio 54 or New York, New York, but at Mel Quinn's on 42nd Street and Club 371 in the Bronx, where a young Harlemite who called himself D.J. Hollywood spun on the weekends. It wasn't unusual for black club jocks to talk to their audiences in the jive style of the old personality deejays. Two of the top black club spinners of the day, Pete (D.J.) Jones and Maboya, did so. Hollywood, just an adolescent when he started, created a more complicated, faster style, with more rhymes than his older mentors and call-and-response passages to encourage reaction from the dancers. At local bars, discos, and many illegal after-hours spots frequented by street people, Hollywood developed a huge word-of-mouth reputation. Tapes of his parties began appearing around the city on the then new and incredibly loud Japanese portable cassette players flooding into America. In Harlem, Kurtis Blow, Eddie Cheeba, and D.J. Lovebug Star-ski; in the Bronx, Junebug Star-ski, Grandmaster Flash, and Melle Mel; in Brooklyn, two kids from the projects called Whodini; and in Queens, Russell and Joey, the two youngest sons from the middle-class Simmons household—all shared a fascination with Hollywood's use of the rhythmic breaks in his club mixes and his verbal dexterity. These kids would all grow up to play a role in the local clubs and, later, a few would appear on the national scene to spread Hollywood's style. Back in the 1970s, while disco reigned in the media, the Black Main Streets of New York were listening to D.J. Hollywood, and learning.
>
> —Nelson George, *The Death of Rhythm and Blues*

WHY USE CAUSE-EFFECT ANALYSIS?

Some causes and effects are not very complicated; at least their explanation requires only a simple statement. New parking facilities are not built because a college (or town) lacks the money in its budget. But frequently a much more thorough analysis is required. New parking facilities are not built partly because of expense and partly because they simply seem to encourage more traffic and rapidly become jammed. The college (or town) delays the project until it can study *why* parking facilities quickly become overloaded. In writing, cause-effect as an expository pattern helps address these kinds of complicated relationships.

Writers often respond to puzzling or intriguing phenomena with causal explanations. In its simplest form, the strategy consists of a description of a puzzling phenomenon (the persistence of alcoholism in families, for example) followed by an explanation or an examination of possible causes. The simplicity of this pattern gives it considerable power and flexibility. Writers speculating about social patterns and individual behavior often use the strategy or vary it to consider possible consequences. In dealing with effects, the strategy consists of discussion of a new or previously unnoticed phenomenon whose consequences are unfamiliar followed by consideration of its likely effects, or it begins with discussion of desired effects followed by examination of actions or arrangements most likely to produce these consequences.

Causal explanations appear frequently in academic and research writing. Scholars often look for a particularly puzzling element in a subject or for a point over which there has been much disagreement and then build an essay in an attempt to explain the phenomena: "Perhaps the most interesting feature of early jazz is. . . ."; "Over the last decade researchers have argued about the role of aggressive behavior in corporate organizations. . . ."

CHOOSING A STRATEGY

To explain fully the causes of a phenomenon, writers must seek not only *immediate* causes (the ones encountered first) but also *ultimate* causes (the basic, underlying factors that help to explain the more apparent ones). Business or professional people, as well as students, often have a pressing need for this type of analysis. How else could they fully understand or report on a failing sales campaign, diminishing church membership, a local increase in traffic accidents, or a decline in crime and the use of drugs? The immediate cause of a disastrous warehouse fire could be faulty electrical wiring, but this might be attributed in turn to the company's unwise economic measures, which might be traced even further to undue pressures on the management to show large profits. The written analysis might logically stop at any point of course, with the actual strategy a writer employs depending on the purpose of the writing and the audience for which it is intended.

Similarly, both the immediate and ultimate *effects* of an action or situation may, or may not, need to be fully explored. If a 5 percent pay raise is granted, what will be the immediate effect on the cost of production, leading to what ultimate effects on prices and, in some cases, on the economy of a business, a town, or perhaps the entire region?

Whatever the extent of the reasoning your writing task demands, you need to make certain strategic choices. Will you focus on causes, effects, or both? Will you focus on a single clear chain of causes and effects or provide a more general discussion, highlighting many contributing factors? How will you use the opening of your writing to convince readers of the importance of understanding the causes or effects of a phenomenon or situation and interest them in reading about the topic?

Because causes and effects often form intricate, potentially confusing relationships, you should develop a straightforward plan for your writing—an organization that will help readers understand the order you have discovered within the complexity. This is particularly important when a phenomenon has multiple causes, as in the following example.

Introduction: Example of a diverse audience at a horror movie responding with both fear and pleasure to the film

  Tentative thesis: People choose to watch horror films for many different reasons, each depending on the individual's taste and psychological makeup.

Cause 1: The "thrill" of being shocked and scared

  Support: Some people are psychologically disposed to get pleasure from danger, especially when it is imaginary.

  Support: Certain people's brain chemistry may mean that they (like people who engage in extreme sports) get a feeling of well-being after feeling that they have placed themselves in danger.

Cause 2: The twists and turns of the plot

  Support: Many people enjoy the kinds of complicated, surprising plots they find in horror movies (similar in some ways to the kinds of plots people enjoy in adventure stories).

Cause 3: The pleasure of "escape"

  Support: The dangers faced by characters in the films allow viewers to escape for a short time from their somewhat less serious but more real everyday problems.

Cause 4: Fashion

Support: Horror movies are popular. Going to them with friends and talking about them afterwards is a pleasant social experience.

Summary

Your writing will need to do more than identify causes and effects. It will need to provide readers with evidence that you have correctly identified the relationships. As a result, much writing that employs this pattern relies on detailed research. Printed sources, television documentaries, and interviews can provide you with useful information. You should keep such research focused, however, so you don't stray too far into areas that are interesting but not really related to the causes or consequences you will be discussing.

DEVELOPING CAUSE-EFFECT ANALYSIS

Discussions of causes and effects can easily become complex and confusing, so consider using the following strategies for alerting readers to the relationships among causes and effects. A concise statement near the beginning of an essay can point out relationships you plan to examine. Statements in the body of an essay can remind readers of the points you are making and the supporting details and reasoning you are providing. Likewise, terms that identify causes and effects or that indicate their relationships can help guide readers' attention:

result	effect	accomplishment	development
outcome	antecedent	source	first
cause	instrument	as a result	second
means	thus	motive	third
consequence	reason	agent	next

When you analyze causes and effects, your readers must always have confidence in the thoroughness and logic of your reasoning. Here are some ways to avoid the most common faults in causal reasoning:

1. Never mistake the fact that something happens with or after another occurrence as evidence of a causal relationship—for example, that a black cat crossing the road caused the flat tire a few minutes later, or that a course in English composition caused a student's nervous breakdown that same semester.

2. Consider all possible relevant factors before attributing causes. Perhaps studying English did result in a nervous breakdown, but the cause may also have been ill health, trouble at home, the stress of working while attending college, or the anguish of a love affair. (The composition course, by providing an "emotional" outlet, may even have helped postpone the breakdown!)
3. Support the analysis by more than mere assertions: offer evidence. It would not often be enough to *tell* why Shakespeare's wise Othello believed the villainous Iago—the dramatist's lines should be used as evidence, possibly supported by the opinions of at least one literary scholar. If you are explaining that capital punishment deters crime, do not expect the reader to take your word for it—give before-and-after statistics or the testimony of reliable authorities.
4. Be careful not to omit any links in the chain of causes or effects unless you are certain that the readers for whom the writing is intended will automatically make the right connections themselves—and this is frequently a dangerous assumption. To unwisely omit one or more of the links might leave the reader with only a vague, or even erroneous, impression of the causal connection, possibly invalidating all that follows and thus making the entire writing ineffective.
5. Be honest and objective. Writers (or thinkers) who bring their old prejudices to the task of casual analysis, or who fail to see the probability of *multiple* causes or effects, are almost certain to distort their analyses or to make them so superficial, so thin, as to be almost worthless.

Student Essay

As an expository pattern, cause-effect can explore personal matters as well as those of broader public interest. Aware of her difficulties in coming to terms with her mother's death, Sarah Egri used the pattern to explore one possible reason for her feelings.

How a Public Document Affected My Life by Sarah Egri

Public documents are a part of everyday life. The presence of these documents can affect a person's life in many different ways. However, the *absence* of such documents may also affect a person's life, such as my

Gives topic an interesting twist: an absence

own. I believe the absence of my mother's death certificate has affected my life.

rather than a presence is the cause.

Thesis statement

Background to help readers understand the cause and the effects

When I was around 12 years old, my mother became very ill with cancer. She was diagnosed with lymphoma, which is cancer within the lymph nodes. She sought several types of medical treatment, but nothing seemed to help her. During this time, the doctor told my family that my mom did not have much longer to live. The doctor also told my mom this, but she did not believe him, nor did she want to. At this point, I did not know what was happening. Since I was so young, I did not understand. I listened to my mom and believed her because I did not want her to die. She and I were quite close. I was able to talk to her about anything and everything. There was still so much I had to learn from her, still so many more memories to be made.

When I was 14 years old my mother passed away. I will never forget that night, for it seemed like a dream; it seemed as though it were not really happening. I awoke to a phone call at one-thirty in the morning saying that my mom had passed away. No more would I be able to talk with her, or learn from her, or make precious memories. She was gone, yet it felt like it was not real. I could not grasp the concept that she would no longer be a part of my life. The years passed by and I only got *used* to my mom not being there; I never faced the fact that she had died. The day that my mother died, I never saw her death certificate. Perhaps if I had seen it, her death would have seemed more realistic.

One of the effects

The cause

Now as I think back, I *never* saw my mother's death certificate. A death certificate is a document that is signed by a doctor, giving information about the time, place, and cause of a person's death. This document finalizes everything. It may be that since I never saw this document, I never came to the realization that she had passed. Since I did not believe she *would* die, I cannot bring myself to believe that she *did* die. If I had seen the death certificate, I would have come to terms with her death.

Examines and explains the cause

Generalizes about the effects

How can such a *small* document make such a *big* difference in my life? All a death certificate is, is a small piece of paper with a person's name on it. I think it might have made a difference because it's an *official* notification of my mom's death. It's a *real,* physical thing; it is more real than just *thinking* someone has died.

Explains the force and importance of public documents

My mother's death certificate has affected my life, even though I never did see it. The absence of this document affects my life, because if I had seen it, I would have come to the realization that she is really gone. If I had seen that document, her death would have been finalized in my mind and I would not just be *used to* her not being around; I would *know* that she has passed and is no longer with us. The death certificate finalizes a person's death, and if I had seen my mom's it would have finalized her death for me. Since I did not see this document, I have not brought my mom's death to a close. Perhaps the *absence* of some documents, such as my mother's death certificate, can affect a person's life more than the presence of other documents.

Explores effects

Ends with a contrast between absence and presence

SUSAN PERRY AND JIM DAWSON

SUSAN PERRY is a former staff writer for Time-Life, Inc., and now works full-time as a freelance writer specializing in health, business, and women's issues. Her articles have appeared in such publications as *Ms.*, the *Washington Post,* and the *Minneapolis Star-Tribune.* She is the author of *Nightmare* (1985) and *Natural Menopause* (1992).

JAMES DAWSON is a science reporter who writes regularly for the *Minneapolis Star-Tribune.* Perry and Dawson coauthored *The Secrets Our Body Clocks Reveal* (1988).

What's Your Best Time of Day?

This essay, published as a magazine article, is drawn from *The Secrets Our Body Clocks Reveal.* The piece opens with examples of some puzzling behaviors, looks at their causes in the rhythms of our bodies, then examines some further effects of these rhythms. The authors make use of examples, classification, and process to support the cause-effect pattern and provide practical advice for taking advantage of the biological patterns that help govern our lives.

Every fall, Jane, a young mother and part-time librarian, begins to eat more and often feels sleepy. Her mood is also darker, especially when she awakens in the morning; it takes all her energy just to drag herself out of bed. These symptoms persist until April, when warmer weather and longer days seems to lighten her mood and alleviate her cravings for food and sleep. 1

Joseph, a 48-year-old engineer for a Midwestern computer company, feels cranky early in the morning. But as the day progresses, he becomes friendlier and more accommodating. 2

All living organisms, from mollusks to men and women, exhibit biological rhythms. Some are short and can be measured in minutes or hours. Others last days or months. The peaking of body temperature, which occurs in most people every evening, is a daily rhythm. The menstrual cycle is a monthly rhythm. The increase in sexual drive in the autumn—not in the spring, as poets would have us believe—is a seasonal, or yearly, rhythm. 3

The idea that our bodies are in constant flux is fairly new—and goes against traditional medical training. In the past, many doctors were taught to believe the body has a relatively stable, or homeostatic, 4

internal environment. Any fluctuations were considered random
and not meaningful enough to be studied.

As early as the 1940s, however, some scientists questioned the 5
homeostatic view of the body. Franz Halberg, a young European scientist working in the United States, noticed that the number of white
blood cells in laboratory mice was dramatically higher and lower at
different times of day. Gradually, such research spread to the study
of other rhythms in other life forms, and the findings were sometimes startling. For example, the time of day when a person receives
X-ray or drug treatment for cancer can affect treatment benefits and
ultimately mean the difference between life and death.

This new science is called chronobiology, and the evidence sup- 6
porting it has become increasingly persuasive. Along the way, the
scientific and medical communities are beginning to rethink their
ideas about how the human body works, and gradually what had
been considered a minor science just a few years ago is being studied
in major universities and medical centers around the world. There
are even chronobiologists working for the National Aeronautics and
Space Administration, as well as for the National Institutes of Health
and other government laboratories.

With their new findings, they are teaching us things that can liter- 7
ally change our lives—by helping us organize ourselves so we can
work *with* our natural rhythms rather than against them. This can enhance our outlook on life as well as our performance at work and play.

Because they are easy to detect and measure, more is known of 8
daily—or circadian (Latin for "about a day")—rhythms than other
types. The most obvious daily rhythm is the sleep/wake cycle. But
there are other daily cycles as well: temperature, blood pressure, hor-
mone levels. Amid these and the body's other changing rhythms,
you are simply a different person at 9 A.M. than you are at 3 P.M. How
you feel, how well you work, your level of alertness, your sensitivity
to taste and smell, the degree with which you enjoy food or take pleasure in music—all are changing throughout the day.

Most of us seem to reach our peak of alertness around noon. 9
Soon after that, alertness declines, and sleepiness may set in by
midafternoon.

Your short-term memory is best during the morning—in fact, 10
about 15 percent more efficient than at any other time of day. So,
students, take heed: when faced with a morning exam, it really does
pay to review your notes right before the test is given.

Long-term memory is different. Afternoon is the best time for 11
learning material that you want to recall days, weeks or months

later. Politicians, business executives or others who must learn speeches would be smart to do their memorizing during that time of day. If you are a student, you would be wise to schedule your more difficult classes in the afternoon, rather than in the morning. You should also try to do most of your studying in the afternoon, rather than late at night. Many students believe they memorize better while burning the midnight oil because their short-term recall is better during the wee hours of the morning than in the afternoon. But short-term memory won't help them much several days later, when they face the exam.

By contrast, we tend to do best on cognitive tasks—things that require the juggling of words and figures in one's head—during the morning hours. This might be a good time, say, to balance a checkbook. 12

Your manual dexterity—the speed and coordination with which you perform complicated tasks with your hands—peaks during the afternoon hours. Such work as carpentry, typing or sewing will be a little easier at this time of day. 13

What about sports? During afternoon and early evening, your coordination is at its peak, and you're able to react the quickest to an outside stimulus—like a baseball speeding toward you at home plate. Studies have also shown that late in the day, when your body temperature is peaking, you will *perceive* a physical workout to be easier and less fatiguing—whether it actually is or not. That means you are more likely to work harder during a late-afternoon or early-evening workout, and therefore benefit more from it. Studies involving swimmers, runners, shot-putters and rowing crews have shown consistently that performance is better in the evening than in the morning. 14

In fact, all of your senses—taste, sight, hearing, touch and smell—may be at their keenest during late afternoon and early evening. That could be why dinner usually tastes better to us than breakfast and why bright lights irritate us at night. 15

Even our perception of time changes from hour to hour. Not only does time seem to fly when you're having fun, but it also seems to fly even faster if you are having that fun in the late afternoon or early evening, when your body temperature is also peaking. 16

While all of us follow the same general pattern of ups and downs, the exact timing varies from person to person. It all depends on how your "biological" day is structured—how much of a morning or night person you are. The earlier your biological day gets going, the earlier you are likely to enter—and exit—the peak 17 times for performing various tasks. An extreme morning person and an extreme night person may have circadian cycles that are a few hours apart.

Each of us can increase our knowledge about our individual rhythms. Learn how to listen to the inner beats of your body; let them set the pace of your day. You will live a healthier—and happier—life. As no less an authority than the Bible tells us, "To every thing there is a season, and a time to every purpose under heaven." 18

Meanings and Values

1. What cause(s) and effect(s) do the writers discuss in this selection?
2. According to the explanations in this essay, what are the best times to undertake the following activities, and why?

   a. Play a sport

   b. Balance a checkbook

   c. Learn a speech

   d. Prepare for an exam

Expository Techniques

1. What functions do the examples that open the essay perform for readers? (See "Guide to Terms": *Introductions.*)
2. Where in the essay do the authors use classification? Why? Where do the authors use process analysis? Why?
3. Would this essay be more effective if discussions of the causes and the effects were more clearly separated? Why, or why not? (Guide: *Evaluation.*)
4. Discuss the arrangement of Paragraphs 9–12, paying special attention to parallel structures and transitions within and between paragraphs. (Guide: *Unity; Parallel Structure.*)

Diction and Vocabulary

1. In what ways does the diction in Paragraphs 1 and 2 emphasize the contrasts being illustrated? (Guide: *Diction.*)
2. Discuss how the authors provide explanations of the following scientific or otherwise unfamiliar terms in the text so that readers will not have to pause to look them up: *homeostatic* (Par. 4); *circadian* (8); *cognitive tasks* (12); *manual dexterity* (13).

3. Does the allusion that concludes the essay seem appropriate? Why, or why not? Try looking up the passage in the Bible (Ecclesiastes 3:1) to see if its original meaning is similar to the one it has in the context of this essay.

Read to Write

1. **Collaborating:** Assume for a moment that Perry and Dawson's view of the cause-effect relationship of body cycles and behavior is accurate. In a group, discuss how typical academic or work schedules might need to be altered to take into account the patterns described by the authors. What common practices seem particularly in need of change given the information provided here? As a group, plan an essay with such practical consequences as its topic.
2. **Considering Audience:** In a magazine like *Discover* or *Scientific American,* read an article that offers a physical explanation of human behavior. Or in a magazine like *Psychology Today,* read an article that offers a psychological or social explanation of behavior. Then prepare a brief analysis of the different kinds of audiences to which this article and Perry and Dawson's essay are directed.
3. **Developing an Essay:** Perry and Dawson use numerous examples to explain and confirm the effects of body cycles. Do your experiences agree with what the authors say about the cycles that guide our behavior? In an essay of your own, provide examples that either support or contradict their conclusions, or that do the same for some other well-known explanation of behavior.

(NOTE: Suggestions for topics requiring development by analysis of CAUSE AND EFFECT are on pp. 302–303 at the end of this chapter.)

MARY ROACH

MARY ROACH is a freelance writer specializing in science who has published three books, *Stiff: The Curious Lives of Human Cadavers* (2003), *Spook: Science Tackles the Afterlife* (2005) and *Bonk: The Curious Coupling of Science and Sex* (2008). She was born in New Hampshire, earned a B.A. from Wesleyan University, and currently lives in San Francisco.

My Father the Geezer

In "My Father the Geezer," Mary Roach begins with the assumption that most readers hold negative views about the likely effects of having older parents, then goes on to undermine them by presenting in often humorous detail the consequences in her own life of having a "geezer" for a parent. This essay first appeared in the *New York Times Magazine.*

My father was 65 when I was born. Even to myself, the statement sits funny, like one of those how-so brain teasers with the hidden loophole—the boy's mother is the doctor. But there is no loophole. He was my biological father, 20 years older than my mother. He had children late because he married late. I came in under the wire. 1

People invariably want to know what it was like growing up with an old father. Some want to know because they're coming to parenthood relatively late themselves and wonder how it will affect their children. Most are just rubbernecking. There's a "Good God!" in their tone, as though I'd been suckled by wolves. Who fed whom, they're wondering. Did I dress him or did he dress me? To which I reply that he was a young 65, white-haired but red-blooded. 2

Granted, my upbringing seemed a little odd. I could recite the names of all the members of the Lawrence Welk musical family. I practiced phonemes by reading aloud from *Modern Maturity.* My first paying job, at age 7, was to sit on my father's lap with a pair of tweezers and cull overgrown ear hairs for 2 cents a pluck. 3

One thing I didn't do was engage in those "When I'm age X, he'll be X" calculations. Children live in the moment. If he was around next Saturday to drive me to the riding ring, that was good enough. We'd deal with the strangeness when we got to it. How will an 82-year-old cope with a 16-year-old? As best he could, and with frequent naps. 4

Fortunately for all involved, I wasn't a particularly difficult teen-ager. I remember one summer afternoon, walking out of the 5

A&P with a roll of "Ripe for Tonight" avocado stickers I'd swiped from a stockboy's cart. My father, who'd been waiting in the car, said, "What's under your sweatshirt?" "Nothing," I lied. He just shook his head and went back to his newspaper. For whatever reason, I never moved on to the big stuff: jewelry, clothing, actual avocados. I like to think my father's indifference took the thrill out of shoplifting. More likely, he was just lucky.

In the end, what most people fixate on is that my father was too 6
old to—as they often put it—play ball with me. This is true. I can't recall ever seeing him run. He didn't swim or ride a bicycle or rollerskate. The extent of my father's physical activity was an evening constitutional to the end of Dogford Road, in his Irish tweed hat, whistling a tune and swinging a Hanover Hardware yardstick as if it were a brass-tipped cane. Perhaps that's why I didn't learn to swim as a child, why I was chosen last for gym teams. Perhaps, and who cares. Show me the support group for children of sedentary parents.

What stands out about my father are not the things he couldn't 7
do but the things he did. That most of them were done from a sitting position hardly seems to matter. My father was an artist, a storyteller, a character. When I was 11, he painted a life-size elephant on the basement floor because elephants were my favorite animal. He taught me to draw, making a squiggle on a sheet of paper and challenging me to finish the picture. He framed my finger paintings and hung them on the living room wall, and when guests commented, he'd make up the name of "a noted abstract artist" and wink at me. My father, in short, was a very cool dad. So he mixed Metamucil in his orange juice. So he turned the TV up loud. So his hands shook on the steering wheel. Of all the undesirable things fathers can be (absent, cruel, cold, immature), old is pretty weak poison.

Parenthood over 60 has its advantages. My father spent a good 8
deal more time with me than the average 30-year-old father can afford to. Retirement is like endless paternity leave. Pop was my day care, my baby sitter, my play date. We didn't break a sweat together, but we had a lot of fun.

To be sure, it could easily have been otherwise. Old fathers are 9
more likely to be invalid fathers, senile fathers, dead fathers. (I like to think I kept mine young at heart.) Sixty-five is not the ideal age to have a baby. You can be too old to be a parent. You can also be too young. Neither has all that much to do with years.

Would my father have been a better parent had he been 30 at the 10
time I was born? Probably not. My father spent his 30's on the road with a theater troupe. He would have resented my arrival, the

shelved aspirations, the loss of freedom I represented. As it was, I was a gift (or so I like to think), an unexpected coda on a long, full life.

Meanings and Values

1. Why does Roach point out that people "fixated" on the fact that her father was "too old to play ball" (Par. 1)? What is the traditional value placed on children playing ball with their fathers? What activities "replaced" this for Roach?
2. Why is the phrase "retirement is endless paternity leave" (Par. 8) significant for readers today who often come from homes with two working parents?
3. What is the significance of the last line of the essay? Why is the musical reference appropriate for an essay on Roach's father?

Expository Techniques

1. Roach tells us that her father married late and consequently was an older parent (Par. 1). Only at the end of the essay does the reader learn what career Roach's father had and the potential reason that he may have settled into marriage later in life. Is it important for the reader to know why Roach's father had children later in life early on in the essay? Would it have been more effective? Why might Roach have waited to share that information with her readers?
2. What positive and negative effects of having an older father does Roach list in this essay? Do they support her response to people that she shares with her readers at the end of Paragraph 2 ("to which I reply that he was a young 65, white-haired but red-blooded")?

Diction and Vocabulary

1. What is the tone of Roach's essay? Does she make light of a serious topic, or is her use of humor very deliberate? Explain. (See "Guide to Terms": *Tone.*)
2. At what point does she take on a serious voice? Why might she have chosen this spot?
3. What kinds of readers might enjoy this piece? Explain.

Read to Write

1. **Collaborating:** Roach shares particular memories of episodes and events with her father. Individually, write a list of the times that you

remember the most with one of your parents. Compare your list with a partner and look for any common threads or activities that you might have. Then look at what you did differently. Write an individual comparison and contrast essay of the memories that you and your partner have with your respective parents. Be sure to include a cause-effect analysis explaining the differences.

2. **Considering Audience:** How would readers who have grown up without a father in the household respond to this essay? Would it have the same impact? Rewrite this essay for a reader who might better identify with a mother or some other woman who was a strong role model. Use a woman in your life as the basis for the essay.

3. **Developing an Essay:** Choose a role model in your life who may have been somewhat different from role models in your friends' lives (i.e., Roach's father was different because of his age). Write an essay similar in style sharing with your reader the experiences that you remember. Be sure that the experiences reflect the different quality that the person you choose possesses.

(NOTE: Suggestions for topics requiring development by analysis of CAUSE AND EFFECT are on pp. 302–303 at the end of this chapter.)

WILLIAM SEVERINI KOWINSKI

WILLIAM SEVERINI KOWINSKI grew up in Greensburg, Pennsylvania. In 1964, the year before the first mall was built in Greensburg, he left to attend Knox College in Illinois. While attending Knox he spent a semester studying in the fiction and poetry workshops at the University of Iowa. Kowinski was a writer and editor for the Boston *Phoenix* and the Washington *Newsworks* and has written articles for a number of national newspapers and magazines including *Esquire, New Times,* and the *New York Times Magazine.* His book *The Malling of America: An Inside Look at the Great Consumer Paradise* (1985) is based on his travels to malls throughout the United States and Canada.

Kids in the Mall: Growing Up Controlled

Over the past 30 years, the number, size, and variety of suburban shopping malls have grown at astonishing rates, replacing, in many cases, both plazas and urban shopping districts. They are now important economic and cultural forces in American and Canadian society. In this chapter from *The Malling of America,* Kowinski looks at some of the ways malls have affected the teenagers who spend much of their time shopping, working, or just hanging around at the mall.

Butch heaved himself up and loomed over the group. "Like it was different for me," he piped. "My folks used to drop me off at the shopping mall every morning and leave me all day. It was like a big free baby-sitter, you know? One night they never came back for me. Maybe they moved away. Maybe there's some kind of a Bureau of Missing Parents I could check with."

—Richard Peck, *Secrets of the Shopping Mall,* a novel for teenagers

From his sister at Swarthmore, I'd heard about a kid in Florida whose mother picked him up after school every day, drove him straight to the mall, and left him there until it closed—all at his insistence. I'd heard about a boy in Washington who, when his family moved from one suburb to another, pedaled his bicycle five miles every day to get back to his old mall, where he once belonged. 1

Their stories aren't unusual. The mall is a common experience for the majority of American youth; they have probably been going there all their lives. Some ran within their first large open space, saw their first fountain, bought their first toy, and read their first book in 2 a mall. They may have smoked their first cigarette or first joint or turned them down, had their first kiss or lost their virginity in the mall parking lot. Teenagers in America now spend more time in the mall than anywhere else but home and school. Mostly it is their choice, but some of that mall time is put in as the result of two-paycheck and single-parent households, and the lack of other viable alternatives. But are these kids being harmed by the mall?

I wondered first of all what difference it makes for adolescents to experience so many important moments in the mall. They are, after all, at play in the fields of its little world and they learn its ways; they adapt to it and make it adapt to them. It's here that these kids get their street sense, only it's mall sense. They are learning the ways of a large-scale artificial environment: its subtleties and flexibilities, its particular pleasures and resonances, and the attitudes it fosters. 3

The presence of so many teenagers for so much time was not something mall developers planned on. In fact, it came as a big surprise. But kids became a fact of mall life very early, and the International Council of Shopping Centers found it necessary to commission a study, which they published along with a guide to mall managers on how to handle the teenage incursion. 4

The study found that "teenagers in suburban centers are bored and come to the shopping centers mainly as a place to go. Teenagers in suburban centers spent more time fighting, drinking, littering and walking than did their urban counterparts, but presented fewer overall problems." The report observed that "adolescents congregated in groups of two to four and predominantly at locations selected by them rather than management." This probably had something to do with the decision to install game arcades, which allow management to channel these restless adolescents into naturally contained areas away from major traffic points of adult shoppers. 5

The guide concluded that mall management should tolerate and even encourage the teenage presence because, in the words of the report, "The vast majority support the same set of values as does shopping center management." *The same set of values* means simply that mall kids are already preprogrammed to be consumers and that the mall can put the finishing touches to them as hard-core, lifelong shoppers just like everybody else. That, after all, is what the mall is about. So it shouldn't be surprising that in spending a lot of time there, adolescents find little that challenges the assumption that the goal of life is to make money and buy products, or that just about everything else in life is to be used to serve those ends. 6

7 Growing up in a high-consumption society already adds inestimable pressure to kids' lives. Clothes consciousness has invaded the grade schools, and popularity is linked with having the best, newest clothes in the currently acceptable styles. Even what they read has been affected. "Miss [Nancy] Drew wasn't obsessed with her wardrobe," noted *Wall Street Journal.* "But today the mystery in teen fiction for girls is what outfit the heroine will wear next." Shopping has become a survival skill and there is certainly no better place to learn it than the mall, where its importance is powerfully reinforced and certainly never questioned.

8 The mall as a university of suburban materialism, where Valley Girls and Boys from coast to coast are educated in consumption, has its other lessons in this era of change in family life and sexual mores and their economic and social ramifications. The plethora of products in the mall, plus the pressure on teens to buy them, may contribute to the phenomenon that psychologist David Elkind calls "the hurried child": kids who are exposed to too much of the adult world too quickly, and must respond with a sophistication that belies their still-tender emotional development. Certainly the adult products marketed for children—form-fitting designer jeans, sexy tops for preteen girls—add to the social pressure to look like an adult, along with the home-grown need to understand adult finances (why mothers must work) and adult emotions (when parents divorce).

9 Kids spend so much time at the mall partly because their parents allow it and even encourage it. The mall is safe, it doesn't seem to harbor any unsavory activities, and there is adult supervision; it is, after all, a controlled environment. So the temptation, especially for working parents, is to let the mall be their babysitter. At least the kids aren't watching TV. But the mall's role as a surrogate mother may be more extensive and more profound.

10 Karen Lansky, a writer living in Los Angeles, has looked into the subject and she told me some of her conclusions about the effects on its teenaged denizens of the mall's controlled and controlling environment. "Structure is the dominant idea, since true 'mall rats' lack just that in their homelives," she said, "and adolescents about to make the big leap into growing up crave more structure than our modern society cares to acknowledge." Karen pointed out some of the elements malls supply that kids used to get from their families, like warmth (Strawberry Shortcake dolls and similar cute and cuddly merchandise), old-fashioned mothering ("We do it all for you," the fast-food slogan), and even home cooking (the "homemade" treats at the food court).

The problem in all this, as Karen Lansky sees it, is that while families nurture children by encouraging growth through the assumption of responsibility and then by letting them rest in the bosom of the family from the rigors of growing up, the mall as a structural mother encourages passivity and consumption, as long as the kid doesn't make trouble. Therefore all they learn about becoming adults is how to act and how to consume. 11

Kids are in the mall not only in the passive role of shoppers—they also work there, especially as fast-food outlets infiltrate the mall's enclosure. There they learn how to hold a job and take responsibility, but still within the same value context. When *CBS Reports* went to Oak Park Mall in suburban Kansas City, Kansas, to tape part of their hour-long consideration of malls, "After the Dream Comes True," they interviewed a teenaged girl who worked in a fast-food outlet there. In a sequence that didn't make the final program, she described the major goal of her present life, which was to perfect the curl on top of the ice-cream cones that were her store's specialty. If she could do that, she would be moved from the lowly soft-drink dispenser to the more prestigious ice-cream division, the curl on top of the status ladder at her restaurant. These are the achievements that are important at the mall. 12

Other benefits of such jobs may also be overrated, according to Laurence D. Steinberg of the University of California at Irvine's social ecology department, who did a study on teenage employment. Their jobs, he found, are generally simple, mindlessly repetitive and boring. They don't really learn anything, and the jobs don't lead anywhere. Teenagers also work primarily with other teenagers; even their supervisors are often just a little older than they are. "Kids need to spend time with adults," Steinberg told me. "Although they get benefits from peer relationships, without parents and other adults it's one-sided socialization. They hang out with each other, have age-segregated jobs, and watch TV." 13

Perhaps much of this is not so terrible or even so terribly different. Now that they have so much more to contend with in their lives, adolescents probably need more time to spend with other adolescents without adult impositions, just to sort things out. Though it is more concentrated in the mall (and therefore perhaps a clearer target), the value system there is really the dominant one of the whole society. Attitudes about curiosity, initiative, self-expression, empathy, and disinterested learning aren't necessarily made in the mall; they are mirrored there, perhaps a bit more intensely—as through a glass brightly. 14

Besides, the mall is not without its educational opportunities. There are bookstores, where there is at least a short shelf of classics at great prices, and other books from which it is possible to learn more than how to do sit-ups. There are tools, from hammers to VCRs, and products, from clothes to records, that can help the young find and express themselves. There are older people with stories, and places to be alone or to talk one-on-one with a kindred spirit. And there is always the passing show. 15

The mall itself may very well be an education about the future. I was struck with the realization, as early as my first forays into Greengate,[1] that the mall is only one of a number of enclosed and controlled environments that are part of the lives of today's young. The mall is just an extension, say, of those large suburban schools—only there's Karmelkorn instead of chem lab, the ice rink instead of the gym: It's high school without the impertinence of classes. 16

Growing up, moving from home to school to the mall—from enclosure to enclosure, transported in cars—is a curiously continuous process, without much in the way of contrast or contract with unenclosed reality. Places must tend to blur into one another. But whatever differences and dangers there are in this, the skills these adolescents are learning may turn out to be useful in their later lives. For we seem to be moving inexorably into an age of preplanned and regulated environments, and this is the world they will inherit. 17

Still, it might be better if they had more of a choice. One teenaged girl confessed to *CBS Reports* that she sometimes felt she was missing something by hanging out at the mall so much. "But I'm here," she said, "and this is what I have." 18

Meanings and Values

1. Do teenagers who spend their time in malls display any obviously unusual behavior? If so, in what ways do they behave? If not, how might one describe their behavior?
2. What question does this essay attempt to answer? Where in the essay is the question asked? Other than providing an answer to the question, what purpose or purposes does this selection have? (See "Guide to Terms": *Purpose.*)

[1]Greengate Mall in Greensburg, Pennsylvania, where Kowinski began his research on malls (Editors' note).

3. What does Kowinski see as the major effects of malls on teenagers? What other, less important effects (if any) does he identify? Discuss whether or not the author presents enough evidence to convince most readers that he has correctly identified the effects.
4. Where in the essay does Kowinski consider causes other than the mall environment for the attitudes and behaviors of teenagers? Explain how the alternative explanation either undermines or adds to his view of the malls.

Expository Techniques

1. What strategies does the author employ in the introduction (Pars. 1–3) to help convince readers of the importance of reading and thinking about what happens to teenagers as a result of the time they spend at malls? (Guide: *Introductions.*)
2. Discuss how the author uses examples, quotations from authorities, and various strategies of emphasis in Paragraphs 8, 9, 11, 13, and 14 to indicate whether or not the effects of malls can be considered harmful. (Guide: *Emphasis.*)
3. Which chapters of the essay are devoted *primarily* to exploring the effects of the mall environment? Which are devoted *primarily* to discussing whether or not the effects are harmful?
4. What use does the author make of qualification in presenting his conclusions in Paragraphs 15 and 17–19? (Guide: *Qualification.*) Explain why this strategy adds to or weakens your confidence in his conclusions.
5. Explain how parallelism in Paragraphs 17 and 18 helps emphasize similarities in the environments. (Guide: *Parallel Structure.*)

Diction and Vocabulary

1. Who is the Nancy Drew alluded to in Paragraph 8? (Guide: *Figures of Speech.*) What is the purpose of this allusion?
2. What transitional devices are used to tie together Paragraphs 7–9? (Guide: *Transition.*) Which are used to link Paragraphs 10–13?
3. If you do not know the meaning of some of the following words, look them up in the dictionary: *loomed, piped* (Par. 1); *viable* (3); *resonances, fosters* (4); *incursion* (5); *inestimable* (8); *mores, ramifications, plethora* (9); *surrogate* (10); *denizens* (11); *nurture* (12); *socialization* (14); *impositions, empathy, disinterested* (15); *kindred* (16); *forays, impertinence* (17); *inexorably* (18).

Read to Write

1. **Collaborating:** Working in a group, use these questions to help develop a topic and plan for an essay: Were malls as important to you

as they were to the people Kowinski describes in his essay? Based on your experience and observations, does Kowinski appear to be overstating the effects of malls on teenagers? What other influences on the lives of teenagers are as important or more important than malls (or than shopping in general)? Are malls important in people's lives because of the special experiences they offer, or simply because they bring together large numbers of people and offer work to many individuals?

2. **Considering Audience:** Kowinski takes a partly negative view of malls and the work they provide. Are readers in general likely to agree or disagree with him? What do you think? Prepare a brief essay analyzing readers' likely reactions to the essay.

3. **Developing an Essay:** What experiences and activities condition us for success or failure? Which ones give us important goals for work, personal relationships, and civic responsibility? Taking an approach similar to the one Kowinski employs in "Kids in the Mall," criticize the influence of the activities that characterize contemporary teenage life. Or, reverse Kowinski's approach and praise the effects of particular activities and experiences.

(NOTE: Suggestions for topics requiring development by analysis of CAUSE AND EFFECT are on pp. 302–303 at the end of this chapter.)

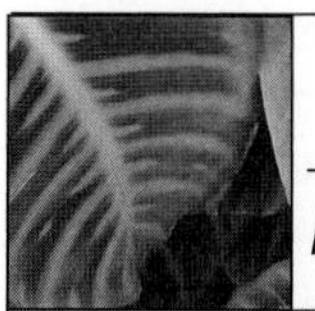

Issues and Ideas

Natural Darkness and Artificial Light

- Cullen Murphy, *Hello, Darkness*
- Verlyn Klinkenborg, *Our Vanishing Night*

Night and day—darkness and lightness—are such regular parts of our day that we seldom take special note of them, much less think of them as human creations. At most we think of them as opportunities (time to look at the stars) or as inconveniences (daylight comes too early and wakes me up). Yet with a little thought we can identify the many ways their alternation shapes our lives. As diurnal (day/night) creatures, our biological and social lives follow specific patterns. When we break these patterns, researchers tell us, we may not like the consequences. People with night jobs, for example, sometimes experience illnesses at a greater rate than those with day jobs.

If we stop for a moment to think about darkness and light, we can see how questions about cause and effect can enlarge our understanding and lead to surprising insights, even if we do not approach the topic from a scientific perspective. We assume that darkness and light are natural, but what if we ask about artificial darkness and artificial light. What is special about a darkened theater, a candlelit dinner, or a sporting event played under the lights? How do these events affect us in special or unusual ways? What causes some people to prefer the night and others the day? Does artificial daylight have the same effects as natural daylight?

A little bit of research can uncover further insights. What are the biological consequences of too much (or too little) light? What causes the difference between natural and artificial light, and what happens as a result of this difference? To say "What is the cause?" or "What is the effect?" opens up all sorts of additional interesting questions.

Both the essays that follow offer some surprising conclusions while opening as many questions as they answer. Cullen Murphy's "Hello, Darkness" looks at the effects of our modern habit of turning the night into day: less sleep, more activity, and an often frantic life style and contrasts it with the times that came before artificial lighting, the lightbulb in particular. Along the way, it points out that our way of living is not inevitable but is the cause of specific technical developments. These developments have created a sharp divide between our lives and those of people living only two hundred years ago. Whether these developments are advances is something Murphy leaves up to readers and to other writers willing to pick up the topic.

Verlyn Klinkenborg, in "Our Vanishing Night," encourages us to see the contemporary split between dark and light not as something natural but as something humans have created. He shows us how the light we have created is changing our world physically as well as socially and asks us to consider the likely effects of the environment we are building. In asking readers to adopt what will be to many a fresh perspective, Klinkenborg follows many contemporary writers in asking people to regard their surroundings not as something natural but as something we continue to create. Focusing on causes and effects helps him raise important questions, leaving it up to readers to pursue answers.

Both essays illustrate what a flexible tools an investigation of causes and effects can be for exploring complicated topics, developing fresh insights, and presenting information and ideas to readers. Though they look at similar topics, each essay takes its own pathway. Each leaves the reader to consider other explanations and other effects as well.

CULLEN MURPHY

CULLEN MURPHY grew up in Greenwich, Connecticut, and attended school in both Greenwich and Dublin, Ireland. He received a B.A. from Amherst College in 1974 and soon after began working in the production department of *Change* magazine. In 1977 he was named editor of the *Wilson Quarterly,* and he has been managing editor of the *Atlantic Monthly* since 1985. In his parallel career, he has written the comic strip *Prince Valiant* since the middle 1970s (a comic strip that his father draws). Murphy is an essayist and nonfiction writer as well. His essays on many different topics have appeared in the *Atlantic Monthly* and other magazines, including *Harper's.* His first book, *Rubbish!* (with William Rathje), appeared in 1992; a collection of his essays, *Just Curious,* was published in 1995; and *The World According to Eve* appeared in 1998.

Hello, Darkness

"Hello, Darkness" was first published in the *Atlantic Monthly* in 1996. With touches of humor, Murphy looks at a subject that troubles many people: lack of sleep. His explanations of a phenomenon that most of us view as a matter of personal behavior may at first seem surprising; nonetheless, they point convincingly to technology and social change as the culprits who have stolen sleep.

Americans today have plenty of reasons to be thankful that they were not Americans a hundred years ago, but they also have more than a few reasons to wish they had been. On the one hand, a hundred years ago there was no Voting Rights Act, no penicillin, and no zipper, and the first daily comic strip was still more than a decade away. On the other hand there was no income tax, no nuclear bomb, and no Maury Povich. Also on the plus side, the average American a hundred years ago was able to sleep 20 percent longer than the average American today. 1

That last figure, supported by various historical studies over the years, comes from a report released by the Better Sleep Council. Americans in the late 1800s are believed to have slept an average of about nine and a half hours a night. The average today is about seven and a half hours. A survey by the Better Sleep Council reveals that on a typical weeknight almost 60 percent of Americans get *less* than seven hours of sleep. Other evidence seems to indicate that the rate of sleep loss is in fact accelerating. 2

Some may argue that the Better Sleep Council's news should be discounted, on the grounds that the council has an interest in the story—it is supported (comfortably?) by the mattress industry. 3

I would counter that the data simply confirm what anecdotal evidence already suggests is true. Independent experts at universities and hospitals speak as one on the subject, observing that as a nation we are laboring under a large and increasingly burdensome "sleep deficit," defined as the difference between how much sleep we need and how much we get. 4

Would that we could pass this particular deficit on to our children! But the only way we can pay it back, the experts say, is by getting more sleep ourselves. Apparently, we're trying. A recent article in *The Wall Street Journal* took note of the growing phenomenon of employees napping at work, but I suspect that this barely covers the interest payments, which go right to Japan. (As you may have noticed, the Japanese are asleep most of the time that we're awake.) 5

Why, by degrees, are we banishing sleep? In a handful of instances, arguably, the cause has been government over-regulation. I am thinking of the recent case of Sari Zayed, of Davis, California. Ms. Zayed, after being overheard by a neighbor, was awakened at 1:30 A.M. by a municipal "noise-abatement officer" who gave her a $50 citation for snoring too loudly. The amount of money that Ms. Zayed subsequently received in damages from the city of Davis would allow her to pay for nightly snoring citations from now to the end of the year. 6

America's sleep deficit, though, is surely a systemic phenomenon. Many commentators would blame it on what might be called the AWOL factor—that is, the American Way of Life. We are by nature a busy and ambitious people whom tectonic social forces—declining average wage, high rate of divorce, two-paycheck families, instant telecommunications, jet travel across time zones, growing popularity of soccer for everyone older than four—have turned into a race of laboratory rats on a treadmill going nowhere ever faster. And there is obviously something to this explanation. It is noteworthy that television shows like *Seinfeld* and *Cheers,* on which nobody seems to have any real responsibilities (circumstances that accord more fully with most viewers' fantasies than with their actual lives), have come to constitute a distinct broadcast genre known as "time porn." 7

It is hard not to credit the importance of the AWOL factor, but I wonder if the driving force behind the sleep deficit is in fact more pervasive, and indeed global in nature: the triumph of light. I am by 8 no means a romantic or a Luddite when it comes to electricity (anyone who is should read Robert Caro's *The Years of Lyndon Johnson* for its haunting description of life in west Texas in the days before rural electrification), and I also don't subscribe to the fashionable opinion that electronic labor-saving devices (personal computers possibly excepted) end up consuming more labor than they save. Yet electricity's ubiquitous and seemingly most innocuous use—to power the common light bulb—could not help exacting a price in sleep. Electricity made it possible for the first time in history for masses of humanity to vanquish darkness.

I had never given much thought to the role of darkness in ordinary human affairs until I read a monograph prepared by John Staudenmaier, a historian of technology and a Jesuit priest, for a recent conference at MIT. (The essay appears in a book called *Progress: Fact or Illusion,* edited by Leo Marx and Bruce Mazlish.) Staudenmaier makes the point—obvious when brought up, though we've mostly lost sight of it—that from the time of the hominid Lucy, in Hadar, Ethiopia, to the time of Thomas Edison, in West Orange, New Jersey, the onset of darkness sharply curtailed most kinds of activity for most of our ancestors. He writes, 9

> Living with electric lights makes it difficult to retrieve the experience of a non-electrified society. For all but the very wealthy, who could afford exorbitant arrays of expensive artificial lights, nightfall brought the works of daytime to a definitive end. Activities that need good light—where sharp tools are wielded or sharply defined boundaries maintained; purposeful activities designed to achieve specific goals; in short, that which we call work—all this subsided in the dim light of evening. Absent the press of work, people typically took themselves safely to home and were left with time in the evening for less urgent and more sensual matters: storytelling, sex, prayer, sleep, dreaming.

Staudenmaier's comments on electric light occupy only a few passages. His larger subject is Western intellectual history, and how metaphors of "enlightenment" came to be associated with orderliness, objectivity, and progress, even as metaphors of darkness came to signify the chaotic, the nonrational, the terrifying. He argues that we have lost, to our detriment, the medieval view that some aspects of life and understanding are not necessarily helped by clarity or harmed by ambiguity. Observing that Enlightenment ideals have "taken a fair beating" in the course of this century, Staudenmaier wonders if it is time to rediscover the metaphysical dark, that place "where visions are born and human purpose renewed." 10

I'll leave that thought where it is. But the implication of electricity in the sleep deficit seems hard to argue with. Whatever it is that we wish or are made to do—pursue leisure, earn a living—there are simply far more usable hours now in which to do it. Darkness was once an ocean into which our capacity to venture was greatly limited; now we are wresting vast areas of permanent lightness from the darkness, much the way the Dutch have wrested polders of dry land from the sea. So vast are these areas that in composite satellite photographs of the world at night the contours of civilization are clearly illuminated—the boundaries of continents, the metastases of cities. Even Wrigley Field, once a reliable pool of nocturnal darkness, would now show up seventeen nights during the baseball season. In the United States at midnight more than five million people are at work at full-time jobs. Supermarkets, gas stations, copy shops—many of these never close. I know of a dentist in Ohio who decided to open an all-night clinic, and has had the last laugh on friends who believed that he would never get patients. The supply-side theory may not have worked in economics, but it has certainly worked with regard to light: the more we get, the more we find ways to put it to use. And, of course, the more we get, the more we distance ourselves from the basic diurnal rhythm in which our evolution occurred. 11

Thomas Edison, famous for subsisting on catnaps, would have wanted it this way. In contrast, Calvin Coolidge, a younger man with an older temperament, slept at least ten and often as much as eleven hours a day. Two world views collide here, and somewhere between them is a balance waiting to be struck. Where and how? The only useful contribution I can make is to recall life in Ireland in the mid-1960s. One of the elements that made it so congenial was a shared expertise among engineers at the Electricity Supply Board which resulted in regular but unpredictably occurring blackouts. The relentless march of time would suddenly be punctuated by a limbo of uncertain duration. Lights were extinguished. Clocks stopped. Television screens went black. Drivers became hesitant and generous at traffic signals. Society and all its components took a blessed time out. 12

There was also something in Ireland called "holy hour," a period in the afternoon when all the pubs would close. Perhaps what Americans need is a holy hour in the form of a blackout—a brief caesura in our way of life that might come every day at perhaps nine-thirty or ten at night. Not the least of the holy hour's benefits, I might add, would be an appealing new time slot for Maury Povich. 13

Meanings and Values

1. The writer mentions "anecdotal evidence" of a "'sleep deficit'" (Par. 4) but does not present it directly. Why do you think he chose not to offer it in detail? Is the essay weakened—or perhaps strengthened—by this omission? Explain. (See "Guide to Terms": *Evaluation.*)
2. Are we to take the example in Paragraph 6 seriously? If not, what is its role in the essay? Is it an indication that we should not take other examples in the essay seriously? Why or why not?
3. Explain why the author might be justified in referring to certain television shows as "time porn." Do you think most readers will agree or disagree with his conclusion? Why?
4. According to this essay, what was lost when electricity made it possible to "vanquish darkness" (8)?

Expository Techniques

1. Where does Murphy first announce the phenomenon he wishes to explain? Should this announcement be considered a thesis? Why or why not? (Guide: *Thesis.*)
2. What is the role of the rhetorical question that opens Paragraph 6? (Guide: *Rhetorical Questions.*)
3. Which causes of the sleep deficit does the author consider most important, and how does he signal their importance to readers? Which of the strategies for creating emphasis does he use with frequency in this essay? (Guide: *Emphasis.*)
4. Where in the essay does the author begin discussing the effects of electricity?
5. What is the role of the extended discussion of Staudenmaier's work in Paragraphs 10 and 11? To what extent do these paragraphs contradict or complement Murphy's tone and approach in the rest of the essay? (Guide: *Style/Tone.*)
6. What strategy does the writer use to conclude the essay? (Guide: *Closings.*) How effective is the conclusion?

Diction and Vocabulary

1. To what does the title allude? (Guide: *Figures of Speech.*) How is the allusion related to the rest of the essay? Discuss how repetition of the word "darkness," beginning with the title, serves to create unity and coherence in the essay. (Guide: *Unity; Coherence.*) Is the title effective even for readers who do not recognize the allusion? Why or why not?
2. What choices of words and phrases does the writer make in Paragraph 8 to indicate the importance of electricity as one of the causes of the sleep deficit and the disappearance of "darkness" in our

daily lives? (Guide: *Diction.*) Do you think the diction in this paragraph is appropriate to its purposes, or is it excessive? Explain. (Guide: *Evaluation.*)

3. If you do not know the meaning of some of the following terms, look them up in a dictionary: *anecdotal* (Par. 4); *systemic, tectonic* (7); *Luddite, innocuous, vanquish* (8); *hominid, curtailed* (9); *metastases, diurnal* (11); *subsisting, limbo, duration* (12); *caesura* (13).

Read to Write

1. **Collaborating:** In a group, think of other modern inventions (airplanes, television, the Internet, credit cards) and the ways they have changed our society and shaped our lives. The inventions can be seemingly insignificant (cup holders in automobiles, telephone calling cards, zippers, or Velcro) and still be topics worth exploring because of their consequences, both good and bad. Then plan an essay exploring the consequences of one or more of the inventions.
2. **Considering Audience:** This essay is partly humorous, partly serious. Prepare an essay analyzing the role of each element and discussing how readers are likely to respond to the combination.
3. **Developing an Essay:** This essay makes effective use of the concept of a "deficit," that is, the difference between what we have and what we ought to have. Use a similar strategy to begin an essay of your own by introducing some other kind of "deficit" whose causes and consequences are worth exploring.

(NOTE: Suggestions for topics requiring development by analysis of CAUSE AND EFFECT are on pp. 302–303 at the end of this chapter.)

VERLYN KLINKENBORG

VERLYN KLINKENBORG was born in 1952 in Meeker, Colorado, attended Pomona College, and received a Ph.D. from Princeton University. During the 1980s and the early 1990s, he taught literature and creative writing at Fordham University, St. Olaf College, Bennington College, and Harvard University. Since 1997, Klinkenborg has held a position on the editorial board for *The New York Times*, and has published a number of notable opinion pieces, many of which center on the topic of rural farm life. His books include *Making Hay* (1986), *The Rural Life* (2002), *The Last Fine Time* (2004), and *Timothy, or, Notes of an Abject Reptile* (2006). In 2007, he received a Guggenheim Fellowship, which is being used to fund his forthcoming book about the English farmer and journalist, William Cobbett.

Our Vanishing Night

"Our Vanishing Night" appeared in *National Geographic* in 2008. In this article, Klinkenborg addresses the relatively recent concern regarding "light pollution" and describes the impact that our careless use of artificial light has had on the natural rhythms and biological processes of many species. He then goes on to relate this scientific data to a number of similar effects on human life in order to illustrate the fact that the dangers of this phenomenon are not limited to non-human species. His explanation of an issue with which many of us are probably not familiar delivers the unsettling message that progress and technological innovation have caused us to divorce ourselves from "our evolutionary and cultural patrimony."

If humans were truly at home under the light of the moon and stars, we would go in darkness happily, the midnight world as visible to us as it is to the vast number of nocturnal species on this planet. Instead, we are diurnal creatures, with eyes adapted to living in the sun's light. This is a basic evolutionary fact, even though most of us don't think of ourselves as diurnal beings any more than we think of ourselves as primates or mammals or Earthlings. Yet it's the only way to explain what we've done to the night: We've engineered it to receive us by filling it with light. 1

This kind of engineering is no different than damming a river. Its benefits come with consequences—called light pollution—whose effects scientists are only now beginning to study. Light pollution is 2 largely the result of bad lighting design, which allows artificial light to shine outward and upward into the sky, where it's not wanted, instead of focusing it downward, where it is. Ill-designed lighting washes out the darkness of night and radically alters the light levels—and light rhythms—to which many forms of life, including ourselves, have adapted. Wherever human light spills into the natural world, some aspect of life—migration, reproduction, feeding—is affected.

For most of human history, the phrase "light pollution" would 3
have made no sense. Imagine walking toward London on a moonlit night around 1800, when it was Earth's most populous city. Nearly a million people lived there, making do, as they always had, with candles and rushlights and torches and lanterns. Only a few houses were lit by gas, and there would be no public gaslights in the streets or squares for another seven years. From a few miles away, you would have been as likely to *smell* London as to see its dim collective glow.

Now most of humanity lives under intersecting domes of re- 4
flected, refracted light, of scattering rays from overlit cities and suburbs, from light-flooded highways and factories. Nearly all of nighttime Europe is a nebula of light, as is most of the United States and all of Japan. In the south Atlantic the glow from a single fishing fleet—squid fishermen luring their prey with metal halide lamps—can be seen from space, burning brighter, in fact, than Buenos Aires or Rio de Janeiro.

In most cities the sky looks as though it has been emptied of 5
stars, leaving behind a vacant haze that mirrors our fear of the dark and resembles the urban glow of dystopian science fiction. We've grown so used to this pervasive orange haze that the original glory of an unlit night—dark enough for the planet Venus to throw shadows on Earth—is wholly beyond our experience, beyond memory almost. And yet above the city's pale ceiling lies the rest of the universe, utterly undiminished by the light we waste—a bright shoal of stars and planets and galaxies, shining in seemingly infinite darkness.

We've lit up the night as if it were an unoccupied country, when 6
nothing could be further from the truth. Among mammals alone, the number of nocturnal species is astonishing. Light is a powerful biological force, and on many species it acts as a magnet, a process being studied by researchers such as Travis Longcore and Catherine Rich, co-founders of the Los Angeles-based Urban Wildlands Group. The effect is so powerful that scientists speak of songbirds and seabirds being "captured" by searchlights on land or by the light from gas flares on marine oil platforms, circling and circling in

the thousands until they drop. Migrating at night, birds are apt to collide with brightly lit tall buildings; immature birds on their first journey suffer disproportionately.

Insects, of course, cluster around streetlights, and feeding at those insect clusters is now ingrained in the lives of many bat species. In some Swiss valleys the European lesser horseshoe bat began to vanish after streetlights were installed, perhaps because those valleys were suddenly filled with light-feeding pipistrelle bats. Other nocturnal mammals—including desert rodents, fruit bats, opossums, and badgers—forage more cautiously under the permanent full moon of light pollution because they've become easier targets for predators. 7

Some birds—blackbirds and nightingales, among others—sing at unnatural hours in the presence of artificial light. Scientists have determined that long artificial days—and artificially short nights—induce early breeding in a wide range of birds. And because a longer day allows for longer feeding, it can also affect migration schedules. One population of Bewick's swans wintering in England put on fat more rapidly than usual, priming them to begin their Siberian migration early. The problem, of course, is that migration, like most other aspects of bird behavior, is a precisely timed biological behavior. Leaving early may mean arriving too soon for nesting conditions to be right. 8

Nesting sea turtles, which show a natural predisposition for dark beaches, find fewer and fewer of them to nest on. Their hatchlings, which gravitate toward the brighter, more reflective sea horizon, find themselves confused by artificial lighting behind the beach. In Florida alone, hatchling losses number in the hundreds of thousands every year. Frogs and toads living near brightly lit highways suffer nocturnal light levels that are as much as a million times brighter than normal, throwing nearly every aspect of their behavior out of joint, including their nighttime breeding choruses. 9

Of all the pollutions we face, light pollution is perhaps the most easily remedied. Simple changes in lighting design and installation yield immediate changes in the amount of light spilled into the atmosphere and, often, immediate energy savings. 10

It was once thought that light pollution only affected astronomers, who need to see the night sky in all its glorious clarity. And, in fact, some of the earliest civic efforts to control light pollution—in Flagstaff, Arizona, half a century ago—were made to protect the view from Lowell Observatory, which sits high above that city. Flagstaff has tightened its regulations since then, and in 2001 it was declared the 11 first International Dark Sky City. By now the effort to control light pollution has spread around the globe. More and more cities and even entire countries, such as the Czech Republic, have committed themselves to reducing unwanted glare.

Unlike astronomers, most of us may not need an undiminished view of the night sky for our work, but like most other creatures we do need darkness. Darkness is as essential to our biological welfare, to our internal clockwork, as light itself. The regular oscillation of waking and sleep in our lives—one of our circadian rhythms—is nothing less than a biological expression of the regular oscillation of light on Earth. So fundamental are these rhythms to our being that altering them is like altering gravity. 12

For the past century or so, we've been performing an open-ended experiment on ourselves, extending the day, shortening the night, and short-circuiting the human body's sensitive response to light. The consequences of our bright new world are more readily perceptible in less adaptable creatures living in the peripheral glow of our prosperity. But for humans, too, light pollution may take a biological toll. At least one new study has suggested a direct correlation between higher rates of breast cancer in women and the nighttime brightness of their neighborhoods. 13

In the end, humans are no less trapped by light pollution than the frogs in a pond near a brightly lit highway. Living in a glare of our own making, we have cut ourselves off from our evolutionary and cultural patrimony—the light of the stars and the rhythms of day and night. In a very real sense, light pollution causes us to lose sight of our true place in the universe, to forget the scale of our being, which is best measured against the dimensions of a deep night with the Milky Way—the edge of our galaxy—arching overhead. 14

Meanings and Values

1. How does this essay define "light pollution" (Par. 2)?
2. Where does the writer first outline the consequences of human-generated light spreading into the natural world, and what does he name as the general kinds of effects?
3. What are the negative consequences of excessive light that the writer discusses in detail in this essay?

EXPOSITORY TECHNIQUES

1. a. What pronoun does the writer use throughout the essay to refer to himself: *I, we*, or *he*? What pronoun does he use to refer to readers: *you, they*, or *we*?

   b. In what ways are these choices related to the overall theme? (See "Guide to Terms": *Unity.*)

2. Is the discussion in this essay neatly divided between causes and effects? If so, where is the dividing line? If not, which sections are primarily devoted to causes and which to effects?

DICTION AND VOCABULARY

1. The word *light* often has positive connotations. In this essay, what other words does the writer associate with *light* to give it negative connotations and what negative synonyms does he use for *light*? Hint: Look at Paragraphs 2, 4, 5, 6, 9, and 11. (Guide: *Connotation/Denotation.*)
2. If you do not know the meaning of some of the following words, look them up in a dictionary: *diurnal* (Par. 2): *refracted, nebula, halide* (4); *dystopian, pervasive* (5); *priming* (8); *predisposition, gravitate* (9); *oscillation, circadian* (12); *peripheral* (13); *patrimony* (14).

READ TO WRITE

1. **Collaborating:** In a group, brainstorm a list of modern advancements (airplanes or televisions, for example) whose consequences have been negative (rapid spread of diseases or changes in social patterns, for instance) as well as positive. Choose three advances and list negative consequences for each. Then use one of the subjects and its effects and plan an essay using this content.
2. **Considering Audience:** As displayed in this essay, environmental thinking encourages us to consider the harmful as well as helpful effects of our actions. Prepare an essay suggesting to readers the need to consider ther full range of consequences for actions they generally consider positive. You need not limit yourself to environmental issues; even personal behaviors like honesty and hard work can have a variety of outcomes.
3. **Developing an Essay:** This essay uses the term *pollution* to turn a positive term, *light*, into a negative one, *light pollution*. Use a similar strategy to develop an essay of your own. Try terms like *music, sports,* or *food* to look at the downside of these subjects.

(NOTE: Suggestions for topics requiring development by analysis of CAUSE and EFFECT follow.)

Writing Suggestions for Chapter 8

Cause and Effect

Analyze the immediate and ultimate causes and/or effects of one of the following subjects or another suggested by them. (Be careful that your analysis does not develop into a mere listing of superficial "reasons.")

1. The ethnic makeup of a neighborhood
2. Some *minor* discovery or invention
3. The popularity of some modern singer or other celebrity
4. The popularity of some fad of clothing or hairstyle
5. The widespread fascination for antique cars (or guns, furniture, dishes, motorcycles, old bottles, etc.)
6. The decision of some close acquaintance to enter the religious life
7. Some unreasonable fear or anxiety that afflicts you or someone you know well
8. The popularity of computer games
9. The mainstreaming of handicapped children
10. The appeal of a recent movie or current television series
11. The willingness of some people to sacrifice personal relationships for professional success
12. The disintegration of a marriage or family
13. A trend in the national economy
14. The concern with diet and physical fitness
15. Attention to gender roles
16. Willingness to take risks, even extreme ones

Collaborative Exercises

1. As a group, research the causes of a war or other armed conflict. Decide collectively which causes were most central, and together write an essay showing how the combination of such causes led to the conflict. Look at immediate (direct) causes as well as indirect causes.

2. Split into teams of four. Divide each team into two halves, one that will analyze the causes and one that will analyze the effects of number 12 (p. 302). Create a thesis based on your analyses that would work as a claim for an essay on the topic.
3. Perform the same task for the above question for the topic of "the high percentage of women in the workforce."

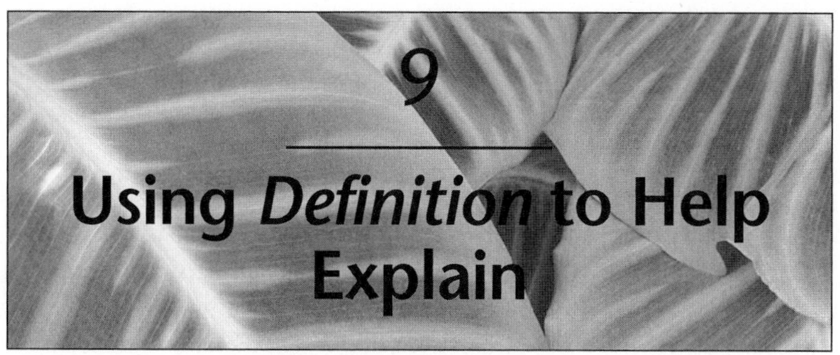

9

Using *Definition* to Help Explain

Few barriers to communication are as great as those created by key terms or concepts that have various meanings or shades of meaning. For this reason, expository writing often provides definitions of words and ideas whose precise meaning is important to the writer's purpose. Sometimes **definitions** merely clarify meanings of concrete or noncontroversial terms. This simple process is similar to that often used in dictionaries:

1. providing a synonym, for example

   cinema: a motion picture

   or
2. placing the word in a class and then showing how it differs from others of the same class, for example

Term	Class	Details
metheglin:	an alcoholic liquor	made of fermented honey

Often, however, definitions specify the meanings of abstract, unusual, or newly minted terms. Definitions of this sort are particularly useful when the experiences or knowledge of readers does little to help them with the meaning of a term or idea that is nonetheless a key element of an overall explanation.

Sometimes a term or concept (or perhaps a process, a natural phenomenon, a group of people, or a relationship) is itself the subject of an explanation, leading to an *extended definition,* as in the following example.

> This is *orienteering,* a mixture of marathon, hike, and scavenger hunt, a cross-country race in which participants must locate a series of markers set in unfamiliar terrain by means of map and compass. The course, which may range from an acre of city park to twenty square miles of wilderness, is dotted with anywhere from four to fifteen "controls," red-and-white flags whose general locations are marked on the map by small circles. At each control there is a paper punch that produces a distinctive pattern on a card the racer carries. In most events the order in which the card must be punched is fixed; the route taken to reach each control, however, is up to the participant.
>
> —Linton Robinson, "Marathoning with Maps"

Extended definitions may take a paragraph or two or may be the primary pattern for all or most of an essay, depending on the complexity of the subject being defined, the amount of controversy or confusion it has generated, the likely interest of readers in the discussion, and the writer's purpose.

WHY USE DEFINITION?

When your subject requires you to write about terms, ideas, or phenomena likely to be unfamiliar to your audience, or when the concepts and words you are using have conflicting or controversial meanings, then you probably need to prepare an extended definition for your readers. For years, discussions of how much people work each week excluded housework and other time spent on activities important to home and family. The definition of *work* included only labor outside the home for a specific wage. Women were rightly angered by this definition, which excluded the hours many of them labored creating homes and maintaining families. If you were to write today about how much work people do in an average week, you would need to provide an extended definition of work including such activities. Few people would argue your definition, but they would expect you to be aware of the different (and conflicting) meanings of the term and to make your choice among them clear. If some readers are likely to disagree with your choice, however, you will need to present reasons for it. You might even need to stipulate (or dictate) the meaning of the term as you use it in the essay so that your audience will not misread your essay by substituting their preferred meaning for your own.

When your writing focuses on a fashion, artistic trend, social phenomenon, political movement, or set of ideas or behaviors whose impact is widespread enough to interest most readers but new enough to require definition, you might consider creating an essay that presents an *informative definition,* one that explores and explains the various aspects of your subject. In contrast, when your readers already have some ideas about your subject, but you think these ideas (or perspectives) need to be changed, you could create a *redefinition* essay. A redefinition begins with the ideas readers hold and tries to substitute new and different ones. For example, people often try to make pets of wild animals because they consider the creatures cute, cuddly, or amusing. You might attempt to redefine the favorable images people hold of animals like koala bears, monkeys, boa constrictors, ocelots, or raccoons to show that these and similar creatures are likely to make troublesome, unpleasant, or even dangerous pets.

CHOOSING A STRATEGY

Extended definitions, unlike the simple dictionary type, follow no set pattern. Often when extended definitions are part of an essay, readers are not specifically aware of the process of definition. This lack of specific awareness arises because the definitions are frequently part of the overall subject, are written in the same tone as the rest of the exposition, and are closely tied to the writer's thesis and purpose.

When an extended definition is the primary pattern for an essay, however, the essay itself may follow one of several broad strategies. An informative definition often begins by explaining the reason for the subject's current importance as well as the need to define it. It may then move to a brief, sometimes formal definition; continue with a discussion of the historical background and present instances; and conclude with a review of the subject's features. The following informal plan for an essay includes these strategies in an order appropriate to the subject.

Introduction
- Tentative thesis: If you look carefully at your calendar for the month of December, you are likely to come across the holiday Kwanzaa, which may be unfamiliar to you but which is celebrated each year by an increasing number of your friends, coworkers, and neighbors.
- Current importance: Examples

Definition
- Brief formal definition
- Historical background

Features: Seven principles, various activities, clothing, participants, meaning of celebration, food, stories, and materials and resources
Present instances: Current and growing popularity
Conclusion: Summary and sources for further information

A redefinition essay grows from the assumption that readers already have some ideas about the subject but these ideas should be modified or discarded altogether. Redefinitions often begin in the same matter as informative definitions—by creating interest in the topic. Then they generally proceed to mention the ways the subject is normally interpreted, following each with an alternate interpretation, or redefinition. Or they review various aspects of the subject and suggest fresh ways of looking at each.

DEVELOPING DEFINITIONS

A definition helps writers and readers agree on the meaning of a term, concept, or phenomenon by providing answers to some important questions. As you develop a definition, try keeping in mind the questions you will need to address in order to help readers understand your subject. These sample questions can provide a start.

For subjects that can be observed, measured, and known:

What are its features?

What is its history?

What does it do?

What doesn't it do?

For concepts, values, or terms whose meaning depends on the ways people use them:

How do people use it?

What has its meaning been historically, and how has the meaning changed?

How is this set of values or concepts different from others? Similar?

Definitions use many familiar techniques of expository writing, including examples, comparisons, and classifications. There are, however, some techniques peculiar to definition. You can give the *background* of a word, answering the question "What is the history of the term or concept?" (that is, its *etymology*) and providing valuable hints to its meanings. For example, *catholic* originally, in ancient times, meant pertaining to the universal Christian church. Its present meaning—of or concerning the Roman Catholic Church—retains some of the original force because the Roman Catholic Church views itself as the direct descendant of the ancient, undivided Christian church.

You can also enumerate the *characteristics* of the term or subject, sometimes isolating an essential one for special treatment. In defining a social group, such as triathletes, for example, you might list the physical qualities they share (endurance, strength, versatility, and exceptional fitness), their mental qualities (high endurance for pain, desire to exceed normal levels of achievement, and pleasure in physical exertion), and their social preferences (tolerance for solitary training routines, desire to excel, and preference for individual achievement rather than group membership). In so doing, you would be explaining the common elements that define the group and distinguish it from other groups.

You might define by *negation,* sometimes called "exclusion" or "differentiation," by showing what is *not* the meaning of the term, concept, or phenomenon. (This is an important technique for a redefinition essay.) To do this, you answer the question, "What is it *not?*": "*Intelligence* is neither a puzzle-solving activity that enables people to do well on a standardized example like the SAT or ACT, nor the ability to remember columns of facts and figures that may have no real use." If you employ this technique, however, remember that readers will expect you also to provide a positive definition, indicating what the definition *is* as well as what it *is not.*

But perhaps the most dependable techniques for defining are basic expository patterns. You can illustrate the meaning of a term or define a phenomenon by drawing *examples* from your own experience, from newspaper or online reports, from books and magazines, or from interviews and surveys. For instance, you might help explain the range of behaviors included in the term *deviant behavior* by offering examples not only of thieves, drug dealers, and pornographers, but also of people who live alone in the wilderness for spiritual enlightenment or who participate in dangerous sports. You might even include yourself in the category by telling how you climbed the side of a glacier or parachuted from a bridge into a river gorge. Or you might define by *classifying,* sorting kinds of deviant behavior into those that are socially acceptable, even honorable (the search for spiritual enlightenment); those that are harmful only to the individual (dangerous sports); and those that harm other people (thievery and other activities generally considered criminal).

Comparisons are useful, too, both those that identify *synonyms* (*naïve* means innocent, unsophisticated, natural, unaffected, and artless) or that distinguish among concepts with similar, though not identical, meanings, such as *consensus* (general agreement among a group of people on their attitude toward an issue or problem) and *dissensus* (general agreement among a group of people on the ways their attitudes toward an issue or problem differ). Comparisons respond to the question, "What is the subject like or unlike?" So, too, do *similes* and *metaphors,* two techniques that are especially useful in defining concepts and attitudes that are difficult to grasp directly ("an *epiphany* is a moment of sudden clarity and insight, like the moment your eyes become accustomed to the dark and you can suddenly see your surroundings," "a *transition* in writing is a bridge between ideas").

A narrative or an account of a process can also help you define. An explanation of *courage,* for example, might include the story of a 10-year-old saving a friend from drowning in an icy pond. A discussion of *open-heart surgery* might include a description of the process.

Few extended definitions would use all these methods, but the extent to which you use them should depend on three factors: (1) the term or concept itself, since some are more elusive and subject to misunderstanding than others; (2) the function the term serves in your writing, since it is foolish to develop several pages defining a term that serves only a casual or unimportant purpose; and (3) your prospective audience, since the extent of your readers' knowledge and their likely responses to your definition of a disputed or controversial concept or phenomenon should lead you to choose the most convincing or persuasive strategies for the particular audience.

Finally, remember that reference works can be valuable sources for definition. The *Oxford English Dictionary,* for example, traces the meanings of a word during various historical periods; the *Dictionary of Slang and Unconventional English* or the *Encyclopedia of Pop, Rock, and Soul* can provide you with surprising and useful information. A reference librarian or an Internet search engine can provide you with many more sources.

Student Essay

In the following essay, Lori L'Heureux uses a variety of definition techniques to define and redefine *stars.*

Stars

by Lori L'Heureux

How many of us as children longed to be famous when we grew up? Many of us admired a certain celebrity and wanted to be just like him or her when we got older. We wanted to be a star.

Importance of term

Word/concept to be defined

The word "star," used to describe a celebrity, first came into use around 1830. Before this, there was no special term to label performers who, on their own, could draw large numbers of spectators to a performance or an athletic contest. The lack of a term for such a celebrity probably reflected a greater emphasis on the performance or athletic event than on the individual performer or athlete. But as the role of talented individuals became more important, a word for it was needed. Many words, old or newly fashioned, might have served, but the noun borrowed from gazing at the night sky somehow captured the emerging role (Braudy 9).

Background and history

Stars, indeed, have an enormous impact on our lives. They are recognized throughout society, observed closely onstage and off, thought about, talked about, emulated, even dreamed about. Stardom is a vital force in our culture.

Effects and importance

Because so many people perceive the work stars do as a form of upgraded play, they understand only imperfectly the work life of celebrity entertainers. According to Jib Fowles, many stars resent the stereotypes that have been created for them over the last century. Many people, thinking that the majority of stars spend the hours of the day at leisure, imagine them living a lavish lifestyle characterized by money and glamour. Stars are thought to be greedy and to associate only with people whose social status matches their own. Stars are frequently imagined as leading relaxed lives: this one reclining in a chaise lounge, reading a script; that one stretched out on a massage table, getting worked on by a team's trainer; several others poolside and prone. But in reality, the life of most stars is quite the opposite (Fowles 59).

Define by negation

I conducted a survey of my own to see if most people hold these misconceptions of celebrities' lives. I asked 15 people to tell me what type of lives they felt celebrities lead. Twelve people said that stars were rich and had easy careers. Only three said celebrities led hard lives in the public eye and had difficult jobs. Two people added that they were never tempted to become stars (L'Heureux).

What readers believe

But what exactly is a star? Is there a downside to being constantly in the public eye? Is being a star really a lot of work? What is the cost of being famous?

Rhetorical questions provide structure

It must be understood that being a star is a social role that an individual adopts. Every day of our lives, we, too, take on social roles; we accept the obligations and behaviors of being an employee, a parent, a spouse, and so forth. Celebrity performers are similar; they wake up in the morning and step into the star role.

A star's talent delights audiences of all ages. A star acts or sings or cracks jokes or even just poses, and does these things with such style that we are fascinated and refreshed. We pay attention to stars because their performances are so successful at entertaining us. Because the audience for television shows, films, and recordings has become so large and so appreciative, the acclamation a star receives has become greater and more ferocious in recent decades. Through ticket sales, high ratings, and fan mail, an audience makes known its jubilant or waning response to a star's performance. When the response is good, the flow of good tidings certifies a star in public regard and elevates him or her to a special glory. At some moments for certain stars and their captivated fans, the reaction can be manic, as when the Beatles first toured the U.S. in 1964.

Examples

Becoming a star is sometimes a difficult task. Trying to become known in the industry, to be liked by directors, and to get parts, hopefuls embark on endless rounds of auditions. Most will spend more time at auditions than they ever will before the camera. Athletes struggling to become star players generally spend many years in the minor leagues (or the equivalent) waiting for a call to "the show."

Redefining star

Examples

Meanwhile, between roles, struggling actors have to sustain themselves. Usually this means menial jobs of one sort or another. For example, Marilyn Monroe labored in a wartime defense plant where she packed parachutes. For aspiring athletes, a job in the off-season is generally a necessity.

Example

Fame may require much in the way of disappointment, strain, and heartache. Since so many people are striving to become stars, and since so few will make it, the typical aspirant's work life is a ceaseless round of rejection and exclusion. He or she may attempt to maintain motivation with visions of ultimate stardom, but the daily experience of trudging from audition to audition can prove devastating. Celebrity George C. Scott commented about acting, "I think it is a psychologically damaging profession, just too much rejection to cope with every day of your life."

Redefining

Example and quote

Aspirants may initially set themselves on the path to stardom because, in their rosy view, fame promises freedom beyond compare. But in fact the job of the celebrity performer is subject to suffocating impositions and strangling constraints. Asked what it means to become a star, Cary Grant replied, "Does it mean happiness? Yeah, for a couple of days. And then what happens? You find out that your life is not your own anymore, and that you're on show every time you step out on the street."

Example and quote

According to Yoti Lane, such a reaction is altogether typical, for "one of the most characteristic symptoms of having actually become a celebrity is a certain disillusionment, which sets in—after the first thrill of seeing one's name in headlines—upon discovering the obligations and inconveniences of being known by everyone everywhere" (130).

Underestimated by the public, a star's work is one of the most strenuous occupations that a person can have. Fred Astaire commented, "People will come up to me and say, 'Boy, it must have been fun making those old MGM musicals.' Fun? I suppose you could have considered them that—if you like beating your brains and feet out."

Redefinition continues

Knocking oneself out to deliver first-rate performances to the public, time after time, is the fate of those ensconced in the star role. The occupation calls for extraordinary effort and ceaseless toil.

For most stars, the preparation for performing begins with a general readiness. Professional athletes work out for countless hours to maintain their physical condition. Singers exercise their voices daily, practicing their delivery and keeping their vocal cords in shape. Actors take classes to strengthen their performance or spend time carefully observing others. **Process**

From a base of readiness, the star prepares for the performance. The rock band practices its songs for a concert, the comedian works on new material, and the actor concentrates on a new character to become familiar with it. Actors must go over their lines again and again, working to get them right. Before going on, the star has to be costumed and made up, a process that can be very time-consuming.

The hard work for a star truly begins when he or she must concentrate on the task at hand. What a performer must do is create wonderfully and completely, on cue. The star has been engaged to deliver, within the framework of the performance, the right act at the right moment. The audience expects the comedian to have the perfect punchline, the center fielder to catch the ball in the sun, and the actress to cry when required.

Being a star can also be dangerous. Actor Sylvester Stallone calculates that in making some of his action films he has broken his nose three times, his hand twice, and has suffered a concussion and a ruptured stomach. Also a danger to stars is their public. Fan letters pour in by the thousands each day, and the letter writers often want to enter into some sort of transaction with their idols. This can be dangerous when fans strive to encounter a star in person, pushing and shoving for contact, or when outraged fans try to injure a star. **Effects of stardom**

For the privilege of staring at a star, fans will follow an entertainer into parties, restaurants, and even bathrooms. Sometimes stars have to live with the unremitting presence of fans camped at their front doors. The romance and obsession that are in a fan's mind can lead them to stalk an idol. Brooke Shields was the object of the affections of one Mark Bailey, who attempted to break into her New Jersey home; the judge put him on five years' probation. While David Letterman was on the West Coast, a mentally ill woman who claimed to be his wife installed herself in his East Coast home (Fowles 310).

The media can also invade the privacy of a star. Interviews may seem endless and prove to be very draining. The press tends to emphasize personal questions that make the subject of an interview understandably uncomfortable. Magazines such as *The National Enquirer* strive to create rumors about different stars, often relying on questionable sources and rumors that later prove to be unfounded. A personal problem that any of us could easily encounter and that most of us would like to face in privacy frequently ends up on the front pages of newspapers, creating stress and embarrassment for the celebrity and threatening his or her career.

Summary

Even if their lives do not fit within stereotypes, stars are not people who lead normal lives. Celebrities are widely admired and often receive considerable money for their work, yet they must face situations that the general public does not fully understand. Stars face danger; give up their privacy; and work long, hard hours. Referring to celebrities as "stars" is quite appropriate because their lives are as far from ours as the stars are distant from the ground we stand on.

Works Cited

Braudy, Leo. *Frenzy of Renown: Fame and Its History.* New York: Oxford UP, 1986. Print.

Fowles, Jib. *Starstruck.* Chicago: Smith-sonian, 1992. Print.

Lane, Yoti. *The Psychology of the Actor.* Westport: Greenwood, 1959. Print.

L'Heureux, Lori. Survey. U of Rhode Island, Kingston., 7–10 Nov. 1995. TS.

JOHN BERENDT

John Berendt was born in Syracuse, New York, in 1939. He was a student at Harvard and received his B.A. in 1961. A journalist, essayist, and writer of nonfiction, he has also worked as an editor and columnist at *Esquire,* an editor at *Holiday* and *New York* magazines, and as an associate producer of the *David Frost Show* and the *Dick Cavett Show.* His essays and articles have appeared in numerous magazines, including *Forbes, Publisher's Weekly, Esquire, Architectural Digest,* and the *New Yorker.* His best-selling book, *Midnight in the Garden of Good and Evil* (1994) is a nonfiction account of unusual characters and scandalous goings-on in Savannah, Georgia.

The Hoax

In this essay, first published in *Esquire,* Berendt takes a relatively straightforward approach to definition, yet through skillful writing and wit, he manages to offer a fresh and insightful understanding of a familiar term and the behavior it designates.

When the humorist Robert Benchley was an undergraduate at Harvard eighty years ago, he and a couple of friends showed up one morning at the door of an elegant Beacon Hill mansion, dressed as furniture repairmen. They told the housekeeper they had come to pick up the sofa. Five minutes later they carried the sofa out the door, put it on a truck, and drove it three blocks away to another house, where, posing as deliverymen, they plunked it down in the parlor. That evening, as Benchley well knew, the couple living in house A were due to attend a party in house B. Whatever the outcome—and I'll get to that shortly—it was guaranteed to be a defining example of how proper Bostonians handle social crises. The wit inherent in Benchley's practical joke elevated it from the level of prank to the more respectable realm of hoax. 1

To qualify as a hoax, a prank must have magic in it—the word is derived from *hocus-pocus,* after all. Daring and irony are useful ingredients, too. A good example of a hoax is the ruse perpetrated by David Hampton, the young black man whose pretense of being Sidney Poitier's son inspired John Guare's *Six Degrees of Separation.* Hampton managed to insinuate himself into two of New York's most sophisticated households—one headed by the president of 2 the public-television station *WNET,* the other by the dean of the Columbia School of Journalism. Hampton's hoax touched a number of sensitive themes: snobbery, class, race, and sex, all of which playwright Guare deftly exploited.

Hampton is a member of an elite band of famous impostors that includes a half-mad woman who for fifty years claimed to be Anastasia, the lost daughter of the assassinated czar Nicholas II; and a man named Harry Gerguson, who became a Hollywood restaurateur and darling of society in the 1930s and 1940s as the ersatz Russian prince Mike Romanoff. 3

Forgeries have been among the better hoaxes. Fake Vermeers painted by an obscure Dutch artist, Hans van Meegeren, were so convincing that they fooled art dealers, collectors, and museums. The hoax came to light when van Meegeren was arrested as a Nazi collaborator after the war. To prove he was not a Nazi, he admitted he had sold a fake Vermeer to Hermann Göring for $256,000. Then he owned up to having created other "Vermeers," and to prove he could do it, he painted *Jesus in the Temple* in the style of Vermeer while under guard in jail. 4

In a bizarre twist, a story much like van Meegeren's became the subject of the book *Fake!*, by Clifford Irving, who in 1972 attempted to pull off a spectacular hoax of his own: a wholly fraudulent "authorized" biography of Howard Hughes. Irving claimed to have conducted secret interviews with the reclusive Hughes, and McGraw-Hill gave him a big advance. Shortly before publication, Hughes surfaced by telephone and denied that he had ever spoken with Irving. Irving had already spent $100,000 of the advance; he was convicted of fraud and sent to jail. 5

As it happens, we are used to hoaxes where I come from. I grew up just a few miles down the road from Cardiff, New York—a town made famous by the Cardiff Giant. As we learned in school, a farmer named Newell complained, back in 1889, that his well was running dry, and while he and his neighbors were digging a new one, they came upon what appeared to be the fossilized remains of a man twelve feet tall. Before the day was out, Newell had erected a tent and posted a sign charging a dollar for a glimpse of the "giant"—three dollars for a longer look. Throngs descended on Cardiff. It wasn't long before scientists determined that the giant had been carved from a block of gypsum. The hoax came undone fairly quickly after that, but even so—as often happens with hoaxes—the giant became an even bigger attraction *because* it was a hoax. 6

P. T. Barnum offered Newell a fortune for the giant, but Newell refused, and it was then that he got his comeuppance. Barnum simply made a replica and put it on display as the genuine Cardiff Giant. Newell's gig was ruined.

The consequences of hoaxes are what give them spice. Orson Welles's lifelike 1938 radio broadcast of H. G. Well's *War of the Worlds* panicked millions of Americans, who were convinced that martians had landed in New Jersey. The forged diary of Adolf Hitler embarrassed historian Hugh Trevor-Roper, who had vouched for its authenticity, and *Newsweek* and the *Sunday Times* of London, both of which published excerpts in 1983 shortly before forensic tests proved that there were nylon fibers in the paper it was written on, which wouldn't have been possible had it originated before 1950. The five-hundred-thousand-year-old remains of Piltdown man, found in 1912, had anthropologists confused about human evolution until 1953, when fluoride tests exposed the bones as an elaborate modern hoax. And as for Robert Benchley's game on Beacon Hill, no one said a word about the sofa all evening, although there it sat in plain sight. One week later, however, couple A sent an anonymous package to couple B. It contained the sofa's slipcovers. 7

Meanings and Values

1. State Berendt's definition of a hoax in your own words, and indicate the difference between a hoax and a practical joke or prank. Look up *hoax* in a dictionary, and tell how Berendt's definition differs, if at all, from the one you encounter there.
2. Restate the meaning of this sentence, "The consequences of hoaxes are what give them spice" (Par. 7), and discuss whether the examples that follow it provide satisfactory support for the writer's conclusion. (See "Guide to Terms": *Evaluation.*)
3. Other than defining the term *hoax,* what purposes do you think the writer had in mind for this essay? (Guide: *Purpose.*)

Expository Techniques

1. Discuss how the way Berendt presents the examples in Paragraphs 2, 3, and 6 makes them seem imaginative (and somewhat harmless) escapades rather than criminal frauds or deceptions.
2. Determine what definition strategies Berendt uses in this essay. Which seem most effective, and why? (Guide: *Evaluation.*)

3. Evaluate the strategy Berendt uses to open and close the essay. What makes it successful or unsuccessful?

Diction and Vocabulary

1. To what extent does Berendt's presentation of the hoaxes described in Paragraphs 2, 3, and 6 as escapades rather than crimes depend on the terms he uses to present them? (See Expository Techniques, Question 1.) (Guide: *Diction.*)
2. If you do not know the meaning of some of the following terms, look them up in a dictionary: *perpetrated* (Par. 2); *ersatz* (3); *reclusive* (5); *gypsum, gig* (6); *vouched, forensic* (7).

Read to Write

1. **Collaborating:** Pranks, jokes, humorous events, adventures, and absurd occurrences make enjoyable examples in essays, and they often reveal a good deal about human beings and their relationships. Working in a group, make a list of possible examples of this sort. Then freewrite individually about the examples as a way of discovering a possible topic and thesis for an essay of your own.
2. **Considering Audience:** Make a list of words that most readers are likely to believe imply some sort of trickery and deception. Then prepare an essay in which you *redefine* one of the words and attempt to alter readers' views of its meaning.
3. **Developing an Essay:** Using Berendt's essay as a general pattern, create a definition of your own about a very different subject—such as the greatest loss, the most difficult task, or the biggest disappointment.

(Note: Suggestions for topics requiring development by definition are on pp. 349–350 at the end of this chapter.)

DAGOBERTO GILB

DAGOBERTO GILB was born in Los Angeles in 1950 and has lived for many years in Texas, first in El Paso, now in Austin. He spent sixteen years in construction, twelve years as a highrise carpenter with the United Brotherhood of Carpenters. His collection of stories, *The Magic of Blood* (1994) won the PEN/Hemingway Award. He has also published a novel, *The Last Known Residence of Mickey Acuna* (1995) and another collection of stories, *Woodcuts of Women* (2000). His collection of essays, *Gritos,* appeared in 2003.

Pride

In medieval times, pride was considered one of the seven deadly sins. (The others were gluttony, envy, sloth, lechery, wrath, and greed.) In this essay, from his collection *Gritos,* Dagoberto Gilb treats pride as a positive trait—a virtue. He also focuses on the actions of ordinary people in everyday circumstances, treating them as sources of pride.

It's almost time to close at the northwest corner of Altura and Copia in El Paso. That means it is so dark that it is as restful as the deepest unremembering sleep, dark as the empty space around this spinning planet, as a black star. Headlights that beam a little cross-eyed from a fatso American car are feeling around the asphalt road up the hill toward the Good Time Store, its yellow plastic smiley face bright like a sugary suck candy. The loose muffler holds only half the misfires, and, dry springs squeaking, the automobile curves slowly into the establishment's lot, swerving to avoid the new self-serve gas pump island. Behind it, across the street, a Texas flag—out too late this and all the nights—pops and slaps in a summer wind that finally is cool. 1

A good man, gray on the edges, an assistant manager in a brown starched and ironed uniform, is washing the glass windows of the store, lit up by as many watts as Venus, with a roll of paper towels and the blue liquid from a spray bottle. Good night, m'ijo! he tells a young boy coming out after playing the video game, a Grande Guzzler the size of a wastebasket balanced in one hand, an open bag of Flaming Hot Cheetos, its red dye already smearing his mouth and the hand not carrying the weight of the soda, his white T-shirt, its 2 short sleeves reaching halfway down his wrists, the whole XXL of it billowing and puffing in the outdoor gust.

A plump young woman steps out of that car. She's wearing a party dress, wide scoops out of the top, front, and back, its hemline way above the knees. 3

Did you get a water pump? the assistant manager asks her. Are you going to make it to Horizon City? He's still washing the glass of the storefront, his hand sweeping in small hard circles. 4

The young woman is patient and calm like a loving mother. I don't know yet, she tells him as she stops close to him, thinking. I guess I should make a call, she says, and her thick-soled shoes, the latest fashion, slap against her heels to one of the pay phones at the front of the store. 5

Pride is working a job like it's as important as art or war, is the happiness of a new high score on a video arcade game, of a pretty new black dress and shoes. Pride is the deaf and blind confidence of the good people who are too poor but don't notice. 6

A son is a long time sitting on the front porch where he played all those years with the squirmy dog who still licks his face, both puppies then, even before he played on the winning teams of Little League baseball and City League basketball. They sprint down the sidewalk and across streets, side by side, until they stop to rest on the park grass, where a red ant, or a spider, bites the son's calf. It swells, but he no longer thinks to complain to his mom about it—he's too old now—when he comes home. He gets ready, putting on the shirt and pants his mom would have ironed but he wanted to iron himself. He takes the ride with his best friend since first grade. The hundreds of moms and dads, abuelos y abuelitas, the tios and primos, baby brothers and older married sisters, all are at the Special Events Center for the son's high school graduation. His dad is a man bigger than most, and when he walks in his dress eel-skin boots down the cement stairs to get as close to the hardwood basketball-court floor and ceremony to see—m'ijo!—he feels an embarrassing sob bursting from his eyes and mouth. He holds it back, and with his hands, hides the tears that do escape, wipes them with his fingers, because the chavalitos in his aisle are playing and laughing and they are so small and he is so big next to them. And when his son walks to the stage to get his high school diploma and his dad wants to scream his name, he hears how many others, from the floor in caps and gowns and from around the arena, are already 7 screaming it—could be any name, it could be any son's or daughter's: Alex! Vanessa! Carlos! Veronica! Ricky! Tony! Estella! Isa!—and sees his boy waving back to all of them.

Pride hears gritty dirt blowing against an agave whose stiff fertile stalk, so tall, will not bend—the love of land, rugged like the people who live on it. Pride sees the sunlight on the Franklin Mountains in the first light of morning and listens to a neighbor's gallo—the love of culture and history. Pride smells a sweet, musky drizzle of rain and eats huevos con chile in corn tortillas heated on a cast-iron pan—the love of heritage. 8

Pride is the fearless reaction to disrespect and disregard. It is knowing the future will prove that wrong. 9

Seeing the beauty: look out there from a height of the mountain and on the north and south of the Rio Grande, to the far away and close, the so many miles more of fuzz on the wide horizon, knowing how many years the people have passed and have stayed, the ancestors, the ones who have medaled, limped back on crutches or died or were heroes from wars in the Pacific or Europe or Korea or Vietnam or the Persian Gulf, the ones who have raised the fist and dared to defy, the ones who wash the clothes and cook and serve the meals, who stitch the factory shoes and the factory slacks, who assemble and sort, the ones who laugh and the ones who weep, the ones who care, the ones who want more, the ones who try, the ones who love, those ones with shameless courage and hardened wisdom, and the old ones still so alive, holding their grandchildren, and the young ones in their glowing prime, strong and gorgeous, holding each other, the ones who will be born from them. The desert land is rock-dry and ungreen. It is brown. Brown like the skin is brown. Beautiful brown. 10

Meanings and Values

1. What purposes do you think the writer is trying to achieve in this essay? (See "Guide to Terms": *Purpose.*)
2. Explain the extent to which you believe most readers are likely to feel Gilb succesfully achieves his purposes in this essay. (Guide: *Evaluation.*)
3. Does Gilb focus on a particular ethnic group in this essay? If so, which one? Do his ideas apply to other groups as well or to people in general? Why, or why not?

4. In your own words, state the definition of *pride* this essay offers. (Hint: Be ready to take more than one sentence to present your definition.)

Expository Techniques

1. Which paragraphs in the essay provide definition in the form of extended examples?
2. Which paragraphs in the essay provide definition in the form of brief statements or examples?
3. What advantages (if any) does the writer's stratagy of providing multiple (though related) definitions of *pride* have over the more familiar strategy of providing a single, detailed definition followed by supporting examples. What disadvantages does it have? (Guide: *Evaluation.*)
4. Identify the parallel structures in Paragraphs 6, 8, and 9, and discuss the role they play in conveying the central theme of the essay. (Guide: *Unity.*)

Diction and Vocabulary

1. Point out the concrete words in Paragraphs 2 and 7. Discuss what these words contribute to the examples presented in the paragraph. (Guide: *Concrete/Abstract.*)
2. If you do not know the meaning of some of the following words, look them up in a dictionary, either English or English/Spanish, as appropriate: *m'ijo* (par. 2); *abuelos y abuelitas, tios, primos, chavalitos* (7); *gallo, huevos con chile* (8).

Read to Write

1. **Collaborating:** Working in a group, create a list of examples of behavior that illustrate and define a virtue (such as kindness or loyalty) or that help readers understand the positive sides of more questionable behaviors such as stubbornness or anger. Choose two examples and write three brief paragraphs (total) defining and explaining the behavior.
2. **Considering Audience:** Rewrite parts of Gilb's essays by substituting examples from your own experience or from a social, cultural, or ethnic group to which you belong. Or use the essay as a model for a discussion of other kinds of behavior.
3. **Developing an Essay:** Gilb finds positive traits and values in everyday behavior. Take a similar approach in an essay of your own by looking at everyday behaviors and ordinary people and emphasizing qualities within them deserving praise and admiration.

(Note: Suggestions for topics requiring development by use of DEFINITION are on pp. 349–350 at the end of this chapter.)

ANNE FADIMAN

ANNE FADIMAN was born in New York City in 1953 and attended Harvard University, where she served as the undergraduate columnist for *Harvard Magazine.* She later wrote for both *Life* and *Civilizations,* and she has received two National Magazine Awards for Reporting and Essays. She also received the National Book Critics Circle Award for her 1997 book, *The Spirit Catches You and You Fall Down.* Her other works include two collections of essays entitled *Ex-Libris: Confessions of a Common Reader* (1998) and *At Large and At Small: Familiar Essays* (2007). Fadiman currently serves as the Francis Chair in nonfiction writing at Yale University.

Coffee

Caffeine is perceived by many as a necessary crutch that is used to get us through early mornings, interminable hours at the office, and many of the other stressful situations that arise on a daily basis. In this essay, Anne Fadiman traces the transformation of coffee from the stigmatized ambrosia of the overworked to a kind of miracle drug that raised English society out of its drunken haze, inspired the feverishly brilliant writings of Balzac, fostered a public discourse that led to some of the great intellectual advances of the seventeenth and eighteenth centuries, and personally enabled her to survive on of the greatest emotional challenges of her life.

When I was a sophomore in college, I drank coffee nearly every evening with my friends Peter and Alex. Even though the coffee was canned; even though the milk was stolen from the dining hall and refrigerated on the windowsill of my friends' dormitory room, where it was diluted by snow and adulterated by soot; even though Alex's scuzzy one-burner hot plate looked as if it might electrocute us at any moment; and even though we washed our *batterie de cuisine* in the bathroom sink and let it air-dry on a pile of paper towels next to the toilet—even though Dunster F-13 was, in short, not exactly Escoffier's kitchen, we considered our nightly coffee ritual the very acme and pitch of elegance. And I think that in many ways we were right. 1

Alex came from Cambridge, but Peter was alluringly international. He had a Serbian father, an American mother, and a French coffeemaker. At my home in Los Angeles, the coffee-making process had taken about three seconds: you plunked a spoonful of Taster's Choice freeze-dried crystals in a cup, added hot water, and stirred. 2

With Peter's *cafetière à piston,* you could easily squander a couple of hours on the business of assembling, heating, brewing, pouring, drinking, disassembling, and cleaning (not to mention talking), all the while telling yourself that you weren't really procrastinating, because as soon as you were fully caffeinated you would be able to study like a fiend. The *cafetière* had seven parts: a cylindrical glass beaker; a four-footed metal frame; a chrome lid impaled through its center by a plunger rod topped with a spherical black knob; and three metal filtration discs that screwed onto the tip of the plunger in a sequence for whose mastery our high SAT scores had somehow failed to equip us. After all the pieces were in place, you dolloped some ground coffee into the beaker, poured in boiling water, and waited precisely four minutes. (In the title sequence of *The Ipcress File,* special agent Harry Palmer unaccountably fails to carry out this crucial step. As an eagle-eyed critic for *The Guardian* once observed, Palmer grinds his beans and pops them into his *cafetière,* but *fails to let the grounds steep before he depresses the plunger*. How could any self-respecting spy face his daily docket of murder and mayhem fueled by such an anemic brew?) Only then did you apply the heel of your hand to the plunger knob and ram the grounds to the bottom of the beaker, though the potable portion always retained a subtle trace of Turkish sludge. What a satisfying operation! The plunger fit *exactly* into its glass tunnel, presenting a sensuous resistance when you urged it downward; if you pressed too fast, hot water and grounds would gush out the top. The whole process involved a good deal of screwing and unscrewing and trying not to make too much of a mess. Truth to tell, it was a lot like sex (another mystery into which I was initiated that year, though not by Peter or Alex), and as soon as you'd done it once, you wanted to do it again and again and again.

Disdaining the dining hall's white polystyrene cups, most of 3
which had gone a little gray around the rim, each of us had procured our own china mug. Mine had a picture of a polka-dotted pig on it, an allusion to the frequency with which it was refilled. I stirred its contents with a silver demitasse spoon whose bowl was engraved with the name of my hometown. "Firenze" or "Cap d'Antibes" would have been preferable to "Los Angeles," but I did like the feel of the calligraphy against my tongue. Although the whole point of coffee-drinking was to be grown up—no Pepsi-Cola for bohemian intellectuals like *us!*—the amount of milk and sugar with which we undermined our sophisticated brew suggested that we needed to regress as much as we yearned to evolve. The end product resembled melted coffee ice cream.

It was the last time in my life that coffee slowed the hours rather than speeding them up. Those long, lazy nights—snow falling outside on Cowperthwaite Street, the three of us huddled inside in a warm, bright room, talking of literature and politics until the rest of Dunster House was asleep—were an essential part of my college curriculum. After all, wasn't education a matter of infusing one's life with flavorful essences, pressing out the impurities, and leaving only a little sludge at the bottom? 4

It is said that around the seventh century, somewhere near the Red Sea—whether it was Ethiopia or Yemen is a subject of debate—a herd of goats ate the magenta berries of a local shrub and began to act strangely. In a classic 1935 study called *Coffee: The Epic of a Commodity,* the German journalist Heinrich Eduard Jacob described their behavior thus: 5

> All night, for five nights in succession—nay, for seven or eight—they clambered over rocks, cutting capers, chasing one another, bleating fantastically. They turned their bearded heads hither and thither; with reddened eyes they gambolled convulsively when they caught sight of the goatherds, and then they darted off swift as arrows speeding from the bow.

Having observed the frisky goats, the imam of a nearby monastery—a sort of medieval Carlos Castaneda—roasted the berries in a chafing dish, crushed them in a mortar, mixed them with boiling water, and drank the brew. When he lay down, he couldn't sleep. His heartbeat quickened, his limbs felt light, his mood became cheerful and alert. "He was not merely thinking," wrote Jacob. "His thoughts had become concretely visible. He watched them from the right side and from the left, from above and from below. They raced like a team of horses." The imam found that he could juggle a dozen ideas in the time it normally took to consider a single one. His visual acuity increased; in the glow of his oil lamp, the parchment on his table looked unusually lustrous and the robe that hung on a nearby peg seemed to swell with life. He felt strengthened, as Jacob put it, "by heavenly food brought to him by the angels of Paradise." 6

Whoa! Little did the hopped-up imam know that while he and the goats were happily tripping, 1,3,7-trimethylxanthine (otherwise known as caffeine) was coursing through their veins, stimulating brain activity by blocking the uptake of adenosine, a neurotransmitter that, if left to its own devices, makes people (and goats) sleepy and depressed. Just enough of the stuff and you feel you've been fed by the angels of Paradise; too much, and Mr. Coffee 7

Nerves (a diabolical cartoon character with a twirly mustache who graced Postum ads in the 1930s) gets you in his grip.

Caffeine was first isolated in 1819, when the elderly Johann Wolfgang von Goethe, who had swallowed oceans of coffee in his younger days and regretted his intemperance, handed a box of Arabian mocha coffee beans to a chemist named Friedlieb Ferdinand Runge and enjoined him to analyze their contents. Runge extracted an alkaloid that, as Jacob put it, "presents itself in the form of shining, white, needle-shaped crystals, reminding us of swansdown and still more of snow." Caffeine is so toxic that laboratory technicians who handle it in its purified state wear masks and gloves. In *The World of Caffeine,* by Bennett Alan Weinberg and Bonnie K. Bealer, there is a photograph of the label from a jar of pharmaceutical-grade crystals. It reads in part: 8

> Warning! May be harmful if inhaled or swallowed. Has caused mutagenic and reproductive effects laboratory animals. Inhalation causes rapid heart rate, excitement, dizziness, pain, collapse, hypotension, fever, shortness of breath. May cause headache, insomnia, nausea, vomiting, stomach pain, collapse and convulsions.

Anyone who doubts that caffeine is a drug should read some of 9
the prose composed under its influence. Many of the books on coffee that currently crowd my desk share a certain . . . *velocity,* as if their authors, all terrifically buzzed at 3:00 A.M., couldn't get their words out fast enough and had to resort to italics, hyperbole, and sentences so long that by the time you get to the end you can't remember the beginning. (But that's only if you're uncaffeinated when you read them; if you've knocked back a couple of *cafés noirs* yourself, keeping pace is no sweat.) Heinrich Eduard Jacob boasts that his narrative was "given soul by a coffee-driven euphoria." Gregory Dicum and Nina Luttinger claim that while they were writing *The Coffee Book: Anatomy of an Industry from Crop to the Last Drop,* they

> sucked down 83 double Americanos, 12 double espressos, 4 perfect ristrettos, 812 regular cups (from 241 French press-loads, plus 87 cups of drip coffee), 47 Turkish coffees, a half-dozen regrettable cups of flavored coffee, 10 pounds of organic coffee, 7 pounds of fair trade coffee, a quarter pound of chicory and a handful of hemp seeds as occasional adjuncts, 1 can of ground supermarket coffee (drunk mostly iced), 6 canned or bottled coffee drinks, 2 pints of coffee beer, a handful of mochas, 1 pint of coffee concentrate, a couple of cappuccinos, 1 espresso soda, and, just to see, a lone double tall low-fat soy orange decaf latte.

Their book contains only 196 pages and doesn't look as if it took 10
very long to write; that decaf latte aside, the authors' caffeine quota per day must have been prodigious. (But note their exactitude: coffee makes you peppy, but it doesn't make you sloppy.)

The contemporary master of the genre is Stewart Lee Allen, 11
known as "the Hunter S. Thompson of coffee journalism," whose gonzo masterwork, *The Devil's Cup,* entailed the consumption of "2,920 liters of percolated, (drip, espresso, latte, cappuccino, macchiato, con panna, instant and americana." (It isn't very long, either. By the time Allen finished, his blood must have been largely composed of 1, 3, 7-trimethylxanthine.) Following the historical routes by which coffee spread around the globe, Allen gets wired in Harrar, Sant'a, Istanbul, Vienna, Munich, Paris, Rio de Janeiro, and various points across the United States, attempting to finance his travels and his coffee habit with complicated transactions involving forged passports and smuggled art. He ends up on Route 66, in search of the worst cup of coffee in America, in a Honda Accord driveaway filled with every form of caffeine he can think of: Stimu-Chew, Water Joe, Krank, hi-caf candy, and a vial of caffeine crystals (scored from an Internet site that features images of twitching eyeballs) whose resemblance to cocaine occasions some exciting psychopharmacological plot twists when a state trooper pulls him over in Athens, Tennessee.

But in the realm of twitching eyeballs, even Stewart Lee Allen 12
can't hold a candle to Honoré de Balzac, the model for every espresso-swilling writer who has followed in his jittery footsteps. What hashish was to Baudelaire, opium to Coleridge, cocaine to Robert Louis Stevenson, nitrous oxide to Robert Southey, mescaline to Aldous Huxley, and Benzedrine to Jack Kerouac, caffeine was to Balzac. The habit started early. Like a preppie with an expensive connection, he ran up alarming debts with a concierge who, for a price, was willing to sneak contraband coffee beans into Balzac's boarding school. As an adult, grinding out novels eighteen hours a day while listening for the rap of creditors at the door, Balzac observed the addict's classic regimen, boosting his doses as his tolerance mounted. First he drank one cup a day, then a few cups, then many cups, then forty cups. Finally, by using less and less water, he increased the concentration of each fix until he was eating dry coffee grounds: "a horrible, rather brutal method," he wrote, "that I recommend only to men of excessive vigor, men with thick black hair and skin covered with liver spots, men with big square hands and legs shaped like bowling pins." Although the recipe was hell on the stomach, it dispatched caffeine to the brain with exquisite efficiency.

> From that moment on, everything becomes agitated. Ideas quick-march into motion like battalions of a grand army to its legendary fighting ground, and the battle rages. Memories charge in, bright flags on high; the cavalry of metaphor deploys with a magnificent gallop; the artillery of logic rushes up with clattering wagons and cartridges; on imagination's orders, sharpshooters sight and fire; forms and shapes and characters rear up; the paper is spread with ink.

Could that passage have been written on decaf? 13

Balzac's coffeepot is displayed at 47 rue Raynouard in Paris, 14
where he lived for much of his miserable last decade, writing *La Cousine Bette* and *Le Cousin Pons,* losing his health, and escaping bill collectors through a secret door. My friend Adam (who likes his espresso strong but with sugar) visited the house a few years ago. "The coffeepot is red and white china," he wrote me, "and bears Balzac's monogram. It's an elegant, neat little thing, almost nautical in appearance. I can imagine it reigning serenely over the otherwise-general squalor of his later life, a small pharos of caffeine amid the gloom."

When I was fifteen, I went to Paris myself. I didn't realize it at 15
the time, but that summer I stood at a fateful crossroads. One way led to coffee, the other to liquor.

I was a student on a high school French program in an era when 16
the construction of *in loco parentis* was considerably looser than it is now. I began each day with a *café au lait* at a local patisserie and ended it with a *crème de menthe frappé* at a bar. One afternoon, after we had left Paris and were traveling through southern France, the director of the program invited me to lunch at a three-star restaurant in Vienne, where we shared *pâté de foie gras en brioche, mousse de truite Périgueux, turbot á la crème aux herbes, pintadeau aux herbes, gratin dauphinois, fromages, gâteau aux marrons, petits fours,* and a Brut Crémant '62. I'd never drunk half a bottle of wine before. Afterward, en route to Avignon in Monsieur Cosnard's Mercedes, I was asked to help navigate, a task that appeared inexplicably difficult until I realized I was holding the map upside down.

The conclusion was clear: *Why would anyone want to feel like this?* 17
Although I never became a teetotaler, I knew—especially when I woke up the next morning with a hangover—that I would cast my lot with caffeine, not with alcohol. Why would I wish my senses to be dulled when they could be sharpened? Why would I wish to forget when I could remember? Why would I wish to mumble when I could scintillate? Of course, since even in those days I was a loquacious workaholic who liked to stay up late, you might think I'd pick

a drug that would nudge me closer to the center of the bell curve instead of pushing me farther out on the edge—but of course I didn't. Who does? Don't we all just keep doing the things that make us even more like ourselves?

As I lay in bed with a godawful headache, sunlight streamed through the open window, and so did the smell of good French coffee from the hotel kitchen downstairs. 18

Heinrich Eduard Jacob called coffee the "anti-Bacchus." By the middle of the seventeenth century, when it had filtered westward from the Middle East and begun to captivate Europe, its potential consumers were in dire need of sobering up. "The eyes, the blood-vessels, the senses of the men of those days were soused in beer," observed Jacob. "It choked their livers, their voices, and their hearts." The average Englishman drank three liters of beer a day—nearly two six-packs—and spent a lot of time bumping into lampposts and falling into gutters. Coffee was hailed as a salubrious alternative. As an anonymous poet put it in 1674, "When foggy Ale, leavying up mighty trains/Of muddy vapours, had besieg'd our Brains,/Then Heaven in Pity . . ./First sent amongst us this All-healing Berry." 19

Between 1645 and 1750, as coffeehouses sprang up in Paris, Vienna, Leipzig, Amsterdam, Rome, and Venice, the All-healing Berry defogged innumerable Continental brains. But until tea gained the upper hand around 1730, the English were the undisputed kings of coffee. By the most conservative estimates, London had five hundred coffeehouses at the turn of the eighteenth century. (If New York City were similarly equipped today, it would have nearly eight thousand.) These weren't merely places to drink the muddy liquid that one critic likened to "syrup of soot or essence of old shoes." In the days when public libraries were nonexistent and journalism was in its embryonic stages, they were a vital center of news, gossip, and education—"penny universities" whose main business, in the words of a 1657 newspaper ad, was "PUBLICK INTERCOURSE." 20

London had a coffeehouse for everyone (as long as you were male). If you were a gambler, you went to White's. If you were a physician, you went to Garraway's or Child's. If you were a businessman, you went to Lloyd's, which later evolved into the great insurance house. If you were a scientist, you went to the Grecian, where Isaac Newton, Edmund Halley, and Hans Sloane once staged a public dissection of a dolphin that had been caught in the Thames. If you were a journalist, you went to Button's, where Joseph 21

Addison had set up a "Reader's Letter-box" shaped like a lion's head; you could post submissions to *The Guardian* in its mouth. And if you were a man of letters, you—along with Pope, Pepys, and Dryden—went to Will's, where you could join a debate on whether Milton should have written *Paradise Lost* in rhymed couplets instead of blank verse. These coffeehouses changed the course of English social history by demonstrating how pleasant it was to hang out in a place where (according to a 1674 set of Rules and Orders of the Coffee House) "Gentry, Tradesmen, all are welcome hither, / and may without affront sit down together." And they changed the course of English literature by turning monologuists into conversationalists. A 1705 watercolor that now hangs in the British Museum depicts a typical establishment, a high-ceilinged room dominated by a huge black coffee cauldron that simmers over a blazing fire. The periwigged patrons are sipping coffee, smoking pipes, reading news-sheets, and scribbling in notebooks, but most of all—you can tell from their gesticulations—they are talking.

Looking back, I see that my evenings in Dunster House were a penny university in miniature. It therefore saddens me to report that these days my coffee-drinking is usually a solitary affair, a Balzacian response to deadlines (though in smaller doses) rather than an opportunity for PUBLICK INTERCOURSE. Time is scarcer than it used to be; I make my coffee with a disposable paper filter stuffed into a little plastic cone, not in a *cafetière a piston*. My customary intake is only a cup or two a day—still with milk and sugar—though I ratchet up my consumption when I'm writing. In the spirit of participatory journalism, every word of this essay has been written under the influence of 1, 3, 7-trimethylxanthine, in quantities sufficient to justify the use, after a respite of thirty years, of the mug with the polka-dotted pig. 22

My coffee is in every way a weaker brew than it once was, but I could never give it up entirely. This is not just a matter of habit, sentiment, or taste; it is more akin to the reasons that, long ago, the Galla people of Ethiopia ate ground coffee mixed with animal fat before they went off to fight, or that the night before every battle of the Civil War, you would have seen hundreds of campfires flickering in the darkness, each surmounted by a pot of thick, black, courage-inducing coffee. 23

I remember a morning five years ago when I took a dawn flight to Fort Myers, Florida. My father had just been hospitalized with what looked like and in fact turned out to be—terminal cancer, and the task of dealing with doctors, nurses, and hospice workers had fallen to me. I'd been up all night, and I stumbled off the plane so 24 bleary I could hardly walk. There, shimmering like a mirage at the end of the jetway, in the midst of what on my last visit had been a wasteland of Pizza Huts and Burger Kings, stood a newly opened Starbucks.

I know, I know. Heartless corporate giant. Monster of coast-to- 25
coast uniformity. Killer of mom-and-pop cafés. But that's not what I thought at that moment. I thought: I'm going to order a grande latte with whole milk. I'm going to pour in two packets of Sugar in the Raw, and stir really well so there are no undissolved crystals at the bottom. I'm going to sit down and drink it slowly. Then I'm going to drive to the hospital.

As I walked toward the counter, I said to myself: *I can do this.* 26

Meanings and Values

1. Paragraphs 1–4 focus on the writer's college experiences. What other sections does the essay have, and what subject areas do they cover as a way of defining *coffee*, its meanings, and its roles for people?
2. Why are Paragraphs 1–4 filled with sophisticated, unfamiliar terms along with extensive attention to trivial details?
3. What does the history of coffee and its uses in Paragraphs 5–14 add to the definition of coffee?

Expository Techniques

1. The writer opens each of these sections with references to time: 15–18, 19–21, and 22–26. What are these references? How do they serve to tie the parts of the essay together? What other sections open in similar ways? (See "Guide to Terms": *Transitions.*)
2. Which definition strategies does the writer use in this essay, and where? (See "Developing Definitions," pp. 308–310.)
3. At times in the essay, the writer indicates more or less directly the effects of coffee and its meaning for coffee drinkers. Identify these statements.
4. Does the essay seem to indicate that it is possible to provide a concise definition of coffee? If so, state it in your own words. If not, explain where in the essay the writer comes closest to defining the meaning of coffee.

DICTION AND VOCABULARY

1. In the last sentence of Paragraph 4, Fadiman offers an extended comparison (an analogy). State it in your own words, and explain why you find it accurate and effective, or not. (See the introduction to Chapter 6 for a discussion of Analogy; see also Guide: *Analogy.*)
2. a. The opening four paragraphs of the essay contain many allusions. Identify as many as you can. (Guide: *Figures of Speech.*)

   b. Do you think readers are expected to understand these allusions? If not, why did the writer put them in the text?
3. This essay contains words likely to be unfamiliar to many readers. Some are used to indicate the writer's state of mind at the time of events. Others add an exotic or far-away feel to the essay. If you do not know the meaning of them, look them up in a dictionary.

READ TO WRITE

1. **Collaborating:** Coffee isn't the only substance or activity that people make an important part of their lives. Working in a group, brainstorm other such substances or activities as possible topics for papers, and choose one to list details that might be used in an essay that provides a definition of the topic.
2. **Considering Audience:** Are Anne Fadiman's college experiences or her love of coffee typical of college students today? In a paragraph or two, indicate how you would revise the essay so that it more clearly reflects the interests, attitudes, and values of the majority of contemporary college students.
3. **Developing an Essay:** Using Fadiman's approach, define something you love by its good effects in various times and places so that others can understand why you consider it so important.

(NOTE: Suggestions for essays requiring development by means of DEFINITION are on pp. 349–350 at the end of this chapter.)

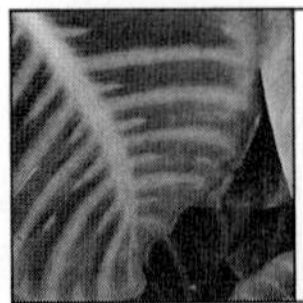

Issues and Ideas

Defining Values and Roles

- Stephen L. Carter, *The Insufficiency of Honesty*
- Veronica Chambers, *Mother's Day*

Leave It to Beaver represents for many people a time and a culture whose values, relationships, and roles were simple, clear, and unchanging. Things were probably never that simple, though the television program certainly made them appear that way. Nonetheless, values, identities, and relationships are certainly undergoing more changes and redefinition now than they were five decades ago. The changes involve not only the development of new identities but also the recognition that all our identities are constructed from multiple—and sometimes seemingly incompatible—elements. Stephen Carter, in "The Insufficiency of Honesty," reminds us of the complexity of values and identities, even those as often praised as honesty.

Though we are always the children of our parents, sometimes we end up playing parental roles toward them, offering advice or counsel, just as Veronica Chambers explains in her essay, "Mother's Day." Though we might like to think of ourselves as typically middle class, Midwestern, or business/labor minded in our values and outlooks, few, if any, of us are so easily defined. Even such seemingly clear roles as "mother" and "father" can be filled by many different people and by more than one person, especially in this age of blended families.

These two essays remind us that the need to understand our values, identities, and roles in relation to other people makes definition an important pattern of thought and analysis. Each essay also demonstrates many other expository patterns.

STEPHEN L. CARTER

STEPHEN L. CARTER is professor of law at Yale Law School and the author of several controversial but highly respected and tightly reasoned books that explore issues in contemporary ethics, politics, and social relationships. After graduating from Yale Law School, he had a variety of professional experiences, including clerking for U.S. Supreme Court Justice Thurgood Marshall and working in a prestigious law firm. Carter's books are *Reflections of an Affirmative Action Baby* (1992), *The Culture of Disbelief: How American Law and Politics Trivialize Religious Devotion* (1994), *The Confirmation Mess: Cleaning Up the Federal Appointments Mess,* (1995), *Integrity* (1997), and *Civility* (1999) (nonfiction); and *The Emperor of Ocean Park* (2002) (a novel).

The Insufficiency of Honesty

Integrity is not simply a term or idea. It refers to a way of acting and of discerning the qualities of our actions. Integrity may be something we all claim to admire and wish to have ourselves, but as Stephen L. Carter points out in this essay first published in the *Atlantic Monthly,* it can be very difficult to achieve.

A couple of years ago I began a university commencement address by telling the audience that I was going to talk about integrity. The crowd broke into applause. Applause! Just because they had heard the word "integrity": that's how starved for it they were. They had no idea how I was using the word, or what I was going to say about integrity, or, indeed, whether I was for it or against it. But they knew they liked the idea of talking about it. 1

Very well, let us consider this word "integrity." Integrity is like the weather: every body talks about it but nobody knows what to do about it. Integrity is that stuff that we always want more of. Some say that we need to return to the good old days when we had a lot more of it. Others say that we as a nation have never really had enough of it. Hardly anybody stops to explain exactly what we mean by it, or how we know it is a good thing, or why everybody needs to have the same amount of it. Indeed, the only trouble with integrity is that everybody who uses the word seems to mean something slightly different. 2

For instance, when I refer to integrity, do I mean simply "honesty"? The answer is no; although honesty is a virtue of importance, 3 it is a different virtue from integrity. Let us, for simplicity, think of honesty as not lying; and let us further accept Sissela Bok's definition of a lie: "any intentionally deceptive message which is *stated*." Plainly, one cannot have integrity without being honest (although, as we shall see, the matter gets complicated), but one can certainly be honest and yet have little integrity.

When I refer to integrity, I have something very specific in mind. Integrity, as I will use the term, requires three steps: discerning what is right and what is wrong; acting on what you have discerned, even at personal cost; and saying openly that you are acting on your understanding of right and wrong. The first criterion captures the idea that integrity requires a degree of moral reflectiveness. The second brings in the ideal of a person of integrity as steadfast, a quality that includes keeping one's commitments. The third reminds us that a person of integrity can be trusted. 4

The first point to understand about the difference between honesty and integrity is that a person may be entirely honest without ever engaging in the hard work of discernment that integrity requires: she may tell us quite truthfully what she believes without ever taking the time to figure out whether what she believes is good and right and true. The problem may be as simple as someone's foolishly saying something that hurts a friend's feelings; a few moments of thought would have revealed the likelihood of the hurt and the lack of necessity for the comment. Or the problem may be more complex, as when a man who was raised from birth in a society that preaches racism states his belief in one race's inferiority as a fact, without ever really considering that perhaps this deeply held view is wrong. Certainly the racist is being honest—he is telling us what he actually thinks—but his honesty does not add up to integrity. 5

Telling Everything You Know

A wonderful epigram sometimes attributed to the filmmaker Sam Goldwyn goes like this: "The most important thing in acting is honesty; once you learn to fake that, you're in." The point is that honesty can be something one *seems* to have. Without integrity, what passes for honesty often is nothing of the kind; it is fake honesty—or it is honest but irrelevant and perhaps even immoral. 6

Consider an example. A man who has been married for fifty years confesses to his wife on his deathbed that he was unfaithful thirty-five years earlier. The dishonesty was killing his spirit, he says. Now he has cleared his conscience and is able to die in peace. 7

The husband has been honest—sort of. He has certainly unburdened himself. And he has probably made his wife (soon to be his widow) quite miserable in the process, because even if she forgives him, she will not be able to remember him with quite the vivid image of love and loyalty that she had hoped for. Arranging his own emotional affairs to ease his transition to death, he has shifted to his wife the burden of confusion and pain, perhaps for the rest of her life. Moreover, he has attempted his honesty at the one time in his life when it carries no risk; acting in accordance with what you think is right and risking no loss in the process is a rather thin and unadmirable form of honesty. 8

Besides, even though the husband has been honest in a sense, he has now twice been unfaithful to his wife: once thirty-five years ago, when he had his affair, and again when, nearing death, he decided that his own peace of mind was more important than hers. In trying to be honest he has violated his marriage vow by acting toward his wife not with love but with naked and perhaps even cruel self-interest. 9

As my mother used to say, you don't have to tell people everything you know. Lying and nondisclosure, as the law often recognizes, are not the same thing. Sometimes it is actually illegal to tell what you know, as, for example, in the disclosure of certain financial information by market insiders. Or it may be unethical, as when a lawyer reveals a confidence entrusted to her by a client. It may be simple bad manners, as in the case of a gratuitous comment to a colleague on his or her attire. And it may be subject to religious punishment, as when a Roman Catholic priest breaks the seal of the confessional—an offense that carries automatic excommunication. 10

In all the cases just mentioned, the problem with telling everything you know is that somebody else is harmed. Harm may not be the intention, but it is certainly the effect. Honesty is most laudable when we risk harm to ourselves; it becomes a good deal less so if we instead risk harm to others when there is no gain to anyone other than ourselves. Integrity may counsel keeping our secrets in order to spare the feelings of others. Sometimes, as in the example of the wayward husband, the reason we want to tell what we know is precisely to shift our pain onto somebody else—a course of action dictated less by integrity than by self-interest. Fortunately, integrity and self-interest often coincide, as when a politician of integrity is rewarded with our votes. But often they do not, and it is at those moments that our integrity is truly tested. 11

Error

Another reason that honesty alone is no substitute for integrity is that if forthrightness is not preceded by discernment, it may result in the expression of an incorrect moral judgment. In other words, I may be honest about what I believe, but if I have never tested my beliefs, I may be wrong. And here I mean "wrong" in a particular sense: the proposition in question is wrong if I would change my mind about it after hard moral reflection. 12

Consider this example. Having been taught all his life that women are not as smart as men, a manager gives the women on his staff less-challenging assignments than he gives the men. He does this, he believes, for their own benefit: he does not want them to fail, and he believes that they will if he gives them tougher assignments. Moreover, when one of the women on his staff does poor work, he does not berate her as harshly as he would a man, because he expects nothing more. And he claims to be acting with integrity because he is acting according to his own deepest beliefs. 13

The manager fails the most basic test of integrity. The question is not whether his actions are consistent with what he most deeply believes but whether he has done the hard work of discerning whether what he most deeply believes is right. The manager has not taken this harder step. 14

Moreover, even within the universe that the manager has constructed for himself, he is not acting with integrity. Although he is obviously wrong to think that the women on his staff are not as good as the men, even were he right, that would not justify applying different standards to their work. By so doing he betrays both his obligation to the institution that employs him and his duty as a manager to evaluate his employees. 15

The problem that the manager faces is an enormous one in our practical politics, where having the dialogue that makes democracy work can seem impossible because of our tendency to cling to our views even when we have not examined them. As Jean Bethke Elshtain has said, borrowing from John Courtney Murray, our politics are so fractured and contentious that we often cannot even reach *disagreement.* Our refusal to look closely at our own most cherished principles is surely a large part of the reason. Socrates thought the unexamined life not worth living. But the unhappy truth is that few of us actually have the time for constant reflection on our views—on public or private morality. Examine them we must, however, or we will never know whether we might be wrong. 16

None of this should be taken to mean that integrity as I have described it presupposes a single correct truth. If, for example, your integrity-guided search tells you that affirmative action is wrong, and my integrity-guided search tells me that affirmative action is right, we need not conclude that one of us lacks integrity. As it happens, I believe—both as a Christian and as a secular citizen who struggles toward moral understanding—that we *can* find true and sound answers to our moral questions. But I do not pretend to have found very many of them, nor is an exposition of them my purpose here. 17

It is the case not that there aren't any right answers but that, given human fallibility, we need to be careful in assuming that we have found them. However, today's political talk about how it is wrong for the government to impose one person's morality on somebody else is just mindless chatter. *Every* law imposes one person's morality on somebody else, because law has only two functions: to tell people to do what they would rather not or to forbid them to do what they would. 18

And if the surveys can be believed, there is far more moral agreement in America than we sometimes allow ourselves to think. One of the reasons that character education for young people makes so much sense to so many people is precisely that there seems to be a core set of moral understandings—we might call them the American Core—that most of us accept. Some of the virtues in this American Core are, one hopes, relatively noncontroversial. About 500 American communities have signed on to Michael Josephson's program to emphasize the "six pillars" of good character: trustworthiness, respect, responsibility, caring, fairness, and citizenship. These virtues might lead to a similarly noncontroversial set of political values: having an honest regard for ourselves and others, protecting freedom of thought and religious belief, and refusing to steal or murder. 19

Honesty and Competing Responsibilities

A further problem with too great an exaltation of honesty is that it may allow us to escape responsibilities that morality bids us bear. If honesty is substituted for integrity, one might think that if I say I am not planning to fulfill a duty, I need not fulfill it. But it would be a peculiar morality indeed that granted us the right to avoid our moral responsibilities simply by stating our intention to ignore them. Integrity does not permit such an easy escape. 20

Consider an example. Before engaging in sex with a woman, her lover tells her that if she gets pregnant, it is her problem, not his. 21

She says that she understands. In due course she does wind up pregnant. If we believe, as I hope we do, that the man would ordinarily have a moral responsibility toward both the child he will have helped to bring into the world and the child's mother, then his honest statement of what he intends does not spare him that responsibility.

This vision of responsibility assumes that not all moral obligations stem from consent or from a stated intention. The linking of obligations to promises is a rather modern and perhaps uniquely Western way of looking at life, and perhaps a luxury that only the well-to-do can afford. As Fred and Shulamit Korn (a philosopher and an anthropologist) have pointed out, "If one looks at ethnographic accounts of other societies, one finds that, while obligations everywhere play a crucial role in social life, promising is not preeminent among the sources of obligation and is not even mentioned by most anthropologists." The Korns have made a study of Tonga, where promises are virtually unknown but the social order is remarkably stable. If life without any promises seems extreme, we Americans sometimes go too far the other way, parsing not only our contracts but even our marriage vows in order to discover the absolute minimum obligation that we have to others as a result of our promises. 22

That some societies in the world have worked out evidently functional structures of obligation without the need for promise or consent does not tell us what *we* should do. But it serves as a reminder of the basic proposition that our existence in civil society creates a set of mutual responsibilities that philosophers used to capture in the fiction of the social contract. Nowadays, here in America, people seem to spend their time thinking of even cleverer ways to avoid their obligations, instead of doing what integrity commands and fulfilling them. And all too often honesty is their excuse. 23

Meanings and Values

1. Most readers are likely to consider honesty a good trait. Why, therefore, do you think Carter created a definition that points out its shortcomings? What do you think was his overall purpose in writing the essay? Do you believe the essay has more than one purpose? If so, what are they? (See "Guide to Terms": *Purpose.*)

2. List the reasons the author gives for considering honesty insufficient. State in your own words why the author believes that the men in Paragraphs 7–9 and 21 have honesty but lack integrity.

3. Does this essay have a thesis statement? If so, where is it? Does it adequately sum up the main idea of the entire essay? Why, or why not? If the essay does not have a thesis statement, is it nonetheless organized around a main idea or theme? What is it? (Guide: *Thesis.*) Explain why you consider the essay unified or not unified. (Guide: *Unity.*)

Expository Techniques

1. If one of the main purposes of this essay is to define *integrity,* why does the writer spend so much time discussing the meaning of *honesty?* In formulating your answer, take into account various definition strategies and the likely responses of readers to concepts like honesty.

2. What is the main definition strategy Carter employs in this essay? How is the organization of the essay related to this strategy? Be specific in answering this question. What other definition patterns does the writer employ, and where in the essay does he use them?

3. Which paragraphs in the essay are devoted wholly, or mostly, to qualification? (Guide: *Qualification.*) What role(s) do they play in helping develop the definitions? Why would the essay be weaker without them?

4. Where in the essay does the writer use transitions at the beginnings of paragraphs to highlight the essay's organization and indicate the definition strategy he is employing? (Guide: *Transition.*)

Diction and Vocabulary

1. Throughout the essay, Carter uses contrasting words and concepts to explain the difference between honesty and integrity. Sometimes the contrasts involve the denotation of words and sometimes the connotations. (Guide: *Connotation/Denotation.*) Discuss the contrasts as they appear in Paragraphs 6, 8, and 9, and explain the use Carter makes of them. (Guide: *Diction.*) Explain the extent to which Carter reinforces the contrasts through sentence structure. (Guide: *Syntax.*)

2. In the course of the essay, Carter repeats a small number of words quite frequently, often varying their form. What are the words? How are they related to the essay's thesis (or theme)? How do they contribute to the essay's coherence? (Guide: *Coherence.*)

3. If you do not know the meanings of some of the following terms, look them up in a dictionary: *discerning, criterion, steadfast* (Par. 4); *epigram* (6); *gratuitous, excommunication* (10); *laudable, counsel* (11); *forthrightness* (12); *contentious* (16); *presupposes* (17); *fallibility, impose* (18); *parsing* (22).

READ AND WRITE

1. **Collaborating:** Working in a group, create a list of terms naming qualities that most people would agree are virtues (like *honesty* and *integrity*). Choose two and write three brief examples for each word that help define it. Choose examples that indicate what the term means and also some that indicate what it does not or should not mean. Include examples focusing on women as well as men.
2. **Considering Audience:** Rewrite Carter's essay by substituting examples from women's experiences, or use the essay as a model for a discussion of moral concepts as they apply to both men and women.
3. **Developing an essay:** Carter's title, "The Insufficiency of Honesty," suggests both a focus for the essay and an interesting approach to explaining why a particular quality is inadequate. Borrow this approach for an essay. Explain why your subject is inadequate, insufficient, or incomplete.

(NOTE: Suggestions for topics requiring development by use of DEFINITION are on pp. 340–350 at the end of this chapter.)

VERONICA CHAMBERS

VERONICA CHAMBERS is a writer living in New York City. She was a contributing editor for *Glamour* and *Esquire* and has published a memoir, *Mama's Girl* (1996).

Mother's Day

In this selection from her book *Mama's Girl,* also published as an essay in *Glamour* magazine, Chambers uses a variety of expository patterns (comparison, example, narrative, cause and effect) to help understand why her Mother's Day gift received such a cool reception. As she considers the differences between her perspective as an African American professional woman and college-educated writer with that of her mother, who struggled to raise her child on a secretary's salary in the days when educational and occupational opportunities for African Americans were strictly limited, Chambers comes to a deeper appreciation of her mother's achievements.

A couple of years ago, I earned a good salary for the first time and I wanted to do something special for my mother. So I sent her a gift certificate for a day at Elizabeth Arden. Included were a massage, facial, sauna and makeover—the works, plus tips. My mother wouldn't have to spend a dime, only the subway token it would take to get her there. I called her up on Mother's Day, all excited about the gift. She was excited, too, and described how it had come gift-wrapped with a big red bow. Then she asked me a question that broke my heart in two. "Vee?" she whispered. "Do they allow black people in those places?" 1

It was 1992 and my mother was asking whether Elizabeth Arden would slam the red door in her black face. "Of course they allow black people!" I said, using an angry voice to conceal how hurt I felt. "I've paid for everything, including a tip for everyone who touches your body. So if anybody so much as looks at you funny, you tell me!" 2

Months went by and my mother did not use the gift certificate. "*You* use it," she would tell me. "You work so hard. Burning the candle at both ends. . . ." Finally, I got furious with her and made some empty threat about refusing to talk to her until she went to Elizabeth Arden. She wouldn't budge. 3

In my frustration I reimagined the situation as a Daliesque fantasy in which I was an avenging angel pushing my mother through 4 the Red Door. When a friend suggested that perhaps my mother did not want to go to Elizabeth Arden alone, I sent her neighbor a gift certificate too, but it didn't help: She turned out to be just as afraid to go as my mother.

Finally, almost a year later, my mother called and said, "Guess where I've just been? Elizabeth Arden." 5

My heart almost stopped. "How was it?" I asked. 6

"Nice . . . but everyone there was just like you," she said coyly. 7

"Just like *me?*" I repeated disbelievingly, picturing the Fifth Avenue crowd of older white women laid out on massage tables. 8

"Professionals. Upper-class women. You know," she replied. 9

While I was thrilled that she'd gone, that exchange made me wonder what my mother saw when she looked at me. I wondered if everything about me that she chose to see as being white—my education, my career, my social activities—obscured everything about me that was black—my family, my community, my mother herself. I always knew she saw me as different from her, but not until she went to Elizabeth Arden did I realize how different. 10

I never stop feeling that I want to make things up to my mother—make up for her difficulties with my father, from whom she was eventually divorced, for my brother's failure to do well in school or in a job, for the ways in which we all left her. So I buy her things. If I'm shopping and I buy myself a suit, I'll get my mother a blouse. I send her vases and candles and antique dolls. One of the first questions I ask when I enter a store is: "Can you ship this somewhere for me?" I'd be a liar if I said my generosity was only about bestowing kindnesses on my mother. It is also about easing my own guilt. 11

I am more aware now of how my schooling and experiences separate us, but I cannot get used to the distance. She is so much a part of me that I half felt I graduated college for both of us. To me, the newfound abundance of the money I can earn has meaning for both of us. But my mother sees things differently. We are separated by education and economics. 12

When I was in college, my mother once called me an Oreo—black on the outside, white on the inside. The word, so cruel when it comes from a black person's peers, was like a punch in the face coming from my mother—as if I were a total stranger and not her own child. Later, when I told her how much it had hurt me, she said, "But I was just joking!" 13

Now that I am working, she is fond of calling me a Buppie. I hate it, I tell her, and ask her to stop. But if I talk about wanting to 14 see a certain play or deliberate over whether to buy a painting, she can't help but let it slip: "You're such a Buppie." There is a texture of affection and pride in her voice that suggests she's glad I'm not as poor as she was when she was my age, but it is a pride I have trouble absorbing. Her voice says, "I am proud of you—but you are now an entirely different being than I am."

Going from poor to middle class was both the longest and the 15
shortest transition I have ever made. Long, because every day that I went without was just one of an unending stretch of days in which I'd always done without. Once I'd craved things so deeply that I kept myself away from malls and shops, so as not to preoccupy myself with what I could not have. In college I collected mail-order catalogs, marking them up with stars and circling the outfits I liked in the colors and sizes I wanted. Desire became a game and playing the game was satisfying in its own way. At the end of freshman year, a friend asked, "Why do you always mark up those catalogs when you never order anything?" I hadn't realized that anyone noticed what had become a mindless habit, and I didn't know what to say. Was he being cruel?

"I don't know," I said, feigning dumbness and vowing to keep 16
the catalogs out of sight.

But the jump from poverty to solvency seemed short and sud- 17
den because it was one I made alone. It was just me in an apartment, staring at a paycheck that was bigger than any I'd ever seen. Who could I call, without it sounding like I was bragging? Who wouldn't immediately ask for a loan? Who would understand how a thousand dollars could feel so much like a million? I wanted my mother there on the other end of the phone.

But I also felt guilty, because I felt she was much more deserv- 18
ing of that check than I was. I watched my mother work all her life with no reward greater than a cost-of-living raise; she was always just getting by. I knew that hard work was no guarantee of success. Success was only a dream—the big payoff that never came from my father's get-rich-quick schemes, or a winning lottery number that came to you in a vision. My life had been different. And even after going to college, even after years of hard work, I still felt deep inside that I was more lucky than successful. As if I had dreamed of a number and that number had come in.

My mother was neither lucky nor successful. She believed in the 19
promise of the civil rights movement, but never really thought what those rights would mean to her. She taught her children the importance of equality and pride, but never expected to live in equality herself.

I can see now that although she was affected by the benefits of integration—no more sitting in the back of the bus, no more separate water fountains—most of the triumphs of the movement remained for my mother events that happened on TV. In 1970, my mother gave birth to me and worked as a secretary. In the 1990s, my mother is still a secretary. She's worked hard all her life, mostly for white people, and the civil rights movement did not change that. What it changed was me, and I wasn't some bright, young black woman that my mother saw on TV. I was her daughter. My success brought the benefits of integration through her front door, and that scared her. She could call me an Oreo and a Buppie and try to keep what I represented at a safe distance, but the things I bought her, the restaurants I took her to, forced her to consider life differently. Maybe it wouldn't take a winning lottery ticket for her to be able to lead a better life. 20

I called my mother recently and had a long talk about money. My mother is only 45. She has so much life ahead of her. I was hoping that I could use some of what I've learned about saving and investing to make her life more comfortable, so I began to ask her questions: What do your retirement savings look like? What are your financial goals? She had to stop and think. 21

"You mean goals besides paying the rent and putting dinner on the table?" She laughed nervously. 22

"Yes," I said. "What do you want to own? What trips do you want to take?" 23

There wasn't much she wanted to own. What she really wanted to do was travel. She wanted to go to Jamaica, Ghana, and Brazil. The tentativeness in her voice was so clear, as if just by speaking her wishes aloud, she might cause the genie to dive back into its bottle. My mother had never been able to see further ahead than the next day or next month. I knew then why it had scared her when, as a ten-year-old, I started talking about college. She didn't know what we were going to eat for the next seven days, much less where she would find tuition in seven years. 24

Now as we discussed *her* money for the first time, I told my mother that if she didn't dream, if she didn't think about what she wanted to have, then she was going to wake up and another 20 years would be gone. "There's nothing to save," she said, I asked if I could see her weekly budget. I told her I knew it was personal, but I needed to know exactly how much she and my stepfather made and where it was going. "What budget?" she said. 25

I wrote down all my mother's figures—how much she owed, what little she had saved, how much she and my stepfather made. I 26 did a budget and a savings plan and outlined a retirement plan that would give her some sort of nest egg.

"It's not a lot," I told her. "You'd probably still need to work. But maybe you could save enough to open a business." I wrote out the plan and mailed it to her. When she called me back, I could tell she was impressed. She told me that she and my stepfather had gone over my plan and they thought they could stick to it. 27

My mother told me she had tried to save money when we were little, but often she was too embarrassed to take a five dollar bill up to the teller's window and deposit it, so she would keep it in an envelope. By the next week, it would be gone. 28

"I feel like I can really be hopeful now," she said. "Like I have something to look forward to besides bills." Then she paused and added, "I'm still going to play the lottery, and if I hit it, then to hell with your savings plan." I laughed and said that would be fine. 29

For the first time in my life, I hear in my mother's voice that she is more than just coping, more than just figuring out how to get by. When I hear my mother talk, I can hear her dreaming and it's the sweetest sound in the world to me. 30

Meanings and Values

1. In what ways does the author's mother define her daughter? In what ways does the author define her mother? In what ways does the author define herself?
2. What social movements and changes in values and attitudes make necessary the redefinition of identity and roles the author undertakes in this essay? How many of these social movements are mentioned in the essay, and where are they mentioned?
3. How are readers likely to react to the question at the end of Paragraph 1? What might determine the ways different readers react? What proportion of readers do you think are likely to react as the writer does? Why?

Expository Techniques

1. In what ways does the question at the end of Paragraph 1 act as a justification for the redefining of roles that Chambers undertakes in this essay? Does it provide justification for most readers as well as for the writer? If not, how else does the writer justify the need for new definitions?

2. Can the sentence at the end of Paragraph 1 be considered a thesis statement? Why, or why not? If not, where else in the essay does the author make plain the purpose or thesis (main theme) of the piece? (See "Guide to Terms": *Thesis; Purpose.*)
3. Which paragraphs in the essay use comparison as an expository pattern? What do they contribute to the process of definition?

Diction and Vocabulary

1. Many of the paragraphs in this essay discuss conflicting definitions and misunderstandings. Discuss how the writer uses transitions in Paragraphs 12–14 and 17–20 to emphasize such conflicts and contrasting perspectives. (Guide: *Transition; Emphasis.*)
2. To what does the word "Daliesque" in Paragraph 4 allude? (Guide: *Figures of Speech.*) What does this reveal about the speaker's attitudes and perspective? What is a "Buppie"? Why would the writer be offended by the term?
3. If you do not know the meaning of some of the following words, look them up in a dictionary: *sauna* (Par. 1); *disbelievingly* (8); *bestowing* (11); *tentativeness* (24).

Read to Write

1. **Collaborating:** Working with a partner, discuss some aspect of your individual upbringings that distinguishes you from each other. Discuss the differences, and plan an essay comparing the definition of your childhood lifestyle with that of your partner.
2. **Considering Audience:** Throughout her essay, Chambers employs definitions of race, education, socioeconomic class, and even gender to explain the differences between her thinking and that of her mother. Choose one of these categories or another, similar one to help you better understand some of the differences between you and a member of your immediate family from a previous generation. Write an essay on parent-child relationships that addresses the feelings and values of readers who are in your age group.
3. **Developing an Essay:** In what ways are college-educated children likely to view the world differently from parents who have not attended college? Are there likely differences in the perspective between children who have attended graduate school and parents who attended college? Do differences in careers and kinds of work also lead to different perspectives? Consider exploring these and other contrasting outlooks (or definitions of values and identities) in an expository essay.

(Note: Suggestions for topics requiring development by DEFINITION follow.)

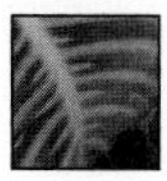

Writing Suggestions for Chapter 9

DEFINITION

Develop a composition for a specified purpose and audience, using whatever methods and expository patterns will help convey a clear understanding of your meaning of one of the following terms:

1. Country music
2. Conscience
3. Religion
4. Bigotry
5. Success
6. Empathy
7. Family
8. Hypocrisy
9. Humor
10. Sophistication
11. Naïveté
12. Cowardice
13. Wisdom
14. Integrity
15. Morality
16. Greed
17. Social poise
18. Intellectual (the person)
19. Pornography
20. Courage
21. Patriotism
22. Equality (or equal opportunity)
23. Loyalty
24. Stylishness (in clothing or behavior)
25. Fame
26. Obesity

27. Cheating
28. Hero
29. Feminine
30. Masculine

Collaborative Exercise

Working in a group, choose a term from the list below. Have each member of your group define the term for a reader/audience of a particular age group. As a group, compare your choices of definition strategies based on each intended audience.

a. Success
b. Family
c. Cowardice
d. Loyalty
e. Hero
f. Integrity

10

Explaining with the Help of *Description*

You can make your expository writing more vivid, and hence more understandable, with the support of **description,** sometimes even using the pattern as the basic plan for an exposition. In writing, you can use sensory details—sight, sound, touch, taste, and smell—to re-create *places:* a portrait of the steamy closeness of the Brazilian jungle; the gray stone, narrow streets, tall houses, and church spires of an Eastern European city. You can create portraits of *people, qualities, emotions,* or *moods:* a beloved aunt whose cheerfulness was part of a long fight against pain and illness, the physical and spatial on-court "intelligence" of a star basketball player, the despair of a child crying for her puppy just killed by a car, or the contrasting moods of a city where excited theatergoers pass a drunk slumped against a building.

Descriptive writing depends on detail, and your first and most important job as a writer employing description is to select the details to be included. There are usually many from which to choose, and it is easy to become so involved in a subject—especially one that is visually or emotionally intriguing—that you lose sight of the expository purpose of your writing. As you draft and revise, therefore, you need to keep in mind the kind of picture you want to paint with words, one that accomplishes *your* purpose for *your* intended audience. Such a word picture need not be entirely visual, for the dimensions of sound, smell, and even touch can create a vivid and effective image in your readers' minds.

When used as a pattern for much or all of an expository essay, description does more than set a mood, add a vivid touch to an explanation, or provide an occasional supporting detail. It becomes the primary strategy for explaining a subject or supporting a thesis, as in the following example.

> It's not winter without an icestorm. When Robert Frost gazed at bowed birch trees and tried to think that boys had bent them playing, he knew better: "Icestorms do that." They do that and a lot more, trimming disease and weakness out of the tree—the old tree's friend, as pneumonia used to be the old man's. Some of us provide life-support systems for our precious shrubs, boarding them over against the ice, for the icestorm takes the young or unlucky branch or birch as well as the rotten or feeble. One February morning we look out our windows over yards and fields littered with kindling, small twigs and great branches. We look out at a world turned into one diamond, ten thousand carats in the line of sight, twice as many facets. What a dazzle of spinning refracted light, spider webs of cold brilliance attacking our eyeballs! All winter we wear sunglasses to drive, more than we do in summer, and never so much as after an icestorm, with its painful glaze reflecting from maple and birch, granite boulder and stone wall, turning electric wires into bright silver filaments. The snow itself takes on a crust of ice, like the finish of a clay pot, that carries our weight and sends us swooping and sliding. It's worth your life to go for the mail. Until sand and salt redeem the highway, Route 4 is quiet. We cancel the appointment with the dentist, stay home, and marvel at the altered universe, knowing that midday sun will strip ice from tree and roof and restore our ordinary white winter world.
>
> —Donald Hall, *Seasons at Eagle Pond*

WHY USE DESCRIPTION?

Descriptions help readers create mental images of a subject or scene. To do this, the writer uses concrete, specific detail ("The floodwater turned the carpet into a slippery mess that smelled like dead fish and covered the electronic insides of the TV with a thin coat of black mud") rather than abstract, general impressions ("The flood soaked everything in the living room"). You can put descriptive detail to work for a variety of purposes, however.

You might choose to focus on a particular place or scene, using description to convey and support your thoughts and conclusions about it. Writing of this sort often appears in brief essays focusing on a limited scene: a beach in winter, a small corner of the Sonoran Desert, or a mall parking lot just before Christmas, for example. On the other hand, a description of a typical family apartment in Cairo might provide important conclusions and support for a study of family structure in Egypt, or descriptions of the Arctic landscape might contribute to an understanding of the habits of polar bears. When used for such expository purposes, descriptive writing goes beyond simply recording details to offering conclusions and explanations of the effects of a setting on those who live in it.

You might also use descriptive writing to create a portrait of a person. To do this, you combine descriptive detail with narration (see Chapter 11), usually in the form of brief but representative incidents. Your aim is to highlight the characteristics of your subject: details of appearance, speech, action, and feeling. In such a context, descriptive detail serves to support and convey your understanding of an individual's outlook and motivation, a sense of his or her personality, and your insight into the individual's influence on others.

Technical descriptions, common in scientific and professional writing, are another use for descriptive writing. In this form of writing, you provide a precise understanding of the elements of a subject and their relationship, and in so doing you convey necessary information or evidence to support your conclusions. Biologists, for example, might describe features of a frog that are marks of evolution or function; art historians might focus on color, line, shape, and brush stroke as a way of supporting a thesis about an artist or a particular painting.

CHOOSING A STRATEGY

Descriptive writing generally follows one of two strategies—*objective* description or *subjective* description—though some overlapping is also common. In objective description you aim at conveying the details of a subject thoroughly and accurately without suggesting your feelings or biases and without trying to evoke an emotional response from readers. Scientific papers, business reports, and academic writing often take this stance. In choosing details, writers of objective descriptions aim at precision and try to avoid emotional overtones. In arranging the details for presentation, writers either pay attention to the need to support a conclusion or to the function of the object or process being presented, as in the following example.

Cathode Ray Tube

The most familiar example is a television picture tube, and the simplest kind is the black and white. The inside of the tube is coated with a *phosphor*, a substance that glows when struck by electrons. At the rear of the tube (the neck) is an electron gun that shoots a beam of

> electrons toward the front. Electromagnetic coils or electrically charged metal plates direct this stream from side to side and top to bottom, forming a glow-picture of the "message" being received by the cathode ray tube. Color tubes are similar except that the face is coated with thousands of groups of dots. Each group, called a *pixel* (picture element), consists of three dots, one for each of the three primary colors—red, green, and blue.
>
> —Herman Schneider and Leo Schneider, *The Harper Dictionary of Science in Everyday Language*

In subjective description, however, you make your values and feelings clear and often encourage readers to respond emotionally. Often, instead of describing how something *is* objectively, you describe how it *seems* subjectively. To do this, you may make occasional use of direct statement, but you are likely to find it more effective to rely on a choice of vivid, concrete, or emotionally laden detail or on the connotations of words. *Connotations* are the feelings or associations that accompany a word, not its dictionary or literal meaning. Subjective descriptions express your conclusions about a subject or your attitudes toward it. Thus, in arranging details for presentation, you should pay attention to the dominant impression or interpretation you wish to convey as well as to the arrangement of details in the setting (right to left, top to bottom, for example).

In creating a subjective description, pay attention to the dominant impression you create, making sure it conveys and supports your overall purpose or interpretation. In the following passage, for example, the dominant impression clearly conveys the writer's insights into the effects of atmosphere—in this case, fog—on human perceptions, even though she does not directly state this conclusion.

> It begins in late afternoon, a wall of gray blocking the entrance to the harbor, moving imperceptibly, closing in. The sun becomes a bright thing in the sky for a moment before a thick grayness takes over. Trails of vapor drift by. Roads taper off into mist. Pine trees, encircled by the fog, take on different shapes. Inside vacation houses, people make tea, read books, play cards with old decks. Outside, the air smells of soaked wharves. Down by the rocks the surf crashes, but it is a muffled sound, heard while asleep. Bay bushes hunch together, woolly and wet. Walking through fields of Queen Anne's lace, lupine, and goldenrod, their colors muted, is like moving through dreamland. A foghorn blows. Other people are out—a figure appears near the raspberry bushes, spectral, with a basket. A dog runs by, and from the leaves drops fall.
>
> —Susan Minot, "Lost in the Light of Gray"

DEVELOPING DESCRIPTION

The first and most important job in descriptive writing is to select the details. The questions you ask about a subject can help you identify significant details and suggest ways of interpreting it.

For scenes or objects:

- What does it look like (colors, shapes, height, depth)?
- What does it sound like (loud, soft, rasping, soothing, musical, like a lawn mower)?
- What does it smell like (smoky, acrid, like gasoline, like soap, like a wood fire)?
- What does it feel like (smooth, sticky, like a cat's fur, like a spider's web, like grease)?
- What does it taste like (bitter, salty, like grass, like feathers)?

For emotions or ideas:

- What effect does it have on behavior (anger: red face, abrupt gestures)?
- What is it like (freedom: like taking a deep breath of air after leaving a smoky room)?

For people:

- What does the person look like (hair neatly combed, rumpled blouse, muddy boots)?
- What are some characteristic behaviors (rubs hands on skirt, picks ear)?
- What has the person done or said (cheated on a chemistry test, said cruel things to friends)?
- How do others respond to the person (turn to her for advice, call him a "slob")?

Successful subjective descriptions generally focus on a single *dominant impression,* which can act in place of a conclusion or thesis. To create a dominant impression, you select those details that will help create a mood or atmosphere or emphasize a feature or quality. But more than the materials themselves are involved in creating a dominant impression. The words you choose, and both their literal and suggestive meanings (denotations and connotations), convey an impression. So, too, do the arrangements of words in sentences, as in the use of short, hurried sentences to help convey a sense of urgency or excitement.

The actual arrangement of the material is perhaps less troublesome in description than in most other expository patterns. Nonetheless, you need to follow a sequence that is clear to your reader and that helps you achieve your purpose or support your thesis. A clear spatial organization, for example, will help readers understand a visually complex subject. You can move from left to right, top to bottom, or near to far. You can describe a person from head to toe, or vice versa, or begin with the most noticeable feature and work from there. Or you could start with an overall view of a scene and then move to a focal point.

A chronological arrangement enables you to look at a scene from several perspectives: early morning, midday, and night, for example, or in different weather conditions. Such a strategy allows you to make a point by contrasting the scenes, and it provides variety and interest. A thematic organization emphasizes the dominant impression or thesis through focus and repetition. You might emphasize by repeating clusters of key words (grim, grasping, hard, short-tempered) or images (pink ribbons, the scent of violets). You might also arrange segments of the description by increasing order of importance or in another manner that best supports a thesis.

You can also choose a point of view, either first person ("I looked . . .") or third person ("He sighed . . . . ," "It moved . . . ."). You might also choose a perspective, including the location of the observer and any limitation on the observer's ability to see and understand, perhaps observing a familiar family scene from a child's perspective to provide a new understanding of relationships.

Whatever techniques you choose, however, try to avoid excessive description, which creates confusion and boredom, or description without a clear purpose, which offers your readers no goal or reward for their effort.

Student Essay

In preparing the following essay, Carey Braun tried to combine technical descriptions of the effects of light with her subjective responses and perceptions. In linking the two, she makes some interesting observations about the way we humans are linked to the natural world.

Bright Light
by Carey Braun

The sun woke me by sneaking its way through the narrow cracks of the vertical blinds. I squinted at the bright sun, then kept my eyes closed and enjoyed its warmth on my face and shoulders. After a time, I slid across the bed to the window and peeked through the blinds to look out on a day that reminded me of *my* version of Andrew Lloyd Webber's song, "*Light*" changes everything"—or at least the sun does.

Initial setting
Time: morning

Thesis—stated somewhat indirectly

What better place to see light, feel light, and become one with the sun, I thought, than at the beach? I rushed out of bed, got dressed, had a bite of breakfast, grabbed my bathing suit and suntan lotion, and headed for the beach.

As I stepped out of the car in the parking lot, I felt a sunwarmed breeze across my face. It blew my hair across my cheek and made me wonder what it would be like to be a bird, about to skim across the waves of wind with the sun on my back. I hurried down the walkway. On each side of the path, dilapidated summer cottages managed to look fresh and new in the early morning rays. Crossing the hot sand, I stepped gingerly on it, a recognition that even this early in the day we need to shape our actions to the sun's heat and power.

Observer moves from place to place—observations show the effect of light at different times of day

Observer is also participant

I sat on the blanket and rubbed the suntan lotion over my body. My skin shined, reflecting the sun's rays and making me seem for a moment like a second source of light. But soon I began to feel like a frying pan that would sizzle if a drop of water hit me. In the background I could hear the sound of many boom boxes blending together forming a lighthearted hymn that took away thoughts of everything else but this time and place. People were splashing the water, sending luminous drops into the air and breaking the surface of the water into a million mirroring pieces. During brief breaks in the music and the sounds of splashing, I could hear the sound of birds singing.

Detailed, specific observations

Time: Midday

The sun's heat relaxed me so that I fell asleep. When I woke, there was sweat covering my face and my arms and refracting the sun's rays. If I looked just right, I could see rainbow dots on the surface of my skin. I woke up slowly and decided to head for the cool, refreshing water in front of me. I could feel my body temperature dropping as it moved into the water. As I dove into a wave, chills went through my body like shock waves. I was ready to move back to the beach and the sun.

Appeals to a variety of senses

I couldn't taste the sun, but as I walked back to my blanket, I licked the salt off my lips, which had dried quickly in the heat. Salt, I decided, must be the taste of light, at least this morning. The salt on my skin made it feel like stretched leather, tight across my cheekbones and shoulders and stiffening at my joints. I walked across the glinting sand, through midday air heated to luminous, shimmering waves, to the outdoor shower.

More senses

As I let the water wash away the salt, I looked at the sky and realized that the sun was beginning to descend. The subtle change in light made me feel cooler even though the sand was just as hot as I returned to my blanket. As the light turned to afternoon, people began looking at each other, perhaps noticing the growing shadows and the loss of brilliance. Light now turned to haze, luminous and bright, but still haze. People began straggling up the sand, looking as if their energy, too, had begun to wane. The music left and the song that remained was the crash of waves, glinting here and there as the growing fog broke to let through a stray ray.

Transition to late afternoon

Change in mood and effects of light

I gathered my belongings and shook all the sand off. As I drove away, I took one last look in the mirror to mourn the passing of the sun's power and light; startled by the electrifying colors of reds, yellows, and oranges spreading from the horizon through the sky, I realized once again the power of light to change everything.

Restates thesis

GARY SOTO

GARY SOTO was born in 1952 in Fresno, California, and currently teaches at the University of California, Berkeley. He has won numerous awards for his poetry and novels as well as for his essays and other nonfiction writing. These include ten volumes of poetry and two novels. *Nickel and Dime* (2000) and *Poetry Lover* (2001). His essays have been collected in *Small Faces* (1982), *Lesser Evils* (1988), *A Summer Life* (1995), and *The Effects of Knut Hamsun on a Fresno Boy* (2000) as well as in periodicals such as the *Iowa Review, El Andar,* and *American Literary History.* His memoir, *Living up the Street* (1985), received an American Book Award.

The Jacket

"The Jacket" was first published in *Small Faces.* It illustrates the subjective form of description that is generally known as impressionistic description. At the same time, the writer seems to stand outside the scenes and brief incidents, making the reader aware of what the jacket reveals about the psychological and social dimensions of growing up. In this way, the description serves an expository purpose.

My clothes have failed me. I remember the green coat that I wore in fifth and sixth grades when you either danced like a champ or pressed yourself against a greasy wall, bitter as a penny toward the happy couples. 1

When I needed a new jacket and my mother asked what kind I wanted, I described something like bikers wear: black leather and silver studs with enough belts to hold down a small town. We were in the kitchen, steam on the windows from her cooking. She listened so long while stirring dinner that I thought she understood for sure the kind I wanted. The next day when I got home from school, I discovered draped on my bedpost a jacket the color of day-old-guacamole. I threw my books on the bed and approached the jacket slowly, as if it were a stranger whose hand I had to shake. I touched the vinyl sleeve, the collar, and peeked at the mustard-colored lining. 2

From the kitchen mother yelled that my jacket was in the closet. I closed the door to her voice and pulled at the rack of clothes in the closet, hoping the jacket on the bedpost wasn't for me but my mean brother. No luck. I gave up. From my bed, I stared at the jacket. I wanted to cry because it was so ugly and so big that I knew I'd have 3 to wear it a long time. I was a small kid, thin as a young tree, and it would be years before I'd have a new one. I stared at the jacket, like an enemy, thinking bad things before I took off my old jacket whose sleeves climbed halfway to my elbow.

I put the big jacket on. I zipped it up and down several times, and rolled the cuffs up so they didn't cover my hands. I put my hands in the pockets and flapped the jacket like a bird's wings. I stood in front of the mirror, full face, then profile, and then looked over my shoulder as if someone had called me. I sat on the bed, stood against the bed, and combed my hair to see what I would look like doing something natural. I looked ugly. I threw it on my brother's bed and looked at it for a long time before I slipped it on and went out to the backyard, smiling a "thank you" to my mom as I passed her in the kitchen. With my hands in my pockets I kicked a ball against the fence, and then climbed it to sit looking into the alley. I hurled orange peels at the mouth of an open garbage can and when the peels were gone I watched the white puffs of my breath thin to nothing. 4

I jumped down, hands in my pockets, and in the backyard on my knees I teased my dog, Brownie, by swooping my arms while making bird calls. He jumped at me and missed. He jumped again and again, until a tooth sunk deep, ripping an L-shaped tear on my left sleeve. I pushed Brownie away to study the tear as I would a cut on my arm. There was no blood, only a few loose pieces of fuzz. Damn dog, I thought, and pushed him away hard when he tried to bite again. I got up from my knees and went to my bedroom to sit with my jacket on my lap, with the lights out. 5

That was the first afternoon with my new jacket. The next day I wore it to sixth grade and got a D on a math quiz. During the morning recess Frankie T., the playground terrorist, pushed me to the ground and told me to stay there until recess was over. My best friend, Steve Negrete, ate an apple while looking at me, and the girls turned away to whisper on the monkey bars. The teachers were no help: they looked my way and talked about how foolish I looked in my new jacket. I saw their heads bob with laughter, their hands half-covering their mouths. 6

Even though it was cold, I took off the jacket during lunch and played kickball in a thin shirt, my arm feeling like braille from the goose bumps. But when I returned to class I slipped the jacket on and shivered until I was warm. I sat on my hands, heating them up, while my teeth chattered like a cup of crooked dice. Finally warm, I slid out of the jacket but a few minutes later put it back on when the fire bell rang. We paraded out into the yard where we, the sixth 7 graders, walked past all the other grades to stand against the back fence. Everybody saw me. Although they didn't say out loud, "Man, that's ugly," I heard the buzz-buzz of gossip and even laughter that I knew was meant for me.

And so I went, in my guacamole-colored jacket. So embarrassed, so hurt, I couldn't even do my homework. I received Cs on quizzes, and forgot the state capitals and rivers of South America, our friendly neighbor. Even the girls who had been friendly blew away like loose flowers to follow the boys in neat jackets. 8

I wore that thing for three years until the sleeves grew short and my forearms stuck out like the necks of turtles. All during that time no love came to me—no little dark girl in a Sunday dress she wore on Monday. At lunchtime I stayed with the ugly boys who leaned against the chainlink fence and looked around with propellers of grass spinning in our mouths. We saw girls walk by alone, saw couples, hand in hand, their heads like bookends pressing air together. We saw them and spun our propellers so fast our faces were blurs. 9

I blame that jacket for those bad years. I blame my mother for her bad taste and her cheap ways. It was a sad time for the heart. With a friend I spent my sixth-grade year in a tree in the alley, waiting for something good to happen to me in that jacket, which had become the ugly brother who tagged along wherever I went. And it was about that time that I began to grow. My chest puffed up with muscle and, strangely, a few more ribs. Even my hands, those fleshy hammers, showed bravely through the cuffs, the fingers already hardening for the coming fights. But that L-shaped rip on the left sleeve got bigger, bits of stuffing coughed out from its wound after a hard day of play. I finally Scotch-taped it closed, but in rain or cold weather the tape peeled off like a scab and more stuffing fell out until that sleeve shriveled into a palsied arm. That winter the elbows began to crack and whole chunks of green began to fall off. I showed the cracks to my mother, who always seemed to be at the stove with steamed-up glasses, and she said that there were children in Mexico who would love that jacket. I told her that this was America and yelled that Debbie, my sister, didn't have a jacket like mine. I ran outside, ready to cry, and climbed the tree by the alley to think bad thoughts and watch my breath puff white and disappear. 10

But whole pieces still casually flew off my jacket when I played hard, read quietly, or took vicious spelling tests at school. When it became so spotted that my brother began to call me "camouflage," I flung it over the fence into the alley. Later, however, I swiped the jacket off the ground and went inside to drape it across my lap and mope. 11

I was called to dinner; steam silvered my mother's glasses as she said grace; my brother and sister with their heads bowed made ugly faces at their glasses of powdered milk. I gagged too, but eagerly ate big rips of buttered tortilla that held scooped-up beans. Finished, I went outside with my jacket across my arm. It was a cold sky. The faces of clouds were piled up, burting. I climbed the fence, jumping down with a grunt. I started up the alley and soon slipped into my jacket, that green ugly brother who breathed over my shoulder that day and ever since. 12

Meanings and Values

1. What is the general tone of this writing? (See "Guide to Terms": *Style/ Tone.*)
2. At what points in the essay are readers likely to notice a difference between the feelings and perceptions of the boy and those of the writer as an adult? In what ways does this contrast contribute to what the writer has to say about the process of growing up?
3. Discuss the possible meanings of the last sentence. "I started up the alley and soon slipped into my jacket, that green ugly brother who breathed over my shoulder that day and ever since."
4. Has this author avoided the excesses of sentimentality? Try to discover how. (Guide: *Sentimentality.*) If not, where does he fail?

Expository Techniques

1. Can the jacket be considered a symbol as well as a concrete object? Is it a natural, conventional, or personal symbol? (Guide: *Symbol.*)
2. Should this writing be classed as primarily impressionistic, rather than objective? If so, what is the dominant impression? Or should it be classed as having a double perspective, impressionistic and objective? Why, or why not? Does the jacket function as object or as symbol depending on whether the emphasis is on impressionistic or objective description? Explain your answer.
3. a. Analyze the role that selection of details plays in creating the dominant impression in Paragraphs 2, 7, 9, 10, and 12. Provide examples of the type of details that could have been included but were not. Are such omissions justifiable?

   b. Discuss the extent to which the details in these paragraphs reflect the social and economic circumstances in which the writer grew up.
4. Identify the paragraphs in this essay that can be viewed as examples (see Chapter 3, "Example"). Explain how this pattern of exposition supports the purpose of the essay. (Guide: *Purpose.*)

Diction and Vocabulary

1. Discuss the ways in which the simple (often one-syllable) words and short sentences convey the perceptions and feelings of the writer as a young boy. (Guide: *Diction.*)
2. Discuss how the choice of words and the relatively complicated sentence structures in Paragraphs 10 and 12 reflect the writer's perceptions as an older boy and his perspective as an adult. (Guide: *Diction; Syntax.*) Pay particular attention to the use of parallel structures in Paragraph 10. (Guide: *Parallel Structure.*)

Read to Write

1. **Collaborating:** Working with a group to identify and explore topics for writing, think about some common childhood experiences (schooling, loss of a parent or friend, sibling relationships, choice of clothing or toys, sports, and the like) that reflect important stages in social and psychological development. The stages and the quality of the experiences may vary greatly according to individual experience and social or cultural background, of course. Put the group's thoughts in the form of questions you could attempt to answer in an essay. Here are three questions to get you started: What kinds of clothing or other objects are likely to play important roles in childhood and adolescent development or to reflect different stages of development? What kinds of behavior, appearance, or background are likely to play a role in the social groupings common in schools or neighborhoods? What kinds of childhood memories are likely to remain vivid and laden with emotion into adulthood?
2. **Considering Audience:** Soto's essay begins with some forceful, slightly puzzling statements whose meaning becomes clearer in the course of the selection. Use a similar reader-centered strategy to begin an essay of your own. Start with statements or conclusions about the objects, incidents, people, relationships, or things you plan to explain and describe, and go on to discuss and explore them in the body of your essay.
3. **Developing an Essay:** A description is not a form of exposition unless it is used for expository purposes, as in "The Jacket." Follow Soto's lead by using detailed description in an essay to explain a relationship, problem, or phenomenon. Consider focusing on a subject whose importance and possible consequences may not be immediately apparent to readers, or consider using description to encourage readers to critically view actions and attitudes they take for granted.

(Note: Suggestions for topics requiring development by use of description are on pp. 402–403 at the end of this chapter.)

DONNA TARTT

DONNA TARTT was born in 1963 in Greenwood, Mississippi. She attended the University of Mississippi and Bennington College. Her first novel, *The Secret History,* was published in 1992 and her second, *The Little Friend,* in 2003, winning the WHSmith Literary Award and making the list of finalists for the Orange Prize for fiction. She has also published nonfiction essays and short stories.

A Garden Party

The power of childhood experiences over your values and perspectives as well as the briefness of life (and beauty) are some of the ideas explored through description in this essay, originally published in the *Guardian* (U.K.) newspaper and in *When We Were Young: An Anthology of Childhood.* Instead of describing a single scene in this essay, Tartt presents several detailed examples, each related to the central theme.

Not long ago, my little godson came to stay with me for the first time: his first summer vacation, and also his first trip to the countryside. Though still an infant, not yet able to speak, his eyes were round and ringing with astonishment all weekend long. Everything at my house was shocking and utterly new: velvet sofa cushions, purple flowers, elderly pug (bigger than he was, a frightening but friendly lion). In the photographs from that weekend (swimming pool; absurd yellow kiddie float) his face is alight with violent wonder—an expression very similar to the dazed, incredulous joy that I remember on the faces of some somber little hill-children in India at the watermelon sparklers I gave them. These were a racy treat of my American childhood—clear candies of a biting, gorgeous pink, deliciously sour, smooth and sparkling like jewels when you took them out of your mouth and held them up to the light after you'd sucked on them for a while. But though they are pretty enough to look at, their taste is the real stunner—an overpowering electric tang to make a grown-up's eyes water, but that children adore. As a child I craved these candies, was driven mad by them, saved my nickels and dimes for them—all the children on my school bus did—but there, in the high Himalayas, they were unheard of, pure magic: I might as well have been handing out rubies. 1

Of course, it's not at all remarkable that children are captivated by new things, because to children everything is new. But what is re- 2 markable is how fleeting impressions of childhood delight can linger and change and vanish and re-appear unexpectedly over the years, winking like fireflies throughout the arduous and complicated darks of a lifetime. It has been remarked that a poet's most powerful, passionate metaphors—the ones that recur again and again, the ones that carry the deepest personal meaning—are fixed irrevocably in the mind before the age of 12. So, too, I think, for the rest of us. Someday, long after I am dead, my little godson may be an old man of 80 or 90 sitting in a deck chair in Miami Beach, inexplicably transfixed with a wordless pang of joy at a striped beach ball, at dazzling turquoise pool water—just as someday (I hope) a particular impossible shade of watermelon pink, glimpsed in passing, may perhaps strike an old lady in a Himalayan hill village as the very sweetness of youth.

Quite often there's a pattern to these haphazard and apparently random flashes of childhood memory—a pattern that doesn't emerge or make itself known until later in life. One particularly vivid memory that has stayed with me throughout my life, and will be with me until I die, is of the first time I saw a hummingbird. The incident was inconsequential enough; I was about four years old, and had accompanied my beloved great-grandmother (then in her late 70s) to a garden party given for a distant relative: a young bride-to-be. It was springtime; the azaleas were in spectacular bloom; the astonishing little ruby-throated creature flew right in front of me—down at my eye level, practically in front of my face—and hovered there for some moments before it buzzed forward, then backward, then flew away across the green lawn for ever. 3

That was all. It can have lasted no more than 10 seconds, yet this tiny incident has left a much more intense and lasting impression on me than many of the great landmark events of my childhood. For many years, I wondered exactly why I remembered this specific incident so vividly and not some thing else, something more powerful. Why the hummingbird? What was it trying to tell me? Why had this memory, and not some other, struck me so forcefully in the first place; why does it come back to me so persistently, in memory and in dream? 4

Only now—at mid-life, in my 40th year—am I starting to realise what the hummingbird means, and why, at unexpected moments, it returns to me still. It is a premonition of heaven, and of death. My great-grandmother (who was leaning beside me, holding my hand, as the hummingbird paused in mid-air before me) did not have long to live. Nor did the bride herself—lovely laughing Ginger, who died young, of cancer. I couldn't have understood it then, and scarcely 5 understand it now, but my entire subsequent impressions of death, and beauty, and mutability, and the brevity of life itself are somehow crystallised perfectly in those few moments, when the tiny iridescent hummingbird darted before my face, hovered briefly, then flew away. All I know of the sublime is somehow encapsulated and encoded in that instant: flowers everywhere, white-gloved ladies in pastel dresses. Then beautiful Ginger, in an apple-green dress, kneeling to say hello.

Meanings and Values

1. Where in the essay does the writer announce the central theme (thesis)? (See "Guide to Terms": *Thesis.*) State the central theme in your own words.
2. Why should this essay be regarded as expository in purpose rather than simply a vivid recreation of experiences? (Guide: *Purpose.)*
3. If you have read E.B. White's essay, "Once More to the Lake" (beginning on p. 393), compare Tartt's views on death, beauty, and life's briefness with White's.

Expository Techniques

1. What "fleeting impressions of childhood delight" does the writer present as examples in this essay?
2. Where does the writer locate the statement of the essay's central theme (thesis) in relationship to the two main examples? Why do you think she chose this location?
3. Can the watermelon candy and the hummingbird be considered symbols? (Guide: *Symbol.*) If so, what does each symbolize?

Diction and Vocabulary

1. Identify the words and phrases the writer uses in Paragraph 1 to help readers imagine the taste and appearance of the watermelon candy. How effective are her choices in conveying the candy's qualities? (Guide: *Diction.*)
2. What words does the writer use in Paragraph 5 to emphasize the briefness and fragility of life and beauty? (Guide: *Diction.*)

3. If you do not know the meaning of some of the following words, look them up in the dictionary: *pug, incredulous, somber* (Par. 1); *captivated, arduous, irrevocably, inexplicably, transfixed* (2); *haphazard, inconsequential* (3); *premonition, subsequent, mutability, brevity, iridescent, sublime, encapsulated* (5).

READ TO WRITE

1. **Collaborating:** Working in a group, use the following questions and make up others like them in order to examine the relationship among places, childhood experiences, and values, and develop a list of possible topics for writing. Do many people today have a chance to return to the homes or neighborhoods in which they grew up, which helped shape their values and personalities? Are experiences with food, weather, natural settings, animals, or social events likely to be central to people's values? How are the childhood memories of people who grew up in settings unlike those described by Tartt likely to differ? Are their values likely to differ also?
2. **Considering Audience:** Consider how readers who grew up in settings very different from those describe by Tartt likely to respond to her essay. Write an essay describing the likely reactions of such readers, focusing especially on passages they might not fully appreciate or to which they might respond negatively.
3. **Developing an Essay:** Preparing an essay describing one or more experiences you had as a child, paying particular attention to the physical and sensory details. Follow Tartt's lead and deal with questions of change, loss, growth, continuity, death, and beauty, offering your insights, of course, and not Tartt's.

(NOTE: Suggestions for topics requiring development by use of DESCRIPTION are on pp. 402–403 at the end of this chapter.)

GEORGE SIMPSON

GEORGE SIMPSON, born in Virginia in 1950, received his B.A. in journalism from the University of North Carolina at Chapel Hill. He went to work for *Newsweek* in 1972, and in 1978 he became public affairs director for that magazine. Before joining *Newsweek,* Simpson worked for two years as a writer and editor for the *Carolina Financial Times* in Chapel Hill, North Carolina, and as a reporter for the *News-Gazette* in Lexington, Virginia. He received the Best Feature Writing award from Sigma Delta Chi in 1972 for a five-part investigative series on the University of North Carolina football program. He has written stories for the *New York Times, Sport, Glamour,* the *Winston-Salem* (North Carolina) *Journal,* and *New York.*

The War Room at Bellevue

"The War Room at Bellevue" was first published in *New York* magazine. The author chose, for good reason, to stay strictly within a time sequence as he described the emergency ward. This essay is also noteworthy for its cumulative descriptive effect, which was accomplished almost entirely with objective details.

Bellevue. The name conjures up images of an indoor war zone: the wounded and bleeding lining the halls, screaming for help while harried doctors in blood-stained smocks rush from stretcher to stretcher, fighting a losing battle against exhaustion and the crushing number of injured. "What's worse," says a longtime Bellevue nurse, "is that we have this image of being a hospital only for . . ." she pauses, then lowers her voice, "for crazy people." 1

Though neither battlefield nor Bedlam is a valid image, there is something extraordinary about the monstrous complex that spreads for five blocks along First Avenue in Manhattan. It is said best by the head nurse in Adult Emergency Service: "If you have any chance for survival, you have it here." Survival—that is why they come. Why do injured cops drive by a half-dozen other hospitals to be treated at Bellevue? They've seen the Bellevue emergency team in action. 2

9:00 P.M. It is a Friday night in the Bellevue emergency room. The after-work crush is over (those who've suffered through the day, only to come for help after the five-o'clock whistle has blown) and it is nearly silent except for the mutter of voices at the admitting desk, where administrative personnel discuss who will go for coffee. 3

Across the spotless white-walled lobby, ten people sit quietly, passively, in pastel plastic chairs, waiting for word of relatives or to see doctors. In the past 24 hours, 300 people have come to the Bellevue Adult Emergency Service. Fewer than 10 percent were true emergencies. One man sleeps fitfully in the emergency ward while his heartbeat, respiration, and blood pressure are monitored by control consoles mounted over his bed. Each heartbeat trips a tiny bleep in the monitor, which attending nurses can hear across the ward. A half hour ago, doctors in the trauma room withdrew a six-inch stiletto blade from his back. When he is stabilized, the patient will be moved upstairs to the twelve-bed Surgical Intensive Care Unit.

9:05 P.M. An ambulance backs into the receiving bay, its red and yellow lights flashing in and out of the lobby. A split second later, the glass doors burst open as a nurse and an attendant roll a mobile stretcher into the lobby. When the nurse screams, "Emergency!" the lobby explodes with activity as the way is cleared to the trauma room. Doctors appear from nowhere and transfer the bloodied body of a black man to the treatment table. Within seconds his clothes are stripped away, revealing a tiny stab wound in his left side. Three doctors and three nurses rush around the victim, each performing a task necessary to begin treatment. Intravenous needles are inserted into his arms and groin. A doctor draws blood for the lab, in case surgery is necessary. A nurse begins inserting a catheter into the victim's penis and continues to feed in tubing until the catheter reaches the bladder. Urine flows through the tube into a plastic bag. Doctors are glad not to see blood in the urine. Another nurse records pulse and blood pressure. 4

The victim is in good shape. He shivers slightly, although the trauma room is exceedingly warm. His face is bloodied, but shows no major lacerations. A third nurse, her elbow propped on the treatment table, asks the man a series of questions, trying to quickly outline his medical history. He answers abruptly. He is drunk. His left side is swabbed with yellow disinfectant and a doctor injects a local anesthetic. After a few seconds another doctor inserts his finger into the wound. It sinks in all the way to the knuckle. He begins to rotate his finger like a child trying to get a marble out of a milk bottle. The patient screams bloody murder and tries to struggle free. 5

Meanwhile in the lobby, a security guard is ejecting a derelict who has begun to drink from a bottle hidden in his coat pocket. "He's a regular, was in here just two days ago," says a nurse. "We checked him pretty good then, so he's probably okay now. Can you 6 believe those were clean clothes we gave him?" The old man, blackened by filth, leaves quietly.

9:15 P.M. A young Hispanic man interrupts, saying his pregnant girl friend, sitting outside in his car, is bleeding heavily from her vagina. She is rushed into an examination room, treated behind closed doors, and rolled into the observation ward, where, much later in the night, a gynecologist will treat her in a special room—the same one used to examine rape victims. Nearby, behind curtains, the neurologist examines an old white woman to determine if her headaches are due to head injury. They are not. 7

9:45 P.M. The trauma room has been cleared and cleaned mercilessly. The examination rooms are three-quarters full—another overdose, two asthmatics, a young woman with abdominal pains. In the hallway, a derelict who has been sleeping it off urinates all over the stretcher. He sleeps on while attendants change his clothes. An ambulance—one of four that patrol Manhattan for Bellevue from 42nd Street to Houston, river to river—delivers a middle-aged white woman and two cops, the three of them soaking wet. The woman has escaped from the psychiatric floor of a nearby hospital and tried to drown herself in the East River. The cops fished her out. She lies on a stretcher shivering beneath white blankets. Her eyes stare at the ceiling. She speaks clearly when an administrative worker begins routine questioning. The cops are given hospital gowns and wait to receive tetanus shots and gamma globulin—a hedge against infection from the befouled river water. They will hang around the E.R. for another two hours, telling their story to as many as six other policemen who show up to hear it. The woman is rolled into an examination room, where a male nurse speaks gently: "They tell me you fell into the river." "No," says the woman, "I jumped. I have to commit suicide." "Why?" asks the nurse. "Because I'm insane and I can't help [it]. I have to die." The nurse gradually discovers the woman has a history of psychological problems. She is given dry bedclothes and placed under guard in the hallway. She lies on her side, staring at the wall. 8

The pace continues to increase. Several more overdose victims arrive by ambulance. One, a young black woman, had done a striptease on the street just before passing out. A second black woman is semiconscious and spends the better part of her time at Bellevue alternately cursing at and pleading with the doctors. Attendants find a plastic bottle coated with methadone in the pocket of a Hispanic O.D. The treatment is routinely the same, and sooner or later involves vomiting. Just after doctors begin to treat 9 the O.D., he vomits great quantities of wine and methadone in all directions. "Lovely business, huh?" laments one of the doctors. A young nurse confides that if there were other true emergencies, the overdose victims would be given lower priority. "You can't help thinking they did it to themselves," she says, "while the others are accident victims."

10:30 P.M. A policeman who twisted his knee struggling with an "alleged perpetrator" is examined and released. By 10:30, the lobby is jammed with friends and relatives of patients in various stages of treatment and recovery. The attendant who also functions as a translator for Hispanic patients adds chairs to accommodate the overflow. The medical walk-in rate stays steady—between eight and ten patients waiting. A pair of derelicts, each with battered eyes, appear at the admitting desk. One has a dramatically swollen face laced with black stitches. 10

11:30 P.M. The husband of the attempted suicide arrives. He thanks the police for saving his wife's life, then talks at length with doctors about her condition. She continues to stare into the void and does not react when her husband approaches her stretcher. 11

Meanwhile, patients arrive in the lobby at a steady pace. A young G.I. on leave has lower-back pains; a Hispanic man complains of pains in his side; occasionally parents hurry through the adult E.R. carrying children to the pediatric E.R. A white woman of about 50 marches into the lobby from the walk-in entrance. Dried blood covers her right eyebrow and upper lip. She begins to perform. "I was assaulted on 28th and Lexington, I was," she says grandly, "and I don't have to take it *anymore.* I was a bride 21 years ago and, God, I was beautiful then." She has captured the attention of all present. "I was there when the boys came home—on Memorial Day—and I don't have to take this kind of treatment." 12

As midnight approaches, the nurses prepare for the shift change. They must brief the incoming staff and make sure all reports are up-to-date. One young brunet says, "Christ, I'm gonna go home and take a shower—I smell like vomit." 13

11:50 P.M. The triage nurse is questioning an old black man about chest pains, and a Hispanic woman is having an asthma attack, when an ambulance, its sirens screaming full tilt, roars into the receiving bay. There is a split-second pause as everyone drops what he or she is doing and looks up. Then all hell breaks loose. Doctors and nurses are suddenly sprinting full-out toward the trauma room. The glass doors burst open and the occupied stretcher is literally run past me. Cops follow. It is as if a comet has whooshed by. In the 14 trauma room it all becomes clear. A half-dozen doctors and nurses surround the lifeless form of a Hispanic man with a shotgun hole in his neck the size of your fist. Blood pours from a second gaping wound in his chest. A respirator is slammed over his face, making his chest rise and fall as if he were breathing. "No pulse," reports one doctor. A nurse jumps on a stool and, leaning over the man, begins to pump his chest with her palms. "No blood pressure," screams another nurse. The ambulance driver appears shaken, "I never thought I'd get here in time," he stutters. More doctors from the trauma team upstairs arrive. Wrappings from syringes and gauze pads fly through the air. The victim's eyes are open yet devoid of life. His body takes on a yellow tinge. A male nurse winces at the gunshot wound. "This guy really pissed off somebody," he says. This is no ordinary shooting. It is an execution. IV's are jammed into the body in the groin and arms. One doctor has been plugging in an electrocardiograph and asks everyone to stop for a second so he can get a reading. "Forget it," shouts the doctor in charge. "No time." "Take it easy, Jimmy," someone yells at the head physician. It is apparent by now that the man is dead, but the doctors keep trying injections and finally they slit open the chest and reach inside almost up to their elbows. They feel the extent of the damage and suddenly it is all over. "I told 'em he was dead," says one nurse, withdrawing. "They didn't listen." The room is very still. The doctors are momentarily disgusted, then go on about their business. The room clears quickly. Finally there is only a male nurse and the still-warm body, now waxy-yellow, with huge ribs exposed on both sides of the chest and giant holes in both sides of the neck. The nurse speculates that this is yet another murder in a Hispanic political struggle that has brought many such victims to Bellevue. He marvels at the extent of the wounds and repeats, "This guy was really blown away."

15 Midnight. A hysterical woman is hustled through the lobby into an examination room. It is the dead man's wife, and she is nearly delirious. "I know he's dead, I know he's dead," she screams over and over. Within moments the lobby is filled with anxious relatives of the victim, waiting for word on his condition. The police are everywhere asking questions, but most people say they saw nothing. One young woman says she heard six shots, two louder than the other four. At some point, word is passed that the man is, in fact, dead. Another woman breaks down in hysterics; everywhere young Hispanics are crying and comforting each other. Plainclothes detectives make a quick examination of the body, check on the time of

pronouncement of death, and begin to ask questions, but the bereaved are too stunned to talk. The rest of the uninvolved people in the lobby stare dumbly, their injuries suddenly paling in light of a death.

12:30 A.M. A black man appears at the admissions desk and says he drank poison by mistake. He is told to have a seat. The ambulance brings in a young white woman, her head wrapped in white gauze. She is wailing terribly. A girl friend stands over her, crying, and a boyfriend clutches the injured woman's hands, saying, "I'm here, don't worry, I'm here." The victim has fallen downstairs at a friend's house. Attendants park her stretcher against the wall to wait for an examination room to clear. There are eight examination rooms and only three doctors. Unless you are truly an emergency, you will wait. One doctor is stitching up the eyebrow of a drunk who's been punched out. The friends of the woman who fell down the stairs glance up at the doctors anxiously, wondering why their friend isn't being treated faster. 16

1:10 A.M. A car pulls into the bay and a young Hispanic asks if a shooting victim has been brought here. The security guard blurts out, "He's dead." The young man is stunned. He peels his tires leaving the bay. 17

1:20 A.M. The young woman of the stairs is getting stitches in a small gash over her left eye when the same ambulance driver who brought in the gunshot victim delivers a man who has been stabbed in the back on East 3rd Street. Once again the trauma room goes from 0 to 60 in five seconds. The patient is drunk, which helps him endure the pain of having the catheter inserted through his penis into his bladder. Still he yells, "That hurts like a bastard," then adds sheepishly, "Excuse me, ladies." But he is not prepared for what comes next. An X-ray reveals a collapsed right lung. After just a shot of local anesthetic, the doctor slices open his side and inserts a long plastic tube. Internal bleeding had kept the lung pressed down and prevented it from reinflating. The tube releases the pressure. The ambulance driver says the cops grabbed the guy who ran the eight-inch blade into the victim's back. "That's not the one," says the man. "They got the wrong guy." A nurse reports that there is not much of the victim's type blood available at the hospital. One of the doctors says that's okay, he won't need surgery. Meanwhile blood pours from the man's knife wound and the tube in his side. As the nurses work, they chat about personal matters, yet they respond immediately to orders from either doctor. "How ya doin'?" the doctor asks the patient. "Okay," he says. His blood spatters on the floor. 18

So it goes into the morning hours. A Valium overdose, a woman who fainted, a man who went through the windshield of his car. More overdoses. More drunks with split eyebrows and chins. The doctors and nurses work without complaint. "This is nothing, about normal, I'd say," concludes the head nurse. "No big deal." 19

Meanings and Values

1. What is the author's point of view? (See "Guide to Terms": *Point of View.*) How is this reflected by the tone? (Guide: *Style/Tone.*)
2. Does Simpson ever slip into sentimentality—a common failing when describing the scenes of death and tragedy? (Guide: *Sentimentality.*) If so, where? If not, how does he avoid it?
3. Cite at least six facts learned from reading this piece that are told, not in general terms but by specific, concrete details—for example, that a high degree of cleanliness is maintained at Bellevue, illustrated by "the spotless white-walled lobby" (Par. 3) and "the trauma room has been cleared and cleaned mercilessly" (Par. 8). What are the advantages of having facts presented in this way?

Expository Techniques

1. Do you consider the writing to be primarily objective or impressionistic? What is the dominant impression, if any?
2. What is the value of using a timed sequence in such a description?
3. Does it seem to you that any of this description is excessive—that is, unnecessary to the task at hand? If so, how might the piece be revised?
4. List, in skeletal form, the facts learned about the subject from reading the two-paragraph introduction. How well does it perform the three basic purposes of an introduction? (Guide: *Introductions.*)
5. What is the significance of the rhetorical question in Paragraph 2? (Guide: *Rhetorical Questions.*) Why is it rhetorical?
6. Is the short closing effective? (Guide: *Closings.*) Why, or why not?

Diction and Vocabulary

1. Cite the clichés in Paragraphs 4, 5, 8, and 14. (Guide: *Clichés.*) What justification, if any, can you offer for their use?
2. Cite the allusion in Paragraph 2, and explain its meaning and source. (Guide: *Figures of Speech.*)

3. Simpson uses some slang and other colloquialisms. Cite as many of these as you can. (Guide: *Colloquial Expressions.*) Is their use justified? Why, or why not?

Read to Write

1. **Collaborating:** Working in a group, discuss a job or an activity (sport, organization) that to an outsider might seem hectic or hazardous. Consider describing it in an essay so that readers can come to understand it more clearly.
2. **Considering Audience:** Descriptive writing can create events for readers who have not experienced it. Much of the power of Simpson's writing comes from the sensational nature of the subjects he describes and his careful selection of detail. If you have witnessed or participated in some other kind of "extreme" experience, help your readers understand it by describing and explaining it with the same mix of detail and commentary that Simpson offers.
3. **Developing an Essay:** Consider arranging an expository essay of your own by using a time frame as Simpson does. Your purposes for using this device need not be the same, however, and you can use this strategy for expository patterns other than description.

(Note: Suggestions for topics requiring development by use of description are on pp. 402–403 at the end of this chapter.)

DANIEL THOMAS COOK

DANIEL THOMAS COOK teaches at Rutgers University/Camden in the Department of Childhood Studies. His research focuses on children as consumers, and he has published widely on this topic. His books include *The Commodification of Childhood: The Children's Clothing Industry and the Rise of the Child Consumer* (2004), *Symbolic Childhood* (2002) and *The Lived Experiences of Public Consumption* (2008). He is also the founder of The Consumer Studies Research Network for the exchange of information about the ways in which commodification and market logic pervade our lives and interactions.

Children of the Brand

Description can play an important role in expository writing even if it takes up only part of an essay. Daniel Thomas Cook uses the pattern to introduce his topic and to provide support for his generalizations in "Children of the Brand." In addition, his descriptions suggest similar experiences that readers can bring with them to the essay to help understand his conclusions and judge their value.

As I sat in the café of a Borders bookstore in Chicago huddled over my laptop and struggling to write about children and commercialism, I was interrupted by an annoying clamor of loud talk, screams and laughter. I looked over and to my horror discovered it was a group of . . . kids! How dare children disrupt my ruminations on childhood! 1

Accepting my fate, I behaved like a social researcher: I observed the 2
scene. "Welcome to Borders Explorers," exclaimed their hostess in a voice intended for seven-year-olds. "We are excited to have you here.
We have a lot of fun things planned for your stay with us." On each table 3
stood a cardboard cutout of the "Border Explorer"—a goofy-looking cartoon character sporting winged goggles and an outfit that intimated a '50s version of a "futuristic" space suit. Clearly a boy (explorers are still male, apparently), the character displayed a gigantic "B" on his belt.

As the students colored in an image of the Borders Explorer character, the staff member explained the morning's plan. Each table would be given several topics, such as "seals" and "mountains," to be divided among the students, who would then go to the children's section and find books on the topic.

The children's section was clearly "kid-themed," with an entranceway in colorful "kid letters," a soft stars-and-planets carpet, 4

Daniel Thomas Cook, "Children of the Brand." This article is reprinted with permission from *In These Times* magazine, December 25, 2006, and is available at www.inthesetimes.com

floor level displays and a nonlinear arrangement of bookshelves. The iconography and organization of the section revealed the same method of age ascendance that I had found in my historical research on the rise of the child consumer. The books and small toys intended for the youngest children were situated in the back corner; the age ladder progressively moved up toward the entrance area where items intended for the oldest children (9 and 10-year-olds) were displayed. Such an arrangement is designed to avoid exposing the older children to undesirable "babyish" things—which could "pollute" them by association—while giving the younger children, who must pass through this area, a feeling of maturity, perhaps even of desire.

Brands and branding

Delightful and insidious at once, Borders endeavors to brand the expe- 5
rience of reading and exploring ideas. Paradoxically, Borders strives, on the one hand, to stimulate the children's curiosity and, on the other, to numb their critical faculties with characters, arts-and-crafts activities and merchandise placement. They're encouraged to explore everything about Borders—except of course the company's brand strategy.

Branding resides, first and foremost, in the realm of design. The 6
quintessential marriage of art and commerce, branding, when it works best, is inspired by aesthetic sensibility and intuition, and guided by market research. Brands—their iconography, acoustics, tastes, physical feelings and smells—coax us to react but not to analyze. Every moment is to be infused not just with "style" or "beauty," but with emotional bonding to a corporate entity. At least, this is the dream of brand managers. Art, in its most general sense, serves as an ideal vehicle for connecting human emotions to a material object because it strikes us at a pre-analytic level. We experience it and react to it before we can reflect on it.

However, corporate ingenuity and the colonization of art and 7
design for promotional effect is not the entire story. Children and adults, after all, want things, buy things and identify with things. We are not completely helpless creatures, but active beings searching for meaning and significance.

Meaning-full brands

The kids' market has proven lucrative (well into $100 billion annu- 8
ally), in large part because both kids and parents derive personal wellbeing from the goods and images of contemporary consumer capitalism. When asked why she put "Blues Clues" characters on

her four-year-old's birthday cake, a 33-year-old mother told me that a simple "Happy Birthday" was generic and not special.

Brands—in their artful presence as icons, images and styles—seek to accomplish the somewhat contradictory task of allowing people to forge personal identities out of mass-produced, mass-distributed, readily available goods and images. To grasp the power of brand appeal, one need only think of those who tattoo the Nike swoosh on their bodies, name their kids after global brands like Puma or spend hours blogging about their favorite products. 9

Retailers, designers, marketers and merchandisers have known for the better part of a century something that social scientists are now just learning. To cultivate a consumer market at a deep level, beyond simple functional need, consumers must be approached and addressed as having desires and aspirations that transcend the specific product at hand. For many of us, as brand managers have discovered, the "need" for belonging, for intimacy, for respect, for individuality and for being seen as someone worthy in the eyes of others is what drives consumption and brand attachment. Some of the key "needs" of children, who by default are relatively powerless economically (but quite powerful emotionally), include recognition, aspiration and a sense of ownership over their world. 10

Kids aspire to be older than they are at whatever age because, early in life, they recognize their position on the lower rungs of the social ladder. Hence retailers, like Borders, design spaces that encode both aspiration to older, more autonomous identities and distance from younger, undesirable selves. Any savvy package designer knows that a child's product, if it is to have any chance on the market, must appear to appeal to the age group just older than the intended end-user. Something intended for a six-year-old boy will probably not do well if a six-year-old is pictured on it—better an eight-year-old. 11

Making such appeals directly to a child is, historically speaking, new and revolutionary. The recognition and appeasement of the child's point of view in commercial contexts began in the '30s and marked a change not only in marketing and merchandising, but in parent-child relations as well. The child's view now must be acknowledged, addressed and satisfied in many arenas of social life. For a parent to do otherwise is to set themselves up as morally suspect. 12

The strongest institutional urge to "know" and speak to the child's view comes from the world of marketing, branding and design. It is marketers, often more than parents, who are in tune with kids and their worlds. They visit children's bedrooms and query 13 them about their decorating, clothing and music choices. They attend girls' sleepover parties and convene focus groups to observe "tweens" discussing the benefits of various products. In doing so, marketers venerate children's commercial choices as a democratic exercise. They insist that, in this way, they are "empowering" children.

These children certainly appeared to be "empowered" as they 14
actively delved into the books. But, I had to wonder, if it is the kind of power that will transcend its corporate inspired origins and help the kids navigate contemporary life, or if this "category management" will serve only to infuse brand attachment into the minds of those just learning about the world. It is almost criminal to discourage the next generation from reading and engaging with books. This day, however, was not about books or reading for the young Explorers. It was about engineering the Borders™ experience and cultivating consumers, ultimately re-empowering those who already have the power to produce experiences in addition to products.

Meanings and Values

1. What setting does the writer describe in Paragraph 4? State in your own words the interpretation he offers of the setting.
2. What does the writer explain as the goal of branding?
3. According to the essay, what do brands provide for people?
4. In your own words, explain the "contradictory task" (Par. 9) that brands achieve.

Expository Techniques

1a. What does the writer describe in Paragraph 1? How does this description contrast with the descriptions in the paragraphs that follow?

 b. Which description does the writer wish us to view positively and which negatively?

2. Paragraphs 1–4 provide descriptions the writer echoes elsewhere in the text. Where does he do so?

3. What examples does the writer provide in Paragraphs 8, 9, and 13? Does he provide an appropriate balance of generalization and examples in these paragraphs? (See "Guide to Terms": *Evaluation.*)

4. In general, does the essay provide enough balance between description and interpretation so that the overall aim can be called *expository*?
5. Where, if at all, does the writer argue for a particular point of view on branding and similar activities?

Diction and Vocabulary

1. What does the author mean when he says Borders is "Delightful and insidious at once . . ." (Par. 5)? In what way is this a paradox, as the writer suggests elsewhere in the paragraph. (Guide: *Paradox*.)
2. If you do not know the meaning of some of the following terms, look them up in a dictionary: *ruminations* (Par. 1); *iconography, ascendance* (4); *insidious* (5); *quintessential, acoustics* (6); *lucrative, generic* (8); *aspirations, transcend, default* (10); *appeasement* (12); *query* (13).

Read to Write

1. **Collaborating:** Working in a group, prepare a description of some other setting (such as a store, a camp, a bank, or a library) in which the arrangement of space, the objects, and the colors or sounds conveys messages about what is most important and what is less important.
2. **Considering Audience:** Has this writer done enough to take into account people who might not agree with his conclusions? What other perspectives can you imagine people having on the scenes he describes? Write out these perspectives or objections to his conclusions. Then write out what you think the author might say in response to them.
3. **Developing an Essay:** Go to a store that children are likely to visit. Take notes on the setting and on the behavior of the children you see at the store. Use these notes to create an essay that, like Cook's, draws conclusions from a description.

(Note: Suggestions for topics requiring development by means of DESCRIPTION are on pp. 402–403 at the end of this chapter.)

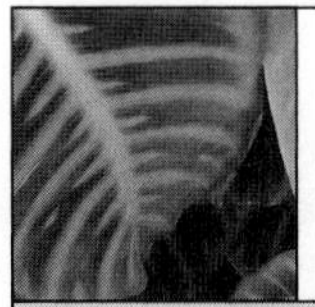

Issues and Ideas

Place and Person

- Barry Lopez, *A Passage of Hands*
- E. B. White, *Once More to the Lake*

Our environments shape us, but we in turn shape them, in large ways and small. This probably seems so obvious to you that you seldom stop to notice the many relationships between place and person. This, however, is exactly what the next essays ask you to do. Barry Lopez's "A Passage of Hands," and E.B. White's "Once More to the Lake" offer three rather different perspectives on the relationship of people and their surroundings.

Though a feeling of nostalgia—a sense of fond memories and loss—might seem most appropriate for journeys back to childhood settings, the tone Barry Lopez creates is far more complex. E. B. White also asks readers to move beyond sentimental responses in his descriptions of places from the past. Indeed, when description is used as an expository strategy, it goes beyond simple re-creation of a setting to analysis and explanation.

BARRY LOPEZ

BARRY LOPEZ was born in 1945 in Port Chester, New York. He attended the University of Notre Dame and the University of Oregon and works as a writer and photographer specializing in natural subjects. His writing and photography have been published in *Audubon, National Wildlife, Harper's, National Geographic,* and many other magazines. Among his books are *Desert Notes: Reflections in the Eye of the Raven* (1976), *Of Wolves and Men* (1978), *River Notes:The Dance of the Herons* (1979), *Winter Count* (1982), *Arctic Dreams* (1986) (winner of the National Book Award), *The Rediscovery of North America* (1990), and *About This Life* (1998).

A Passage of Hands

In this essay, first published in the collection *About This Life,* Barry Lopez links a number of descriptions as a way of recording and exploring changes in his life as well as the development of his values and a growing sense of self. Though the hands remain physical objects throughout, engaged in all sorts of activities, they simultaneously act as symbols summing up the meaning Lopez discovers in the various activities in which the hands are engaged.

My hands were born breech in the winter of 1945, two hours before sunrise. Sitting with them today, two thousand miles and more from that spot, turning each one slowly in bright sunshine, watching the incisive light raise short, pale lines from old cuts, and seeing the odd cant of the left ring finger, I know they have a history, though I cannot remember where it starts. As they began, they gripped whatever might hold me upright, surely caressed and kneaded my mother's breasts, yanked at the restrictions of pajamas. And then they learned to work buttons, to tie shoelaces and lift the milk glass, to work together. 1

The pressure and friction of a pencil as I labored down the spelling of words right-handed raised the oldest permanent mark, a callus on the third joint of the middle finger. I remember no trying accident to either hand in these early years, though there must have been glass cuts, thorn punctures, spider bites, nails torn to the cuticle, scrapes from bicycle falls, pin blisters from kitchen grease, splinters, nails blackened from door pinches, pain lingering from having all four fingers forced backward at once, and the first true weariness, 2 coming from work with lumber and stones, with tools made for larger hands.

3 It is from these first years, five and six and seven, that I am able to remember so well, or perhaps the hands themselves remember, a great range of texture—the subtle corrugation of cardboard boxes, the slickness of the oilcloth on the kitchen table, the shuddering bend of a horse's short-haired belly, the even give in warm wax, the raised oak grain in my school-desk top, the fuzziness of dead bumblebees, the coarseness of sheaves immediate to the polished silk of unhusked corn, the burnish of rake handles and bucket bails, the rigidness of the bony crest rising beneath the skin of a dog's head, the tackiness of flypaper, the sharpness of saws and ice picks.

4 It is impossible to determine where in any such specific memory, of course, texture gives way to heft, to shape, to temperature. The coolness of a camellia petal seems inseparable from that texture, warmth from the velvet rub of a horse's nose, heft from a brick's dry burr. And what can be said, as the hand recalls the earliest touch and exploration, or how texture changes with depth? Not alone the press of the palm on a dog's head or fingers boring to the roots of wool on a sheep's flank, but of, say, what happens with an orange: the hands work in concert to disassemble the fruit, running a thumb over the beaded surface of the skin, plying the soft white flay of the interior, the string net of fiber clinging to the translucent skin cases, dividing the yielding grain of the flesh beneath, with its hard, wrinkled seeds. And, further, how is one to separate these textures from a memory of the burst of fragrance as the skin is torn, or from the sound of the sections being parted—to say nothing of the taste, juice dripping from the chin, or the urge to devour, then, even the astringent skin, all initiated by the curiosity of the hands?

5 Looking back, it's easy to see that the education of the hands (and so the person) begins like a language: a gathering of simple words, the assembly of simple sentences, all this leading eventually to the forging of instructive metaphors. Afterward nothing can truly be separated, to stand alone in the hands' tactile memory. Taking the lay of the dog's fur, the slow petting of the loved dog is the increasingly complicated heart speaking with the hand.

6 Still, because of an occasional, surprising flair of the hands, the insistence of their scarred surfaces, it is possible for me to sustain the illusion that they have a history independent of the mind's perception, the heart's passion; a history of gathering what appeals, of expressing exasperation with their own stupidity, of faith in the

accrual of brute work. If my hands began to explore complex knowledge by seeking and sorting texture—I am compelled to believe this—then the first names my memory truly embraced came from the hands' differentiating among fruits and woven fabrics.

Growing on farms and in orchards and truck gardens around 7
our home in rural California was a chaos of fruit: navel and Valencia oranges, tangerines, red and yellow grapefruit, pomegranates, lemons, pomelos, greengage and damson plums, freestone and cling peaches, apricots, figs, tangelos, Concord and muscadine grapes. Nectarines, Crenshaw, casaba, and honeydew melons, watermelons, and cantaloupes. My boyish hands knew the planting, the pruning, and picking, and the packing of some of these fruits, the force and the touch required. I sought them all out for the resilience of their ripeness and knew the different sensation of each—pips, radius, cleavage. I ate even tart pomegranates with ardor, from melons I dug gobs of succulent meat with mouth and fingers. Slicing open a cantaloupe or a melon with a knife, I would hesitate always at the sight of the cleft fistula of seeds. It unsettled me, as if it were the fruit's knowing brain.

The fabrics were my mother's. They were stacked in bolts 8
catawampus on open shelves and in a closet in a room in our small house where she both slept and sewed, where she laid out skirts, suits, and dresses for her customers. Lawn, organdy, batiste, and other fine cottons; cambric and gingham; silks—moiré, crepe de chine, taffeta; handkerchief and other weights of linen; light wools like gabardine; silk and cotton damasks; silk and rayon satins; cotton and wool twills; velvet; netted cloths like tulle. These fabrics differed not only in their texture and weave, in the fineness of their threads, but in the way they passed or reflected light, in their drape, and, most obviously from a distance, in their color and pattern.

I handled these fabrics as though they were animal skins, open- 9
ing out bolts on the couch when Mother was working, holding them against the window light, raking them with my nails, crumpling them in my fist, then furling them as neatly as I could. Decades later, reading "samite of Ethnise" and "uncut rolls of brocade of Tabronit" in a paperback translation of Wolfram von Eschenbach's *Parzival,* I watched my free hand rise up to welcome the touch of these cloths.

It embarrassed and confounded me that other boys knew so lit- 10
tle of cloth, and mocked the knowledge; but growing up with orchards and groves and vine fields, we shared a conventional, peculiar intimacy with fruit. We pelted one another with rotten

plums and the green husks of walnuts. We flipped gourds and rolled melons into the paths of oncoming, unsuspecting cars. The prank of the hand—throwing, rolling, flipping—meant nothing without the close companionship of the eye. The eye measured the distance, the crossing or closing speed of the object, and then the hand—the wrist snapping, the fingers' tips guiding to the last—decided upon a single trajectory, measured force, and then a rotten plum hit someone square in the back or sailed wide, or the melon exploded beneath a tire or rolled cleanly to the far side of the road. And we clapped in glee and wiped our hands on our pants.

In these early years—eight and nine and ten—the hands became attuned to each other. They began to slide the hafts of pitchforks and pry bars smoothly, to be more aware of each other's placement for leverage and of the light difference in strength. It would be three or four more years before, playing the infield in baseball, I would sense the spatial and temporal depth of awareness my hands had of each other, would feel, short-hopping a sharp grounder blind in front of third base, flicking the ball from gloved-left to bare-right hand, making the cross-body throw, that balletic poise of the still fingers after the release, would sense how mindless the beauty of it was. 11

I do not remember the ascendancy of the right hand. It was the one I was forced to write with, though by that time the right hand could already have asserted itself, reaching always first for a hammer or a peach. As I began to be judged according to the performance of my right hand alone—how well it imitated the Palmer cursive, how legibly it totaled mathematical figures—perhaps here is where the hands first realized how complicated their relationship would become. I remember a furious nun grabbing my six-year-old hands in prayer and wrenching the right thumb from under the left. Right over left, she insisted. *Right over left*. Right over left in praying to God. 12

In these early years my hands were frequently folded in prayer. They, too, collected chickens' eggs, contended with the neat assembly of plastic fighter planes, picked knots from bale twine, clapped chalkboard erasers, took trout off baited hooks, and trenched flower beds. They harbored and applauded homing pigeons. When I was eleven, my mother married again and we moved east to New York. The same hands took on new city tasks, struggled more often with coins and with tying the full Windsor knot. Also, now, they pursued a more diligent and precise combing of my hair. And were in anxious anticipation of touching a girl. 13

And that caress having been given, one hand confirmed the memory later with the other in exuberant disbelief. They overhauled and pulled at each other like puppies.

I remember from these years—fourteen and fifteen and sixteen— 14
marveling at the dexterity of my hands. In games of catch, one hand tipped the falling ball to the other, to be seized firmly in the same instant the body crashed to the ground. Or the hands changed effortlessly on the dribble at the start of a fast break in basketball. I remember disassembling, cleaning, and reassembling a two-barrel carburetor, knowing the memory of where all the parts fit was within my hands. I can recall the baton reversal of a pencil as I wrote then erased, wrote then erased, composing sentences on a sheet of paper. And I remember how the hands, so clever with a ball, so deft with a pair of needle-nose pliers, fumbled attaching a cymbidium orchid so close to a girl's body, so near the mysterious breast.

By now, sixteen or so, my hands were as accustomed to books, 15
to magazines, newspapers, and typing paper, as they were to mechanic's tools and baseballs. A blade in my pocketknife was a shape my fingers had experienced years earlier as an oleander leaf. The shape of my fountain pen I knew first as a eucalyptus twig, drawing make-believe roads in wet ground. As my hands had once strained to bring small bluegills to shore, now they reeled striped bass from the Atlantic's surf. As they had once entwined horses' manes, now they twirled girls' ponytails. I had stripped them in those years of manure, paint, axle grease, animal gore, plaster, soap suds, and machine oil; I had cleaned them of sap and tar and putty, of pond scum and potting soil, of fish scales and grass stains. The gashes and cuts had healed smoothly. They were lithe, strenuous. The unimpeded reach of the fingers away from one another in three planes, their extreme effective span, was a subtle source of confidence and wonder. They showed succinctly the physical intelligence of the body. They expressed so unmistakably the vulnerability in sexual desire. They drew so deliberately the curtains of my privacy.

One July afternoon I stood at an ocean breakwater with a friend, 16
firing stones one after another in long, beautiful arcs a hundred feet to the edge of the water. We threw for accuracy, aiming to hit small breaking waves with cutting *thwips*. My friend tired of the game and lay down on his towel. A few moments later I turned and threw in a single motion just as he leaped to his feet. The stone caught him full in the side of the head. He was in the hospital a month with a fractured skull, unable to speak clearly until he was operated on. The following summer we were playing baseball together again, but I

could not throw hard or accurately for months after the accident, and I shied away completely from a growing desire to be a pitcher.

My hands lost innocence or gained humanity that day, as they 17
had another day when I was pulled off my first dog, screaming, my hands grasping feebly in the air, after he'd been run over and killed in the road. Lying awake at night I sometimes remember throwing the near deadly stone, or punching a neighbor's horse with my adolescent fist, or heedlessly swinging a 16-gauge shotgun, leading quail—if I hadn't forgotten to switch off the trigger safety, I would have shot an uncle in the head. My hands lay silent at my sides those nights. No memory of their grace or benediction could change their melancholy stillness.

While I was in college I worked two summers at a ranch in 18
Wyoming. My hands got the feel of new tools—foot nips, frog pick, fence pliers, skiving knife. I began to see that the invention, dexterity, and quickness of the hands could take many directions in a man's life; and that a man should be attentive to what his hands loved to do, and so learn not only what he might be good at for a long time but what would make him happy. It pleased me to smooth every wrinkle from a saddle blanket before I settled a saddle squarely on a horse's back. And I liked, too, to turn the thin pages of a Latin edition of the *Aeneid* as I slowly accomplished them that first summer, feeling the impression of the type. It was strengthening to work with my hands, with ropes and bridles and hay bales, with double-bitted axes and bow saws, currying horses, scooping grain, adding my hands' oil to wooden door latches in the barn, calming horses at the foot of a loading ramp, adjusting my hat against the sun, buckling my chaps on a frosty morning. I'd watch the same hand lay a book lovingly on a night table and reach for the lamp's pull cord.

I had never learned to type, but by that second summer, at nine- 19
teen, I was writing out the first few stories longhand in pencil. I liked the sound and the sight of the writing going on, the back pressure through my hand. When I had erased and crossed out and rewritten a story all the way through, I would type it out slowly with two or sometimes four fingers, my right thumb on the space bar, as I do to this day. Certain keys and a spot on the space bar are worn through to metal on my typewriters from the oblique angles at which my fingernails strike them.

Had I been able to grasp it during those summers in Wyoming, 20
I might have seen that I couldn't get far from writing stories and

physical work, either activity, and remain happy. It proved true that in these two movements my hands found their chief joy, aside from the touching of other human beings. But I could not see it then. My hands only sought out and gave in to the pleasures.

I began to travel extensively while I was in college. Eventually I 21
visited many places, staying with different sorts of people. Most worked some substantial part of the day with their hands. I gravitated toward the company of cowboys and farmers both, to the work of loggers and orchardists, but mostly toward the company of field biologists, college-educated men and women who worked long days open to the weather, studying the lives of wild animals. In their presence, sometimes for weeks at a time, occasionally in stupefying cold or under significant physical strain, I helped wherever I could and wrote in my journal what had happened and, sometimes, what I thought of what had happened. In this way my hands came to know the prick and compression of syringes, and the soldering of radio collars, the arming of anesthetizing guns, the setting of traps and snares, the deployment of otter trawls and plankton tows, the operation of calipers and tripod scales, and the manipulation of various kinds of sieves and packages used to sort and store parts of dead animals, parts created with the use of skinning and butchering knives, with bone saws, teasing needles, tweezers, poultry shears, and hemostatic clamps. My hands were in a dozen kinds of blood, including my own.

Everywhere I journeyed I marveled at the hands of other crea- 22
tures, at how their palms and digits revealed history, at how well they performed tasks, at the elegant and incontrovertible beauty of their design. I cradled the paws of wolves and polar bears, the hooves of caribou, the forefeet of marine iguanas, the foreflippers of ringed seals and sperm whales, the hands of wallabies, of deer mice. Palpating the tendons, muscles, and bones beneath the skin or fur, I gained a rough understanding of the range of ability, of expression. I could feel where a broken bone had healed and see from superficial scars something of what a life must have been like. Deeper down, with mammals during necropsy, I could see how blood vessels and layers of fat in a paw or in a flipper were arranged to either rid the creature of its metabolic heat or hoard it. I could see the evidence of arthritis in its phalanges, how that could come to me.

I have never touched a dead human, nor do I wish to. The living 23
hands of another person, however, draw me, as strongly as the eyes. What is their history? What are their emotions? What longing is

there? I can follow a cabinetmaker's hands for hours as they verify and detect, shave, fit, and rub; or a chef's hands adroitly dicing vegetables or shaping pastry. And who has not known faintness at the sight of a lover's hand? What man has not wished to take up the hands of the woman he loves and pore over them with reverence and curiosity? Who has not in reverie wished to love the lover's hands?

Years after my mother died I visited her oldest living friend. We were doing dishes together and she said, "You have your mother's hands." Was that likeness a shade of love? And is now I say out of respect for my hands I would buy only the finest tools, is that, too, not love? 24

The hands evolve, of course. The creases deepen and the fingers begin to move two or three together at a time. If the hands of a man are put to hard use, the fingers grow blunt. They lose dexterity and the skin calluses over like hide. Hardly a pair of man's hands known to me comes to mind without a broken or dislocated finger, a lost fingertip, a permanently crushed nail. Most women my age carry scars from kitchen and housework, drawer pinches, scalds, knife and glass cuts. We hardly notice them. Sunlight, wind, and weather obscure many of these scars, but I believe the memory of their occurrence never leaves the hands. When I awaken in the night and sense my hands cupped together under the pillow, or when I sit somewhere on a porch, idly watching wind crossing a ripening field, and look down to see my hands nested in my lap as if asleep like two old dogs, it is not hard for me to believe they know. They remember all they have done, all that has happened to them, the ways in which they have been surprised or worked themselves free of desperate trouble, or lost their grip and so caused harm. It's not hard to believe they remember the heads patted, the hands shaken, the apples peeled, the hair braided, the wood split, the gears shifted, the flesh gripped and stroked, and that they convey their feelings to each other. 25

In recent years my hands have sometimes been very cold for long stretches. It takes little cold now to entirely numb thumbs and forefingers. They cease to speak what they know. When I was thirty-one, I accidentally cut the base of my left thumb, severing nerves, leaving the thumb confused about what was cold, what was hot, and whether or not it was touching something or only thought so. When I was thirty-six, I was helping a friend butcher a whale. We'd been up for many hours under twenty-four-hour arctic daylight and 26 were tired. He glanced away and without thinking drove the knife into my wrist. It was a clean wound, easy to close, but with it I lost the nerves to the right thumb. Over the years each thumb has regained some sensitivity, and I believe the hands are more sympathetic to each other because of their similar wounds. The only obvious difference lies with the left hand. A broken metacarpal forced a rerouting of tendons to the middle and ring fingers as it healed and raised a boss of carpal bone tissue on the back of the hand.

At the base of the right thumb is a scar from a climbing accident. On the other thumb, a scar the same length from the jagged edges of a fuel-barrel pump. In strong sunlight, when there is a certain tension in the skin, as I have said, I can stare at my hands for a while, turning them slowly, and remember with them the days, the weather, the people present when some things happened that left scars behind. It brings forth affection for my hands. I recall how, long ago, they learned to differentiate between cotton and raw silk, between husks of the casaba and the honeydew melon, and how they thrilled to the wire bristle of a hog's back, how they clipped the water's surface in swimming-pool fights, how they painstakingly arranged bouquets, how they swung and lifted children. I have begun to wish they would speak to me, tell me stories I have forgotten. 27

I sit in a chair and look at the scars, the uneven cut of the nails, and reminisce. With them before me I grin as though we held something secret, remembering bad times that left no trace. I cut firewood for my parents once, winter in Alabama, swamping out dry, leafless vines to do so. Not until the next day did I realize the vines were poison ivy. The blisters grew so close and tight my hands straightened like paddles. I had to have them lanced to continue a cross-country trip, to dress and feed myself. And there have been days when my hands stiffened with cold so that I had to quit the work being done, sit it out and whimper with pain as they came slowly back to life. But these moments are inconsequential. I have looked at the pale, wrinkled hands of a drowned boy, and I have seen handless wrists. 28

If there were a way to speak directly to our hands, to allow them a language of their own, what I would most wish to hear is what they recall of human touch, of the first exploration of the body of another, the caresses, the cradling of breast, of head, of buttock. Does it seem to them as to me that we keep learning, even when the caressed body has been known for years? How do daydreams of an idealized body, one's own or another's affect the hands' first tentative inquiry? Is the 29 hand purely empirical? Does it apply an imagination? Does it retain a man's shyness, a boy's clumsiness? Do the hands anguish if there is no one to touch?

30 Tomorrow I shall pull blackberry vines and load a trailer with rotten timber. I will call on my hands to help me dress, to turn the spigot for coffee, to pull the newspaper from its tube. I will put my hands in the river and lift water where the sunlight is brightest, a playing with fractured light I never tire of. I will turn the pages of a book about the history of fire in Australia. I will sit at the typewriter, working through a story about a trip to Matagorda Island in Texas. I will ask my hands to undress me. Before I turn out the light, I will fold and set my reading glasses aside. Then I will cup my hands, the left in the right, and slide them under the pillow beneath my head, where they will speculate, as will I, about what we shall handle the next day, and dream, a spooling of their time we might later remember together and I, so slightly separated from them, might recognize.

Meanings and Values

1. Lopez uses his hands as the thread for an autobiographical essay. Why might he have chosen hands to represent the changes in his life? (See "Guide to Terms": *Symbol.*)
2. Lopez says, "Looking back, it's easy to see that the education of the hands (and so the person) begins like a language: a gathering of simple words, the assembly of simple sentences, all this leading eventually to the forging of instructive metaphors" (Par. 5). Why might he have chosen such a simile? What is the connection between hands and language as Lopez explains it?
3. Find all of Lopez's references to writing in the essay. What theme emerges from the repetitive use of the physical act of writing?

Expository Techniques

1. Identify where Lopez uses transition to represent the passage of time. How does he use the subject of hands to link stages in his life? (Guide: *Transitions.*)
2. Does Lopez primarily use concrete or abstract images in this essay? Point to examples of each and analyze their success. (Guide: *Evaluation.*)
3. Compare the references to dogs in Paragraph 5 ("Taking the lay of the dog's fur, the slow petting of the loved dog is the increasingly complicated heart speaking with the hand") to that in Paragraph 17

("My hands lost innocence or gained humanity that day, as they had another day when I was pulled off my first dog, screaming, my hands grasping feebly in the air, after he'd been run over and killed in the road"). How do these acts of placing hands on a dog differ? How has the author grown as a result of these experiences?

Diction and Vocabulary

1. Compare the tasks of the hands in Paragraphs 1 and 30. What words and actions are repeated? Explain the significance of Lopez's linked introduction and conclusion in this essay. (Guide: *Introductions; Conclusions.*)
2. Why does Lopez emphasize his right hand throughout the essay? What connotation does the left hand evoke in many readers? (Guide: *Denotation/Connotation.*)
3. Look up any of the following words with which you are unfamiliar: *heft* (Par. 4); *casaba* (7); *cambric* (8); *hafts* (11); *necropsy* (22).

Read to Write

1. **Collaborating:** Lopez "grows up" in this essay. Consider the various stages in your own lives. List those stages in an outline. Working in a group, identify the specific passages that indicate a new phase of Lopez's life and outline them. Compare Lopez's stages with your own and with those of other group members. Write a paragraph analyzing the similarities and differences among your choices.
2. **Considering Audience:** Lopez shares many experiences with his audience. With how many of these experiences might a majority of his readers be familiar? Can you think of any personal experiences with your hands that could be added and that readers would readily understand? Choose one and write a paragraph that could fit into Lopez's essay.
3. **Developing an Essay:** "A Passage of Hands" relies on clear description of touch. Choose one of your other senses and write an autobiographical essay similar to Lopez's.

(Note: Suggestions for topics regarding development by use of DESCRIPTION are on pp. 402–403 at the end of this chapter.)

E. B. WHITE

E. B. WHITE, distinguished essayist, was born in Mount Vernon, New York, in 1899 and died in 1985 in North Brooklin, Maine. A graduate of Cornell University, White worked as a reporter and advertising copywriter, and in 1926 he joined the staff of the *New Yorker* magazine. After 1937 he did most of his writing at his farm in Maine, for many years contributing a regular column, "One Man's Meat," to *Harper's* magazine and freelance editorials for the "Notes and Comments" column of the *New Yorker.* White also wrote children's books, two volumes of verse, and, with James Thurber, *Is Sex Necessary?* (1929). With his wife, Katherine White, he compiled *A Subtreasury of American Humor* (1941). Collections of his own essays include *One Man's Meat* (1942), *The Second Tree from the Corner* (1953), *The Points of My Compass* (1962), and *Essays of E. B. White* (1977). In 1959 he revised and enlarged William Strunk's *The Elements of Style,* a textbook still widely used in college classrooms. White received many honors and writing awards for his crisp, highly individual style and his sturdy independence of thought.

Once More to the Lake

In this essay White relies primarily on description to convey his sense of the passage of time and the power of memory. The vivid scenes and the clear yet expressive prose in this essay are characteristic of his writing.

August 1941

One summer, along about 1904, my father rented a camp on a lake in Maine and took us all there for the month of August. We all got ringworm from some kittens and had to rub Pond's Extract on our arms and legs night and morning, and my father rolled over in a canoe with all his clothes on; but outside of that the vacation was a success and from then on none of us ever thought there was any place in the world like that lake in Maine. We returned summer after summer—always on August 1 for one month. I have since become a salt-water man, but sometimes in summer there are days when the restlessness of the tides and the fearful cold of the sea water and the incessant wind that blows across the afternoon and into the evening make me wish for the placidity of a lake in the woods. A few weeks ago this feeling got so strong I bought myself a couple of bass hooks and a spinner and returned to the 1 lake where we used to go, for a week's fishing and to revisit old haunts.

I took along my son, who had never had any fresh water up his nose and who had seen lily pads only from train windows. On the journey over to the lake I began to wonder what it would be like. I wondered how time would have marred this unique, this holy spot—the coves and streams, the hills that the sun set behind, the camps and the paths behind the camps. I was sure that the tarred road would have found it out, and I wondered in what other ways it would be desolated. It is strange how much you can remember about places like that once you allow your mind to return into the grooves that lead back. You remember one thing, and that suddenly reminds you of another thing. I guess I remembered clearest of all the early mornings, when the lake was cool and motionless, remembered how the bedroom smelled of the lumber it was made of and of the wet woods whose scent entered through the screen. The partitions in the camp were thin and did not extend clear to the top of the rooms, and as I was always the first up I would dress softly so as not to wake the others, and sneak out into the sweet outdoors and start out in the canoe, keeping close along the shore in the long shadows of the pines. I remembered being very careful never to rub my paddle against the gunwale for fear of disturbing the stillness of the cathedral. 2

The lake had never been what you would call a wild lake. There were cottages sprinkled around the shores, and it was in farming country although the shores of the lake were quite heavily wooded. Some of the cottages were owned by nearby farmers, and you would live at the shore and eat your meals at the farmhouse. That's what our family did. But although it wasn't wild, it was a fairly large and undisturbed lake and there were places in it that, to a child at least, seemed infinitely remote and primeval. 3

I was right about the tar: it led to within half a mile of the shore. But when I got back there, with my boy, and we settled into a camp near a farmhouse and into the kind of summertime I had known, I could tell that it was going to be pretty much the same as it had been before—I knew it, lying in bed the first morning, smelling the bedroom and hearing the boy sneak quietly out and go off along the shore in a boat. I began to sustain the illusion that he was I, and therefore, by simple transposition, that I was my father. This sensation persisted, kept cropping up all the time we were there. It was not an entirely new feeling, but in this setting it grew much stronger. I seemed to be living a dual existence. I would be in the middle of 4 some simple act, I would be picking up a bait box or laying down a table fork, or I would be saying something, and suddenly it would be not I but my father who was saying the words or making the gesture. It gave me a creepy sensation.

We went fishing the first morning. I felt the same damp moss 5
covering the worms in the bait can, and saw the dragonfly alight on the tip of my rod as it hovered a few inches from the surface of the water. It was the arrival of this fly that convinced me beyond any doubt that everything was as it always had been, that the years were a mirage and that there had been no years. The small waves were the same, chucking the rowboat under the chin as we fished at anchor, and the boat was the same boat, the same color green and the ribs broken in the same places, and under the floorboards the same fresh-water leavings and débris—the dead helgramite, the wisps of moss, the rusty discarded fishhook, the dried blood from yesterday's catch. We stared silently at the tips of our rods, at the dragonflies that came and went. I lowered the tip of mine into the water, tentatively, pensively dislodging the fly, which darted two feet away, poised, darted two feet back, and came to rest again a little farther up the rod. There had been no years between the ducking of this dragonfly and the other one—the one that was part of memory. I looked at the boy, who was silently watching his fly, and it was my hands that held his rod, my eyes watching. I felt dizzy and didn't know which rod I was at the end of.

We caught two bass, hauling them in briskly as though they 6
were mackerel, pulling them over the side of the boat in a businesslike manner without any landing net, and stunning them with a blow on the back of the head. When we got back for a swim before lunch, the lake was exactly where we had left it, the same number of inches from the dock, and there was only the merest suggestion of a breeze. This seemed an utterly enchanted sea, this lake you could leave to its own devices for a few hours and come-back to, and find that it had not stirred, this constant and trustworthy body of water. In the shallows, the dark, water-soaked sticks and twigs, smooth and old, were undulating in clusters on the bottom against the clean ribbed sand, and the track of the mussel was plain. A school of minnows swam by, each minnow with its small individual shadow, doubling the attendance, so clear and sharp in the sunlight. Some of the other campers were in swimming, along the shore, one of them with a cake of soap, and the water felt thin and clear and unsubstantial. Over the years there had been this person with the cake of soap, this cultist, and here he was. There had been no years.

Up to the farmhouse to dinner through the teeming, dusty field, the road under our sneakers was only a two-track road. The middle track was missing, the one with the marks of the hooves and the splotches of dried, flaky manure. There had always been three tracks to choose from in choosing which track to walk in; now the choice was narrowed down to two. For a moment I missed terribly the middle alternative. But the way led past the tennis court, and something about the way it lay there in the sun reassured me; the tape had loosened along the backline, the alleys were green with plantains and other weeds, and the net (installed in June and removed in September) sagged in the dry noon, and the whole place steamed with midday heat and hunger and emptiness. There was a choice of pie for dessert, and one was blueberry and one was apple, and the waitresses were the same country girls, there having been no passage of time, only the illusion of it as in a dropped curtain—the waitresses were still fifteen; their hair had been washed, that was the only difference—they had been to the movies and seen the pretty girls with the clean hair. 7

Summertime, oh, summertime, pattern of life indelible, the fade-proof lake, the woods unshatterable, the pasture with the sweetfern and the juniper forever and ever, summer without end; this was the background, and the life along the shore was the design, their tiny docks with the flagpole and the American flag floating against the white clouds in the blue sky, the little paths over the roots of the trees leading from camp to camp and the paths leading back to the outhouses and the can of lime for sprinkling, and at the souvenir counters at the store the miniature birch-bark canoes and the postcards that showed things looking a little better than they looked. This was the American family at play, escaping the city heat, wondering whether the newcomers in the camp at the head of the cove were "common" or "nice," wondering whether it was true that the people who drove up for Sunday dinner at the farmhouse were turned away because there wasn't enough chicken. 8

It seemed to me, as I kept remembering all this, that those times and those summers had been infinitely precious and worth saving. There had been jollity and peace and goodness. The arriving (at the beginning of August) had been so big a business in itself, at the railway station the farm wagon drawn up, the first smell of the pine-laden air, the first glimpse of the smiling farmer, and the great importance of the trunks and your father's enormous authority in such matters, and the feel of the wagon under you for the long ten-mile haul, and at the top of the last long hill catching the first view of 9 the lake after eleven months of not seeing this cherished body of water. The shouts and cries of the other campers when they saw you, and the trunks to be unpacked, to give up their rich burden. (Arriving was less exciting nowadays, when you sneaked up in your car and parked it under a tree near the camp and took out the bags and in five minutes it was all over, no fuss, no loud wonderful fuss about trunks.)

10 Peace and goodness and jollity. The only thing that was wrong now, really, was the sound of the place, an unfamiliar nervous sound of the outboard motors. This was the note that jarred, the one thing that would sometimes break the illusion and set the years moving. In those other summertimes all motors were inboard; and when they were at a little distance, the noise they made was a sedative, an ingredient of summer sleep. They were one-cylinder and two-cylinder engines, and some were make-and-break and some were jump-spark, but they all made a sleepy sound across the lake. The one-lungers throbbed and fluttered, and the twin-cylinder ones purred and purred, and that was a quiet sound, too. But now the campers all had outboards. In the daytime, in the hot mornings, these motors made a petulant, irritable sound; at night, in the still evening when the afterglow lit the water, they whined about one's ears like mosquitoes. My boy loved our rented outboard, and his great desire was to achieve single-handed mastery over it, and authority, and he soon learned the trick of choking it a little (but not too much), and the adjustment of the needle valve. Watching him I would remember the things you could do with the old one-cylinder engine with the heavy flywheel, how you could have it eating out of your hand if you got really close to it spiritually. Motorboats in those days didn't have clutches, and you would make a landing by shutting off the motor at the proper time and coasting in with a dead rudder. But there was a way of reversing them, if you learned the trick, by cutting the switch and putting it on again exactly on the final dying revolution of the flywheel, so that it would kick back against compression and begin reversing. Approaching a dock in a strong following breeze, it was difficult to slow up sufficiently by the ordinary coasting method, and if a boy felt he had complete mastery over his motor, he was tempted to keep it running beyond its time and then reverse it a few feet from the dock. It took a cool nerve, because if you threw the switch a twentieth of a second too soon you would catch the flywheel when it still had speed enough to go up past center, and the boat would leap ahead, charging bull-fashion at the dock.

We had a good week at the camp. The bass were biting well and the sun shone endlessly, day after day. We would be tired at night and lie down in the accumulated heat of the little bedrooms after the long hot day and the breeze would stir almost imperceptibly outside and the smell of the swamp drift in through the rusty screens. Sleep would come easily and in the morning the red squirrel would be on the roof, tapping out his gay routine. I kept remembering everything, lying in bed in the mornings—the small steamboat that had a long rounded stern like the lip of a Ubangi, and how quietly she ran on the moonlight sails, when the older boys played their mandolins and the girls sang and we ate doughnuts dipped in sugar, and how sweet the music was on the water in the shining night, and what it had felt like to think about girls then. After breakfast we would go up to the store and the things were in the same place—the minnows in a bottle, the plugs and spinners disarranged and pawed over by the youngsters from the boys' camp, the Fig Newtons and the Bee-man's gum. Outside, the road was tarred and cars stood in front of the store. Inside, all was just as it had always been, except there was more Coca-Cola and not so much Moxie and root beer and birch beer and sarsaparilla. We would walk out with the bottle of pop apiece and sometimes the pop would backfire up our noses and hurt. We explored the streams, quietly, where the turtles slid off the sunny logs and dug their way into the soft bottom; and we lay on the town wharf and fed worms to the tame bass. Everywhere we went I had trouble making out which was I, the one walking at my side, the one walking in my pants. 11

One afternoon while we were there at that lake a thunderstorm came up. It was like the revival of an old melodrama that I had seen long ago with childish awe. The second-act climax of the drama of the electrical disturbance over a lake in America had not changed in any important respect. This was the big scene, still the big scene. The whole thing was so familiar, the first feeling of oppression and heat and a general air around camp of not wanting to go very far away. In mid-afternoon (it was all the same) a curious darkening of the sky, and a lull in everything that had made life tick; and then the way the boats suddenly swung the other way at their moorings with the coming of a breeze out of the new quarter, and the premonitory rumble. Then the kettle drum, then the snare, then the bass drum and cymbals, then crackling light against the dark, and the gods grinning and licking their chops in the hills. Afterward the calm, the rain steadily 12 rustling in the calm lake, the return of light and hope and spirits, and the campers running out in joy and relief to go swimming in the rain, their bright cries perpetuating the deathless joke about how they were getting simply drenched, and the children screaming with delight at the new sensation of bathing in the rain, and the joke about getting drenched linking the generations in a strong indestructible chain. And the comedian who waded in carrying an umbrella.

When the others went swimming, my son said he was going in, 13
too. He pulled his dripping trunks from the line where they had hung all through the shower and wrung them out. Languidly, and with no thought of going in, I watched him, his hard little body, skinny and bare, saw him wince slightly as he pulled up around his vitals the small, soggy, icy garment. As he buckled the swollen belt, suddenly my groin felt the chill of death.

Meanings and Values

1. In what ways have the lake and its surroundings remained the same since White's boyhood? In what ways have they changed? Be specific.
2. Can the lake be considered a personal symbol for White? (See "Guide to Terms": *Symbol.*) If so, what does it symbolize?
3. At one point in the essay, White says, "I seemed to be living a dual existence" (Par. 4). What is the meaning of this statement? How does this "dual existence" affect his point of view in the essay? (Guide: *Point of View.*) Is the dual existence emphasized more in the first half of the essay or the second half? Why?
4. Where in the essay does White link differences between the lake now and in his youth with a difference between his son's outlooks and his own? Is this distance between father and son caused by changes in the world around them or merely the passage of time? Explain.
5. After spending a day on the lake, White remarks, "There had been no years" (Par. 6). What other direct or indirect comments does he make about time and change? Be specific.
6. What is the tone of the essay? (Guide: *Style/Tone.*) Does the tone change or remain the same throughout the essay?
7. What is meant by the closing phrase of the essay, "suddenly my groin felt the chill of death" (Par. 13)? Is this an appropriate way to end the essay? Why, or why not?

Expository Techniques

1. In the first part of the essay, White focuses on the unchanged aspects of the lake; in the second part, he begins acknowledging the passage of time. Where does this shift in attitude take place? What strategies, including transitional devices, does White use to signal to the reader the shift in attitude? Be specific.
2. How does White use the discussion of outboard motors and inboard motors (Par. 10) to summarize the differences between life at the lake in his youth and at the time of his return with his son?
3. Many of the descriptive passages in this essay convey a dominant impression, usually an emotion or mood. Discuss how the author's choice of details and the author's comments suggest that the impressions are more a reflection of the observer's perspective than an objective description of the lake. (Guide: *Syntax; Diction.*)
4. In many places the author combines description and comparison. Select a passage from the essay and discuss in detail how he combines the patterns. In what ways is the combination of description and comparison appropriate to the theme and the point of view of the essay?

Diction and Vocabulary

1. How much do the connotations of the words used in Paragraph 8 contribute to the dominant impression the author is trying to create? (Guide: *Connotation/Denotation.*) In Paragraph 10? What do these connotations suggest about the relation of person to place? Of observer to subject of observation?
2. Is the diction in this passage sentimental: "Summertime, oh, summertime, pattern of life indelible, the fade-proof lake, the woods unshatterable, the pasture with the sweetfern and the juniper forever and ever, summer without end. . . ." (Par. 8)? (Guide: *Sentimentality.*) If so, why would the author choose to use this style in the passage? Does the passage contain an allusion? If so, what is alluded to and why? (Guide: *Figures of Speech.*)
3. In what sense can a tennis court steam "with midday heat and hunger and emptiness" (Par. 7)?
4. What kind of paradox is presented in this passage: "the waitresses were the same country girls, there having been no passage of time, only the illusion of it as in a dropped curtain—the waitresses were still fifteen; their hair had been washed, that was the only difference—they had been to the movies and seen the pretty girls with the clean hair" (Par. 7)? (Guide: *Paradox.*)
5. Study the author's uses of the following words, consulting the dictionary as needed: *incessant, placidity* (Par. 1); *gunwale* (2); *primeval* (3); *transposition* (4); *helgramite, pensively* (5); *petulant* (10); *premonitory* (12); *languidly* (13).

Read to Write

1. **Collaborating:** Working with a group, make a list of your memorable vacations and holidays, then choose three and develop for each a tentative thesis statement that sums up the meaning of the event.
2. **Considering Audience:** In his descriptions, White creates symbols to convey his ideas about the passing of time. How else might readers respond to the incidents White describes? To what extent might responses be shaped by differing religious, social, economic, or cultural backgrounds? Prepare a short essay considering the possible range of reactions.
3. **Developing an Essay:** Drawing on the strategies White employs in "Once More to the Lake," choose some place you remember from your childhood and have seen recently, and write a description of it comparing its present appearance with your memories of it. As you write, take into account the relationships of place and person, permanence and change, and the effect of experience on perception.

(Note: Suggestions for topics requiring development by use of description follow.)

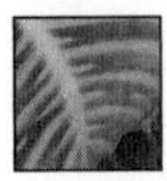

Writing Suggestions for Chapter 10

Description

1. Primarily by way of impressionistic description that focuses on a single dominant impression, show and explain the mood or atmosphere of one of the following:

    a. A country fair

    b. A ball game

    c. A rodeo

    d. A wedding

    e. A funeral

    f. A busy store

    g. A ghost town

    h. A cave

    i. A beach in summer (or winter)

    j. An antique shop

    k. A party

    l. A family dinner

    m. A traffic jam

    n. Reveille

    o. An airport (or a bus depot)

    p. An automobile race (or a horse race)

    q. A home during one of its rush hours

    r. The last night of holiday shopping

    s. A natural scene at a certain time of day

    t. The campus at examination time

    u. A certain person at a time of great emotion—for example, joy, anger, or grief

2. Using objective description as your basic pattern, explain the functional qualities or the significance of one of the following:

    a. A house for sale

    b. A public building

    c. A dairy barn

    d. An ideal workshop (or hobby room)

    e. An ideal garage

f. A fast-food restaurant
g. The layout of a town (or airport)
h. The layout of a farm
i. A certain type of boat
j. A sports complex

Settings

Some settings give us insights into human behavior. Choose a kind of behavior from the list below and create a description of a setting and any activity within it that offers insights into the behavior.

1. How children develop values
2. How family conflicts develop
3. How we learn compassion
4. How we develop ways to reduce conflict
5. How we learn to recognize beauty
6. How we develop an appreciation for hard work
7. How we come to recognize personality in animals
8. How people come to understand the effects of their anger
9. How films, paintings, or music affect people in different ways
10. How sporting events draw varied reactions from people

Collaborative Exercises

1. Have each member of your team brainstorm a list of words that describe the mood or atmosphere he or she feels when attending any one of the events listed in 1a–c. From your individual lists, look for similar experiences and moods. Collaboratively write an essay based on one of those events and the team similarities.
2. Have each member of the group describe a designated building on campus. Compare and contrast your descriptions.
3. Consider an ideal gymnasium or dormitory. Have each student in the group research this building by talking to other students on campus. Share your results and write a collaborative essay incorporating each member's research.

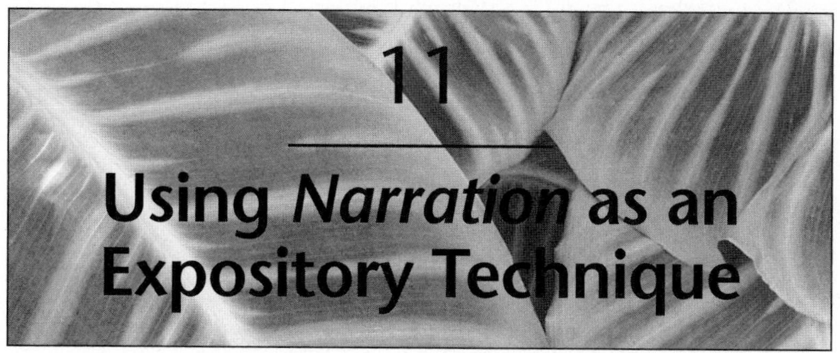

11

Using *Narration* as an Expository Technique

When is narration a pattern of exposition rather than a story told for its own purposes? The answer: when it serves to explain a subject, present conclusions, or support an interpretation or a thesis. For example, a writer who wishes to explain the role of risk-taking individuals (rather than corporations) in developing new ideas and products might tell the story of an entrepreneur who perfected the frozen French fry in the early 1950s only to discover that there was little demand for his product. The story would emphasize his perseverance in struggling to develop a market for the product—a perseverance that paid off for all concerned a decade later when the rapidly growing fast-food industry discovered the usefulness of frozen fries for ready-in-a-minute menus.

Whether you use narration as the pattern for an entire essay or for support and explanation within an essay, your readers will expect you to do certain things. They will expect your narrative to help them understand *what happened,* including the *who, where, what,* and *to whom* of events. They will expect the narrative to *re-create* events, showing (through concrete detail or the actual words of participants) rather than merely telling what happened (through summary). Finally, your readers will expect your narrative to help them understand the *significance* of the events. They will look for the point you are making, for what you have to say about the events, or for the way the events support your thesis.

In a book explaining the extraordinary character and physical courage of early Antarctic explorers, the writer Edwin Mickleburgh offers the following narrative to support his thesis about the explorer

Ernest Shackleton's abilities as a leader and about the courage of his crew.

> For anyone who has looked up from the sullen South Georgia shore [an island near Antarctica] towards the soaring, razor-edged peaks and the terrible chaos of glaciers topped by swirling clouds and scoured by mighty winds, the knowledge of the crossing made by these three men adds a wider dimension to an already awe inspiring sight. How they did it, God only knows, but they crossed the island in thirty-six hours. They were fortunate that the weather held, although many times great banks of fog rolled in from the open sea, creeping toward them over the snow and threatening to obscure their way. Confronted by precipices of ice and walls of rock they had often to retrace their steps adding many miles to the journey. They walked almost without rest. At one point they sat down in an icy gully, the wind blowing the drift around them, and so tired were they that Worseley and Crean fell asleep immediately. Shackleton, barely able to keep himself awake, realized that to fall asleep under such conditions would prove fatal. After five minutes he woke the other two, saying that they had slept for half an hour.
>
> —Edwin Mickleburgh,
> *Beyond the Frozen Sea: Visions of Antarctica*

Introduces narrative and its relation to writer's main point

Narrative

WHY USE NARRATION?

Perhaps the most familiar form of expository narrative is the personal narrative, based on personal experience or observation, that offers insights into events or conclusions about relationships and the importance of certain kinds of experience. These include memoirs focusing on the author's personal and intellectual development, on an unusual and significant childhood event, or on other experiences. They include autobiographies of media stars, politicians, and other well-known people, especially those that shed light on the fields in which they have worked or on the important events they have witnessed. And they include personal narratives embedded in other kinds of works in order to give the works a sense of authenticity.

Another use of narrative is to present a profile on an unfamiliar or unusual activity or the people involved in it. Typically, such a narrative begins by presenting an interesting person in action (a day in the life of a computer game creator, for example) or by focusing on an activity (workers changing light bulbs on the spire of the Empire State Building; divers searching in deep water for wreckage from an airplane crash). As a way of creating drama and interest, such narratives frequently reveal surprising tensions or contradictions, such as the quiet home life and personal kindness of an offshore boat racer also known for his fearlessness, abrasiveness, spectacular crashes, and narrow escapes from death.

A narrative can also provide a framework for commentary and analysis, with passages of narrative interspersed with discussions of the significance and implications of the events. Or narratives can add convincing detail or emotional force to explanations built around some other expository pattern, such as comparison (Chapter 5), cause-and-effect (Chapter 8), or definition (Chapter 9).

CHOOSING A STRATEGY

A narrative is a chronological account of events. You do not always have to present the events in chronological order or give them all equal emphasis. When you are creating an event for expository purposes, begin your planning process with questions like these:

- What events are most important to my purpose for writing?
- What ideas and emotions surrounding the events are worth sharing with my readers?
- What point do I want to make with this narrative?

Your answers to questions like these should help you limit the time frame of your narrative and focus on the most important events of the story. Many writers are gripped by a compulsion to get all the details of a story down—important and unimportant. Radical surgery often helps. Instead of covering a whole week or day, consider focusing on the single most important incident—the four or five minutes when all the forces came together—and summarizing the rest.

Remember that you can arrange the events to suit your purpose(s). In basic form, a narrative sets the scene; introduces characters; presents, in chronological order, episodes that introduce a conflict or prepare for the central event; then, finally, explores in detail the most important incident in which the conflict is resolved or the writer's outlook is made clear. Yet the chronological approach can make it hard to emphasize the most important element. You may instead want to start in the middle of things, perhaps at the climactic episode, and fill in prior events through flashbacks. Or you might stop in the middle of events to provide important background information or comment on the characters and their actions.

And you need to choose whether to provide an explicit thesis statement to organize your narrative and direct commentary on the events, or to let the events speak for themselves, assuming that their relationship to your main point will be sufficiently clear to readers.

DEVELOPING A NARRATIVE

As you draft and revise a narrative, pay attention to the following concerns that can contribute to the success (or failure) of your efforts.

- **Selection of Details.** You will probably have many more details you might include in a narrative than you need. Keep in mind that too many details can overwhelm readers, making them lose sight about the point the narrative is making or the explanation it is offering. Focused, unified writing makes use only of those details that are most relevant to the writer's purpose and desired effect. Whenever possible, try to include concrete, specific details that make the narrative vivid and believable and that will be likely to hold your readers' interest.
- **Time Order.** You can employ straight chronology, relating events as they happened, or the flashback method, leaving the sequence temporarily in order to go back and relate some now-significant happening of a time prior to the main action. If you use flashback, do so deliberately, not merely because you neglected to mention the episode earlier.
- **Transitions.** Watch out for overly simple and repetitive transitions between events in the narrative: "And then we. . . . And then she. . . . And then we . . ." As you revise, make a conscious effort to create variety in transitions: "next," "following," "subsequently," "as a consequence," "reacting to," "later," "meanwhile," "at the same time," "concurrently," and the like.
- **Point of View.** Decide whether you want to tell the story from the point of view of a participant, such as yourself or a character, or from the overall perspective of a spectator. The vividness and immediacy possible from a participant's point of view can make

the narrative more dramatic, but the spectator's point of view can allow for an easier transition from narrative to commentary and may be especially useful in expository writing. Whichever point of view you choose, keep it consistent throughout the narrative.

- **Dialogue.** Remember that quoting the words of participants can help make narrative more convincing and dialogue, which can reveal conflicting perspectives among the participants, can also be a springboard to your commentary on the meaning of the events.

Student Essay

One important use of narrative in expository writing is to explore values and the ways they change. In the following essay, Hrishikesh Unni uses flashback and a dream sequence to explain a set of personal values—love of ivory and of ivory carvings—that may be unfamiliar to many of his readers. He then returns to the main narrative of his encounter with a herd of elephants in Zambia and uses it to explain his change in attitude toward ivory collecting.

Elephants, Ivory, and an Indelible Experience
by Hrishikesh Unni

Opening incident—starts in the middle of events

Unusual, exotic—gets readers' attention

Appeals to senses

The roar of the engine increased to a crescendo as the driver revved the engine of the open van. This sound broke the monotonous atmosphere of the dry and deserted African grassland of the Luangwa Valley in Zambia and made me shift in my rear seat. I had been sitting there for at least three hours since noon and had not seen any game, apart from the impala and zebra that intermittently spotted the grasslands. These creatures are a common sight in all national parks in Zambia, including the Luangwa. The drought had taken its toll. What was once a land filled with green vegetation was turned into a brown and heavily scorched area by the menacing October sun that was callously beating down on my back. I clutched my Canon camera even more firmly and could feel the heat radiating from the surface of its black case.

Uses quotation

"You sure are unlucky, aren't you, Hrishi? No elephants yet!" said Musa, the guide, who was the only other person in the spacious van besides Banda.

Banda was a local driver who could only speak the local language, Nyanga. I merely nodded to this statement, admitting my disappointment. I had come all the way from Ndola (another town in Zambia) to see the well-known elephants of the Luangwa National Park. I had given up hope because it was the third and final day of my visit, and I had not seen any so far. What irritated me was the fact that I had lost a long-awaited opportunity to see these beasts. To overcome my disappointment, I looked at the metallic body of the van that was painted white. It blazed in the sun and blinded my eyes. It reminded me of something I had once loved and treasured: ivory.

Fills in background of events

I had an affinity for ivory. I loved its color, texture, and appearance. My positive feelings for this substance had begun after I received my first ivory carving for my ninth birthday from a Zambian friend. It was a superb carving of a baby elephant, and I instantly liked it. I would gaze at it, admiring its dominant white color and its smooth texture. Also, its different shades of light brown never seemed to bore me. Since receiving that gift, I had bought every ivory item I could get my hands on and had a magnificent collection that I kept in my room.

Uses key word to set off flashbacks

Introduces his values

Flashbacks—source of values

My eyes could no longer take the glare and in an attempt to reduce the strain, I allowed my eyelids to drop over them. I realized how tired I was when I closed my eyes. Every muscle in my body seemed to be screaming in desperation, ordering my brain to sleep. I felt sleep gradually overtake me like an ivy conquering an old dilapidated castle. Soon I was fast asleep and dreaming of the time. . . .

Back to main narrative

Dream event

I entered my room and switched on my titanium-white tube light. I stared in awe as the light fell on my ivory collection, enhancing its already immaculate white coating. The furniture in my room consisted of a bed, a table, a chair, and a couple of shelves that were attached to the wall. It was decorated with my extravagant ivory collection. I stood at the doorway and began surveying the room, casting my eyes on each and every piece of ivory. I admired and absorbed every detail of the carvings and was aware of the hours of work involved in creating a single delicate carving from a long curved elephant tusk. The dexterity and skill the African craftsmen possessed amazed me, and I never got tired of looking at my collection. I saw a variety of things: old traditional men, dogs, a range of birds, daggers, kudu, impala, elephants, rhino, leopards, cheetahs—all in ivory. My eyes finally came to rest on the carving I admired the most—an elephant bull, which I had named Tusker Bull. It was the largest piece I had. Its place on the highest shelf and its majestic posture gave it an authority over the other animals in my collection. Its ominous, evil eyes and its cocked ears portrayed tyranny. I had a sudden urge to look into its lifeless eye. I daringly did this and saw a look I had never seen before. It was one of anger and rage. This look sent a chill down my spine as I wondered if my imagination was mocking me. The look in its eye seemed to be saying. . . .

Explains values; love of ivory helps readers understand appeal of art that may be unfamiliar to them

"Wake up, Hrishi, elephants!" shouted the guide.

Brief transition paragraph

I awoke with a jump, expecting to see my room, but the heat waves of the national park that enveloped me made me aware that I was a long way away from there. The painful process of adjusting to the amber sunlight took quite a while. The sky was an orange-yellow, and the ground seemed to have darkened to a beige color. It was nearly dusk, and I realized I had been sleeping for at least two hours. Musa repeated the word "elephant," the word I longed to hear. I knew he had spotted a couple of them.

Back to main narrative

"Where?" I asked anxiously.

He pointed in between two brown-colored thickets and said, "By that dry waterhole."

He was right, and I could see the posterior of two African elephants. I could not see the entire waterhole because the dry trees and scrub that had adapted to drought conditions partially obliterated our view. I was filled with excitement as images of elephants and my ivory collection flashed in my mind. I quickly set my camera to "operate" as the driver steered the van toward the elephants. We took an unorthodox and meandering path toward the elephants. As the van cut through the dry scrub, I could hear the twigs being crushed by its enormous tires and the dry grass, grazing and caressing the sides of the van. We finally reached the brown-colored thicket, and the driver deftly steered around it enabling us to see the entire expanse of the waterhole that merely had shallow puddles of water.

What we saw shocked us. There were not two elephants; there were two thousand of them! From where we were before, we could only get a glimpse of this enormous herd.

"What a sight! Ten years in this business, and I have not seen this many at once!" exclaimed Musa.

"Hitut, hitut!" said Banda, in awe.

Experience of seeing elephants more dramatic and moving than their representations in ivory

Everywhere I looked, I only saw elephants. They completely superimposed the entire landscape, which now looked like a dark gray Persian carpet. The faint sunlight that reflected off the elephants transformed the color of their bodies to a stone-gray. It was an absolutely fantastic and awesome sight! I began surveying them in the manner I surveyed my ivory collection in my dream, slowly and meticulously, but this time I wasn't looking at elephant ivory carvings but at real elephants. My eyes swept across the herd, and I was amazed at the unique behavior of each individual elephant I saw. There were numerous bulls with gigantic tusks. Their white tusks contrasted with their black bodies and made me think of ivory. From our position the tusks looked like curved toothpicks. The females were nurturing and tending to their playful calves. The elephants were of different sizes, but all the bulls were above eleven feet. Their postures conveyed a strong sense of magnanimity as they marched slowly in unison, every step serving a purpose. I admired the ease with which they moved, taking all the time in the world. They deliberately swung their trunks from side to side, like pendulums, and their tails moved naturally to their rhythmic walk. The mild deep grunts of the bulls were amplified by the wind that blew toward us. This natural sound enabled them to coax the members of the herd that were extremely slow. The pitch of this sound was lower than the sound the baby elephants made, which was like notes played on a trumpet that was not in tune. The calves pranced around playfully and used their trunks to mock and tease each other, not aware of their vulnerability to predators. A huge bull raised its head and arched its trunk in a form of imperious salute. He was definitely the largest and seemed to be leading the herd, ready to admonish the herd of any potential danger. I wanted a photo of this elephant.

Concrete details appeal to senses throughout narrative

"Let's get closer, I want a photo of that bull," I said, pointing to the conspicuous animal.

Dialogue

"I think we'll be asking for trouble if we get any closer. This herd is definitely overprotective because there are so many young," replied Musa.

"Oh, come on, this is the only opportunity we've had of seeing so many elephants. I mean, this is a rare sight, and we haven't seen any all day. I want that bull. We must get closer," I persisted.

Musa and Banda conversed in the local language about my idea. I could tell Banda was not pleased, but finally he reluctantly nodded his head in apparent consent.

"Okay, but Banda says only a couple of meters," he said firmly.

I gave them both a "thumbs up" sign showing my appreciation. Banda furtively drove the van toward the herd that had not noticed us yet, and he stopped near it. As a precaution he left the engine on and did not remove his foot from the accelerator, establishing a ready position to take off if something went terribly wrong. From the expressions on Banda's and Musa's faces, I could tell that they were not pleased. I was told that the elephants were used to the sound of the van, and if you maintained a safe distance, you would be fine even if they were aware of you. I knew the elephants had seen us because some turned their heads in our direction.

Now we were a dangerous fifteen meters from the herd, and I was now in a position to take a photo of the largest elephant that was closer to us than the rest of the herd. I set the flash on my camera and peered at the bull through the eyepiece. It was out of focus, and I had the lateral view of the elephant. I quickly brought it into focus and waited, hoping it would turn toward me. I had to wait for approximately forty seconds until the moment I longed for arrived, but it was a moment I have never forgotten to this day. The bull turned its head towards me, and I stared into its eye the way I stared into the eye of the elephant carving in my dream. I saw the same look of rage and anger in its eye. The menacing look seemed to be accusing me of an unforgivable crime I seemed to have committed. I avoided its eyes and pressed the button on my camera. This was a big mistake because the flash disturbed the elephant, and it let out an ear-shattering sound that I had never heard before. This sound seemed to be the warning alarm because it caused the whole herd to simultaneously bellow in this fashion. It sounded like a loud never-ending echo, which punished our ears. The ground reverberated beneath us as they moved impetuously and tried to form a cordon around their young. There were so many of them, causing them to nearly trample on each other. Some began running away from us, while others advanced toward us, their ears flapping rapidly and fervently in a form of defense. What had once been a calm and benign atmosphere turned into a calamitous one at the push of a camera button.

Link to dream sequence—effect on his values

I was speechless and could hear Musa shouting, "Tieni, tieni fast!" to the driver. Instinctively, Banda slammed the foot on the accelerator causing the engine to roar strongly, but this sound was barely audible due to the louder angry grunts of the elephants. He then turned the van away from the herd in an attempt to reach safety.

"Abuil abuil ei tiuti hamba isa tieni tieni fast!" shouted Musa frantically to Banda as he ducked below a seat. I did not know what this had meant, but I soon

Dramatic climax of narrative

found out. The massive bull, which I had tried to photograph, began charging at us from the rear, flapping its ears vigorously and grunting vehemently. Its tusks were raised, like a tank with two white-colored barrels, ready for battle. I had a clear view of its tusks and they made me think of ivory—yet not as a smooth and attractive substance, as I once did, but as something dangerous to be in possession of. Now the thought of ivory did not amaze me but frightened me. I have never seen ivory the same way since that day. At that moment, the image of Tusker Bull, my biggest piece in the ivory collection, flashed into my mind. It seemed as if it had come alive and was after me. I was surprised at the pace the bull was running because I didn't expect such a large animal to run at such a fast speed. I honestly thought I was going to die and was terrified because it was merely ten feet away from the van and was gaining on us. I held on to the side of the van and shut my eyes, not looking behind me. Yet, I could see the elephant in my mind, charging angrily at us. Banda was doing his best to escape from this animal, but his efforts seemed to be futile.

Reference to dream sequence and to underlying discussion of values

It seemed hours had passed when suddenly Musa yelled in relief, "It's stopped! It's stopped!" pointing at the elephant that had become stationary.

It gave an indignant salute that meant to say, "Don't ever come near my herd again. We are much more powerful than you."

Warning symbolic of writer's changed perspectives

"Hiny in hyi it fl, ungo," replied Banda in a tone of relief.

"Are you all right?" Musa asked me.

Since I was in a state of shock, I did not say a word and merely nodded.

"We'll be at the lodge soon so don't worry. It's over, and everything will be all right," said Musa.

I responded to him with a slight smile and then closed my eyes, while thinking of my close brush with death. The roar of the engine increased to a crescendo as the driver revved the engine of the open van and followed the dusty route to Mfuwe Lodge of the Luangwa National Park of Zambia.

Discussion of changed values—summarizes main ideas of essay

The ten-minute encounter with the elephants and the charging bull changed my perspective of elephants and gave me second thoughts about collecting ivory. This frightening experience made me aware of how protective an elephant community is and of the similarities in its character to that of a human society. It was during this time that I realized the natural power these animals possess and that a human is only able to overpower them with the use of guns and other weapons. My respect for these animals and nature in general has increased. I felt that the elephants were trying to make me aware of the cruelty of people and how they have killed elephants to get ivory. Just the fact that I collected ivory betrayed my insensitivity toward these creatures. I burned my collection when I got home, and now I am no longer interested in collecting ivory. Now I don't value my collection in terms of money but in terms of the amount of life that was wasted in obtaining every piece that was present in my collection. I was taught a lesson by the victims that I feel is the best way to be punished. I will never collect ivory again, and I am planning to become part of the organization that plans to ban ivory and abolish poaching. Yes, the actual substance of ivory I will continue to admire, but differently, because I now think that ivory looks best on an elephant and not as carvings placed on a shelf in my room.

MARTIN GANSBERG

MARTIN GANSBERG was born in Brooklyn, New York, in 1920 and received a Bachelor of Social Sciences degree from St. John's University. He was an editor and reporter for the *New York Times,* including a three-year period as editor of its international edition in Paris. He also served on the faculty of Fairleigh Dickinson University. Gansberg wrote for many magazines, including *Diplomat, Catholic Digest, Facts,* and *U.S. Lady.*

38 Who Saw Murder Didn't Call the Police

"38 Who Saw Murder . . ." was written for the *New York Times* in 1964, and for obvious reasons it has been anthologized frequently since then. Cast in a deceptively simple news style, it still provides material for serious thought, as well as a means of studying the use and technique of narration.

For more than half an hour 38 respectable, law-abiding citizens in Queens watched a killer stalk and stab a woman in three separate attacks in Kew Gardens. 1

Twice their chatter and the sudden glow of their bedroom lights interrupted him and frightened him off. Each time he returned, sought her out, and stabbed her again. Not one person telephoned the police during the assault; one witness called after the woman was dead. 2

That was two weeks ago today. 3

Still shocked is Assistant Chief Inspector Frederick M. Lussen, in charge of the borough's detectives and a veteran of 25 years of homicide investigations. He can give a matter-of-fact recitation on many murders. But the Kew Gardens slaying baffles him—not because it is a murder, but because the "good people" failed to call the police. 4

"As we have reconstructed the crime," he said, "the assailant had three chances to kill this woman during a 35-minute period. He returned twice to complete the job. If we had been called when he first attacked, the woman might not be dead now." 5

This is what the police say happened beginning at 3:20 A.M. in the staid, middle-class, tree-lined Austin Street area: 6

Twenty-eight-year-old Catherine Genovese, who was called Kitty by almost everyone in the neighborhood, was returning home from 7

---

her job as manager of a bar in Hollis. She parked her red Fiat in a lot adjacent to the Kew Gardens Long Island Rail Road Station, facing Mowbray Place. Like many residents of the neighborhood, she had parked there day after day since her arrival from Connecticut a year ago, although the railroad frowns on the practice.

She turned off the lights of her car, locked the door, and started 8
to walk the 100 feet to the entrance of her apartment at 82–70 Austin Street, which is in a Tudor building, with stores in the first floor and apartments on the second.

The entrance to the apartment is in the rear of the building be- 9
cause the front is rented to retail stores. At night the quiet neighborhood is shrouded in the slumbering darkness that marks most residential areas.

Miss Genovese noticed a man at the far end of the lot, near a 10
seven-story apartment house at 82–40 Austin Street. She halted. Then, nervously, she headed up Austin Street toward Lefferts Boulevard, where there is a call box to the 102nd Police Precinct in nearby Richmond Hill.

She got as far as a street light in front of a bookstore before the 11
man grabbed her. She screamed. Lights went on in the 10-story apartment house at 82–67 Austin Street, which faces the bookstore. Windows slid open and voices punctuated the early-morning stillness.

Miss Genovese screamed: "Oh, my God, he stabbed me! Please 12
help me! Please help me!"

From one of the upper windows in the apartment house, a man 13
called down: "Let that girl alone!"

The assailant looked up at him, shrugged and walked down 14
Austin Street toward a white sedan parked a short distance away. Miss Genovese struggled to her feet.

Lights went out. The killer returned to Miss Genovese, now try- 15
ing to make her way around the side of the building by the parking lot to get to her apartment. The assailant stabbed her again.

"I'm dying!" she shrieked, "I'm dying!" 16

Windows were opened again, and lights went on in many apart- 17
ments. The assailant got into his car and drove away. Miss Genovese staggered to her feet. A city bus, Q-10, the Lefferts Boulevard line to Kennedy International Airport, passed. It was 3:35 A.M.

The assailant returned. By then, Miss Genovese had crawled to 18
the back of the building, where the freshly painted brown doors to the apartment house held out hope for safety. The killer tried the first door; she wasn't there. At the second door, 82–62 Austin Street,

he saw her slumped on the floor at the foot of the stairs. He stabbed her a third time—fatally.

It was 3:50 by the time the police received their first call, from a man who was a neighbor of Miss Genovese. In two minutes they were at the scene. The neighbor, a 70-year-old woman, and another woman were the only persons on the street. Nobody else came forward. 19

The man explained that he had called the police after much deliberation. He had phoned a friend in Nassau County for advice and then he had crossed the roof of the building to the apartment of the elderly woman to get her to make the call. 20

"I didn't want to get involved," he sheepishly told the police. 21

Six days later, the police arrested Winston Moseley, a 29-year-old business-machine operator, and charged him with homicide. Moseley had no previous record. He is married, has two children and owns a home at 133–19 Sutter Avenue, South Ozone Park, Queens. On Wednesday, a court committed him to Kings County Hospital for psychiatric observation. 22

When questioned by the police, Moseley also said that he had slain Mrs. Annie May Johnson, 24, of 146–12 133rd Avenue, Jamaica, on Feb. 29 and Barbara Kralik, 15, of 174–17 140th Avenue, Springfield Gardens, last July. In the Kralik case, the police are holding Alvin L. Mitchell, who is said to have confessed to that slaying. 23

The police stressed how simple it would have been to have gotten in touch with them. "A phone call," said one of the detectives, "would have done it." The police may be reached by dialing "O" for operator or SPring 7–3100. 24

Today witnesses from the neighborhood, which is made up of one-family homes in the $35,000 to $60,000 range with the exception of the two apartment houses near the railroad station, find it difficult to explain why they didn't call the police. 25

A housewife, knowingly if quite casually, said, "We thought it was a lover's quarrel." A husband and wife both said, "Frankly, we were afraid." They seemed aware of the fact that events might have been different. A distraught woman, wiping her hands on her apron, said, "I didn't want my husband to get involved." 26

One couple, now willing to talk about that night, said they heard the first screams. The husband looked thoughtfully at the bookstore where the killer first grabbed Miss Genovese. 27

"We went to the window to see what was happening," he said, "but the light from our bedroom made it difficult to see the street." The wife, still apprehensive, added: "I put out the light and we were able to see better." 28

Asked why they hadn't called the police, she shrugged and replied: "I don't know." 29

A man peeked out from the slight opening in the doorway to his apartment and rattled off an account of the killer's second attack. Why hadn't he called the police at the time? "I was tired," he said without emotion. "I went back to bed." 30

It was 4:25 A.M. when the ambulance arrived to take the body of Miss Genovese. It drove off. "Then," a solemn police detective said, "the people came out." 31

Meanings and Values

1. What is Gansberg's central (expository) theme? How might he have developed this theme without using narration at all? Specify what patterns of exposition he could have used instead. Would any of them have been as effective as narration *for the purpose?* Why, or why not?
2. Why has this narrative account of old news (the murder made its only headlines in 1964) retained its significance to this day? Are you able to see in this event a paradigm of any larger condition or situation? If so, explain, using examples as needed to illustrate your ideas.

Expository Techniques

1. What standard introductory technique is exemplified in the first paragraph? ("Guide to Terms": *Introductions.*) How effective do you consider it? If you see anything ironic in the fact stated there, explain the irony. (Guide: *Irony.*)
2. Where does the main narration begin? What, then, is the function of the preceding paragraphs?
3. Study several of the paragraph transitions within the narration itself to determine Gansberg's method of advancing the time sequence (to avoid overuse of "and then") What is the technique? Is another needed? Why, or why not?
4. What possible reasons do you see for the predominant use of short paragraphs in this piece? Does this selection lose any effectiveness because of the short paragraphs?
5. Undoubtedly, the author selected with care the few quotations from witnesses that he uses. What principle or principles do you think applied to his selection?
6. Explain why you think the quotation from the "solemn police detective" was, or was not, deliberately and carefully chosen to conclude the piece. (Guide: *Closings.*)

7. Briefly identify the point of view of the writing. (Guide: *Point of View.*) Is it consistent throughout? Show the relation, as you see it, between this point of view and the author's apparent attitude toward his subject matter.

Diction and Vocabulary

1. Why do you think the author used no difficult words in this narration? Do you find the writing at all belittling to college people because of this fact? Why, or why not?

Read to Write

1. **Collaborating:** Gansberg's narration is written as a news account except that it clearly editorializes about the apathetic attitude of citizens. Working in a group, identify the places in the essay that Gansberg injects his bias. With your group, rewrite those sections where Gansberg expresses his perspective, taking the opposite point of view—supporting people who do not get involved in a situation like the one presented in the essay.
2. **Considering Audience:** The general plot of this story is as believable for audiences of the twenty-first century as it was for audiences of the 1960s—perhaps even more so because levels of violence in society have increased in the intervening decades. However, how might the behaviors of the people involved have been different if the incident had occurred today? Write out your answer and a brief explanation of it.
3. **Developing an Essay:** Though he certainly has his own view of the events he reports, Gansberg allows readers to question the motivations of the observers and to make their own judgments about the lack of involvement. Prepare an account of some incident you witnessed and use a similar approach. Call attention to the various motivations expressed by the participants, to any inconsistencies in their behavior, and to any other elements you wish readers to analyze and question. The event itself need not be of more than local significance (an account of a meeting or a sports event can offer interesting insights, for example), but your exposition should offer readers insights worth considering.

(NOTE: Suggestions for topics requiring development by NARRATION are on pp. 445–446 at the end of this chapter.)

GEOFFREY CANADA

GEOFFREY CANADA is the President/CEO of the Harlem Children's Zone in New York City.

Pain

"Pain," an excerpt from the book *Reaching Up for Manhood,* draws on the writer's training and experience as a psychologist. He uses the narrative to explain the power of memory in our lives, especially memory of painful experiences. His particular focus is on boys and on the ways they are taught to repress the wounds caused by painful experiences. Nonetheless, it should be easy for readers to apply his insights to the experiences of girls.

Boys are taught to suffer their wounds in silence. To pretend that it doesn't hurt, outside or inside. So many of them carry the scars of childhood into adulthood, never having come to grips with the pain, the anger, the fear. And that pain can change boys and bring doubts into their lives, though more often than not they have no idea where those doubts come from. Pain can make you afraid to love or cause you to doubt the safety of the ground you walk on. I know from my own experience that some pain changes us forever. 1

It all started because there was no grass. Actually, there was grass, you just couldn't walk on it. 2

In the late fifties and early sixties, the projects were places people moved to get away from tenement buildings like mine. We couldn't move into the projects because my mother was a single parent. Today most projects are crammed full of single parents, but when I was a child your application for the projects was automatically rejected if that was your situation. The projects were places for people on the way up. They had elevators, they were well maintained, and they had grass surrounding them. Grass like we had never seen before. The kind of grass that was like walking on carpet. Grass that yelled out to little girls and boys to run and tumble and do cartwheels and roll around on it. There was just one problem, it was off limits to people. All the projects had signs that said "Keep Off the Grass." And there were men keeping their eyes open for children who dared even think of crossing the single-link chain that 3 enclosed it. The projects didn't literally have the only grass we could find in the Bronx. Crotona Park, Pelham Bay Park, and Van Cortland Park were available to us. But the grass in those parks was a sparse covering for dirt, rocks, and twigs. You would never think about rolling around in that grass, because if you did you'd likely be rolling in dog excrement or over a hard rock.

There was one other place where we found grass in our neighborhood. Real grass. Lawn-like grass. It was in the side yard of a small church that was on the corner of Union Avenue and Home Street. The church was small and only open on Sundays. The yard and its precious grass were enclosed by a four-foot-high fence. We were not allowed in the yard by the pastor of the church. 4

Occasionally we would sneak in to retrieve a small pink Spaulding ball that had gone off course during a game of stickball or punch ball, but if we were seen climbing the fence there would be a scene, with screams, yells, and threats to tell our parents. So although we often looked at that soft grass with longing, the churchyard was off limits. 5

It would have stayed off limits if it had not been for football. Football came into my life one fall when I was nine years old, and I played it every fall for the rest of my childhood and adolescence. But football in the inner city looked very different than football played other places. The sewer manhole covers were the end zones. Anywhere in the street was legal playing territory, but not the sidewalk. There could be no tackling on pavement, so the game was called two-hand touch. If you touched an opponent with both hands, play had to stop. The quarterback called colorful plays: "Okay now. David, you go right in front of the blue Chevy. I'm gonna fake it to you. Geoff, see the black Ford on the right? No, don't look, stupid—they're gonna know our play. You go there, stop, then cross over toward William's stoop. I'll look for you short. Richard, go to the first sewer and turn around and stop. I'll pump it to you, go long, Geoff, you hike on three. Ready! Break!" 6

All we needed was grass. All our eyes were drawn to the churchyard. A decision had to be made. Rory was the first to bring it up. "We should sneak into the churchyard and play tackle." 7

We all walked over to Home Street and, out of sight of front windows, climbed over the fence and walked onto the grass. A thick carpet of grass that felt like falling on a mattress. We were in heaven. 8

Football in the churchyard was everything we had imagined. We could finally block and tackle and not worry about falling on the 9 hard concrete or asphalt streets. We didn't have to worry about cars coming down the block the way we did when we played two-hand touch. And because we were able to tackle, we could have running plays. We loved it. We played for hours on end.

There was one problem with our football field, which was about thirty yards long and fifteen yards wide: at the far end there was a built-in barbecue pit, right in the middle of the end zone. If we were running with the football, or going out for a pass, we had to avoid the barbecue pit with its metal rods along the top, set into its concrete sides. We knew that no matter what you were doing when in that area of the yard, you had to keep one eye on the barbecue pit. To run into its concrete sides—or, even worse, the metal bars—would be very painful and dangerous. 10

I was fast and crafty. I loved to play split end on the offense. I could fake out the other kids and get free to catch the ball. I had one problem, though—I hadn't mastered catching a football thrown over my head. To do this you have to lean your head back and watch as the football descends into your hands. Keep your eye on the ball, that's the trick to catching one over the shoulder. We all wanted to go deep for "the bomb"—a ball thrown as far as possible, where a receiver's job is to run full speed and catch it with outstretched hands. It took me forever to learn to concentrate on the football, with my head back as far as it would go, while running full speed. But finally I mastered it. I was now a truly dangerous receiver. If you played too far away from me I could catch the ball short, and if you came too close I could run right by the slower boys and catch the bomb. 11

The move I did on Ned was picture perfect. I ran ten yards, turned around, and faced Walter. He pumped the ball to me. I felt Ned take a step forward, going for the fake as I turned and ran right by him. Walter launched the bomb. As the football left his hand I stopped looking over my shoulder at him and started my sprint to the end zone. After running ten yards I tilted my head back and looked up at the bright blue fall sky. Nothing. I looked forward again and ran harder, then looked up again. There it was, the brown leather football falling in a perfect arc toward the earth, toward where I would be in three seconds, toward the winning touchdown. 12

And then pain. The bar of the barbecue pit caught me in midstride in the middle of my shin. I went down in a flurry of ashes, legs and arms flying every which way. The pain was all-enveloping. I grabbed my leg above and below where it had hit; I couldn't bear to 13 touch the place where it had slammed into the bar. The pain was too much. I lay flat on the ground, trying to cry out. I could only make a humming sound deep in the back of my throat. My friends gathered around and I tried to act like a big boy, the way I had been taught. I tried not to cry. Then the pain consumed me and I couldn't see any of my friends anymore. I howled and then cried and then howled some more. The boys saw the blood seeping through my dungarees and my brother John said, "Let me see. Be still. Let me see." He rolled my pants leg up to my knee to look at the damage. All the other boys who had been playing or watching were in a circle around me. They all grimaced and turned away. I knew it was bad then, and I howled louder.

Catching the metal bar in full stride with my shin had crushed a quarter-sized hole in my leg. The skin was missing and even to this day I can feel the indentation in my shinbone where the bar gouged out a small piece of bone. I was off my feet for a few days and it took about two weeks for my shin to heal completely. Still, I was at the age where sports and friends meant everything to me. I couldn't wait to play football in the churchyard again, but I was a much more cautious receiver than before. 14

Several years later, when I finished the ninth grade at a junior high school in the South Bronx and was preparing to go to high school, I knew that my life had reached a critical juncture. My high school prospects were grim. I didn't pass the test to get into the Bronx High School of Science (I was more interested in girls than prep work), so my choices were either Morris High School or Clinton High School. Both of these were poor academically and suffered from a high incidence of violence. I asked my mother if I could stay with my grandparents in the house they had just built in Wyandanch, a quiet, mostly African-American town on Long Island. She agreed and they agreed, so I went there for my three years of high school. 15

That first year I went out for the junior varsity football team at Wyandanch High and played football as a receiver. I was a good receiver. The years of faking out kids on the narrow streets of the Bronx made me so deceptive that I couldn't be covered in the wide-open area of a real football field. But I had one problem—I couldn't catch the bomb. My coach would scream at me after the ball had slipped through my fingers or bounced off my hands. "Geoff! What's the matter with you? Concentrate, goddamn it! Concentrate!" I couldn't. No matter how I tried to focus on the ball coming down out of the sky, at the last minute I would have 16 to look down. To make sure the ground wasn't playing tricks on me. No hidden booby traps. What happened in the churchyard would flash into my mind and even though I knew I was in a wide-open field, I'd have to glance down at the ground. I never made it as a receiver in high school. I finished my career as quarterback. Better to be looking at your opponent, knowing he wanted to tackle you, sometimes even getting hit without seeing it coming, but at least being aware of that possibility. Never again falling into the trap of thinking you were safe, running free, only you and the sky and a brown leather ball dropping from it.

Boys are conditioned not to let on that it hurts, never to say, 17
"I'm still scared." I've written here only about physical trauma, but every day in my work I deal with boys undergoing almost unthinkable mental trauma from violence or drug abuse in the home, or carrying emotional scars from physical abuse or unloving parents. I have come to see that in teaching boys to deny their own pain we inadvertently teach them to deny the pain of others. I believe this is one of the reasons so many men become physically abusive to those they supposedly love. Pain suffered early in life often becomes the wellspring from which rage and anger flow, emotions that can come flooding over the banks of restraint and reason, often drowning those unlucky enough to get caught in their way. We have done our boys an injustice by not helping them to acknowledge their pain. We must remember to tell them "I know it hurts. Come let me hold you. I'll hold you until it stops. And if you find out that the hurt comes back, I'll hold you again. I'll hold you until you're healed."

Boys are taught by coaches to play with pain. They are told by 18
parents that they shouldn't cry. They watch their heroes on the big screen getting punched and kicked and shot, and while these heroes might groan and yell, they never cry. And even some of us who should know better don't go out of our way to make sure our boys know about our pain and tears, and how we have healed ourselves. By sharing this we can give boys models for their own healing and recovery.

Even after I was grown I believed that ignoring pain was part of 19
learning to be a man, that I could get over hurt by simply willing it away. I had forgotten that when I was young I couldn't run in an open field without looking down, that with no one to talk to me about healing, I spent too many years unable to trust the ground beneath my feet.

Meanings and Values

1. What is the main expository point (thesis) of the essay, and where does the writer state it? (See "Guide to Terms": *Unity.*)
2. What desires or aspirations did grass represent for the writer as a young man?
3. a. What, according to the writer, are the consequences of painful experiences (physical or emotional) suffered in youth?

   b. Why might the writer have chosen to focus on the consequences of pain for boys? How might the essay's conclusions be applied to or adapted for understanding the experiences of girls?

Expository Techniques

1. Which paragraphs in the essay are devoted primarily to retelling events? Which focus on analyzing the events and generalizing about behavior?
2. Why do you think the writer waited until the end of the essay to offer an extended discussion of the psychological consequences of painful events? Where else in the essay might he have undertaken such an explanation?
3. Discuss the strategies the writer employs to create transitions between the paragraphs in the following pairs: 1 and 2, 5 and 6, 6 and 7, 12 and 13, and 17 and 18.

Diction and Vocabulary

1. Discuss the use of the repetition of the word *pain* and its synonyms in Paragraph 17 to provide emphasis for the writer's main ideas. (Guide: *Emphasis.*)
2. For what purposes does the writer employ repetition and parallel structures in Paragraph 3? (Guide: *Parallel Structures.*)
3. Look up in a dictionary any of the following words with which you are unfamiliar: *excrement* (Par. 3); *grimaced* (13); *trauma, wellspring* (17).

Read to Write

1. **Collaborating:** Working in a group, list and describe briefly the earliest recollections that each group member has of a painful event, either physical or emotional. From the list, choose several that your group finds particularly intriguing and plan a narrative essay around each one.

2. **Considering Audience:** How might girls' (and women's) experiences of pain differ from the experience described in Canada's essay? Write a brief essay exploring the similarities and differences between boys' and girls' experiences of pain.
3. **Developing an Essay:** Think of some central event from your youth that continues to affect your behavior today, positively or negatively. Write a narrative similar to Canada's, emphasizing that distinguishing part of your experience and commenting on the way such experiences are likely to affect many other people. To expand your perspective on the events, include your point of view, then and now, and describe the reactions of others to the events.

(NOTE: Suggestions for topics requiring development by NARRATION are on pp. 445–446 at the end of this chapter.)

PAT CONROY

PAT CONROY was born in Atlanta, Georgia in 1945. He is well known for having been heavily influenced by his Southern upbringing and military education, both of which remain regular themes in many of his works. A number of his novels draw on his dysfunctional—and often strained—relations with several family members, resulting in both personal controversy and critical acclaim. Conroy received a humanitarian award from the Natinal Education Association for his novel *The Water is Wide*, which was adapted as a feature film. Other works include *The Great Santini* (1976), *The Lords of Discipline* (1980), *The Prince of Tides* (1986), and *Beach Music* (1994), several of which have also become popular films.

Chili Cheese Dogs, My Father and Me

This essay, first published in *Parade* magazine, offers several narratives tied together by hot dogs—especially chili cheese dogs. These short narratives are interesting in themselves, yet Conroy takes them further. He uses them to explore important topics such as family dynamics, parent-child relationships, and the role of food in culture. These are large orders, but Conroy accomplishes them gracefully and in a short space.

When I was growing up and lived at my grandmother's house in Atlanta, my mother would take us after church to The Varsity, an institution with more religious significance to me than any cathedral in the city. Its food was celebratory, fresh, and cleansing to the soul. It still remains one of my favorite restaurants in the world. 1

I had then what I order now—a habit that has not deviated since my sixth birthday in 1951, when my grandmother, Stanny, ordered for me what she considered the picture-perfect Varsity meal: a chili cheese hot dog, onion rings and a soft drink called "The Big Orange." 2

On that occasion, when my family had finished the meal, my mother lit six candles on a cupcake she had made, and Stanny, Papa Jack, my mother and my sister Carol sang "Happy Birthday" as I blushed with pleasure and surprise. I put together for the first time that the consumption of food and celebration was a natural and fitting combination. It was also the first time I realized that no one in my family could carry a tune. 3

When my father returned home from the Korean War, he refused to believe that The Varsity—or the American South, for that matter— 4

Pat Conroy, "Chili Cheese Dogs, My Father and Me." Initially published in *Parade* Magazine, November 14, 2004.

could produce a hot dog worthy of consumption. My Chicago–born father was a fierce partisan of his hometown, and he promised me that he would take me to eat a real "red hot" after we attended my first White Sox game.

That summer, we stayed with my dad's parents on the South 5 Side of Chicago. There, I met the South Side Irish for the first time on their own turf. My uncles spent the summer teasing me about being a Southern hick as they played endless games of pinochle with my father. Then my father took me for the sacramental rite of passage: my first major league baseball game. We watched the White Sox beat the despised Yankees.

After the game, my father drove my Uncle Willie and me to a 6 place called Superdawg to get a red hot. He insisted that the Superdawg sold the best red hots in the city. When my father handed me the first red hot I had ever eaten, he said, "This will make you forget The Varsity for all time." That summer, I learned that geography itself was one of the great formative shapers of identity. The red hot was delicious, but in my life time I will never forsake the pleasure of The Varsity chili cheese dog.

When my father was dying of colon cancer in 1998, he would 7 spend his days with me at home on Fripp Island, S. C., then go back to Beaufort at night to stay with my sister Kathy, who is a nurse and was in charge of his medications. Since I was responsible for his daily lunch, I told him I would cook him anything he wanted as long as I could find it in a South Carolina supermarket.

"Anything, pal?" my father asked. 8

"Anything," I said. 9

Thus the last days between a hard-core Marine and his edgy 10 son, who had spent his career writing about horrific father-son relationships, became our best days as we found ourselves united by the glorious subject of food.

My father was a simple man with simple tastes, but he was 11 well-traveled, and he began telling me his life story as we spent our long hours together. The first meal he ordered was an egg sandwich, a meal I had never heard of but one that kept him alive during the Depression. He told me, "You put a fried egg on two slices of white bread which have been spread with ketchup."

"It sounds repulsive," I said. 12

"It's delicious," he replied. 13

When Dad spoke of his service in Korea, I fixed him kimchi (spicy 14 pickled vegetables), and when he talked about his year-long duty on an aircraft carrier on the Mediterranean, I made spaghetti carbonara or gazpacho. But most of the time I made him elaborate sandwiches: salami or baloney tiered high with lettuce, tomatoes and red onions. The more elaborate I made them, the more my father loved them.

He surprised me one day by asking me to make him some red hots, done "the Chicago way, pal." That day I called Superdawg and was surprised that it was still in business. A very pleasant woman told me to dress the red hots with relish, mustard, onion and hot peppers with a pickle on the side. "If you put ketchup on it, just throw it in the trash," she added. 15

The following week he surprised me again by ordering up some chili cheese dogs, "just like they make at The Varsity in Atlanta." So I called The Varsity and learned step by step how to make one of their scrumptious chili cheese dogs. 16

When my father began his quick, slippery descent into death, my brothers and sisters drove from all directions to sit six-hour shifts at his bedside. We learned that watching a fighter pilot die is not an easy thing. 17

One morning I arrived for my shift and heard screaming coming from the house. I raced inside and found Carol yelling at Dad: "Dad, you've got to tell me you love me. You've got to tell me you're proud of me. You've got to do it before you die." 18

I walked Carol out of the bedroom and sat her down on the sofa. "That's Don Conroy in there, Carol—not Bill Cosby," I said. "You've got to learn how to translate Dad. He says it, but in his own way." 19

Two weeks before my father died, he presented me with a gift of infinite price. I made him the last chili cheese dog from The Varsity's recipe that he would ever eat. When he finished, I took the plate back to the kitchen and was shocked to hear him say, "I think the chili cheese dog is the best red hot I've ever eaten." 20

There is a translation to all of this, and here is how it reads: In the last days of his life, my father was telling me how much he loved me, his oldest son, and he was doing it with food. 21

Meanings and Values

1. Conroy uses the words "translate" (Par. 21) and "translation" (Par. 23) to mean *interpret* or *find the meaning of*. In your own words, *translate* this essay by explaining what insights it offers into the meaning of food for family and cultures.

2. What examples does the writer offer of the importance of family relationships despite the imperfections of individual family members?

Expository Techniques

1. Which paragraphs contain the first narrative in this essay? the second? the third? Are there any others? If so, where are they in the essay?
2. What events or objects tie these narratives together? (See "Guide to Terms": *Unity*.)
3. In your own words, state the theme or thesis that links the narratives. (Guide: *Unity*.)

Diction and Vocabulary

1. In Paragraph 1, the writer explains how The Varsity has a religious significance for him. Look up *Figures of Speech* in the Guide to Terms and explain why or why not this explanation is a metaphor (or simile).
2. If you do not know the meaning of some of the following terms, look them up in a dictionary: *celebratory* (Par. 1); *deviated* (2); *pinochle, sacramental* (5).

Read to Write

1. **Collaborating:** Working in a group, make individual lists of foods that have special meaning for you or your family. Then combine these lists, making note of foods that have significance for more than one member of the group. Then ask each member of the group to write out briefly what one of the foods means to him or her.
2. **Considering Audience:** Foods from different ethnic groups (Italian, Korean, Chinese, Brazilian, Indian, or German foods, for example) may hold special meanings for people from other ethnic groups. Create an essay explaining what a food from an ethnic group other than your own means to you, and include at least one narrative as part of your explanation.
3. **Developing an Essay:** Follow Conroy's lead and create an essay about your family (or another group to which you belong) explaining the importance of some event or cultural phenomenon (including food) for the group. Use narration, description, or any other patterns you find helpful for your task.

(Note: Suggestions for topics requiring development by use of NARRATION are on pp. 445–446 at the end of this chapter.

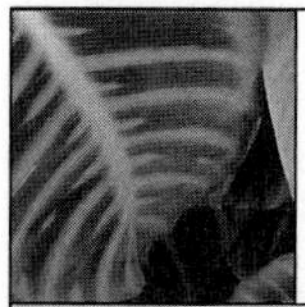

Issues and Ideas

Stories and Values

- George Orwell, *A Hanging*
- Wayne Worcester, *Arms and the Man*

Sometimes speaking directly about our values or perspectives does not clarify or convey them effectively. The situation that gives rise to a particular moral judgment or that leads to an ethical perspective can give someone else a better understanding than a detailed definition or even a careful comparison of differing perspectives. The more complex the idea or outlook, the more we may need to know about the events surrounding it. A detailed narrative can perhaps give readers a better understanding of causes and effects than an explanation that attempts to isolate them from the surrounding details.

The three essays that follow demonstrate the effectiveness of narration as an expository pattern for dealing with questions of value. Capital punishment has been the subject of many argumentative and expository essays, but few have offered the kind of insight into the minds of the prisoner and of those responsible for carrying out the sentence that George Orwell provides in "A Hanging." And few essays explore the moral ambiguities surrounding the practice as well as Orwell does.

Wayne Worcester's "Arms and the Man" provides an insider's view of some of the values associated with gun ownership and use. Although his perspective is in one way linked to his (and his friend's) experience, it nonetheless gains power and depth for others from the same experience.

GEORGE ORWELL

GEORGE ORWELL (1903–1950), whose real name was Eric Blair, was a British novelist and essayist well known for his satire. He was born in India and educated at Eton in England; he was wounded while fighting in the Spanish Civil War. Later he wrote the books *Animal Farm* (1945), a satire on Soviet history; and *1984* (1949), a vivid picture of life in a projected totalitarian society. He was, however, also sharply aware of injustices in democratic societies and was consistently socialistic in his views. Many of Orwell's essays are collected in *Critical Essays* (1946), *Shooting an Elephant and Other Essays* (1950), and *Such, Such Were the Joys* (1953).

A Hanging

"A Hanging" is typical of Orwell's essays in its setting—Burma—and in its subtle but biting commentary on colonialism, on capital punishment, and even on one aspect of human nature itself. Although he is ostensibly giving a straightforward account of an execution, the author masterfully uses descriptive details and dialogue to create atmosphere and sharply drawn characterizations. The essay gives concrete form to a social message that is often delivered much less effectively in abstract generalities.

It was in Burma, a sodden morning of the rains. A sickly light, like yellow tinfoil, was slanting over the high walls into the jail yard. We were waiting outside the condemned cells, a row of sheds fronted with double bars, like small animal cages. Each cell measured about ten feet by ten and was quite bare within except for a plank bed and a pot for drinking water. In some of them brown, silent men were squatting at the inner bars, with their blankets draped round them. These were the condemned men, due to be hanged within the next week or two. 1

One prisoner had been brought out of his cell. He was a Hindu, a puny wisp of a man, with a shaven head and vague liquid eyes. He had a thick, sprouting mustache, absurdly too big for his body, rather like the mustache of a comic man on the films. Six tall Indian warders were guarding him and getting him ready for the gallows. Two of them stood by with rifles and fixed bayonets, while the others handcuffed him, passed a chain through his handcuffs and fixed it to their belts, and lashed his arms tight to his sides. They crowded very close about him, with their hands always on him in a careful, 2 caressing grip, as though all the while feeling him to make sure he was there. It was like men handling a fish which is still alive and may jump back into the water. But he stood quite unresisting, yielding his arms limply to the ropes, as though he hardly noticed what was happening.

Eight o'clock struck and a bugle call, desolately thin in the wet 3
air, floated from the distant barracks. The superintendent of the jail, who was standing apart from the rest of us, moodily prodding the gravel with his stick, raised his head at the sound. He was an army doctor, with a grey toothbrush mustache and a gruff voice. "For God's sake, hurry up, Francis," he said irritably. "The man ought to have been dead by this time. Aren't you ready yet?"

Francis, the head jailer, a fat Dravidian in a white drill suit and 4
gold spectacles, waved his black hand. "Yes sir, yes sir," he bubbled. "All iss satisfactorily prepared. The hangman iss waiting. We shall proceed."

"Well, quick march, then. The prisoners can't get their breakfast 5
till this job's over."

We set out for the gallows. Two warders marched on either side 6
of the prisoner, with their rifles at the slope; two others marched close against him, gripping him by arm and shoulder, as though at once pushing and supporting him. The rest of us, magistrates and the like, followed behind. Suddenly, when we had gone ten yards, the procession stopped short without any order or warning. A dreadful thing had happened—a dog, come goodness knows whence, had appeared in the yard. It came bounding among us with a loud volley of barks and leapt round us wagging its whole body, wild with glee at finding so many human beings together. It was a large woolly dog, half Airedale, half pariah. For a moment it pranced around us, and then, before anyone could stop it, it had made a dash for the prisoner, and jumping up tried to lick his face. Everybody stood aghast, too taken aback even to grab the dog.

"Who let that bloody brute in here?" said the superintendent 7
angrily. "Catch it, someone!"

A warder detached from the escort, charged clumsily after the 8
dog, but it danced and gambolled just out of his reach, taking everything as part of the game. A young Eurasian jailer picked up a handful of gravel and tried to stone the dog away, but it dodged the stones and came after us again. Its yaps echoed from the jail walls. The prisoner, in the grasp of the two warders, looked on incuriously, as though this was another formality of the hanging. It was several minutes before someone managed to catch the dog. Then we put my

handkerchief through its collar and moved off once more, with the dog still straining and whimpering.

It was about forty yards to the gallows. I watched the bare brown back of the prisoner marching in front of me. He walked clumsily with his bound arms, but quite steadily, with that bobbing gait of the Indian who never straightens his knees. At each step his muscles slid neatly into place, the lock of hair on his scalp danced up and down, his feet printed themselves on the wet gravel. And once, in spite of the men who gripped him by each shoulder, he stepped lightly aside to avoid a puddle on the path. 9

It is curious; but till that moment I had never realized what it means to destroy a healthy, conscious man. When I saw the prisoner step aside to avoid the puddle, I saw the mystery, the unspeakable wrongness, of cutting a life short when it is in full tide. This man was not dying, he was alive just as we are alive. All the organs of his body were working—bowels digesting food, skin renewing itself, nails growing, tissues forming—all toiling away in solemn foolery. His nails would still be growing when he stood on the drop, when he was falling through the air with a tenth-of-a-second to live. His eyes saw the yellow gravel and the grey walls, and his brain still remembered, foresaw, reasoned—even about puddles. He and we were a party of men walking together, seeing, hearing, feeling, understanding the same world; and in two minutes, with a sudden snap, one of us would be gone—one mind less, one world less. 10

The gallows stood in a small yard, separate from the main grounds of the prison, and overgrown with tall prickly weeds. It was a brick erection like three sides of a shed, with planking on top, and above that two beams and a crossbar with the rope dangling. The hangman, a greyhaired convict in the white uniform of the prison, was waiting beside his machine. He greeted us with a servile crouch as we entered. At a word from Francis the two warders, gripping the prisoner more closely than ever, half led, half pushed him to the gallows and helped him clumsily up the ladder. Then the hangman climbed up and fixed the rope round the prisoner's neck. 11

We stood waiting, five yards away. The warders had formed in a rough circle round the gallows. And then, when the noose was fixed, the prisoner began crying out to his god. It was a high, reiterated cry of "Ram! Ram! Ram! Ram!" not urgent and fearful like a prayer or cry for help, but steady, rhythmical, almost like the tolling of a bell. The dog answered the sound with a whine. The hangman, still standing on the gallows, produced a small cotton bag like a flour bag and drew it down over the prisoner's face. But the sound, 12 muffled by the cloth, still persisted, over and over again: "Ram! Ram! Ram! Ram! Ram!"

The hangman climbed down and stood ready, holding the lever. Minutes seemed to pass. The steady, muffled crying from the prisoner went on and on, "Ram! Ram! Ram!" never faltering for an instant. The superintendent, his head on his chest, was slowly poking the ground with his stick; perhaps he was counting the cries, allowing the prisoner a fixed number—fifty, perhaps, or a hundred. Everyone had changed colour. The Indians had gone grey like bad coffee, and one or two of the bayonets were wavering. We looked at the lashed, hooded man on the drop, and listened to his cries—each cry another second of life; the same thought was in all our minds; oh, kill him quickly, get it over, stop that abominable noise! 13

Suddenly the superintendent made up his mind. Throwing up his head he made a swift motion with his stick. "Chalo!" he shouted almost fiercely. 14

There was a clanking noise, and then dead silence. The prisoner had vanished, and the rope was twisting on itself. I let go of the dog, and it galloped immediately to the back of the gallows; but when it got there it stopped short, barked, and then retreated into a corner of the yard, where it stood among the weeds, looking timorously out at us. We went round the gallows to inspect the prisoners's body. He was dangling with his toes pointed straight downwards, very slowly revolving, as dead as a stone. 15

The superintendent reached out with his stick and poked the bare brown body; it oscillated slightly. "*He's* all right," said the superintendent. He backed out from under the gallows, and blew out a deep breath. The moody look had gone out of his face quite suddenly. He glanced at his wrist-watch. "Eight minutes past eight. Well, that's all for this morning, thank God." 16

The warders unfixed bayonets and marched away. The dog, sobered and conscious of having misbehaved itself, slipped after them. We walked out of the gallows yard, past the condemned cells with their waiting prisoners, into the big central yard of the prison. The convicts, under the command of warders armed with lathis, were already receiving their breakfast. They squatted in long rows, each man holding a tin pannikin, while two warders with buckets marched around ladling out rice; it seemed quite a homely, jolly scene, after the hanging. An enormous relief had come upon us now that the job was done. One felt an impulse to sing, to break into a run, to snigger. All at once everyone began chattering gaily. 17

The Eurasian boy walking beside me nodded towards the way we had come, with a knowing smile. "Do you know, sir, our friend (he meant the dead man) when he heard his appeal had been dismissed, he pissed on the floor of his cell. From fright. Kindly take one of my cigarettes, sir. Do you not admire my new silver case, sir? From the boxwallah, two rupees eight annas. Classy European style." 18

Several people laughed—at what, nobody seemed certain. 19

Francis was walking by the superintendent, talking garrulously: "Well, sir, all has passed off with the utmost satisfactoriness. It was all finished—flick! Like that. It iss not always so—oah, no! I have known cases where the doctor was obliged to go beneath the gallows and pull the prissoner's legs to ensure decease. Most disagreeable!" 20

"Wriggling about, eh? That's bad," said the superintendent. 21

"Ach, sir, it iss worse when they become refractory! One man, I recall, clung to the bars of hiss cage when we went to take him out. You will scarcely credit, sir, that it took six warders to dislodge him, three pulling at each leg. We reasoned with him, 'My dear fellow,' we said, 'think of all the pain and trouble you are causing to us!' But no, he would not listen! Ach, he wass very troublesome!" 22

I found that I was laughing quite loudly. Everyone was laughing. Even the superintendent grinned in a tolerant way. "You'd better all come out and have a drink," he said quite genially. "I've got a bottle of whisky in the car. We could do with it." 23

We went through the big double gates of the prison into the road. "Pulling at his legs!" exclaimed a Burmese magistrate suddenly, and burst into a loud chuckling. We all began laughing again. At that moment Francis' anecdote seemed extraordinarily funny. We all had a drink together, native and European alike, quite amicably. The dead man was a hundred yards away. 24

Meanings and Values

1. What was the real reason for the superintendent's impatience?
2. On first impression it may have seemed that the author gave undue attention to the dog's role in this narrative. Why was the episode such a "dreadful thing" (Par. 6)? Why did the author think it worth noting that the dog was excited at "finding so many human beings together"? Of what significance was the dog's trying to lick the prisoner's face?
3. Explain how the prisoner's stepping around a puddle could have given the author a new insight into what was about to happen (Par. 10).

4. Why was there so much talking and laughing after the hanging was finished?
5. What is the broadest meaning of Orwell's last sentence?

Expository Techniques

1. Cite examples of both objective and impressionistic description in the first paragraph.
2. What is the primary time order used in this narrative? If there are any exceptions, state where.
3. Considering the relatively few words devoted to them, several of the characterizations in this essay are remarkably vivid—a result, obviously, of highly discriminating selection of details from the multitude of those that must have been available to the author. For each of the following people, list the character traits that we can observe, and state whether these impressions come to us through details of description, action, and/or dialogue.

    a. The prisoner

    b. The superintendent

    c. Francis

    d. The Eurasian boy
4. Why do you think the author included so many details of the preparation of the prisoner (Par. 2)? Why did he include so many details about the dog and his actions? What is gained by the assortment of details in Paragraph 10?
5. How would your characterize the tone of this selection? (Guide: *Style/Tone.*)

Diction and Vocabulary

1. A noteworthy element of Orwell's style is his occasional use of figurative language. Cite six metaphors and similes, and comment on the author's choice of them and on their effectiveness. (Guide: *Figures of Speech.*)
2. Orwell was always concerned with the precise effects that words could give to meaning and style. Cite at least six nonfigurative words that seem to you particularly well chosen for their purpose. Show what their careful selection contributes to the description of atmosphere or to the subtle meanings of the author. (Guide: *Style/Tone.*)

Read to Write

1. **Collaborating:** Discuss in a group people who have jobs that place their "duty" in conflict with their "conscience." Choose one such

person or profession and write a collaborative essay similar in style to Orwell's. You may choose to make group members responsible for one or two concrete examples each, to be combined into a unified paper.

2. **Considering Audience:** Orwell's approach in his essay makes his discussion of capital punishment approachable even to readers who may be in disagreement with his views. Identify places in the essay where Orwell deals with opposing views, and prepare an analysis of his success in dealing with them.

3. **Developing an Essay:** Draw on Orwell's expository technique in an essay of your own by recounting a minor incident (like the actions of the dog in "A Hanging") that led to much deeper insight. Or use a minor incident to reveal and emphasize insights that readers probably have not considered before.

(NOTE: Suggestions for topics requiring development by NARRATION are on pp. 445–446 at the end of this chapter.)

WAYNE WORCESTER

WAYNE WORCESTER is a former newspaper reporter and editor. He now teaches journalism at the University of Connecticut.

Arms and the Man

In "Arms and the Man," first published as a newspaper essay, Wayne Worcester narrates a brief incident, largely through dialogue, that explores a variety of values and issues associated with guns and their personal use.

In an especially rural part of southern New Hampshire, where the hills in early spring roll to mottled green and the roads turn to deep mud-brown, I have two old friends who live as they please. 1

He drives a truck. She works in a dentist's office. They have three children, and on most days the kids' toys sprawl in abandon across the living-room floor, directly in front of the gun cabinet, which has no lock. 2

"Doesn't it bother you?" I asked on a recent visit. "The kids' playing around the gun cabinet?" 3

"Nope. We brought 'em up to not touch it." 4

He handed me his newest gun. It was flat and small, only slightly larger than my hand, and the room's bright light died on its coal-black barrel. No reflection. Not a hint. 5

"Isn't that a sweetheart?" 6

"Very small." 7

"It's hers, but it's got real stoppin' power. Great protection." 8

I popped the magazine out, and saw the stack of bullets. 9

"You always keep it loaded?" I asked. 10

"Course." 11

"She carry it?" 12

"No point havin' it, she gonna leave it to home." 13

"She works for a dentist, for Chrissake! He use this instead of Novocain? What's she need a gun for?" 14

His lips went tight, as though I'd insulted him, which I had. 15

"You never know." 16

"How did she get a permit?" 17

"A what? C'mon." 18

"Well, why's she carrying?" 19

"I told you. Protection." 20

"Right. What else have you got in there?" 21

"Couple rifles. Shotgun. My AR 15. God, that's fun. Last year, me and a couple guys from work, we just went out and set up a target on a red oak out back, and we hit it with the AR so many times the damned tree just broke in half like we'd sawed it off. Thing just toppled right over." 22

"Your neighbor must love you." 23

"Yeah, he called the cops up, but they didn't do nothing—just checked to see we was on our own property." 24

"'Live free or die,' right? What'd the neighbor do?" 25

"Bout three days later, he comes over. His wife's bein' a pain in the ass. He says, 'We're moving in two months, but if you keep the shootin' down till then, you can have this.'" 26

From the top shelf of the cabinet, my friend took down a long-barreled, chrome-plated .357-magnum, the kind of handgun that'll stop a speeding car, or most anything else. 27

"But this one here's my pride 'n' joy," he said. It was a .22-caliber handgun, jet black with a long, heavy barrel. 28

"Real accurate. Wanna try her out?" 29

We walked to the edge of the woods, and he set a bright-blue Maxwell House can swinging from a tree limb. 30

For a small-caliber weapon, the gun was bone-heavy, and in the palm of my hand it felt oddly substantial, as though it were even more than its true weight. I walked slowly back toward the house, flipped off the safety, turned—quickly, for some reason—and squeezed the trigger the instant the barrel fell in line with the target. The shot was loud. It was sharp and clear and flat, as though it had hard, cutting edges, and before the sound had died the can had jumped and the chamber slide had recoiled and kicked out a casing with that matchlessly pleasing sound that metal on metal can make only when the parts have been properly and ever-so-precisely machined. I was pleased, and I fired again, and then, quickly in the echo, twice again, and I could smell the shots and feel the recoil of the bone-weight as though it were an extension of me, and I squeezed the trigger again, and then again in affirmation, counting silently in the loud and hard flat noise and clink-sliding of the chamber—seven shots now—and the can danced some more and in a far shadow I thought I could see old man Bergevin, whom I'd worked for as a teenager and hated and do to this day, though he is long dead and not thought of in years. I considered him in his grave, all scraps and maggoty bone, and was glad. Eight shots, and the can finally fell to 31 the ground, and I lowered the gun toward the fallen target and squeezed the trigger for the ninth time and sent the can skittering.

We were quiet on the way back. I was still listening to the gun, feeling its weight, thinking about a quip I'd overheard: "You know what N.R.A. stands for? Not a Rational Adult." I chuckled aloud. 32

"What?" my friend asked. 33

"Just thinking. You ever wonder who you really need protecting from?" 34

He just smiled. 35

Meanings and Values

1. Why, in Paragraph 2, does Worcester discuss the parents' careers, present a description of the toys, and mention the gun cabinet? What is the significance of these three topics mentioned in conjunction with each other?
2. Worcester says, "His lips went tight as though I'd insulted him, which I had" (Par. 14). What did he say that was potentially offensive? Was his friend justified in being insulted? Why, or why not?
3. What is the overall meaning of the last four paragraphs of the essay (31–34)? Who needs protecting, and from whom?

Expository Techniques

1. Worcester uses dialogue to present much of his narrative. How does this dialogue provide a context for the only substantially nonconversational section (Par. 30)? Is this heavy use of dialogue an effective technique? Please explain.
2. Identify the descriptive details in Paragraph 30. What ideas or qualities do they emphasize? (See "Guide to Terms": *Emphasis.*) How does this paragraph serve to unify the essay? (Guide: *Unity.*)

Diction and Vocabulary

1. Why does Worcester use few difficult words in this essay? Who is his target audience? Is it fair to say that he is belittling the characters in this essay by using such relatively simple language? Why, or why not?

Read to Write

1. **Collaborating:** "Arms and the Man" could serve as an introduction to a larger research essay on gun control. Working in a group, choose

another controversial issue and write an anecdote similar in style to Worcester's (either fiction or nonfiction) that could be an introduction to an essay on that issue.

2. **Considering Audience:** What does Worcester assume about the attitude most of his readers will have toward gun use? Identify those places in the essay where he makes his assumptions about his audience clear. Then prepare an essay analyzing the way Worcester addresses, identifies, and interacts with his audience's attitudes.

3. **Developing an Essay:** Think of a time you disagreed with the course of behavior or values of a friend because of the implications of the action or behavior. Write an essay about that relationship, similar to Worcester's essay, and incorporate dialogue and detailed description in your narration.

(NOTE: Suggestions for topics requiring development by NARRATION follow.)

Writing Suggestions for Chapter 11

Narration

Set 1

Use narration as a primary or partial pattern (e.g., in developed examples or in comparison) for one of the following expository themes or another suggested by them. Avoid the isolated personal account that has little broader significance. Remember, too, that development of the essay should itself make your point, without excessive moralizing.

1. People can still succeed without a college education.
2. The frontiers are not all gone.
3. When people succeed in communicating, they can learn to get along with each other.
4. Even with "careful" use of capital punishment, innocent people can be executed.
5. Sports don't always build character.
6. Physical danger can make us more aware of ourselves and our values.
7. Conditioning to the realities of the job is as important for police officers as it is in professional training.
8. It is possible for employees themselves to determine when they have reached their highest level of competence.
9. Wartime massacres are not a new development.
10. "Date rape" and sexual harassment on the job are devastating and generally unexpected.
11. Both heredity and environment shape personality.
12. Physical and mental handicaps can be overcome in some ways, but they are still a burden.
13. Toxic wastes pose a problem for many communities.
14. Hunting is a worthwhile and challenging sport.
15. Lack of money places considerable stress on a family or a marriage.
16. Exercise can become an obsession.
17. People who grow up in affluent surroundings don't understand what it is like to worry about money, to be hungry, or to live in a dangerous neighborhood.
18. Some jobs are simply degrading, either because of the work or because of the fellow workers.

Set 2

Some events in our lives are so important that they suggest generalizations about larger issues. Develop an expository essay built around one of these events, and use the narration to make a larger point of significance to readers.

a. A first kiss
b. Staying away from home for several days for the first time
c. Learning to swim (or some other challenging activity)
d. Being rejected
e. Rejecting someone
f. Losing a parent
g. A major operation
h. A serious accident
i. Being humiliated
j. Winning

Collaborative Exercises

1. Consider item 6 from the list of writing suggestions. Have each member of a group relate a story of physical danger and self-awareness that affected the group member or a friend. Each group member can then combine the examples into a unified paper narrating the effects that physical dangers may have upon people. When the papers are completed, group members can compare them and discuss the different choices the writers made.
2. Item 9 from the list of writing suggestions addresses analyzing wartime massacres. Have each member of your group choose some wartime atrocity (e.g., from the Gulf War, the Holocaust, or the like). Group members can then choose from these examples to create unified narratives.

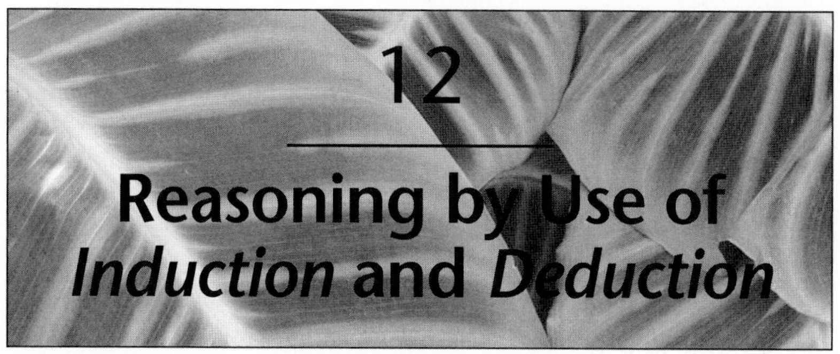

12

Reasoning by Use of *Induction* and *Deduction*

Sometimes you can best explain a subject by asking readers to follow the line of reasoning you use to *understand it:* either *inductive reasoning* or *deductive reasoning. Induction* is the process by which we accumulate evidence until, at some point, we can make the "inductive leap" and thus reach a useful *generalization.* The science laboratory employs this technique: hundreds of tests and experiments and analyses may be required before the scientist will generalize, for instance, that a disease is caused by a certain virus. It is also one of the primary techniques of the prosecuting attorney who presents pieces of inductive evidence, asking the jury to make the inductive leap and conclude that the accused did indeed kill the victim.

Whereas induction is the method of reaching a potentially useful generalization (for example, people attending meetings after lunch are invariably less attentive than those at morning meetings), *deduction* is the method of *using* such a generality, now accepted as a fact (for example, because we need an attentive audience, we had better schedule this meeting at 10:30 A.M. rather than 1:00 P.M.). Working from a generalization already formulated—by ourselves, by someone else, or by tradition—we may deduce that a specific thing or circumstance that fits into the generality will act the same. Hence, if we are convinced that orange-colored food tastes bad, we will be reluctant to try pumpkin pie.

A personnel manager may have discovered over the years that electrical engineering majors from Central College are invariably well trained in their field. His induction may have been based on the evidence of observations, records, and opinions of people at his company; and, perhaps without realizing it, he has made the usable generalization about the training of Central College electrical engineering majors. Later, when he has an application from Nancy Ortega, a graduate of Central College, his deductive process will probably work as follows: Central College turns out well-trained electrical engineering majors; Ortega was trained at Central; therefore, Ortega must be well trained. Here he has used a generalization for a specific case.

In written form, you can use inductive reasoning to help readers explore the details of a subject and arrive at the same conclusion or interpretation you do, as in the following paragraph.

> Roaming the site, I can't help noticing that when men start cooking, the hardware gets complicated. Custom-built cookers—massive contraptions of cast iron and stainless steel—may cost $15,000 or more; they incorporate the team's barbecue philosophy. "We burn straight hickory under a baffle," Jim Garts, coleader of the Hogaholics, points out as he gingerly opens a scorching firebox that vents smoke across a water tray beneath a 4-by-8-foot grill. It's built on a trailer the size of a mobile home. Other cookers have been fashioned from a marine diesel engine; from a '76 [Nissan], with grilling racks instead of front seats, a chimney above the dash, and coals under the hood; and as a 15-foot version of Elvis Presley's guitar (by the Graceland Love Me Tenderloins). It's awesome ironmongery.

Preliminary observation states topic

Inductive evidence/ details

Inductive generalization

—Daniel Cohen,
"Cooking-Off for Fame and Fortune"

You can use deductive reasoning to help readers use a generalization as a way of understanding a complex situation or complicated evidence and details, as in this paragraph.

> It is an everyday fact of life that competitors producing similar products claim that their own goods or services are better than those of their rivals. Every product advertised—from pain relievers to fried chicken—is claimed to be better than its competitor's. If all these companies sued for libel, the courts would be so overloaded with cases that they would grind to a halt. For years courts dismissed criticisms of businesses, products, and performances as expressions of

Background for generalization

Deductive generalizations

opinion. When a restaurant owner sued a guidebook to New York restaurants for giving his establishment a bad review, he won a $20,000 verdict in compensatory damages and $5 in punitive damages. But this was overturned by the court of appeals. The court held that, with the exception of one item, the allegedly libelous statements were expressions of opinion, not fact. Among these statements were that the "dumplings, on our visit, resembled bad ravioli . . . chicken with chili was rubbery and the rice . . . totally insipid. . . ." Obviously, it would be impossible to prove the nature of the food served at that particular meal. What is tender to one palate may be rubbery to another. The one misstatement of fact, that the Peking duck was served in one dish instead of three, was in my opinion, a minor and insignificant part of the entire review. Had the review of the restaurant been considered as a whole . . . , this small misstatement of fact would have been treated as *de minimis*. That is a well established doctrine requiring that minor matters not be considered by the courts. In this case, the court held that the restaurant was a public figure and had failed to prove actual malice.

Specific instance to be explained using the generalizations

—Lois G. Forer,
A Chilling Effect: The Mounting Threat of Libel and Invasion of Privacy Actions to the First Amendment

WHY USE INDUCTION AND DEDUCTION?

One useful way to think of induction and deduction is as a way of arriving at a generalization (induction) and of applying a generalization as an explanatory strategy (deduction). Once you start thinking of the patterns this way, you can develop questions to help you decide when to employ them in your writing. You might ask, for example, "Why should I lead readers through the process of arriving at a generalization when I could simply announce it at the beginning of an essay and then provide examples, comparisons, and other kinds of evidence to explain the generalization and show how reasonable it is?" One answer is that you employ deduction whenever the process of arriving at a generalization is as important as the conclusion itself. For example, in explaining a particular kind of childhood behavior, you may also wish to model for readers a way of drawing conclusions about such behavior.

Another occasion when induction is an appropriate pattern of explanation is when the evidence leading to your conclusion is quite complicated or your conclusion is unusual or surprising. In such cases, readers may be more likely to understand and agree with your conclusion if you lead them through the process of reasoning. Inductive reasoning is also appropriate when you want to create tension or drama by building toward your conclusion or when you want to arrive at it by considering and rejecting other explanations until you arrive at a satisfactory one.

Before employing deduction as an explanatory strategy, you might ask, "How will my readers benefit if I use deductive reasoning to guide my explanation?" The importance of deductive reasoning as an explanatory pattern lies in the careful logic (and hence reliability) it can lend to conclusions. Put in simplified form (which, in writing, it seldom is), the deductive process is also called a "syllogism"—with the beginning generality known as the "major premise" and the specific that fits into the generality known as the "minor premise." For example:

Major premise—Orange-colored food is not fit to eat.
Minor premise—Pumpkin pie is orange-colored.
Conclusion—Pumpkin pie is not fit to eat.

As this example makes clear, however, deductive reasoning can be only as reliable as the original generalizations that were used as deductive premises. If the generalizations themselves were based on flimsy or insufficient evidence, any future deduction using them is likely to be erroneous.

Working together, induction and deduction can be good strategies for exploring an unfamiliar or complicated topic. Inductive reasoning can suggest a generalization about the topic; deductive reasoning can use the generalization to explore and explain whatever details, applications, and consequences call for understanding.

CHOOSING A STRATEGY

The organization of writing employing induction, deduction, or both generally parallels the process of reasoning. The following example may make this clear. Suppose that after a careful process of reasoning, you concluded that your family's dog treats you and other family members as if they were part of her own dog pack. This would be a somewhat startling conclusion for many readers, so to help make your explanation convincing, you might wish to follow an inductive-deductive pattern.

Tentative Thesis (to be presented in full at the end of the essay): My family's dog treats my parents and my siblings as if we were all members of the same pack of dogs.

Inductive Explanation: Dogs behave in ways that surprise humans.

1. They often try to sleep with their owners or members of the family. Dogs in packs like to sleep together.
2. Dogs often like to carry around bits of smelly clothing (ugh!) from their owners or family members. Dogs in packs recognize and relate to each other through scent.
3. Dogs choose one family member as most important and others as less so. Dog packs are strictly hierarchical; a dog is content when he or she can recognize the "Alpha" dog and his or her own place in the pack.

4, 5, 6. . . .

Inductive Generalization: Dogs relate to humans in ways similar to the ways they relate to other dogs in a pack.

Deductive Explanation: Much of my dog's behavior can be explained by considering my family as her pack.

1. Every time one of the family sits down, our female beagle comes over and falls asleep on one of our feet. She's "cuddling" with us and feeling comfortable when she is literally "in touch" with her pack.
2. I have lots of single socks; the dog has the other ones, which she chews, then "lovingly" drapes over her head or muzzle when she falls asleep in her bed. My dog isn't trying to be a pest or to cause me trouble. She's "complimenting" me by letting me know that my scent is an important element in her life.
3. My mother says that even though she feeds and walks the dog, our beagle still thinks my father and my brothers are the most important people in the house. Beagles aren't politically correct; the lead dog is still generally a male, even if the "dog" walks on two legs.

4, 5, 6. . . .

One particularly effective and familiar pattern of induction in writing is the "process of elimination." If it can be shown, for instance, that "A" does not have the strength to swing the murder weapon, that "B" was in a drunken sleep at the time of the crime, and that "C" had recently become blind and could not have found her way to the boathouse, then we may be ready for the inductive leap—that the foul deed must have been committed by "X," the only other person on the island. This organization can help you explain to readers why a particular explanation or interpretation of a subject is the only reasonable one.

Details of the subject to be explained
Explanation 1
    Strengths and weaknesses
Explanation 2
    Strengths and weaknesses
Explanation 3
    Strengths and weaknesses
Explanation 4, 5. . . .
Deductive Generalization
    This explanation is the only one with significant strengths and few significant weaknesses. It is probably the most accurate one.

DEVELOPING INDUCTION AND DEDUCTION

To develop an explanation using induction and deduction, you need to pay attention to the logic of your reasoning. These two faults are common in induction: (1) the use of *flimsy* evidence—mere opinion, hearsay, or analogy, none of which can support a valid generalization—instead of verified facts or opinions of reliable authorities; and (2) the use of *too little* evidence, leading to a premature inductive leap. The amount of evidence needed in any situation depends, of course, on purpose and audience. The success of two Central College graduates might be enough to convince some careless personnel director that all Central College electrical engineering graduates would be good employees, but two laboratory tests would not convince medical researchers that they had learned anything worthwhile about a disease-causing virus.

Deductive reasoning can fall victim to questionable premises or any of a number of flaws in logic. Induction and deduction are highly logical processes, and any trace of weakness can seriously undermine an exposition that depends on their reasonableness. Although no induction or deduction ever reaches absolute, 100 percent certainty, we should try to get from these methods as high a degree of *probability* as possible.

Student Essay

In the following essay, Sheilagh Brady shows how an essay can use induction and deduction to organize a complicated explanation in a way readers will consider clear and easy to understand. She takes readers through the history of MADD, leading up to some of its key positions, then explores the positions in detail.

Mad About MADD

Sheilagh Brady

Background

On May 3, 1980, Cari Lightner was walking through a suburban neighborhood on her way to a church carnival in Fair Oaks, California, when she was killed by a hit-and-run drunk driver. The driver was Clarence Busch, 46 years old with four prior arrests for drunk driving. Busch had just been released on bail for a hit-and-run drunk-driving charge a week before.

Cari's mother, Candy Lightner, was 33 at the time, a divorced mother of two other children working as a real estate agent. She was told by two police officers investigating the accident that Busch would probably receive little jail time, if any, because "'That's the way the system works'" (Lightner and Hathaway 224).

Events in the history of MADD and its efforts lead up to the inductive conclusion

Faced with these circumstances, many of us might have concluded that the only possible responses were despair and frustrated rage. Candy Lightner reached another conclusion. Mulling over the police officers' words during dinner the same night, Lightner conceived of the organization that eventually became MADD, Mothers Against Drunk Driving. She felt the need to do something to take away her pain. MADD became a way for her to use her anger and to come to terms with the death of her daughter. For the next five years, Lightner devoted her time and effort to the creation of MADD.

Lightner moved to Dallas, Texas, the eventual headquarters of MADD, to begin working on organizing the new group. In March 1983, NBC aired a documentary, "Mothers Against Drunk Driving: The Candy Lightner Story." According to James B. Jacobs, MADD chapters doubled across the United States by 1985, and in the same year *Time* magazine reported that there were 320 chapters nationwide, and 600,000 volunteers and donors (Otto 41).

MADD's response to drunk driving has been to emphasize jail sentences and legislation. MADD members get angry when people feel "that a killer drunk driver deserves a lesser penalty than other homicidal offenders" (Jacobs). MADD has been successful in focusing public attention on the problems associated with drinking and driving and mobilizing legal changes to create stiffer penalties for drunk driving. MADD aims to have these stiffer penalties made mandatory and plea bargaining abolished (Voas and Lacey 126–27).

Not only has MADD focused public attention but it has also had considerable effect on local, state, and federal governments. In 1988, S. Ungerleider and S. A. Bloch did an evaluation of MADD that has been summarized as concluding that MADD was "more successful in state legislatures where a large number of laws were enacted in an effort to produce more severe sanctions for the drunk driving offense" (qtd. in Voas and Lacey 137).

Yet according to Dave Russel, a member of the Rhode Island Chapter of MADD, the past few years have been difficult. During the 1980s legislation was passed quickly because of the sudden public support through pressure groups concerned about drinking and driving. Since then, the progress of drunk-driving legislation has slowed considerably. Russel says that the number of deaths per year has steadily decreased since 1980 but that alcohol related accidents still take close to 19,000 lives each year. As a response to this situation, MADD chapters nationally have concluded that there is still a need for more drunk-driving legislation, even if legislators do not see it.

Inductive generalization

Having reached this conclusion, MADD chapters nationwide have decided to submit three different bills annually to their state legislatures. Some states have turned these bills into laws, but many have not. Just what are these MADD chapters proposing? Are the laws they want enacted reasonable or unreasonable?

First deductive explanation

One bill aims to reduce the BAC (blood alcohol content) level from .10 to .08 as the legal limit of intoxication. In 1988 in a report focusing on BAC levels, researchers Moskowitz and Robinson found that although theoretically impairment begins with the first drink, significant impairment occurs in most people at .05 BAC or lower. At the Surgeon General's Workshop, December 14–16, 1988, C. Everett Koop called for lowering the BAC limit in all states to .08, as did the National Highway Transportation Safety Administration in reports sent to the United States Congress. According to MADD's national office, lowering the BAC level to .09 will reduce drunk driving by making it more likely that drunk drivers will be caught, and also by acting to discourage driving under the influence. If research evidence and reliable authorities suggest reducing the BAC level from .10 to .08 will save lives, then most of us are likely to conclude that the legislative proposal seems reasonable.

Second deductive explanation

Another bill is the ALR Bill or the Administrative License Revocation Bill. This law would eliminate the period between the arrest of a drunk driver and the hearing suspending the license. Right now, in many states, that period is supposed to be around 30 days but inevitably becomes much longer, a delay that allows the drunk driver to continue driving for that much longer legally under a valid license. The ALR would be a process that would allow the police officer to take the drunk driver's license if there is a refusal to take the breathalyzer test. In return, the driver would be given a temporary permit, good for ten to 15 days, following an appearance at a hearing. If the driver does not appear for the hearing or cannot provide reasonable evidence for refusing the test, the license is suspended. In the case of a "no show," the driver must appear later to answer to the charge against him or her, but what is important is that the license will have already been suspended.

The Administrative License Revocation was recommended by the Presidential Commission on Drunk Driving, which developed the National Commission Against Drunk Driving. According to several researchers, "Administrative revocation has widespread support among researchers, highway safety experts, and the public in general because it has been shown to be an effective administrative action that protects innocent drivers" in an experiment conducted in California, Washington, and Minnesota (Peck, Sadler, and Perrine). Most of us would probably conclude that ALR is a reasonable procedure, yet 17 states have not yet turned the ALR bill into a law.

Third deductive explanation

Last, MADD chapters propose annually an Open Container Law requiring that open containers of alcohol not be allowed in the passenger compartments of vehicles. According to MADD's national chapter, it is fundamental to separate drinking and driving because this separation is essential to the public interest and to the public's understanding of the crisis created by drunk driving. MADD argues that banning open containers of alcoholic beverages in a vehicle is one way to make sure drivers do not start drinking while driving or to become even more intoxicated while driving. Moskowitz and Robinson, in *Effects of Low Doses of Alcohol on Driving Skills*, report that drinking while driving is dangerous because ingesting even a small amount of alcohol begins the impairment process. For most of us, the Open Container Law probably also seems quite reasonable.

Even though the bills proposed by MADD chapters are likely to seem reasonable to most people, many states have not turned them into laws. At the same time, the combination of alcohol and driving remains a problem. Nineteen thousand deaths per year may be lower than in previous years, but this is still too many avoidable tragedies. One appropriate response is for each of us to become involved in working for a solution. If MADD's three proposals seem reasonable to you, if they are not yet law in your state, and if you want these policies in place to protect you, your family, and your friends, call your local MADD chapter and ask what you can do to help.

Works Cited

Jacobs, James B. *Drunk Driving: An American Dilemma.* Chicago: U of Chicago P, 1989. Print.

Lightner, Candy, and Nancy Hathaway. "The Other Side of Sorrow." *Ladies' Home Journal* Sept. 1990: 158–224. Print.

Moskowitz, H., and C. D. Robinson. *Effects of Low Doses of Alcohol on Driving Skills.* Washington: National Highway Traffic Safety Administration, 1988. Print.

Otto, Friedrich. "Seven Who Succeeded." *Time* 7 Jan. 1985: 40. Print.

Peck, Raymond C., D. D. Sadler, and M. W. Perrine. "The Comparative Effectiveness of Alcohol Rehabilitation and Licensing Control Actions for Drunk Driving Offenders: A Review of the Literature." *Alcohol, Drugs and Driving: Abstracts and Reviews* 1.1 (1985): 15–39. Print.

Russel, Dave. Personal interview. 19 Nov. 1993. MS.

Voas, Robert B., and John H. Lacey. "Drunk Driving Enforcement Adjudication, and Sanctions in the United States." *Drinking and Driving: Advances in Research and Prevention.* Ed. Robert E. Mann and R. Jean Wilson. New York: Guilford, 1990. 130–45. Print.

NANCY FRIDAY

NANCY FRIDAY is the author of numerous books, including *My Mother, My Self: The Daughter's Search for Identity* (1977); *My Secret Garden: Women's Sexual Fantasies* (1988); *Jealousy* (1997); and *Our Looks, Our Lives: Sex, Beauty, Power, and the Need to Be Seen* (1999).

The Age of Beauty

In "The Age of Beauty," first published in the *New York Times Magazine*, Friday uses induction and deduction to explain a parallel process of personal discovery and change. Her effective use of the pattern illustrates its versatility.

I had stood, all eagerness and impatience, while my sister's old evening dress was pinned on me before that fateful dance at the yacht club. I didn't even know enough to look critically at the mirror and see that the strapless gown didn't suit me, especially after the dark brown velvet straps had been added to keep the dress up on my flat chest. I placed no value on looks. Having not had this rite of passage explained to me, I hadn't a clue that beauty was *the* prerequisite to adolescent stardom. Certainly, this new longing for boys had made me awkward in their presence; but I had noticed that they were awkward, too. Accustomed to being chosen first for any team of girls, I didn't question success that night, couldn't remember failure, so carefully had I buried nursery angers under trophies of recent accomplishments. I'm sure I was prepared to solve any hesitancy the boys might have in approaching us girls by taking the initiative myself. Assuming responsibility was who I was. In recent years my life had been a great adventure, in which there had been no comparisons made to my mother and sister. In my mind, they were boring in their tedious arguing over my sister's looks and her evenings with boys. 1

That night at the yacht club marked the end of childhood, the finish of that adventure story with me as heroine. In one momentous night I took it all in and made my concession speech to myself. I watched my friends, whose leader I had been for years, watched them happy in the arms of desirable boys, and I recognized what they had that I lacked; saw it so clearly that I can recreate the film today, frame by frame: they had a look I lacked that went beyond beauty. It wasn't curls, breasts, prettiness, but a quality of acquiescence: the 2 agreeable offer to be led instead of to lead. My own face was too eager, too open, too sure of itself. I needed a mask. I needed a new face that belied the intelligent leader inside and portrayed the little girl, no, the tiny, helpless baby who hadn't been held enough in the first years of life and had been waiting all these years for boys now to care for her.

I stood in my horrible dress, shoulder blades pressing into the wall, watching my dear friends dance by in the arms of handsome boys, with a frozen, ghastly smile on my face, denying I needed to be rescued. Why, even the girl who couldn't hit a ball danced by. Though they all whispered for me to hide in the ladies' room, I stood my ground. 3

Miserable as I was, I recognized the work ahead: the girl I had invented, so full of words waiting to be spoken and skills to be mastered, she had to be pushed down like an ugly jack-in-the-box. No boy was going to take a package like me. 4

A part of me was filled with rage at having to abandon what I thought to be a fine person. But I had no voice for rage. I belonged to a family of women who wept, and by not weeping I had made myself different from my mother and sister. But that night I became a woman; I wept and wept after someone's father drove me home while the rest of my group went off to a late party with boys. I showed my grief but not my rage. I did what most women still do: I swallowed anger, choked on it. I bowed my head, in part to be shorter, but also, like a cornered cow, to signal I had given up. 5

By morning I had buried and mourned my 11-year-old self, the leader, the actress, the tree climber, and had become an ardent beauty student. From now on I would ape my beautiful friends, smile the group smile, walk the group walk and, what with hanging my head and bending my knees, approximate as best I could the group look. 6

I have a photograph of myself taken in our yard on what looks like The First Day of Adolescence. I am sitting in a white wicker chair, hunched forward, staring at the ground, hands tightly clasped in my lap, swathed in the loser's agony of defeat. I remember the box camera aimed at me and that awful skirt and sweater, which had been my sister's—as had the awful dress at the yacht club, fine for a beauty but oh, so wrong for the tomboy I had been. 7

Twenty years later, I would go through countless hours of physical therapy to realign my spine, which has never recovered from the bent-leg posture I mastered in learning the art of being less. Neither professional success, great friendships nor the love of men 8 could recapture the self-confidence, the inner vision and, yes, the kindness of generosity I owned before I lost myself in the external mirrors of adolescence.

Meanings and Values

1. In Paragraph 2, Friday says, "That night at the yacht club marked the end of childhood, the finish of that adventure story with me as the heroine." Explain the significance of that one evening. What did it symbolize for Friday? (See "Guide to Terms": *Symbol.*)
2. What does Friday mean when she says, "It wasn't curls, breast, prettiness, but a quality of acquiescence: the agreeable offer to be led instead of to lead" (Par. 2)? How is Friday defining the "role" of a successful woman from her adolescent perspective?
3. Why did Friday have to undergo physical therapy for her spine (Par. 8)? What is the significance of this reference as the conclusion of her essay?

Expository Techniques

1. What inductive generalizations does the adolescent Friday make? Does the author still regard that generalization as valid? Why, or why not?
2. Throughout the essay, the author uses masculine imagery to describe her youthful self, for example "adventure story" (Par. 2), "the girl who couldn't hit a ball" (3), and "the loser's agony of defeat" (7). Why might she have used such masculine and athletic references?
3. What is the tone of Friday's essay? (Guide: *Tone.*) Is it successful in supporting the inductive pattern that she presents?

Diction and Vocabulary

1. Look up any of the following words with which you may be unfamiliar: *tedious* (Par. 1); *acquiescence* (2); *ardent* (6); *swathed* (7).

Read to Write

1. **Collaborating:** In a group, share stories from your adolescence that had a particular impact on the way that you defined yourself. Do group members share any similar experiences? Write a collaborative essay using one of those similar experiences as a basis for an inductive essay.

2. **Considering Audience:** Most women who read this essay would have some understanding of Friday's experiences. The image of the dress, the moving from "tomboy" to adolescent "girl," and the effort to "fit" are somewhat universal examples for young women. What images might be universal for men? Think of experiences that young boys have that mark their adolescence. Write an essay similar to Friday's looking at some adult male behaviors that may be outcomes of adolescent experiences. You may have to do some research in the form of interviews.
3. **Developing an Essay:** Think of something physical or emotional that is part of your adult character and that developed as a result of adolescent experiences. Write an essay incorporating an inductive generalization like Friday's to help your reader understand the impact of adolescence on your life.

(NOTE: Essays requiring development by means of INDUCTION and DEDUCTION are on p. 477 at the end of this chapter.)

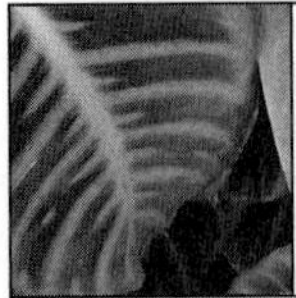

Issues and Ideas

Digital Realities

- Maia Szalavitz, *A Virtual Life*
- J. C. Herz, *Superhero Sushi*

To some people, computers may be simply one more appliance whose effects on daily life seem to b°e minimal. However, the number of people who can avoid working on computers seems to be shrinking, just as computer influence seems to be growing. Computers, the software they run, and their many networked connections change the way we run our lives. They alter the time we need to spend at a task, the kind of tasks we can undertake, and our creative abilities. They alter our schedules, our places of work and play, and maybe even our friendships and personal relationships.

We can say that computers create new realities for us, digital realities. The essays that follow use inductive and deductive reasoning to explore these digital realities. Maia Szalavitz, in "A Virtual Life," considers her experiences as a computer user, sums them up, and then reviews her experiences to see if her perceptions and values have indeed changed as much as she suspects. J. C. Herz, in "Superhero Sushi," shows how cultures blend in remarkable ways once they are drawn into cyberspace. Both authors are a bit tentative in their conclusions because new digital realities may emerge in just a few years.

MAIA SZALAVITZ

MAIA SZALAVITZ, formerly a television producer, now spends her time as a writer and is co-author of *Recovery Options: The Complete Guide, How You and Your Loved Ones Can Understand and Treat Alcohol and Other Drug Problems.* She lives in New York City. She has also written numerous articles for magazines, newspapers, and online publications.

A Virtual Life

In this essay from the *New York Times Magazine,* Szalavitz uses induction and deduction to explore digital reality and its consequences. Along the way, she compares the digital world to the "real" world, acknowledging the attractions of the electronic dimension.

After too long on the Net, even a phone call can be a shock. My boyfriend's Liverpudlian accent suddenly becomes indecipherable after the clarity of his words on screen; a secretary's clipped tonality seems more rejecting than I'd imagined it would be. Time itself becomes fluid—hours become minutes, and alternately seconds stretch into days. Weekends, once a highlight of my week, are now just two ordinary days. 1

For the last three years, since I stopped working as a producer for Charlie Rose, I have done much of my work as a telecommuter. I submit articles and edit them via E-mail and communicate with colleagues on Internet mailing lists. My boyfriend lives in England, so much of our relationship is also computer-mediated. 2

If I desired, I could stay inside for weeks without wanting anything. I can order food, and manage my money, love and work. In fact, at times I have spent as long as three weeks alone at home, going out only to get mail and buy newspapers and groceries. I watched most of the blizzard of '96 on TV. 3

But after a while, life itself begins to feel unreal. I start to feel as though I've merged with my machines, taking data in, spitting them back out, just another node on the Net. Others on line report the same symptoms. We start to feel an aversion to outside forms of socializing. It's like attending an A.A. meeting in a bar with everyone holding a half-sipped drink. We have become the Net naysayers' worst nightmare. 4

What first seemed like a luxury, crawling from bed to com- 5
puter, not worrying about hair, and clothes and face, has become an evasion, a lack of discipline. And once you start replacing real human contact with cyber-interaction, coming back out of the cave can be quite difficult.

I find myself shyer, more circumspect, more anxious. Or, con- 6
versely, when suddenly confronted with real live humans, I get manic, speak too much, interrupt. I constantly worry if I'm dressed appropriately, that perhaps I've actually forgotten to put on leggings and walked outside in the T-shirt and underwear I sleep and live in.

At times, I turn on the television and just leave it to chatter in 7
the background, something that I'd never done previously. The voices of the programs soothe me, but then I'm jarred by the commercials. I find myself sucked in by soap operas, or compulsively needing to keep up with the latest news and the weather. *Dateline, Frontline, Nightline,* CNN, New York 1, every possible angle of every story over and over and over, even when they are of no possible use to me. Work moves from foreground to background. I decide to check my E-mail.

On line, I find myself attacking everyone in sight. I am irritable, 8
and easily angered. I find everyone on my mailing list insensitive, believing that they've forgotten that there are people actually reading their invective. I don't realize that I'm projecting until after I've been embarrassed by someone who politely points out that I've flamed her for agreeing with me.

When I'm in this state, I fight with my boyfriend as well, misin- 9
terpreting his intentions because of the lack of emotional cues given by our typed dialogue. The fight takes hours, because the system keeps crashing. I say a line, then he does, then crash! And yet we keep on, doggedly.

I'd never realized how important daily routine is: dressing for 10
work, sleeping normal hours. I'd never thought I relied so much on co-workers for company. I began to understand why long-term unemployment can be so insidious, why life without an externally supported daily plan can lead to higher rates of substance abuse, crime, suicide.

To counteract my life, I forced myself back into the real world. 11
I call people, set up social engagements with the few remaining friends who haven't fled New York City. I try to at least get to the gym, so as to differentiate the weekend from the rest of my week.

I arrange interviews for stories, doctor's appointments—anything to get me out of the house and connected with others.

But sometimes, just one engagement is too much. I meet a friend and her ripple of laughter is intolerable—the hum of conversation in the restaurant, overwhelming. I make my excuses and flee. I re-enter my apartment and run to the computer as though it were a sanctuary. 12

I click on the modem, the once-grating sound of the connection now as pleasant as my favorite tune. I enter my password. The real world disappears. 13

Meanings and Values

1. What is the inductive generalization the author arrives at after spending "too long on the Net" (Par. 1)? Where does she state it?
2. In which paragraphs does she apply this generalization in a deductive manner?
3. Explain the meaning of the following phrases: "just another node on the Net" (Par. 4); "I've flamed her for agreeing with me" (8); and "The fight takes hours, because the system keeps crashing" (9).

Expository Techniques

1. How does the essay's conclusion reinforce the inductive generalization arrived at earlier in the essay? What strategy does the writer employ to conclude the essay? (See "Guide to Terms": *Closings.*)
2. What do the beginning sentences of Paragraphs 6–13 have in common in terms of wording or structure? (Guide: *Syntax.*) In what ways are these similarities related to the inductive generalization? Discuss how they help create coherence in the essay. (Guide: *Coherence.*)
3. Discuss the use of parallelism to provide emphasis in the sentences in Paragraphs 3 and 11. (Guide: *Parallel Structure.*)

Diction and Vocabulary

1. Discuss the essay's use of computer terminology and slang used by people familiar with computers. Does this add to or detract from most readers' understanding of the essay? How would the essay be different if the terminology and slang were not used? (Guide: *Colloquial Expressions.*)

2. If you do not know the meaning of some of the following words, look them up in a dictionary: *mediated* (Par. 2); *aversion* (4); *evasion, cyber* (5); *circumspect, manic* (6); *invective* (8); *doggedly* (9); *insidious* (10); *counteract* (11).

READ TO WRITE

1. **Collaborating:** Freewrite about your computer experiences or about typical behaviors of computer users that you have observed. Compare your freewrite with other members of a group. As a team, focus on one or two particularly interesting areas, examples, or topics that you have in common. Develop these areas into passages that might be collected for a collaborative essay.
2. **Considering Audience:** Most readers have probably experienced the online environment to which Szalavitz refers in her essay. Most, therefore, would understand her references to the "virtual life." List other mechanical/technical devices that have removed people from human contact in past generations. Choose one with which you are familiar and write an essay similar to Szalavitz's, making an inductive generalization about the consequences of this other device.
3. **Developing an Essay:** Draw on Szalavitz's comparisons of the digital and the physical world in order to develop further comparisons in an essay of your own.

(NOTE: Suggestions for essays requiring development by INDUCTION and DEDUCTION are on p. 477 at the end of this chapter.)

J. C. HERZ

J. C. HERZ was a graduate student at Harvard University when she set out to explore the world of video games. Her reports on this virtual world have appeared in numerous magazines and in two books, *Surfing on the Internet* (1995) and *Joystick Nation: How Videogames Ate Our Quarters, Won Our Hearts, and Rewired Our Minds* (1997).

Superhero Sushi

For J. C. Herz, induction and deduction serve to explain the complicated mixture of American and Japanese characteristics and cultures that appear in the figures of video game heroes. The essay is a detailed and sometimes disturbing (though entertaining) exploration of the worlds of virtual reality and their complex relationships to everyday life. This essay first appeared in *Joystick Nation.*

After walloping her opponent, *Tekken 2*'s heroine, Michelle Chang, swivels within the videogame arena and turns to face the camera, the viewer, the players. And it's a disconcerting moment, because she looks at you intelligently, and there are so many polygons in her face that she almost seems real, and because she is such a confusing mix of signals. She's a slender girl who beats up rippling hypermasculine bruisers. She's computer generated, yet more true-to-life than most of the silicon-enhanced, digitally retouched dreamgirls staring vacantly out from real world magazine racks. She's got an Asian name but ambiguous features—a Western nose, almond-shaped eyes. If you saw her on the street, you'd peg her as Amerasian. 1

In a way, she is a perfect metaphor for videogames themselves. She's a hybrid, of mixed Asian and American heritage, a creature made possible by the technological innovation of two hemispheres. Videogame characters are a bicontinental crossbreed of American and Japanese pop culture, with elements of Japanese comic books (manga) and animation as well as Western comics and science fiction. 2

On the Pacific side, videogames' family resemblance to manga and Japanimation are undeniable. In some cases, the games themselves are playable translations of popular Japanese comic books and animated films. In the last decade, hundreds of manga titles 3 have been made into videogames in Japan, crossing over into the United States as manga shifts from cult status to mass acceptance, mostly via MTV. *Dragonball* alone has spawned six arcade games, a dozen titles for the Super Famicon (the Japanese equivalent of the Super NES), and a *Dragonball* Game Boy cartridge.

The salient feature of manga heroes—and the game characters 4
based on them—is a preternatural cuteness and almost freakish babylike quality, which takes the form of oversized heads, tiny noses, and saucerlike, impossibly liquid eyes. This way of drawing characters translated easily into early videogames, which didn't have the graphic resolution to represent characters with adult proportions. Small, cute characters had fewer pixels per inch and were easier to use, and so videogames borrowed, for reasons of expediency, what manga had developed as a matter of convention. Even a character like Mario the Plumber, who's supposed to be an adult, with facial hair no less, is rendered with the roly-poly proportions of a child, like a manga character. You would expect characters to take on mature dimensions as technology enables videogame manufacturers to animate large, complex, realistic forms. But instead, companies like Sega hew even closer to the babyland aesthetic. To paraphrase Gordon Gekko in *Wall Street,* cuteness is good. Cuteness works.

The reason cuteness works, as Scott McCloud notes in *Under-* 5
standing Comics,[1] is that abstraction fosters identification. It is only because an animated character is abstract and cartoony that we can project our own expressions onto him. We can't really map ourselves onto truly realistic characters—we see them as objects, separated from us by their details. To use an annoying but useful postmodern term, they read as the Other. The most realistically rendered characters in videogames are usually enemies. The good guys are rounded, simplified, and childlike, a puttylike visual glove into which our own hands and faces fit. If anything, early videogames were especially powerful in this sense. The more photorealistic characters become, the less we relate to them. Seeing a cast of TV actors in a full-motion video makes you into more of a spectator or an editor than a part of the story, whereas the polygon people in *Tekken 2* are easy to slide into, and a character like Mario or Sonic is even easier to identify with. A primitive, completely minimal figure like Pac-Man takes this link between pixel and personality to the nth degree.

[1]Scott McCloud, *Understanding Comics: The Invisible Art* (New York: HarperCollins, 1993).

Characters in *Mortal Kombat* have fingers and stubble. You watch them. Pac-Man has one black dot for an eye, and you *become* him.

Videogame companies are well aware of this, which is why their figureheads are all round and minimal and cute, just like, well, jeepers, just like Mickey Mouse. Sega is even working on a version of *Virtua Fighter 2* called *Virtua Fighter Kizu* ("kizu" is Japlish for "kids") where all the adult martial arts characters are rendered with gigantic toddler heads. From a distance, it looks like ferocious dueling lollipops. If you count the height of their hair, the giant toddlers' heads are as tall as the rest of their bodies. The eyes are bigger than their flying fists. 6

Americans usually read these saucer eyes as Western, as a sign of whiteness. After all, the reasoning goes, Western eyes are bigger and rounder than Asian eyes. This must be the way that they see us. And for some strange reason, they're drawing us all over their comic books. But actually, that's not the case, says Matt Thorn, a doctoral candidate at Columbia University who is writing his dissertation on teen-girl comic books in Japan. "Japanese readers don't think of the characters as white," he says. "Of course, they have these huge eyes. And so to us, the characters do look white, because Westerners expect that the Japanese will represent themselves the way that Westerners represent them. That is, we have these certain standardized ways of indicating to a viewer this character is Asian or this character is black or this character is anything but white, including the slanty eyes and the black hair. And of course, the Japanese don't draw themselves that way. Those characters aren't white, and the readers don't think of them as being white, despite those features. There's a concept in linguistics called the unmarked category. And in the West, which is white-dominated, white is the unmarked category. Everything else is marked and has to be indicated, but white is taken for granted. But in Japan, Japanese is the unmarked category, the one that's taken for granted. They've developed that style with the huge eyes—that's the way that they've developed for drawing people, which means Japanese people. And when they want to indicate that a character is not Japanese, they have different ways of doing it. Like, for white people and black people they use exaggerated features. Like for white people, they'll have big noses or really big bodies or really sharply defined eyelashes." 7

So within a typical martial arts videogame, the racial continuum is deceptive. It's not a simple matter of ethnic blur. It's a matter of reading the signs in completely different ways. All the indeterminate characters that to Western eyes would read as white look 8

Japanese to kids playing the games in Tokyo. Figuratively speaking, we read these faces left to right. The Japanese read them up and down. This isn't their way of drawing us. It's their way of drawing themselves. Meanwhile, both sets of videogame players look at the screen and think the characters look native. It's counterintuitive. But when you think about it, really, *no one* has eyes that big.

There are characters in videogames that are visibly Asian, the 9
way Westerners would draw Asians. But these characters are never supposed to be from Japan. They are supposed to be from China or Korea or Mongolia or some other part of Asia. "The irony," says Thorn, "is that the techniques that Westerners use to draw Asians are the same techniques the Japanese use when they're drawing Asians other than themselves. So you'll have a manga in which there are Japanese characters, which to us read as white. And then you'll have a Chinese character, and the Chinese character is drawn in such a way as to indicate to players that this character is not Japanese but Chinese. And they'll use the same kinds of techniques that we use: the straight black hair, the slanty eyes, etc."

And Americans? Usually, when a videogame character hails 10
from the United States, he's blond. He's broad. He's buff. And he's larger than life, or at least larger than the other videogame characters. He looks more like an American comic book character than a manga hero. And he's not nearly as unassuming and cute. In fact, the more videogames borrow from American comic books, the less cute they get. Whereas Japanese manga characters are generally childlike and unassuming, American cartoon heroes in the Marvel/DC vein are, if anything, hyperadult. "In America," writes comic book historian Fred Schodt, "almost every comic book hero is a 'superhero' with bulging biceps (or breasts, as the case may be), a face and physique that rigidly adhere to the classical traditions, invincibly accompanied by superpowers, and a cloying, moralistic personality."[2] Like the drawings in a Western superhero comic, American characters in Japanese fighting games have wildly distorted, hyperrealistic, hypersexual bodies. And in American software houses, where Superman takes native precedence over Speed Racer and Astro Boy, the videogames themselves are absolutely devoid of blinking sweetness, offering instead the beloved stateside menagerie of larger-than-life comic book mutants. Capcom's *Marvel*

[2]Frederik Schodt, *Manga Manga: The World of Japanese Comics* (Tokyo: Kodansha, 1983), 77, 78.

Superheroes arcade cabinet, which is seven feet tall and physically towers over its Japanese counterparts, pumps out sound effects at blockbuster volume and stars veiny, spandex-clad standbys like the Incredible Hulk, Spiderman, and Captain America. The arcade game is, essentially, a moving comic book that replaces Pow! Boom! Zap! bubbles with gut-rattling audio effects. In this way, a Marvel Comics videogame is a more intense comic book experience than the paper it's based on. Comic book characters have always been drawn swooping and swinging and flying through the air. Now they can do it in real time. Comic book videogames are comic books squared. And with this added dimension the blurry line between comic books and videogames finally dissolves.

This blur between media is epitomized by *Comix Zone,* a videogame for the Sega Saturn. The premise, whose only precedent is Swedish pop group A-Ha's *Take on Me* video, is that your character, Sketch, is trapped in a Marvelesque comic book universe and forced to battle through it, panel by panel, combating enemies drawn by Mortus, an evil comic book artist. Along the way, helper characters yell out from the corner of the screen ("Watch out, Sketch!") in comic book dialogue boxes. The object, ultimately, is to defeat the evil illustrator and rip yourself out of his two-dimensional paper universe. It's like an Escher drawing, where you break out of one trompe l'oeil tableau only to find yourself in another impossible illusion. Beyond the simulated comic book page is a simulated TV cartoon, when, really, there aren't any pages, or any television, for that matter. There are only the conventions of paper and television, twined around each other, to float the action of a videogame. 11

Of course, to kids playing *Comix Zone* or *Marvel Superheroes* or *Tekken 2,* the distinction between comic book and videogame or Asian and Western is completely irrelevant. The only categories they recognize are "fun" and "not fun." If you walk into an arcade, you don't see white kids choosing white characters and black kids choosing black characters. Kids routinely choose any and all of these options and don't think twice about it, because the only factor in their decision is a given character's repertoire of kick-ass fighting moves. Ironically, all considerations of race, sex, and nationality are shunted aside in the videogame arena, where the only goal is to clobber everyone indiscriminately. 12

But on a deeper level, the kids playing these games intuitively understand that they're operating in a disembodied environment 13 where your virtual skin doesn't have to match your physical one, and that you can be an Okinawan karate expert, a female Thai kick-boxer, a black street fighter from the Bronx, or a six-armed alien from outer space, all within the span of a single game. Members of the previous generation might have a problem with the idea of playing a Japanese schoolgirl in a combat game. At the very least, they would be aware of their decision to choose this character, and maybe even a little smug about being enlightened enough to do so. For kids of the eighties and nineties, shuffling videogame bodies and faces is like playing with a remote control. The game starts, cycles through a bunch of avatars, and you punch the fire button when you see one you like. It's channel surfing.

In this milieu, the classic distinctions between heroes and villains break down. In older videogames, and in all previous media, the good guys look one way and the bad guys look another. It may be as simple as black hats and white hats or as fraught as cowboys and Indians. In movies and TV shows, we know what the hero and the villain are supposed to look like, and those images are very loaded. Heroes talk like midwestern news anchors and own dogs. Bad guys speak with foreign accents and stroke cats. Heroines are slender and blond and adorably helpless. Bad girls have dark hair and red nails and hips and guns they're ready to use. And because of the way these people look, and the way they're lit, it's clear for whom you're supposed to root. 14

But in an arcade fighting game like *Virtua Fighter 2*, you can't do that, because those categories don't exist at all. You can play any character, and it's every gladiator for himself. This type of videogame doesn't label opposing forces as evil or good, because that would imply a scripted outcome, that the designated "hero" is supposed to win, when really no one is supposed to win. Everyone is supposed to play. It's the skill of the competitors that determines who wins and who loses. In a videogame, unlike in novels or movies or other fictions like history, no one—not even the game designer—knows the outcome of a given contest. And so it's impossible to cast a moral hair light on one character versus another.[3] There are no heroes and villains in a round-robin martial arts game. There are only combatants, each with his or her own special weapons, attributes, 15

[3]This becomes patently obvious when you play a game like *Tekken 2*, where even the more wholesome characters are monstrously broad-shouldered, earnest, square-jawed, and monumental in the style of socialist realism. This is when you realize that monstrosity is in the eye of the beholder. This is also when you realize that most of the superheroes we hold up for children to admire are freaks.

and fighting style. In the post–Cold War world, this seems an even-handed approach. Everyone's a hero. Everyone is also a monster.

Or, to paraphrase the Red Dog beer motto, you are your own monster. Now that the videogame hero is freed from the cosmetic constraints of gallant poster boyhood, you can play a whole menagerie of creatures, from werewolves to ice creatures to dinosaurs. Superhuman strength and/or demonic powers seem to be the only prerequisites for inclusion in the videogame bestiary, which draws from martial arts movies, Arthurian legend, the Greek pantheon, science fiction, Norse mythology, and Jurassic Park. And that's just *Primal Rage,* one of the hotter fighting games of 1996. 16

Primal Rage is mythic stuff. It's a fight-to-the-death among angry, violent demigods who are also dinosaurs. According to the epic back story, "Before there were humans, gods walked the earth. They embodied the essence of Hunger, Survival, Life, Death, Insanity, Decay, Good, and Evil. They fought countless battles up through the Mesozoic Wars." When these conflicts threatened to destroy the planet, a wiser, more mature deity in another dimension decided to launch a kind of mythological NATO peacekeeping mission to shut them up. "He was not powerful enough to kill the gods," the story goes, "so instead he banished one to a rocky tomb within the moon. This disrupted the fragile balance between the gods; pandemonium ensued, and a great explosion threw clouds of volcanic dust into the atmosphere. The dinosaurs died out, and the surviving gods went into suspended animation. Now, the impact of a huge meteor strikes the Earth. Its destructive force wipes out civilization, rearranges the continents, and frees the imprisoned gods. Get ready to rumble . . . ." 17

The game ensues, throwing you into a kind of fossil fantasy Ragnarok scenario where you choose one of these reptilian gods to fight against all the others. Each of them has its own repertoire of decay-related weapons, most of which involve bodily functions. The God of Survival is a crafty velociraptor lacking in brute strength but incredibly agile and slippery. 18

In addition to its personal eccentricities, each character also has a coordinated epic backdrop. The fire-breathing Tyrannosaurus rex dukes it out in the Inferno, an active volcanic island oozing lava. The serpentine Goddess of Insanity fights on a Stonehengian knoll under a full moon with petrified enemies planted like lawn sculptures in the background. And, if you make it through all these themed battlegrounds, the final scene of *Primal Rage* is set in a dinosaur graveyard littered with the bones of fallen reptiles. Red cracks split the 19 ground, and a huge vortex swirls in the sky as you leap, bite, and strike as best you can against a very scary-looking, dragonish God of Death. It's a perfect frappé of paleontology and the supernatural, prehistory and the apocalypse. Like the science fiction universe, videogames are where technology melts into the occult. This is a place where missile launchers and mojo are both legitimate weapons. All the old monsters, harpies, dragons, and divinities are excavated from their mythological sediment, sampled, looped, remixed, cross-faded, and digitally recycled. Videogames do to dusty legends what deejays do to vintage vinyl. They weave the old grooves into something accessible to teenagers.

And increasingly, it doesn't matter where those teenagers are. 20
The same way a transcendent house mix leaps from a mixing board in London to sound systems in Tokyo, Los Angeles, and Helsinki, good videogames have a way of becoming popular everywhere. It's all digital. And a certain echelon of global youth all have access to the technology. So if it's fun, it quickly goes transnational. And in the process, it ceases to connote nationality. A successful dance track or videogame doesn't read Japanese or American, German, or British. It's all just pop. And it's yours for fifty cents.

The finest digital architects on the planet have built these play- 21
grounds out of comic books, Hong Kong cinema, scroll paintings and music videos, ancient monsters and digital technology. They pour in their myths and suck out quarters.

And this is what it's about, finally, as the cultural streams of 22
East and West swirl into the Tastee-Freez of global entertainment. Mythic figures resonate, all the more if they're engaged in some kind of combat or action adventure, real or simulated, the most popular forms being basketball and video games. They resonate for the same reasons mythic figures have always resonated. Only now, the audience numbers in the millions, and the object is not to celebrate ancestors or teach lessons or curry favor with the spirits. It's commerce. And the people transmitting their stories to the next generation aren't priests or poets or medicine women. They're multinational corporations. And they are not trying to appease the gods. They are trying to appease the shareholders. It's not just videogames. It's everything, with the possible exception of the Internet. All the mythic pop stars in Hollywood, the NBA, and MTV are purchasable commodities. Videogames are just the logical extreme, because all the superheroes in them are computer generated for maximum resonance and marketing kick. Unlike sports stars or actors, they don't get addicted, arrested, or petulant. They

perform. They may look and act superhuman. They may throw lightning or breathe fire. And when you're in the game, they may really inspire or scare you. But unlike the mythic monsters that preceded them, videogame demons are caged in their arcade cabinets, firmly under the control of their corporate wardens. Demigods used to make people docile. Now it's the other way around. It is Sega and Namco and Capcom and Williams Entertainment, finally, that have tamed the dragons.

Meanings and Values

1. Explain the significance of the title of the essay. How does it connect to Herz's message?
2. Why does Herz open with a description of a female, Japanese video character? What is significant about this character as opposed to other characters that Herz might have chosen to use in an introduction?
3. What is the significance of Paragraph 4? Does technology control other images that we see? Can it define or create stereotypes? Please explain.
4. In the first section of this essay (Par. 1–11), Herz explains the different images of heroes from different nations. But in Paragraph 12, she makes a clear shift into limiting the importance of gender, race, and nationality. What is the significance of this shift?

Expository Techniques

1. Herz repeatedly uses comparison and contrast in this essay. Identify the different things that she compares. How successful is this technique for a reader who may have limited knowledge of video games?
2. What is the thesis of this essay? (See "Guide to Terms": *Thesis.*) What type of reasoning (inductive, deductive, or a combination of both) does Herz employ to clarify and support the thesis?
3. Herz uses the second person (*you*) at various points in the essay. How effective is this? Why might she have chosen that technique in the places that she did?

Diction and Vocabulary

1. Identify slang and jargon in "Superhero Sushi." (Guide: *Slang.*) Is the use of such language excessive? Could a person unfamiliar with

video games and the language associated with them understand the essay? Please explain.

2. To what age group(s) is this essay targeted? Explain how Herz's language helps to define the age of her intended audience.

READ TO WRITE

1. **Collaborating:** List as many video game characters as you can think of and identify their race, gender, nationality, or species (if appropriate). Working with a group, compare your lists. Write a plan for an essay analyzing the various trends in video game characters.
2. **Considering Audience:** This essay clearly will be more easily understood by readers who have played video games or at least observed others play them. Using Herz's thesis as the basis for an essay, write a similar piece for an audience that might be less familiar with such technology.
3. **Developing an Essay:** Choose two or three virtual characters with which you are familiar, then go to a local arcade and study the newest games. Write an essay similar to Herz's that uses these characters collectively as a basis for an inductive generalization about the latest trends in video game characters.

(NOTE: Suggestions for essays requiring development by INDUCTION and DEDUCTION follow.)

Writing Suggestions for Chapter 12

Induction and Deduction

Choose one of the following unformed topics and shape your central theme from it. This could express the view you prefer or an opposing view. Develop your composition primarily by use of induction, alone or in combination with deduction. Unless otherwise directed by your instructor, be completely objective and limit yourself to exposition, rather than engaging in argumentation.

1. Little League baseball (or the activities of 4-H clubs, Boy Scouts, Girl Scouts, etc.) as a molder of character
2. Conformity as an expression of insecurity
3. Pop music as a mirror of contemporary values
4. The status symbol as a motivator to success
5. The liberal arts curriculum and its relevance to success in a career
6. Student opinion as the guide to better educational institutions
7. The role of public figures (including politicians, movie stars, and business people) in shaping attitudes and fashions
8. The values of education, beyond dollars and cents
9. Knowledge and its relation to wisdom
10. The right of individuals to select the laws they obey
11. Television commercials as a molder of morals
12. The "other" side of one ecological problem
13. The value of complete freedom from worry
14. Homosexuality as inborn or as voluntary behavior
15. Raising mentally challenged children at home
16. Fashionable clothing as an expression of power (or as a means of attaining status)

Collaborative Exercise

Using number 3, 5, or 10 from the Writing Suggestions list above, have each member of your group write an inductive generalization for the topic. Then as a group, create a plan for a unified essay that presents one of the inductive generalizations.

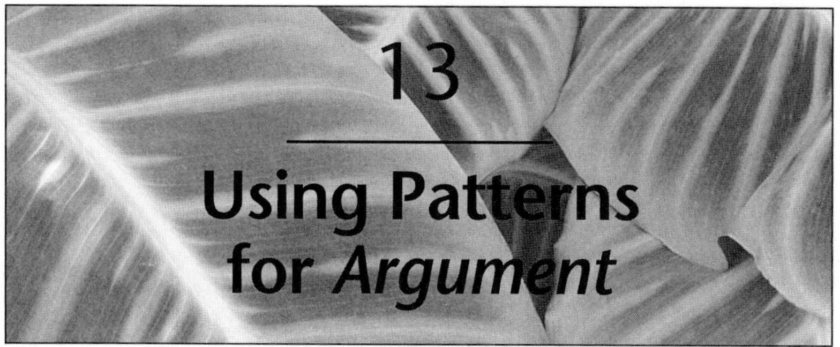

13 Using Patterns for *Argument*

Argument and exposition have many things in common. They both use the basic patterns of exposition; they share a concern for the audience; and they often deal with similar subjects, including social trends (changing social relationships, the growth of the animal rights movement), recent developments (the creation of new strains of plants through genetic manipulation, developments in health care), and issues of widespread concern (the quality of education, the effects of pollution). As a result, the study of argument is a logical companion to the study of exposition. Yet the two kinds of writing have very different purposes.

Expository writing shares information and ideas; it explores issues and explains problems. Argumentative writing has a different motivation. It asks readers to choose one side of an issue or take a particular action, whether it is to choose a career, vote for a candidate, or build a new highway. In exposition we select facts and ideas to give a clear, interesting, and thorough picture of a subject. In argument we select facts and ideas that provide strong support for our point of view and arrange this evidence in the most logical and persuasive order, taking care to provide appropriate background information and to acknowledge and refute opposing points of view.

The evidence we choose for an argument is determined to a great extent by the attitudes and needs of the people we are trying to persuade. For example, suppose you want to argue successfully for a new approach to secondary education in your community—an approach that enrolls students in "mini-schools" according to their interests. Your essay would need to provide enough examples, facts, and reasons to convince parents and community leaders that the approach would be best for *their* children, not just for children in general. You would need to show that the community could afford the approach and that the benefits would justify the added expense. To be effective, moreover, your essay would also need to answer possible objections to the proposal and demonstrate that it is preferable to other approaches a reasonable school board and community might consider.

Your argumentative writing needs to focus on your thesis: the opinion you wish readers to share, the action you want them to undertake, or the assertion you wish them to endorse. The twin poles of argumentative writing—your thesis and the needs and values of your readers—need to be linked by evidence and reasoning. Evidence and reasoning extend your thesis to readers, and they bring readers closer to it.

WHY USE ARGUMENT?

Argumentative writing responds to situations in which there are two or more conflicting points of view. An argument attempts to resolve or at least modify disagreements by encouraging people to agree upon an action or a point of view. You can recognize an argumentative thesis and an argumentative essay by the writer's evident awareness of opposing perspectives. When readers are likely to require good reasons before they will agree with your thesis or when they are likely to resist your point of view, your situation is one that calls for argumentative writing.

In addition, a simple argumentative essay can serve one of three purposes. Some essays ask readers to agree with a *value judgment* ("The present daycare system is inadequate and inefficient"). Others propose a *specific action* ("Money from the student activity fee at this college should be used to establish and staff a fitness program available to all students"). And still others advance an *opinion* quite different from that held by most people ("The supposed 'revolution' of Web shopping is no more than the logical next step in catalog retailing").

In situations calling for more complex arguments, however, you should feel free to combine these purposes as long as the relationship among them is made clear to the reader. In a complex argument, for instance, you might *first* show that the city government is inefficient and corrupt and *then* argue that it is better to change the city charter to eliminate the opportunities for the abuse of power than it is to try to vote a new party into office or to support a reform faction within the existing political machine.

Some people draw a distinction between situations calling for *logical argument* (usually called, simply, *argument*) and *persuasive argument* (usually termed *persuasion*). Whereas logical argument appeals to reason, persuasive argument appeals to the emotions. The aim of both, however, is to convince, and they are nearly always blended into whatever mixture seems most likely to do the convincing. After all, reason and emotion are both important human elements. The two often work together, with reason helping to change minds and emotion helping to prompt action.

CHOOSING A STRATEGY

Argument begins with an issue, moves to a thesis (or assertion) addressing the issue, and concludes with evidence and reasoning to convince readers and deal with opposing perspectives. This is an admittedly oversimplified view of the components of an argument (and the process of composing), yet it serves to point out that choosing strategies for an argumentative essay calls for a number of different activities.

First, you need to *identify an issue* that you can effectively address through argument. Without an issue—a difference in point of view—you have nothing to argue about. Some issues will take a clear shape before you begin writing: matters of social justice, environmental regulation, civil and criminal law, education, community relationships, and the like are filled with familiar and significant matters of disagreement and difference. In preparing to address such an issue, you need to make sure that you understand them well enough to present them in clearly defined form to readers and to provide appropriate background. You should be ready to stress the significance of an issue and the need to make a judgment or take an action.

Some familiar issues have been argued so often that readers are not likely to be receptive to further argument; others are matters of taste that are beyond argument. For instance, no amount of reasoning is likely to convince people who dislike action movies to begin enjoying them. And some issues involve matters of deeply held religious or ethical beliefs that are difficult, if not impossible, to address through logical argument.

Many issues will take a clear shape only when you think and write about them, however. Perhaps you have been irritated for some time by the concert arrangements at a local civic center, and you believe other people share your irritation. Your irritation is not itself an issue, but it can point to one. If you propose changing the arrangements, and you realize that your proposals are not the only ones that ought to be considered, then you have begun to shape an issue. As you write, you need to be ready to explain the issue to your readers, perhaps drawing on their own irritation with the arrangements to stress the importance of considering changes. Of course, when an issue takes shape in your writing, the opposing points of view are probably not well developed, if at all. For instance, you may not be aware of any alternate concert arrangements that other people have proposed, but you can probably think of some plausible alternatives to your own. In exploring them for readers, however, you identify the opposing points of view that create the issue.

Next, you need to *articulate your stance.* At the heart of an argumentative essay is the opinion you want readers to share or the action you are proposing they undertake. Being able to state this *thesis* (or *proposition*) concisely and clearly to yourself is essential to developing your strategy for an argumentative essay. Conveying your thesis in convincing form is, after all, the main purpose of the essay. Expressing your stance concisely and clearly in a *thesis statement* is perhaps the best way to alert readers to the point of your argument.

Some writers like to arrive at a sharply focused thesis statement early in the process of composing and use it to guide the selection and arrangement of evidence, for example,

> The inconvenience and discontent that accompanies concerts at the Civic Center can be greatly reduced by moving the box office further away from the main entrance doors, doubling the number of rest rooms, improving the lighting, and removing the temporary seating that partially obstructs the central aisles.

Other writers settle on a tentative ("working") thesis, which they revise as an essay takes shape. In either case, checking frequently to see that factual evidence and supporting ideas or arguments are clearly linked to the thesis is a good way for writers to make sure their finished essays are coherent, unified arguments.

Finally, you need to develop evidence and reasoning that supports your thesis and arrange it in ways that readers will consider clear and convincing. Variety in evidence gives writers a chance to present an argument fully and persuasively. Examples, facts and figures, statements from authorities, personal experience, or the experience of other people—all these can be valuable sources of support. The basic patterns of exposition, too, can be supporting strategies.

For example, to persuade people to take driving lessons at an automobile racing school, you might tell the story of someone whose life was saved through the evasive maneuver she learned in her first day at such a school. Or you might follow this narrative example with a classification of the most common kinds of accidents, comparing them, in turn, with the parallel kinds of safety lessons the schools provide.

The expository patterns can also be easily adapted to argumentative purposes. Writers frequently turn to example, comparison and contrast, cause and effect, definition, and induction or deduction to organize arguments. A series of *examples* can be an effective way of showing that a government social policy does not work and in fact hurts the people it is supposed to serve. *Comparison and contrast* can guide choices among competing products, among ways of disposing toxic waste, or among ways of revising student loan policies. *Cause and effect* can organize an argument over who is to blame for a problem or over the possible consequences of a new program. *Definition* is helpful when a controversy hinges on the interpretation of a key term or when the meaning of an important word is itself the subject of disagreement. *Induction* and *deduction* are useful in argument because they provide the kind of careful, logical reasoning necessary to convince many readers, especially those who may at first have little sympathy for the writer's opinion.

An argument need not be restricted to a single pattern. The choice of a pattern or a combination of patterns depends on the subject, the specific purpose, and the kinds of evidence needed to convince the audience to which the essay is directed. Some arguments about complicated, significant issues use so many patterns that they can be called *complex arguments.*

In arranging your evidence and reasoning, you should also consider the potential impact on readers. Three common and effective arrangements from which you can choose are ascending order, refutation-proof, and pro-con. In an *ascending order* arrangement, the strongest, most complex, or most emotionally moving evidence comes last, where it can build on the rest of the evidence in the essay and is likely to have the greatest impact on readers, as in the following example.

Introduction: The issue—some people are trying to have genetically altered farm products banned while others are arguing for an increase in the number of such products.

Tentative thesis: Despite a few drawbacks, genetically altered farm products are a great benefit to us all.

Support 1: The regulations governing genetic alteration and extensive testing means the products are generally quite safe; problems have been minor and worries have not been warranted by experience.
Support 2: Genetic alteration can create crops that are less resistant to disease and that are easier to cook and digest.
Support 3: Genetic alteration can make farms more productive and in so doing lower food costs, make more food available, and help fight undernourishment throughout the world [strongest, most moving support; even if there are some problems, these benefits may outweigh them].
Conclusion: Sums up, restates, and reinforces the thesis and the evidence.

In a *refutation-proof* arrangement, the writer acknowledges opposing points of view early in the essay and then goes on to show why the author's outlook is superior.

Tentative thesis: Genetically altered farm products benefit farmers and consumers.
Opposing points of view: Genetically engineered products are often less tasty and less nutritious; they can have unintended health consequences for farmers and consumers.
Refutation: The products can be engineered to be both tasty and nutritious—the choice is up to the producers and consumers; all natural products can have unintended consequences, and we forget this when dealing with "scientific products"; more extensive testing can help us deal with any unfortunate consequences.
Support 1: Genetically altered products can be more disease and pest-resistant, reducing the dangers of exposure to pesticides and other chemicals.
Support 2: Genetically altered products provide greater variety for consumers and choices for farmers looking for products appropriate for their soil and climate.
Support 3, 4, 5. . . .
Conclusion

A *pro-con* arrangement allows the writer to present an opposing point of view and then refute it, continuing until all opposition has been dealt with and all positive arguments voiced. This strategy is particularly useful when there is a strong opposition to the writer's thesis.

Tentative thesis: The benefits of genetically altered farm products far outweigh the liabilities.

Con 1: The engineered products may end up replacing "natural" ones.

Pro 1: Some "natural" products may be less common, but the success of organic and other specialty products indicates that there will be a demand for both "new" and "natural" foods.

Con 2: Genetically altered products are often designed for the needs of large corporate farms and will contribute to the demise of smaller, family farms.

Pro 2: The shift to larger farms and agribusinesses has been occurring for many reasons other than genetic engineering of crops; the new crops will have only a small effect, if any.

Con 3, 4, 5. . . .

Pro 3, 4, 5. . . .

Conclusion

DEVELOPING ARGUMENTS

In developing an argument, you need to pay attention to your choice of evidence and to make sure your reasoning is clear and logical. It is never possible to arrive at absolute proof—argument, after all, assumes that there are at least two sides to the matter under discussion—yet a carefully constructed case will convince many readers.

One way to construct arguments is to follow the pattern of *data-warrant-claim reasoning* as outlined by the philosopher Stephen Toulmin. *Data* correspond to your evidence and *claim* to your thesis or assertion. *Warrant* refers to the mental process by which a reader connects the data to the claim. To argue effectively, you need to show your readers how the warrant connects the data to your claim, as in the following sequence.

Data: Children's books are relatively expensive, generally costing between ten and thirty dollars.

Warrant: Buying children a variety of books can be very expensive.

Warrant: Children learn to love books by reading; playing with books on a regular basis is something that helps them become good readers.

Warrant: Children get easily bored with a book, so they need a variety of books to keep them occupied—though the book that bores them today will interest them tomorrow and the day after.

Claim: The high cost of children's books keeps many children from learning to love books and becoming better readers.

At the same time, a flaw in logic can undermine an otherwise reasonable argument and destroy a reader's confidence in its conclusions. The introduction to Chapter 12, "Reasoning by Use of *Induction* and *Deduction*," discusses some important errors to avoid in reasoning or in choosing evidence. Here are some others:

Post hoc ergo propter hoc ("After this therefore because of this")—Just because one thing happened *after* another does not mean that the first event caused the second. In arguing without detailed supporting evidence that a recent drop in the crime rate is the result of a newly instituted anticrime policy, a writer might be committing this error, because there are other equally plausible explanations: a drop in the unemployment rate, for example, or a reduction in the number of people in the 15–25 age bracket, the segment of the population that is responsible for a high proportion of all crimes.

Begging the question—A writer "begs the question" when he or she assumes the truth of something that is still to be proven. An argument that begins this way, "The recent, unjustified rise in utility rates should be reversed by the state legislature," assumes that the rise is "unjustified," though this important point needs to be proven.

Ignoring the question—A writer may "ignore the question" by shifting attention away from the issue at hand to some loosely related or even irrelevant matter: for example, "Senator Jones's plan for encouraging new industries cannot be any good because in the past he has opposed tax cuts for corporations" (this approach shifts attention away from the merits of Senator Jones's proposal). A related problem is the *ad hominem* (toward the person) argument, which substitutes personal attack for a discussion of the issue in question.

Student Essay

In recent years, many new foods have been developed, including some that are substitutes for "natural foods." The development of these products has gone hand-in-hand with growing controversies over their safety, with most people willing to at least listen to the criticisms on the grounds that food safety is one of the most important public health issues all of us face. In the face of such controversy, Julie Richardson sets out to defend an "artificial" food, olestra, in her essay, "The Fight on Fat Controversy."

The Fight on Fat Controversy
by Julie Richardson

Background

Today, Americans are realizing the importance of a healthy lifestyle, which includes exercising and following a balanced diet. Reducing fat in the diet decreases the risk of health problems such as heart disease and obesity and is a vital step in achieving an improved lifestyle. Food manufacturers are responding to the consumer's needs by adding more reduced-fat foods to product lines. A trip down the grocery aisle is evidence of the increased "better-for-you" products, tempting the consumer with less salt, less sugar, and sugarless, lower fat, and nonfat items.

Importance of topic for readers

Information about specific issue/disagreement

After nine years of research, the U.S. Food & Drug Administration (FDA) approved a fat-free cooking oil known as olestra to be used in frying savory snacks. Olestra has been hailed as a breakthrough solution for millions of Americans who are looking to reduce fat and calories from the foods they want to eat without sacrificing the quality of taste. Excitement, curiosity, and confusion have followed the new lineup of products made with olestra. This new discovery is slowly, yet dramatically changing food processing, and consumers need to educate themselves on the facts surrounding this innovative alternative to fat.

"Confusion" suggests potential disagreements

Olestra, marketed by Procter & Gamble as Olean, is made from vegetable oil and sugar, then used in place of regular cooking oils or fats. This revolutionary fat substitute does not break down like other fats; instead, it passes through the stomach and intestines without being digested or absorbed by the body. As a result, olestra provides all the taste of vegetable oil but none of the calories or harmful saturated fats of regular vegetable oils. The results are snacks that taste great with no fat and half of the calories.

Concise statement of issue

Heralded as a waistline-whittling savior by millions of consumers, olestra has been condemned by others as a nutritional saboteur with distressing gastrointestinal side effects. The Center for Science in the Public Interest (CSPI) believes there are serious health risks when products made with olestra are consumed. This nonprofit health group believes the FDA should ban olestra or, at the very least, require a prominent warning label on the front of packages stating that olestra can cause severe side effects. Currently there is only a small warning on the back of packaging, warning consumers that they could experience soft stools when consuming olestra.

Arguments against the product

Challengers of olestra also advocate that the body is robbed of vitamins or carotenoids (found in fresh fruits and vegetables) that have already been digested. Michael Jacobson, executive director of CSPI, reveals that carotenoids protect against chronic diseases. Jacobson also states that long-term use of olestra in snack foods is likely to cause thousands of cases of cancer and heart disease each year. Opponents of olestra believe additional research should be completed to ensure the protection of consumers' health.

More arguments against

Proponents of olestra, including Procter & Gamble and the FDA, are quick to point out the fallacy of olestra "robbing" the body of vitamins and carotenoids that have already been digested, as Jacobson implies. Olestra can only interact with vitamins or carotenoids that are in the digestive system at the exact same time as the olestra; and even then, the level of interaction has not been outside the acceptable range. Results from the FDA Advisory Committee review in June 1998 determined there is no direct evidence that carotenoids are responsible for lower risk of disease, which disproves Jacobson's theory that carotenoids protect against chronic diseases. These results also show the absurdity of Jacobson's claim that long-term use of olestra causes cancer.

Arguments and evidence for the product—refuting opponents of olestra

Frito-Lay has been allowed to fortify their WOW! Chips with extra vitamins to insure there is no net loss or reduction in vitamin levels due to normal absorption. However, the FDA is preventing Frito-Lay from adding extra carotenoids to their WOW! Chips because the jury in the scientific community is still out as to whether or not carotenoids are actually good or bad. In a study conducted in Sweden, a compelling argument raises the possibility of carotenoids actually causing cancer.

Admits to some validity in worries about the product

Michael Jacobson's research is anecdotal and unscientific. Most of his research is obtained through questionnaires completed on the CSPI Web site, not in a laboratory by scientists. In contrast, P&G has spent 25 years and $200 million researching olestra, in one of the most comprehensive reviews of any food additive in history. The FDA received 150,000 pages of data from studies of 8,000 adults and children. Results from a follow-up study were reviewed in June 1998 by a FDA panel of leading health, medical, and nutrition experts who overwhelmingly reaffirmed the safety of Olean. The committee also discussed the possibility of removing or rewording the warning label on Frito-Lay's WOW! Chips.

Direct refutation of major objections supported by statistics and authoritative testimony

Another issue of concern with olestra rivals is the labeling of "fat-free" on snacks made with olestra. Opponents feel the packaging is misleading to consumers since olestra is an indigestible fat. I do understand the dispute over labeling, even though olestra technically is a fat substitute and does not have the same effect as regular fat in the body.

Agrees with objections to packaging of product

Side effects from olestra in some people have given way for public scrutiny. Olestra's larger and tighter molecules pass through the body undigested. Since the olestra is mixed in with other food products in the digestive system, it may physically soften the stool, similar to adding oil or water to bread dough. The symptoms experienced may depend on consumption, other eaten foods, and the individual body reaction.

Another objection

Followed by two paragraphs of refutation

Prior to olestra's approval, it was determined that digestive symptoms were common among the general population. As recorded in the FDA's report on olestra in 1996, 40 precent of adults noted that they experienced some digestive effect within the past month. Also, a study published in the *Journal of the American Medical Association* (January 1998) said that potato chips made with Olean are no more likely to cause digestive changes than potato chips made with regular vegetable oil.

Common digestive symptoms are caused by a range of other foods, such as beans, some milk products, and fruit, especially in those who eat too much. Usually when people determine that certain foods do not agree with them, they avoid them. To ban olestra since it may cause diarrhea in some instances is like banning milk because it causes illness for those that are lactose intolerant.

Opponents of olestra, namely the CSPI group, have fought loud and hard at attacking the new fat substitute by relying on the media to circulate their allegations. They have become the nation's most familiar nutrition watchdog group; however, some people may view CSPI's intentions as being more interested in publicity rather than protecting the public's interest. Let's face it, the media loves drama brought on by interest groups representing "victims," and CSPI is good at digging out victims from their Web site. According to a *Reader's Digest* article titled, "Attack of the Food Police," Jacobson has not only thrashed olestra, but has also attempted bans on movie theater popcorn and Chinese food.

Questions motivation of opponents

CSPI has also petitioned the Federal Trade Commission to stop deceptive multimillion-dollar advertising campaigns for Olean and products made with it. As a result, Michael Jacobson persuaded *The New England Journal of Medicine* to pull Olean advertisements on the basis that *NEJM* was biased and had received funds from manufacturer, Procter & Gamble, for its support.

The truth of the matter is that *NEJM* elected to discontinue the Olean ad because it did not want to compromise its position while receiving advertising money from P&G. It is common for prestigious magazines to make decisions such as this to protect their interests; however, it was even more critical with Olean. The backlash and rhetoric the magazine would receive from Jacobson if it were to publish a positive report on olestra while still accepting ad funds from P&G would be damaging to its credibility. This is a good example of the effectiveness of Jacobson's scare tactics and persuasiveness.

Refutes the reasoning of criticisms of the product

Since Olean's approval, tens of millions of people have eaten over half-a-billion servings of new snacks made with this ingredient. These consumers have avoided more than 10 million pounds of fat and 40 billion calories, fat and calories they would have eaten in full-fat snacks. That's particularly noteworthy, considering the country's struggle with obesity and concern for cardiovascular diseases.

Pro-evidence of safety (facts)

Proctor & Gamble is continuing to study olestra, including possible nutrient depletion, and will report its findings to the FDA. The company has signed agreements with 12 other firms interested in making olestra snacks. P&G has tested olestra in several other foods, such as ice cream and mayonnaise, and states it will submit another application to the FDA for olestra's use within a year.

Evidence of trustworthiness of the manufacturer

I believe the protests made by opponents of olestra to be exaggerated, unfounded, and sensationalized. The Center for Science in the Public Interest is leading the crusade against olestra in its typical melodramatic fashion by twisting and eliminating the true facts. Consumers owe it to themselves to be aware of the organizations supporting olestra, such as The Food & Drug Administration, The American Medical Association, The American Dietetics Association, The American Academy of Pediatrics, and The National Consumer League.

Argumentative proposition implied throughout—now stated directly

The evidence from years of research has proven that olestra can be worked into a healthy diet, just like any other food. Olestra has confirmed its safety and effectiveness to the medical and scientific community as well as gained momentum in the consumer's "fight on fat" battle. Olestra alone is not the answer to trim the fat off America's belly; however, it is a safe and effective way to enjoy favorite foods without sacrificing the taste. Olestra has opened the doors; now it's up to the American people to open their eyes to the truth. As Abraham Lincoln said "Truth is generally the best vindication against slander," and the truth of olestra's safety will prevail over Michael Jacobson and the CSPI group.

Summarizes evidence for and ends with a quotation summing up the writer's opinion of critics

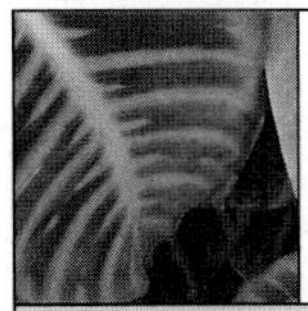

Issues and Ideas

Current Controversies

- Christopher B. Daly, *How the Lawyers Stole Winter*
- Stephanie Mills, *Could You Live with Less?*
- Anna Quindlen, *The Drug That Pretends It Isn't*
- Andrew O' Hehir, *The Myth of Media Voilence*
- Elizabeth Svoboda, *I Am Not a Puzzle, I Am a Person*
- Barbara Lawrence, *Four-Letter Words Can Hurt You*
- Sarah Min, *Language Lessons*

An issue is a subject on which there is more than one point of view. Since arguments address differences and disagreements, they necessarily begin with an issue. When an issue disappears, however, so does the usefulness and relevance of an argument—unless, of course, the argument is expressed in language so moving and effective or with reasoning so precise and convincing that it remains admirable even though the immediate concerns of the author and the audience may pass away.

The essays in this chapter address contemporary questions, though the issues themselves have been around in some form for quite a while and are likely to remain with us in coming years. Christopher B. Daly's "How the Lawyers Stole Winter" focuses not only on concerns about children's safety and legal liability, but also on the much larger issue of personal responsibility. Stephanie Mills's "Could You Live with Less?" focus on issues resulting from our current ways of living and interacting with nature and our environments. Anna Quindlen's "The Drug That Pretends It Isn't" redefines a behavior that many resist labeling as extreme because it is something they enjoy. Andrew O'Hehir "The Myth of Media Violence" addresses the linking of media violence and actual violence. Elizabeth Svoboda's "I Am Not a Puzzle, I Am a Person" argues for new definitions that re-shape our notions of autism and autistic people. Barbara Lawrence's essay, "Four-Letter Words Can Hurt You," was first published a little more than 20 years ago. Nonetheless, although the particular words we use may have changed somewhat, the issues are still alive. Sarah Min, in "Language Lessons," takes a personal and refreshing approach to the issue of bilingualism.

ARGUMENT THROUGH COMPARISON AND CONTRAST

CHRISTOPHER B. DALY

CHRISTOPHER B. DALY grew up in Medford, Massachusetts. He now lives with his family in Newton, Massachusetts, and is a freelance writer and contributor to magazines.

How the Lawyers Stole Winter

In this essay, which appeared first in *Atlantic Monthly,* Daly uses comparison to make the case that in our attempts to prevent dangerous accidents, we (and, in particular, the lawyers among us) have not only stolen some enjoyment from our lives but also lessened responsibility for our own actions. He suggests that the result may be more danger, not less.

When I was a boy, my friends and I would come home from school each day, change our clothes (because we were not allowed to wear "play clothes" to school), and go outside until dinnertime. In the early 1960s in Medford, a city on the outskirts of Boston, that was pretty much what everybody did. Sometimes there might be flute lessons, or an organized Little League game, but usually not. Usually we kids went out and played. 1

In winter, on our way home from the Gleason School, we would go past Brooks Pond to check the ice. By throwing heavy stones onto it, hammering it with downed branches, and, finally, jumping on it, we could figure out if the ice was ready for skating. If it was, we would hurry home to grab our skates, our sticks, and whatever other gear we had, and then return to play hockey for the rest of the day. When the streetlights came on, we knew it was time to jam our cold, stiff feet back into our green rubber snow boots and get home for dinner. 2

I had these memories in mind recently when I moved, with my wife and two young boys, into a house near a lake even closer to Boston, in the city of Newton. As soon as Crystal Lake froze over, I grabbed my skates and headed out. I was not the first one there, though: the lawyers had beaten me to the lake. They had warned the town recreation department to put it off limits. So I found a sign that said DANGER. THIN ICE. NO SKATING. 3

Knowing a thing or two about words myself, I put my own gloss on the sign. I took it to mean *When the ice is thin, there is danger* 4 *and there should be no skating.* Fair enough, I thought, but I knew that the obverse was also true: *When the ice is thick, it is safe and there should be skating.* Finding the ice plenty thick, I laced up my skates and glided out onto the miraculous glassy surface of the frozen lake. My wife, a native of Manhattan, would not let me take our two boys with me. But for as long as I could, I enjoyed the free, open-air delight of skating as it should be. After a few days others joined me, and we became an outlaw band of skaters.

What we were doing was once the heart of winter in New England—and a lot of other places, too. It was clean, free exercise that needed no StairMasters, no health clubs, no appointments, and hardly any gear. Sadly, it is in danger of passing away. Nowadays it seems that every city and town and almost all property holders are so worried about liability and lawsuits that they simply throw up a sign or a fence and declare that henceforth there shall be no skating, and that's the end of it. 5

As a result, kids today live in a world of leagues, rinks, rules, uniforms, adults, and rides—rides here, rides there, rides everywhere. It is not clear that they are better off; in some ways they are clearly *not* better off. 6

When I was a boy skating on Brooks Pond, there were no grown-ups around. Once or twice a year, on a weekend day or a holiday, some parents might come by with a thermos of hot cocoa. Maybe they would build a fire (which we were forbidden to do), and we would gather round. 7

But for the most part the pond was the domain of children. In the absence of adults, we made and enforced our own rules. We had hardly any gear—just some borrowed hockey gloves, some hand-me-down skates, maybe an elbow pad or two—so we played a clean form of hockey, with no high-sticking, no punching, and almost no checking. A single fight could ruin the whole afternoon. Indeed, as I remember it, thirty years later, it was the purest form of hockey I ever saw—until I got to see the Russian national team play the game. 8

But before we could play, we had to check the ice. We became serious junior meteorologists, true connoisseurs of cold. We learned that the best weather for pond skating is plain, clear cold, with starry nights and no snow. (Snow not only mucks up the skating surface but also insulates the ice from the colder air above.) And we learned that moving water, even the gently flowing Mystic River, is a lot less likely to freeze than standing water. So we skated only on the pond. We learned all the weird whooping and cracking sounds that ice makes as it expands and contracts, and thus when to leave the ice. 9

Do kids learn these things today? I don't know. How would they? We don't let them. Instead we post signs. Ruled by lawyers, cities and towns everywhere try to eliminate their legal liability. But try as they might, they cannot eliminate the underlying risk. Liability is a social construct; risk is a natural fact. When it is cold enough, ponds freeze. No sign or fence or ordinance can change that. 10

In fact, by focusing on liability and not teaching our kids how to take risks, we are making their world more dangerous. When we were children, we had to learn to evaluate risks and handle them on our own. We had to learn, quite literally, to test the waters. As a result, we grew up to be savvier about ice and ponds than any kid could be who has skated only under adult supervision on a rink. 11

When I was a boy, despite the risks we took on the ice no one I knew ever drowned. The only people I heard about who drowned were graduate students at Harvard or MIT who came from the tropics and were living through their first winters. Not knowing (after all, how could they?) about ice on moving water, they would innocently venture out onto the half-frozen Charles River, fall through, and die. They were literally out of their element. 12

Are we raising a generation of children who will be out of their element? And if so, what can we do about it? We cannot just roll back the calendar. I cannot tell my six-year-old to head down to the lake by himself to play all afternoon—if for no other reason than that he would not find twenty or thirty other kids there, full of the collective wisdom about cold and ice that they had inherited, along with hockey equipment, from their older brothers and sisters. Somewhere along the line that link got broken. 13

The whole setting of childhood has changed. We cannot change it again overnight. I cannot send my children out by themselves yet, but at least some of the time I can go out there with them. Maybe that is a start. 14

As for us, last winter was a very unusual one. We had ferocious cold (near-zero temperatures on many nights) and tremendous snows (about a hundred inches in all). Eventually a strange thing happened. The town gave in—sort of. Sometime in January the recreation department "opened" a section of the lake, and even dispatched a snowplow truck to clear a good-sized patch of ice. The boys and I skated during the rest of winter. Ever vigilant, the town officials kept the THIN ICE signs up, even though their own truck could safely drive on the frozen surface. And they brought in "lifeguards" and all sorts of rules about the hours during which we could skate and where we had to stay. 15

But at least we were able to skate in the open air, on real ice. And it was still free. 16

Meanings and Values

1. Summarize in your own words the issue the author is addressing in this essay. In what ways is this issue representative of similar issues in other settings and climates? Explain. Does this "representativeness" make the argument significant and interesting for people who are not worried about thin ice and have no interest in skating? Why, or why not? (See "Guide to Terms": *Evaluation.*)
2. Daly presents his examples of growing up in the early 1960s as illustrations of a good way to teach children responsibility and to allow them to have healthy fun. Does he succeed in doing so? If so, what details in the examples or statements of interpretation are most convincing? If not, what keeps the examples from being successful?
3. What opposing points of view, if any, does Daly acknowledge? Would the essay be more (or less) effective if he spent more time dealing with possible objections to his argument? Make a list of possible objections to his argument and evidence that could be used to support them.
4. Does the writer offer possible answers to the problem he identifies? If so, what are they? Does the essay make a clear case that lawyers are to blame for the problem? If not, does this weaken the essay? Why, or why not?

Argumentative Techniques

1. Why does the writer wait until Paragraph 6 to offer an argumentative proposition (thesis)? What role(s) do the opening paragraphs play? Do they explain an issue or problem? Do they provide evidence that can be used to support the thesis? Be specific in your answer, and point to specific evidence to support your conclusions. (Guide: *Introductions.*)
2. Which sentence or sentences state the argumentative proposition (thesis)? (Guide: *Thesis.*) Restate it in your own words. Are all parts of the essay clearly related to this thesis? If not, what are the functions of any parts not clearly related to the thesis? (Guide: *Unity.*) How is the comparison-contrast pattern related to the thesis? Explain. Would another arrangement of ideas and evidence be likely to provide more convincing development and support for the thesis? What arrangement, and why?
3. In what ways does the concluding sentence "echo" the beginning of the essay? Which paragraphs should be considered the conclusion of the essay? What functions do they perform? (Guide: *Closings.*)

Diction and Vocabulary

1. The effectiveness of this essay depends to a considerable extent on the writer's ability to make the account of his childhood experiences seem like a realistic ideal and not merely a sentimental, nostalgic excursion. How does the diction in Paragraphs 1–2 and 7–9 aid him in staying away from too much sentimentality while at the same time making the experience seem attractive and worth reclaiming? If you think the examples are overly sentimental, explain why. (Guide: *Sentimentality.*)
2. What words with positive connotations does Daly associate with skating and playing hockey (see Pars. 4 and 8)? (Guide: *Connotation/ Denotation.*) How do the connotations of these words help support his thesis?
3. If you do not know the meaning of some of the following words, look them up in a dictionary: *gloss, obverse* (Par. 4); *high-sticking, checking* (8); *meteorologists, connoisseurs* (9); *liability, construct* (10); *vigilant* (15).

Read to Write

1. **Collaborating:** Working in a group, make a list of other valuable childhood activities that have been curtailed, limited, or threatened by legal concerns. Should we ignore these concerns, find a way to accommodate them, or come up with different and less dangerous activities? Consider making an issue from this general subject area the focus of an argumentative essay.
2. **Considering Audience:** Using Daly's essay as a model, argue that in an attempt to deal with a problem, threat, or danger, we have taken steps that create more problems and dangers by taking away the need to be responsible for our actions. In developing the essay, acknowledge that many readers have legitimate fears, and avoid being too critical of such readers.
3. **Developing an Essay:** Begin an argumentative essay of your own with examples of how things should be, then develop your argument by contrasting how they are with how they ought to be.

(Note: Suggestions for topics requiring development by ARGUMENT are on pp. 533–534 at the end of this chapter.)

ARGUMENT THROUGH EXAMPLE

STEPHANIE MILLS

STEPHANIE MILLS is an activist and writer. She has written and edited a number of books on environmental and social issues, including *In Praise of Nature* (ed.) (1991); *In Service of the Wild: Restoring and Reinhabiting Damaged Land* (1995); *Turning Away from Technology: A New Vision for the 21st Century* (ed.) (1997); and *Epicurean Simplicity* (2002).

Could You Live with Less?

The examples in this essay, first published in *Glamour* magazine, are drawn from Mills's experience and, she suggests, are arguments intended primarily to justify her frugal, natural lifestyle. It should be clear to most readers, however, that she intends them to encourage readers to take seriously the choices she has made and perhaps even make similar choices themselves. What helps make this essay more than a statement of personal belief is the time Mills spends dealing with potential objections to her reasoning. In appearing to deal with objections, she is actually arguing in favor of her outlook—and addressing these arguments to readers, hoping to persuade them to agree with her.

Compared to the lifestyle of the average person on Earth, my days are lush with comfort and convenience: I have a warm home, enough to eat, my own car. But compared to most of my urban American contemporaries, I live a monastically simple life. 1

Since 1984 I've made my home outside a small city in lower Michigan, where the winters are snowy but not severely cold. My snug 720-square-foot house is solar- and wood-heated. No thermostat, just a cast-iron stove. There's electric lighting, indoor plumbing, a tankless water heater, a secondhand refrigerator and range—but no microwave oven, no dishwasher, no blow-dryer, no cordless phone. My gas-sipping compact station wagon has 140,000 miles on it and spreading patches of rust. I've never owned a television set. My home entertainment center consists of a thousand books, a CD-less stereo system, a picture window and two cats. 2

Part of the reason I live the way I do is that as a freelance writer, my income is unpredictable and at best fairly unspectacular. Thus it behooves me to keep in mind the difference between wants and 3 needs. Like all human beings, I have some needs that are absolute: about 2,500 calories a day, a half a gallon of water to drink, a sanitary means of disposing of my bodily wastes, water to bathe in, something muscular to do for part of the day and a warm, dry place to sleep. To stay sane I need contact with people and with nature, meaningful work and the opportunity to love and be loved.

I don't need, nor do I want, to complicate my life with gadgets. 4
I want to keep technology at the periphery rather than at the center of my life, to treat it like meat in Chinese cuisine—as a condiment rather than as a staple food. Technology should abet my life, not dominate or redefine it. A really good tool—like a sharp kitchen knife, a wheelbarrow or a baby carrier, all of which have been with us in some form for thousands of years—makes a useful difference but doesn't displace human intelligence, character or contact the way higher technologies sometimes do. Working people need the tools of their trade, and as a writer, I do have a fax, but I've resisted the pressure to buy a personal computer. A manual typewriter has worked well for me so far. Noticing that the most computer-savvy people I know are always pining for more megabytes and better software, I've decided not to climb on the purchasing treadmill of planned obsolescence.

Doing with less is easier when I remember that emotional needs 5
often get expressed as material wants, but can never, finally, be satisfied that way. If I feel disconnected from others, a cellular phone won't cure that. If I feel like I'm getting a little dowdy, hours on a tanning bed can't eradicate self-doubt.

Why live in a snowy region when I don't use central heat? I 6
moved here for love several years ago, and while that love was brief, my affection for this place has grown and grown. I like the roots I've put down; living like Goldilocks, moving from chair to chair, seems like not much of a life to me.

Being willfully backward about technology suits my taste—I like 7
living this way. Wood heat feels good, better than the other kinds. (Central heating would make my home feel like it was just anywhere.) Fetching firewood gets me outdoors and breathing (sometimes gasping) fresh air in the wintertime when it's easy to go stale. It's hard, achy work to split and stack the eight or 12 cords of stove wood I burn annually. I've been known to seek help to get it done. But the more of it I do myself, the more I can brag to my city friends.

My strongest motivation for living the way I do is my knowl- 8
edge, deep and abiding, that technology comes at a serious cost to the planet and most of its people. Burning fossil fuels has changed the

Earth's climate. Plastics and pesticides have left endocrine-disrupting chemicals everywhere—in us and in wildlife, affecting reproductive systems. According to Northwest Environment Watch in Seattle, the "clean" computer industry typically generates 139 pounds of waste, 49 of them toxic, in the manufacture of each 55-pound computer.

I refuse to live as if that weren't so. In this, I'm not unique. 9
There are many thousands of Americans living simply, questioning technology, fighting to preserve what remains of nature. We're bucking the tide, acting consciously and succeeding only a little. Yet living this way helps me feel decent within myself—and that, I find, is one luxury worth having.

Meanings and Values

1. To what extent does the title of this essay act as a statement of the argumentative thesis (admittedly an *indirect* statement)? Is the thesis stated anywhere else in the essay? If not, does it need to be? (See "Guide to Terms": *Unity.*)
2. Summarize in your own words the issue the author is addressing in this essay. What evidence is there in the essay that the writer's purpose is to take a stand on the issue rather than simply to make a statement of personal belief? (Guide: *Purpose.*)
3. What opposing points of view does Mills acknowledge? Identify each and tell how effective you think she is at rebutting it. (Guide: *Evaluation.*) Do you think other readers are likely to agree with your estimate of Mills's success or failure? Why? What kinds of readers would be likely to disagree with you, if any?

Argumentative Techniques

1. Why does the writer not announce her argumentative proposition (thesis) clearly in the opening paragraphs of the essay? What role(s) do the opening paragraphs play? Do they explain an issue or problem? Do they provide evidence that can be used to support the thesis? Be specific in your answer, and point to specific evidence to support your conclusions. (Guide: *Introductions.*)
2. Examine the opening sentences of Paragraphs 3–8. How are they related to the argumentative thesis? Which parts of the essay, if any, do not support or explain the thesis? Could the essay be revised in any way to make it more unified? (Guide: *Thesis; Unity.*)
3. In what ways does the concluding paragraph sentence "echo" or refer to the beginning of the essay? What appeal to readers to agree with her does Mills offer in the conclusion? (Guide: *Closings.*)

Diction and Vocabulary

1. The effectiveness of this essay depends to a considerable extent on the writer's ability to make her way of living seem like a realistic ideal and not merely an impractical, foolish, or sentimental exercise. How do the diction and the details in Paragraphs 3–4 and 7–8 emphasize the realistic and practical side of her way of living and help her stay away from too much sentimentality or nostalgia in portraying a lifestyle many will see as pointing back to the "good old times"? If you think the examples are overly sentimental, explain why. (Guide: *Sentimentality.*)
2. What words with positive connotations does Mills associate with her lifestyle (see Pars. 3, 4, 6, 7, and 8)? (Guide: *Connotation/Denotation.*) How do the connotations of these words help support her thesis?

Read to Write

1. **Collaborating:** Working in a group, list other ways of living that most people might not endorse immediately. Decide with your group which patterns of development might be used for an essay defending one of these ways of living.
2. **Considering Audience:** Envision yourself as a modern suburban or urban dweller reading Mills's essay (this will not be much of a stretch for many people). Write a letter to the editor of the magazine in which it appeared (*Glamour*), responding to the issue from your perspective.
3. **Developing an Essay:** Mills clearly lets her readers know how she feels without excessive moralizing. Choose a controversial issue and write an essay similar to Mills's in which you share your belief without judging harshly or openly criticizing those in opposition.

(Note: Suggestions for essays requiring development by ARGUMENT are on pp. 533–534 at the end of this chapter).

ARGUMENT THROUGH DEFINITION

ANNA QUINDLEN

ANNA QUINDLEN has been a reporter and columnist for the *New York Times* and a columnist for *Newsweek*. She has written four novels: *Object Lessons* (1991), *One True Thing* (1994), *Black and Blue* (1998), and *Blessings* (2002). Her books of nonfiction essays include *Living Out Loud* (1988), *Thinking Out Loud* (1993), *How Reading Changed My Life* (1998), and *Loud and Clear* (2004).

The Drug That Pretends It Isn't

In this essay, Quindlen employs a particularly useful (and flexible) argument strategy: choose a definition about which most people agree, and then show that a controversial subject or issue fits within the definition. Quindlen begins by pointing out that most people see illegal drug use as a big problem, and then argues that we need to view alcohol as a drug and its misuse as a significant problem. She builds on this framework, too, paying attention to arguments and evidence likely to be most persuasive to her readers.

Spring break in Jamaica, and the patios of the waterfront bars are so packed that it seems the crowds of students must go tumbling into the aquamarine sea, still clutching their glasses. Even at the airport one drunken young man with a peeling nose argues with a flight attendant about whether he can bring his Red Stripe, kept cold in an insulated sleeve, aboard the plane heading home. 1

The giggle about Jamaica for American visitors has always been the availability of ganja; half the T-shirts in the souvenir shops have slogans about smoking grass. But the students thronging the streets of Montego Bay seem more comfortable with their habitual drug of choice: alcohol. 2

Whoops! Sorry! Not supposed to call alcohol a drug. Some of the people who lead antidrug organizations don't like it because they fear it dilutes the message about the "real" drugs, heroin, cocaine, and marijuana. Parents are offended by it: as they try to figure out which vodka bottle came from their party and which from their teenager's, they sigh and say, "Well, at least it's not drugs." And naturally the lobbyists for the industry hate it. They're power guys, these guys: The wine guy is George W.'s brother-in-law, the beer guy meets regularly with House majority whip Tom DeLay. When you lump a cocktail in with a joint, it makes them crazy. 3

And it's true: Booze and beer are not the same as illegal drugs. They're worse. A policy research group called Drug Strategies has produced a report that calls alcohol "America's most pervasive drug problem" and then goes on to document the claim. Alcohol-related deaths outnumber deaths related to drugs four to one. Alcohol is a factor in more than half of all domestic violence and sexual assault cases. Between accidents, health problems, crime, and lost productivity, researchers estimate alcohol abuse costs the economy $167 billion a year. In 1995 four out of every ten people on probation said they were drinking when they committed a violent crime, while only one in ten admitted using illicit drugs. Close your eyes and substitute the word blah-blah for alcohol in any of those sentences, and you'd have to conclude that an all-out war on blah-blah would result. 4

Yet when members of Congress tried to pass legislation that would make alcohol part of the purview of the nation's drug czar, the measure failed. Mothers Against Drunk Driving faces opposition to both its education programs and its public service ads from principals and parents who think illicit drugs should be given greater priority. The argument is this: Heroin, cocaine, and marijuana are harmful and against the law, but alcohol is used in moderation with no ill effects by many people. 5

Here's the counterargument: There are an enormous number of people who cannot and will never be able to drink in moderation. And what they leave in their wake is often more difficult to quantify than DWIs or date rapes. In his memoir *A Drinking Life,* Pete Hamill describes simply and eloquently the binges, the blackouts, the routine: "If I wrote a good column for the newspaper, I'd go to the bar and celebrate; if I wrote a poor column, I would drink away my regret. Then I'd go home, another dinner missed, another chance to play with the children gone, and in the morning, hung over, thick-tongued, and thick-fingered, I'd attempt through my disgust to make amends." Hamill and I used to drink, when we were younger, at a dark place down a short flight of stairs in the Village called the Lion's Head. There were book jackets covering the walls that I used to look at covertly with envy. But then I got older, and when I passed the Head I sometimes thought of how many books had never been written at all because of the drinking. 6

Everyone has a friend/an uncle/a coworker/a spouse/a neighbor who drinks too much. A recent poll of seven thousand adults found that 82 percent said they'd even be willing to pay more for a drink if the money was used to combat alcohol abuse. New Mexico and Montana already use excise taxes on alcohol to pay for treatment 7 programs. It's probably just coincidence that, as Drug Strategies reports, the average excise tax on beer is nineteen cents a gallon, while in Missouri and Wisconsin, homes to Anheuser-Busch and Miller, respectively, the tax is only six cents.

A wholesale uprising in Washington against Philip Morris, which owns Miller Brewing and was the largest donor of soft money to the Republicans in 1998, or against Seagram's, which did the same for the Democrats in 1996, doesn't seem likely. Homeschooling is in order, a harder sell than even to elected officials, since many parents prefer lessons that do not require self-examination. Talking about underage drinking and peer pressure lets them off the hook by suggesting that it's all about sixteen-year-olds with six-packs. But the peer group is everywhere, from the frogs that croak "Bud" on commercials to those tiresome folks who behave as if wine were as important as books (it's not) to parents who drink to excess and teach an indelible life lesson. 8

Prohibition was cooked up to try to ameliorate the damage that drinking does to daily life. It didn't work. But there is always self-prohibition. It's not easy, since all the world's a speakeasy. "Not even wine?" Hamill recalls he was asked at dinner parties after he stopped. Of course, children should not drink, and people who sell them alcohol should be prosecuted. Of course, people should not drink and drive, and those who do should be punished. But twenty-one is not a magic number, and the living room is not necessarily a safe place. There is a larger story that needs to be told, loud and clear, in homes and schools and on commercials given as much prominence and paid for in the same way as those that talk about the dangers of smack or crack: that alcohol is a mind-altering, mood-altering drug, and that lots of people should never start to drink at all. "I have no talent for it," Hamill told friends. Just like that. 9

Meanings and Values

1. Summarize the reasons why, as this essay claims, people resist viewing alcohol as a drug.
2. Summarize the arguments and evidence the essay offers in favor of viewing alcohol as a drug.
3. Where in this essay does the writer offer readers a definition of illegal drugs, and in what ways does she provide this definition? Will the definition be precise enough so that most readers will be able to follow the argument? Why, or why not? (See "Guide to Terms": *Evaluation*.)

Argumentative Techniques

1. Identify the thesis statement in this essay. Tell why you find it either clear, focused, and appropriately limited in scope or unclear, vague, and too broad (or too narrow). (Guide: *Thesis.*)
2. What strategy does the writer employ to introduce opposing points of view? What strategies does she employ to introduce her refutation of the opposing points of view?
3. Identify the elements of this essay that are consistent with a refutation proof organization (see p. 497). Does the essay, in general, follow a refutation-proof pattern? Why, or why not?
4. Can this essay be said to combine strategies of definition and refutation-proof? If so, why? If not, why not?

Diction and Vocabulary

1. Discuss how the author's choice of words in Paragraphs 3 and 8 is a strategy for criticizing people and groups unwilling to take strong measures against alcohol use and abuse. (Guide: *Diction.*)
2. Analyze the use of the words "blah-blah" in Paragraph 4 as a strategy consistent with the author's use of definition for purposes of argument.
3. What words or phrases in Paragraph 7 are used ironically? (Guide: *Irony.*)
4. If you do not know the meaning of some of the following words, look them up in a dictionary: *aquamarine* (Par. 1); *lobbyists* (2); *purview* (5); *eloquently, amends, covertly* (6); *excise* (7).

Read to Write

1. **Collaborating:** Working in a group, focus on drinking or some other activity some people may regard as "recreational" and others as "dangerous." List as many reasons as you can for each judgment. Summarize these *pro* and *con* perspectives in a brief informative essay.
2. **Considering Audience:** The range of responses to Quindlen's essay is likely to be broad, depending on a reader's experiences, values, and background. Identify four kinds of people likely to have differing responses, and summarize briefly the likely responses from each kind of reader as well as reasons for the responses.
3. **Developing an Essay:** Using Quindlen's essay as a model, develop an argumentative essay of your own about how a particular activity generally regarded in either a positive or negative light should be redefined as the opposite.

(Note: Suggestions for topics requiring development by ARGUMENT are on pp. 533–534, at the end of this chapter.)

ANDREW O'HEHIR

ANDREW O'HEHIR has written both film and book reviews for *Salon.com* and *Sight and Sound*. He is primarily interested in "indie" films. O'Hehir currently lives in Brooklyn, New York, with his wife and children.

The Myth of Media Violence

This serious argument, published online at *Salon.com,* has nonetheless an often informal tone. It addresses an issue about which people have strong opinions which often run contrary to facts and research, as this writer points out. One of the writer's main tactics in this essay is to look at the reasoning commonly used about media violence (both induction and deduction) and point out its many faults.

Kids these days. They're all wasting their spare hours, or so we're told, with immoral trash like *Grand Theft Auto,* the now-notorious series of slickly decorated and powerfully addictive video games. As Senator Hillary Clinton explained at a forum hosted by the Kaiser Family Foundation, "They're playing a game that encourages them to have sex with prostitutes and then murder them." 1

Fans of "GTA" claim this is a typical nongamer's misinterpretation—it might be possible to kill hookers in the game, but it won't necessarily help you win—but let's let that go. There's no doubt that GTA allows you, for example, to play the role of an ex-con trying to take over a vice-addled city by gunning down drug lords, cops, low-flying aircraft and pretty much everything and everybody else. These games revel in their pseudo-noir amorality, and they're basically designed to be loathed by parents, school principals and tweedy psychologists. 2

Clinton's attack on the latest manifestation of the Media Demon—you know, the evil force within video games, action movies, rap songs, comic books, dime novels, Judas Priest records played backward and, I don't know, Javanese puppet theater and cave hieroglyphics—is a depressingly familiar ploy in American politics. When you can't make any progress against genuine social problems, or, like Senator Clinton, you seem religiously committed to triangulating every issue and halving the distance between yourself and Jerry Falwell, you go after the people who sell fantasy to teenagers. 3

What might be most interesting about this latest vapidity, in fact, is what Clinton didn't say. Five years ago, in the wake of the Columbine massacre, we were told that there was no serious debate about whether media violence contributed to teenage crime in the real world. A clear link had been established, the case was closed, and the only question was what we were going to do about it. By contrast, Clinton's comments were surprisingly mild and almost entirely subjective. She called violent and debauched entertainment a "silent epidemic," essentially arguing that it has effects, but we don't quite know what they are. 4

Over the long haul, Clinton said, violent media might teach kids "that it's okay to dis people because they're women or they're a different color or they're from a different place." Perhaps more to the point, she added: "Parents worry their children will not grow up with the same values they did because of the overwhelming presence of the media." That was it—no claims that we were breeding a nation of perverts and murderers, and no mention of all the supposed science indicating a link between simulated mayhem and the real thing. Playing GTA and watching Internet porn might lead your kids to "dis" somebody, or to grow up with different values from yours (or anyway to make you concerned that they might). Katy, bar the door! 5

As dopey as Clinton's remarks are, I don't mean to ridicule parents and educators for their legitimate concerns. Of course, I'm not certain that violent movies and games (or, for that matter, dumb-ass sitcoms and vapid reality shows) are harmless. My own kids are still too young for this question to matter much, but of course, I hold onto the naive hope that they'll spend their formative years hiking the Appalachians and reading about the Byzantine Empire, rather than vegetating in media sludge. But it's long past time to face the fact that, while it's legitimate not to like violent media, or to believe it's psychologically deadening in various ways, the case that it directly leads to real-life violence has pretty much collapsed. 6

Hillary Clinton's equivocation may be something of a compulsive family trait, but it also reflects how muddy this issue has become since the summer of 2000, when the American Medical Association, the American Psychiatric Association, the American Academy of Child and Adolescent Psychiatry, and several other professional busybody organizations issued a joint statement proclaiming that "well over 1,000 studies" had shown a direct connection between media violence and "juvenile aggression." In 2002, Harvard psychologist Steven Pinker wrote that it had become an 7 article of faith "among conservative politicians and liberal health professionals alike . . . that violence in the media is a major cause of American violent crime."

Actually, there never was any such consensus in the academic fields of psychology, criminology, or media studies. And there weren't well over a thousand studies of media violence either—that was one of the many myths and legends that sprung up around this question. In the years since then, the mavericks have been increasingly heard from. Even in the theatrical United States Senate hearings convened a few days after the Columbine shootings in 1999, MIT professor Henry Jenkins observed that the idea that violent entertainment had consistent and predictable effects on viewers was "inadequate and simplistic," adding almost poetically that most young people don't absorb entertainment passively, but rather move "nomadically across the media landscape, cobbling together a personal mythology of symbols and stories taken from many different places." 8

Jenkins was a lonely voice at the time, but more recently the edifice of mainstream certainty has begun to crumble. Psychologists like Pinker, Jonathan Freedman, Jonathan Kellerman, and Melanie Moore have counterattacked against their own establishment, arguing that media-violence research to date has been flawed and inconclusive at best, and a grant-funding scam at worst. Some have gone further, suggesting that violent entertainment provides a valuable fantasy outlet for the inevitable rage of childhood and adolescence, and probably helps more children than it hurts. . . . 9

We've also heard from criminologists, lawyers, and literary scholars as the tide of counterarguments has swelled. The latest of these last is Harold Schechter, a professor at Queens College in New York whose book, *Savage Pastimes*, provides an eye-opening survey of gruesome entertainment throughout the history of Western civilization. Schechter's main point concerns what scholars call the "periodicity" of campaigns like Senator Clinton's latest screed. Every time a technological shift occurs (such as from books to movies, radio to TV, movies to video games), he argues, it produces a new medium for gruesome entertainment aimed at adolescent audiences, and produces a renewed outrage among the self-appointed guardians of civilization. 10

One remarkable example not cited by Schecter: In 1948, there was an enormous uproar in Canada over a meaningless killing committed by two boys, ages 13 and 11. Pretending to be highwaymen, they hid near a road with a stolen rifle and shot at a passing car, killing a 11 passenger. When it was revealed that they were avid readers of crime comic books, the anticomics movement swelled. This story bears an uncanny similarity to a recent case, examined in *Salon*, in which two boys, ages 15 and 13, stole their father's rifle, hid near a highway, and shot at a passing car, killing a passenger. The youths defended themselves on the grounds that playing *Grand Theft Auto* made them do it.

The Jeremiahs who condemn violent entertainment, whether crime comics or *Grand Theft Auto*, also invariably lament the passage of a golden age, generally contemporaneous with their own childhoods, when entertainment was healthful and wholesome, suitable for infants and grannies alike. I don't mean to impugn Granny, who may have a healthy appetite for phony bloodshed, but these moral guardians' sunny views of the past either reflect fuzzy memories or whopping hypocrisy. 12

Schechter offers an amusing catalog of the outrageous bloodshed and mayhem found in popular entertainment since time immemorial, from the classics (as he observes, the onstage blinding of Gloucester in "King Lear"—"out, vile jelly"—is one of the most traumatic acts of violence in any medium) to the pornographic sadism of Grand-Guignol theater, the lurid sensationalism of turn-of-the-century "penny papers," and the ugly misogyny of Mickey Spillane's best-selling pulp novels. Undoubtedly Hillary Clinton would prefer that today's kids read books instead of playing GTA, and Schechter might suggest *Seth Jones: or, The Captives of the Frontier*, a wilderness adventure that was one of the best-selling kids' books of the nineteenth century. In one scene, the hero comes upon the corpse of a man who has been tied to a tree by Indians and burned to death: "Every vestige of the flesh was burned off to the knees, and the bones, white and glistening, dangled to the crisp and blackened members above! The hands, tied behind, had passed through the fire unscathed, but every other part of the body was literally roasted!" Seth is greatly relieved, however, to discover that the victim was not a white man. As Schechter says, it's impossible to imagine anyone publishing this as kiddie lit today, both for its gore quotient and its casual racism. 13

In another dime novel of the period, a rattling Western adventure called *Deadwood Dick on Deck*, Schechter reports that more than 100 people are killed in the first two chapters, a figure that fans of *Resident Evil* and *Doom* can only view with awe and veneration. Then there's the gruesome "comic" yarn Schechter digs up from 1839, in which that authentic American hero, Davy Crockett, engages in a "scentiforous fight" with an individual referred to as "a pesky great 14 bull nigger" (and also as "Blackey," "Mr. Nig" and "snow-ball"). Crockett ends the battle by gouging out one of his adversary's eyes, feeling "the bottom of the socket with end of my thum."

Schechter knows what you're thinking: At least those kids were reading, and as reprehensible by our standards as those books may have been, there's really no comparison between the printed page and the "hyperkinetic visuals of movies and computer games." The only answer to this is maybe and maybe not; critics of pop culture always assume that new technologies have rendered kids incapable of telling the difference between reality and fantasy, and so far they've always been wrong. Schechter writes that for children who had never seen a movie or a video game, "the printed page was a PlayStation, and penny dreadfuls were state-of-the-art escapism, capable of eliciting a shudder or thrill every bit as intense as the kind induced by today's high-tech entertainment." The relativist position that each generation is equally affected by the media available to it is supported by ample historical evidence, from the way that the audiences at early film screenings rose in panic when on-screen trains bore down upon them to the wildly Dionysian effect of that hypersexual, morals-corroding music, swing. 15

If Senator Clinton might prefer an outdoor family activity in the sunny American heartland, there's always the example of Owensboro, Kentucky, where on August 14, 1936, some 20,000 citizens of all ages crowded into the courthouse square. It was a "jolly holiday," according to newspaper reports. Hot dogs, popcorn, and soft drinks were sold, and there was a mixture of cheers and catcalls—but no general disorder, as the local paper angrily insisted—when sheriff's deputies brought a man named Rainey Bethea out to the scaffold, where he was hanged. 16

Schechter cites the infamous opening pages of Michel Foucault's *Discipline and Punish*, which recount the horrible tortures inflicted in 1757 on Robert François Damiens, the attempted assassin of Louis XV. In 1305 in London, Scottish rebel William Wallace was hanged and revived, castrated and disemboweled while still alive, and finally decapitated and dismembered, with the pieces coated in boiling tar and strung up in various public places. (When Mel Gibson played Wallace in *Braveheart*, we saw none of that.) Sometimes it's the little things that tell the story: During the Reign of Terror in revolutionary France, children were given 2-foot-tall toy guillotines they could use to behead birds and mice. 17

Schechter doesn't bring up the Bethea execution to paint white Kentuckians of the Depression as depraved rubes; his point is that we 18 actually have come a long way in seven decades. We're free to regard violent movies and video games as loathsome, but we also have to admit they reflect at least a partially successful sublimation of what William James called "our aboriginal capacity for murderous excitement." Few of us are eager for the return of public executions (except perhaps the programming executives at Fox) and no real cops or prostitutes were harmed during the creation of *Grand Theft Auto.* Although a few juveniles charged with murder, or their victims' families, have argued that video games were responsible for murder, kids who play video-game shooters aren't outside gunning down the neighbors, possibly because that would mean getting off their butts and leaving behind the overlit universe of their TV or computer screen.

As Schechter says, there are two linked assumptions that underpin all the hysteria about purported media-influenced violence in the last 20 years, if not longer. Assumption No. 1 is that we live in an especially violent time in human history, surrounded by serial killers, hardened teenage "superpredators," genocidal atrocities, and all sorts of amoral mayhem. Assumption No. 2 is that our popular entertainment is far more violent than the entertainment of the past, and presents that violence in more graphic and bloodthirsty detail. For critics of media violence, from the Clintons to Dave Grossman to the leadership of the child-psychiatry establishment, these assumptions go essentially unchallenged, and the conclusion they draw is that there is a causal or perhaps circular relationship between these "facts": Media violence breeds real violence, which leads to ever more imaginative media violence, and so on. 19

A longtime crime buff who has written several books about notorious murderers, Schechter mounts an impressive case in *Savage Pastimes* that, if anything, our pop culture is less bloody-minded than that of the past. Anyone who looks back at the 1950s, when Schechter himself was a child, and remembers only *Leave It to Beaver* and Pat Boone needs to read his discourse on the hugely popular *Davy Crockett* miniseries of 1954, "whose level of carnage," he writes, "remains unsurpassed in the history of televised children's entertainment." This series, with its barrage of "shootings, stabbings, scalpings, stranglings," was broadcast on Wednesday nights at 7:30 PM, and presented as the acme of wholesome family fare. 20

In fact, as Schechter demonstrates, fifties TV was profoundly rooted in guns and gunfire, to a degree that would provoke widespread outrage today. But there are factors he doesn't consider, or considers only in passing, that fuel people's perceptions that the past was less violent, both in real and symbolic terms. Those fifties 21

TV shows were mostly westerns, of course, which meant that they presented themselves as instructive fables of American history in [their] most masculine, individualistic form. They were racially and politically uncomplicated; *Gunsmoke* and *Bonanza* developed a social conscience in the sixties, but the white screen cowboys of the fifties were heroes, and the whites, Indians, and Mexicans around them were clearly divided into good guys and bad.

In other words, while *Davy Crockett* and *Have Gun Will Travel* and 22 *The Rifleman* were loaded with violence, it was mostly reassuring violence, presented without splatter and without moral consequences. The graphic media violence of our age, whether in *Taxi Driver* or *Reservoir Dogs* or *CSI* or *Grand Theft Auto*, is deliberately unsettling, meant to fill viewers with dread and remind them that life is an uncertain, morally murky affair. This might put us closer to the murder-obsessed Victorian age than to the scrubbed fifties, and in examining both eras, it's important to remember that this message can be delivered badly or well, used for a cheap roller-coaster effect or a tremendous *King Lear* catharsis. (It's also worth pointing out that Jib Fowles disagrees with Schecter, arguing, "It does appear that television violence has been slowly growing in volume and intensity since 1950.")

But if Assumption No. 2 looks questionable, Assumption No. 1 is 23 just flat-out false. As Fowles painstakingly details in *The Case for Television Violence*, violence has clearly been decreasing in the Western world for the last 500 years; as far as we can tell from uneven record keeping, the murder rate in medieval Europe was several times higher than it is today, even in relatively violent societies like the United States. While the twentieth century has seen some spikes in violent crime—correlating less to the arrival of television than to the proportion of young men in the population—the downward trend since about 1980 has reinforced the general tendency. As Rhodes puts it, "We live in one of the least violent eras in peacetime human history."

Again, there are some complicating ambiguities here, although 24 they don't make the absolute numbers look any different. If you're convinced that we live amid a psychotic crime wave, well, blame the media. Murder has become an increasingly rare crime, and most of it is pretty unglamorous—poor people, many of them black and brown, killing each other in petty disputes over love affairs or insultingly small amounts of money. But whenever something truly ghoulish happens—a serial killer hacks up some white girls or a mom drowns her kids in the tub—we're exposed to so many pseudo-news stories and movies of the week that it seems as if society is totally out of its gourd and such things are happening every day.

I don't think there's any question that the sense of dislocation this produces, while unmeasurable by social science, can be profound. We know this as the "mean world" syndrome, and it's the reason why, for instance, my wife's 90-something grandparents not only don't go outside after dark but also refuse to answer the phone. (Apparently the depraved criminals roaming the suburban streets can teleport themselves through the phone lines.) Our obsession with violent crime may indeed be at an all-time high, even as crime itself keeps becoming rarer. Perhaps TV has made us so frightened that we've mostly stopped killing each other. 25

There's far more that one could and perhaps should say about the essentially adolescent character of our civilization, fatally torn between the impulses of Eros and Thanatos. But the point I'm struggling toward is that while you can't prove that media violence *doesn't* lead to real violence—and only an idiot would assert that no one has ever been inspired to commit a crime by a book or movie or video game—our definitions of "media" and "violence" may need some rethinking. And as a general proposition, the simplistic consensus of a few years ago stands on exceedingly shaky ground. "This whole episode of studying television violence," as Fowles told Rhodes in 2000, "is going to be seen by history as a travesty. It's going to be used in classes as an example of how social science can just go totally awry." 26

Most likely it will be seen in the same way that we now see psychologist Frederic Wertham's infamous fifties campaign against horror comics—as an understandable, if in retrospect laughable, response to the unknown. Wertham interviewed juvenile offenders and found that most of them read comic books; ergo, comics led to juvenile crime. There was widespread panic about juvenile delinquency in that decade (which actually saw record lows in crime of all kinds), and he had found an appropriately disreputable scapegoat. While Wertham focused his ire on the gore-drenched horror comics, with their rotting zombies and sadistic scientists, he also wrote that Wonder Woman was a lesbian, Batman and Robin were a man-boy couple and Superman was a fascist. (So he got those right, at least.) 27

Attorney and author Marjorie Heins has pointed out that the conflict between pop culture and its critics is literally as old as Western civilization: Plato thought that unsavory art should be censored, while Aristotle argued that violent and upsetting drama had a cathartic effect and helped purge the undesirable emotions of spectators. Jib Fowles suggests that these periodic culture wars are mostly a way of displacing anxieties about class, race, and gender, as well as, most obviously, a proxy war between middle-aged adults and the succeeding generations whose culture they can't quite understand. 28

Perhaps the most sensible words on this subject that I've discovered come from comics author Gerard Jones, in a 2000 *Mother Jones* article that became, in part, the basis for his book *Killing Monsters.* "I'm not going to argue that violent entertainment is harmless," he wrote. "I am going to argue that it's helped hundreds of people for every one it's hurt, and that it can help far more if we learn to use it well. I am going to argue that our fear of `youth violence' isn't well-founded on reality, and that the fear can do more harm than the reality. We act as though our highest priority is to prevent our children from growing up into murderous thugs—but modern kids are far more likely to grow up too passive, too distrustful of themselves, too easily manipulated." 29

That expresses, I suspect, exactly what many parents of more or less my generation feel about their kids and the media. To be fair, I also think it's a more honest, less red-state-coded version of what Hillary Clinton was trying to say. We know that the media stew most of us marinate in is tremendously powerful, but we don't understand its power, so we fear it. Furthermore, even if violent entertainment has always been with us, as Harold Schechter argues, it's *supposed* to scare us, because it calls up emotions and impulses we don't usually want to think about, because it summons demons from below our conscious minds and before our approved history. That's its job. 30

Ultimately, we can't protect our kids from being frightened or unsettled by things they will inevitably encounter, whether while reading Dostoevsky or playing the latest zombie-splattering incarnation of *Resident Evil.* We can't stop them from forging their own culture out of fragments and shards they collect along the way, a culture specifically intended to confuse and alienate us. But I think Jones is right: Most of us don't have to worry about breeding little homicidal maniacs. What's far more plausible, and more dangerous, is that well raise a pack of sedentary, cynical little button-pushing consumption monsters who never go outside. Now that's scary. 31

Meanings and Values

1. How would you describe the tone of this essay? (See "Guide to Terms": *Tone.*) Does it vary anywhere in the essay? If so, where.
2. To what extent does the tone support or undermine the purpose and argumentative proposition of the essay? (Guide: *Purpose, Thesis.*)
3. What argumentative proposition does the writer advance in this essay? Where does he state it?

ARGUMENTATIVE TECHNIQUES

1a. Which sections of this essay are taken up by summaries and refutations of points of view that differ from the writer's?

b. Does the writer spend too much time on other points of view? Why, or why not? (Guide: *Evaluation.*)

2. Discuss the use of transitions at the beginnings of Paragraphs 28, 29, 30, 31, 35, and 36. (Guide: *Transitions.*) How do they advance the argument and guide the reader? Are they effective? (Guide: *Evaluation.*)

3. This essay uses a number of detailed examples. Make a list of them, and indicate which you think are particularly effective or ineffective and why?

DICTION AND VOCABULARY

1. Tell what the specific, concrete diction contributes to the effectiveness of the examples in Paragraphs 11, 19, and 23. (Guide: *Concrete/Abstract, Diction.*)

2. Does the offensiveness of some of the language in Paragraphs 11, 19, and 23 undermine the writer's purpose? Why, or why not? (Guide: *Purpose, Evaluation.*)

3. If you do not know the meaning of some of the following terms, look them up in a dictionary: *pseudo-noir* (Par. 1); *debauched* (4); *consensus, nomadically* (8); *brazen* (12); *Jeremiahs* (16); *Grand-Guignol* (18); *hyperkinetic* (20); *disembowled* (23); *simplistic* (32); *unsavory* (34).

READ TO WRITE

1. **Collaborating:** Most of us have experience with media violence. Working with a group, ask each person to write a paragraph about specific examples of media violence they have witnessed and the effects (or lack of them) that this violence had for them.

2. **Considering Audience:** Do different people with different personalities respond to media violence in varied ways? Prepare a questionnaire about media violence and ask your friends or classmates to respond to it, then summarize the results.

3. **Developing an Essay:** Follow O'Hehir's approach, and argue against many of the widely-held opinions on an issue, criticizing them using tactics similar to O'Hehir's.

(NOTE: Suggestions for topics requiring development by use of ARGUMENT are on pp. 533–534, at the end of this chapter.)

ELIZABETH SVOBODA

ELIZABETH SVOBODA was born in the suburbs of Western New York. She graduated from Yale University in 2003 and now writes for various publications on a number of eclectic topics, which she approaches from a unique and often unorthodox perspective. She currently lives in San Jose, California, with her husband.

I Am Not a Puzzle, I Am a Person

In this essay, first published online at *Salon.com*, the writer reports on a controversy over the appropriate definition and treatment of autism. Though the aim at first seems expository, it is in fact argumentative. The writer structures the essay as an argument and advances a particular perspective on autism through the people whose experiences and ideas she describes—without taking an explicit position herself. Clearly, however, she agrees with those parents who take a moderate approach in favor of "neurodiversity."

Long before her son Michelangelo's first birthday, Dana Commandatore began to suspect he was different. The other babies she knew babbled animatedly to everyone in sight. Michelangelo, though, never took much interest in children his age, and by the time he was 18 months old, he still wasn't speaking. Determined to find out what was wrong, Commandatore took her son to the pediatrician. "They sent us for a hearing test. The technicians were trying to put the headphones on and Michelangelo wouldn't let them do it," she recalls. "One tech said to the other, 'It seems more like autism than a hearing problem.' I turned around and said, 'What?'" 1

When Michelangelo's autism diagnosis was confirmed soon after, the verdict was more of a relief than anything else—it seemed to suggest a clear course of action. "We knew who he was," Commandatore says. "Now we knew what to do." In the process of scouring the Internet, she stumbled across Web sites run by autistic adults who advocated a school of thought they called "neurodiversity." Autism was not a "disease," their reasoning went, but a "neurological variation" that ought to be as respected as a difference like skin color or sexual orientation. The Centers for Disease Control and Prevention estimates that the prevalence of autism spectrum disorders in the U.S. is about 1 in every 150 8-year-olds. 2

Elizabeth Svoboda, "I am not a puzzle, I am a person," *Salon.com*, April 27, 2009. This article first appeared in Salon.com, at http://www.Salon.com. An online version remains in the Salon archives. Reprinted with permission.

The advocates' core message—that autistic people should be 3
celebrated for their uniqueness, not aggressively "normalized"—struck a chord with Commandatore. She began learning more about the movement and went to hear Ari Ne'eman, president of the Autistic Self Advocacy Networt, give a lecture. "I am not a person at all who joins groups. I'm not religious," Commandatore says. "But when I found Ari's Web site and saw him speak, he put into words what I had been thinking."

Like the deaf culture movement before it, the so-called autistic 4
culture movement continues to gain traction, boasting thousands of adherents among parents, patients and healthcare professionals. And the rhetoric is often as strident as anything out of the deaf-pride movement. Some autistic people even use the pejorative term "curebie" to refer to people who hope for a cure for the condition. Organizations like Autism Network International view efforts to cure autism as similar to misguided efforts to cure homosexuality and left-handedness.

As its associated swag—buttons and T-shirts proclaiming "I am 5
not a puzzle, I am a person"—suggests, the movement aims to redefine autism as something to be valued and protected, not obliterated. Proponents insist that forcing autistic people to behave like "neurotypicals," a term that borders on insulting, squelches the very qualities that make them unique. "The real ends for autistic people should be quality of life, full access in society, the kinds of things we support and are working for," Ne'eman says. "Parents have been told that the way to approach these things is to support research for a cure, but our belief is that that's not the most effective paradigm."

In other words, Jenny McCarthy can go jump off a cliff. While 6
the Hollywood comedian's claims that childhood shots cause autism may be well-intentioned, Ne'eman says, her message has a pernicious and probably untrue implication: If we stopped giving kids "toxic" vaccines, autism wouldn't exist. Not only does this message distract from pragmatic efforts to get autistic kids the social support they need, it implies that autistic children are inherently less valuable than their normal counterparts. The cure paradigm sends a message that there is somehow a normal person under the autistic person, and that's a significant denial of who we are."

But it's not just anti-vaccine diatribes that raise autistic culture 7
crusaders' ire. Their primary target is something much broader and more insidious: the general therapeutic approach to autism in the medical community. Many autistic rights advocates have spoken out against applied behavioral analysis (ABA), the most common

type of autism therapy, developed by UCLA psychologist Ivar Lovaas in the 1960s and '70s, with the goal of helping autistic children achieve "normal intellectual and educational" functioning. The therapy, which uses repetition and rewards to reinforce new skills, is geared toward extinguishing autistic behaviors such as "stimming" (making repetitive body movements) and failing to make eye contact. One sign of the treatment's success, Lovaas suggested, might be for school personnel to perceive an autistic child as "indistinguishable" from his or her normal peers.

Approaches like this miss the point entirely, says Kathleen Seidel, the webmaster of Neurodiversity.com and the mother of a child on the autism spectrum. Instead of trying to coerce autistic kids to behave like "neurotypicals," therapists should focus on helping them deal more effectively with the non-autistic world. "A person's nervous system is not fundamentally going to change—an autistic person is going to remain autistic throughout his or her lifetime," Seidel says. "And it can be very problematic and a source of stress for an autistic child to have to suppress certain mannerisms." 8

Equally problematic, says Dora Raymaker, a Portland, Ore., artist with autism, is the tendency for medical professionals to impose "normal" behaviors on autistic people—even when those behaviors do not necessarily improve their ability to function. Rather than undergoing continual and grueling speech therapy, Raymaker has fought to express herself via text chat, the communication medium with which she feels most at home. "If we'd done this interview on the telephone you would have been lucky to get much more than disjointed, stuttering, completely non sequitur responses from me," she told me in an instant-message conversation. "But because you allowed me to do this interview through text-only media where I can slow down, really understand you, and bypass my difficulties with spoken language, I'm able to give you intelligent, on topic answers." 9

The key assumption that underlies much autistic culture discourse is that any autism-related limitations can be worked around 10 and dealt with in a way that does not compromise the autistic individual's core "personhood." When such workarounds are found, Raymaker asserts, the concept of a "cure" becomes irrelevant. "Do I need a pill to make me suddenly able to have phone conversations, or do I need you to be able to find a middle ground that bypasses my disabilities?"

Some parents and therapists counter that this kind of active opposition to suppressing autistic symptoms is a niche crusade—one mounted by a small, visible group of high-functioning autistics who 11 don't represent the autistic population at large. If a child stages screaming outbursts in the classroom or has trouble stringing together a complete sentence, New Brunswick lawyer Harold Doherty argues, does it really make sense to treat that child's condition as "a different neurological way of being," instead of a disease that imposes severe limitations?

"Some of these advocates oppose a cure and they appear in court proceedings. In all these cases, they're talking about other people's children," says Doherty, whose son Conor is autistic. "Who gives them the authority to represent autistics? What does Ari Ne'eman know about Conor? He has no real investment in my son's life. There's a denial in this movement of the challenges of more autistic individuals. It's not a feel-good story to talk about kids who are smashing their heads into things." 12

The question of whether autism should be considered a medical condition or a variation in neural wiring isn't just one of semantics. If autistic-rights advocates win their court battles, many treatment programs could stop receiving government money. In 2004, for instance, autistic-rights crusader Michelle Dawson convinced the Canadian Supreme Court to overturn an appeal that would have provided state funding for ABA therapy. If similar legal efforts succeed in the U.S., says Massachusetts psychologist Teresa Bolick, autistic children could be hampered in acquiring the skills they need to interact with the world. 13

"One of the main dangers of saying, 'This is not a developmental disorder,' is that federal and state governments don't usually fund intervention for differences," Bolick says. "Parents say, 'But what if his natural personality is to be a hermit? What if my son just wants to be like Thoreau?' I say, 'You know what, if he wants to be Thoreau, that's terrific.' But we need to give people the skills so they can choose whether to be like Thoreau or like a more social person." 14

Bolick adds that the justification many autistic culture advocates give for slamming ABA—that the therapy is condescending and attempts to turn autistic children into people they're not—is strained and largely outmoded. "If we look at contemporary ABA, we see tremendous attention to the individual and tremendous appreciation for personality," she says. "Old-fashioned behavior modification has the reputation of using aversives and denying individual freedoms, but that's not the way good treatments are anymore. For the most part, reinforcement is driven by what the kid wants to do. One kid loves it when his teaching assistant draws for him, so he'll do anything if she'll draw." 15

Ne'eman disputes the accuracy of this portrayal, citing cases in which autistic children were abused and restrained in the name of "therapy." "There are very significant problems with the way in which intervention is approached," he says. "The founders of ABA quite unabashedly practiced the use of aversives, including electric shock, and this is something that continues to this day." 16

In some cases, inappropriate therapeutic interventions may be a catalyst for antisocial behavior, says Ann Bauer, a Salon essayist who recently wrote about her autistic son Andrew's violent outbursts. "I believe deeply that one contributor to Andrew's recent behavior is a system that treats him inappropriately," Bauer says. "We had an overworked and apathetic state caseworker who consistently placed my son in homes developed for people with IQs of 70 or below because she couldn't see the difference between this and high-functioning autism. I'm not sure I wouldn't have gone insane myself if housed in such a place." Still, she does not solely blame the system for Andrew's furious rampages. "This is not to say that I don't hold my son responsible for his behaviors. He behaves cognitively and socially in a way that is completely out of sync with the rest of our world. I guess what I'm saying is, it's complicated. Is there something wrong with him or something wrong with society or both?" 17

In theory, neurodiversity advocates fall squarely into the something-wrong-with-society camp. The problem isn't that they or their children are defective, their thinking goes, but that society simply isn't capable yet of giving them the accommodations they need. In practice, though, many pro-neurodiversity families take a more nuanced stance on therapy and treatment than heated message-board debates might suggest. Safeguarding a child's dignity and teaching him to navigate a neurotypical world, they reason, don't have to be mutually exclusive. "Michelangelo has had a form of ABA three times a week," Commandatore says, "but it is so loose and we control and guide it. We just say, 'Look, we don't stop any stimming behavior.' But that doesn't mean you let him do whatever he wants. If he's stimming and hurting something, you have to stop that. You have to realize what is important and what isn't." 18

Arriving at such realizations is easier said than done. While the autistic culture movement may come off as dogmatic at times, Commandatore says the question of how to raise autistic kids in the spirit of neurodiversity has no clear-cut answer. Her child-rearing strategies don't radiate from a single ideological core—they're more cobbled-together, day-by-day solutions to various issues that crop up. Instead of trying to train her son out of his personality quirks, 19 such as strong reactions to loud and sudden noises, she says, "We've given him headphones that he can use in public, these big 1970s speaker headphones. If he starts to panic, he asks for his headphones and we give them to him." She and her husband have also taught Michelangelo how to do deep-breathing exercises whenever he finds himself in a stressful situation, as he did this winter when his first-grade class began preparations for a holiday singing performance. "He was nervous. He said, 'Mama, I don't want to sing.'"

20 Rather than making her son practice the songs over and over until they became rote, as some therapists might recommend, Commandatore decided to give him a choice. "I said, 'Look, if you don't want to try this, you don't have to. I just want you to go up there and stand with your friends, and remember that Mama and Papa love you and we will be here for you.'" Though Michelangelo was skeptical, he agreed to give it a shot. When it came time for his moment in the limelight, he closed his eyes and took a deep breath. A smile slowly spread across his face as he burst into song.

Meanings and Values

1. Which paragraphs outline the issue addressed in this essay? State it in your own words.

2a. With which person in the essay does the writer seem to agree most fully? Please support your answer with specific evidence from the text.

b. State in your own words the thesis or argumentative proposition endorsed by the person you identified in answering *a*, above. (See "Guide to Terms": *Thesis*.)

3. State any objections to the argumentative proposition that the writer presents in this essay.

Argumentative Techniques

1a. What perspective on the issue does the writer present in Paragraphs 1–5?

b. Why do you think the writer chose to begin this way?

2. Paragraphs 6–12 look at other approaches to autism and argue why they are wrong or inappropriate. Which paragraphs provide summaries? Which provide arguments against? Which provide both?

3. In what ways does the title of the essay attract readers' attention? In what ways does it summarize the argumentative proposition?

Diction and Vocabulary

1. Describe how the writer uses diction to make Dana Commandatore and her stand on the issue seem sensible and sympathetic?
2. If you do not know the meaning of some of the terms used in the essay, look them up in a dictionary.

Read to Write

1. **Collaborating:** Working in a group, create a list of the qualities you think most people associate with autism (or alcoholism, schizophrenia, or some other named condition). Then make a note of how the lists of people in the group might differ based on their experience or knowledge.
2. **Considering Audience:** Sometimes readers need to learn a good deal more about an issue before they can form an opinion or agree with an argumentative proposition. Choose two important issues, and write out in brief form what you think most readers will need to learn about each before they can form an opinion or agree with an argumentative proposition.
3. **Developing an Essay:** Using Svoboda's approach, report on an issue in such a way that the people whose ideas, words, and experiences you report help convince readers to share their perspective.

(Note: Suggestions for topics requiring development by argument are on pp. 533–534 at the end of this chapter.)

ARGUMENT THROUGH DEFINITION

BARBARA LAWRENCE

BARBARA LAWRENCE was born in Hanover, New Hampshire. After receiving a B.A. in French literature from Connecticut College, she worked as an editor on *McCall's, Redbook, Harper's Bazaar,* and the *New Yorker.* During this period she also took an M.A. in philosophy from New York University. Currently a professor of humanities at the State University of New York's College at Old Westbury, Lawrence has published criticism, poetry, and fiction in *Choice, Commonweal, Columbia Poetry,* the *New York Times,* and the *New Yorker.*

Four-Letter Words Can Hurt You

"Four-Letter Words Can Hurt You" first appeared in the *New York Times* and was later published in *Redbook.* In arguing against the "earthy, gut-honest" language often preferred by her students, Lawrence also provides a thoughtful, even scholarly, extended definition of *obscenity* itself. To accomplish her purpose, the author makes use of several other patterns as well.

Why should any words be called obscene? Don't they all describe natural human functions? Am I trying to tell them, my students demand, that the "strong, earthy, gut-honest"—or, if they are fans of Norman Mailer, the "rich, liberating, existential"—language they use to describe sexual activity isn't preferable to "phony-sounding, middle-class words like 'intercourse' and 'copulate'"? "Cop You Late!" they say with fancy inflections and gagging grimaces. "Now, what is *that* supposed to mean?" 1

Well, what is it supposed to mean? And why indeed should one group of words describing human functions and human organs be acceptable in ordinary conversation and another, describing presumably the same organs and functions, be tabooed—so much so, in fact, that some of these words still cannot appear in print in many parts of the English-speaking world? 2

The argument that these taboos exist only because of "sexual hangups" (middle-class, middle-age, feminist), or even that they are a result of class oppression (the contempt of the Norman conquerors for the language of their Anglo-Saxon serfs), ignores a much more likely explanation, it seems to me, and that is the sources and functions of the words themselves. 3

The best known of the tabooed sexual words, for example, comes from the German *ficken,* meaning "to strike"; combined, according to Partridge's etymological dictionary *Origins,* with the Latin sexual verb *futuere:* associated in turn with the Latin *fustis,* "a staff or cudgel"; the Celtic *buc,* "a point, hence to pierce"; the Irish *bot,* "the male member"; the Latin *battuere,* "to beat"; the Gaelic *batair,* "a cudgeller"; the Early Irish *bualaim,* "I strike"; and so forth. It is one of what etymologists sometimes called "the sadistic group of words for the man's part in copulation." 4

The brutality of this word, then, and its equivalents ("screw," "bang," etc.) is not an illusion of the middle class or a crotchet of Women's Liberation. In their origins and imagery these words carry undeniably painful, if not sadistic, implications, the object of which is almost always female. Consider, for example, what a "screw" actually does to the wood it penetrates; what a painful, even mutilating, activity this kind of analogy suggests. "Screw" is particularly interesting in this context, since the noun, according to Partridge, comes from words meaning "groove," "nut," "ditch," "breeding sow," "scrofula" and "swelling," while the verb, besides its explicit imagery, has antecedent associations to "write on," "scratch," "scarify," and so forth—a revealing fusion of a mechanical or painful action with an obviously denigrated object. 5

Not all obscene words, of course, are as implicitly sadistic or denigrating to women as these, but all that I know seem to serve a similar purpose: to reduce the human organism (especially the female organism) and human functions (especially sexual and procreative) to their least organic, most mechanical dimension; to substitute a trivializing or deforming resemblance for the complex human reality of what is being described. 6

Tabooed male descriptives, when they are not openly denigrating to women, often serve to divorce a male organ or function from any significant interaction with the female. Take the word "*testes,*" for example, suggesting "witnesses" (from the Latin *testis*) to the sexual and procreative strengths of the male organ; and the obscene counterpart of this word, which suggests little more than a mechanical shape. Or compare almost any of the "rich," "liberating" sexual verbs, so fashionable today among male writers, with that much-derived Latin word "copulate" ("to bind or join together") or even that Anglo-Saxon phrase (which seems to have had no trouble surviving the Norman Conquest) "make love." 7

How arrogantly self-involved the tabooed words seem in comparison to either of the other terms, and how contemptuous of the 8 female partner. Understandably so, of course, if she is only a "skirt," a "broad," a "chick," a "pussycat" or a "piece." If she is, in other words no more than her skirt, or what her skirt conceals; no more than a breeder, or the broadest part of her; no more than a piece of a human being or a "piece of tail."

The most severely tabooed of all the female descriptives, incidentally, are those like a "piece of tail," which suggests (either explicitly or through antecedents) that there is no significant difference between the female channel through which we are all conceived and born and the anal outlet common to both sexes—a distinction that pornographers have always enjoyed obscuring. 9

This effort to deny women their biological identity, their individuality, their humanness, is such an important aspect of obscene language that one can only marvel at how seldom, in an era preoccupied with definitions of obscenity, this fact is brought to our attention. One problem, of course, is that many of the people in the best position to do this (critics, teachers, writers) are so reluctant today to admit that they are angered or shocked by obscenity. Bored, maybe, unimpressed, aesthetically displeased, but—no matter how brutal or denigrating the material—never angered, never shocked. 10

And yet how eloquently angered, how piously shocked many of these same people become if denigrating language is used about any minority group other than women; if the obscenities are racial or ethnic, that is, rather than sexual. Words like "coon," "kike," "spic," "wop," after all, deform identity, deny individuality and humanness in almost exactly the same way that sexual vulgarisms and obscenities do. 11

No one that I know, least of all my students, would fail to question the values of a society whose literature and entertainment rested heavily on racial or ethnic pejoratives. Are the values of a society whose literature and entertainment rest as heavily as ours on sexual pejoratives any less questionable? 12

Meanings and Values

1. Explain the meaning of *irony* by use of at least one illustration from the latter part of this essay. (See "Guide to Terms": *Irony.*)
2. Inasmuch as the selection itself includes many of the so-called "strong, earthy, gut-honest" words, could anyone logically call it obscene?

Why, or why not? To what extent, if at all, does the author's point of view help determine your answer? (Guide: *Point of View.*)

3. Compose, in your own words, a compact statement of Lawrence's thesis. (Guide: *Thesis.*) Are all parts of the essay completely relevant to this thesis? Justify your answer.
4. Evaluate this composition by use of our three-question system. (Guide: *Evaluation.*)

Argumentative Techniques

1. What is the purpose of this essay? (Guide: *Purpose.*)
2. What objection to her opinion does the author refute in Paragraph 3, and how does she refute it? (Guide: *Refutation.*) Where else in the essay does she refute opposing arguments?
3. Are the evidence and supporting arguments in this essay arranged in a refutation-proof pattern? If not, describe the arrangement of the essay.
4. Which of the methods "peculiar to definition alone" (see the introduction to Chapter 9) does the author employ in developing this essay? What other patterns of exposition does she also use?
5. Which of the standard techniques of introduction are used? (Guide: *Introductions.*) Which methods are used to close the essay? (Guide: *Closing.*)

Diction and Vocabulary

1. How, if at all, is this discussion of words related to *connotation?* (Guide: *Connotation/Denotation.*) To what extent would connotations in this matter depend on the setting and circumstances in which the words are used? Cite illustrations to clarify your answer.
2. In view of the fact that the author uses frankly many of the "gut-honest" words, why do you suppose she plainly avoids others, such as in Paragraphs 4 and 7?
3. The author says that a "kind of analogy" is suggested by some of the words discussed (Par. 5). If you have studied Chapter 6 of this book, does her use of the term *analogy* seem in conflict with what you believed it to mean? Explain.
4. Study the author's uses of the following words, consulting the dictionary as needed: *existential, grimaces* (Par. 1); *etymological, cudgel* (4); *sadistic* (4–6); *crotchet, scrofula, explicit, antecedent, scarify* (5); *denigrated* (5–7, 10–11); *aesthetically* (10); *pejoratives* (12).

Read to Write

1. **Collaborating:** Why do people use obscene language? Are these reasons satisfactory enough to keep from stigmatizing it or considering it impolite? Have our views of obscene language undergone any

recent changes? Should we discourage the use of obscene language in more social situations than we currently do? Working in a group, continue this list of questions until you have identified several possible topics for an essay. Words characterizing ethnic groups are likely to get strong responses from readers.

2. **Considering Audience:** Does the author make a justifiable comparison between obscene words and ethnic pejoratives? Using illustrations for specificity, carry the comparison further to show why it is sound, or explain why you consider it a weak comparison.
3. **Developing an Essay:** Following Lawrence's lead, discuss some other closely related group of terms and its significance, and suggest ways we should alter the way we use these terms.

(NOTE: Suggestions for topics requiring development by ARGUMENT are on pp. 533–534 at the end of this chapter.)

ARGUMENT THROUGH NARRATIVE

SARAH MIN

SARAH MIN works at *Glamour* magazine.

Language Lessons

Issues of bilingualism and bilingual education along with proposals for "English Only" in government and schools have drawn much interest over the past decade. Sarah Min takes a somewhat different, and personal, approach to bilingualism, arguing for its importance through her own story.

Even though I could understand only snippets of their conversation, I comprehended enough to know that the manicurists at the nail salon were talking about me. 1

What a shame! Another Korean who cannot speak the language, the woman filing my fingernails said to her colleague, both of them shaking their heads in disapproval. Her remark hit me, and I stumbled for the right words to defend myself. 2

The fact is, I traded my own Korean voice to give my parents their English ones: My mom and dad came to this country 27 years ago with an English vocabulary dominated by brand names like Tropicana and Samsonite. But they were determined to master the language of their new home. When I was in grade school, my dad read my English textbooks and asked me to give him the same lessons I had learned that day. On long car trips, my parents spent the confined hours in our Impala station wagon practicing their pronunciation aloud. My brother and I, captive tutors, led them in oral exercises, repeating the difficult distinction between *ear* and *year, war* and *wore.* 3

As my parents' fluency increased, their use of Korean dwindled. Though they spoke to each other in their native tongue, with my brother and me they used only one language: English. They didn't want us to speak Korean, they said, because they didn't want even a trace of an accent to infect our American-style speech. 4

Still, I absorbed bits and pieces of Korean, important phrases like "Oh-mo-mo" and "Whey-goo-deh?"—the equivalent of "Oh no!" and "What's your problem?"—subtleties that can't be precisely 5

---

translated but are understood as readily as "oy vey" or "cool." In private, I'd practice the sound effects—the gasps and clucks that are a part of the Korean language.

In public, though, I was reluctant to speak. My words sounded clunky, choppy, unlike the rhythmic cadences of my mother's voice. Once when I attempted conversation with a Korean-speaking woman in my neighborhood, my efforts were clearly unimpressive: She snickered at my accent and answered me in English. By the time I was in college, I had stopped trying to speak Korean, a decision only I noticed. No one expected me to speak the language anyway. 6

Yet I always felt that a part of me had been silenced. As I got older and moved to a city where I met more Koreans, I began to feel as the women in the nail salon did: That those of us who didn't speak Korean had something to be ashamed of, that we were distancing ourselves from our cultural heritage. Language, after all, involves much more than the ability to communicate. It conveys a desire to understand and participate in a culture, to make it one's own. Could I ever fully understand and appreciate my heritage if I couldn't speak the language of my ancestors? 7

So I registered for a course in Korean at an adult education school. I expected my classmates to be Americans who were going abroad, but I discovered most of the students had come for the same reason that I had: to find their Korean voices. 8

To my surprise, I picked up the language quickly. Even though my vocabulary was limited and my grammar was rough, I realized I knew quite a bit, as if the Korean words had been lurking somewhere in a quiet corner of my brain. The teacher taught phrases that sounded familiar and came to me effortlessly; I practiced the new tongue placements and inflections to hide my American accent. The first time I called my parents and said, in flawless Korean, "Hello, we haven't spoken in such a long time," I was 24 years old, but they reacted as proudly as if I were a toddler who had just uttered her first words. And when I walked into a Korean restaurant and casually greeted the waiter, who responded in Korean that I could sit anywhere I liked, I knew he took me for the genuine article. 9

Now whenever I visit my parents, I ask them to speak Korean with me at least some of the time. Although I'm still struggling, still studying so I can become more fluent, I know enough now that my parents can tell me stories, jokes and proverbs that would otherwise have gotten garbled in the static of translation. Eagerly, I listen, laugh and nod in full understanding. 10

Being able to speak Korean has some surprising bonuses: In American restaurants, my dad and I figure the tip right in front of the waiter. And among Koreans, knowing the language forges an almost instant camaraderie. 11

That day at the nail salon, when I finally worked up the courage to respond to the manicurist, I spoke slowly, but confidently: *I understand you and yes, it is shameful that I can only speak a little.* 12

The young woman polishing my fingernails paused. She looked up at me and smiled, as if she were seeing me for the first time. And, for the first time, I too was seeing a new part of myself: a proud Korean American who could finally hear her own voice. 13

Meanings and Values

1. Min devotes much of Paragraphs 3 and 4 in her essay to a discussion of her parents' efforts to learn English and to encourage their children to speak English. Explain why her parents may have felt they needed to do this. As a young girl, how does Min react to her parents' effort?
2. What feelings inspired Min to take adult education courses in Korean (Par. 8)? Is she justified in her concerns about heritage? How important are these cultural issues in the contemporary America?

Argumentative Techniques

1. The anecdote in Min's introduction (Pars. 1 and 2) is readdressed in her conclusion. What element of surprise does she incorporate into this story? Does she convince her reader of the importance of her conversation with the manicurists?
2. Much of Min's argument is in the form of narrative. How effective is this technique? Why do you think she chose a first-person narrative for this topic?

Diction and Vocabulary

1. Are there any words in this essay with which you are unfamiliar? Why might Min have used a basic vocabulary for this piece? Who might her target audience include?
2. Min writes this as an autobiographical narrative. Point to specific uses of transitions, dialogue, and other techniques that help the narrative have a storylike quality.

READ TO WRITE

1. **Collaborating:** Working in a group, list the native languages of your ancestors. How many of you still speak that language? Discuss with your teammates the reasons why you feel that your family no longer speaks in the native tongue, or if your family still does, why the members have chosen to continue. Compare your reasons and look for underlying cultural connections regarding the maintenance of native tongues. Keeping in mind your group discussions, write an individual paper in a style similar to Min's discussing your use or lack of use of your family's native tongue. If your ancestry is of English-speaking people, write about a friend or someone you know who has had this issue arise in his or her family.
2. **Considering Audience:** Min says, "And among Koreans, knowing the language forges an almost instant camaraderie" (Par. 11). Would non-Korean readers identify with this statement? Does her point apply to others besides Koreans? Write a short analysis explaining your response.
3. **Developing an Essay:** Min's essay clearly encourages the maintaining of a native tongue, but not at the sacrifice of learning English when living in the United States. This is one facet of a debate on language. Research the question of whether or not the United States should have a unified language and the impact of maintaining a native tongue in some capacity. Consider the unifying qualities of language both inside and outside of the cultural boundaries. Write an argumentative essay employing multiple patterns of development in which you address the issue of either the adoption of a national language, the use of native languages in the household, or the acceptance of bilingualism or multilingualism in society.

(NOTE: Suggestions for essays requiring development by use of ARGUMENT follow.)

Writing Suggestions for Chapter 13

ARGUMENT

Choose one of the following topic areas, identify an issue (a conflict or problem) within it, and prepare an essay that tries to convince readers to share your opinion about the issue and to take any appropriate action. Use a variety of evidence in your essay, and choose any pattern of development you consider proper for the topic, for your thesis, and for the intended audience.

1. Gun control
2. The quality of education in American elementary and secondary schools
3. Treatment of critically ill newborn babies
4. Hunting
5. Euthanasia
6. Censorship in public schools and libraries
7. College athletics
8. The problem of toxic waste or a similar environmental problem
9. Careers versus family responsibilities
10. The separation of church and state
11. Law on the drinking age or on drunk driving
12. Evolution versus creationism
13. Medical ethics
14. Government spending on social programs
15. The quality of television programming
16. The impact of divorce
17. The effects of television viewing on children
18. Professional sports
19. Violence in service of an ideal or belief
20. Scholarship and student loan policies
21. Low pay for public service and the "helping" professions
22. Cheating in college courses
23. Drug and alcohol abuse
24. Product safety and reliability
25. Government economic or social policy

Collaborative Activities

As you prepare an essay on one of the given topics (1–25) or on some other topic, make a list of the evidence for your opinion. Share the list with one or more readers. Ask the reader to rank each piece of evidence for persuasiveness, using a scale of 1 (unpersuasive) to 5 (very persuasive).

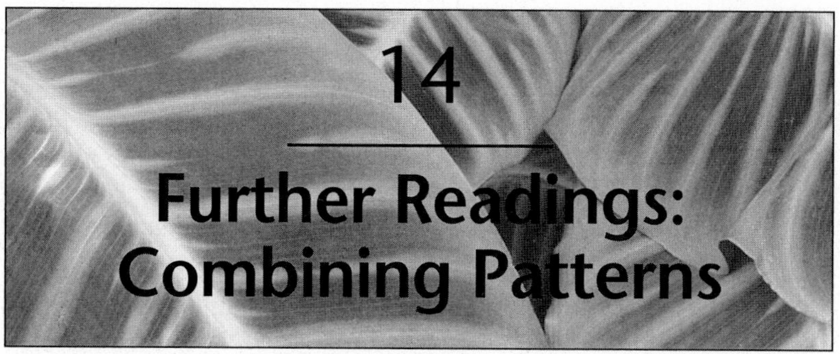

14

Further Readings: Combining Patterns

JASON KELLY

JASON KELLY'S articles that have appeared in a number of publications, including *The Atlanta Journal Constitution, The European, Forbes ASAP*, and the online magazine *PopPolitics*. He currently lives in Atlanta, Georgia.

The Great TV Debate

In "The Great TV Debate" (published by *PopPolitics* in 2001), Jason Kelly addresses a topic that is familiar to many parents: how much television is too much? Using persuasive logic, comparison, and cause-and-effect analysis, Kelly conveys a message about the importance of finding a middle ground while simultaneously expressing his own ambivalence about where the line should be drawn.

I worry about a lot of things related to my son. September 11 brought almost more than I could bear. Today, for instance, I'm worried that he's pushing other kids at his day care center. Alas, there are a few constant worries, including this one: Am I already letting him turn his brain to mush? 1

When I got this assignment, I set out to try and understand the latest salvos in the great TV debate. I'd planned to do a sensibly journalistic, fully objective treatment of both sides. Then I realized that, especially as a dad, that's nearly, if not totally, impossible. 2

My wife and I have operated under the notion that I'd ascribe to most people—we allow our son, Owen, age 2, to watch some television, though we worry about him watching too much. We'll give into the pressure a little too often, pushing in a Teletubbies or Elmo video when we need a mental break, or need to actually get something done. 3

It's worth confessing here that I like TV, and maybe slightly more than the average bear. I watch enough shows regularly to have strong opinions about, and feelings for, fake people: Carrie on *Sex and the City*, Jack on *Will and Grace*, Donna on *West Wing*. I do feel like I know them. I, of course, hide behind my occupation as a "writer," tricking myself (but not others, I'm afraid) into thinking that watching these shows is really work, as if talking about them in important terms—"Sorkin's gift for writing that crisp, banter-y dialogue makes these shows feel more like plays than movies"—will make them important, will turn them into high art. 4

And so, actually, I feel slightly ashamed of my own viewing habits. Why not include my son in my neuroses ("Paging Dr. Frasier Crane")? These overlapping guilts lead to a creeping sense of hypocrisy, whereby I deprive my son of watching *Clifford: The Big Red Dog* but, when he leaves the room, quickly switch over to *Today*, so I can see Katie banter with Matt about listening to the *Shrek* soundtrack in her minivan. At least Clifford's got a "big idea of the day"—usually something like "respect" or "sharing"—on at the end of every show. Katie and Matt just have Willard and his jelly jars every few days. 5

In the great American spirit of rationalization, I've convinced myself that my son—who goes to day care during the week—actually watches less TV than a kid who stays at home full-time with a parent or a nanny. I know that occasionally his teachers roll in the television and slip in a video, but it's certainly not every day. Owen has always been somewhat fickle about watching TV, and in this I see the tendencies that stay with you through adulthood. Sometimes, the dude just wants to chill out and watch the Teletubbies (or, in his lingo, simply "Tubbies"). Other times, he's far too busy, and actually walks over and turns it off in favor of reading a book, coloring or building Lego towers. 6

I spent hours on the Web sifting through searches on "Kids and TV," looking for guidance. While on the Cartoon Network site, I came across a link for "TV Parental Guidelines." That's the site for the classification system that puts the little box on the screen that says "TV-MA (mature audiences only)," for example. The guidelines, at least for me, have become more or less invisible; they're 7 pretty broad and based on the quite-flawed Motion Picture Association of America guidelines, which say it's okay for 13-year-olds to both see and hear the F-bomb.

The Fox Kids TV site was suitably frightening to me, with its animation and teasers—"It's the stinkiest Ripping Friends ever!!" The site for the PBS shows (for better or worse, the only shows we let Owen watch) was similarly predictable in its "We're really about education here" language. Drilling through the Teletubbies, I noted the repeated use of carefully chosen words like "safe," "friendly," and "stimulating." 8

After wading through the positive messages from the purveyors themselves, I found the Washington, D.C.-based TV-Turnoff Network, which appears to have a reputable staff and advisory board. I gave them a call, and they mailed me a packet of materials supporting a TV-free lifestyle, including the requisite bumper stickers. The one that made me chuckle was designed to mimic the warnings on cigarette boxes: "Surgeon General's Warning: Television Promotes Illiteracy." They also feature some startling statistics, like the fact that the average 2- to 17-year-old viewer watches nearly 20 hours of TV per week. And that 73 percent of American parents would like to limit their kids' TV-watching. 9

Writing this story forced the topic to the front of my mind, and as I chatted with friends and colleagues, even interview subjects for other stories, about various other topics, I often tried to sneak this one in. One friend told me that his kids watch about an hour of TV a month. It took me a full minute to stop saying "Wow." He and his wife both work and have had a full-time nanny since their now-7- and 9-year-old children were born. The nanny knows that no TV is the rule. "And the nanny's a TV junkie" in her off-hours, my friend tells me. 10

In an odd turn of events, two days later we go with another family on a Sunday outing, loading three adults and three kids comfortably into their family minivan, one of the new, decked-out Honda Odysseys. The high-end versions of these veritable cruise ships on wheels have a VCR and video screen installed; the player sits in the middle console up front, and the screen flips down from the ceiling just behind the front seats. Our hour-plus trip was nearly silent. We could've ridden for days it seemed, despite the fact that we had three sub-6-year-olds in the car. 11

Somewhere in the middle of these two extremes is where I fall, and, by the looks of it, so does a lot of America. Schools across the country embrace the idea of using TV as a learning tool and are 12 aided by groups like Cable in the Classroom and Channel One, which provide special programming. The latter is the much-ballyhooed 11-year-old network that broadcasts to roughly 12,000 American middle, junior, and high schools; the network claims those schools represent more than 8 million students and 400,000 educators. There is, however, a catch: Channel One also broadcasts commercials. So while the kids are learning more about, say, life in space, they're also being told to eat Mars bars.

More pointedly, many of the kids TV shows—led by the granddaddy of educational TV, *Sesame Street*—encourage kids to read. *Clifford the Big Red Dog*, we're told at the end of his PBS show, wants us to "be the best-read dog on the block." And in fact, Clifford was born as a book character himself, then migrated to PBS. *Teletubbies* and others took the reverse path. But they all stress the value of reading. My own son seems to have no problem reading and watching TV, often at the same time. It's a brand of multitasking I'm sure my wife and I have encouraged by example, as we talk on the phone, listen to the radio, cook dinner, and read a magazine, all in one fluid, continuous motion. 13

I'm starting to come to grips with the idea that this is just how it is, that we live in an information and media-drenched society. We can't stop it, as the wise man said, we can only hope to contain it. Then, as I'm putting all my thoughts together, I come across one more thing that makes me throw my hands up. 14

Neil Postman's *Amusing Ourselves to Death* is a book I read in college that paints a stark picture of what TV is doing to us and our children. He spends 163 pages undermining just about every idea set forth by the Cable in the Classrooms and PBS's of the world, namely that "educational television" is a contradiction in terms. While his data is old—the book was published in 1985—his arguments likely have more, not less, relevance. 15

And his voice, while somewhat histrionic, does echo in my ears: "Like the alphabet or the printing press, television has by its power to control the time, attention, and cognitive habits of our youth gained the power to control their education." 16

And so I end much like I began—pretty damn confused, with my finger poised uncertainly in front of the "play" button. 17

MARGARET ATWOOD

MARGARET ATWOOD was born in Ottawa, Ontario, in 1939. After attending college in Canada, she went to graduate school at Harvard University. She has had a distinguished career as a novelist, poet, and essayist, and is generally considered to be one of the central figures in contemporary Canadian literature and culture. Atwood's international reputation as a writer rests on her novels, including *The Edible Woman* (1960), *Surfacing* (1972), *Life Before Man* (1979), *Bodily Harm* (1982), *The Handmaid's Tale* (1986), *Cat's Eye* (1989), *The Robber Bride* (1993), *Alias Grace* (1996), *The Blind Assassin* (2000), and her short stories, including *Bluebeard's Egg and Other Stories* (1986) and *Good Bones* (1992), though she has written poetry, television plays, and children's books as well. Her essays were collected in the volume *Second Words* (1982) and have continued to appear in newspapers and magazines such as *Ms., Harper's, Globe and Mail, The Nation, Maclean's, Washington Post, Harvard Educational Review, The Humanist, The New Republic,* and *Architectural Digest.* As an essayist, Atwood frequently writes about issues in contemporary culture and society, including the nature of Canadian culture and relationships between Canada and the United States.

Pornography

In the following essay, Atwood addresses the question of pornography with a directness and originality that are characteristic of her work. This essay originally appeared in *Chatelaine Magazine,* a mass-circulation women's magazine. As you read the selection, consider how well it addresses both the concerns of its original audience and the concerns about pornography a somewhat wider audience might have. Note also how she makes use of definition and a number of other expository patterns.

When I was in Finland a few years ago for an international writers' conference, I had occasion to say a few paragraphs in public on the subject of pornography. The context was a discussion of political repression, and I was suggesting the possibility of a link between the two. The immediate result was that a male journalist took several large bites out of me. Prudery and pornography are two halves of the same coin, said he, and I was clearly a prude. What could you expect from an Anglo-Canadian? Afterward, a couple of pleasant Scandinavian men asked me what I had been so worked up about. All "pornography" means, they said, is graphic depictions of whores, and what was the harm in that? 1

Not until then did it strike me that the male journalist and I had two entirely different things in mind. By "pornography," he meant naked bodies and sex. I, on the other hand, had recently been doing the research for my novel *Bodily Harm,* and was still in a state of shock from some of the material I had seen, including the Ontario Board of Film Censors' "outtakes." By "pornography," I meant women getting their nipples snipped off with garden shears, having meat hooks stuck into their vaginas, being disemboweled; little girls being raped; men (yes, there are some men) being smashed to a pulp and forcibly sodomized. The cutting edge of pornography, as far as I could see, was no longer simple old copulation, hanging from the chandelier or otherwise: it was death, messy, explicit and highly sadistic. I explained this to the nice Scandinavian men. "Oh, but that's just the United States," they said. "Everyone knows they're sick." In their country, they said, violent "pornography" of that kind was not permitted on television or in movies; indeed, excessive violence of any kind was not permitted. They had drawn a clear line between erotica, which earlier studies had shown did not incite men to more aggressive and brutal behavior toward women, and violence, which later studies indicated did. 2

Some time after that I was in Saskatchewan, where, because of the scenes in *Bodily Harm,* I found myself on an open-line radio show answering questions about "pornography." Almost no one who phoned in was in favor of it, but again they weren't talking about the same stuff I was, because they hadn't seen it. Some of them were all set to stamp out bathing suits and negligees, and, if possible, any depictions of the female body whatsoever. God, it was implied, did not approve of female bodies, and sex of any kind, including that practiced by bumblebees, should be shoved back into the dark, where it belonged. I had more than a suspicion that *Lady Chatterley's Lover,* Margaret Laurence's *The Diviners,* and indeed most books by most serious modern authors would have ended up as confetti if left in the hands of these callers. 3

For me, these two experiences illustrate the two poles of the emotionally heated debate that is now thundering around this issue. They also underline the desirability and even the necessity of defining the terms. "Pornography" is now one of those catchalls, like "Marxism" and "feminism," that have become so broad they can mean almost anything, ranging from certain verses in the Bible, ads for skin lotion and sex tests for children to the contents of *Penthouse,* Naughty '90s postcards and films with titles containing the word *Nazi* that show vicious scenes of torture and killing. It's easy to say 4 that sensible people can tell the difference. Unfortunately, opinions on what constitutes a sensible person vary.

But even sensible people tend to lose their cool when they start 5
talking about this subject. They soon stop talking and start yelling, and the name-calling begins. Those in favor of censorship (which may include groups not noticeably in agreement on other issues, such as some feminists and religious fundamentalists) accuse the others of exploiting women through the use of degrading images, contributing to the corruption of children, and adding to the general climate of violence and threat in which both women and children live in this society; or, though they may not give much of a hoot about actual women and children, they invoke moral standards and God's supposed aversion to "filth," "smut" and deviated *perversion,* which may mean ankles.

The camp in favor of total "freedom of expression" often comes 6
out howling as loud as the Romans would have if told they could no longer have innocent fun watching the lions eat up Christians. It too may include segments of the population who are not natural bedfellows: those who proclaim their God-given right to freedom, including the freedom to tote guns, drive when drunk, drool over chicken porn and get off on videotapes of women being raped and beaten, may be waving the same anticensorship banner as responsible liberals who fear the return of Mrs. Grundy, or gay groups for whom sexual emancipation involves the concept of "sexual theater." *Whatever turns you on* is a handy motto, as is *A man's home is his castle* (and if it includes a dungeon with beautiful maidens strung up in chains and bleeding from every pore, that's his business).

Meanwhile, theoreticians theorize and speculators speculate. Is 7
today's pornography yet another indication of the hatred of the body, the deep mind-body split, which is supposed to pervade Western Christian society? Is it a backlash against the women's movement by men who are threatened by uppity female behavior in real life, so like to fantasize about women done up like outsize parcels, being turned into hamburger, kneeling at their feet in slave-like adoration or sucking off guns? Is it a sign of collective impotence, of a generation of men who can't relate to real women at all but have to make do with bits of celluloid and paper? Is the current flood just a result of smart marketing and aggressive promotion by the money men in what has now become a multibillion-dollar industry? If they were selling movies about men getting their testicles stuck full of knitting needles by women with swastikas on their sleeves, would they do as well, or is this penchant somehow peculiarly male? If so, why? Is pornography

a power trip rather than a sex one? Some say that those ropes, chains, muzzles and other restraining devices are an argument for the immense power female sexuality still wields in the male imagination: you don't put these things on dogs unless you're afraid of them. Others, more literary, wonder about the shift from the 19th-century Magic Woman or Femme Fatale image to the lollipop-licker, airhead or turkey-carcass treatment of women in porn today. The proporners don't care much about theory; they merely demand product. The antiporners don't care about it in the final analysis either; there's dirt on the street, and they want it cleaned up, now.

It seems to me that this conversation, with its *You're-a-prude/ You're-a-pervert* dialectic, will never get anywhere as long as we continue to think of this material as just "entertainment." Possibly we're deluded by the packaging, the format: magazine, book, movie, theatrical presentation. We're used to thinking of these things as part of the "entertainment industry," and we're used to thinking of ourselves as free adult people who ought to be able to see any kind of "entertainment" we want to. That was what the First Choice pay-TV debate was all about. After all, it's only entertainment, right? Entertainment means fun, and only a killjoy would be antifun. What's the harm? 8

This is obviously the central question: *What's the harm?* If there isn't any real harm to any real people, then the antiporners can tsk-tsk and/or throw up as much as they like, but they can't rightfully expect more legal controls or sanctions. However, the no-harm position is far from being proven. 9

(For instance, there's a clear-cut case for banning—as the federal government has proposed—movies, photos and videos that depict children engaging in sex with adults: real children are used to make the movies, and hardly anybody thinks this is ethical. The possibilities for coercion are too great.) 10

To shift the viewpoint, I'd like to suggest three other models for looking at "pornography"—and here I mean the violent kind. 11

Those who find the idea of regulating pornographic materials repugnant because they think it's Fascist or Communist or otherwise not in accordance with the principles of an open democratic society should consider that Canada has made it illegal to disseminate material that may lead to hatred toward any group because of race or religion. I suggest that if pornography of the violent kind depicted these acts being done predominantly to Chinese, to blacks, to Catholics, it would be off the market immediately, under the present laws. Why is hate literature illegal? Because whoever made the law 12 thought that such material might incite real people to do real awful things to other real people. The human brain is to a certain extent a computer: garbage in, garbage out. We only hear about the extreme cases (like that of American multimurderer Ted Bundy) in which pornography has contributed to the death and/or mutilation of women and/or men. Although pornography is not the only factor involved in the creation of such deviance, it certainly has upped the ante by suggesting both a variety of techniques and the social acceptability of such actions. Nobody knows yet what effect this stuff is having on the less psychotic.

Studies have shown that a large part of the market for all kinds of porn, soft and hard, is drawn from the 16-to-21-year-old population of young men. Boys used to learn about sex on the street, or (in Italy, according to Fellini movies) from friendly whores, or, in more genteel surroundings, from girls, their parents, or, once upon a time, in school, more or less. Now porn has been added, and sex education in the schools is rapidly being phased out. The buck has been passed, and boys are being taught that all women secretly like to be raped and that real men get high on scooping out women's digestive tracts. 13

Boys learn their concept of masculinity from other men: is this what most men want them to be learning? If word gets around that rapists are "normal" and even admirable men, will boys feel that in order to be normal, admirable and masculine they will have to be rapists? Human beings are enormously flexible, and how they turn out depends a lot on how they're educated, by the society in which they're immersed as well as by their teachers. In a society that advertises and glorifies rape or even implicitly condones it, more women get raped. It becomes socially acceptable. And at a time when men and the traditional male role have taken a lot of flak and men are confused and casting around for an acceptable way of being male (and, in some cases, not getting much comfort from women on that score), this must be at times a pleasing thought. 14

It would be naïve to think of violent pornography as just harmless entertainment. It's also an educational tool and a powerful propaganda device. What happens when boy educated on porn meets girl brought up on Harlequin romances? The clash of expectations can be heard around the block. She wants him to get down on his knees with a ring, he wants her to get down on all fours with a ring in her nose. Can this marriage be saved? 15

Pornography has certain things in common with such addictive substances as alcohol and drugs: for some, though by no means for 16 all, it induces chemical changes in the body, which the user finds exciting and pleasurable. It also appears to attract a "hard core" of habitual users and a penumbra of those who use it occasionally but aren't dependent on it in any way. There are also significant numbers of men who aren't much interested in it, not because they're undersexed but because real life is satisfying their needs, which may not require as many appliances as those of users.

For the "hard core," pornography may function as alcohol does 17
for the alcoholic: tolerance develops, and a little is no longer enough. This may account for the short viewing time and fast turnover in porn theaters. Mary Brown, chairwoman of the Ontario Board of Film Censors, estimates that for every one mainstream movie requesting entrance to Ontario, there is one porno flick. Not only the quantity consumed but the quality of explicitness must escalate, which may account for the growing violence: once the big deal was breasts, then it was genitals, then copulation, then that was no longer enough and the hard users had to have more. The ultimate kick is death, and after that, as the Marquis de Sade so boringly demonstrated, multiple death.

The existence of alcoholism has not led us to ban social drink- 18
ing. On the other hand, we do have laws about drinking and driving, excessive drunkenness and other abuses of alcohol that may result in injury or death to others.

This leads us back to the key question: what's the harm? 19
Nobody knows, but this society should find out fast, before the saturation point is reached. The Scandinavian studies that showed a connection between depictions of sexual violence and increased impulse toward it on the part of male viewers would be a starting point, but many more questions remain to be raised as well as answered. What, for instance, is the crucial difference between men who are users and men who are not? Does using affect a man's relationship with actual women, and, if so, adversely? Is there a clear line between erotica and violent pornography, or are they on an escalating continuum? Is this a "men versus women" issue, with all men secretly siding with the proporners and all women secretly siding against? (I think not; there *are* lots of men who don't think that running their true love through the Cuisinart is the best way they can think of to spend a Saturday night, and they're just as nauseated by films of someone else doing it as women are.) Is pornography merely an expression of the sexual confusion of this age or an active contributor to it?

Nobody wants to go back to the age of official repression, when even piano legs were referred to as "limbs" and had to wear pantaloons to be decent. Neither do we want to end up in George Orwell's *1984,* in which pornography is turned out by the State to keep the proles in a state of torpor, sex itself is considered dirty and the approved practice it only for reproduction. But Rome under the emperors isn't such a good model either. 20

If all men and women respected each other, if sex were considered joyful and life-enhancing instead of a wallow in germ-filled glop, if everyone were in love all the time, if, in other words, many people's lives were more satisfactory for them than they appear to be now, pornography might just go away on its own. But since this is obviously not happening, we as a society are going to have to make some informed and responsible decisions about how to deal with it. 21

LESLIE MARMON SILKO

LESLIE MARMON SILKO was born in 1948 in Albuquerque, New Mexico. She was raised on the Laguna Pueblo Reservation and attended the University of New Mexico (B.A., 1969). Formerly on the English faculty of the University of Arizona, Silko now focuses full-time on her writing, for which she has received many awards, including a MacArthur Foundation grant. Much of Silko's writing draws on Native American traditions and myths and on the interactions of Native American cultures and perspectives with the contemporary world. Her novels include the much-praised *Ceremony* (1977), *Almanac of the Dead* (1991), and *Gardens in the Dunes* (1999). She has also published a volume of poetry, *Laguna Woman* (1974); a collection of short stories, *Storyteller* (1981); an autobiography, *Sacred Water* (1993); and a collection of essays, *Yellow Woman and a Beauty of the Spirit* (1996).

Yellow Woman and a Beauty of the Spirit

"Yellow Woman and a Beauty of the Spirit" comes from the book with the same title. In this essay, Silko recalls her differences in appearance from other Laguna Pueblo children, the result of her mixed ancestry, and uses this memory as a springboard to an explanation of the traditional Pueblo disregard of physical appearance and emphasis instead on individual qualities of spirit as the basis of true beauty. She also discusses the Pueblo disregard of fixed gender, work, and family roles, but a correspondingly strong emphasis is on the quality of relationships among people, animals, and the land. As in much of her work, Silko's perspective lies at the center of the intersection between cultures.

From the time I was a small child, I was aware that I was different. I looked different from my playmates. My two sisters looked different too. We didn't look quite like the other Laguna Pueblo children, but we didn't look quite white either. In the 1880s, my great-grandfather had followed his older brother west from Ohio to the New Mexico Territory to survey the land for the U.S. government. The two Marmon brothers came to the Laguna Pueblo reservation because they had an Ohio cousin who already lived there. The Ohio cousin was involved in sending Indian children thousands of miles away from their families to the War Department's big Indian boarding school in Carlisle, Pennsylvania. Both brothers married full-blood Laguna Pueblo women. My great-grandfather 1 had first married my great-grandmother's older sister, but she died in childbirth and left two small children. My great-grandmother was fifteen or twenty years younger than my great-grandfather. She had attended Carlisle Indian School and spoke and wrote English beautifully.

I called her Grandma A'mooh because that's what I heard her say whenever she saw me. *A'mooh* means "granddaughter" in the Laguna language. I remember this word because her love and her acceptance of me as a small child were so important. I had sensed immediately that something about my appearance was not acceptable to some people, white and Indian. But I did not see any signs of that strain or anxiety in the face of my beloved Grandma A'mooh. 2

Younger people, people my parents' age, seemed to look at the world in a more modern way. The modern way included racism. My physical appearance seemed not to matter to the old-time people. They looked at the world very differently; a person's appearance and possessions did not matter nearly as much as a person's behavior. For them, a person's value lies in how that person interacts with other people, how that person behaves toward the animals and the earth. That is what matters most to the old-time people. The Pueblo people believed this long before the Puritans arrived with their notions of sin and damnation, and racism. The old-time beliefs persist today; thus I will refer to the old-time people in the present tense as well as the past. Many worlds may coexist here. 3

I spent a great deal of time with my great-grandmother. Her house was next to our house, and I used to wake up at dawn, hours before my parents or younger sisters, and I'd go wait on the porch swing or on the back steps by her kitchen door. She got up at dawn, but she was more than eighty years old, so she needed a little while to get dressed and to get the fire going in the cookstove. I had been carefully instructed by my parents not to bother her and to behave, and to try to help her any way I could. I always loved the early mornings when the air was so cool with a hint of rain smell in the breeze. In the dry New Mexico air, the least hint of dampness smells sweet. 4

My great-grandmother's yard was planted with lilac bushes and iris; there were four o'clocks, cosmos, morning glories, and hollyhocks, and old-fashioned rosebushes that I helped her water. If the garden hose got stuck on one of the big rocks that lined the path in the yard, I ran and pulled it free. That's what I came to do early every morning: to help Grandma water the plants before the heat of the day arrived. 5

Grandma A'mooh would tell about the old days, family stories about relatives who had been killed by Apache raiders who stole the sheep our relatives had been herding near Swahnee. Sometimes she read Bible stories that we kids liked because of the illustrations of Jonah in the mouth of a whale and Daniel surrounded by lions. Grandma A'mooh would send me home when she took her nap, but when the sun got low and the afternoon began to cool off, I would be back on the porch swing, waiting for her to come out to water the plants and to haul in firewood for the evening. When Grandma was eighty-five, she still chopped her own kindling. She used to let me carry in the coal bucket for her, but she would not allow me to use the ax. I carried armloads of kindling too, and I learned to be proud of my strength. 6

I was allowed to listen quietly when Aunt Susie or Aunt Alice came to visit Grandma. When I got old enough to cross the road alone, I went and visited them almost daily. They were vigorous women who valued books and writing. They were usually busy chopping wood or cooking but never hesitated to take time to answer my questions. Best of all they told me the *hummah-hah* stories, about an earlier time when animals and humans shared a common language. In the old days, the Pueblo people had educated their children in this manner; adults took time out to talk to and teach young people. Everyone was a teacher, and every activity had the potential to teach the child. 7

But as soon as I started kindergarten at the Bureau of Indian Affairs day school, I began to learn more about the differences between the Laguna Pueblo world and the outside world. It was at school that I learned just how different I looked from my classmates. Sometimes tourists driving past on Route 66 would stop by Laguna Day School at recess time to take photographs of us kids. One day, when I was in the first grade, we all crowded around the smiling white tourists, who peered at our faces. We all wanted to be in the picture because afterward the tourists sometimes gave us each a penny. Just as we were all posed and ready to have our picture taken, the tourist man looked at me. "Not you," he said and motioned for me to step away from my classmates. I felt so embarrassed that I wanted to disappear. My classmates were puzzled by the tourists' behavior, but I knew the tourists didn't want me in their snapshot because I looked different, because I was part white. 8

In the view of the old-time people, we are all sisters and brothers because the Mother Creator made all of us—all colors and all sizes. We are sisters and brothers, clanspeople of all the living 9 beings around us. The plants, the birds, fish, clouds, water, even the clay—they all are related to us. The old-time people believe that all things, even rocks and water, have spirit and being. They understood that all things want only to continue being as they are; they need only to be left as they are. Thus the old folks used to tell us kids not to disturb the earth unnecessarily. All things as they were created exist already in harmony with one another as long as we do not disturb them.

As the old story tells us, Tse'itsi'nako, Thought Woman, the 10
Spider, thought of her three sisters, and as she thought of them, they came into being. Together with Thought Woman, they thought of the sun and the stars and the moon. The Mother Creators imagined the earth and the oceans, the animals and the people, and the *ka'tsina* spirits that reside in the mountains. The Mother Creators imagined all the plants that flower and the trees that bear fruit. As Thought Woman and her sisters thought of it, the whole universe came into being. In this universe, there is no absolute good or absolute bad; they are only balances and harmonies that ebb and flow. Some years the desert receives abundant rain, other years there is too little rain, and sometimes there is so much rain that floods cause destruction. But rain itself is neither innocent nor guilty. The rain is simply itself.

My great-grandmother was dark and handsome. Her expres- 11
sion in photographs is one of confidence and strength. I do not know if white people then or now would consider her beautiful. I do not know if the old-time Laguna Pueblo people considered her beautiful or if the old-time people even thought in those terms. To the Pueblo way of thinking, the act of comparing one living being with another was silly, because each being or thing is unique and therefore incomparably valuable because it is the only one of its kind. The old-time people thought it was crazy to attach such importance to a person's appearance. I understood very early that there were two distinct ways of interpreting the world. There was the white people's way and there was the Laguna way. In the Laguna way, it was bad manners to make comparisons that might hurt another person's feelings.

In everyday Pueblo life, not much attention was paid to one's 12
physical appearance or clothing. Ceremonial clothing was quite elaborate but was used only for the sacred dances. The traditional Pueblo societies were communal and strictly egalitarian, which means that no matter how well or how poorly one might have dressed, there was no social ladder to fall from. All food and other resources were strictly shared so that no one person or group had

more than another. I mention social status because it seems to me that most of the definitions of beauty in contemporary Western culture are really codes for determining social status. People no longer hide their face-lifts and they discuss their liposuctions because the point of the procedures isn't just cosmetic, it is social. It says to the world, "I have enough spare cash that I can afford surgery for cosmetic purposes."

In the old-time Pueblo world, beauty was manifested in behavior and in one's relationships with other living beings. Beauty was as much a feeling of harmony as it was a visual, aural, or sensual effect. The whole person had to be beautiful, not just the face or the body; faces and bodies could not be separated from hearts and souls. Health was foremost in achieving this sense of well-being and harmony; in the old-time Pueblo world, a person who did not look healthy inspired feelings of worry and anxiety, not feelings of well-being. A healthy person, of course, is in harmony with the world around her; she is at peace with herself too. Thus an unhappy person or spiteful person would not be considered beautiful. 13

In the old days, strong, sturdy women were most admired. One of my most vivid preschool memories is of the crew of Laguna women, in their forties and fifties, who came to cover our house with adobe plaster. They handled the ladders with great ease, and while two women ground the adobe mud on stones and added straw, another woman loaded the hod with mud and passed it up to the two women on ladders, who were smoothing the plaster on the wall with their hands. Since women owned the houses, they did the plastering. At Laguna, men did the basket making and the weaving of fine textiles; men helped a great deal with the child care too. Because the Creator is female, there is no stigma on being female; gender is not used to control behavior. No job was a man's job or a woman's job; the most able person did the work. 14

My Grandma Lily had been a Ford Model A mechanic when she was a teenager. I remember when I was young, she was always fixing broken lamps and appliances. She was small and wiry, but she could lift her weight in rolled roofing or boxes of nails. When she was seventy-five, she was still repairing washing machines in my uncle's coin-operated laundry. 15

The old-time people paid no attention to birthdays. When a person was ready to do something, she did it. When she no longer was able, she stopped. Thus the traditional Pueblo people did not worry about aging or about looking old because there were no social boundaries drawn by the passage of years. It was not remarkable for 16 young men to marry women as old as their mothers. I never heard anyone talk about "women's work" until after I left Laguna for college. Work was there to be done by any able-bodied person who wanted to do it. At the same time, in the old-time Pueblo world, identity was acknowledged to be always in a flux; in the old stories, one minute Spider Woman is a little spider under a yucca plant, and the next instant she is a sprightly grandmother walking down the road.

When I was growing up, there was a young man from a nearby 17
village who wore nail polish and women's blouses and permed his hair. People paid little attention to his appearance; he was always part of a group of other young men from his village. No one ever made fun of him. Pueblo communities were and still are very interdependent, but they also have to be tolerant of individual eccentricities because survival of the group means everyone has to cooperate.

In the old Pueblo world, differences were celebrated as signs of 18
the Mother Creator's grace. Persons born with exceptional physical or sexual differences were highly respected and honored because their physical differences gave them special positions as mediators between this world and the spirit world. The great Navajo medicine man of the 1920s, the Crawler, had a hunchback and could not walk upright, but he was able to heal even the most difficult cases.

Before the arrival of Christian missionaries, a man could dress 19
as a woman and work with the women and even marry a man without any fanfare. Likewise, a woman was free to dress like a man, to hunt and go to war with the men, and to marry a woman. In the old Pueblo worldview, we are all a mixture of male and female, and this sexual identity is changing constantly. Sexual inhibition did not begin until the Christian missionaries arrived. For the old-time people, marriage was about teamwork and social relationships, not about sexual excitement. In the days before the Puritans came, marriage did not mean an end to sex with people other than your spouse. Women were just as likely as men to have a *si'ash,* or lover.

New life was so precious that pregnancy was always appropri- 20
ate, and pregnancy before marriage was celebrated as a good sign. Since the children belonged to the mother and her clan, and women owned and bequeathed the houses and farmland, the exact determination of paternity wasn't critical. Although fertility was prized, infertility was no problem because mothers with unplanned pregnancies gave their babies to childless couples within the clan in open adoption arrangements. Children called their mother's sisters "mother" as well, and a child became attached to a number of parent figures.

In the sacred kiva ceremonies, men mask and dress as women to pay homage and to be possessed by the female energies of the spirit beings. Because differences in physical appearance were so highly valued, surgery to change one's face and body to resemble a model's face and body would be unimaginable. To be different, to be unique was blessed and was best of all. 21

THE TRADITIONAL CLOTHING of Pueblo women emphasized a woman's sturdiness. Buckskin leggings wrapped around the legs protected her from scratches and injuries while she worked. The more layers of buckskin, the better. All those layers gave her legs the appearance of strength, like sturdy tree trunks. To demonstrate sisterhood and brotherhood with the plants and animals, the old-time people make masks and costumes that transform the human figures of the dancers into the animal beings they portray. Dancers paint their exposed skin; their postures and motions are adapted from their observations. But the motions are stylized. The observer sees not an actual eagle or actual deer dancing, but witnesses a human being, a dancer, gradually changing into a woman/buffalo or a man/deer. Every impulse is to reaffirm the urgent relationships that human beings have with the plant and animal world. 22

In the high desert plateau country, all vegetation, even weeds and thorns, becomes special, and all life is precious and beautiful because without the plants, the insects, and the animals, human beings living here cannot survive. Perhaps human beings long ago noticed the devastating impact human activity can have on the plants and animals; maybe this is why tribal cultures devised the stories about humans and animals intermarrying, and the clans that bind humans to animals and plants through a whole complex of duties. 23

We children were always warned not to harm frogs or toads, the beloved children of the rain clouds, because terrible floods would occur. I remember in the summer the old folks used to stick big bolls of cotton on the outside of their screen doors as bait to keep the flies from going in the house when the door was opened. The old folks staunchly resisted the killing of flies because once, long, long ago, when human beings were in a great deal of trouble, a Green Bottle Fly carried the desperate messages of human beings to the Mother Creator in the Fourth World, below this one. Human beings had outraged the Mother Creator by neglecting the Mother Corn altar while they dabbled with sorcery and magic. The Mother Creator disappeared, and with her disappeared the rain clouds, and the plants and the animals too. The people began to starve, and they had no way of reaching the Mother Creator down below. Green Bottle 24

Fly took the message to the Mother Creator, and the people were saved. To show their gratitude, the old folks refused to kill any flies.

THE OLD STORIES demonstrate the interrelationships that the Pueblo people have maintained with their plant and animal clanspeople. Kochininako, Yellow Woman, represents all women in the old stories. Her deeds span the spectrum of human behavior and are mostly heroic acts, though in at least one story, she chooses to join the secret Destroyer Clan, which worships destruction and death. Because Laguna Pueblo cosmology features a female Creator, the status of women is equal with the status of men, and women appear as often as men in the old stories as hero figures. Yellow Woman is my favorite because she dares to cross traditional boundaries of ordinary behavior during times of crisis in order to save the Pueblo; her power lies in her courage and in her uninhibited sexuality, which the old-time Pueblo stories celebrate again and again because fertility was so highly valued. 25

The old stories always say that Yellow Woman was beautiful, but remember that the old-time people were not so much thinking about physical appearances. In each story, the beauty that Yellow Woman possesses is the beauty of her passion, her daring, and her sheer strength to act when catastrophe is imminent. 26

In one story, the people are suffering during a great drought and accompanying famine. Each day, Kochininako has to walk farther and farther from the village to find fresh water for her husband and children. One day she travels far, far to the east, to the plains, and she finally locates a freshwater spring. But when she reaches the pool, the water is churning violently as if something large had just gotten out of the pool. Kochininako does not want to see what huge creature had been at the pool, but just as she fills her water jar and turns to hurry away, a strong, sexy man in buffalo skin leggings appears by the pool. Little drops of water glisten on his chest. She cannot help but look at him because he is so strong and so good to look at. Able to transform himself from human to buffalo in the wink of an eye, Buffalo Man gallops away with her on his back. Kochininako falls in love with Buffalo Man, and because of this liaison, the Buffalo People agree to give their bodies to the hunters to feed the starving Pueblo. Thus Kochininako's fearless sensuality results in the salvation of the people of her village, who are saved by the meat the Buffalo People "give" to them. 27

My father taught me and my sisters to shoot .22 rifles when we were seven; I went hunting with my father when I was eight, and I killed my first mule deer buck when I was thirteen. The Kochininako 28 stories were always my favorite because Yellow Woman had so many adventures. In one story, as she hunts rabbits to feed her family, a giant monster pursues her, but she has the courage and presence of mind to outwit it.

In another story, Kochininako has a fling with Whirlwind Man and returns to her husband ten months later with twin baby boys. The twin boys grow up to be great heroes of the people. Once again, Kochininako's vibrant sexuality benefits her people. 29

The stories about Kochininako made me aware that sometimes an individual must act despite disapproval, or concern for appearances or what others may say. From Yellow Woman's adventures, I learned to be comfortable with my differences. I even imagined that Yellow Woman had yellow skin, brown hair, and green eyes like mine, although her name does not refer to her color, but rather to the ritual color of the east. 30

There have been many other moments like the one with the camera-toting tourist in the schoolyard. But the old-time people always say, remember the stories, the stories will help you be strong. So all these years I have depended on Kochininako and the stories of her adventures. 31

Kochininako is beautiful because she has the courage to act in times of great peril, and her triumph is achieved by her sensuality, not through violence and destruction. For these qualities of the spirit, Yellow Woman and all women are beautiful. 32

MARTIN LUTHER KING JR.

MARTIN LUTHER KING JR. (1929–1968), was a Baptist minister, the president of the Southern Christian Leadership Conference, and a respected leader in the nationwide movement for equal rights for blacks. He was born in Atlanta, Georgia, and earned degrees from Morehouse College (A.B., 1948), Crozer Theological Seminary (B.D., 1951), Boston University (Ph.D., 1955), and Chicago Theological Seminary (D.D., 1957). He held honorary degrees from numerous other colleges and universities and was awarded the Nobel Peace Prize in 1964. Some of his books are *Stride Toward Freedom* (1958), *Strength to Love* (1963), and *Why We Can't Wait* (1964). King was assassinated April 4, 1968, in Memphis, Tennessee.

Letter from Birmingham Jail[1]

This letter, written to King's colleagues in the ministry, is a reasoned explanation for his actions during the civil rights protests in Birmingham. It is a good example of both persuasion and logical argument. Here the two are completely compatible, balancing each other in rather intricate but convincing and effective patterns.

My Dear Fellow Clergymen: 1

While confined here in the Birmingham city jail, I came across your recent statement calling my present activities "unwise and untimely." Seldom do I pause to answer criticism of my work and ideas. If I sought to answer all the criticisms that cross my desk, my secretaries would have little time for anything other than such correspondence in the course of the day, and I would have no time for constructive work. But since I feel that you are men of genuine good will and that your criticisms are sincerely set forth, I want to try to 2

[1]This response to a published statement by eight fellow clergymen from Alabama (Bishop C. C. J. Carpenter, Bishop Joseph A. Durick, Rabbi Hilton L. Grafman, Bishop Paul Hardin, Bishop Holan B. Harmon, the Reverend George M. Murray, the Reverend Edward V. Ramage, and the Reverend Earl Stallings) was composed under somewhat constricting circumstances. Begun on the margins of the newspaper in which the statement appeared while I was in jail, the letter was continued on scraps of writing paper supplied by a friendly Negro trusty, and concluded on a pad my attorneys were eventually permitted to leave me. Although the text remains in substance unaltered, I have indulged in the author's prerogative of polishing it for publication.—*King's note.*

answer your statement in what I hope will be patient and reasonable terms.

I think I should indicate why I am here in Birmingham, since you have been influenced by the view which argues against "outsiders coming in." I have the honor of serving as president of the Southern Christian Leadership Conference, an organization operating in every southern state, with headquarters in Atlanta, Georgia. We have some eighty-five affiliated organizations across the South, and one of them is the Alabama Christian Movement for Human Rights. Frequently we share staff, educational, and financial resources with our affiliates. Several months ago the affiliate here in Birmingham asked us to be on call to engage in a nonviolent direct-action program if such were deemed necessary. We readily consented, and when the hour came, we lived up to our promise. So I, along with several members of my staff, am here because I was invited here. I am here because I have organizational ties here. 3

But more basically, I am in Birmingham because injustice is here. Just as the prophets of the eighth century B.C. left their villages and carried their "thus saith the Lord" far beyond the boundaries of their home towns, and just as the Apostle Paul left his village of Tarsus and carried the gospel of Jesus Christ to the far corners of the Greco-Roman world, so am I compelled to carry the gospel of freedom beyond my own home town. Like Paul, I must constantly respond to the Macedonian call for aid. 4

Moreover, I am cognizant of the interrelatedness of all communities and states. I cannot sit idly by in Atlanta and not be concerned about what happens in Birmingham. Injustice anywhere is a threat to justice everywhere. We are caught in an inescapable network of mutuality, tied in a single garment of destiny. Whatever affects one directly, affects all indirectly. Never again can we afford to live with the narrow, provincial "outside agitator" idea. Anyone who lives inside the United States can never be considered an outsider within its bounds. 5

You deplore the demonstrations taking place in Birmingham. But your statement, I am sorry to say, fails to express a similar concern for the conditions that brought about the demonstrations. I am sure that none of you would want to rest content with the superficial kind of social analysis that deals merely with effects and does not grapple with underlying causes. It is unfortunate that demonstrations are taking place in Birmingham, but it is even more unfortunate that the city's white power structure left the Negro community with no alternative. 6

In any nonviolent campaign there are four basic steps: collection of the facts to determine whether injustices exist; negotiation; self-purification; and direct action. We have gone through all these steps in Birmingham. There can be no gainsaying the fact that racial injustice engulfs this community. Birmingham is probably the most thoroughly segregated city in the United States. Its ugly record of brutality is widely known. Negroes have experienced grossly unjust treatment in the courts. There have been more unsolved bombings of Negro homes and churches in Birmingham than in any other city in the nation. These are the hard, brutal facts of the case. On the basis of these conditions, Negro leaders sought to negotiate with the city fathers. But the latter consistently refused to engage in good-faith negotiation. 7

Then, last September, came the opportunity to talk with leaders of Birmingham's economic community. In the course of the negotiations, certain promises were made by the merchants—for example, to remove the stores' humiliating racial signs. On the basis of these promises, the Reverend Fred Shuttlesworth and the leaders of the Alabama Christian Movement for Human Rights agreed to a moratorium on all demonstrations. As the weeks and months went by, we realized that we were the victims of a broken promise. A few signs, briefly removed, returned; the others remained. 8

As in so many past experiences, our hopes had been blasted, and the shadow of deep disappointment settled upon us. We had no alternative except to prepare for direct action, whereby we would present our very bodies as a means of laying our case before the conscience of the local and the national community. Mindful of the difficulties involved, we decided to undertake a process of self-purification. We began a series of workshops on nonviolence, and we repeatedly asked ourselves: "Are you able to accept blows without retaliating?" "Are you able to endure the ordeal of jail?" We decided to schedule our direct-action program for the Easter season, realizing that except for Christmas, this is the main shopping period of the year. Knowing that a strong economic-withdrawal program would be the by-product of direct action, we felt that this would be the best time to bring pressure to bear on the merchants for the needed change. 9

Then it occurred to us that Birmingham's mayoral election was coming up in March, and we speedily decided to postpone action until after election day. When we discovered that the Commissioner of Public Safety, Eugene "Bull" Connor, had piled up enough votes to be in the run-off, we decided again to postpone action until the 10 day after the run-off so that the demonstrations could not be used to cloud the issues. Like many others, we waited to see Mr. Connor defeated, and to this end we endured postponement after postponement. Having aided in this community need, we felt that our direct-action program could be delayed no longer.

You may well ask, "Why direct action? Why sit-ins, marches, and so forth? Isn't negotiation a better path?" You are quite right in calling for negotiation. Indeed, this is the very purpose of direct action. Nonviolent direct action seeks to create such a crisis and foster such a tension that a community which has constantly refused to negotiate is forced to confront the issue. It seeks so to dramatize the issue that it can no longer be ignored. My citing the creation of tension as part of the work of the nonviolent-resister may sound rather shocking. But I must confess that I am not afraid of the word "tension." I have earnestly opposed violent tension, but there is a type of constructive, nonviolent tension which is necessary for growth. Just as Socrates felt that it was necessary to create a tension in the mind so that individuals could rise from the bondage of myths and half-truths to the unfettered realm of creative analysis and objective appraisal, so must we see the need for nonviolent gadflies to create the kind of tension in society that will help men rise from the dark depths of prejudice and racism to the majestic heights of understanding and brotherhood. 11

The purpose of our direct-action program is to create a situation so crisis-packed that it will inevitably open the door to negotiation. I therefore concur with you in your call for negotiation. Too long has our beloved Southland been bogged down in a tragic effort to live in monologue rather than dialogue. 12

One of the basic points in your statement is that the action that I and my associates have taken in Birmingham is untimely. Some have asked: "Why didn't you give the new city administration time to act?" The only answer that I can give to this query is that the new Birmingham administration must be prodded about as much as the outgoing one, before it will act. We are sadly mistaken if we feel that the election of Albert Boutwell as mayor will bring the millennium to Birmingham. While Mr. Boutwell is a much more gentle person that Mr. Connor, they are both segregationists, dedicated to maintenance of the status quo. I have hoped that Mr. Boutwell will be reasonable enough to see the futility of massive resistance to desegregation. But he will not see this without pressure from devotees of civil rights. My friends, I must say to you that we have not made a single gain in civil rights without determined legal and nonviolent 13 pressure. Lamentably, it is an historical fact that privileged groups seldom give up their privileges voluntarily. Individuals may see the moral light and voluntarily give up their unjust posture; but, as Reinhold Niebuhr has reminded us, groups tend to be more immoral than individuals.

We know through painful experience that freedom is never vol- 14
untarily given by the oppressor; it must be demanded by the oppressed. Frankly, I have yet to engage in a direct-action campaign that was "well timed" in the view of those who have not suffered unduly from the disease of segregation. For years now I have heard the word "Wait!" It rings in the ear of every Negro with piercing familiarity. This "Wait" has almost always meant "Never." We must come to see, with one of our distinguished jurists, that "justice too long delayed is justice denied."

We have waited for more than 340 years for our constitutional 15
and God-given rights. The nations of Asia and Africa are moving with jetlike speed toward gaining political independence, but we still creep at horse-and-buggy pace toward gaining a cup of coffee at a lunch counter. Perhaps it is easy for those who have never felt the stinging darts of segregation to say, "Wait." But when you have seen vicious mobs lynch your mothers and fathers at will and drown your sisters and brothers at whim; when you have seen hate-filled policemen curse, kick, and even kill your black brothers and sisters; when you see the vast majority of your twenty million Negro brothers smothering in an airtight cage of poverty in the midst of an affluent society; when you suddenly find your tongue twisted and your speech stammering as you seek to explain to your six-year-old daughter why she can't go to the public amusement park that has just been advertised on television, and see tears welling up in her eyes when she is told that Funtown is closed to colored children, and see ominous clouds of inferiority beginning to form in her little mental sky, and see her beginning to distort her personality by developing an unconscious bitterness toward white people; when you have to concoct an answer for a five-year-old son who is asking, "Daddy, why do white people treat colored people so mean?"; when you take a cross-country drive and find it necessary to sleep night after night in the uncomfortable corners of your automobile because no motel will accept you; when you are humiliated day in and day out by nagging signs reading "white" and "colored"; when your first name becomes "nigger," your middle name becomes "boy" (however old you are) and your last name becomes "John," and your wife and mother are never given the respected title "Mrs."; when you are

harried by day and haunted by night by the fact that you are a Negro, living constantly at tiptoe stance, never quite knowing what to expect next, and are plagued with inner fears and outer resentments; when you are forever fighting a degenerating sense of "nobodiness"—then you will understand why we find it difficult to wait. There comes a time when the cup of endurance runs over, and men are no longer willing to be plunged into the abyss of despair. I hope, sirs, you can understand our legitimate and unavoidable impatience.

You express a great deal of anxiety over our willingness to break laws. This is certainly a legitimate concern. Since we so diligently urge people to obey the Supreme Court's decision of 1954 outlawing segregation in the public schools, at first glance it may seem rather paradoxical for us consciously to break laws. One may well ask: "How can you advocate breaking some laws and obeying others?" The answer lies in the fact that there are two types of laws: just and unjust. I would be the first to advocate obeying just laws. One has not only a legal but a moral responsibility to obey just laws. Conversely, one has a moral responsibility to disobey unjust laws. I would agree with St. Augustine that "an unjust law is no law at all." 16

Now, what is the difference between the two? How does one determine whether a law is just or unjust? A just law is a man-made code that squares with the moral law or the law of God. An unjust law is a code that is out of harmony with the moral law. To put it in the terms of St. Thomas Aquinas: An unjust law is a human law that is not rooted in eternal law and natural law. Any law that uplifts human personality is just. Any law that degrades human personality is unjust. All segregation statutes are unjust because segregation distorts the soul and damages the personality. It gives the segregator a false sense of superiority and the segregated a false sense of inferiority. Segregation, to use the terminology of the Jewish philosopher Martin Buber, substitutes an "I-it" relationship for an "I-thou" relationship and ends up relegating persons to the status of things. Hence segregation is not only politically, economically, and sociologically unsound, it is morally wrong and sinful. Paul Tillich has said that sin is separation. Is not segregation an existential expression of man's tragic separation, his awful estrangement, his terrible sinfulness? Thus it is that I can urge men to obey the 1954 decision of the Supreme Court, for it is morally right; and I can urge them to disobey segregation ordinances, for they are morally wrong. 17

Let us consider a more concrete example of just and unjust laws. An unjust law is a code that a numerical or power majority 18 group compels a minority group to obey but does not make binding on itself. This is *difference* made legal. By the same token, a just law is a code that a majority compels a minority to follow and that it is willing to follow itself. This is *sameness* made legal.

Let me give another explanation. A law is unjust if it is inflicted on a minority that, as a result of being denied the right to vote, had no part in enacting or devising the law. Who can say that the legislature of Alabama which set up that state's segregation laws was democratically elected? Throughout Alabama all sorts of devious methods are used to prevent Negroes from becoming registered voters, and there are some counties in which, even though Negroes constitute a majority of the population, not a single Negro is registered. Can any law enacted under such circumstances be considered democratically structured? 19

Sometimes a law is just on its face and unjust in its application. For instance, I have been arrested on a charge of parading without a permit. Now, there is nothing wrong in having an ordinance which requires a permit for a parade. But such an ordinance becomes unjust when it is used to maintain segregation and to deny citizens the First Amendment privilege of peaceful assembly and protest. 20

I hope you are able to see the distinction I am trying to point out. In no sense do I advocate evading or defying the law, as would the rabid segregationist. That would lead to anarchy. One who breaks an unjust law must do so openly, lovingly, and with a willingness to accept the penalty. I submit that an individual who breaks a law that conscience tells him is unjust, and who willingly accepts the penalty of imprisonment in order to arouse the conscience of the community over its injustice, is in reality expressing the highest respect for the law. 21

Of course, there is nothing new about this kind of civil disobedience. It was evidenced sublimely in the refusal of Shadrach, Meshach, and Abednego to obey the laws of Nebuchadnezzar, on the ground that a higher moral law was at stake. It was practiced superbly by the early Christians, who were willing to face hungry lions and the excruciating pain of chopping blocks rather than submit to certain unjust laws of the Roman Empire. To a degree, academic freedom is a reality today because Socrates practiced civil disobedience. In our own nation, the Boston Tea Party represented a massive act of civil disobedience. 22

We should never forget that everything Adolf Hitler did in Germany was "legal" and everything the Hungarian freedom fighters did in Hungary was "illegal." It was "illegal" to aid and comfort 23 a Jew in Hitler's Germany. Even so, I am sure that, had I lived in Germany at the time, I would have aided and comforted my Jewish brothers. If today I lived in a Communist country where certain principles dear to the Christian faith are suppressed, I would openly advocate disobeying that country's anti-religious laws.

I must make two honest confessions to you, my Christian and Jewish brothers. First, I must confess that over the past few years I have been gravely disappointed with the white moderate. I have almost reached the regrettable conclusion that the Negro's great stumbling block in his stride toward freedom is not the White Citizen's Counciler or the Ku Klux Klanner, but the white moderate, who is more devoted to "order" than to justice; who prefers a negative peace which is the absence of tension to a positive peace which is the presence of justice; who constantly says, "I agree with you in the goal you seek, but I cannot agree with your methods of direct action"; who paternalistically believes he can set the timetable for another man's freedom; who lives by a mythical concept of time and who constantly advises the Negro to wait for a "more convenient season." Shallow understanding from people of good will is more frustrating than absolute misunderstanding from people of ill will. Lukewarm acceptance is much more bewildering than outright rejection. 24

I had hoped that the white moderate would understand that law and order exist for the purpose of establishing justice and that when they fail in this purpose they become the dangerously structured dams that block the flow of social progress. I had hoped that the white moderate would understand that the present tension in the South is a necessary phase of the transition from an obnoxious negative peace, in which the Negro passively accepted his unjust plight, to a substantive and positive peace, in which all men will respect the dignity and worth of human personality. Actually, we who engage in nonviolent direct action are not the creators of tension. We merely bring to the surface the hidden tension that is already alive. We bring it out in the open, where it can be seen and dealt with. Like a boil that can never be cured so long as it is covered up but must be opened with all its ugliness to the natural medicines of air and light, injustice must be exposed, with all the tension its exposure creates, to the light of human conscience and the air of national opinion, before it can be cured. 25

In your statement you assert that our actions, even though peaceful, must be condemned because they precipitate violence. But is this a logical assertion? Isn't this like condemning a robbed man because his possession of money precipitated the evil act of robbery? 26

Isn't this like condemning Socrates because his unswerving commitment to truth and his philosophical inquiries precipitated the act by the misguided populace in which they made him drink hemlock? Isn't this like condemning Jesus because his unique God-consciousness and never-ceasing devotion to God's will precipitated the evil act of crucifixion? We must come to see that, as the federal courts have consistently affirmed, it is wrong to urge an individual to cease his efforts to gain his basic constitutional rights because the quest may precipitate violence. Society must protect the robbed and punish the robber.

I had also hoped that the white moderate would reject the myth 27 concerning time in relation to the struggle for freedom. I have just received a letter from a white brother in Texas. He writes: "All Christians know that the colored people will receive equal rights eventually, but it is possible that you are in too great a religious hurry. It has taken Christianity almost two thousand years to accomplish what it has. The teachings of Christ take time to come to earth." Such an attitude stems from a tragic misconception of time, from the strangely irrational notion that there is something in the very flow of time that will inevitably cure all ills. Actually, time itself is neutral; it can be used either destructively or constructively. More and more I feel that the people of ill will have used time much more effectively than have the people of good will. We will have to repent in this generation not merely for the hateful words and actions of the bad people, but for the appalling silence of the good people. Human progress never rolls in on wheels of inevitability; it comes through the tireless efforts of men willing to be co-workers with God, and without this hard work, time itself becomes an ally of the forces of social stagnation. We must use time creatively, in the knowledge that the time is always ripe to do right. Now is the time to make real the promise of democracy and transform our pending national elegy into a creative psalm of brotherhood. Now is the time to lift our national policy from the quicksand of racial injustice to the solid rock of human dignity.

You speak of our activity in Birmingham as extreme. At first I 28 was rather disappointed that fellow clergymen would see my nonviolent efforts as those of an extremist. I began thinking about the fact that I stand in the middle of two opposing forces in the Negro community. One is a force of complacency, made up in part of Negroes who, as a result of long years of oppression, are so drained of self-respect and a sense of "somebodiness" that they have adjusted to segregation; and in part of a few middle-class Negroes who, because of a degree of academic and economic security and because in some ways they profit by segregation, have become insensitive to the problems of the masses. The other force is one of bitterness and hatred, and it comes perilously close to advocating violence. It is expressed in the various black nationalist groups that are springing up across the nation, the largest and best-known being Elijah Muhammad's Muslim movement. Nourished by the Negro's frustration over the continued existence of racial discrimination, this movement is made up of people who have lost faith in America, who have absolutely repudiated Christianity, and who have concluded that the white man is an incorrigible "devil."

I have tried to stand between these two forces, saying that we need emulate neither the "do-nothingism" of the complacent nor the hatred and despair of the black nationalist. For there is the more excellent way of love and nonviolent protest. I am grateful to God that, through the influence of the Negro church, the way of nonviolence became an integral part of our struggle. 29

If this philosophy had not emerged, by now many streets of the South would, I am convinced, be flowing with blood. And I am further convinced that if our white brothers dismiss as "rabble-rousers" and "outside agitators" those of us who employ nonviolent direct action, and if they refuse to support our nonviolent efforts, millions of Negroes will, out of frustration and despair, seek solace and security in black-nationalist ideologies—a development that would inevitably lead to a frightening racial nightmare. 30

Oppressed people cannot remain oppressed forever. The yearning for freedom eventually manifests itself, and that is what has happened to the American Negro. Something within has reminded him of his birthright of freedom, and something without has reminded him that it can be gained. Consciously or unconsciously, he has been caught up by the *Zeitgeist,* and with his black brothers of Africa and his brown and yellow brothers of Asia, South America, and the Caribbean, the United States Negro is moving with a sense of great urgency toward the promised land of racial justice. If one recognizes this vital urge that has engulfed the Negro community, one should readily understand why public demonstrations are taking place. The Negro has many pent-up resentments and latent frustrations, and he must release them. So let him march; let him make prayer pilgrimages to the city hall; let him go on freedom rides—and try to understand why he must do so. If his repressed emotions are not released in nonviolent ways, they will seek expression through violence; this is not a threat but a fact of history. So I have not said to my 31 people, "Get rid of your discontent." Rather, I have tried to say that this normal and healthy discontent can be channeled into the creative outlet of nonviolent direct action. And now this approach is being termed extremist.

But though I was initially disappointed at being categorized as an extremist, as I continued to think about the matter I gradually gained a measure of satisfaction from the label. Was not Jesus an extremist for love: "Love your enemies, bless them that curse you, do good to them that hate you, and pray for them which despitefully use you, and persecute you." Was not Amos an extremist for justice: "Let justice roll down like waters and righteousness like an ever-flowing stream." Was not Paul an extremist for the Christian gospel: "I bear in my body the marks of the Lord Jesus." Was not Martin Luther an extremist: "Here I stand; I cannot do otherwise, so help me God." And John Bunyan: "I will stay in jail to the end of my days before I make a butchery of my conscience." And Abraham Lincoln: "This nation cannot survive half slave and half free." And Thomas Jefferson: "We hold these truths to be self-evident, that all men are created equal . . .". So the question is not whether we will be extremists, but what kind of extremists we will be. Will we be extremists for hate or for love? Will we be extremists for the preservation of injustice or for the extension of justice? In that dramatic scene on Calvary's hill three men were crucified. We must never forget that all three were crucified for the same crime—the crime of extremism. Two were extremists for immorality, and thus fell below their environment. The other, Jesus Christ, was an extremist for love, truth, and goodness, and thereby rose above his environment. Perhaps the South, the nation, and the world are in dire need of creative extremists. 32

I had hoped that the white moderate would see this need. Perhaps I was too optimistic; perhaps I expected too much. I suppose I should have realized that few members of the oppressor race can understand the deep groans and passionate yearnings of the oppressed race, and still fewer have the vision to see that injustice must be rooted out by strong, persistent, and determined action. I am thankful, however, that some of our white brothers in the South have grasped the meaning of this social revolution and committed themselves to it. They are still all too few in quantity, but they are big in quality. Some—such as Ralph McGill, Lillian Smith, Harry Golden, James McBride Dabbs, Anne Braden, and Sarah Patton Boyle—have written about our struggle in eloquent and prophetic terms. Others have marched with us down nameless streets of the South. They have languished in filthy, roach-infested jails, suffering 33 the abuse and brutality of policemen who view them as "dirty nigger-lovers." Unlike so many of their moderate brothers and sisters, they have recognized the urgency of the moment and sensed the need for powerful "action" antidotes to combat the disease of segregation.

Let me take note of my other major disappointment. I have been so greatly disappointed with the white church and its leadership. Of course, there are some notable exceptions. I am not unmindful of the fact that each of you have taken some significant stands on this issue. I commend you, Reverend Stallings, for your Christian stand on this past Sunday, in welcoming Negroes to your worship service on a nonsegregated basis. I commend the Catholic leaders of this state for integrating Spring Hill College several years ago. 34

But despite these notable exceptions, I must honestly reiterate that I have been disappointed with the church. I do not say this as one of those negative critics who can always find something wrong with the church. I say this as a minister of the gospel, who loves the church; who has nurtured in its bosom; who has been sustained by its spiritual blessings and who will remain true to it as long as the cord of life shall lengthen. 35

When I was suddenly catapulted into the leadership of the bus protest in Montgomery, Alabama, a few years ago, I felt we would be supported by the white church. I felt that the white ministers, priests, and rabbis of the South would be among our strongest allies. Instead, some have been outright opponents, refusing to understand the freedom movement and misrepresenting its leaders; all too many others have been more cautious than courageous and have remained silent behind the anesthetizing security of stained glass windows. 36

In spite of my shattered dreams, I came to Birmingham with the hope that the white religious leadership of this community would see the justice of our cause and, with deep moral concern, would serve as the channel through which our just grievances could reach the power structure. I had hoped that each of you would understand. But again I have been disappointed. 37

I have heard numerous southern religious leaders admonish their worshipers to comply with a desegregation decision because it is the law, but I have longed to hear white ministers declare: "Follow this decree because integration is morally right and because the Negro is your brother." In the midst of blatant injustices inflicted upon the Negro, I have watched white churchmen stand on the sideline and mouth pious relevancies and sanctimonious trivialities. In 38 the midst of a mighty struggle to rid our nation of racial and economic injustice I have heard many ministers say: "Those are social issues, with which the gospel has no real concern." And I have watched many churches commit themselves to a completely otherworldly religion which makes a strange, un-Biblical distinction between body and soul, between the sacred and the secular.

I have traveled the length and breadth of Alabama, Mississippi, 39
and all the other southern states. On sweltering summer days and crisp autumn mornings I have looked at the South's beautiful churches with their lofty spires pointing heavenward. I have beheld the impressive outlines of her massive religious-education buildings. Over and over I have found myself asking: "What kind of people worship here? Who is their God? Where were their voices when the lips of Governor Barnett dripped with words of interposition and nullification? Where were they when Governor Wallace gave a clarion call for defiance and hatred? Where were their voices of support when bruised and weary Negro men and women decided to rise from the dark dungeons of complacency to the bright hills of creative protest?"

Yes, these questions are still in my mind. In deep disappoint- 40
ment I have wept over the laxity of the church. But be assured that my tears have been tears of love. There can be no deep disappointment where there is not deep love. Yes, I love the church. How could I do otherwise? I am in the rather unique position of being the son, the grandson, and the great-grandson of preachers. Yes, I see the church as the body of Christ. But, oh! How we have blemished and scarred that body through social neglect and through fear of being nonconformists.

There was a time when the church was very powerful—in the 41
time when the early Christians rejoiced at being deemed worthy to suffer for what they believed. In those days the church was not merely a thermometer that recorded the ideas and principles of popular opinion; it was a thermostat that transformed the mores of society. Whenever the early Christians entered a town, the people in power became disturbed and immediately sought to convict the Christians for being "disturbers of the peace" and "outside agitators." But the Christians pressed on, in the conviction that they were "a colony of heaven," called to obey God rather than man. Small in number, they were big in commitment. They were too God-intoxicated to be "astronomically intimidated." By their effort and example they brought an end to such ancient evils as infanticide and gladiatorial contests.

Things are different now. So often the contemporary church is a weak, ineffectual voice with an uncertain sound. So often it is an archdefender of the status quo. Far from being disturbed by the presence of the church, the power structure of the average community is consoled by the church's silent—and often even vocal—sanction of things as they are. 42

But the judgment of God is upon the church as never before. If today's church does not recapture the sacrificial spirit of the early church, it will lose its authenticity, forfeit the loyalty of millions, and be dismissed as an irrelevant social club with no meaning for the twentieth century. Every day I meet young people whose disappointment with the church has turned into outright disgust. 43

Perhaps I have once again been too optimistic. Is organized religion too inextricably bound to the status quo to save our nation and the world? Perhaps I must turn my faith to the inner spiritual church, the church within the church, as the true *ekklesia*[2] and the hope of the world. But again I am thankful to God that some noble souls from the ranks of organized religion have broken loose from the paralyzing chains of conformity and joined us as active partners in the struggle for freedom. They have left their secure congregations and walked the streets of Albany, Georgia, with us. They have gone down the highways of the South on tortuous rides for freedom. Yes, they have gone to jail with us. Some have been dismissed from their churches, have lost the support of their bishops and fellow ministers. But they have acted in the faith that right defeated is stronger than evil triumphant. Their witness has been the spiritual salt that has preserved the true meaning of the gospel in these troubled times. They have carved a tunnel of hope through the dark mountain of disappointment. 44

I hope the church as a whole will meet the challenge of this decisive hour. But even if the church does not come to the aid of justice, I have no despair about the future. I have no fear about the outcome of our struggle in Birmingham, even if our motives are at present misunderstood. We will reach the goal of freedom in Birmingham and all over the nation, because the goal of America is freedom. Abused and scorned though we may be, our destiny is tied up with America's destiny. Before the pilgrims landed at Plymouth, we were here. Before the pen of Jefferson etched the majestic words of the Declaration of Independence across the pages of history, we were 45

[2]The Greek New Testament word for the early Christian church. (Editor's note.)

here. For more than two centuries, our forbears labored in this country without wages; they made cotton king; they built the homes of their masters while suffering gross injustice and shameful humiliation—and yet out of a bottomless vitality they continued to thrive and develop. If the inexpressible cruelties of slavery could not stop us, the opposition we now face will surely fail. We will win our freedom because the sacred heritage of our nation and the eternal will of God are embodied in our echoing demands.

Before closing I feel impelled to mention one other point in your statement that has troubled me profoundly. You warmly commended the Birmingham police force for keeping "order" and "preventing violence." I doubt that you would have so warmly commended the police force if you had seen its dogs sinking their teeth into unarmed, nonviolent Negroes. I doubt that you would so quickly commend the policemen if you were to observe their ugly and inhumane treatment of Negroes here in the city jail; if you were to watch them push and curse old Negro women and young Negro girls; if you were to see them slap and kick old Negro men and young boys; if you were to observe them, as they did on two occasions, refuse to give us food because we wanted to sing our grace together. I cannot join you in your praise of the Birmingham police department. 46

It is true that the police have exercised a degree of discipline in handling the demonstrators. In this sense they have conducted themselves rather "nonviolently" in public. But for what purpose? To preserve the evil system of segregation. Over the past few years I have consistently preached that nonviolence demands that the means we use must be as pure as the ends we seek. I have tried to make clear that it is wrong to use immoral means to attain moral ends. But now I must affirm that it is just as wrong, or perhaps even more so, to use moral means to preserve immoral ends. Perhaps Mr. Connor and his policemen have been rather nonviolent in public, as was Chief Pritchett in Albany, Georgia, but they have used the moral means of nonviolence to maintain the immoral end of racial injustice. As T.S. Eliot has said, "The last temptation is the greatest treason: To do the right deed for the wrong reason." 47

I wish you had commended the Negro sit-inners and demonstrators of Birmingham for their sublime courage, their willingness to suffer, and their amazing discipline in the midst of great provocation. One day the South will recognize its real heroes. They will be the James Merediths, with the noble sense of purpose that enables 48 them to face jeering and hostile mobs, and with the agonizing loneliness that characterizes the life of the pioneer. They will be old, oppressed, battered Negro women, symbolized in a seventy-two-year-old woman in Montgomery, Alabama, who rose up with a sense of dignity and with her people decided not to ride segregated buses, and who responded with ungrammatical profundity to one who inquired about her weariness: "My feets is tired, but my soul is at rest." They will be the young high school and college students, and young ministers of the gospel and a host of their elders, courageously and nonviolently sitting in at lunch counters and willingly going to jail for conscience' sake. One day the South will know that when these disinherited children of God sat down at lunch counters, they were in reality standing up for what is best in the American dream and for the most sacred values in our Judaeo-Christian heritage, thereby bringing our nation back to those great wells of democracy which were dug deep by the founding fathers in their formulation of the Constitution and the Declaration of Independence.

Never before have I written so long a letter. I'm afraid it is much too long to take your precious time. I can assure you that it would have been much shorter if I had been writing from a comfortable desk, but what else can one do when he is alone in a narrow jail cell, other than write long letters, think long thoughts, and pray long prayers? 49

If I have said anything in this letter that overstates the truth and indicates an unreasonable impatience, I beg you to forgive me. If I have said anything that understates the truth and indicates my having a patience that allows me to settle for anything less than brotherhood, I beg God to forgive me. 50

I hope this letter finds you strong in the faith. I also hope that circumstances will soon make it possible for me to meet each of you, not as an integrationist or a civil-rights leader but as a fellow clergyman and a Christian brother. Let us all hope that the dark clouds of racial prejudice will soon pass away and the deep fog of misunderstanding will be lifted from our fear-drenched communities, and in some not too distant tomorrow the radiant stars of love and brotherhood will shine over our great nation with all their scintillating beauty. 51

Yours for the cause of Peace and Brotherhood, 52

MARTIN LUTHER KING JR. 53

A Guide to Terms

Abstract (See *Concrete/Abstract.*)

Allusion (See *Figures of Speech.*)

Analogy (See Chapter 6.)

Argument is writing that uses factual evidence and supporting ideas to convince readers to share the author's opinion on an issue or to take some action the writer considers appropriate or necessary. Like exposition, argument conveys information; however, it does so not to explain but to induce readers to favor one side in a conflict or to choose a particular course of action.

Some arguments appeal primarily to reason, others primarily to emotion. Most, however, mix reason and emotion in whatever way is appropriate for the issue and the audience. (See Chapter 13.)

Support for an argument can take a number of forms:

1. *Examples*—Real-life examples or hypothetical examples (used sparingly) can be convincing evidence if they are typical and if the author provides enough of them to illustrate all the major points in the argument or combines them with other kinds of evidence. (See Daly, Mills, Svoboda, and Min.) Some examples are *specific,* referring to particular people or events. (See Daly.) Others are *general,* referring to kinds of events or people, usually corresponding in some way to the reader's experiences. (See O'Hehir.)

2. *Facts and figures*—Detailed information about a subject, particularly if presented in statistical form, can help convince readers by showing that the author's perspective on an issue is consistent with what is known about the subject. (See O'Hehir and Quindlen.) But facts whose accuracy is questionable or statistics that are confusing can undermine an argument.

3. *Authority*—Supporting an argument with the ideas or the actual words of someone who is recognized as an expert can be an effective strategy as long as the author can show that the expert is a reliable witness and can combine the expert's opinion with other kinds of evidence that point in the same direction.

4. *Personal experience*—Examples drawn from personal experience or the experience of friends can be more detailed and vivid (and hence

more convincing) than other kinds of evidence, but a writer should use this kind of evidence sparingly because readers may sometimes suspect that it represents no more than one person's way of looking at events. When combined with other kinds of evidence, however, examples drawn from personal experience can be an effective technique for persuasion. (See Daly, Svoboda.)

In addition, all the basic expository patterns can be used to support an argument. (See Chapter 13.)

Cause (See Chapter 8.)

Central Theme (See *Unity.*)

Classification (See Chapter 4.)

Clichés are tired expressions, perhaps once fresh and colorful, that have been overused until they have lost most of their effectiveness and become trite or hackneyed. The term is also applied, less commonly, to trite ideas or attitudes.

We may need to use clichés in conversation, of course, when the quick and economical phrase is an important and useful tool of expression—and when no one expects us to be constantly original. We are fortunate, in a way, to have a large accumulation of clichés from which to draw. To describe someone, without straining our originality very much, we can always declare that he is *as innocent as a lamb, as thin as a rail,* or *as fat as a pig;* that she is *as dumb as an ox, as sly as a fox,* or *as wise as an owl;* that he is *financially embarrassed* or *has a fly in the ointment* or that *her ship has come in;* or that, *last but not least, in this day and age,* the *Grim Reaper* has taken him to *his eternal reward.* There is indeed *a large stockpile* from which we can draw for ordinary conversation. But the trite expression, written down on paper, is a permanent reminder that the writer is either lazy or not aware of the dullness of stereotypes—or, even more damaging, it is a clue that the ideas themselves may be threadbare and therefore can be adequately expressed in threadbare language.

Occasionally, of course, a writer can use obvious clichés deliberately (see Lawrence, Par. 1; Frazier). But usually to be fully effective, writing must be fresh and should seem to have been written specifically for the occasion. Clichés, however fresh and appropriate at one time, have lost these qualities.

Closings are almost as much of a problem as introductions, and they are equally important. The function of a closing is simply "to close," of course, but this implies somehow tying the entire writing into a neat package, giving the final sense of unity to the whole endeavor, and thus leaving the reader with a sense of satisfaction instead of an uneasy feeling that there ought to be another page.

There is no standard length for closings. A short composition may be effectively completed with one sentence—or even without any real closing at all, if the last point discussed is a strong or climactic one. A longer piece of writing, however, may end more slowly, perhaps through several paragraphs.

A few types of weak endings are so common that warnings are in order here. Careful writers will avoid these faults: (1) giving the effect of suddenly tiring and quitting; (2) ending on a minor detail or an apparent afterthought; (3) bringing up a new point in the closing; (4) using any new qualifying remark in the closing (if writers want their opinions to seem less dogmatic or generalized, they should go back to do their qualifying where the damage was done), and (5) ending with an apology of any kind (authors who are not interested enough to become at least minor experts in their subject should not be wasting the reader's time).

Of the several acceptable ways of giving the sense of finality to a paper, the easiest is the *summary,* but it is also the least desirable for most short papers. Readers who have read and understood something only a page or two before probably do not need to have it reviewed for them. Such a review is apt to seem merely repetitious. Longer writings, of course, such as research or term papers, may require thorough summaries.

Several other closing techniques are available to writers. The following ones which do not represent all the possibilities, are useful in many situations, and they can frequently be employed in combination:

1. *Using word signals*—for example, *finally, at last, thus, and so,* and *in conclusion,* as well as more original devices suggested by the subject itself. (See Simpson.)

2. *Changing the tempo*—usually a matter of sentence length or pace. This is a very subtle indication of finality, and it is difficult to achieve. (For examples of modified use, see Simpson, Fadiman, and Walker.)

3. *Restating the central idea of the writing*—sometimes a "statement" so fully developed that it practically becomes a summary itself. (See Catton, Carter, and Buczynski.)

4. *Using climax*—a natural culmination of preceding points or, in some cases, the last major point itself. This is suitable, however, only if the materials have been so arranged that the last point is outstanding. (See Catton, Lawrence, Conroy, Walker, and Szalavitz.)

5. *Making suggestions,* perhaps mentioning a possible solution to the problem being discussed—a useful technique for exposition as well as for argument, and a natural signal of the end. (See Miles.)

6. *Showing the topic's significance,* its effects, or the universality of its meaning—a commonly used technique that, if carefully handled, is an excellent indication of closing. (See Quindlen, Klinkenborg, and Lawrence.)

7. *Echoing the introduction*—a technique that has the virtue of improving the effect of unity by bringing the development around full circle, so to speak. The echo may be a reference to a problem posed or

a significant expression, quotation, analogy, or symbol used in the introduction or elsewhere early in the composition. (See Min and Berendt.)

8. *Using some rhetorical device*—a sort of catchall category, but a good supply source that includes several very effective techniques: pertinent quotations, anecdotes and brief dialogues, metaphors, allusions, ironic comments, and various kinds of witty or memorable remarks. All, however, run the risk of seeming forced and hence amateurish; but properly handled, they make for an effective closing. (See White, Lopate, Lawrence, Simpson, and King.)

Coherence is a quality of good writing that results from the presentation of all parts in logical and clear relations.

Coherence and unity are usually studied together and, indeed, are almost inseparable. But whereas unity refers to the relation of parts to the central theme (see *Unity*), coherence refers to their relations with each other. In a coherent piece of writing, each sentence, each paragraph, and each major division seem to grow out of those preceding them.

Several transitional devices (see *Transition*) help to make these relations clear, but far more fundamental to coherence is the sound organization of materials. From the first moment of visualizing the subject materials in pattern, the writer's goal must be clear and logical development. If it is, coherence is almost ensured.

Colloquial Expressions are characteristic of conversation and informal writing, and they are normally perfectly appropriate in those contexts. However, most writing done for college, business, or professional purposes is considered "formal" writing; for such usage, colloquialisms are too informal, too *folksy* (itself a word most dictionaries would label "colloq.").

Some of the expressions appropriate only for informal usage are *kid* (for child), *boss* (for employer), *flunk, buddy, snooze, gym, a lot of, phone, skin flicks,* and *porn.* In addition, contractions such as *can't* and *I'd* are usually regarded as colloquialisms and are never permissible in, for instance, a research or term paper.

Slang is defined as a low level of colloquialism, but it is sometimes placed "below" colloquialism in respectability; even standard dictionaries differ as to just what the distinction is. (Some of the examples in the preceding paragraph, if included in dictionaries at all, are identified both ways.) At any rate, slang generally comprises words either coined or given novel meanings in an attempt at colorful or humorous expression. Slang often becomes limp with overuse, however, losing whatever vigor it first had. In time, slang expressions either disappear completely or graduate to more acceptable colloquial status and thence, possibly, into standard usage. (This is one way in which our language is constantly changing.) But until their "graduations," slang and colloquialisms have an appropriate place in formal writing only if used sparingly and for special effect. Because dictionaries frequently differ in matters of usage, the student should be sure to use a standard edition approved by the instructor. (For further examples, see Conroy, Frazier, and Simpson, Pars. 8, 16, and 17.)

Comparison (See Chapter 5.)

Conclusions (See *Closings.*)

Concrete and **Abstract** words are both indispensable to the language, but a good rule in most writing is to use the concrete whenever possible. This policy also applies, of course, to sentences that express only abstract ideas, which concrete examples can often make clearer and more effective. Many expository and argumentative paragraphs are constructed with an abstract topic sentence and its concrete support. (See *Unity.*)

A concrete word names something that exists as an entity in itself, something that can be perceived by the human senses. We can see, touch, hear, and smell a horse—hence *horse* is a concrete word. But a horse's *strength* is not. We have no reason to doubt that strength exists, but it does not have an independent existence: something else must *be* strong or there is no strength. Hence *strength* is an abstract word.

Purely abstract reading is difficult for average readers; with no concrete images provided, they are constantly forced to make their own. Concrete writing helps readers to visualize and is therefore easier and faster to read. (See *Specific/General* for further discussion.)

Connotation and **Denotation** both refer to the meanings of words. Denotation is the direct, literal meaning of a word as it would be found in a dictionary, whereas connotation refers to the response a word *really* arouses in the reader or listener. (See Fadiman, Par. 14; Daly; and Lawrence.)

There are two types of connotation: personal and general. Personal connotations vary widely, depending on the experiences and moods that an individual associates with the word. (This corresponds with personal symbolism; see *Symbol.*) *Waterfall* is not apt to have the same meaning for the happy young honeymooners at Yosemite as it has for the grieving mother whose child has just drowned in a waterfall. General connotations are those shared by many people. *Fireside,* far beyond its obvious dictionary definition, generally connotes warmth, security, and good companionship. *Mother,* which denotatively means simply "female parent," means much more connotatively.

A word or phrase considered less distasteful or offensive than a more direct expression is called a *euphemism,* and this is also a matter of connotation. (See Mitford.) The various expressions used instead of the more direct "four-letter words" referring to daily bathroom events are examples of euphemisms. *Remains* is often used instead of *corpse,* and a few newspapers still report people *passing away* and being *laid to rest* rather than *dying* and being *buried.*

But a serious respect for the importance of connotations goes far beyond euphemistic practices. Young writers can hardly expect to know all the different meanings of words for all their potential readers, but they can at least be aware that words do *have* different meanings. Of course, this is most important in persuasive writing—in political speeches, in advertising copywriting, and in any endeavor where some sort of public image is being created. When President Franklin Roosevelt began his series of informal radio talks, he called them "fireside chats," thus putting connotation to work. An advertising copywriter trying to evoke the feeling of love and tenderness associated with motherhood is not seriously tempted to use *female parent* instead of *mother.*

In exposition, where the primary purpose is to explain, the writer ordinarily tries to avoid words that may have emotional overtones, unless these can somehow be used to increase understanding. In argument, however, a writer may on occasion wish to appeal to the emotions.

Contrast (See Chapter 5.)

Deduction (See Chapter 12.)

Denotation (See *Connotation/Denotation.*)

Description (See Chapter 10.)

Diction refers simply to "choice of words," but, not so simply, it involves many problems of usage, some of which are explained under several other headings in this guide, for example, *Clichés, Colloquial Expressions, Connotation/Denotation,* and *Concrete/Abstract*—anything, in fact, that pertains primarily to word choices. But the characteristics of good diction may be more generally classified as follows:

1. *Accuracy*—the choice of words that mean exactly what the author intends

2. *Economy*—the choice of the simplest and fewest words that will convey the exact meaning intended

3. *Emphasis*—the choice of fresh, strong words, avoiding clichés and unnecessarily vague or general terms

4. *Appropriateness*—the choice of words that suit the subject matter, the prospective reader-audience, and the purpose of the writing

(For contrasts of diction see Frazier, Conroy, Graham, Walker, King, Murphy, Svoboda, and Carter.)

Division (See Chapter 4.)

Effect (See Chapter 8.)

Emphasis is almost certain to fall *somewhere,* and the author should be the one to decide where. A major point, not some minor detail, should be emphasized.

Following are the most common ways of achieving emphasis. Most of them apply to the sentence, the paragraph, or the overall writing—all of which can be seriously weakened by emphasis in the wrong places.

1. By *position*—The most emphatic position is usually at the end, the second most emphatic at the beginning. (There are a few exceptions, including news stories and certain kinds of scientific reports.) The middle, therefore, should be used for materials that do not deserve special emphasis. (See Catton, Par. 16; Fadiman for a final statement of considerable emotional effect.)

A sentence in which the main point is held until the last is called a *periodic sentence,* for example, "After a long night of suspense and horror, the cavalry arrived." In a *loose sentence,* the main point is disposed of earlier and followed by dependencies, for example, "The cavalry arrived after a long night of suspense and horror."

2. By *proportion*—Ordinarily, but not necessarily, important elements are given the most attention and thus automatically achieve a certain emphasis.

3. By *repetition*—Words and ideas may sometimes be given emphasis by reuse, usually in a different manner. If not cautiously handled, however, this method can seem merely repetitious, not emphatic. (See Atwood, who repeats words to give them varied meanings and highlight their importance.)

4. By *flat statement*—Although an obvious way to achieve emphasis is simply to *tell* the reader what is most important, it is often least effective, at least when used as the only method. Readers have a way of ignoring such pointers as "most important" and "especially true." (See Catton, Par. 16.)

5. By *mechanical devices*—Emphasis can be achieved by using italics (underlining), capital letters, or exclamation points. But too often these devices are used, however unintentionally, to cover deficiencies of content or style. Their use can quickly be overdone and their impact lost.

6. By *distinctiveness of style*—The author can emphasize subtly with fresh and concrete words or figures of speech, crisp or unusual structures, and careful control of paragraph or sentence lengths. (These methods are used in many essays in this book: see Tyler; Seip; Twain, who changes style radically for the second half of his essay; Catton; Frazier, who parodies many different styles; and Fadiman.) *Verbal irony* (see *Irony*), including *sarcasm* (see Seip, Frazier, and Atwood) and the rather specialized form known as *understatement,* is another valuable means of achieving distinctiveness of style and increasing emphasis. (See Mitford.)

Essay refers to a brief prose composition on a single topic, usually, but not always, communicating the author's personal ideas and impressions. Beyond this, because of the wide and loose application of the term, no satisfactory definition has been universally accepted.

Classifications of essay types have also been widely varied and sometimes not very meaningful. One basic and useful distinction, however, is between *formal* and *informal* essays, although many defy classification even in such broad categories as these. It is best to regard the two types as opposite ends of a continuum, along which most essays may be placed.

The formal essay usually develops an important theme through a logical progression of ideas, with full attention to unity and coherence, and in a serious tone. Although the style is seldom completely impersonal, it is literary rather than colloquial. (For examples of essays that are somewhere near the "formal" end of the continuum, see Fadiman, Cook, Klinkenborg, Catton, Kilbourne, and Lawrence.)

The informal, or personal, essay is less elaborately organized and more chatty in style. First-person pronouns, contractions, and other colloquial or even slang expressions are often freely used. Informal essays are less serious in apparent purpose than formal essays. Although most do contain a worthwhile message or observation of some kind, an important purpose of many is to entertain. (See Ventura, Seip, and Tartt.)

The more personal and intimate informal essays may be classifiable as *familiar* essays, although, again, there is no well-established boundary. Familiar essays pertain to the author's own experience, ideas, or prejudices, frequently in a light and humorous style. (See Buczynski, Conroy, White, and Murphy.)

Evaluation of a literary piece, as for any other creative endeavor, is meaningful only when based on the answers to three questions: (1) What was the author's purpose? (2) How successfully was it fulfilled? and (3) How worthwhile was it?

An architect could hardly be blamed for designing a poor gymnasium if the commission had been to design a library. Similarly, an author who is trying to explain for us why women are paid less than men cannot be faulted for failing to make the reader laugh. An author whose purpose is simply to amuse (a worthy goal) should not be condemned for teaching little about trichobothria. (Nothing prevents the author from trying to explain pornography through the use of humor, or trying to amuse by comparing two Civil War generals, but in these situations the purpose has changed—and grown almost unbearably harder to achieve.)

An architect who was commissioned to design a gymnasium, and who, in fact, designed one, however, could be justifiably criticized on whether the building is successful and attractive *as a gymnasium.* If an author is examining matters of cognition and personality, the reader has a right to expect sound reasoning and clear expository prose; and varied, detailed support ought to be expected in an essay that looks at the physical basis of human behavior (see Perry and Dawson).

Many things are written and published that succeed very well in carrying out the author's intent—but simply are not worthwhile. Although this is certainly justifiable grounds for unfavorable criticism, readers should first make full allowance for their own limitations and perhaps their narrow range of interests, and they should evaluate the work as nearly as possible from the standpoint of the average reader for whom the writing was intended.

Figures of Speech are short, vivid comparisons, either stated or implied, but they are not literal comparisons (e.g., "Your car is like my car," which is presumably a plain statement of fact). Figures of speech are more imaginative. They imply analogy but, unlike analogy, are used less to inform than to make quick and forceful impressions. All figurative language is a comparison of unlikes, but the unlikes do have some interesting point of likeness, perhaps one never noticed before.

A *metaphor* merely suggests the comparison and is worded as if the two unlikes are the same thing—for example, "the language of the river" and "was turned to blood" (Twain, Par. 1) and "a great chapter in American life" (Catton, Par. 1). (For another example in this book, see King.)

A *simile* (which is sometimes classified as a special kind of metaphor) expresses a similarity directly, usually with the word *like* or *as* (Lopate, Par. 12).

A *personification,* which is actually a special type of either metaphor or simile, is usually classified as a "figure" in its own right. In personification, inanimate things are treated as if they had the qualities or powers of a person. Some people would also label as personification any characterization of inanimate objects as animals or of animals as humans.

An *allusion* is literally any casual reference, any alluding, to something, but rhetorically it is limited to a figurative reference to a famous or literary person, event, or quotation, and it should be distinguished from the casual reference that has a literal function in the subject matter. Hence casual mention of Judas Iscariot's betrayal of Jesus is merely a reference, but calling a modern traitor a "Judas" is an allusion. A rooster might be referred to as "the Hitler of the barnyard," or a lover as a "Romeo." Many allusions refer to mythological or biblical persons or places. (See Simpson, Par. 2, for a discussion of some commonly employed allusions.)

Irony and paradox (both discussed under their own headings) and analogy (see Chapter 6) are also frequently classed as figures of speech, and there are several other less common types that are really subclassifications of those already discussed.

General (See *Specific/General.*)

Illustration (See Chapter 3.)

Impressionistic Description (See Chapter 10.)

Induction (See Chapter 12.)

Introductions give readers their first impressions, which often turn out to be the lasting ones. In fact, unless an introduction succeeds in somehow attracting a reader's interest, he or she probably will read no further. The importance of the introduction is one reason that writing it is nearly always difficult.

When the writer remains at a loss for how to begin, it may be a good idea to forget about the introduction for a while and go ahead with the main body of the writing. Later the writer may find that a suitable introduction has suggested itself or even that the way the piece begins is actually introduction enough.

Introductions may vary in length from one sentence in a short composition to several paragraphs or even several pages in longer and more complex expositions and arguments, such as research papers and reports of various kinds.

Good introductions in expository writing have at least three and sometimes four functions.

1. *To identify the subject and set its limitations,* thus building a solid foundation for unity. This function usually includes some indication of the central theme, letting the reader know what point is to be made about the subject. Unlike the other forms of prose, which can often benefit by some degree of mystery, exposition has the primary purpose of explaining, so the reader has a right to know from the beginning just *what* is being explained.

2. *To interest the readers,* and thus ensure their attention. To be sure of doing this, writers must analyze their prospective readers and the readers' interest in their subject. The account of a new X-ray technique would need an entirely different kind of introduction if written for doctors than if written for the campus newspaper.

3. *To set the tone* of the rest of the writing. (See *Style/Tone.*) Tone varies greatly in writing, just as the tone of a person's voice varies with the person's mood. One function of the introduction is to let the reader know the author's attitude since it may have a subtle but important bearing on the communication.

4. *Frequently,* but not always, *to indicate the plan of organization.* Although seldom important in short, relatively simple compositions and essay examinations, this function of introductions can be especially valuable in more complex papers.

These are the necessary functions of an introduction. For best results, keep these guidelines in mind: (1) Avoid referring to the title or even assuming that the reader has seen it. Make the introduction do all the introducing. (2) Avoid crude and uninteresting beginnings, such as "This paper is about . . . ." (3) Avoid going too abruptly into the main body—a smooth transition is at least as important here as anywhere else. (4) Avoid overdoing the introduction, either in length or in extremes of style.

Fortunately, there are many good ways to introduce expository writing (and argumentative writing), and several of the most useful are illustrated by the selections in this book. Many writings, of course, combine two or more of the following techniques for interesting introductions.

1. *Stating the central theme,* which is sometimes fully enough explained in the introduction to become almost a preview summary of the exposition or argument to come. (See Quart.)

2. *Showing the significance of the subject,* or stressing its importance. (See Catton, Graham, Klinkenborg, and Simpson.)

3. *Giving the background of the subject,* usually in brief form, in order to bring the reader up-to-date as early as possible for a better understanding of the matter at hand. (See Stone and Lynn.)

4. *"Focusing down" to one aspect of the subject,* a technique similar to that used in some movies, showing first a broad scope (of subject area, such as a landscape) and then progressively narrowing views until the focus is on one specific thing (perhaps the name "O'Grady O'Connor" on a mailbox by a gate). (See also Rooney.)

5. *Using a pertinent rhetorical device* that will attract interest as it leads into the main exposition—for example, an anecdote, analogy, allusion, quotation, or paradox. (See Conroy and Simpson.)

6. *Using a short but vivid comparison or contrast* to emphasize the central idea. (See Lynn.)

7. *Posing a challenging question,* the answering of which the reader will assume to be the purpose of the writing. (See Lawrence and Buczynski.)

8. *Referring to the writer's experience with the subject,* perhaps even giving a detailed account of that experience. Some writings are simply continuations of experience so introduced, perhaps with the expository purpose of making the telling entirely evident only at the end or slowly unfolding it as the account progresses. (See White, Cook, and Daly.)

9. *Presenting a startling statistic or other fact* that will indicate the nature of the subject to be discussed.

10. *Making an unusual statement* that can intrigue as well as introduce. (See Frazier and Gansberg.)

11. *Making a commonplace remark* that can draw interest because of its very commonness in sound or meaning.

Irony, in its verbal form sometimes classed as a figure of speech, consists of saying one thing on the surface but meaning exactly (or nearly) the opposite—for example, "this beautiful neighborhood of ours" may mean that it is a dump. (For other illustrations, see Frazier, Mitford, and Walker.)

Verbal irony has a wide range of tones, from the gentle, gay, or affectionate to the sharpness of outright *sarcasm* (see Seip), which is always intended to cut. It may consist of only a word or phrase, it may be a simple *understatement* (see Mitford), or it may be sustained as one of the major components of satire.

Irony can be an effective tool of exposition if its tone is consistent with the overall tone and if the writer is sure that the audience is bright enough to recognize it. In speech, a person usually indicates by voice or eye expression that he or she is not to be taken literally; in writing, the words on the page have to speak for themselves. (See Stone for the use of parentheses to indicate ironic or humorous statements.)

In addition to verbal irony, there is also an *irony of situation,* in which there is a sharp contradiction between what is logically expected to happen and what does happen—for example, a man sets a trap for an obnoxious neighbor and then gets caught in it himself. Or the ironic situation may simply be some discrepancy that an outsider can see while those involved cannot. (See Lawrence, Pars. 11–12)

Logical Argument (See Chapter 13.)

Loose Sentence (See *Emphasis.*)

Metaphor (See *Figures of Speech.*)

Narration (See Chapter 11.)

Objective writing and **Subjective** writing are distinguishable by the extent to which they reflect the author's personal attitudes or emotions. The difference is usually one of degree, as few writing endeavors can be completely objective or subjective.

Objective writing, seldom used in its pure form except in business or scientific reports, is impersonal and concerned almost entirely with straight narration, with logical analysis, or with the description of external appearances. (For somewhat objective writing, see Simpson; and Staples, Par. 1.)

Subjective writing (in description called "impressionistic"—see Chapter 10) is more personalized, more expressive of the beliefs, ideals, or impressions of the author. Whereas in objective writing the emphasis is on the object being written about, in subjective writing the emphasis is on the way the author sees and interprets the object. (For some of the many examples in this book, see Twain; Lopate; Tartt; Mitford; Svoboda; Lawrence; and Staples, after Par. 1.)

Paradox is a statement or remark that, although seeming to be contradictory or absurd, actually contains some truth. Many paradoxical statements are also ironic.

Paragraph Unity (See *Unity.*)

Parallel Structure refers in principle to the same kind of "parallelism" that is studied in grammar: the principle that coordinate elements should have coordinate presentation, as in a pair or a series of verbs, prepositional phrases, or gerunds. It is often as much a matter of "balance" as it is of parallelism.

But the principle of parallel structure, far from being just a negative "don't mix" set of rules, is also a positive rhetorical device. Many writers use it as an effective means of stressing variety of profusion in a group of nouns or modifiers, or of emphasizing parallel ideas in sentence parts, in two or more sentences, or even in two or more paragraphs. At times it can also be useful stylistically to give a subtle poetic quality to the prose.

Periodic Sentence (See *Emphasis.*)

Persona refers to a character created as the speaker in an essay or the narrator of a story. The attitudes and character of a persona often differ from those of the author, and their persona may be created as a way of submitting certain values or perspectives to examination and criticism.

Personification (See *Figures of Speech.*)

Point of View in *argument* means the author's opinion on an issue or the thesis being advanced in an essay. In *exposition,* however, point of view is simply the position of the author in relation to the subject matter. Rhetorical point of view in exposition has little in common with the grammatical sort, and it differs somewhat from point of view in fiction.

A ranch in a mountain valley is seen differently by the ranch hand working at the corral, by the gardener deciding where to plant the petunias, by the artist or poet viewing the ranch from the mountainside, and by the geographer in a plane above, map-sketching the valley in relation to the entire range. It is the same ranch, but the positions and attitudes of the viewers are different.

So it is with expository prose. The position and attitude of the author are the important lens through which the reader sees the subject. Consistency is important, because if the lens is changed without sufficient cause and explanation, the reader will become disconcerted, if not annoyed.

Obviously, since the point of view is partially a matter of attitude, the tone and often the style of writing are closely linked to it. (See *Style/Tone.*)

The expository selections in this book provide examples of numerous points of view. Twain's are those of an authority in his own fields of experience, Mitford's is as the debunking prober, and Cook's is that of both a participant and a researcher. In each of these (and the list could be extended to include all the selections in the book), the subject would seem vastly different if seen from some other point of view.

Process Analysis (See Chapter 7.)

Purpose that is clearly understood by the author before beginning to write is essential to both unity and coherence. A worthwhile practice, certainly in the training stages, is to write down the controlling purpose before even beginning to outline. Some instructors require both a statement of purpose and a statement of central theme, or thesis. (See *Unity; Thesis.*)

The most basic element of a statement of purpose is the commitment to "explain" or, in some assignments, to "convince" (argument). But the statement of purpose, whether written down or only decided upon, goes further—for example, "to argue that 'dirty words' are logically offensive because of the sources and connotations of the words themselves" (Lawrence).

Qualification is the tempering of broad statements to make them more valid and acceptable, the authors themselves admitting the probability of exceptions. This qualifying can be done inconspicuously, to whatever degree needed, by the use of *possibly, nearly always, most often, usually, frequently, sometimes,* or *occasionally.* Instead of saying, "Chemistry is the most valuable field of study," it would probably be more accurate and defensible to say that it is for *some* people or that it *can* be the most valuable.

Refutation of opposing arguments is an important element in most argumentative essays, especially when the opposition is strong enough or reasonable enough to provide a real alternative to the author's opinion. A refutation consists of a brief summary of the opposing point of view along with a discussion of its inadequacies, a discussion that often helps support the author's own thesis.

Here are three commonly used strategies for refutation:

1. *Pointing out weaknesses in evidence*—If an opposing argument is based on inaccurate, incomplete, or misleading evidence, or if the argument does not take into account some new evidence that contradicts it, then the refutation should point out these weaknesses. (See Baumeister.)

2. *Pointing out errors in logic*—If an opposing argument is loosely reasoned or contains major flaws in logic, then the refutation should point these problems out to the reader.

3. *Questioning the relevance of an argument*—If an opposing argument does not directly address the issue under consideration, then the refutation should point out that even though the argument may well be correct, it is not worth considering because it is not relevant.

Refutations should always be moderate in tone and accurate in representing opposing arguments; otherwise, readers may feel that the writer has treated the opposition unfairly and as a result judge the author's own argument more harshly.

Rhetorical Questions are posed with no expectation of receiving an answer; they are merely structural devices for launching or furthering a discussion or for achieving emphasis. (See Lawrence.)

Sarcasm (See *Irony.*)

Satire, sometimes called "extended irony," is a literary form that brings wit and humor to the serious task of pointing out frailties or evils of human institutions. It has thrived in Western literature since the time of the ancient Greeks, and English literature of the eighteenth century was particularly noteworthy for the extent and quality of its satire. Broadly, two types are recognized: *Horatian satire,* which is gentle and smiling, and which aims to correct by invoking laughter and sympathy; and *Juvenalian satire,* which is sharper and points with anger, contempt, and/or moral indignation to corruption and evil.

Sentimentality, also called *sentimentalism,* is an exaggerated show of emotion, whether intentional or caused by lack of restraint. An author can sentimentalize almost any situation, but the trap is most dangerous when writing of timeworn emotional symbols or scenes—for example, a broken heart, mother love, a lonely death, or the conversion of a sinner. However sincere the author may be, if readers are not fully oriented to the worth and uniqueness of the situation described, they may be either resentful or amused at any attempt to play on their emotions. Sentimentality is, of course, one of the chief characteristics of melodrama. (For examples of writing that, less adeptly handled, could easily have slipped into sentimentality, see Buczynski, Twain, Catton, Staples, Gilb, Simpson, and Gansberg.)

Simile (See *Figures of Speech.*)

Slang (See *Colloquial Expressions.*)

Specific and **General** terms, and the distinctions between the two, are similar to concrete and abstract terms (as discussed under their own heading), and for our purpose there is no real need to keep the two sets of categories separated. Whether *corporation* is thought of as "abstract" and *Ajax Motor Company* as "concrete," or whether they are assigned to "general" and "specific" categories, the principle is the same: in most writing, *Ajax Motor Company* is better.

But "specific" and "general" are relative terms. For instance, the word *apple* is more specific than *fruit* but less so than *Winesap.* And *fruit,* as general as it certainly is in one respect, is still more specific than *food.* Such relationships are shown more clearly in a series, progressing from general to specific: *food, fruit, apple, Winesap;* or *vehicle, automobile, Ford, Mustang.* Modifiers and verbs can also have degrees of specificity: *bright, red, scarlet;* or *moved, sped, careened.* It is not difficult to see the advantages to the reader—and, of course, to the writer who needs to communicate an idea clearly—in "the scarlet Mustang careened through the pass" instead of "the bright-colored vehicle moved through the pass."

Obviously, however, there are times when the general or the abstract term or statement is essential—for example, "A balanced diet includes some fruit" or "There was no vehicle in sight." But the use of specific language whenever possible is one of the best ways to improve diction and thus clarity and forcefulness in writing.

(Another important way of strengthening general, abstract writing is, of course, to use examples or other illustrations. See Chapter 3.)

Style and **Tone** are so closely linked and so often even elements of each other that it is best to consider them together.

But there is a difference. Think of two young men, each with his girlfriend on separate moonlit dates, whispering in nearly identical tender and loving tones of voice. One young man says, "Your eyes, dearest, reflect a thousand sparkling candles of heaven," and the other says, "Them eyes of yours—in this light—they sure do turn me on." Their *tones* were the same; their *styles* were considerably different.

The same distinction exists in writing. But, naturally, with more complex subjects than the effect of moonlight on a lover's eyes, there are more complications in separating the two qualities, even for the purpose of study.

The tone is determined by the *attitude* of writers toward their subject and toward their audience. Writers, too, may be tender and loving, but they may be indignant, solemn, playful, enthusiastic, belligerent, contemptuous—the list could be as long as a list of the many "tones of voice." (In fact, wide ranges of tone may be illustrated by essays in this book. Compare, for example, those of the two parts of Twain; Tyler and Lynn; and Staples and Seip.)

Style, on the other hand, expresses the author's individuality through choices of words (see *Diction*), sentence patterns (see *Syntax*), and selection and arrangement of details and basic materials. (All these elements of style are illustrated in the contrasting statements of the moonstruck lads.) These matters of style are partially prescribed, of course, by the adopted tone, but they are still bound to reflect the writer's personality, mood, education, and general background.

(Some of the more distinctive styles—partially affected by and affecting tone—represented by selections in this book are those of Frazier, Fadiman, Tartt, Conroy, Seip, White, Silko, Murphy, Staples, and Walker.)

Subjective Writing (See *Objective/Subjective.*)

Symbol refers to anything that although real itself also suggests something broader or more significant—not just in greater numbers, however. A person would not symbolize a group or even humankind itself, although a person might be typical or representative in one or more abstract qualities. On the most elementary level, even words are symbols—for example, *bear* brings to mind the furry beast itself. But more important is that things, persons, or even acts may also be symbolic if they invoke abstract concepts, values, or qualities apart from themselves or their own kind. Such symbols, in everyday life as well as in literature and the other arts, are generally classifiable according to three types, which, although terminology differs, we may label *natural, personal,* and *conventional.*

In a natural symbol, the symbolic meaning is inherent in the thing itself. The sunrise naturally suggests new beginnings to most people, an island is almost synonymous with isolation, and a cannon automatically suggests war; hence these are natural symbols. It does not matter that some things, by their nature, can suggest more than one concept. Although a valley may symbolize security to one person and captivity to another, both meanings, contradictory as they might seem, are inherent, and in both respects the valley is a natural symbol.

The personal symbol, depending as it does on private experience or perception, is meaningless to others unless they are told about it or allowed to see its significance in context (as in literature). Although the color green may symbolize the outdoor life to the farm boy trapped in the gray city (in this respect perhaps a natural symbol), it can also symbolize romance to the young woman proposed to while wearing her green blouse, or dismal poverty to the woman who grew up in a weathered green shanty; neither of these meanings is suggested by something *inherent* in the color green, so they are personal symbols. Anything at all could take on private symbolic meaning, even the odor of marigolds or the sound of a lawnmower. The sunrise itself could mean utter despair, instead of fresh opportunities, to the man who has long despised his daily job and cannot find another.

Conventional symbols usually started as personal symbols, but continued usage in life or art permits them to be generally recognized for their broader meanings, which depend on custom rather than any inherent quality—for example, the olive branch for peace, the flag for love of country, the cross for Christianity, and the raised fist for revolutionary power.

Symbols are used less in expository and argumentative writing than in fiction and poetry, but a few authors represented in this book have either referred to the subtle symbolism of others or made use of it in developing their own ideas.

Syntax is a very broad term—too broad, perhaps, to be very useful—referring to the arrangement of words in a sentence. Good syntax implies the use not only of correct grammar but also of effective patterns. These patterns depend on sentences with good unity, coherence, and emphasis; on the use of subordination and parallel construction as appropriate; on economy; and on a consistent and interesting point of view. A pleasing variety of sentence patterns is also important in achieving effective syntax.

Theme (See *Unity.*)

Thesis In an argumentative essay, the central theme is often referred to as the thesis, and to make sure that readers recognize it, the thesis is often summed up briefly in a *thesis statement.* In a very important sense, the thesis is the center of an argument because the whole essay is designed to make the reader agree with it and, hence, with the author's opinion. (See *Unity.*)

Tone (See *Style/Tone.*)

Transition is the relating of one topic to the next, and smooth transition is an important aid to the coherence of a sentence, a paragraph, or an entire piece of writing. (See *Coherence.*)

The most effective coherence, of course, comes about naturally with sound development of ideas, one growing logically into the next—and that depends on sound organization. But sometimes beneficial even in this situation, particularly in going from one paragraph to the next, is the use of appropriate transitional devices.

Readers are apt to be sensitive creatures, easy to lose. (And, of course, the writers are the real losers since they are the ones who presumably have something they want to communicate.) If the readers get into a new paragraph and the territory seems familiar, chances are that they will continue. But if there are no identifying landmarks, they will often begin to feel uneasy and will either start worrying about their slow comprehension or take a dislike to the author and the subject matter. Either way, a communication block arises, and very likely the author will soon have fewer readers.

A good policy, then, unless the progression of ideas is exceptionally smooth and obvious, is to provide some kind of familiar identification early in the new paragraph to keep the reader feeling at ease with the different ideas. The effect is subtle but important. These familiar landmarks or transitional devices are sometimes applied deliberately but more often come naturally, especially when the prospective reader is kept constantly in mind at the time of writing.

An equally important reason for using some kinds of transitional devices, however, is a logical one: while functioning as bridges between ideas, they also assist the basic organization by pointing out the *relationship* of the ideas—and thus contributing still further to readability.

Transitional devices useful for bridging paragraph changes (and, some of them, to improve transitional flow within paragraphs) may be roughly classified as follows:

1. *Providing an "echo"* from the preceding paragraph. This may be the repetition of a key phrase or word, a pronoun referring back to such a word, or a casual reference to an idea. (See Lopate, last two paragraphs; Conroy, in the words referring to hot dogs; and Mitford.) Such an echo cannot be superimposed on new ideas, but must, by careful planning, be made an organic part of them.

2. *Devising a whole sentence or paragraph* to bridge other important paragraphs or major divisions.

3. *Using parallel structure* in an important sentence of one paragraph and the first sentence of the next. This is a subtle means of making the reader feel at ease in the new surroundings, but it is seldom used because it is much more limited in its potential than the other methods of transition. (See Lawrence, Pars. 1 to 2.)

4. *Using standard transitional expressions,* most of which have the additional advantage of indicating relationship of ideas. Only a few of those available are classified below, but nearly all the selections in this book amply illustrate such transitional expressions:

Time—soon, immediately, afterward, later, meanwhile, after a while
Place—nearby, here, beyond, opposite
Result—as a result, therefore, thus, consequently, hence
Comparison—likewise, similarly, in such a manner
Contrast—however, nevertheless, still, but, yet, on the other hand, after all, otherwise
Addition—also, too, and, and then, furthermore, moreover, finally, first, second, third
Miscellaneous—for example, for instance, in fact, indeed, on the whole, in other words

Trite (See *Clichés.*)

Unity in writing is the same as unity in anything else—in a picture, a musical arrangement, or a campus organization—and that is a *one*-ness in which all parts contribute to an overall effect.

Many elements of good writing contribute in varying degrees to the effect of unity. Some of these are properly designed introductions and closings; consistency in point of view, tone, and style; sometimes the recurring use of analogy or thread of symbolism; and occasionally the natural time boundaries of an experience or event, as in the selections of Mitford, Simpson, Gansberg, and Orwell.

But in most expository and argumentative writing the only dependable unifying force is the *central theme,* which every sentence and every word must somehow help to support. (The central theme is also called the *central idea* or the *thesis* when pertaining to the entire writing, and it is almost always called the *thesis* in argument. In an expository or argumentative paragraph it is the same as the *topic sentence,* which may be implied or, if stated, may be located anywhere in the paragraph but is usually placed first.) As soon as anything appears that is not related to the central idea, there are *two* units instead of one. Hence unity is basic to all other virtues of good writing, even to coherence and emphasis, the other two organic essentials. (See *Coherence; Emphasis.*)

An example of unity may be found in a single river system (for a practical use of analogy), with all its tributaries, big or little, meandering or straight, flowing into the main stream and making it bigger—or at least flowing into another tributary that finds its way to the main stream. This is *one* river system, an example of unity. Now picture another stream nearby that does not empty into the river but goes off in some other direction. There are now two systems, not one, and there is no longer unity.

It is the same way with writing. The central theme is the main river, flowing along from the first capital letter to the last period. Every drop of information or evidence must find its way into this theme-river, or it is not a part of the system. It matters not even slightly if the water is good, the idea-stream perhaps deeper and finer than any of the others: if it is not a tributary, it has no business pretending to be relevant to *this* theme of writing.

And that is why most students are required to state their central idea or thesis, usually in solid sentence form, before even starting to organize their ideas. If the writer can use only tributaries, it is very important to know from the start just what the river is.

Credits

Salman Akhtar, from *Objects of Our Desire* by Salman Akhtar, M.D., copyright © 2005 by Salman Akhtar. Used by permission of Harmony Books, a division of Random House, Inc.

Margaret Atwood, "Pornography," from *Chatelaine Magazine*. Copyright © 1983 by Margaret Atwood. Reprinted by permission of Phoebe Larmore, Literary Agent.

Amy Bell, "Perception of Truth." Reprinted by permission.

John Berendt, "The Hoax," *Esquire*, 1994. Reprinted by permission of International Creative Management, Inc. Copyright © 1994 by John Berendt, for *Esquire*.

Adrian Boykin wrote "Overcoming an Impediment: A Rite of Passage" while taking first-year English at the University of Denver.

Sheilagh Brady, "Mad About MADD." Reprinted by permission.

Carey Braun, "Bright Light." Reprinted by permission.

Alan Buczynski, "Iron Bonding," *The New York Times Magazine*, July 19, 1992. © 1992, Alan Buczynski. Reprinted by permission.

Joe Buhler and Ron Graham, "Give Juggling a Hand!" *The Sciences*, January/February 1984. Reprinted with the permission of the New York Academy of Sciences, 7 World Trade Center, 250 Greenwich St., 40th Floor, New York, NY 10007. www.nyas.org

Geoffrey Canada, "Pain." From *Reaching Up for Manhood* by Geoffrey Canada. Copyright © 1998 by Geoffrey Canada. Reprinted by permission of Beacon Press, Boston.

Matt Carmichael, "Radical Rest," *Resurgence*, Issue 248 (May-June 2008); as excerpted in *Utne Reader* (January–February 2009) titled "Get Radical. Get Some Rest." Reprinted by permission of Resurgence magazine.

Stephen L. Carter, "The Insufficiency of Honesty," from *The Atlantic Monthly*, February 1996. Copyright © 1996 by Stephen L. Carter. Reprinted by permission of the author.

Bruce Catton, "Grant and Lee: A Study in Contrasts," from *The American Story*, Earl Schenck Miers, editor. Copyright © 1956 by Broadcast Music, Inc. Copyright Renewed, 1984. Reprinted by permission of the U.S. Capitol Historical.

Veronica Chambers, "Mother's Day Present," from *Mama's Girl* by Veronica Chambers, copyright © 1996 by Veronica Chambers. Used by permission of Riverhead Books, an imprint of Penguin Group (USA) Inc.

Lan Samantha Chang, "Like Robinson Crusoe" by Lan Samantha Chang, from *Prime Times: Writers on Their Favorite TV Shows*, edited by Douglas Bauer, copyright © 2004 by Douglas Bauer. Used by permission of Crown Publishers, a division of Random House, Inc.

Pat Conroy, "Chili Cheese Dogs, My Father and Me." © 2004 Pat Conroy. Initially published in *Parade* Magazine, November 14, 2004. All rights reserved.

Daniel Thomas Cook, "Children of the Brand." This article is reprinted with permission from *In These Times* magazine, December 25, 2006, and is available at www.inthesetimes.com.

Christopher B. Daly, "How the Lawyers Stole Winter" from *The Atlantic Monthly*, March 1995. Copyright © 1995 by Christopher B. Daly. Reprinted by permission of Christopher B. Daly.

Sarah Egri, "How a Public Document Affected My Life." Reprinted by permission.

Anne Fadiman, "Coffee" from *At Large and At Small: Familiar Essays* by Anne Fadiman. Copyright © 2007 by Anne Fadiman. Reprinted by permission of Farrar, Straus and Giroux, LLC.

Heather Farnum, "Piano Recitals." Reprinted by permission.

Ian Frazier, "How to Operate the Shower Curtain" from *Lamentations of the Father: Essays* by Ian Frazier. Copyright © 2008 by Ian Frazier. Reprinted by permission of Farrar, Straus and Giroux, LLC. Originally published in *The New Yorker*, January 8, 2007.

Nancy Friday, pages 205–207, 173–174 from *The Power of Beauty* by Nancy Friday (edited version as it appeared in *The New York Times Magazine*, May 17, 1996). Copyright © 1996 by Nancy Friday. Reprinted by permission of HarperCollins Publishers.

Karin Gaffney, "Losing Weight." Reprinted by permission.

Martin Gansberg, "38 Who Saw Murder Didn't Call the Police." From *The New York Times*, March 17, 1964. © 1964 The New York Times. All rights reserved. Used by permission and protected by the Copyright Laws of the United States. The printing, copying, redistribution, or retransmission of the Material without express written permission is prohibited.

Dagoberto Gilb, "Pride" from *Gritos: Essays* by Dagoberto Gilb. Copyright © 2003 by Dagoberto Gilb. Reprinted by permission of Witherspoon Associates.

Jennifer Graham, "How to Decorate a Dorm Room on a Budget." Courtesy of eHow.com. http://www.eHow.com.

Wil Haygood, "Underground Dads," from *The New York Times Magazine*, January 30, 1997. Copyright © 1997 by The New York Times. Reprinted by permission of the author.

J. C. Herz, "Superhero Sushi" from *Joystick Nation: How Videogames Ate Our Quarters, Won Our Hearts, and Rewired Our Minds*. Reprinted by permission of International Creative Management, Inc. Copyright © 1997 by J. C. Herz.

Mary Karr, "Dysfunctional Nation," *The New York Times*, May 12, 1996. Reprinted by permission of International Creative Management, Inc. Copyright © 1996 by Mary Karr for *The New York Times*.

Jason Kelly, "The Great TV Debate," *PopPolitics.com*, December 2001. Reprinted by permission of the author.

Jean Kilbourne, "Beauty...And the Beast of Advertising." Copyright © 1989 by Jean Kilbourne. Reprinted by permission of the author.

Martin Luther King Jr., "Letter from Birmingham Jail." Reprinted by arrangement with The Heirs to the Estate of Martin Luther King Jr., c/o Writers House as agent for the proprietor New York, NY. Copyright 1963 Dr. Martin Luther King Jr; copyright renewed 1991 Coretta Scott King.

Barbara Kingsolver, "High Tide in Tucson" from *High Tide in Tucson: Essays from Now or Never* by Barbara Kingsolver. Copyright © 1995 by Barbara Kingsolver. Reprinted by permission of HarperCollins Publishers.

Verlyn Klinkenborg, "Our Vanishing Night," *National Geographic*, November 2008. Reprinted by permission of National Geographic Society.

William Severini Kowinski, "Kids in the Mall: Growing Up Controlled" from *The Malling of America* by William Severini Kowinski. Copyright © 1985, 2002 by William Severini Kowinski. By permission of the author.

Lori L'Heureux, "Stars." Reprinted by permission.

Sarah Lake, "Welcome to the Gym!" Reprinted by permission.

Barbara Lawrence, "Four-Letter Words Can Hurt You," *The New York Times*, October 27, 1973. © 1973, The New York Times. Reprinted by permission.

Jonah Lehrer, excerpt from "The Uses of Reason" from *How We Decide* by Jonah Lehrer. Copyright © 2009 by Jonah Lehrer. Reprinted by permission of Houghton Mifflin Harcourt Publishing Company. All rights reserved.

Phillip Lopate, "A Nonsmoker with a Smoker" from *Against Joie de Vivre: Personal Essays*. Reprinted by permission of The Wendy Weil Agency, Inc. First published by Poseidon Press. © 1989 by Phillip Lopate.

Barry Lopez, "A Passage of the Hands." From *About This Life* by Barry Lopez, copyright © 1998 by Barry Holstun Lopez. Used by permission of Alfred A. Knopf, a division of Random House, Inc.

Bill McKibben, "Old MacDonald Had a Farmer's Market," *In Character*, Winter 2007. www.incharacter.org. Reprinted by permission of the author.

Stephanie Mills, "Could You Live with Less?" First published in *Glamour* Magazine, May 1998. Reprinted by permission of the author.

Sarah Min, "Language Lessons." Copyright © 1997 Condé Nast Publications. All rights reserved. Originally published in *Glamour*, November 1997. Reprinted by permission.

Jessica Mitford, "To Dispel Fears of Live Burial" from *The American Way of Death*. Reprinted by permission of The Estate of Jessica Mitford. Copyright © 1963, 1978 by Jessica Mitford, all rights reserved.

Cullen Murphy, "Hello, Darkness," from *The Atlantic Monthly*, March 1996. Copyright © 1996 by Cullen Murphy. Reprinted by permission of the author.

Kevin Nomura, "Life Isn't Like Baseball." Reprinted by permission.

Andrew O'Hehir, "The Myth of Media Violence," *Salon.com*, March 17, 2005. This article first appeared in Salon.com, at http://www.Salon.com. An online version remains in the Salon archives. Reprinted with permission.

George Orwell, "A Hanging" from *Shooting an Elephant and Other Essays* by George Orwell, copyright 1950 by Sonia Brownell Orwell and renewed 1978 by Sonia Pitt-Rivers, reprinted by permission of Houghton Mifflin Harcourt Publishing Company.

Sridhar Pappu, *Deranged Marriage*, www.Salon.com, June 29, 2000. Reprinted by permission.

Susan Perry and Jim Dawson, "What's Your Best Time of Day?" Reprinted with the permission of Scribner, a Division of Simon & Schuster, Inc. from *The Secrets Our Body Clocks Reveal* by Susan Perry and Jim Dawson. Copyright © 1988 Susan Perry and Jim Dawson.

Brenda Peterson, "Life Is a Musical," from *Nature and Other Mothers*. Copyright © 1992 by Brenda Peterson. Reprinted by permission of Sanford J. Greenburger & Associates.

Alissa Quart, from "Cinema of the In-Crowd" from *Branded: The Buying and Selling of Teenagers* by Alissa Quart. Copyright © 2003 by Alissa Quart. Reprinted by permission of Basic Books, a member of Perseus Books Group.

Anna Quindlen, "The Drug That Pretends It Isn't" from *Loud and Clear*. New York: Random House, 2004. Reprinted by permission of International Creative Management, Inc. Copyright © 2004 by Anna Quindlen.

Julie Richardson, "The Fight on Fat Controversy," from *Exit 17*. Reprinted by permission of the author.

Mary Roach, "My Father the Geezer," from *The New York Times Magazine*, June 15, 1997. Copyright © 1997 by The New York Times. Reprinted by permission of the author.

Andy Rooney, "In and of Ourselves We Trust." © Tribune Media Services, Inc. All Rights Reserved. Reprinted with permission.

Catherine Seipp, "Meet Today's Dad," from *National Review*, June 16, 2004. Copyright © 2004 by National Review Online, www.nationalreview.com. Reprinted by permission.

Leslie Marmon Silko, "Yellow Woman and a Beauty of the Spirit." Reprinted with the permission of Simon & Schuster, Inc., from *Yellow Woman and a Beauty of the Spirit* by Leslie Marmon Silko. Copyright © 1996 by Leslie Marmon Silko. All rights reserved.

George Simpson, "The War Room at Bellevue." Copyright © 1983 by News Group Publications, Inc. Reprinted by permission of *The New York Magazine*.

Gary Soto, "The Jacket," copyright © 1983, 1988, 2000 by Gary Soto, from *The Effects of Knut Hamsun on a Fresno Boy: Recollections and Short Essays* by Gary Soto. Reprinted by permission of the publisher, Persea Books, Inc., New York.

Brent Staples, "Just Walk on By." Reprinted by permission of the author.

Elizabeth Svoboda, "I am not a puzzle, I am a person," *Salon.com*, April 27, 2009. This article first appeared in Salon.com, at http://www.Salon.com. An online version remains in the Salon archives. Reprinted with permission.

Maia Szalavitz, "A Virtual Life," from *The New York Times Magazine*, June 26, 1996. Copyright © 1996 by The New York Times. Reprinted by permission of the author.

Donna Tartt, "A Garden Party," *The Guardian*, October 2, 2004. Reprinted by permission of International Creative Management, Inc. Copyright © 2004 by Donna Tartt for *The Guardian*.

Hrishikesh Unni wrote "Elephants, Ivory, and an Indelible Experience" when he was enrolled in first-year English at the University of Denver.

Michael Ventura, "Taboo: Don't Even Think About It!" *Psychology Today*, January/February 1998. Reprinted with permission from *Psychology Today* Magazine, (Copyright © 1998 Sussex Publishers, LLC.).

Nicholas Wade, "Method and Madness: How Men and Women Think," *The New York Times*, June 12, 1994. © 1994, The New York Times. Reprinted by permission.

Alice Walker, "Am I Blue?" from *Living by the Word: Selected Writings 1973–1987*, copyright © 1986 by Alice Walker, reprinted by permission of Houghton Mifflin Harcourt Publishing Company.

E. B. White, "Once More to the Lake," from *One Man's Meat*. Text copyright © 1941 by E. B. White. Copyright renewed. Reprinted by permission of Tilbury House, Publishers, Gardiner, Maine.

Tom Wolfe, excerpt from "O Rotten Gotham – Sliding Down into the Behavioral Sink" from *The Pump House Gang* by Tom Wolfe. Copyright © 1968, renewed 1996 by Tom Wolfe. Reprinted by permission of Farrar, Straus and Giroux, LLC.

Wayne Worcester, "Arms and the Man," from *Rhode Islander Magazine*, May 30, 1993. Wayne Worcester is a former newspaper reporter and editor, magazine freelance writer, essayist and the author of two novels and a short story. He is a professor of journalism at the University of Connecticut. Reprinted by permission of the author.

Index